The Services
of the Christian Year

THE COMPLETE LIBRARY
OF
CHRISTIAN WORSHIP

THE COMPLETE LIBRARY
OF
CHRISTIAN WORSHIP

Volume 5, The Services of the Christian Year

ROBERT E. WEBBER, EDITOR

The Complete Library of Christian Worship, Vol. 5, The Services of the Christian Year.

Hendrickson Publishers, Inc.
P. O. Box 3473
Peabody, Massachusetts 01961–3473

Printed in the United States of America

Hendrickson Publishers' edition
ISBN 1–56563–191–9
Hendrickson edition published by arrangement with Star Song Publishing Group, a division of
Jubilee Communications, Inc.
2325 Crestmoor, Nashville, Tennessee 37215.

CONTENTS

Part 8:   THE SEASON AFTER PENTECOST AND OTHER COMMEMORATIONS

List of Illustrations

Board of Editorial Consultants

Betty Carr Pulkingham
  Community of Celebration, Aliquippa,
    Pennsylvania

John Rempel
  Manhattan Mennonite Fellowship, New York, New
    York

James Rosenthal
  Anglican Consultative Council, London, UK

Donald Saliers
  Candler School of Theology, Atlanta, Georgia

Frank C. Senn
  Immanuel Lutheran Church (ELCA), Evanston,
    Illinois

Robert Shaper
  Fuller Theological Seminary, Pasadena, California

Dan Sharp
  St. Andrews Presbyterian Church, Newport,
    California

Stephen Shoemaker
  Broadway Baptist Church, Dallas, Texas

Ron Sprunger
  Ashland Theological Seminary, Ashland, Ohio

Gilbert W. Stafford
  Anderson University, Anderson, Indiana

Howard Stevenson
  Evangelical Free Church, Fullerton, California

Sonja M. Stewart
  Western Theology Seminary, Holland, Michigan

Thomas Troeger
  Iliff School of Theology, Denver, Colorado

Terry Howard Wardle
  Simpson Graduate School, Reading, California

Keith Watkins
  Christian Theological Seminary, Indianapolis,
    Indiana

John Weborg
  North Park Theological Seminary, Chicago, Illinois

John Westerhoff, III
  Duke University, Durham, North Carolina

James F. White
  Notre Dame University, Notre Dame, Indiana

Susan J. White
  Westcott House, Cambridge, England

James Wilde
  Oregon Catholic Press, Portland, Oregon

Gregory Wilde
  University of Notre Dame, Notre Dame, Indiana

Benjamin Williams
  Antiochian Orthodox Church, Archdiocese of North
    America, Draper, Utah

William Willimon
  Duke University Chapel, Durham, North Carolina

Contributing Editors

Jean Ackerman
  Diocese of Memphis, Memphis, Tennessee

Doug Adams
  Pacific School of Religion, Graduate Theological
    Union, Berkeley, California

Marlin Adrian
  Wheaton College, Wheaton, Illinois

J. Neil Alexander
  General Theological Seminary, New York City, New
    York

Patrick H. Alexander
  Hendrickson Publishers, Peabody, Massachusetts

Ronald Allen
  Western Theological Seminary, Portland, Oregon

Ronald J. Allen
  Christian Theological Seminary, Indianapolis,
    Indiana

Timothy Allen
  Evangelical Free Church, Naperville, Illinois

Lora Allison
  Celebration Ministries, La Porte, Texas

Chester Alwes
  University of Illinois, Champaign-Urbana, Illinois

Patti Amsden
  Son-Life Church, Collinsville, Illinois

Rubén P. Armendáriz
  McCormick Theological Seminary, Chicago, Illinois

Anton Armstrong
  St. Olaf College, Northfield, Minnesota

Kerchal Armstrong
  Faith Missionary Church, Indianapolis, Indiana

Brent Assink
  Calvary CRC, Minneapolis, Minnesota

Diane S. George Ayer
  Canadian Theological Seminary, Regina,
    Saskatchewan, Canada

Edith Bajema
  Grand Rapids, Michigan

John D. Baker
  Druid Hills Baptist Church, Atlanta, Georgia

Judith Wall Baker
  Atlanta, Georgia

Randall Bane
  Kansas City, Missouri

Henry Baron
  Calvin College, Grand Rapids, Michigan

Andrew R. Jesson
Rienking Community Church, Redding, California.

Calvin Johansson
Evangel College, Springfield, Missouri

Jakob Joez
Wycliff Colege, University of Toronto, Toronto, Canada

Todd Johnson
University of Notre Dame, Notre Dame, Indiana

Susan Jorgensen
Spiritual Life Center, Burlington, Connecticut

Thomas Kane
Weston School of Theology, Cambridge, Massachusetts

Catherine Kapikian
Wesley Theological Seminary, Washington, D.C.

Angela Kauffman
ACTA Publications, Chicago, Illinois

David Kauffman
ACTA Publications, Chicago, Illinois

Aidan Kavanagh
Divinity School, Yale, New Haven, Connecticut

Ralph A. Keifer
St. Mary's Seminary and University, Baltimore, Maryland

Duane Kelderman
Neland Avenue Christian Reformed Curch, Grand Rapids, Michigan

Jeff Kemper
Mt. St. Mary's Seminary, Cincinnati, Ohio

Graham Kendrick
Make Way Music, Pevensey, East Sussex, UK

Joseph Kennan
Philadelphia, Pennsylvania

LeRoy E. Kennell
Christ Community Mennonite Church, Schaumburg, Illinois

Jeffrey Keyes
St. Edward's Parish, Newark, California

Jeannie Kienzle
Grace—St. Luke's Episcopal Church, Memphis, Tennessee

Martha Ann Kirk
Incarnate Word, San Antonio, Texas

Marlene Kropf
Mennonite Board of Congregational Ministries, Elkhart, Indiana

Jill Knuth
Bethany Lutheran Church, Menlo Park, California

Theresa Koernke
Washington Theological Union, Silver Spring, Maryland

Rex A. Koivisto
Multnomah School of the Bible, Portland, Oregon

David T. Koyzis
Redeemer College, Ancaster, Ontario, Canada

Tom Kraeuter
Outreach Ministries, Hillsboro, Missouri

Carolyn Krantz
Diocese of Lafayette, Lafayette, Louisiana

Eleanor Kreider
London Mennonite Center, Manchester, UK

Catherine Krier
Christ on the Mountain Parish, Lakewood, Colorado

John M. Kubiniec
Office of Liturgy, Rochester, New York

Ron Kydd
Central Pentecostal College, Keene, Ontario, Canada

Clements E. Lamberth
Church of the Covenant, Washington, Pennsylvania

John R. Landgraf
Midwest Commission on the Ministry, ABC Clergy

Craig Brian Larson
Leadership, *Carol Stream, Illinois*

Jan Larson
Archdiocese of Seattle, Seattle, Washington

Lloyd Larson
Church of God, Anderson, Indiana

Lizette Larson-Miller
Loyola Marymount College, Los Angeles, California.

Gordon Lathrop
The Lutheran Theological Seminary, Philadelphia, Pennsylvania

Michael Lawler
Creighton University, Omaha, Nebraska

Katherine Lawrence
Bethany Theological Seminary, Lombard, Illinois

Cathy Lee
Corinthians VI, Australia

Janice E. Leonard
Laudemont Ministries, Arlington Heights, Illinois

John Brooks Leonard
Center for Pastoral Liturgy, Notre Dame University, Notre Dame, Indiana

Richard C. Leonard
Laudemont Ministries, Arlington Heights, Illinois

List of Cooperating Publishers

BOOK PUBLISHERS

Abbott-Martyn Press
2325 Crestmoor Road
Nashville, TN 37215

Abingdon Press
201 8th Avenue South
Nashville, TN 37202

Agape
Hope Publishing
Carol Stream, IL 60187

Alba House
2187 Victory Boulevard
Staten Island, NY 10314

**American Choral
Directors Association**
502 Southwest 38th
Lawton, Oklahoma 73505

**Asian Institute for
Liturgy & Music**
P.O. Box 3167
Manila 1099 Philippines

Augsburg/Fortress Press
426 S. Fifth Street
Box 1209
Minneapolis, MN 55440

Ave Maria Press
Notre Dame, IN 46556

Baker Book House
P.O. Box 6287
Grand Rapids, MI 49516-6287

Beacon Hill Press
Box 419527
Kansas City, MO 64141

Bethany House Publishers
6820 Auto Club Road
Minneapolis, MN 55438

The Brethren Press
1451 Dundee Avenue
Elgin, IL 60120

Bridge Publishing, Inc.
200 Hamilton Blvd.
South Plainfield, NJ 07080

Broadman Press
127 Ninth Avenue, North
Nashville, TN 37234

C.S.S. Publishing Company
628 South Main Street
Lima, OH 45804

Cathedral Music Press
P.O. Box 66
Pacific, MO 63069

**Catholic Book
Publishing Company**
257 W. 17th Street
New York, NY 10011

CBP Press
Box 179
St. Louis, MO 63166

Celebration
P.O. Box 309
Aliquippa, PA 15001

Channing L. Bete Company
South Deerfield, MA 01373

Choristers Guild
2834 W. Kingsley Road
Garland, TX 75041

Christian Literature Crusade
701 Pennsylvania Avenue
Box 1449
Ft. Washington, PA 19034

Christian Publications
3825 Hartzdale Drive
Camp Hill, PA 17011

**The Church
Hymnal Corporation**
800 Second Avenue
New York, NY 10017

The Columba Press
93 Merise
Mount Merrion
Blackrock, Dublin

Concordia Publishing House
3558 S. Jefferson Avenue
St. Louis, MO 63118

Covenant Publications
3200 West Foster Avenue
Chicago, IL 60625

Cowley Publications
980 Memorial Drive
Cambridge, MA 02138

CRC Publications
2850 Kalamazoo SE
Grand Rapids, MI 49560

**Creative Communications
for The Parish**
10300 Watson Road
St. Louis, MO 63127

**Crossroad Publishing
Company**
575 Lexington Avenue
New York, NY 10022

Crossroad/Continuum
370 Lexington Avenue
New York, NY 10017

Dominion Press
7112 Burns Street
Ft. Worth, TX 76118

Duke Univesity Press
Box 6697 College Station
Durham, NC 27708

Faith and Life Press
724 Main Street
Box 347
Newton, KS 67114

The Faith Press, Ltd.
7 Tufton Street
Westminster, S.W. 1
England

Fleming H. Revell Company
184 Central Avenue
Old Tappen, N.J. 07675

Folk Music Ministry
P.O. Box 3443
Annapolis, MD 21403

Franciscan Communications
1229 South Santee Street
Los Angeles, CA 90015

Georgetown University Press
111 Intercultural Center
Washington, D.C. 20057

GIA Publications
7404 S. Mason Avenue
Chicago, IL 60638

Great Commission Publications
7401 Old York Road
Philadelphia, PA 19126

Grove Books
Bramcote Notts
England

Harper & Row Publishers
Icehouse One-401
151 Union Street
San Francisco, CA 94111-1299

Harvard University Press
79 Garden Street
Cambridge, MA 02138

Harvest Publications
Baptist General Conference
2002 S. Arlington Heights Road
Arlington Heights, IL 60005

Hendrickson Publishers, Inc.
P.O. Box 3473
Peabody, MA 01961-3473

Herald Press
616 Walnut Avenue
Scottdale, PA 15683

Hinshaw Music Incorporated
P.O. Box 470
Chapel Hill, NC 27514

Holt, Rinehart & Winston
111 5th Avenue
New York, NY 10175

Hope Publishing Company
Carol Stream, IL 60188

Hymn Society of America
Texas Christian University
P.O. Box 30854
Ft. Worth, TX 76129

Indiana University Press
10th & Morton
Bloomington, IN 47405

Integrity Music
P.O. Box 16813
Mobile, AL 36616

J.S. Paluch Company, Inc.
3825 Willow Road
P.O. Box 2703
Schiller Park, IL 60176

**The Jewish Publication
Society of America**
1930 Chestnut Street
Philadelphia, PA 19103

Judson Press
P.O. Box 851
Valley Forge, PA 19482-0851

**Light and Life Publishing
Company**
P.O. Box 26421
Minneapolis, MN 55426

Liguori Publications
One Liguori Drive
Liguori, MO 63057

Lillenas Publishing Company
Box 419527
Kansas City, MO 64141

The Liturgical Conference
1017 Twelfth Street, N.W.
Washington, D.C. 20005-4091

The Liturgical Press
St. John's Abbey
Collegeville, MN 56321

Liturgy Training Publications
1800 North Heritage Avenue
Chicago, IL 60622-1101

**Macmillan Publishing
Company**
866 Third Avenue
New York, NY 10022

Maranatha! Music
25411 Cabot Road
Suite 203
Laguna Hills, CA 92653

Mel Bay Publications
Pacific, MO 63969-0066

Meriwether Publishing, Ltd.
885 Elkton Drive
Colorado Springs, CO 80907

Michael Glazier, Inc.
1723 Delaware Avenue
Wilmington, Delaware 19806

Morehouse-Barlow
78 Danbury Road
Wilton, CT 06897

Multnomah Press
10209 SE Division Street
Portland, OR 97266

**National Association
of Pastoral Musicians**
25 Sheridan Street, NW
Washington, DC 20011

NavPress
P.O. Box 6000
Colorado Springs, CO 80934

New Skete
Cambridge, NY 12816

**North American
Liturgical Resources**
1802 N. 23rd Avenue
Phoenix, AZ 85029

Oxford University Press
16-00 Pollitt Drive
Fair Lawn, NJ 07410

The Pastoral Press
225 Sheridan Street, NW
Washington, D.C. 20011

Paulist Press
997 McArthur Boulevard
Mahwah, NJ 07430

The Pilgrim Press
132 West 31st Street
New York, NY 10001

Psalmist Resources
9820 E. Watson Road
St. Louis, MO 63126

Pueblo Publishing Company
100 West 32nd Street
New York, NY 1001-3210

Regal Books
A Division of Gospel Light
  Publications
Ventura, CA 93006

Resource Publications, Inc.
160 E. Virginia Street #290
San Jose, CA 95112

The Scarecrow Press
52 Liberty Street
Box 416
Metuchen, NJ 08840

Schocken Books
62 Cooper Square
New York, NY 10003

**Schuyler Institute for
Worship & The Arts**
2757 Melandy Drive, Suite 15
San Carlos, CA 94070

SCM Press Ltd.
c/o Trinity Press International
3725 Chestnut Street
Philadelphia, PA 19104

Servant Publications
P.O. Box 8617
Petersham, MA 01366-0545

The Sharing Company
P.O. Box 2224
Austin, TX 78768-2224

Sheed & Ward
115 E. Armour Boulevard
P.O. Box 414292
Kansas City, MO 64141-0281

Shofar Publications, Inc
P.O. Box 88711
Carol Stream, IL 60188

SPCK
Holy Trinity Church
Marylebone Road
London, N.W. 4D4

St. Anthony Messenger Press
1615 Republic Street
Cincinnati, OH 45210

St. Bede's Publications
P.O. Box 545
Petersham, MA 01366-0545

St. Mary's Press
Terrace Heights
Winona, MN 55987

St. Vladimir Seminary Press
575 Scarsdale Road
Crestwood, NY 10707-1699

Thomas Nelson Publishers
P.O. Box 141000
Nashville, TN 37214

Twenty Third Publications
P.O. Box 180
Mystic, CT 06355

Tyndale House Publishers
351 Executive Drive
Carol Stream, IL 60188

United Church of Christ
Office of Church Life and
  Leadership
700 Prospect
Cleveland, OH 44115

United Church Press
132 West 31st Street
New York, NY 10001

**The United Methodist
Publishing House**
P.O. Box 801
Nashville, TN 37202

**United States
Catholic Conference**
Office of Publishing and
  Promotion Services
1312 Massachusetts Avenue, NW
Washington, DC 20005-4105

University of California Press
1010 Westward Blvd.
Los Angeles, CA 90024

**University of Notre
Dame Press**
Notre Dame, IN 46556

The Upper Room
1908 Grand Avenue
P.O. Box 189
Nashville, TN 37202

Victory House Publishers
P.O. Box 700238
Tulsa, OK 74170

Westminster John Knox Press
100 Witherspoon Street
Louisville, KY 40202-1396

**William B. Eerdmans
Publishing Company**
255 Jefferson S.E.
Grand Rapids, MI 49503

**William C. Brown
Publishing Company**
2460 Kerper Boulevard
P.O. Box 539
Dubuque, IA 52001

William H. Sadlier, Inc.
11 Park Place
New York, NY 10007

Winston Press
P.O. Box 1630
Hagerstown, MD 21741

Word Books
Tower-Williams Square
5221 N. O'Conner Blvd. Suite
  1000
Irving, TX 75039

**World Council of
Churches Publications**
P.O. Box 66
150 Route de Ferney
1211 Geneva 20, Switzerland

**World Library
Publications, Inc.**
3815 N. Willow Road
P.O. Box 2701
Schiller Park, IL 60176

**The World
Publishing Company**
Meridian Books
110 E. 59th Street
New York, NY 10022

Yale University Press
302 Temple Street
New Haven, CN 06510

Zion Fellowship
236 Gorham Street
Canadagina, NY 14424

**Zondervan Publishing
Company**
1415 Lake Drive S.E.
Grand Rapids, MI 49506

PERIODICAL PUBLISHERS

**The American Center for
Church Music Newsletter**
3339 Burbank Drive
Ann Arbor, MI 48105

American Organist
475 Riverside Drive, Suite 1260
New York, NY 10115

**ARTS: The Arts in Religious
and Theological Studies**
United Theological Seminary of
the Twin Cities
3000 5th Street, NW
New Brighton, MN 55112

Arts Advocate
The United Church of Christ
Fellowship in the Arts
73 S. Palvuse
Walla Walla, WA 99362

The Choral Journal
American Choral Directors
Association
P.O. Box 6310
Lawton, OK 73506

Choristers Guild Letters
2834 W. Kingsley Road
Garland, TX 75041

Christians in the Visual Arts
(newsletter)
P.O. Box 10247
Arlington, VA 22210

Church Music Quarterly
Royal School of Church Music
Addington Palace
Croyden, England CR9 5AD

The Church Musician
Southern Baptist Convention
127 9th Avenue N.
Nashville, TN 37234

Contemporary Christian Music
CCM Publications
P.O. Box 6300
Laguna Hills, CA 92654

Diapason
380 E. Northwest Highway
Des Plaines, IL 60016

Doxology
Journal of the Order of St. Luke in
the United Methodist Church

1872 Sweet Home Road
Buffalo, NY 14221

Environment and Art Letter
Liturgy Training Publications
1800 N. Hermitage Avenue
Chicago, IL 60622

GIA Quarterly
7404 S. Mason Avenue
Chicago, IL 60638

Grace Notes
Association of Lutheran Church
Musicians
4807 Idaho Circle
Ames, IA 50010

The Hymn
Hymn Society of the United States
and Canada
P.O. Box 30854
Fort Worth, TX 76129

Journal
Sacred Dance Guild
Joyce Smillie, Resource Director
10 Edge Court
Woodbury, CT 06798

Journal of Ritual Studies
Department of Religious Studies
University of Pittsburgh
Pittsburgh, PA 15260

Let the People Worship
Schuyler Institute for Worship and
the Arts
2757 Melendy Drive, Suite 15
San Carlos, CA 94070

Liturgy
The Liturgical Conference
8750 Georgia Avenue, S., Suite
123
Silver Spring, MD 20910

Liturgy 90
Liturgy Training Publications
1800 N. Hermitage Avenue
Chicago, IL 60622

Modern Liturgy
Resource Publications
160 E. Virginia Street, Suite 290
San Jose, CA 95112

Music in Worship
Selah Publishing Company
P.O. Box 103
Accord, NY 12404

Newsnotes
The Fellowship of United
Methodists in Worship, Music,
and Other Arts
P.O. Box 54367
Atlanta, GA 30308

Pastoral Music
225 Sheridian Street, NW
Washington, D.C. 20011

PRISM
Yale Institute of Sacred Music
409 Prospect Street
New Haven, CT 06510

The Psalmist
9820 E. Watson Road
St. Louis, MO 63124

Reformed Liturgy and Music
Worship and Ministry Unit
100 Witherspoon Street
Louisville, KY 40202

Reformed Music Journal
Brookside Publishing
3911 Mt. Lehman Road
Abbotsford, BC V2S 6A9

Reformed Worship
CRC Publications
2850 Kalamazoo Avenue, SE
Grand Rapids, MI 49560

Rite Reasons
Biblical Horizons
P.O. Box 1096
Niceville, FL 32588

**St. Vladimirs Theological
Quarterly**
757 Scarsdale Road
Crestwood, NY 10707

Studia Liturgica
Department of Theology
University of Notre Dame
Notre Dame, IN 46556

Today's Liturgy
Oregon Catholic Press
5536 NE Hassalo
Portland, OR 97213

Worship
The Liturgical Press
St. John's Abbey
Collegeville, MN 56321

Worship Leader
CCM Communications, Inc.
107 Kenner Avenue
Nashville, TN 37205

Worship Today
600 Rinehard Road
Lake Mary, FL 32746

Additional Contributors

Christopher Beatty
The Upright Foundation, Lindale, Texas

Bill Rayborn
TCMR Communications, Grapevine, Texas

Preface to Volume 5

Twentieth-century worship renewal has brought forth the recovery of the Christian year. The restoration of the Christian year began with the Catholics in the sixties, then spread to the mainline churches in the seventies and the eighties. In the 1990s, this practice spread rapidly within the free-church movement and among other Protestant churches.

The Catholics were the first to recognize that the Christian year grew out of the life, death, and resurrection of Jesus. Recognizing that the foundation of the Christian year was the celebration of the saving events of Jesus led the Catholics into a major reshaping of the Christian year. The most notable change was the removal of many saints' days from the calendar, allowing Advent, Christmas, Epiphany, Lent, Holy Week, Easter, and Pentecost to become more visible. Consequently, the worshiper could experience more fully the power of these saving events.

It was this evangelical reform of the Christian year that broke down the wall of prejudice built by the Protestants against the Christian year. Since the Reformation, perhaps the major argument against the practice of the Christian year was the plethora of saints' days that obscured the centrality of Jesus Christ. Once this obstacle was removed, Protestants were able to see the Christocentric nature of the Christian year and its importance to the corporate faith of the church. One by one, the mainline Protestant churches officially restored the Christian year to its rightful place in worship. Nevertheless, the practice of the Christian year has not yet gained a firm foothold in many local congregations.

More recently, the free-church movement and contemporary churches have begun to rediscover the significance of the Christian year. These churches have a firm grasp on a Christocentric Christianity, and worship is focused primarily on the character of God. There is relatively little emphasis on worship as those words and signs that remember God's saving deeds through the proclamation of the Word and enactment of the Eucharist. The revived interest in the Christian year may yet lead these churches to embrace God's mighty acts of salvation through the seasons of the Christian calendar.

The Services of the Christian Year is a book that will help pastors, music ministers, worship leaders, and worship committees introduce the practice of the Christian calendar in their churches. Planners will discover the biblical roots, the historical development, and the theological meaning of the Christian year. Planners will also be delighted to discover every major service of the Christian year laid out in complete form with explanatory notes and suggestions for introducing unfamiliar customs.

I hope you will find this volume useful not only for your planning ministry but also a source of guidance for your personal spirituality and corporate piety.

Robert Webber, Editor

Introduction

The *Complete Library of Christian Worship* has been designed to meet a need in the church. Christian leaders and congregations are becoming increasingly interested in the subjects of worship and worship renewal in the local church. Often, however, they lack adequate biblical and historical perspective or the necessary materials and resources to engage in the renewal process.

To fulfill the demand for worship resources, publishing houses, particularly those of specific denominations, have been producing materials for the local church. While these materials may find use within the constituency of a particular denomination, only a few break across denominational barriers and become known throughout the church at large.

The Complete Library of Christian Worship draws from more than one hundred publishing houses and the major Christian denominations of the world in order to bring those resources together in a seven-volume work, making them readily available to all.

The purpose of this introductory material is to acquaint the reader with *The Complete Library of Christian Worship* and to help him or her to use its information and resources in the local church.

First, the reader needs to have some sense of the scope of worship studies and renewal that are addressed by *The Complete Library of Christian Worship* (see section 101 below). Second, it is important to learn how to use the *Library* (see section 102). Finally, there is a need to understand the precise content of Volume 4, *Music and the Arts in Christian Worship*.

These three introductory entries are a key to the whole concept of the *Library,* a concept that brings together instruction in worship and vital resources for use in worship. The *Library* also directs the reader to a vast array of books, audio tapes, videotapes, model services, and resources in music and the arts. It seeks to provide direction and inspiration for everything the church does in worship.

101 • Introduction to *The Complete Library of Christian Worship*

The word *library* implies a collection of resources, together with a system of organization that makes them accessible to the user. Specifically, *The Complete Library of Christian Worship* is a comprehensive compilation of information pertaining to the worship of the Christian church. It draws from a large pool of scholars and practitioners in the field, and from more than two thousand books and media resources in print.

The purpose of *The Complete Library of Christian Worship* is to make biblical, historical, and contemporary resources on worship available to pastors, music ministers, worship committees, and the motivated individual worshiper. The *Library* contains biblical and historical information on all aspects of worship and numerous resource materials, as well as suggested resource books, audio tapes, and video instructional material for every worship act in the local church.

The twentieth century, more than any century in the history of Christianity, has been the century for research and study in the origins, history, theology, and practice of Christian worship. Consequently there are seven broad areas in which worship studies are taking place. These are:

1. the biblical foundations of worship;
2. historical and theological development of worship;
3. resources for worship and preaching;
4. resources for music and the arts in worship;
5. resources for the services of the Christian year;
6. resources for sacraments, ordinances, and other sacred acts; and
7. resources for worship and related ministries.

The Complete Library of Christian Worship is organized around these seven areas of worship renewal. In these seven volumes one will find a wide variety of resources for every worship act in the church, and a select but broad bibliography for additional resources.

102 • How to Use *The Complete Library of Christian Worship*

The Complete Library of Christian Worship differs from an encyclopedia, which is often organized alphabetically, with information about a particular subject scattered throughout the book. The *Library* does not follow this pattern because it is a work designed to educate as well as to provide resources. Consequently, all the material in the *Library* is organized under a particular theme or issue of worship.

The difference between the *Library* and an encyclopedia may be illustrated, for example, by examining the topic of environmental art in worship. Some of the themes essential to environmental art are banners, candles, stained glass windows, lighting, pulpit hangings, table coverings, and Communion ware. In a typical encyclopedia these entries would be scattered in the B, C, S, L, P, and T sections. Although this is not a problem for people who know what environmental art is and what needs to be addressed in environmental art, it is a problem for the person whose knowledge about the subject is limited. For this reason *The Complete Library of Christian Worship* has been organized—like a textbook—into chapters dealing with particular issues. Therefore, all the matters dealing with environmental art can be found in the chapter on environmental art (see Volume 4, *Music and the Arts in Christian Worship*). In this way a reader becomes educated on environmental art while at the same time having the advantage of in-depth information on the various matters pertaining to this aspect of worship.

Therefore, the first unique feature of *The Complete Library of Christian Worship* is that each volume can be read and studied like a book.

The second unique feature of the *Library* is that the materials have been organized to follow the actual *sequence in which worship happens*.

For example, Volume 1, *The Biblical Foundations of Christian Worship*, looks at the roots of Christian worship in the biblical tradition, while Volume 2, *Twenty Centuries of Christian Worship*, presents the development of various historical models of worship along with an examination of the theology of worship. Next, Volumes 3 through 7 provide resources for the various acts of worship: Volume 3, *The Renewal of Sunday Worship*, provides resources for the various parts of worship; Volume 4, *Music and the Arts in Christian Worship*, presents resources from music and the arts for the different aspects of worship. Volume 5, *The Services of the Christian Year*, branches out to the services of Advent, Christmas, Epiphany, Lent, Holy Week, Easter, and Pentecost, providing resources for those special services that celebrate the saving acts of God in Jesus Christ. Volume 6, *The Sacred Actions of Christian Worship*, deals with Communion, baptism, funerals, weddings, and other special or occasional acts of worship. Finally, Volume 7, *The Ministries of Christian Worship*, deals with evangelism, spirituality, education, social action, children's worship, and other matters impacted by Christian celebration.

Each volume contains an alphabetical index to the material in the book. This index makes desired information readily available for the reader.

The resources in these volumes are intended for use in every denomination and among all groups of Christians: liturgical, traditional Protestant, those using creative styles, and those in the praise-and-worship tradition. Resources from each of these communities may be found in the various volumes.

It is difficult to find material from the free churches (those not following a historic order of worship) and from the charismatic traditions. These communities function with an oral tradition of worship and therefore do not preserve their material through written texts. Nevertheless, a considerable amount of information has been gathered from these oral traditions. Recently, leaders in these communities have been teaching their worship practices through audio tapes and videotapes. Information on the availability of these materials has been included in the appropriate volumes.

The written texts have been the easiest to obtain. Because of this, *The Complete Library of Christian Worship* may give the appearance of favoring liturgical worship. Due to the very nature of written texts, the appearance of a strong liturgical bent is unavoidable. Nevertheless, the goal of the *Library* is not to make free churches liturgical. Rather, it is to expand the perspective of Christians across a wide range of worship traditions. In this way, liturgical resources may serve as guides and sources of inspiration and creativity for free churches, while insights from free traditions may also enrich the practices and understanding of the more liturgical communities.

In sum, the way to use _The Complete Library of Christian Worship_ is as follows:

1. _Read each volume as you would read a book._ Each volume is full of biblical, historical, and theological information—a veritable feast for the curious, and for all worshipers motivated to expand their horizons.
2. _Use the alphabetical index for quick and easy access to a particular aspect of worship._ The index for each volume is as thorough as the listings for an encyclopedia.
3. _For further information and resources, order books and materials listed in the bibliography of resources._ Addresses of publishers may be found in your library's copy of _Books in Print_.
4. _Adapt the liturgical materials to the setting and worship style of your congregation._ Many of the worship materials in _The Complete Library of Christian Worship_ have been intentionally published without adaptation. Most pastors, worship ministers, and worship committee members are capable of adapting the material to a style suitable to their congregations with effective results.

103 ✦ INTRODUCTION TO VOLUME 5: _THE SERVICES OF THE CHRISTIAN YEAR_

The Services of the Christian Year introduces the reader to the range and depth of Christian observances so that one may understand and practice the Christian year intelligently, sensitively, and joyfully.

Part 1 surveys the practice of the Christian year in more than forty major denominations in North America. Here the reader may glean insights from the Eastern Orthodox, Roman Catholic, mainline Protestant, Anabaptist, Restorationist, Holiness, Pentecostal, evangelical, and charismatic traditions.

Part 2 explains the history and theology of the Christian year. Here the reader will discover not only how the Christian year came to be, but also the theological reasoning that supports it.

Parts 3 through 7 examine in considerable detail the primary seasons of the Christian year: Advent, Christmas, Epiphany, Lent, Holy Week, and the Easter season (including Pentecost). Here the reader will find helpful overviews of every major season, followed by resources for planning appropriate worship. Several articles explain the proper use of the arts for each season. Finally, a number of sample services are provided. Typically a sample liturgical service is followed by a creative service, then a convergence service.

The final section, Part 8, presents resources for the season after Pentecost (also known as ordinary time) as well as important commemoratives of the church (sometimes called the lesser feasts).

Planners will find _The Services of the Christian Year_ to be full of vital information and contemporary resources. We hope that this book will be an indispensable guide to the renewal of worship in your local church, a worship that truly celebrates the saving deeds of Jesus Christ.

PART ONE

The Practice of the Christian Year

ONE

The Christian Year Among the Churches

As this chapter will make clear, Christians differ significantly on the need for observing the Christian year. Nevertheless, there are signs that even those denominations that have traditionally resisted following a Christian calendar are taking a second look at this ancient practice. More traditional churches are also discovering how observing the cycle of Christian seasons contributes to worship renewal.

104 ✦ ADVENTIST CHURCHES

Christmas and Easter celebrations have become increasingly common in Adventist churches. Observance of the Christian year remains rare, but a few congregations are discovering that it is a rewarding source of balance and biblical spirituality in worship.

Historically, the Seventh-day Adventist church has paid no attention to the Christian year. In fact, during the formative years of the church in the mid-nineteenth century, even Christmas and Easter were suspect due to the lack of specific biblical introduction for these celebrations and their association with pagan holidays.

In recent years, however, Adventists have come to celebrate both Christmas and Easter with regularity, recognizing that these two primary events of the Christian faith can be celebrated meaningfully in common with all Christians.

Christmas and Easter Sabbaths

Most Seventh-day Adventist churches have a special worship service on the Sabbath (Saturday) closest to Christmas. It may include a pageant and special musical presentations. Some churches conduct a Christmas candlelight Communion service, though they are more likely to occur on a Friday evening than on Christmas Eve, the latter being thought of primarily as a family night rather than a liturgical event.

An increasing number of Adventist churches regularly plan special Easter events. Typically, the major Resurrection celebration takes place in Sabbath morning worship the day before Easter Sunday. A candlelight Communion service on Good Friday evening can be found here and there; much less often, a service on Maundy Thursday. A very few Adventist churches have sponsored an Easter sunrise service. More frequently, they participate with the other churches of the community in sunrise services.

Introducing the Christian Year

Beyond the celebration of Christmas and Easter, the use of the Christian year in Adventist churches is minimal. However, pastors with a special interest in worship, particularly historical and/or liturgical worship, have introduced additional times from the Christian year to their congregations. Advent is usually the starting point, and its observance has generally been well-received.

Epiphany, Ascension, and Pentecost have also been observed. The most common reaction from worshipers has been surprise, both at the depth of spiritual meaning found in remembering these biblical events on a timely basis, and that no one in their church had ever thought to observe them previously.

Adventist pastors encouraging recovery of the Christian year attempt carefully and gradually to lead their congregations to see that this mode of worship focuses on the gospel story and covers Scripture much more fully than is usually the case with independent choice of text and themes. Most members discover use of the Christian year to be a new and rewarding experience that bring spiritual growth and sense of unity with both past and present Christianity.

Use of visuals has been one of the most effective means of introducing the Christian year in congregations I have served. Table/altar displays to illustrate the sermon, Table/pulpit paraments in seasonal colors, and banners for seasons and days have all been effective. Explanations regarding the music—not only of the hymns but also of the organ pieces—have also been helpful, along with the always necessary verbal and written educational process.

——— Introducing the Lectionary ———

This year (1992) I introduced the Common Lectionary to my Lakeside, California Seventh-day Adventist church. The previous use and explanation of various portions of the Christian year provided excellent background, but in general, the initial reaction was "wait and see." Pointing out the historical precedents as far back as the composition of the Psalms contributed to acceptance, as did explanations of the nature and purpose of the lectionary itself. As members began to understand that Scriptures chosen by a group years ago for a particular week's lection spoke to immediate needs in the congregation, attitudes became very favorable.

My hope is to see many more Seventh-day Adventist churches experiencing the spiritual growth and sense of being part of the ongoing stream of Christianity that can come from the use of the Christian year.

Merle J. Whitney

105 • AFRICAN METHODIST-EPISCOPAL ZION CHURCHES

Although A.M.E. Zion churches do not widely observe the Christian year, some congregations have made attempts to include some of its features in worship. This article describes the efforts of one pastor to revitalize worship, particularly through Advent and Epiphany traditions.

The Christian church year presents the cyclical events in the life of Christ. Its perennial use is a vehicle of *recall association*, much like one's favorite hymn, continually reassuring the believer of Christ's activity in the cycles of their own lives.

Zion Methodism has struggled with its identity as a liturgical church. Vested and stoled clergy and the use of paraments were not the norm until the 1950s. The increased number of seminary-trained clergy and the acceptance of Christian education as a ministry of Zion fostered a greater use of liturgy and the church year. In 1968, the General Conference adopted a resolution to observe the Christian church year as a denomination, but in general the resolution did not receive broad support across Zion.

My resolution to the 1992 General Conference for the adoption of the Christian church year was more than a reissuance of the 1968 resolution. It was also a call for uniformity of liturgical practices where the church year is observed. Mother Methodism, the United Methodist Church, and others from whom Zion sought direction seem, to this writer, to have lost their way. I believe that Zion should reject the use of blue for Advent, for it is the Roman color of the Virgin Mary, the color of the sky. Purple is, was, and evermore shall be right and proper. In like manner, Zion should object to the removal of red for Pentecost. It is clear that the flaming tongues, like fire, could not and therefore should not be symbolized by any other color.

Nevertheless, these arguments for the church year and the use of appropriate colors for the seasons will remain moot (except for theological and liturgical debate) unless and until Zion's episcopal leadership promotes and encourages an appreciation of the benefits of the church year. Clergy and laity must both participate in this discovery, or a liturgical A.M.E. Zion connection will not be a reality.

The Shrewsbury Avenue A.M.E. Zion Church where I pastor was organized in 1827. When I arrived in 1982, I began to emphasize the practice of the Christian church year. Prior to my administration, this church observed denominational special days, Easter, Thanksgiving, and Christmas.

The seasons of the church year I introduced were those used by other Methodists: Advent, Christmastide, Epiphany, Lent, Eastertide, Pentecost, and Kingdomtide.

The reorientation process at Shrewsbury Avenue began with the musicians of the church. We talked about the words in the stanzas of hymns and other musical selections that were appropriate for the seasons of the church year. For example, the singing of hymns and playing of music that relates to the Star of Bethlehem is now reserved for the Sunday nearest the day of Epiphany.

Hymns for morning worship are chosen to emphasize the appropriate season. During Kingdomtide, we sing "I Love Thy Kingdom, Lord" and the "King of Love My Shepherd Is." During Advent we do not sing "O Holy Night" or "As With Gladness Men Of Old," since both point to the Star of Bethlehem.

Unfamiliar hymns are introduced during "The Teaching Minute" each Sunday for a month prior to the season in which the hymn is to be sung during morning worship. The theology of the hymn and/or the story of the writer is shared to show why these hymns should be included in our worship experience. This effort has greatly increased the lively participation of the congregation when these "new" hymns are sung.

We commissioned our Christian education department to make banners relevant to the season and its color. For example, Epiphany's banner is green, with a star and the words "The Wise Still Seek Him." Clergy stoles and paraments are changed along with the banners. The only exception is that, in Zion churches, clergy always use white stoles and robes and white paraments for Communion Sundays.

In addition to the visible seasonal enhancements, I contributed congregational calls to worship, invocations, and prayers to emphasize each season and its theme. These tools also increased the level of participation of the congregation in worship. Zion's current responsive readings for the Sundays of the year have been replaced, when appropriate, with a reading written for the season. We have used most of Zion's special day readings, designed for seasons and days in the church year.

Sermon series were prepared according the theme of a season. For example, an Advent series has been titled "Ready or Not, Here He Comes,"

with the emphasis on the first and second advent of Christ.

These changes have produced musicians, choirs, and congregation more keenly aware of the church year and its importance to the renewed life of the church. Musicians are more sensitive about selecting music that is season-appropriate, and deaconesses and Christian education boards make sure the paraments and banners fit with the theme of the season.

As we reflected on Christ's wilderness experience during Lent, we realized with greater conviction that the church year does not inhibit worship, rather it enhances it with a unity of thought, with *recall association*. He is with us as we travel from the bondage of Egypt, through the wilderness of this life, marching to Zion.

Andrew Foster

106 ❖ AMERICAN BAPTIST CHURCHES IN THE USA

American Baptist congregations are free to choose their own order of worship, and so the observance of the Christian year varies among churches. In the twentieth century, many congregations have followed an American civil calendar and have combined both religious and civil observances. Since the 1960s, however, there has been a strong movement toward recovery of a more distinctly Christian calendar.

The American Baptist Churches in the USA (ABCUSA), like other Baptist denominations, is a voluntary association of autonomous local churches organized for mutual aid and the support of common missions and ministries. Thus, there are American Baptist *churches*, but no American Baptist *church*. In discussing events, trends, and developments among American Baptists, then, one is always constrained to remember that Baptists work together by persuasion, not legislation.

—————— Calendars Discarded ——————

Baptist theology and practice, particularly in worship, are rooted in Scottish and English Calvinism. Thus most early Baptists followed the Calvinists in discarding calendars of "feasts and fasts," and in deemphasizing liturgical ceremony. This approach became so deeply entrenched that, even into the early twentieth century, some Baptists of North America declined to observe Christmas and other Christian festivals and continued to uphold the related principle that every Lord's Day (Sunday) was just like any other. Yet, there has always been a minority who maintain that the worship book, the Christian year, and a more formal liturgy do have an authentic place among Baptists.

Discarding religious calendars created two great voids which profoundly influenced Baptist worship. Loss of a lectionary related to a religious calendar led to topical, situation-dependent sermons, resulting in some of the best—and the worst—of Protestant preaching. Loss of the calendar itself encouraged many churches to drift toward civil religion, substituting an American civil calendar for a distinctly Christian calendar.

——— The American Civil Calendar ———

The American civil calendar combines patriotic holidays such as Memorial, Independence, and Labor Days with commercially oriented celebrations such as Mother's, Valentine's, and Grandparents' days. Three explicitly religious days have a prominent place for Christians—Palm Sunday, Easter, and Christmas. Thanksgiving, *the* American holiday, is distinctive as a civil holiday with a religious theme. All of these observances became the core calendar for many Baptist congregations. Denominational "promotions" were added to the core—fund drives for various missions and days of "recognition" such as graduation, Rally Day, Off-to-College Day, and Camps and Conferences Sunday.

Other than hymnals, American Baptists published no "official" liturgical directories or worship books for use in the pews. However, denominational publishing houses have printed pastors' resource books produced by individual authors. One such book, by G. Edwin Osborn (1953), reflects the influence of the American civil calendar. It contains a suggested lectionary and calendar with "thirteen key dates"—six civil and six religious, along with Thanksgiving. This book, a companion to a hymnal (1953) published jointly by the American Baptists (Judson Press) and the Disciples of Christ (Bethany Press), found limited acceptance in both denominations.

Two other books published for American Baptists have also met with limited success. John Skoglund's 1968 service book, now out of print,

maintained the tradition of those Baptists who did not wholly reject the religious calendar or prayer book. Skoglund utilized liturgies and a calendar similar to those of the pre-1965 American Episcopal and Lutheran churches. He also included resources for use on civil occasions observed in churches, but these are clearly segregated from the religious calendar itself. His calendar-lectionary contains *no* reference to a civil observance and principally follows the 1928 Episcopal *Book of Common Prayer*. However, the book was seldom used in the pew as a worship book. The other book, a pastor's manual and planning resource by Orlando Tibetts (1986), is topically—rather than liturgically—arranged. It contains resources for "special days or seasons" (half from the civil calendar) but is otherwise unhelpful for the pastor-liturgist who is seriously following the Christian year.

——— Recovering a Christian Calendar ———

As a denomination, American Baptists are not classed as "liturgical," yet many of their churches and clergy use worship orders and materials which are indistinguishable from those of their liturgical sisters and brothers. Each American Baptist congregation exercises the right to determine its own and use and practice in worship. This right includes the freedom to use, or to abstain from using, any particular form or style of Christian worship—or any particular book, calendar, or lectionary.

As have other denominations since Vatican II, American Baptists are developing a new understanding of Christian worship and of liturgies ancient and modern. Unlike those denominations that have official national offices or commissions on worship, American Baptist involvement in this renewal has had to rise from the grassroots—from individual congregations and individual laity and clergy. Several unsuccessful attempts were made to form a denomination-wide interest group in liturgy from the 1950s to the 1970s. Finally, in 1989, "Liturgy & Life: the American Baptist Fellowship for Liturgical Renewal," was organized and has begun to emerge as a responsible forum for addressing worship-related issues among American Baptists.

Since 1965, various American Baptist churches began to move away from the civil calendar. Usually, without dropping civil observances, they added some distinctly Christian holy days and times, such as Advent or Lent. Pentecost and Epiphany also began to receive attention, though it is still common for Pentecost to be overshadowed, or excluded altogether, when it occurs at the same time as Mother's Day or Memorial Day. Similarly, many parishioners, exhausted long before noon of Christmas day, have little energy or interest in extending the Nativity festival into the New Year, to Epiphany.

Though there have been positive developments in liturgy for American Baptists, those pastors and congregations who desire to stay attuned to developments in liturgy have had to borrow and adapt resources, calendars, and lectionaries from their brothers and sisters in other denominations and will likely continue to have to do so for some time. Yet, those American Baptists most involved in liturgical renewal are also those in dialogue with their counterparts in other denominations, seeking to cooperate rather than to compete, and to develop and to own a common understanding of Christian liturgy and time.

A denomination-wide program which includes a focus on American Baptist worship is being developed in the 1990s. It is unlikely that this program will produce any official American Baptist worship books, lectionaries, or Christian year calendars, yet there is hope that it will stimulate and intensify interest in worship and liturgy.

Ronald K. Freyer Nicholas

107 • ANGLICAN/EPISCOPAL CHURCHES

Worship in the Anglican Communion is structured by liturgical celebration of the Christian year, centering on Easter. In recent decades, greater emphasis has been placed on the paschal and baptismal nature of the church year and on observing the complete yearly cycle, not just major festivals.

The churches of the Anglican Communion inherited the Christian year from the pre-Reformation church in England. It has been an integral part of the worship of the _Book of Common Prayer_ since 1549, and its use was staunchly defended in the seventeenth-century Anglican-Puritan controversy.

The liturgical movement of the twentieth cen-

tury has brought a renewal and deepening of the theological understanding of the Christian year and the reform of many details in its practice. The Episcopal liturgist Massey H. Shepherd has aptly summarized the theological conception behind such reform.

The Christian year is a mystery through which every moment and all the times and seasons of this life are transcended and fulfilled in that reality which is beyond time. Each single holy day...is of itself a sacrament of the whole gospel. Each single feast renews the fullness and fulfillment of the Feast of Feasts, our death and resurrection with Christ.
(_Liturgy and Education_ [1965], 99)

Celebrating the Paschal Mystery

In the renewed understanding of the year, the weekly celebration of Sunday as the Lord's Day, the day of resurrection, is primary. But the paschal mystery of our dying and rising with Christ is celebrated not only weekly, but in the whole framework of the year. The celebration of Easter, beginning with the Great Vigil in the night between Holy Saturday and Easter day and continuing for fifty days until the day of Pentecost, is the year's theological and structural center. The celebrations of the ascension of Christ on the fortieth day and the descent of the Holy Spirit on the fiftieth day are a part of one overarching celebration.

The forty-day observance of Lent, beginning on Ash Wednesday and continuing through Holy Week, is a season of solemn preparation, expressed in fasting and penitence, for the joy of Easter. Increasingly, Lent is also seen as a time for the preparation of catechumens for Easter baptism. Palm Sunday, the first day of Holy Week, is also the Sunday of Passion and celebrates both the triumphal entry into Jerusalem and the passion and death of Christ. Maundy Thursday commemorates the Last Supper, with its foot washing and institution of the Eucharist. Good Friday celebrates the Crucifixion and Christ's conquest of death. The importance of the Great Vigil, marking the transition from Lent to Easter, is being gradually realized, and the Vigil is appearing in increasing numbers of parish calendars.

The Christmas festival—the twelve days from

Christmas to Epiphany—forms the center of a secondary cycle celebrating redemption viewed through the lens of the incarnation. Christmas is preceded by four weeks of Advent, and its celebration continues until the Baptism of Christ on the Sunday after Epiphany. The seasons after Epiphany and after Pentecost complete the cycle of the year.

In addition, a cycle of major and minor holy days commemorates the saints and heroes of the Christian church on fixed dates throughout the year. These observances also refer back to the main theme of our participation in Christ's resurrection, "since the triumphs of the saints are a continuation and manifestation of the Paschal victory of Christ" (*Lesser Feasts and Fasts* [1979], 58). The major holy days have been a part of the calendar since the sixteenth century but have not always been everywhere observed. Liturgical celebration of the minor holy days began officially in 1963 in the United States and is now quite common.

Recent Changes

Specific changes in the latest service books (the 1985 *Book of Alternative Services* in Canada and the 1979 *Book of Common Prayer* in the United States) include the designation of the Sunday after Epiphany (January 6) as the Baptism of our Lord, the elimination of the seasons of pre-Lent and Passiontide, the inclusion of the former Ascensiontide within the fifty days of Easter, and the designation of the Sundays following Pentecost as Sundays after Pentecost, rather than after Trinity. The central theme of the Advent season has also been changed, no longer emphasizing almost exclusively the eschatological Second Advent. Now, after attention is given to the Second Advent on the last Sunday after Pentecost and the first Sunday of Advent, the focus shifts to the Annunciation and the First Advent on the fourth and final Sunday. This procedure ties the season more obviously to Christmas and Epiphany and makes clearer the nature of the Advent celebration as both the beginning and the end of the Christian year.

Canadian Anglicans and American Episcopalians celebrate the Christian year through the use of a lectionary which, with minor variations, is common to Roman Catholics, Anglicans, Lutherans, and several other North American churches.

Although the celebration of the Christian year has always been a part of Anglican worship, the emphasis on its paschal nature has only been common since the 1960s. Also, the integration of the entire yearly cycle, not just Lent and the major festivals, into Sunday worship has become more general. Over this same period the baptismal nature of the church year has become more apparent. Public baptisms have been incorporated into Sunday services at specific points on the calendar, with the Easter Vigil as the great baptismal day, and secondary baptismal celebrations on Pentecost, the Baptism of Christ, and All Saints' Day (November 1).

The Christian year and its accompanying lectionary are widely used as the framework for educational programs for both children and adults, and an increased emphasis throughout the church on liturgical preaching has made the preaching much more seasonal. A similar emphasis is seen in an increased number of seasonal hymns in *The Hymnal 1982*. The seasons are also marked by the burning of the paschal candle throughout the fifty days of Easter and the lighting of Advent wreaths during that season.

The celebration of the Christian year, and the changes made recently in that celebration, do not seem to have caused any marked reaction throughout the church. Many of these changes in emphasis accompanied the introduction of the new prayer book and hymnal and were not themselves matters of note or controversy. The restoration of the Great Vigil of Easter, however, involving as it does a change in the popular celebration of a major festival, has been accepted more slowly than the other changes.

This emphasis on the church year is by no means new to Anglicanism. However, though many examples of calendar-based piety and devotion survive from the nineteenth century, this mode of worship has not become more central to the life of the whole church, not simply to a liturgically-minded elite. In sum, contemporary Anglican worship is based upon the liturgical celebration of the Christian year and the Feast of Feasts which is its center.

Leonal L. Mitchell

108 • ASSEMBLIES OF GOD CHURCHES

The church calendar in the Assemblies of God includes only some of the major events of the Christian year, but _also designates numerous days for promotion of denominational programs and recognizes national holidays and ecumenical observances. Congregations have considerable freedom in choosing which days to observe and how to observe them. Due in part to the influence of charismatics with backgrounds in the liturgical churches, some Assemblies of God pastors are beginning to incorporate more of the events of the traditional church year into worship._

The monthly minister's magazine, _Advance_, the major channel of communication between Assemblies of God denominational headquarters and local pastors, each year contains in its August issue a thirty-two-page supplement called the "Pastor's Planbook." The planbook reveals much about yearly observances in the Assemblies of God, for it includes a 32" x 22" poster-sized calendar designed to aid the pastor in tracing and evaluating the progress of the church for the next calendar year. The Master Calendar designated 1992, the third year of the denomination's "Decade of Harvest," as the "Year of Action" with the theme of "Win Them by All Means" (1 Cor. 9:22). In addition to the printed designations, the pastor may mark on the calendar what the emphasis will be for the year and what special days and events they will celebrate, sponsor, and promote.

The Planbook Calendar and Liturgical Life

Several features of the planbook and calendar provide insight on the liturgical life of the Assemblies of God. First, the denomination's worship calendar matches that of the calendar year. Our year does not start with Advent as with most other churches.

Second, the only liturgical or solely Christian events printed on the calendar include Palm Sunday, Good Friday, Easter, Pentecost Sunday, Reformation Day, and Christmas. There is no mention of Advent, Epiphany, Lent, Ascension Day, Trinity Sunday, Christ the King Sunday, or any of the other liturgical celebrations of many of the historical Protestant churches or Anglicanism.

Third, by far the most significant number of events are what could be called denominational program days. There is a heavy emphasis on missions in the Assemblies of God liturgical calendar. In the "Pastor's Planbook," the first Sunday of each

month is listed as "Missions Sunday." Also, on the months where there are five Sundays, there is a fundraising program for special missions projects called "Fifth Dimension." Other missions-oriented Sundays—both home and foreign—include Teen Challenge Day, Boys and Girls Missionary Crusade Day (children), New Church Evangelism Day, Light-for-the-Lost Day (men's department program), Intercultural Ministries Day, Chi Alpha Campus Ministries Day, Prison Sunday, and Speed-the-Light Day (youth).

Besides these various missions-oriented Sundays are Sundays designated for promoting and raising funds for a wide range of denominational activities and concerns. Among such days are Men's Day, Women's Ministries Day, Church Membership Day, Cradle Roll Day, Child Care Day, Youth Day, Family Week, Missionettes Week (girl's program), High School Day, Aged Minister's Assistance Day, Military Personnel Day, College Commitment Day (for Assemblies of God schools), National Ministers Day, National Sunday School Day, Royal Ranger Week (boy scouting program), Stewardship Sunday, and "Revivaltime" World Prayer meeting (radio ministry). Another denominational event for the year includes a week of prayer emphasis in January.

Fourth, the calendar reflects an ecumenical dimension of the Assemblies of God. It includes, for example, Sanctity of Human Life Sunday (third week of January), World Day of Prayer (March), National Day of Prayer (May), and Bible Sunday (December).

Fifth, national American holidays are listed, such as New Year's Day, Martin Luther King Day, President's Day, Memorial Day, Independence Day, Labor Day, Columbus Day, Election Day, Veteran's Day, and Thanksgiving Day. Finally, there are civil days of celebration, but which are not considered as holidays, such as Valentine's Day, Mother's Day, Armed Forces Day, Children's Day, Father's Day, Single Adult Day, and Watch Night.

With all of these liturgical, denominational, ecumenical, national and civil emphases, only seventeen Sundays on the 1992 calendar were open, with no special theme recommended. Eight Sundays have two items of emphasis on the same day.

Free Use of the Calendar

The Assemblies of God is in the free-church tradition, which means each congregation is sovereign to govern itself and to establish its own liturgical schedule and style. There are no weekly lectionary or designated Scripture readings, nor use of any of the councilor creeds of the church. Although this freedom allows for a great deal of creativity on the part of pastors and worship leaders, it also makes it difficult to describe the "typical" Assemblies of God pattern of worship. Each church is free to use or refuse any or all denominational emphases recommended in the "Pastor's Planbook" and Master Calendar.

Some Assemblies of God pastors are beginning to incorporate some of the more traditional liturgical events into church life. Just where this influence is coming from is hard to say, but no doubt charismatics moving from the historic churches into the Assemblies of God have made an impact by bringing with them an appreciation for the liturgical practices they had previously known. For example, many Assemblies of God congregations now celebrate the four Sundays of Advent and Epiphany Sunday. Others give some kind of recognition to Lent. Others offer special services during Holy Week and on Christmas Eve. Some churches have found ways to offer Communion more than only once a month. Drama and dance are sometimes being used in worship, although this is still rather controversial. It is likely that various creative endeavors will continue and that many pastors will move toward following more closely the Christian liturgical year and putting less emphasis upon denominational and national themes.

In *A Church with a Promise* (Springfield, Mo.: Gospel Publishing House, 1990), David A. Womack describes the Assemblies of God to the outsider looking for a church home as "a church for our times." He describes our worship as "informal and spontaneous" and observes that we would rather "err on the side of friendliness with each other and confidence in the presence of God than to approach God and His people with a cold or ceremonious attitude." However, in addition to being a church with a promise, we are a church in transition, moving to a new dimension of development and maturity. One sign of that movement, among the larger congregations at least, is a new and deeper appreciation for the historic Christian faith as demonstrated in the observance of the Christian liturgical year.

Jerry L. Sandidge

109 ✦ BAPTIST (EVANGELICAL DENOMINATIONS AND INDEPENDENT BAPTIST CHURCHES)

The Meadow Hills Baptist Church in Aurora, Colorado, provides an exception to the suspicion of the Christian year that generally prevails among independent Baptist churches. This congregation has found practice of the Christian year to be a powerful means of deepening evangelical faith.

Most evangelical Baptist churches have little contact with the Christian year except on the Sunday before Christmas and Easter Sunday. Occasionally one can find a Good Friday service. Many parishioners feel that observance of the Christian year would distract from or even work against the primary mission of the church, which is to implement the Great Commission—making disciples from all nations and baptizing them. Widespread lack of knowledge about most of the themes of the Christian year is combined with a suspicion that those Christians who practice such "non-biblical" activities do so as a dry, unfulfilling ritual, which seems completely irrelevant in our age of spiritual freedom, freshness, and spontaneity from the Holy Spirit. Denominational publishing houses mirror these positions and provide no instruction, not even historical information, on the subject of the Christian year.

—— Discovery of the Christian Year ——

This author's Baptist church is a rare exception to the above profile. Drawing from instructive, if limited exposure to liturgical environments and considerable study of church history and Christian symbols, we have begun to learn the value of periodically focusing on all the major themes of our Christian faith. Our celebration of the Christmas season has expanded to encompass Advent and Epiphany as well as Christmas. And along with Easter, we now observe Lent and Pentecost. After using the Christian year as a primary basis of our worship for five years, our congregation would have it no other way. Such observance gives us a sense of the recurring celebration, anticipation, and challenge to all that our Lord has designed us to be.

Advent is anticipated months before it arrives. We celebrate not only the promise of Jesus' coming as a baby in the manger, but we also rejoice in the anticipation of his second coming. During

Advent we sing primarily carols that invite or promise Jesus' coming to be in our midst. Most Christmas carols are not sung before Christmas Eve. We then sing them for several weeks until Epiphany. As we celebrate the wise men giving gifts to our Lord, we also celebrate the many gifts that God gives to us, including spiritual gifts. In the Lenten season we rediscover the uniqueness of our Christian faith, God's plan for our redemption, the sacrifice of God's Son, Jesus, on the cross. This gives us the opportunity to sing many hymns about the cross and to examine prayerfully all that we are doing both in and outside the church. During Holy Week we read aloud the Scriptures concerning Jesus' triumphal entry into Jerusalem, the Last Supper, and the Crucifixion, and sometimes we reenact these scenes in simple fashion. Reliving these events in Jesus' ministry each year brings fresh appreciation of his great love and sacrifice for us and challenges us to enthusiastic obedience. After the culmination of Holy Week on Easter Sunday, the focus on Christ's resurrection continues several weeks. We then turn attention to God's great gift of the Holy Spirit displayed at Pentecost.

Walking through each of these main events in the experience of Jesus provides an endless list of praise themes, sermon topics and texts. There is no difficulty even connecting the Christian year with many topical series of sermons.

Worship Deepened

Initially, this change from the previous ritual of three hymns, offering, special music, and sermon to themes from the Christian year met with some resistance. However, such resistance was generally from those who had strong resistances to many types of changes, rather than from those who had previously chosen to leave a liturgical environment. The former Catholics, Lutherans, and Episcopalians who have become a part of our congregation have in many cases experienced new meaning in their worship life by bringing their evangelical faith to observance of the Christian year. Those who have their first taste of the Christian year in our congregation often find a sense of stability and continuity in their Christian faith and worship.

Our structure of prayers, confessions, singing (even chanting) of the Psalms, connected by the focus of the Christian year gives just enough structure to our worship to enable each person to offer praise and adoration to our Lord. This pattern provides opportunity for pastoral guidance toward effective worship not afforded by the traditional preaching service. We believe God has richly blessed us in our discovery of the Christian year.

Rev. Larry D. Ellis

110 ✦ Baptist General Conference

Bethlehem Baptist Church in Minneapolis, a congregation in the Baptist General Conference, has in recent years begun to place strong emphasis on observing some seasons of the Christian year. The full traditional year is not observed, however, so that some times may be designated for particular attention to concerns such as missions and family life.

Because congregations are independent from any clerical or denominational hierarchy in Baptist polity, this article will describe the state of the Christian year in the worship renewal in one church of the Baptist General Conference rather than attempting to generalize about the entire denomination.

Historically, Baptists have distanced themselves from many liturgical forms, such as following the Christian year, normally associated with mainline denominations. However, in the last decade Bethlehem Baptist Church has begun to devote attention to certain seasons of the Christian year—Advent, Christmastide, Lent, Eastertide, and Pentecost. The development was largely prompted by the congregation's (and pastor's) belief in the importance of preparation for the high days of Christmas and Easter and that a direct correlation exists between the time one invests in preparation and the intensity one experiences in celebration.

Countering Commercialism

The Advent season was a great time to institute the Christian year because our culture does so much to promote the commercial way of preparing for Christmas. Most Christians, therefore, see the need to offset the influence of commercialism and reclaim the spiritual theme of our Lord's birth. Bethlehem implemented observance of Advent through such means as poems written by the pastor, candles, purple choir stoles, and a large banner. As a result, Advent has become the most beautiful time of the year at the church, and the congregation prepared for more meaningful participation in the annual Christmas Eve Candlelight Ceremony of Lessons and Carols—undoubtedly the most beautiful service of the year.

If Advent was a particularly good point at which to introduce the Christian year, Lent was the season during which implementation of the year was most needed. While our culture exerts a lot of influence (however misdirected) to prepare us for Christmas, all that Madison Avenue has to offer for Easter is eggs and rabbits! Thus, the church faces an even greater challenge in cultivating preparation for what is, theologically, the most important day of the year during the Lenten season.

Observance of Lent is marked by the gradual extinguishing of seven Lenten candles, and the use of banners, purple choir stoles, pulpit tapestries, sculpture, music that is meditative and focused on Passion texts, and visual art of the Crucifixion. Through the use of these symbols and media, Lent has become the most reflective and sobering time of the year, preparing the congregation to experience more fully the meaning of Holy Week. Palm Sunday usually involves our children's choirs with palms and processions. But the exuberance and loudness of Palm Sunday praise soon quiets into the soberness of Maundy Thursday Communion, undoubtedly the most solemn service of the year. The sanctuary is darkly lit, the choir wears no colored stoles. After a silent processional, the music is very meditative and somber. Communion is received in complete silence, the last Lenten candle is extinguished, and all worshipers are asked to leave the sanctuary in silence to ponder all that they have heard and experienced.

Then, on Easter Sunday, we are ready to celebrate all day long, with all of our might. Eastertide has begun! The Easter morning celebrations include choir, brass, and congregational singing of the joyful music of Easter. The sanctuary resounds with the Easter greeting "The Lord is risen! The Lord is risen indeed!" Banners and pulpit tapestries are hung, choir stoles are white, and all of the Lenten candles are lit, signifying that Christ defeated death and lives forever! We then conclude this day of days by gathering back at the church in the evening for the Festival of the Resurrection. The most important event in all of history calls for the most glorious of all celebrations—and that is what the Festival of the Resurrection is intended to be. On this night, we try to "pull out all the stops" in celebration of Christ's triumph over death. The service is led by a 100-voice festival choir with brass and includes a lot of congregational participation in song, litanies, and shouts of praise.

Pentecost Parade

The candles remain lit throughout Eastertide and are on display through Pentecost Sunday. Pentecost marks the end of our church's observance of the Christian year. We try to make this day special by doing something bold. Most recently, we have marched through downtown Minneapolis using one of Graham Kendrick's Praise Processions. Huge colorful banners are carried, music is sung, leaflets are distributed, and the joy of the Lord is seen and experienced in our neighborhood—all in the power and spirit of Pentecost. We conclude the event by gathering in a local park for a picnic with those from the neighborhood who have joined us in the parade.

At this point, it seems unlikely that we will broaden our observances of the Christian year to other seasons or days of the Christian year in the near future. With partial observance of the Christian year, there is still enough flexibility in the calendar for other emphasis we have throughout the year, such as Prayer Week, Family Week, and Missions Week. This approach makes for a balance appropriate for our congregation.

Dean Palermo

111 ◆ BRETHREN (PLYMOUTH) ASSEMBLIES

Powerful theological and historical positions make for continued resistance to the Christian year among the (Plymouth) Brethren. Christmas and Easter are viewed mainly as opportunities for evangelism.

The (Plymouth) Brethren, in the tradition of free-church Protestantism, have historically been adverse to practices such as the Christian year that they cannot justify with a direct appeal to Scripture. They have given minimal recognition to Christmas and Easter as Christian holidays and have observed these days more for their evangelistic potential than as a celebration of the lordship of Christ over time. They reason that since many unbelieving persons in North America still have some consciousness of the importance of going to church on these holidays, Christmas and Easter are opportune times to preach the gospel themes of Incarnation and Crucifixion/Resurrection to a larger-than-normal audience. But, for the most part, the Christian year is completely ignored by the Brethren.

—— Resistance to the Christian Year ——

Several reasons may account for this avoidance. First, the early Brethren were strict biblicists who had little room for extra-biblical traditions. They followed the principle that practices not found in Scripture must be _disallowed_ rather than simply left as a matter of preference. Among their leaders were former Anglicans who were well-acquainted with the ecclesiastical calendar, but the strict model of _sola scriptura_ they adopted left them without justification for following it.

John Nelson Darby, a former Anglican priest and the dominant early Brethren leader, explained their position in a response to a Roman Catholic priest regarding the historic practice of Lent: "tradition is obscure, variable, and establishes nothing—can demonstrate nothing—which Scripture does not prove; and that Scripture is clear and simple. For Lent there is no warrant, and it is not in Scripture . . . " (_Collected Writings,_ 18:76). This kind of thinking was natural to the early Brethren who came from dissenting church bodies (such as Edward Cronin and Edward Wilson) and reinforced their disdain for "unbiblical" traditions.

A second reason why the Brethren disregard the Christian year is their tendency to identify the leading of the Spirit with that which is spontaneous in worship. This conviction led them not only to abandon or minimize any structure and planning in their worship (and sometimes preaching) but also to avoid the use of a liturgical calendar or set prayers. The Spirit of God was understood as only or predominantly manifest in spontaneous and immediate work in the assembly rather than in the planned or humanly-guided actions. If Christ is Lord of the assembly, then _he_ is to lead the worship rather than any human leader who sets a pattern for the year or even the week.

A third factor is the tendency to follow a heavenly/earthly or spiritual/fleshly dichotomy. Liturgical practice is associated with the material or this-worldly, which must be avoided in favor of the "heavenly reality" and the eschatological hope that will at any moment swallow up the "evils of this world." John Darby expressed this bifurcation with this appeal: "It is time to be entirely heavenly, for the earth is far from God, and daily its darkness closes in, but we belong to the light, and await another day" (_Letters,_ 1:188).

A fourth reason for the avoidance of the Christian year can be found in the sectarian emphasis that developed particularly among the Exclusive Brethren under the dominant influence of John Darby and his form of dispensational thought. Darby taught that the church was "in ruins" at the end of its dispensation, simply awaiting the judgment of God. In his thinking, the Brethren were largely those who "came out" of the tradition-infested and degradation-infested ecclesiastical structures to "gather in twos or threes" so as to gather to Christ alone, and to await his soon return (see, in this regard, Darby's 1840 essay "On the Formation of Churches" in his _Collected Writings,_ 1:138-55).

Thus, to "bring over" any ecclesiastical baggage, such as a liturgical calendar that reflects the Christian year, would simply be unacceptable. Since the church is understood to be in ruins, believers ought not even attempt to imitate structures found in the New Testament church, much less the structures of the contaminated descendant of that church in the contemporary world. And this kind of thinking is not restricted to the Exclusive Brethren, in view of the cross-pollination that occurred (especially in North America) between Exclusive and Open Brethren.

A final reason is the dominant Brethren value of "simplicity." To the Brethren, anything highly organized or structured makes the Christian faith too complex, and obscures the need for maintaining a simple and unabashed faith in the Lord Jesus Christ and his Word alone. With this dominating value, motivation toward any kind of liturgical calendar can find no room.

———— Prospects for Change ————

Little change in attitude toward the Christian year has occurred among the Brethren in recent years except for scattered interest by "radical" Open Brethren assemblies that feel free to employ elements from the historic churches that may enhance or broaden their worship experience. But such attempts have brought the authenticity of these more progressive assemblies into question by others in the movement. The use of traditional elements such as the Christian year is viewed, all too often, as retrogressive: it represents what was "left behind" when the Brethren movement emerged.

Therefore, unless there is a fresh resurgence of biblical values among segments of the Brethren that is compatible with historic core values they hold, there is not likely to be much collective appreciation of the Christian year in the near future. Additionally, the absence of an ecclesiastical hierarchy means there is no structure higher than the local congregation to encourage or impose such a practice. And, with the emphasis on lay eldership over theologically-trained leadership, it is unlikely that the Brethren will develop much interest in the broader church's understanding and appreciation of the Christian year and the philosophy behind it.

Rex A. Koiviso

112 ✦ CHARISMATIC CHURCHES

Charismatic churches often began in a reaction against the formalism of historic denominations, and the charismatic movement as a whole has shown little interest in any parts of the traditional Christian year outside of Christmas and Easter. However, many of these churches have begun to recover aspects of the Old Testament festal calendar, and there is renewed interest in the historic Christian calendar as well.

Observance of the traditional Christian year has been all but ignored by the churches in the charismatic tradition, with the exception of the special celebration of the Christmas and Easter seasons. As Christians from various traditions encountered the work of the Holy Spirit in a charismatic way, many clustered themselves into new fellowships and left the Christian year behind. They preferred an open, informal format with little or no structure so that the Spirit would move in whichever direction he wished, regardless of the liturgical season. Many new charismatics who had exited denominations that observed the tra-

ditional liturgical calendar rejected it as part of their former church's "dead form."

In their newfound freedom, however, these charismatic fellowships began to introduce new "seasons" of their own. These seasons were built around the preaching topics or ministry emphases of the local church, such as spiritual gifts, healing, praise, and worship, the end times, the prophetic church, the family, evangelism and outreach, building programs, and so on. The church would focus on these concerns and emphases for several weeks through various means: preaching, worship choruses, special times of prayer, conferences, and visiting speakers or ministries.

The charismatic community has continually valued the "now word" or *rhema* of God in addition to the inscripturated Word or *logos*. As a result, flexibility to the movement of the Spirit has been the watchword, even in the midst of a special series or emphasis. God is given the opportunity to reveal his in-season word for the church, the word that speaks to the need of the hour and the current work the Lord is doing in the body, both locally and globally.

The principal celebrations of Christmas and Easter often involve special cantatas or musical-dramatic productions with a primary focus on evangelism and outreach to the community. Some churches are locally or regionally known for these large-scale productions that run for several nights and draw many from outside the congregation. One such church, Full Faith Church of Love in Kansas City, has in recent years offered the same program every Easter season, "Behold the Lamb." With a large cast, extensive costuming, and elaborate special effects, this event reaches many people with the message of Jesus Christ.

While distancing themselves from the concept of following a liturgical year, many charismatic churches have adopted the celebration of some Jewish feasts. Charismatics have been especially interested in the types and models of the Old Testament, including the spiritual and prophetic significance of the Israelite feasts—a fascination that which has led these churches to be more predisposed to celebrating the festivals of the Old Covenant instead of many of the traditional Christian year. The tabernacle/temple model of worship, with its progression from outer court through the sanctuary into the most holy place, and the proliferation of Messianic congregations have been other factors leading to an interest in the biblical festal calendar. Some charismatic churches have celebrated Passover meals and the Jewish Pentecost in the effort to understand the Hebraic roots of Christianity. Each year in October, thousands of worshipers from around the world gather in Jerusalem for the Christian Feast of Tabernacles, a festival noted for its outstanding music, colorful dance, and high pageantry. Some local churches in North America have also begun to schedule an annual Feast of Tabernacles, a time of heightened celebration of the Lord's glory in praise and worship, incorporating dance and other worship arts.

Resistance to following the traditional liturgical year is still quite strong in charismatic circles. Most leaders fear that a recovery of traditional seasons and days would reintroduce "dead form" to the church. One charismatic pastor who became part of a branch of the historic church responded to this concern by noting that "form isn't dead or alive, it's either true or false; people are dead or alive!"

In recent years a few celebrations, in addition to Christmas and Easter, have begun to be integrated into charismatic worship. Maundy Thursday observances of the Lord's Supper have become more and more common; some churches have used a dramatic reenactment of the Last Supper as a tool in evangelistic outreach. Pentecost is now being observed in some congregations with banners, pageantry, and dance in celebration of the coming of the Holy Spirit and the birth of the body of Christ.

For several reasons, pastors have begun to seriously consider the use of a Christian calendar in worship, as well as other aspects of a more traditional liturgy. They have seen their churches becoming lethargic, with members wondering, "Is this all there is to the Christian life?" People from all segments of the charismatic community are expressing concern to their leaders about a lack of stability and safety in their walk with God, and the need for more substance in their pursuit of a relationship with the Lord. While these concerned worshipers are often unable to articulate exactly what they need, many leaders are identifying a desire to return to the traditional values of the early church while not surrendering the emphasis on the work of the Holy Spirit. The implementation of a Christian calendar is one movement

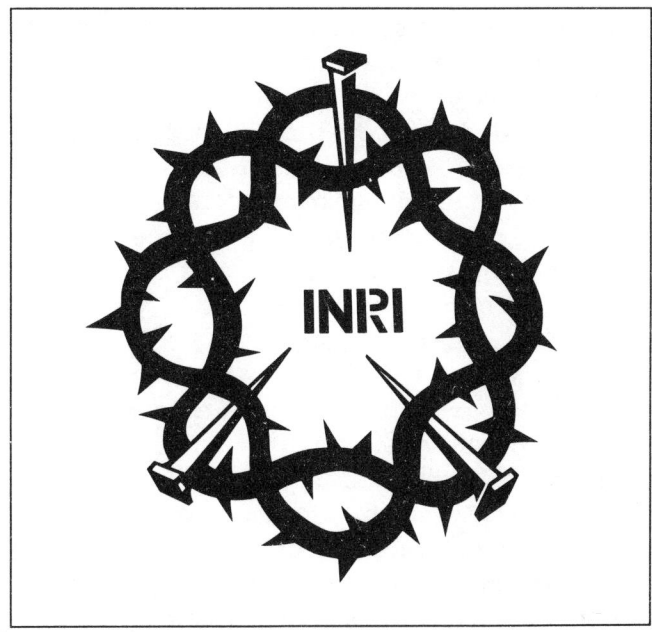

The Crown of Thorns. A well known and ancient symbol of the Passion. Sometimes the crown appears alone. At other times it appears with the nails and the Latin inscription INRI (Jesus of Nazareth, the King of the Jews), like the illustration above.

within the church that is beginning with the clergy. The laity, for their part, are responding in many places with a new enthusiasm for the pattern of the church year, especially where pastors take the time for adequate teaching on the meanings and practices of each season.

The International Worship Symposium, led by its directors, Barry Griffing, Steve Griffing, Larry Dempsey, and David Fisher, has begun to incorporate teaching about the church year into its worship conferences, in the belief this practice needs to be recovered. One of the difficulties encountered is the shortage of people within the charismatic community who are familiar with the church year and able to bridge the gap between traditional practice and the newfound interest among charismatic worshipers.

Another factor inhibiting recover of the liturgical year is the lack of appropriate music in contemporary worship-chorus style. During the Christmas season, for example, many churches seem to abandon their distinctive praise-and-worship format for conventional Christmas carols, resulting in a disconcerting shift in the ambiance and thrust of worship. Charismatic composers need to address this deficiency by creating new music for the various Christian festivals.

Some charismatic leaders are rediscovering the Christian year through personal devotions. They have discovered that a certain amount of structure has added vitality to their individual spiritual life. In the 1970s, use of *The Book of Common Prayer* was instilled in many students at Oral Roberts University by then campus chaplain Bob Stamps. As these men and women went out into prominent ministries, this practice went with them and was passed along to others. In the *BCP* and the Common Lectionary, these charismatic believers discovered an antidote to lack of organization in their personal worship. Since the lectionary readings are based around the traditional church year, the idea of a "year of grace" falls into place through the use of such tools. From their personal pilgrimage through the year in daily devotions, many charismatic Christians have become aware of the value for the whole church in experiencing this journey.

Randolph W. Sly

113 ✦ CHRISTIAN CHURCH (DISCIPLES OF CHRIST)

Worship in the Disciples of Christ denomination was shaped by the conditions of the American frontier during the early nineteenth century. Only in the second half of the twentieth century has widespread use of the Christian year appeared. A worship calendar which became popular in the 1950s helped prepare the way, combining some historic Christian festivals with national and denominational observances. Since the 1960s, Disciples' participation in ecumenical worship renewal has encouraged full embrace of the Christian year.

The early Disciples on the frontier of western Pennsylvania and western Virginia did not use the Christian year as the basis for worship. They followed the style and practice of frontier worship with the exception of participating in the Lord's Supper every Lord's Day. The presence of the Lord's Supper became, and has remained, the defining aspect of Disciples worship. This fact is important for understanding the Disciples recent embrace of the Christian year and the lectionary.

Through the late nineteenth and early twentieth centuries, Disciples joined a number of other churches in evolving an informal calendar that consisted of a combination of Christian holy days and cultural holidays. While these days provided a focus for organizing worship on given Sundays, the week-to-week worship tended not to follow an organized pattern. Preaching tended to be based on random selection of texts or topics.

The Service Book: Preparation for the Christian Year

A landmark for Disciples worship came in 1953 when its denominational publishing house brought out *Christian Worship: A Service Book*, edited by G. Edwin Osborn. The book was not officially authorized by the church's deliberative body—the International Convention of Christian Churches and Churches of Christ—but it did have the approval of the publishing house and a number of leaders in the church's general offices in Indianapolis. While specifically "designed for the voluntary use of nonliturgical churches," the book carried with it the impetus of informal but impressive sanction. Its approach to worship followed the psychological model popularized by von Ogden Vogt a generation earlier. This pattern prevails in some congregations even today.

The Service Book began with a calendar for the Christian year. This calendar included some of the most prominent historical days and seasons of the Christian year such as Advent, Christmas, and Lent, but also virtually canonized national quasi-religious holidays like Memorial Day and Thanksgiving and denominational emphases including Race Relations Sunday, Rural Life Sunday, and Christian Literature Week. The latter components of this calendar were widely followed among Disciples through the 1960s. Few congregations attempted to follow the traditional Christian year in a systematic way.

The Service Book also contained a five-year lectionary that was designed to run from January 1 to December 31. The readings were not closely correlated with the historic lectionary. This lectionary was used in only a handful of pulpits. The bulk of the Service Book consisted of worship materials (e.g., litanies and responsive readings). Some of these materials do relate to the historic Christian year, but most are designed either to serve the calendar in the book or to be used independently.

Whatever its shortcomings, the Service Book helped prepare Disciples for the introduction of the Christian year. Although it respected the freedom of local congregations, the book symbolized a common approach to Disciples worship. It helped Disciples realize that the worship of a local congregation is not idiosyncratic but is a part of a larger ecumenical expression. Through its use of litanies and responsive readings and other printed materials, the Service Book moved Disciples toward a more formal style of worship. It also acquainted them with the basic themes of the Christian year and familiarized the idea of a lectionary.

Convergence with Ecumenical Renewal

Disciples leaders joined leaders of the ecumenical churches in the 1960s in rediscovering the Christian year, the lectionary, and the Hippolytean liturgical tradition. Keith Watkins, a professor of worship at Christian Theological Seminary, took a leading role in adapting the recovery of these traditions to Disciples worship and in adapting Disciples worship to these traditions. In particular, he sought to connect the historically prominent role of the Disciples lay elder at the Lord's Table with the broader Christian tradition.

These developments were welcomed by many Disciples leaders for three reasons. First, the Christian year, the lectionary, and the Hippolytean tradition are all centered in the Lord's Supper. The same is true of Disciples worship. While Disciples practice had customarily been much simpler than the new developments, Disciples had both logical and intuitive affinities with the emergence of the historical perspectives. Second, the emerging developments provided a way for Disciples to embody their ecumenical consciousness. Third, the recovery of the Christian year and the lectionary and Hippolytean liturgy connected with it came at a time when Disciples leaders were becoming aware of increasing lethargy, anemia, and sterility in Disciples worship (as in other denominations which had practiced similar styles of worship). Disciples leaders noticed vitality in worship in the liturgical churches that were recovering these historic patterns.

Thankful Praise and Contemporary Practices

In the late 1960s and 1970s, the denomination's office of worship published occasional materials that helped Disciples appropriate the contemporary renewal of worship. In 1987, the denominational publishing house issued _Thankful Praise_, edited by Keith Watkins. Following the lead of Watkins's earlier work, the book adapted the historic liturgy for Disciples practice and vice versa. It followed the Christian year and included the Common Lectionary. Like _Christian Worship: A Service Book,_ Watkins's volume is not officially sanctioned by the General Assembly, the denomination's central deliberative body. But it does represent an approach that is gaining growing approval among Disciples leaders.

Response to _Thankful Praise_ and the movement it represents has been mixed. Many denominational leaders, ministers, and lay leaders are enthusiastic. Approximately half of Disciples congregations make some use of its approach to the Sunday service. But a good many other leaders and congregations find it too big a step to go from Osborn to Watkins in one movement. Some decry the spirit of _Thankful Praise_ as too formal and stiff for the more easygoing style of recent Disciples worship. However, while many of the latter congregations do not embrace _Thankful Praise_, they do embrace the practice of the Christian year. Some denominational leaders informally estimate that at least three-fourths of Disciples congregations mark some of the major seasons and days. The same leaders estimate that about half of Disciples preachers follow the new Common Lectionary.

A congregation tends to respond positively to the Christian year, lectionary, and Hippolytean approach to worship when the new developments are introduced sensitively and with a program of education that helps the congregation understand their purposes.

The Christian year will likely remain the pattern for Disciples worship for some time. Disciples will discuss, with considerable energy, the degree to which it is appropriate to incorporate the approach to the service represented in _Thankful Praise_. At present, the seminary professors responsible for training in worship as well as the denomination's leaders in its general (i.e., international) offices lean towards _Thankful Praise_. But clergy and the church as a whole have yet to come to a consensus.

Ronald J. Allen

114 ◆ CHRISTIAN CHURCHES AND CHURCHES OF CHRIST

The Christian Churches and Churches of Christ have historically avoided the Christian year as one of the unscriptural practices creating division between denominations—a division which their movement sought to overcome. Most now celebrate Christmas and Easter in worship, but these are among yearly observances based on the civil calendar, not the Christian year. Scattered evidence for increased interest in using visual symbols to deepen worship can be seen, but there is little movement toward following the Christian year.

The Restoration Movement, from which the independent Christian churches and Churches of Christ stem, began about two centuries ago as a reaction against the divisive, human inventions of denominationalism. To this day most of these churches almost completely avoid the church calendar, regarding it as unscriptural, ecclesiastical tradition. Most of the churches of Christ do not use music, recognize no special days, seasons, or observances, other than to meet for the Supper each Lord's Day. On the other hand, many Christian churches from Disciples of Christ backgrounds do observe aspects of the Christian year. But the rank and file of the centrist churches recognize no more than one season (Advent) and perhaps three days (Christmas, Easter, and sometimes Pentecost Sunday).

The Primitive Church as Norm

These churches' rejection of liturgical practice grows more out of their critique of mainline Protestant denominations than an effort to avoid Roman Catholic traditions. They generally do not consider themselves to be Protestant, in the sense of focusing on "protest" against the Catholic church. Rather, they challenge denominationalism as a whole. Many of the Christian churches have recently begun to loosen their separatist position toward evangelical Christianity, but the bias against historical denominations remains nearly unanimous.

The Christian churches look only to biblical and apostolic precedent for their worship practices. Any addition to what they perceive to be the simple and informal practice of the primitive church is seen as a later corruption. Hence, any developments or councilor decisions after the first century would at best be given polite consideration but not considered binding. Sources subsequent to the New Testament writings would be used only to shed light on the practice of the church during the lives of the apostles.

A Cultural Calendar

Most independent Christian churches, to be sure, follow a yearly calendar—the secular calendar of the culture around them. Many, and probably most, of the churches regularly acknowledge Mother's Day, Memorial Day, Father's Day, Graduation Sunday, Independence Day, and sometimes even Boy Scout Sunday and other secular occasions. The motivation is evangelism, not worship. Recognition of such days in worship services, it is thought, creates a point of contact with the unchurched people of the community, while the Christian calendar would not, since it is largely unknown to the community. An evangelistic sermon can then be tied into a secular event.

Sermon series sometimes serve as the organizing principle for the year, rather than the secular calendar. Preachers may give topical or expository series of messages or perhaps dedicate a month to a theme—"Stewardship Month" or "Family Month," for example.

Nearly all of the churches will dedicate at least two weeks to Christmas. However, Christmas is acknowledged not because it is part of the church year, but because of its observance as a holiday in the wider culture. Some of the churches might use the term *Advent,* display a simple wreath, and have some readings. Other seasonal events might include the performance of a cantata, a Sunday School program with the children, or a candlelight Communion service on Christmas Eve. But on the Sunday after Christmas, the service will invariably focus on resolutions and goal setting, thus connecting with the New Year holiday rather than following the traditional church calendar.

The majority of Christian churches also celebrate Easter and Holy Week (although most avoid that term). Easter sunrise services are common, as are Good Friday or Maundy Thursday Communion services. But the structuring of the services is entirely up to the individual congregation, and books or other sources are seldom consulted. A few churches recognize Pentecost Sunday occasionally, but virtually none observe other church days such as Reformation Sunday.

Little support for recovery of the Christian year exists among the rank-and-file membership. Some of the Bible colleges and seminaries offer courses that include a few sessions on the calendar, but there seems to be little more than curiosity about the Christian year among the majority. More than a few preachers have preached from the lectionary schedule for a year without making people aware of it, for they would be opposed to it if they knew.

Though most Christian churches are not moving toward recovery of the Christian year, some preachers and many worship leaders are attempting to deepen the worship vocabulary of their congregations through the use of drama and symbolism, with explanations (on-the-fly catechisms, of sorts) of one element at a time. Mountain Christian Church, located in a highly Catholic area in Joppa, Maryland, has a large gothic-style building with a divided chancel and employs more visual symbolism in worship than most Christian churches. For instance, candles are used every week and a veiling of the cross is conducted on Good Friday. Virtually all of the churches using such acts are historic, large city churches previously associated with the Disciples of Christ.

In sum, broad interest in the Christian year or a liturgical approach to worship is still a long way off.

115 ✦ CHRISTIAN AND MISSIONARY ALLIANCE CHURCHES

Both liturgical and Pentecostal styles of worship have been regarded as extremes to be avoided in the Christian and Missionary Alliance. However, some congregations, though still in the minority, are turning to observance of the Christian year in a quest for worship renewal.

Christian and Missionary Alliance churches have not typically celebrated the Christian year. As an evangelical denomination born in the nineteenth-century Holiness revival, it has often taken the middle ground between the more liturgical churches and the Pentecostal/charismatic movement. This attempt to avoid excess has often robbed Alliance congregations of powerful worship experiences. In recent years a growing hunger for renewal in worship has developed. This

hunger has led to a greater openness to other worship forms and traditions. In particular, there is evidence of a recapturing of the power of the Christian year.

Advent and Christmas

New attention is being given, in at least some congregations, to each of the major days and seasons of the Christian year. Many Alliance churches are developing practices that follow or approximate the high-church tradition of celebrating the Advent season with feasts and various rituals designed to help Christians focus on the importance of the Incarnation. Wreaths with candles lit for each Sunday of Advent are becoming increasingly popular. These Advent wreaths are placed at the front of the worship center. As the service begins a representative of the congregation comes forward to light the candle and explain its significance. This provides the church with a weekly reminder of the Advent season.

Christmas banquets are also becoming a common part of the Advent celebration. One of the most unifying experiences Risen King Community Church has had was the 1990 Christmas banquet. It was a new church that had grown to over four hundred members within a year, and very few people really knew each other. The Christmas banquet provided the opportunity to combine the joy of Christ's coming with genuine fellowship and love. These kinds of practices may very well enable Christian and Missionary Alliance churches to regain the celebrative attitude of the early church toward the birth of our Savior.

Recovering the Primacy of Easter

The Easter season is the highlight of the Christian year, but is celebrated in many Christian and Missionary Alliance churches with far less fanfare than Christmas. Sadly, this may have more to do with cultural influence than with spiritual issues. We are reminded of the coming Christmas season by the materialistic retail shopping season. But the spiritual preparation Lent can provide for the Easter celebration is largely neglected within Alliance churches.

Nevertheless, there is evidence of a growing emphasis on the passion, death and resurrection of our Lord Jesus as a part of the church calendar. Musical presentations and cantatas have always been a part of the Alliance heritage. Now, along with these, one frequently hears of Maundy Thursday Communion services, Good Friday prayer meetings, and Easter sunrise celebrations. A now-retired Christian and Missionary Alliance pastor in New England, Rev. Howard Kingsinger, taught this writer the deep spiritual meaning behind these seasonal services and enriched my understanding of Easter as the primary feast of the Christian year.

Pentecost and Spirit-filled Mission

The Easter season culminates with Pentecost, which celebrates the coming of the Holy Spirit to the early church. Pentecost commemorates the empowerment of Christians to win the world for Christ. For a missionary-minded denomination like the Christian and Missionary Alliance, this ought to be one of the high points of the Christian year. Yet Pentecost Sunday is often completely overlooked by the typical Alliance church.

A renewal of emphasis on the power and work of the Holy Spirit, however, is occurring. Christian and Missionary Alliance churches are once again regaining the Spirit-filled vision of their founder, A. B. Simpson. Perhaps this will result in a renewed experience of the liturgical churches' appreciation for the celebration of Pentecost.

For Risen King Community Church, the Doxology has become far more than ritual. It unites the church of today with the saints of the past five hundred years. In the same way the celebration of the Christian year can be far more than ritual. These events drawn from the church's ancient heritage can be full of meaning and power.

Ron Walborn

116 • CHRISTIAN REFORMED CHURCHES

Prior to the 1960s, the Christian Reformed Church (CRC) practiced a form of worship drawn from its Reformation heritage, which entailed a calendar of observances distinct from the traditional Christian year. In the 1960s, liturgical renewal in the CRC coincided with the worship reforms of Vatican II, leading to widespread recovery of the Christian year in the CRC. However, many congregations still worship in accordance with the tra-
ditional Reformed pattern. Others congregations that have adopted a praise-and-worship style recognize major Christian holidays but do not adhere to the church calendar.

It was not long ago that a church in the Christian Reformed tradition could be identified by its acts of worship. The Sunday morning service always included a reading of the Ten Commandments from either Exodus 20 or Deuteronomy 5. The congregation sang Psalms as well as hymns. Most worshipers referred to the pastoral prayer as "the long prayer" because it occupied nearly fifteen and sometimes even twenty minutes of the service. And the sermon at the first of the two Sunday services was almost always an explication of a Lord's Day section of the Heidelberg Catechism.

Each year every congregation was expected to conduct a worship service on Christmas Day, Ascension Day, Thanksgiving Day, Old and New Year's Days, and the synodically designated Prayer Day. These were unusual worship services in that they almost always took place on a weekday. But most awesome of all worship experiences were the quarterly observances of the Lord's Supper. Each of these services required a prepatory message the week prior and an applicatory message at the service immediately following the sacrament.

In those days, members of the Christian Reformed churches knew little or nothing about the Christian year. The Advent season and the Advent wreath were foreign concepts, as were Epiphany and the season of Lent.

Today, there is so much variety of liturgical expression in Christian Reformed churches that it would be nearly impossible to recognize many of them as having their roots in the Swiss reformation. This changing attitude toward worship cannot be appreciated without some understanding of the concept of worship in the Reformed tradition.

The Reformation Legacy

The Reformed tradition has its origin in the Swiss cities of Zurich and Geneva. Although the Reformation leaders of these two cities, Zwingli in Zurich and Calvin in Geneva, were of different temperament and diverse opinion about worship, they were united in rejecting the worship patterns of the Roman Catholic church.

Instead of following Luther, who devoted his energy to revising the existing patterns of worship, Zwingli and Calvin made a clean break. They decided to begin anew by recovering the pattern of worship of the churches in the New Testament and post-New Testament periods prior to the Constantinian era.

Although Zwingli was an accomplished musician and had a great appreciation for the arts, he believed human artistic expressions belonged to the physical realm and were not intended to convey spiritual realities. According to Zwingli, the grace of God was conveyed only through the faithful proclamation of God's Word. He therefore abandoned the Roman Catholic practice of honoring saints, removed all images from the worship space, rejected the prescribed order for worship, and discontinued the use of music in worship. Zwingli was convinced there was only one means of grace: the Word of God and its faithful proclamation. The Lord's Supper was relegated to the status of being a memorial meal rather than a sacramental action on a par with the Word of God.

Calvin differed markedly from Zwingli in his understanding of worship. He was not nearly as suspicious of signs and symbols as was Zwingli. He recognized the Supper as an effective means of grace, and believed that when the faithful gathered for worship, they should always have the opportunity to participate in both Word and sacrament. He also encouraged the singing of Psalms and other biblical texts in worship. However, he and Zwingli were agreed in their rejection of the Christian year as practiced by the Church of Rome in their day. They were also together in advocating biblical preaching which followed the *lectio continua* method.

Calvin's wishes regarding the frequency of celebrating the Supper were not realized during his lifetime and are still not followed in most Reformed churches today. However, Christians in the Reformed tradition continue to place a strong emphasis on preaching and still attend worship to hear a "good" sermon.

Twentieth-Century Renewal Efforts

In the late 1920s and early 1930s there was an attempt to initiate a new order of worship in Christian Reformed churches. A proposed liturgy was rejected, however, primarily for two reasons: the inclusion of an absolution in the liturgy for the morning worship, and the recommendation that every congregation be required to follow the new liturgy.

The rejection of the proposed order left the churches without liturgical guidance. As a result, nearly every church in the denomination followed a very barren order of worship in which the sermon occupied the dominant position. The other acts of worship—the votum and salutation, the reading of the law, the singing of Psalms, the "long prayer," and the offering—were usually referred to as "preliminaries" to the sermon.

In the mid 1960s, a new attempt at liturgical renewal began. Attention was centered primarily on revising the formularies used for the sacramental and ordination services. A concerted effort was made to create formularies that were somewhat shorter and a bit less didactic than the classic ones. This attempt at renewal had no relationship whatsoever to an observance of the Christian year.

Vatican II and Reformed Worship

While Reformed churches were revising their formularies, the Second Vatican Council of the Roman church was in the process of developing a new concept of worship rooted in the Christian year. Most leaders in the Reformed tradition had no idea at that time that the Christian year and its corresponding lectionary as formulated by Vatican II would one day have a significant influence on the way worship would be done in their churches.

Although there were no representatives from the Christian Reformed denomination involved in the Vatican II study of the liturgy, some of its congregations began to recognize the value of the work done by this commission. The later development of the Common Lectionary was also appealing and proved to be a helpful device for developing a weekly liturgy that celebrated the redemption acts of God on an annual basis.

Thus, by the mid-1980s, a growing number of Christian Reformed congregations were following the Christian year in their worship services. Many members of these churches are still learning about the symbolism of the colors that go with each of the seasons and may not be satisfied that their observance of Lent is as it should be. But they recognize a new depth of spirituality in their worship when the Christian year is observed.

A new quarterly called *Reformed Worship* is being published by CRC Publications. It color-codes the issues to correspond with the seasons of the Christian year. Each issue provides refreshing insights into worship and offers many helpful suggestions on how to create liturgies that follow the Christian year. Calvin Seminary now offers electives to students who wish to know more about the Christian year and the rationale behind the lectionary readings corresponding to the liturgical seasons.

Contemporary Diversity

Some Christian Reformed congregations adhere to the Christian year and follow the Common Lectionary throughout the entire year. Others observe the Christmas and Easter cycles and then depart from the suggested biblical readings of the lectionary during Ordinary Time. Many new congregations being planted by missionaries are following a more spontaneous style of worship sometimes called praise and worship. Even some of the long-established congregations are moving in this direction. These churches do observe the major Christian holidays but would not necessarily consider themselves adherents of the Christian year in their style of worship. The majority of churches in the Christian Reformed denomination continue with a more traditional style of Reformed worship.

A challenge now before this denomination is to determine whether it can remain a unified body while permitting considerable diversity in liturgical practice.

Alvin L. Hoksbergen

117 • CHURCH OF GOD, CLEVELAND, TENNESSEE

Resistance to observance of the Christian year is deeply entrenched in the Church of God, Cleveland, tradition. Such formal worship practices have long been considered a hindrance to the believer's freedom and spontaneity in responding to the power of the Holy Spirit. Little movement toward full adoption of the Christian year exists, but use of modified portions of the yearly calendar is becoming more frequent.

Beyond celebrations of Christmas and Easter, very little observance of the Christian year occurs in the Church of God, Cleveland. It simply isn't part of the thought processes and worship patterns that prevail in the denomination. And this neglect in itself deepens the general lack of understanding of the purpose and benefits of the Christian year.

Rejection of Formalism

The suspicion of the Christian year reflects the concerns that prompted the founding of the denomination in the late nineteenth century and which remain vital today. After several years of prayer, R. G. Spurling, Sr., an elderly pastor in the mountains of eastern Tennessee, organized a fellowship of believers who were seeking spiritual renewal. His action was in response to the lack of spiritual life and dead formalism that dominated his own denomination. The Church of God has since continued to reject those worship practices considered representative of a lower level or absence of spirituality. In so doing, it has tended to discard entire systems of suspect practices without evaluating each part separately.

Moreover, by its very nature, the free style of worship predominant in the Church of God fosters a lack of interest in the Christian year. The freedom to choose what to do and when to do it as the Holy Spirit directs is preferred to a human ecclesiastical calendar.

The relative youthfulness of the denomination may also be a factor in the lack of appreciation for the Christian year. The scarcity of major events in the denomination's history worthy of widespread celebration in the worship setting contributes to an apathy about historical observances, a trend that carries over to neglect of commemorating significant events and people in Christian history.

A final factor is the denomination's approach to ministerial training. Since credentialing has not been dependent upon a formal educational standard, many ministers never took programs of study that would have introduced them to the Christian year. Courses in church history and worship would no doubt have corrected this lack of appreciation.

Perpetuate Pentecost

As in other denominations of Pentecostal and Holiness background, the tradition of ignoring the Christian year in the Church of God runs deep.

Any dramatic change would be viewed as a digression from denominational roots. It also would be seen by some as a deviation from the principle of spontaneity in worship.

Therefore, at this point there is no trend toward introducing the Christian year as part of the denomination's guide for worship and observance. However, the influence of the Christian year is manifested in small ways from time to time. One example is the celebration of Pentecost Sunday, which for decades received only minimal attention in the Church of God. Due to the church's Pentecostal theology and practice, Pentecost was considered a regular emphasis throughout the entire year, not just on one day. However, in 1967 the denominational leadership instituted the Perpetuate Pentecost emphasis for each local church to observe on Pentecost Sunday. A special edition of the _Church of God Evangel_ emphasizing the Day of Pentecost described in Acts 2 and giving specifics of Pentecostal doctrine was developed for members and non-members alike. Though that particular program has changed, the net result has been a heightened emphasis on annual celebration of Pentecost, which has lasted to the present.

—————— Channels for Change ——————

Since each local congregation determines its own pattern of observance and worship emphasis, the door is open for the introduction of aspects of the Christian year. The key factor is the preference of the local pastor. If the pastor understands the purpose and benefit of a particular practice and is willing to put forth the effort, there is a strong possibility of its being incorporated as a permanent observance during his tenure of ministry.

The increasing number of pastors with some academic exposure to the Christian year will likely lead to greater observance of it. The denomination's colleges and seminary have introduced courses in worship during the 1980s, and a broader understanding of worship is slowly beginning to appear. Students have been introduced to the strengths of various styles of worship and the benefits from observance of key events. This results in a new openness to practices which previously had been seen as formal and without spiritual value.

A generally increased understanding and appreciation of our broad Christian heritage is also con-

tributing to changing attitudes about the Christian year. Greater recognition of the men and women of past centuries whose contributions became the foundations for today's Christian church has led a few congregations to emphasize Reformation Sunday and thus look to reference points beyond the denomination's particular history.

A recent trend toward larger local congregations may also open the way to selective use of the Christian year. The performance/participation pattern of worship practiced in these congregations lends itself to such usage. Choral presentations are a particularly likely starting point for introduction of aspects of the Christian year in these churches.

No clearly identifiable movement exists to introduce the Christian year as a whole into local church practice. And it is very doubtful there will be one in the next several decades. However, due to the factors mentioned above, portions of the Christian year will be more frequently observed in an increasing number of Church of God congregations.

Jerald Daffe

118 ✦ CHURCH OF THE BRETHREN

It was protest against the liturgical formalism of the official church which in part gave rise to the Church of the Brethren in the eighteenth century. However, the Brethren always sought to be an authentic worshiping community, and in the twentieth century that historic commitment has resulted in widespread appropriation of the Christian year. The extent and style of such observance, however, varies greatly from congregation to congregation.

On any given Sunday at Stone Church of the Brethren in Huntingdon, Pennsylvania—the county seat and the home of Juniata College—one would find the pulpit, lectern, and Communion table covered with appropriately colored paraments. The bulletin would reflect the Common Lectionary reading for the day. The pastor and choir would be robed with stoles to match the paraments. The order of worship would most likely reflect a theme from the Christian year readings for the day.

At the small rural Church of the Brethren less than twenty miles down the road, the word *parament* is not known. There may be a scarf on the pulpit, but it never changes color. The pastor would not even consider being robed. The celebration of the Christian year would be limited to Christmas, Palm Sunday, Easter, the observance of the Love Feast during Holy Week, and an occasional participation in an ecumenical Lenten series in the community.

The contrasting practices of these two congregations within twenty minutes of each other are indicative of the status of the Christian year in the Church of the Brethren. Some local congregations choose to follow it regularly without being religiously bound to it; others give it little or no recognition.

Transformations in a Worshiping Community

How did a movement which, influenced by Pietism and Anabaptism, emerged early in the eighteenth century protesting against "cold liturgy" and the formalism and dogmatism of the official German church, develop into a denomination with widespread recognition and practice of the Christian year in the twentieth century?

Unlike many radical separatists, Brethren felt the need to be a church—a community of faith. Like the Anabaptists, they viewed the church as a fellowship of believers bound together as obedient disciples of Jesus Christ. Coming together in their homes for prayer and Bible study, they accepted the need for a church order and for observances that would be firmly grounded in the New Testament. Some of those observances became ordinances (as opposed to sacraments) and were faithfully followed in a kind of firm and uniform low-church liturgy. Brethren were never nonliturgical; rather, they strongly desired that their liturgy be alive and meaningful. Such a passion necessitates change as life itself changes. The historic commitment to being a worshiping community, the growing need for places to gather for worship, the conviction that order in worship was more desirable than unrestrained emotionalism, and the deeply felt but often unspoken desire that worship have enough life to move the heart and soul as well as the mind, all helped open the door to changes in Brethren worship practices.

Numerous influences furthered the ongoing process of change in worship: growing support for higher education; the expansion of denominational publications; the move from free to salaried ministers; the acceptance of musical instruments in the church; the growing popularity of Sunday schools; the architectural change from "meetinghouse" to church sanctuary; a strong commitment to and support for ecumenical fraternity; and a growing support for the inclusion of fine arts in the celebrations of the church.

Worship Manuals and the Christian Year

The gradual growth of support for the Christian year in the Church of the Brethren can be traced in the manuals produced by the denomination for use by pastors and church leaders. The earliest of these, H. B. Brumbaugh's *The Church Manual* (1888), and other early manuals, made no mention of the Christian year and included no lectionary or worship resources. The 1946 *Minister's Manual*, although making no mention of the lectionary, carried some orders of service under the heading for "Forms and Ceremonies" and included a one-page discussion of "The Christian Year." The manual declared that "the systematic planning of a church year by an increasing number of churches is a hopeful sign." Observing that one reason Easter is such a great day is that it is observed by all the churches at the same time, the manual urged that other days "should be lifted out of the routine and commonplace into which they have fallen." However, it cautioned that "free churches, such as our own, will not likely choose to go as far as the liturgical churches."

The foreword to the 1953 *Manual of Worship and Polity* spoke favorably of openness to change in worship: "No religious society or movement can long endure which does not adapt and apply itself and its body of faith and program to the living generation." While not specifically named, worship resources related to the Christian year were provided, and mention of a recommended lectionary for those who might desire one.

By the publication of *The Book of Worship, Church of the Brethren* in 1964, enough congregations were using liturgical resources (some in more appropriate fashion than others) that the committee preparing the resource devoted considerable space to educating congregations regarding the Christian year. The index shows a large section of some sixty-five pages on resources for the Christian year, which included an explanation of the year, the advantages of observing it, a description of the days and seasons, guidelines for the use of liturgical colors, and a complete lectionary. "The Christian year is suggested as a guide to worship; it is not to be slavishly followed as an absolute authority. Its intelligent use can enrich our worship." The book reminded pastors that the full sweep of Christian doctrine is covered during the Christian year.

The new manual, _For All Who Minister_, published in 1992, continues strong support for observance of the Christian year and included many new resources and the newly-revised lectionary.

A wide diversity of worship practices will continue in the Church of the Brethren. Not only do congregations differ, as seen in the two Pennsylvania churches within twenty minutes of each other, variations in style may in fact occur from pastor to pastor within a given congregation. But conviction about the centrality of the Bible for life and worship, and the desire to celebrate responsibly the full scope of the Good News will continue to encourage Brethren to selective observance of the Christian year.

Earle W. Fike, Jr.

119 ✦ CHURCH OF THE NAZARENE

An appreciation for the spiritual value of the Christian year is emerging in the Church of the Nazarene, despite a history of general antipathy toward it typical of Holiness groups. Many local pastors, with the encouragement and aid of denominational resources, are rediscovering the traditional observances as a means of building up the congregation in the essentials of the faith.

For decades the Christian year was ignored or deemed ritualistic by many pastors in the Church of the Nazarene. Christmas, Palm Sunday, Easter and Pentecost were often given recognition in worship, but the view that the use of the Christian year symbolized formality and destroyed the freedom of the Spirit was widespread. If one subscribed to the use of the Christian calendar, it was done quietly within one's own parish.

Context for Preaching Christ

In a random survey of a cross section of Nazarene pastors conducted for a doctor of ministry project, I discovered that 20 percent gave no place to the Christian year and 55 gave little place, using only major days such as Christmas and Easter. Only 8 percent indicated they observed the Christian year in its entirety, and 25 percent observed portions of the Christian year. However, a new enthusiasm for the Christian year is slowly emerging as education regarding it breaks down reservations. Many pastors are beginning to realize what they have missed these many years and are becoming convinced that the preaching of "Christ and him crucified" is best done in the context of the Christian year.

The congregation where I serve as pastor had never celebrated the Christian year. We chose Advent as the season to introduce it. We focused on the fact that Christian year follows the theme and substance of early apostolic preaching and that its use was part of the rich heritage of our Christian forbears. We displayed an Advent wreath, lighted by groups and families in the congregation. Many in the congregation commented that they had never heard of Advent before, and response to this "new" practice was positive.

We then went on to observe Epiphany, Lent, Pentecost, and the Time of the Church. Members are coming to understand that faithful observance of the Christian year involves worshipers with the essentials of the Christian faith and brings the community of faith into a dynamic relationship with Christ.

Denominational Resources

Many other Nazarene pastors and congregations are pursuing a similar course. _Worship and Preaching Helps_, developed by the Director of Pastoral Ministries for the Church of the Nazarene and published quarterly, has strongly promoted observance of Christian year. Pastors contributed to the publication, and the response to the helps has been very positive. _A Pastor's Worship Resource_, edited by James Spruce, also encourages and provides guidance for worship based on the Christian year.

As time goes by, those within the Holiness tradition are becoming more and more aware that the Christian year is a tool to enable a more effective worship of God. It will structure worship in an increasing number of Nazarene congregations in coming years.

Curtis Lewis

120 • CHURCHES OF CHRIST

The Christian year was among the practices that the Restoration movement from the Churches of Christ repudiated due to lack of specific New Testament warrant. Today, most members of the Churches of Christ are unfamiliar with it. Recently, however, there has been movement toward partial observance of the year, both for evangelistic purposes and for renewal in the church.

Churches of Christ are largely ignorant of the Christian year, and therefore do not make extensive use of it. Historically, churches from the American Restoration Movement have adhered to a nondenominational, free-church tradition that has endeavored to distinguish itself from many of the practices of denominational churches. One of the slogans popularized in the emergence of the Restoration Movement in the early nineteenth century was: "Where the Scriptures speak, we speak; where they are silent, we are silent." Since the New Testament gives no examples or commands to follow a Christian year, the churches growing out of this tradition did not feel free to make use of this plan. Moreover, the majority of Churches of Christ have never been highly liturgical. Thus, members today are largely unfamiliar with, even unaware of the Christian year.

Evangelistic Motivation

In recent years a growing number of ministers have become aware of the Christian year and are beginning to see value in making some use of its structure. For example, more and more Churches of Christ are planning special services which coincide with the Christmas and Easter seasons. This is being done primarily for evangelistic rather than liturgical reasons, however. People who attend church only at Christmas and Easter might be attracted by special services. *Since religious thoughts are already on people's minds, even unchurched people, during these times of year,* worship leaders reason, *let's capitalize on the situation and try to draw them to a deeper faith in the Lord.*

A Means for Church Renewal

Attitudes toward the Christian year are also changing because younger people with fewer ties to church tradition are now coming into positions of leadership in the congregations. These younger leaders, as they seek renewal in the church, are reevaluating the historical positions of the Restoration Movement to see if they are biblically sound. Many are concluding that some of the old positions are based on more cultural reasons than on scriptural principles. Renewing churches view practices such as the Christian year as methods or means to an end. If it is in keeping with biblical principles, if it can be used beneficially to advance the cause of Christ, and if it helps worshipers praise God more effectively, the Christian year can be used and adapted without reservation.

Another change slowing making its way into the worship planning of renewing churches is the use of the lectionary. This coincides somewhat with the growing use of expository preaching among many preachers in Churches of Christ. Use of the lectionary is not widespread, and such use made of it is likely to be surreptitious. However, an increasing number of ministers and worship leaders understand the need for better long-range planning for worship. Several ministers in renewing churches report that the lectionary assists their worship leaders in providing more balance throughout the year. Worship services and sermons are planned around passages and themes that might be overlooked otherwise.

Use of the Christian year and the lectionary are not likely to take Churches of Christ by storm in the foreseeable future. However, movement in that direction continues to increase slowly and steadily.

Dan Dozier

121 • CONGREGATIONAL CHURCHES

Many of the Congregational churches not part of the United Church of Christ follow a Christian year designed to involve the worshiper with the entire message of Scripture, from Creation to eschatological fulfillment.

The Congregational churches were gathered in a protest against a church calendar cluttered with saint's days and "holy" days. Only later, after about

1860 in North America, did Congregationalists begin to observe Christmas, Easter, and other traditional festivals and seasons. In 1919, the Commission on Evangelism and Devotional Life recommended "devotional services in every church conducted by the pastor during Holy Week with union Good Friday services wherever possible."

Subsequent publications in British and American Congregationalism offered lectionaries and orders of worship for observances of the Christian year. Notable among these was _A Book of Worship for Free Churches_, published in 1948 under the General Council of the Congregational Churches in the United States. It included an introductory essay on "Symbolism in Worship."

Structure for the Whole Message

These publications elicited an ongoing discussion about the role of the traditional Christian year in Congregational worship. It was clear that the restoration of the liturgical year was needed as a way to present a full cycle of God's self-revelation in Scripture. What Congregationalists sought in reconstructing the Christian year was not a quarrying from diverse usages of the past, but a structure through which the whole message of the Bible might speak to the whole of life—personal and society, nurturing diverse moods and needs. For Congregationalists, the Scriptures are the substance of the Christian year.

The _Congregational Worshipbook_, now in its fifth edition, may be taken as representative of much current practice in continuing Congregational churches (those not absorbed into the United Church of Christ). In addition to a lectionary, it provides resources for a variety of acts of Christian worship. The focus is on Sunday as the Lord's Day, the weekly celebration of the Resurrection. As in the ancient practice of the Eastern churches, all seasons begin on Sunday. The Christian year is structured as follows:

Season	_Festival_
Creation (September)	World Communion (first Sunday in October)
Providence (October–November)	Thanksgiving Day
Incarnation/Advent (November–December)	Christmas
Proclamation (January)	Epiphany
Presentation (February)	Covenant Renewal, Baptism (forty days after Christmas)
Preparation/Lent (February–April)	Palm Sunday
The Great Week	Easter
Fellowship (April-May)	Pentecost
Personal Witness (June)	Dedication to Holy Living
World Mission (July-August)	Commissioning of Christian Workers
Fulfillment (August)	Celebration of All Saints

The five-year cycle of Scripture readings in the _Congregational Worshipbook_ had been in use, with revisions, for fifty years. It grew out of the conviction that all of the New Testament and much of the Old must be read in public worship, or else languish in unopened Bibles. The Scripture reading deserves to be heard for its own messages, not just as a springboard to a sermon.

Significance of the Seasons

The Christian year in _Congregational Worshipbook,_ conforming to the biblical order, begins with the season of _Creation_. The season's festival is World Communion Sunday. Harvest Home, or _Providence_, follows, cresting at Thanksgiving.

Incarnation (Advent) rehearses God's varied attempts to restore sinful humanity to himself through nature, law, mighty acts, prophets, apocalyptists, and finally in a Son. Epiphany, January 6, begins the season of _Proclamation_, manifesting Jesus as the Light of the world. Many congregational churches have their annual meetings in January; the real business of such meetings is not the review of financial or procedure minutiae but the effort to make the local church more effective in proclaiming the gospel. Epiphany is a summons to dedicate ourselves and our churches as witnesses to the joy, wonder, and purposes of Jesus Christ. Forty days after Christmas, the ancient churches celebrated the *Presentation* of Jesus in the temple, where he was hailed as the light to the Gentiles and the glory of Israel. Baptisms often occur during this season.

Preparation, or Lent, looks ahead to the Great Week. This season focuses on the life, ministry, teachings and way of salvation in Jesus. The ancient Jerusalem church observed a preparation of forty days, a number occurring frequently in the Bible. This we learn from the testimony of Egeria, a Christian woman from western Europe who visited Jerusalem and other Eastern Christian centers in the years 381–384 and left a record of the daily services of the Great Week, when the Lord's Supper takes place. The Transfiguration of Christ is the gateway to Lent, the drama of the life and teaching of Jesus is the substance thereof, and the culmination comes in the triumph of Palm Sunday.

The Great Week continues the drama of Christ in the cleansing of the temple, the searing truth of his pointed teaching, the solemnity and wonder of the Last Supper in the Upper Room, the terror and mystery of the cross, and the transcendent splendor of the Resurrection.

The Saturday before Easter was recommended as a time for baptism in the ancient church (Cyril of Jerusalem, *Lectures*). In approximation of this practice, *Congregational Worshipbook* incorporates baptism of adults on Palm Sunday and of children on Easter afternoon.

Easter is followed by the season of *Fellowship*— a time of anticipation, of close companionship and common concern. The Scriptures count forty days to Christ's ascension and fifty to Pentecost, which finds the disciples "all together in one place" (Acts 2:1) as the Holy Spirit comes upon them with power to witness. The gift of the Spirit thus calls forth *Personal Witness* to God the Father of our Lord Jesus Christ, as the followers of Jesus are transformed into evangelists, eager to tell what God has done for them in Christ. Following the biblical precedent, new members are enlisted and baptisms are frequent during this season.

Personal witness leads to *World Mission*. Those who have received God's blessings yearn to share them with others, both spiritually and materially. Commissioning of Christian workers—missionaries, public servants, authors, educators—is an appropriate act of this season, fulfilling Christ's mandate of Matthew 28:19.

The scriptural imperative of world mission carries with it the promise of future *Fulfillment*, as believers anticipate the glorious eternal life with the Father of our spirits. Thanksgiving for all saintly souls fittingly crowns this season and the entire Christian year. This practice follows the example of the ancient Eastern churches by giving appropriate attention to the celebration of life "in Christ"—a life that begins here but continues hereafter. In the season of Fulfillment we look to the saints (in the New Testament meaning of the word) of the past and also to the saints of our own gathered church. To remember the great, good, and holy in our own household of faith is to be surrounded by a cloud of witnesses whose faith and example help us to place our own trust in God for fulfillment.

Henry David Gray

122 ✤ Eastern Orthodox Churches

The Orthodox church sanctifies time with daily, weekly, and annual cycles of celebrations that commemorate instances of God's redemptive action in human experience. At the center of the numerous events of the Orthodox church year stands the Easter celebration of the triumph of life over death and light over darkness.

The rhythm of Orthodox Christian worship and spirituality is governed by recognition of the relationship between time an eternity, of the presence of God with us (cf. John 14:16-23), and of the Sunday worship liturgy as a journey to heaven, where we worship God in the presence of and with all the heavenly host (see Alexander Schmemann, *For the Life of the World: Sacraments and Orthodoxy* [Crestwood, N.Y.: St. Vladimir's Seminary Press, 1973], 26–28). The evening-morning cycle of daily life, the recurring sequence of the week, the revolving of the years, and the ongoing stretch of time from one's birth to death are all sanctified by prayer and observance.

From Creation until the End, time is marked by events such as the Fall, the choosing of Abraham, the Exodus, the giving of the Law, the Babylonian captivity and return, and the Incarnation of the Son, which we keep in remembrance as signposts bearing on the work of God with his people and on our own salvation. And for each of us there are those once-in-a-lifetime sacraments and sacramental blessings that affect our lives: baptism, chrismation, marriage (or monastic profession), ordination (if so be our calling), and burial.

Daily and Weekly Cycles

Orthodox prayer life invariably includes evening and morning prayers in which the remembrance of death and resurrection is explicit. In the evening we pray, "Into Your hands, O Lord Jesus Christ, my God, I surrender my spirit and body; bless me, save me, and grant me eternal life." And in the morning: "Arising from sleep, I thank you, O Most Holy Trinity, that, for the sake of Your great kindness and longsufferings, You have not had indignation against me, for I am slothful and sinful. Neither have You destroyed me in my transgressions. . . ."

Additionally, the service books provide corporate prayer services for daily first (6:00 A.M.), third (9:00 A.M.), sixth (noon), and ninth (3:00 P.M.) hours of prayer, as well as daily Matins and Vespers. Few, if any parishes hold all these services, but all observe some of them, and in some monasteries, all the prayers are said.

Within the cycle of the week, there are variations in all the daily services, with certain hymns and emphases allotted for each day of the week. Sunday is a "Little Easter," its theme being the Resurrection. Monday is devoted to the holy angels; Tuesday to St. John the Baptist; Wednesday and Friday, to the Holy Cross; Thursday, to the Apostles; and Saturday to all other saints, particularly the martyrs. Wednesday and Friday are fast days, set aside by the early church in accordance with the tradition of Israel, although different days than the Jewish fast days of Monday and Thursday were chosen.

The Movable Cycle

Upon these cycles are imposed both the observances of the movable cycle of the year centered upon Easter (still called _Pascha_ in the church), and those of the fixed cycle—the feasts which fall upon the same date every year. Though the fixed year "officially" begins on the first day of September, the spiritual heart, center and foundation of the year is Pascha—Easter. For it is the Resurrection of Christ, the triumph of Life over death, of Light over darkness, that everything related to his church begins. Thus, we start there, with the first of the fifty-two Sundays, each of which, we remember, is also a celebration of the Resurrection. On this day time is crossed with eternity and we worship in heaven, at the marriage supper of the Lamb.

But prior to Easter, church continues the tradition of a long period of preparation for the celebration of the Resurrection. Lent is the forty-day period of fasting, prayer, and preparation of our hearts, but we do not enter even Lent unprepared. The following series of Sundays before Lent are assigned scriptural themes designed to show us the way: (1) the Sunday of Zacchaeus; (2) the Sunday of the Publican and the Pharisee; (3) the Sunday of the Prodigal Son; (4) the Sunday of the Last Judgment; and (5) the Sunday of Forgiveness, the day before Lent begins.

And then begins the Forty Days, our journey to Pascha. The structure and content of all the daily service are changed, taking on the flavor of the successive emphases of the weeks of Lent. During these days we devote ourselves, even more than we have, to fasting, to prayer, and to almsgiving. And we progressively prepare ourselves to enter with the Lord into the week before the Cross, through his suffering and death, and to his glorious Resurrection. Lazarus Saturday and the next day, Palm Sunday, are two days of joy, following the weeks of repentance, and which prepare us for Holy Week and its days of darkness and mourning.

Holy Week again changes all the services of the days of the week, and the special content of these days prepares the church to meet the Bridegroom. The services are deep and rich and conclude with service of the burial of our Lord on Holy Friday evening. Then comes the glorious light of Easter morning and the celebration of our Lord's resurrection, as we sing of Christ "risen from the dead, trampling down death by death."

After Easter Sunday we count fifty days till Pentecost, fifty days of celebration in the church. Each Sunday is distinctive. The first is St. Thomas Sunday; the second, that of the women who brought spice to the tomb of Jesus only to then become heralds of his resurrection. The next three Sundays all teach us about baptism and the new life received in the great mystery of grace, focusing successively on the paralytic whom Jesus had healed at the pool of Bethesda (John 5), the Samaritan woman who drank living water (John 4), and the blind man, who washed in the pool of Siloam (John 9). In the middle of the fifth week, on Thursday, we celebrate the Ascension and immediately after, the Sunday of the Holy Fathers of the First Council of Nicea, which the deity of Christ was affirmed. Then comes the Feast of Pentecost, at which we sing of "the presence of the Spirit, the fulfillment of the promise and the completion of hope."

The Fixed Cycle

With the Easter cycle completed, we continue through the year with additional celebrations fixed by date. Pascha is *the* Great Feast, but there are other great feasts to be celebrated, each with its own liturgy of preparation and fulfillment. In examining these fixed feasts, we could start at any point, but most preferable is Christmas, the celebration of the Nativity. Christmas has its own time of preparation, its own forty days of fasting and prayer, called Advent, beginning on November 15th. Once again, the sequence builds, the references to the birth of Christ appear in the services. The second Sunday before Christmas commemorates the ancestors of Christ, and the Sunday following commemorates all righteous men and women who have pleased God from the beginning—from Adam through Joseph, betrothed to Mary. Beginning with December 20th, the texts of the services are all directly concerned with the birth of Christ. Special celebrations are held both Christmas Eve and Christmas day. The day after Christmas commemorates the Lord's Mother. The twelve days from Christmas to Epiphany (January 6th) are filled with yet more commemorations: Stephen, the first martyr, on the 27th; the Holy Innocents, killed by Herod, on the 29th; Joseph the betrothed, David the Prophet and King, and James the Brother of the Lord, on the Sunday after Christmas.

On January 1 we celebrate the circumcision of the Lord, and then begin preparation for Epiphany, also called Theophany, the manifestation of God. At this feast we celebrate not only Christ's appearing but also his baptism, since it is also the occasion for the Great Blessing of the Waters. Christ blessed the waters of the earth once for all by his baptism in the Jordan, and our liturgical services are simply an extension of his act. Following Epiphany the church begins something of great significance to all her people—the annual blessing of each home by a ceremony carried out by the priest and the people of the household.

The fixed cycle includes yet seven more "great feasts": The Birth of the Virgin Mary, Mother of God (September 8th), The Exaltation of the Cross (September 14th), The Presentation of the Virgin Mary, Mother of God, in the Temple (November 21st), The Presentation of our Lord in the Temple (February 2nd), The Annunciation of the Virgin Mary (March 25th), The Transfiguration of our Lord (August 6th), and The Falling Asleep of the Virgin Mary, Mother of God (August 15th). Each is of great significance, and every church celebrates each one, along with its period of preparation.

These do not exhaust the significant church year celebrations, and those mentioned above deserve far more coverage than can be given here. The references below will help the interested reader to gain a broader and deeper understanding of the Orthodox Christian church year: *The Year of Grace of the Lord: A Scriptural and Liturgical Commentary on the Calendar of the Orthodox Church*, by a Monk of the Eastern Church, translated from the French by Deborah Cowan (St. Vladimir's Seminary Press, 1980); *The Festal Menaion*, translated from the original Greek by Mother Mary and Bishop Kallistos Ware (Faber and Faber); *The Lenten Triodion*, translated from the original Greek by Mother Mary and Bishop Kallistos Ware (Faber and Faber); *Divine Prayers and Services of the Catholic Orthodox Church of Christ*, compiled and arranged by the Reverend Seraphim Nassar (Antiochian Orthodox Christian Archdiocese of North America, Englewood, N.J., 1979); *Greek Orthodox Holy Week and Easter Services* (in Greek and English on parallel pages), compiled by Father George L. Papedeas (Daytona Beach, Florida: 1979); Alexander Schmemann, *Liturgy and Life: Christian Development through Liturgical Experience* (Department of Religious Education, Orthodox Church in America, 1974) and Alexander Schmemann, *Great Lent* (St. Vladimir's Seminary Press, 1974).

Dana and Sue Talley

123 ✦ EVANGELICAL COVENANT CHURCHES

The Evangelical Covenant Church emerged from small groups of believers (conventicles) that met to cultivate warm personal piety. It has also—on a customary rather than mandatory basis—sustained observance of the church year, which keeps the Christian story alive and vivid in the community.

The Evangelical Covenant Church originated in the nineteenth-century spiritual renewal movements within the Lutheran church of Sweden. Earlier influences that contributed to this renewal were Pietism and Herrnhutism from Germany, and, to a much lesser extent, Methodism and Puritan devotional literature.

Worship in the Conventicles

Participants in this renewal were called readers because of their commitment to the reading and discussion of Scripture and other devotional texts published in the journal _Pietisten_ (_The Pietist_). These discussions took place in small groups called "conventicles," known for their intimacy, vigorous exchange of ideas, general practice of the priesthood of all believers (a doctrine fundamental to Christians of Lutheran origin), and vigorous singing of the hymns of Lina Sandell, Oscar Ahnfelt, and others. This hymnody is rich in feeling without being sentimental, attentive to human desire and dread without being captive to subjectivity, and anticipates the contemporary recovery of the friendship of Jesus without at the same time collapsing friendship into sheer immanence.

Remarkably for pietistic groups, a "Jesusology" was not permitted to crowd out theology, that is, to neglect the God whose mission Jesus embodied and carried out. God is praised because of Jesus Christ.

The personal and relational elements fostered in the conventicles were not permitted to crowd out the churchly, classical, and transcendent dimensions of the Christian life. This is seen in the preservation of attentiveness to the festivals of the liturgical or church year and the lectionary of readings prescribed for those festivals as they were used in the Lutheran state church. The Covenant Church has no _canonical_ requirement that these festivals be celebrated and these texts read. Rather, the preservation of these festivals and readings is _customary_—an uncodified yet honored stewardship of a gift that is commemorative of the great salvific deeds of God for Israel and the church.

The annual celebration of these events preserves the corporate memory of the people of God. The liturgy ensures that the community's story will not die or be forgotten. The Covenant Church preserved this legacy so that subsequent generations would not be left without the "big picture" of whose they were, whence they came, who were brothers and sisters, and to whom they should go with the story of the God of Jesus Christ.

Worship Books

Practically speaking, this preservation takes two major forms: pastor's handbooks/books of worship and the hymnal. The Covenant church published its first worship handbook in 1900, entitled _Forslag till kristlig gudstajanstordning_ (_A Guide to Christian Worship_). While this book contains no printed lectionary, it refers to "the usual Gospel and Epistle texts," thus assuming access to the customary lectionary. In 1901 the Eastern Preacher's Conference published a _Pastoral Handbook_ which contains the complete lectionary—three sets of readings. The lectionary and liturgical festivals are reprinted with only minor variations in the Covenant's _Pastor's Handbook_ of 1923. The lectionaries contain texts for two Marian days—Purification and Annunciation, John the Baptist's Day, and the festival of the archangel, St. Michael. Some distinctive Swedish uses are also present, such as "Prayer Sunday" preceding the Ascension and the second day celebrations of Christmas, Easter, and Pentecost.

While the _Covenant Ministers' Service Book_ of 1945 contains no lectionary, the _A Book of Worship for Covenant Churches_ (1964) contains a lectionary for a three-year cycle but without the special days listed in the 1923 book. In 1981 _A Book of Worship for Covenant Churches_ was published along with the now current ecumenical Common Lectionary, with some variations for use in a three-year cycle. This book contains a brief paragraph at the beginning of each season of the liturgical year explaining what is commemorated, celebrated, and confessed during that season. Special celebrations include Covenant Founders Day (February 20), Christian Family Day, Reformation Day, Thanksgiving Day, and New Year's Day.

The Transfiguration of Christ is no longer commemorated on August 6 but on the last Sunday in Epiphany. The three pre-Ash Wednesday Sundays—Septuagesima, Sexagisma, and Quinquagesima—are dropped in favor of a longer Epiphany season as is now the common practice, and the long Trinity season is now named the season of Pentecost. This book also contains a carefully crafted statement on the theology of worship and a discussion of the use of colors for banners, stoles, and paraments according to the season.

Hymnals

Hymnals constitute the second set of major influences. *Sionssharpan* (*Zion's Harp*), the antecedent of the first official hymnal of the Covenant Church, was published independently by the Mission Friend's Publishing House in 1890. It combined the chorale tradition of the Lutheran church and the newer music of the readers as sung in the conventicles. It contains eighty-five specific hymns in a section spanning the birth of Christ through Pentecost. In 1909 the Covenant Church published its first official hymnal, *Sions Basun* (*Zion's Trumpet*), bearing clear relationship to the aforementioned antecedent. The section on the church year is slightly expanded to about 100 hymns covering similar material and the full lectionary of the Swedish Church is published, including the two

Basin and Ewer. *This symbol recalls Pilate's act of ordering the basin and water and washing his hands of responsibility for Jesus' death.*

previously noted feast days of Mary, John the Baptist's Day, and the day for Michael the Archangel. In 1931 a new hymnal came out, *The Covenant Hymnal;* it contained little by way of reference to hymns sequenced according to the liturgical year and no lectionary. *The Hymnal* of 1950 has a clearly marked section of hymns devoted to the liturgical year (about one hundred) and contains the lectionary of Gospel and Epistle texts published in *A Book of Worship for Covenant Churches* in 1964.

In *The Covenant Hymnal* (1973) the section on the liturgical calendar was expanded to about 140 hymns, and the lectionary includes a description of each season of the church year to which the readings pertain, together with a general statement about the nature and function of the church year and the lectionaries. This hymnal also contains the lectionary for the special days referred to in the *Covenant Book of Worship* in 1981.

The Evangelical Covenant Church is in the process of publishing a new hymnal, due in 1995, that will present the liturgical year as "The Story We Tell." It is to include a section on "Promise and Covenant" drawing together a more integral relation with the Hebrew scriptures and the story of Israel. No doubt it will also contain a lectionary.

Freedom and independence are not the same. The former seems best achieved in and with a community. The continued use of hymnals and worship books maintains an organic relationship with a heritage that continually calls its heirs to account and thus can save them from both a parochialism that denies the catholicity of the faith and from a novelty that more calls attention to itself than to Christ and the gospel. Covenant churches treasure the liturgical year as generative of our common life but not as our canon law. We enjoy freedom but not independence.

Materials referred to in this article or desired secondary literature may be obtained by writing: *The Covenant Archivist,* c/o North Park Theological Seminary, 3225 W. Foster Avenue, Chicago, Illinois 60625.

John Weborg

124 ◆ EVANGELICAL FREE CHURCHES

In its origins, the Evangelical Free Church sharply rejected practice of the Christian year as part of the rigid structures of the state church. Congregations today usually recognize Advent, Christmas, and Holy Week in some fashion, but formal adherence to the liturgical calendar remains almost nonexistent. A recent renewal of emphasis on worship in general, however, may bring about new attention to the Christian year.

The Evangelical Free Church of America has historically been very good at evangelism and discipleship but somewhat weak in worship. For the most part of the churches of the Evangelical Free Church of America pay virtually no attention to the formal liturgical calendar. However, most do observe some traditional practices and hold special services during Christmas and Easter seasons.

Repudiation of Liturgical Forms

The free-church movement was born out of a desire both to worship freely (that is, free from the state-controlled church of the Scandinavian countries from which they came) and to evangelize the lost. At its inception in America, the movement was primarily under lay leadership, and a great deal more emphasis was placed on studying the Word and evangelizing the world than on worshiping God. Christian societies were formed in the churches for the sole purpose of supporting missionaries.

Rejection of the rigid structure of the state church entailed a radical turn away from the traditional rituals of the liturgical worship, and even anything that would hint at such forms. In years past, it was viewed as almost "sinful" even to print an order of worship. Congregations wanted the Spirit to lead worship and did not want it pre-planned. Of course, the irony of this situation was that even though there was no printed order of worship, the order of worship proceeded with little change from week to week: an opening song, prayer, two more songs, the offering, the sermon, and a closing song.

One factor which keeps free churches in America from observing the Christian church year is the preaching style to which many of our congregations are accustomed. The vast majority of pastors preach in the expository style, taking one book of the Bible at a time and preaching through that book to its conclusion. The theme of the worship service is determined each week not by the church year but rather by the theme of that

particular morning's message. Often these series, which last two or more years, will be interrupted by a special Advent series or Lenten series. Usually, the message is simply adapted to the occasion and themes are drawn from the biblical book being used which lend themselves to the particular season.

Christmas and Easter Traditions

Christmas and Easter have always been a part of our worship traditions. The Advent wreath, with its Scandinavian roots, has become a very key part of the Christmas worship celebration. Thus, the four Sundays in Advent begin to take on a clearer focus. Christmas Eve and even Christmas day services (the Swedish "Jolotta") are common. Many congregations "pray in the new year" on New Year's Eve, often in conjunction with an observance of the Lord's Supper.

Ash Wednesday and the beginning of the Lenten season passes each year barely noticed by members of the Evangelical Free churches. It is not until the Easter Week approaches that attention is drawn to this significant season of worship. Palm Sunday, Maundy Thursday, Good Friday, and Easter Sunday represent virtually the totality of our Lenten season. Palm Sunday lends itself as a great victory celebration. Many of our churches will observe Communion on either Maundy Thursday or Good Friday and conclude the week with a great celebration of Christ's victorious resurrection on Easter Sunday. Elaborate musical presentations are often a part of both the Easter and Christmas celebrations and have become a major focus of ministry for our church musicians.

Thanksgiving also provides a thematic setting for worship as many congregations offer a Thanksgiving Eve or Thanksgiving day service. These services often consist of personal testimonies of God's faithfulness through the year and the observance of the Lord's Supper.

Worship Renewal and the Church Year

An awakening to the importance of worship has emerged in the Evangelical Free Church of America. As our congregations have grown, they have been able to bring worship leaders and musicians on to their paid ministry staff. These men and women have been able to focus their attention more on worship and thus complement the discipling and evangelizing that the church has always done well.

The current Christian music scene contributes to this heightened sensitivity to worship. The great influx of new praise-and-worship choruses are finding their way into worship services. Church members who for years have enjoyed singing the great hymns of faith *about* God are now enjoying singing the praise and worship songs *to* God.

One can only speculate as to how this renewal in worship will affect practice of the Christian year. Because each congregation is independent, the direction each takes in the matters will be strongly influenced by its worship leader. My sense is that while we will never abandon our free worship tradition, we will develop a greater awareness of the different seasons of the church year.

Douglas R. Thiesen

125 ✦ EVANGELICAL LUTHERAN CHURCH IN AMERICA

Full observance of the church year is central to Lutheran spiritual life. Lutherans have been influenced by ecumenical developments, as seen in the Evangelical Lutheran Church in America's adoption of the Roman Catholic calendar and lectionary. They have also influence ecumenical development of the Christian year, particularly in the observance of Advent.

The church year has always had a secure place in the Lutheran tradition. The liturgical seasons (Advent, Christmas, Epiphany, Lent, Easter and Sundays after Pentecost or Trinity), the major festivals (Easter, Ascension, Pentecost, Trinity Sunday, Christmas Day, Epiphany), many lesser festivals (All Saints Day, Holy Cross Day, Reformation Day, and some saints' days), and days of devotion (Ash Wednesday, Maundy Thursday, and Good Friday) have been observed for centuries. The church year lectionary has, for the most part, controlled preaching, hymn, and anthem selection. Paraments and vestments (stole, chasuble) reflect the colors of the liturgical seasons. Banners have highlighted symbols related to days and seasons. The folk practices that Lutherans have retained from various European cultures have been connected with the church year, such as

Advent wreaths and calendars, Christmas trees, Lenten self-denial banks, and Easter eggs. The church year has helped to form a liturgical spirituality within Lutheran congregations and homes.

The major change in recent years has been the adoption of the archetypal Roman Catholic church year calendar and lectionary for Sundays and festivals within the church bodies which formed the ELCA in 1988. The European Lutheran churches have not adopted this calendar and lectionary.

Since the Roman calendar and lectionary constituted a reform of the historic church year, the changes have not been major. They have included dropping Latin tags for the names of Sundays in the church year and clarifying the organization of the church year around the Christmas and Easter cycles. This resulted in dropping the pre-Lenten Sundays (Septuagesima, Sexagesima, and Quinquagesima). The Epiphany season was extended through the Sunday before Ash Wednesday, which is now celebrated as the Feast of the Transfiguration of our Lord (some sixteenth-century Lutheran church orders counted the Transfiguration as an Epiphany event anyway). The last Sunday of the church year is Christ the King rather than Judgment Sunday, as in the older Lutheran observance. Of greater consequence is the recovery of Easter as the focus of Sundays as well as the central festival of the church year.

Lutherans have made their own contribution to the development of the church year. In particular, the Lutheran observance of Advent (originally a Gallican liturgical season rather than a Roman one) has had an ecumenical impact. The Lutheran liturgy provided a proper eucharistic preface for Advent before one was provided in the Roman Sacramentary. The Lutheran use of blue as a liturgical color for Advent rather than purple (thus emphasizing hope more than penitence) has been imitated in some other churches. Lutheran hymnals contain a rich collection of Advent hymns which are awaiting appropriation by other denominations (including "O Lord, How Shall I Meet You," "Come, O Precious Ransom, Come," "Rejoice, Believers," "Prepare the Royal Highway," and "Savior of the Nations, Come," as well as the kingly chorale "Wake, Awake for Night is Flying"). The Advent wreath is virtually a Lutheran invention, since it first emerged in northern Germany in the sixteenth century. All this has helped Lutheran congregations to resist capitulation to the secular Christmas celebrations in American culture. Some pastors have courted martyrdom by insisting that no Christmas carols be sung in church services before Christmas Eve. To a lesser extent Lutherans have made an ecumenical contribution to the celebration of Lent, adding the focus on the Passion of Christ to the catechetical/penitential observance of Lent in the Roman tradition. Again, a number of Lutheran passion chorales await adoption in the hymnals of other denominations, just as the *Lutheran Book of Worship* has been enriched by ecumenical hymn traditions.

Some ritual practices associated with the church year in the *Lutheran Book of Worship* are recoveries of long-abandoned practices. Some of these were abandoned even before the Reformation. The re-introduction of such practices as ashes on Ash Wednesday, the blessing of palms on Palm Sunday, the footwashing on Maundy Thursday, and the veneration of the cross on Good Friday have required patient pastoral teaching and the overcoming of latent anti-Catholic and anti-ritualistic prejudices in American Protestantism and culture. For several decades now there has been a patient but persistent effort to reintroduce the Easter Vigil as the "Queen of Feasts," although it has had to compete with the more typical (and popular) Protestant Easter sunrise services. The recovery of an adult catechumenal process based on the R.C.I.A. will probably go a long way toward recovering the importance of the Easter Vigil in parish life. Special liturgies for Ash Wednesday, Maundy Thursday, Good Friday, and the Easter Vigil are included in the *Lutheran Book of Worship*, Ministers Edition (1978).

Commemoration of Saints
Ancient and Recent

In the instance of a Lutheran recovery of the sanctoral cycle of the church year (the calendar of saints' days), opportunities for creative celebrations have emerged. Lutherans have always observed days of certain biblical saints such as Mary the Mother of our Lord, Mary Magdalene, the Apostles and Evangelists, St. Stephen (and some church orders retained a few post-biblical saints such as St. Lawrence and St. Lucia). In the *Lutheran Book of Worship* the calendar of commemorations is greatly expanded from any previous Lutheran list anywhere. It is also a more balanced list in terms of the catholicity of the

Christian witness in all times and places than that of any other denomination. So it includes not only renewers of the church outside the Lutheran confession, such as John Calvin, John and Charles Wesley, George Fox, and Pope John XXIII, but also some who were only at the fringe of church life, like Dag Hammarskjold. It includes women as well as men, people of color as well as whites. Even a recitation of the names in the calendar for the week in the concluding remembrance of the faithful departed in the Sunday intercessions will expand the congregation's consciousness of the size and extent of the communion of the saints.

Some commemorations may give rise to a festival, such as the Day of Bach, Handel, and Schutz on July 28. Much helpful information for the observance of these days is included in Philip H. Pfatteicher, *Festivals and Commemorations: Handbook to the Calendar in Lutheran Book of Worship* (Minneapolis: Augsburg Publishing House, 1980).

Great headway has been made in congregations in the observance of the festivals and commemorations of the church year since the publication of the *Lutheran Book of Worship* in 1978. One would like to think that this progress will continue, since the church year is such a powerful tool of formation into the life and mission of Christ. This prognosis depends on whether Christian initiation or church growth models prevail in the ELCA in the years to come.

Frank C. Senn

126 • FRIENDS (QUAKERS)

The Quaker rejection of formalism and ceremony in worship extended to the observances of the church calendar. Resistance to formalism remains today, although Evangelical Quakers celebrate portions of the Christian year.

Quakers have historically rejected symbolism, the observance of special days, and other ceremonies and forms as human inventions. They regard such ceremonies and forms as unnecessary when individual believers can experience the Spirit of God directly. In addition, they believe avoidance of such externals protects believers from the idolatry into which humankind so easily falls.

Early Quakers reacted strongly against the formalism of the Anglican church, maintaining that the Reformation had stopped short, leaving Protestant worship ceremonial and ritualistic. Robert Barclay, in his *Apology*, stated the case forcefully: "For we find many branches lopped off by them [the reformers], but the roote yet remaining; to wit, a worship acted in and from man's will and spirit, and not by and from the Spirit of God" (quoted in *Friends Worship in a Pastoral Meeting*, n.d.). It is not unusual, therefore, to find rules like the following from *The Rules of Discipline of the Yearly Meeting. Held on Rhode Island for New England* (1856, 27): "We cannot, therefore, consistently unite with any in the observance of public fasts, feasts, and what they term holy days; or such injunctions and forms as are devised in man's will for divine worship" (quoted by John White in *Protestant Worship: Traditions in Transition*).

Today, little has changed and Quakers for the most part do not observe the Christian year. There continues to be at least a latent fear of formalism, especially among Evangelical Quakers, though the theological rhetoric of the past is largely absent. Most Evangelical Quakers, like their pulpit-centered church neighbors, celebrate Christmas and Easter, and in some cases, Good Friday. Occasionally one finds observance of the Advent sermon with wreath-lighting and Advent sermons. It is unusual, however, to find any further adoption of the Christian year.

127 ✦ INDEPENDENT FUNDAMENTALIST AND EVANGELICAL CHURCHES

During the past decade, interest in a modified observance of the Christian year has been growing in some independent evangelical churches, despite longstanding disdain for liturgy and formalism. Following the Christian year has allowed some congregations to foster Christian maturity in a balanced way.

Many independent churches and other evangelical churches with roots in revivalism have been most suspicious of any observance of liturgy in whatever form, especially observance of the church year. An anti-intellectual, anti-formal, and anti-liturgical mindset is part of the heritage of these churches. At the beginning of the twentieth century, many pastors had little seminary training and many had received their only education in a Bible school. Thus, they had little basis for appreciating liturgy. Hence clerical robes, use of candles, liturgical colors, and so forth were left for certain "formalist denominations" (Lutherans, Methodists, Presbyterians, Episcopalians, and of course, the Roman Catholics). The independent church was not the choicest of soils for germination of worship renewal. Nevertheless, it has occurred and continues to grow.

Change in One Independent Church

Our church, a typical independent church, is one that has found observances of the Christian year to be a source of vitality. While the liturgical calendar has not been fully adopted nor has the lectionary cycle been embraced, serious attention is being given to the seasons of Advent, Christmastide, Lent, Eastertide, and Pentecost. Advent wreaths and banners and an emphasis on Holy Week are some of the most common adaptations. Observance of the Maundy Thursday service has become more frequent as an emphasis on Holy Week strengthens. More and more families in the congregation have begun to celebrate Advent with their own wreaths at home and show genuine interest in family worship, especially during this season of the year.

How did a church that was rather anti-liturgical and baptistic come to the point of enthusiastic participation in a modified version of the Christian year? These observances began when the church hired a minister of music and worship. For the first time, someone was given responsibility for worship. Often senior pastors have so many responsibilities that the organization of the Sunday morning service is left to the last minute. The result is usually a carbon copy of the previous week's service with a few hymns or songs changed.

This church wanted a change, and change has been implemented in a variety of ways. The bulletin each week lists that Sunday's status in the church calendar, e.g. first Sunday in Advent. When appropriate, the hymns, anthems, and additional music are coordinated with the themes of the season, especially during Advent.

The church has been celebrating Communion monthly. The worship leadership decided to mark the beginnings of the seasons with a morning

Communion when possible. The first Sunday in Advent, Lent, and Pentecost were natural times for morning Communion. Special mention was always made of the reason for the season in these services focusing on the Second Advent of Christ, the coming of the Holy Spirit, and so forth.

Since there was a missions conference in the middle of the year, it was natural to make it coincide with Epiphany and the taking of the gospel to the Gentiles. While major emphasis was not placed on Epiphany, the people were exposed to an explanation of the season and its relationship to our church life.

Several in the congregation are Messianic Jews and thus the choir sings music of Jewish origin during the High Holy Days, even though these days are not part of the traditional church year. One year we used a modified prayer from a Yom Kippur service. The service included brief comments on the Jewish roots of Christian worship and the significance of the Atonement.

The minister of music and worship began writing a weekly hundred-word paragraph in the bulletin called "Notes on Worship" which described various aspects of the service. In addition, a thought-provoking devotional paragraph was placed at the top of the bulletin to assist people in their preparation for worship. People began to read the order of worship as it varied slightly from week to week. The bulletin became a key tool in worship.

Over a period of years, the congregation began to assume a more active role in the worship. When that happened, the importance of the church year grew as it opened new avenues of learning, understanding, and experiences in worship. People were given a context for the various worship events.

Response to the Change

Within the evangelical church there is a growing number of people born during the middle years of the twentieth century who are hungry for deeper worship than they have known in the past. They have keen interest in greater understanding of the historical roots and significance of various worship practices. The more common superficial treatment of the profound things of God are not satisfying. For example, many of these people feel cheated of the anticipation, wonder, and celebration of Advent when it is only marked by one

"Christmas service" on the Sunday nearest December 25. People are eager to see, experience, and understand the interconnectedness of time and faith. The observance of the church year does that in a clear way.

Invariably one of the first comments made by newcomers attracted to the church is "we've come because of the sense of worship and reverence here." Over the years the attendance at the Maundy Thursday service in Holy Week, for example, has grown from 250 to around 1000. This service is easily the most intense and serious of the entire year. Yet people appreciate the care with which it is structured. It is a service of darkness, with candles being extinguished gradually during the service. Often it concludes with J. S. Bach's "Come Sweet Death," followed by everyone leaving in silence. A single candle provides light in the emptying sanctuary, a simple reminder of the Resurrection. During the first years, people were concerned that it was too morbid. Yet in time worshipers came to see that after focusing on depth of despair and loneliness in Christ's suffering, the celebration Easter morning becomes all the more glorious.

Modified Observance

A modified observance of the church year may work best for evangelical churches. Observance of the four Sundays of Advent, with the lighting of the Advent candles, use of banners, and gradual decoration of the sanctuary in succeeding weeks culminating in a Christmas Eve service of lessons and carols constitutes a solid beginning. Use of Advent carols throughout the season is also imperative. The hymnal entitled *The Worshiping Church* contains an outstanding collection of material in the evangelical tradition useful for observance of Advent and the entire church year.

Missions and Epiphany may work together. The Lenten season may provide a setting for great choral music. It may also be a time to encourage the congregation to take spiritual inventory, including periods of fasting and praying. Palm Sunday, the various services of Holy Week (perhaps weekday noontime services), Maundy Thursday, Good Friday, and Resurrection Sunday all provide a setting for the great drama of the faith to be recalled in light of the present day circumstances. Eastertide culminating in Pentecost offers a joyous season concluding with a focus on the ministry of the Holy Spirit. The season of Pentecost provides roughly six months of outward-focusing ministry to the world.

The alternation between the life and ministry of Christ and the outward mission of the church each year provides theological and educational balance for congregational life. It is a great protection against ruts.

Frequently, evangelical churches are tempted to make getting more people through the doors the driving motivation in worship planning. While there should be great concern for the unchurched person, too often worship leaders are unwilling to provide genuine worship opportunities for the believer who comes week after week. Participation in the Christian year provides educational and inspirational opportunities for the church of Jesus Christ to grow in faith and maturity.

Daniel L. Sharp

128 ✦ INTERNATIONAL CHURCH OF THE FOURSQUARE GOSPEL

Foursquare churches combine important days from the Christian year with national observances in forming their own church year, one that correlates with the yearly rhythm experienced by its members and the surrounding community. Special Pentecost services emphasizing the church's Pentecostal beliefs were held in its early days and have recently been revived in a different form.

For most of its seventy-year history, the calendar of the Foursquare Church has included the observance of certain religious holidays, such as Good Friday, Easter, Pentecost, and Christmas. In the United States, Foursquare churches have also held rallies on July 4 and Thanksgiving expressing gratefulness to God for the Christian influence in the nation's heritage, and have emphasized family values on Mother's Day, Father's Day, and in some cases, Children's Day.

Holy Week and Easter

In many Foursquare churches, Good Friday services emphasize the suffering and sacrifice of Jesus Christ at Calvary. Communion is served, providing an expression of the believer's identification with the death and burial of the Lord. Usually the service traces the steps of Jesus on the way to his sacrifice for humanity at the cross.

One of the highlights of Easter observance has been sunrise services, conducted with great pageantry and music commemorating the victorious resurrection of the Lord. Many new believers choose this day to be baptized in water. The presentation of cantatas and drama depicting the Resurrection and its eternal impact upon humankind are commonplace.

Christmas remains the most active celebration on the Foursquare Church calendar. As is true during Easter, extensive effort is devoted to presenting the claims of the gospel to the unsaved. Even in congregations that have adopted a relatively low-key pattern of weekly worship, special music ensembles and choirs are formed to present the gospel in music and drama. Church facilities are brightly decorated, and in many congregations a Christmas dinner is held early in December. Renewed emphasis on family life has given special meaning to returning to "Grandma's house" on Christmas Day. Despite the numerous activities during the holiday season, the church schedule is adjusted to allow for quality family time.

Pentecost "Holy Ghost Rallies"

During the earliest days of the Foursquare movement, its founder, Aimee Semple McPherson, and others conducted special services on and around Pentecost Sunday. Called "Holy Ghost Rallies," these services presented the Pentecostal teachings that the Foursquare Church holds dear and offered concentrated opportunity for seekers to be baptized with the Holy Spirit with the evidence of speaking in other tongues, as in the original day of Pentecost described in Acts 2.

During the latter part of the 1950s these rallies began to decline and by the 1980s almost ceased to exist. However, having been influenced by the charismatic revival and the recent "third-wave" of renewal throughout the body of Christ, several of the Foursquare churches are reinstating the special observances of Pentecost into their local calendars. The services are not patterned on the "rallies" of the past, but they do manifest a strong resurgence of teaching and celebration regarding Jesus Christ, the Baptizer with the Holy Spirit.

National Holidays and Observances

National observances provide opportunity for the teaching of responsible, biblical citizenship.

On the weekend surrounding U. S. Independence Day, musicals or other presentations focus on the Christian principles on which the United States was founded. Thanksgiving is an outstanding season to teach and appropriate the biblical teachings on gratefulness, giving, and praise. Foursquare churches in some areas of the nation use this time as a season of "ingathering," wherein offering for missions are taken or other projects take place.

Mother's Day and Father's Day are excellent "teaching moments" regarding Christian family, marriage, and the home. It is during these times that many baby dedications are performed. The manner in which churches celebrate these occasions varies, depending upon the age groups predominating in the membership, circumstances with their homes, and the taste of the pastor. In some congregations, the eldest and the youngest are honored.

As can be seen by the above, rather than following a "liturgical" year with a uniformity of theme and observance, each Foursquare church is admonished to establish a church year that correlates with and complements the "life" year of its members and the community which it serves. It will include certain "religious (Feast) days," but will also incorporate the instruction of Deuteronomy 6:6-9: "You shall maintain God's words in your heart...and teach them diligently to your children, and you shall talk of them when you sit in your house, when you walk by the way, when you lie down, and when you rise up. You shall bind them as a sign on your hand [embracing the past], and they shall be as frontlets between your eyes [envisioning the future]. You shall write them on the doorposts of your house and on your gates [experiencing the present]."

Ronald D. Williams

129 • LUTHERAN CHURCH–MISSOURI SYNOD

The Lutheran Church–Missouri Synod, in continuity with Martin Luther and subsequent confessional Lutheranism, observes the full, traditional Christian year as a vehicle of the gospel. In the 1980s, some Missouri Synod churches moved away from the church year as too restrictive, while others sought an even more thorough appropriation of the church's ancient liturgical heritage.

The Saxon immigrants and pastors who organized the Evangelical Lutheran Synod of Missouri, Ohio, and other states (later, _Lutheran Church–Missouri Synod_) came to North America for the express purpose of establishing congregations which would be specifically Evangelical Lutheran in both doctrine and practice. The writings of Martin Luther and the confessional writings of the _Book of Concord_ (1580) were not only guides along this path; they were regarded as signposts of Lutheran confessionalism and orthodoxy.

Luther and the Church Year

Luther's own understanding of the liturgy, liturgical ceremony, and the provisions of the traditional church year is usually characterized as "conservative." In fact, Luther recognized the value of these observations as not only pedagogical devices but as means by which the church extols and rejoices in the gospel. To Luther, both proclamation and sacramental administration were means by which the gospel offers, communicates, and imparts the grace that Christ has accomplished for sinners by his Incarnation, Passion, Crucifixion, and Resurrection. Where the gospel is rightly taught and proclaimed and the sacraments are rightly given, the provisions of the liturgy in the liturgical year are seen to be of inestimable value to the church and a most appropriate vehicle in the service of the gospel.

Living under the gospel, the church may not be bound, after the manner of the law, to a particular system of observances, readings, and liturgical formulae. Rather, such observances are to be seen as gifts that ought not fall into disuse.

Luther's own preaching, as he himself notes in _An Order of Mass and Communion_ (1523) and the _German Mass and Order of Service_ (1526), puts special emphasis on the proclamation of the traditional Gospel reading of the day at the Sunday celebration of the evangelical Mass. In later years the chorales and cantatas of the orthodox period would draw upon those same Sunday and festival readings for their primary inspiration.

The confessional awakening in nineteenth-century European Lutheranism out of which the Missourians came encompassed not only a revival of appreciation for the evangelical and catholic doctrinal position of the Evangelical Lutheran Church, but also a renewed appreciation for the liturgical heritage of the Lutheran Reformation. Research into the earliest Evangelical Lutheran Church orders (*Kirchen-Ordnungen*) and the traditional liturgical music and chorales came to public attention in the works of Ludwig Amelius Richter, Friedrich Layriz, George Rietschel, and most notably, in the *Agenda for Christian Congregations of the Lutheran Confessions* prepared by Pastor Wilhelm Loehe for the immigrant congregations of the Saginaw Valley of Michigan, northern Indiana, and elsewhere.

The Missourians brought with them an emphatic appreciation for the strong relationship between their own orthodox theology and the liturgical treasures of the period of Lutheran orthodoxy that had culminated in the theological works of Johann Gerhard, Abraham Calov, and others.

The Book of Liturgy

In the newly organized Missouri Synod, Loehe's almost encyclopedic liturgical work was supplanted in 1856 by the publication of the Synod's own *Agende* (*Book of Liturgy*), based upon older Saxon models from a time before rationalistic and unionizing effects had taken their toll. Here, as in Loehe's work, the church year appears as it did in the classical Reformation and orthodox periods, with all the major observances of the cycles of seasons which long antedated the Lutheran Reformation. Collects, Epistles, and Gospels are provided for the Sundays in Advent, the Feast of Christmas (three days), Circumcision, the Epiphany of the Lord, Lent and Palm Sunday (including Confirmation), Maundy Thursday, Good Friday, Easter (three days), Ascension, Pentecost (three days), the Feast of the Holy Trinity, and the Sundays of the Trinity season.

In addition to the *Agende* and other liturgical materials produced for congregational use, devotional materials for use in the home were produced, as in the confessional and orthodox periods, which were based upon the themes and Scripture readings of the church year and included sermons on the Sunday Gospels.

Among the first generations of Missourians, saints' days and special liturgical observances included the traditional days commemorating the apostles and evangelists, and St. Nicholas (Dec. 7), the Presentation of Our Lord and Purification of Mary or Candlemas (Feb. 2), Annunciation (March 25), St. John the Baptist (June 24), Visitation (July 2), St. Mary Magdalene Day (July 22), St. Lawrence Day (August 10), the Exaltation of the Holy Cross (September 14), St. Michael's Day (September 29), the Feast of the Reformation, All Saints (November 1), Anniversary of the Consecration of the Church, the Festival of the Harvest, the Day of Repentance, and special propers for the ending of the church year.

Acculturation and the Liturgical Heritage

In many places, the pattern of congregational life was shaped by these observances. With the passing of time and the adoption of a new language and culture, the pattern of annual observances passed from German into English and a few commemorations were deleted. Although the progressive acculturation of Lutherans brought a general "Protestantizing," causing many of the weekday commemorations and celebrations to fall into disuse in some places, liturgy and the church year continued to characterize Lutheran congregational life.

The publication of *Lutheran Worship* in 1981 as an official liturgy and hymnal of the Missouri Synod brought the restoration of almost all of the days noted in the earlier books. New commemorations were added, including: The Confession of Saint Peter (January 18), St. Timothy, Pastor and Confessor (January 24), St. Titus, Pastor and Confessor (January 26), Martin Luther, Doctor and Confessor (February 18), C. F. W. Walther, Doctor (first President of the Synod, May 7), St. Barnabas, Apostle (June 11), the Presentation of the Augsburg Confession (June 25), St. Mary, Mother of our Lord (August 15), and the Commemoration of the Faithful Departed (November 2). Provision was made for the use of a three-year lectionary based on the Roman Catholic *Ordo Lectionem Missae* or a revised version of the traditional pericopal system. In congregations using *Lutheran Worship* the pre-Lenten Sundays were dropped, and the number of Sundays in the Epiphany season was correspondingly increased, with the Sundays in the non-festal half of the church year being numbered from Pentecost rather than Trinity Sunday. Congregations using the older *The Lutheran Hymnal* have maintained the earlier system.

The observance of the weekday commemorations, although by no means universal, seems to be on the increase. A large number of congregations have day schools, some of which take advantage of the opportunity to keep the entire calendar. In any case, the pattern of the church year and its seasons and cycles are still important to Missouri Synod Lutherans.

In general, although Advent and Lent are no longer kept as closed seasons with no extra-ordinary or festal activities permitted, most congregations observe these seasons with special mid-week devotional services, in many cases with additional weekday celebrations of the Sacrament of the Altar. Epiphany and Ascension services continue as weekday services in many places. Elsewhere their observance is transferred to the following Sunday.

Appointments for the celebration of the Holy Eucharist are provided for every day in Holy Week, including the uniquely Lutheran usage of celebrating the sacrament on Good Friday. There are no appointments for the celebration of the Holy Eucharist on Holy Saturday, but the Easter Vigil, which includes the lighting of the New Fire, the Prophecies, Holy Baptism, the Remembrance of Baptism by the worshiping congregation, and the celebration of the first Eucharist of Easter, is provided.

By the end of the 1980s, at a time when large numbers of Protestants of Reformed and evangelical background were exhibiting a renewed appreciation for liturgical seasons, a vocal minority in the Missouri Synod was expressing concern that the liturgy and the church year are too restrictive and were in any case out of tune with contemporary American culture. They have elected to move away from any observance of the church year excepting such major days as Christmas, Easter, and Pentecost. For others, however, the process has been one of addition rather than subtraction, from a desire to take fuller advantage of this opportunity to use the church's heritage to extol the gospel and guide the ongoing life of the congregation according to its provisions.

Charles J. Evanson

130 ◆ MENNONITE CHURCHES

During the eighteenth and nineteenth centuries, Mennonites followed the Christian year while most American Protestants did not. In the twentieth century, with the transition to use of English in worship, Mennonites dropped the Christian year, which now seemed formalistic and restrictive. Since 1980, many Mennonites have discovered the Christian year as a means of revitalizing worship, though on the whole its use remains irregular.

Prior to 1980, Mennonite churches in twentieth-century America planned and conducted worship with little reference to the Christian year. Apart from the major Christian festivals of Christmas and Easter, neither the days and season of the liturgical calendar nor the lectionary exerted much influence on their patterns of worship. Good Friday was observed in some congregations and Pentecost was often noted, but among many groups, services proper to the seasons were unknown.

Suspicion of Symbol and Ritual

Generally, Mennonites considered the Christian year formulaic and restrictive—appropriate, perhaps to "liturgical" worship but inappropriate to the free worship traditions of the Anabaptists and other like-minded groups. With their emphasis on conversion, discipleship, and daily obedience, Mennonites preferred a style of worship centered around the sermon and focused on texts or topics selected for the day by the preacher. Sermon series sometimes linked Sunday's service to the next; more often, each Sunday's sermon dealt with a different biblical passage or aspect of Christian life. Until the 1960s, "worship" usually referred to the non-sermon part of the service and followed a standard pattern: opening prayers, familiar hymns, and the Scripture reading, followed by a lengthy sermon. While the greater flexibility and variety in worship services appeared in the late sixties and seventies, Mennonites remained unfamiliar with the practices of the Christian year and somewhat suspicious of its general purpose.

Opponents and advocates alike attributed Mennonites' reservations about the Christian year to their suspicion of "liturgy." The origins of that suspicion were traced to the reformer Zwingli, whose opposition to ecclesiastical symbol and ritual shaped early Anabaptist worship. Most Mennonites assumed that from the Reformation forward, Mennonite worship developed outside the influence of the liturgical tradition, free of fixed seasons, Scriptures, or saints' days.

The Mennonite Church Year

Surprisingly, it has not been brought to light that in America, Mennonites were one of the few Protestant groups to observe the Christian year in detail. Under Calvinist Puritan and separatist influences in Britain and Europe, many Protestant groups who eventually emigrated to America rejected the Christian year and its feasts as "abominations." Consequently, most American Protestants limited their observances of the Christian year to Easter and Christmas until the twentieth century. Christmas itself was not observed until the nineteenth century. Meanwhile, a church year was followed in nearly all Mennonite churches to the twentieth century.

While it is unclear when and where Anabaptists first adopted the Christian year as a pattern for worship, a book of sermons published in 1730 by a German Mennonite preacher, Jacob Denner, shows that some Mennonites in Europe observed the Christian year from at least the eighteenth century. Denner's sermons followed the church year, with each section of the book designated for a specific season of the year. By 1800, Denner's sermons had been brought to America and were sold and used widely.

The predominant Mennonite hymnal and worship book of the nineteenth century, the German-language *Gesangbuch,* also included a church calendar. Through the years, these calendars became more elaborate, and the calendar which appears in the *Gesangbuch* includes observances which were not present in Denner's calendar— the Annunciation, Ascension Day, the Visitation of Mary, St. Michael and All Angels, and a Harvest Festival which occurred near the end of September. It is not clear why the Mennonites chose to observe St. Michael's and not other saint's days.

Prior to the turn of the twentieth century, all main feast days were observed, beginning with a period of Advent and continuing with a two or three-day Christmas season. New Year, Epiphany, Lent, Good Friday, Easter Sunday (as well as Easter Monday and sometimes Easter Tuesday), Ascension Day, and finally Pentecost (usually bringing a baptismal service) were also observed. Although one writer of the period suggests that the church year ended at Pentecost and was "resurrected" again at Advent, the *Gesangbuch* calendar includes both Scripture readings and suggested hymns for all of the twenty-seven Sundays after Trinity, as well as special occasions such as the "Day of John the Baptist."

Transitions to English and Loss of the Christian Year

Mennonite observance of the Christian year was discontinued in the first quarter of the twentieth century just as many Protestant groups were experiencing liturgical renewal. Factors within and beyond the Mennonite church accounted for the termination. The great revivals of the nineteenth century and the movements they spawned prompted Mennonites to examine their forms of worship and patterns of life, leading to a renewal of piety within the church. Coupled with Mennonites' historic concern for Christian faithfulness in life, the new piety gradually turned worship and preaching toward the doctrines and disciplines of faith and away from a formal liturgical cycle. Greater mobility among Mennonites and frequent contact with society at large also loosened the connections between worship and community for Mennonites, diminishing the community's engagement with the Christian year cycle and highlighting the need for corporate worship to deal with issues in the lives of individuals.

The shift from German to English as the primary language among Mennonites epitomized the changes which eroded the use of the Christian year in worship. Until the early years of the twentieth century, Mennonites, much like present-day Amish, lived, worked and worshiped within German-speaking communities. Their contact with English-speaking society remained strictly separate from their communal life and most especially from their worship. The use of German in work and in worship stressed their continuity with the European Anabaptist/Mennonite tradition and reinforced their separation from American social and religious groups.

As social and religious developments at the turn of the century increased their contact with the larger world, Mennonites began to evaluate their use of German as a first language. Travel, education, and business dealings expanded contact with English-speakers outside the community, and the renewal of personal religious faith among many Mennonites raised questions about their general reluctance to give witness to their faith verbally. To retain German as a mark of separateness was regressive, many felt, when the church was being newly challenged to reach out to the world. Gradually, in the first decades of the twentieth century, English emerged as a common and then primary language among Mennonites.

The shift to English among Mennonites meant that many of understandings that had supported the use of the Christian year in worship disappeared with the German language. The adoption of English did more than represent a break with tradition; it left Mennonites unable to express in their new liturgical language many of the qualities of worship and life that had grounded their understanding of the Christian year. The structure and sense of the German language had shaped their experience of faith, time, story, and community—aspects of experience that are basic to living out the meaning of the Christian year. For these categories of experience to be reshaped in a "foreign" language meant that the Christian year became more a formal than an experiential reality.

Consequently, English hymnals that replaced the German _Gesangbuch_ after the turn of the century omitted the calendar of the Christian year, the lectionary, and the schedule of hymns for each Sunday's readings. So widespread was this disregard of the church calendar that Mennonites for nearly three-quarters of a century neglected use of the Christian year and forgot their own history of observance. Most Mennonites are even yet convinced that the calendar of the Christian year and the lectionary have never been part of their tradition.

Contemporary Discoveries and Practice

Since 1980, however, ecumenical awareness and a perceived need to revitalize their own worship have led some Mennonites to realize the potential for liturgical renewal in the Christian year, though for most it is a matter of discovery, not recovery. Initially, Mennonites sought the variety and the structure provided by the Christian year. Linking worship to the cycle of the Christian calendar avoided the arbitrariness involved in most worship planning and provided an expanding horizon of texts and themes for Christian worship. For some, the benefits multiplied: the Scriptures were read systematically and informed the entire worship event; resources keyed to the Christian year offered diverse worship expressions; the _story_ of Christ and the church acquired new emphasis; the affective dimension of worship—color, symbol, movement and sound—deepened; the ancient traditions of the church drew nearer; and the Christian year began to create a counter-rhythm to the calendar of secular life.

Adherence to the Christian year is promoted by the denominational offices and seminaries of the Mennonite church. It is not mandatory, however, and observance across the denomination is limited. The church hymnal published in 1992 includes sections of hymns appropriate to the seasons of the Christian year, but is organized around acts of worship rather than the liturgical calendar. It does not include a lectionary, making it difficult for congregations throughout the church to follow the weekly Scriptures. Correspondingly, larger congregations near urban or educational centers are more likely than smaller rural churches to follow the Christian calendar, although the Mennonite Board of Congregational Ministries has published a planning calendar for small churches structured around the Christian year.

Congregations observing the Christian year often do so only during the major seasons and frequently select their own texts and themes for each Sunday. Many congregations, large and small, continue to plan worship without reference to the Christian year or the lectionary, focusing rather on topics and biblical passages pertinent to individual and corporate Christian life.

Notwithstanding their irregular observance, Mennonites have begun to make unique contributions to the practice of the Christian year. Nowhere is the congregational singing tradition stronger than among Mennonites. Their new hymnal, entitled _Hymnal: A Worship Book_ offers extensive resources for congregational song drawn from ancient and contemporary sources, representing a broad range of cultures and worship styles. Though sequenced according to acts of worship, hymns and readings are indexed and cross-referenced with both the Scripture and the Christian year, facilitating comprehensive use through the seasons and special days. Many of the hymns emphasizing Christian community, discipleship, peace, justice, and cultural inclusivity expand the meaning of the gospel and add new dimensions to the traditional themes of the Christian calendar.

In addition to these printed resources, several Mennonite congregations have begun to consider the significance of the Christian year for stewardship, lifestyle, family, social and political action, spirituality, the created order, and community formation. Correspondingly, Mennonite artists, readers, actors, preachers, and storytellers have explored new ways to present the Word.

Currently, the Christian year and the lectionary serve as more of a resource for Mennonite worship than a pattern. In years to come, the strong biblical and Christological focus of the Christian year and its potential for ordering life in Christian community may eventually lead Mennonites to recover the Christian year as a central reality in worship and in life.

Duane M. Sider and Maretta Hershberger

131 ✦ MESSIANIC SYNAGOGUE

Messianic Jews observe the liturgical calendar of the Torah rather than the Christian year. In some instances, they add a Christological tone to the traditional Jewish meaning of these observances.

One of the characteristics shared by all the congregations of the Messianic Jewish movement is a high view of Scripture and a consequent determination to order congregational life according to what was in the 1970s often called biblical *kashrut* and is now more simply designated *Torah*. Therefore, Messianic Jews share a virtually universal adherence to the Jewish liturgical calendar that is mandated in the Torah itself. This approach differs significantly from the older Hebrew Christian philosophy, which taught that, having been set free from the "burden" of the law by the Messiah, it would be wrong to practice the liturgical year whose very existence derives from that law. The Hebrew Christian practice had been to mention at a Sunday service that, during the following week, a Jewish holiday would occur.

―― "Yamim Naraim": The Days of Awe ――

The month of Elul, which ends with the new moon at which the Jewish new year begins, inaugurates a nearly two-month period of introspection, the goal of which is *teshuvah* (repentance). This emphasis intensifies with Rosh Hashanah, at which time God is traditionally pictured sitting in judgment, both on individuals and on the community. The days from Rosh Hashanah to Yom Kippur, and beyond to Sukkot, are referred to as the Days of Awe, for they focus attention on the majesty of the Creator-Judge of the universe sitting on the throne, contemplating us and our sins. Even less liturgically inclined Messianic synagogues tend toward traditional practice at this time of year.

Rosh Hashanah, the Jewish New Year, is derived from the biblical Holy Day *Yom Teruah* (the Feast of Trumpets) or *Yom Hazikaron* (the Day of Repentance), the festival at which the *shofar* (ram's horn) is blown in synagogues the world over. In the early centuries of the common era, problems concerning inaccuracies in determining the date of the new moon prompted the rabbinical authorities to observe the Holy Day for two days instead of one. The custom continues to this day, except among some Reformed congregations and in Israel, where it was never practiced (Hayim Halevia Donin, *To Be a Jew* [New York: Basic, 1972], 210–212).

The two days of Rosh Hashanah are seldom treated equally in Messianic synagogues; the first evening is often observed with a major worship service, as is the following morning. The liturgy for both services, as well as the three service of Yom Kippur, is found in the *Machzor for High Holydays*, which was an editorial priority of the Messianic movement in the late 1970s. The most distinguishing feature of Rosh Hashanah is blowing the *shofar*, the ram's horn or trumpet, which is mandated in the scriptural legislation that established this Holy Day (Lev. 23:23-25; Num. 29:1-6). The *shofar* is blown rhythmically to the commands *tekiah* (a single continuing sound), *teruah* (many staccato sounds), and *shevarim* (a series of somewhat longer sounds). It is a day of rest and of repentance (Maimonides, *Hil. Teshuvah*; Hos. 14:2). The customary New Year's greeting is *Shana Tovah*, an abridgment of the traditional *L'shana tovah tikatev v'taihatem*—"may you be inscribed and sealed for a good year" (Donin, *To Be a Jew*, 246).

The Sabbath between Rosh Hashanah and Yom Kippur continues the theme of repentance. Called *Shabbat Shuvah*—the Sabbath of Repentance—it is dedicated to the renewal of individual relationships with God and relationships among the congregation's members.

A custom traditionally associated with the afternoon of Rosh Hashanah—although some Messianic synagogues practice it on the afternoon of Yom Kippur—is _Tashlikh_ (the casting), a vivid representation of Micah 7:19. In Highland Park, Illinois, for example, many of the worshipers at Congregation V'nai Maccabim go as a group to the edge of Lake Michigan, not far from the synagogue's meeting place, where they cast their sins (represented by pebbles) into the sea (represented by the lake). Orthodox and Messianic congregations both practice _Tashlikh_, although not usually on the same day. For Messianic Jews, the casting is associated with the atonement provided by Yeshua the Messiah, whereas for the Orthodox it is an act of repentance practiced prior to the Day of Judgment (_Yom Hadin_) which is an essential preparation for Yom Kippur (the Day of Atonement). It is an already accomplished fact for the Messianist.

Yom Kippur is the Day of Atonement, mandated in the Torah (cf. discussion of Old Testament holy days in volume 1). In fact, it is _the_ Holy Day—if a Jew visits the synagogue only once a year, it will be on this day. The evening service is called _Kol Nidre_, after a prayer of the same name. The _Kol Nidre_ prayer exists to give comfort to a person suffering from guilt because of failure to live up to the commitments, vows, or promises one has made.

The day itself is largely spent in worship. There are several synagogue services, beginning with _Shaharit_ or _Musaf_ (in more traditional congregations) in the morning. _Yizkor_ (a memorial service) may be then celebrated in the early afternoon, although Messianic congregations have tended either to ignore this service or rewrite it into a memorial of the suffering of Yeshua or the Lord's Supper. The concluding service, _Neilah_ (The Closing of the Gates), signifies that God's patience may come to an end in judgment (Gen. 6:7; Jer. 8:20; Ezek. 22:31), although overall the service is short and joyful, climaxing in the blowing of the _shofar_.

As commanded in the Torah, the Holy Day is observed by fasting, and in accordance with Jewish tradition, the fast lasts from sundown of _Erev Yom Kippur_ (holiday eve) to the following sundown. After the _shofar_ is blown to mark the end of the fast, a festive family or congregational dairy meal is traditional.

Sukkot—the Festival of Booths (Tabernacles)—is also mandated in Scripture. It commemorates God's provision for Israel during their post-Exodus wandering, and like the other major Jewish holidays, lasts eight days with a two-day initial intense period. At some point, often as early as the evening after Yom Kippur, the congregation's _sukkah_ (booth) is built as a center for as much holiday activity as weather permits.

As the week-long holiday draws to an end, traditional Jews observe the "Festival of Great Praise", _Hoshannah Rabbah_. Messianic Jews largely overlook this holiday within a holiday, but they do observe the final day of _Sikkot_, which is called _Simhat Torah_ (The Joy of the Torah). The Law of Moses is celebrated, and the cycle of liturgical readings is concluded and begins again, the Torah scroll is paraded through the synagogue and even danced with as unimpeded exuberance elevates the celebrants to ecstatic heights.

The Winter Festivals

The next holiday is _Chanukah_, the Festival of Light, commemorating the rededication of the Temple after the Maccabees won Judea's freedom from Seleucid Syria. Strangely, the only scriptural mention of this Jewish holiday is found in the New Testament (John 10:22). _Chanukah_ lasts the customary eight days, which are commemorated at home by lighting the _Chanukah_ Menorah—a candelabra with eight candles plus a ninth candle, called the _shamus_, which is used to light the others. The _shamus_ lights one candle the first night, two candles the second night, and so on until all the candles are lit the eighth evening. In the synagogue, on the Sabbath during _Chanukah_, the _megillah_ (scroll of 1 Maccabees) is read.

The lack of any common customs for celebrating the Nativity of Yeshua eloquently illustrates Messianic Judiasm's self-identification as a Jewish movement. Each synagogue has faced independent congregational decisions about whether, and how, to celebrate Christmas (commonly called the Nativity). Possible ways of observance include family celebrations in individual homes with none in the synagogue, referring to the holiday in congregational services with primary celebration taking place in homes, and formal Christmas congregational services.

Late in the winter comes a one-day holiday, _Purim_ which commemorates Israel's survival of

Haman's plans for an ancient holocaust. Another *megillah* (the scroll of Esther) is read in the synagogue, which approaches the holiday in a party mood. In fact, Jews are "required" to "eat, drink, and be merry." Traditional Jews are commanded to get drunk (Megillah 75), and Messianic Jews have yet to develop any custom centered in the celebration this command is designed to foster.

Carnival-style festivals, especially among children, are increasingly popular. Giving charity to poor people and worthy causes has developed as an important way to mark the holiday, and traditionally each person sends "portions," often gifts of food and drink to friends—a custom called *shalach* (or *mishloach*) *manot* ("sending out the portions"). Because sending the "portions" is a private custom, it is hard to quantify the extent to which the Messianic community participates, but there is no reason to doubt that it does do so.

Pesach—the Feast of the Passover

Exodus 12:15-20 commands that the Jewish community observe *Pesach*, the Passover, the Festival of Unleavened Bread (*hag hamatzot*), which commemorates the deliverance from Egyptian slavery. The eating of leavened bread, or any other food containing leaven (*hametz)* is forbidden, (Exod. 12:19-20). Passover is observed for eight days, and the *seder* (Passover supper) is celebrated on the first two evenings. For Messianic Jews, the Seder's connection with the Last Supper is very important. The Seder is more than just a supper; it is a family-centered religious service for which the Messianic movement has developed numerous *haggadot* (Seder prayer books).

Closely associated with *Pesach* is the festival of the Resurrection, which some congregations observe on Easter Sunday, some observe on the Sabbath or Sunday after the first Seder, and still others remember on the third day of Passover, regardless of the day of the week on which it falls. Some of those whose commemoration is on the Sabbath organize their worship service around the Resurrection theme, somewhat like those whose service is on Sunday. However, this is not true of all congregations within the Messianic movement.

The Festivals of Spring

Yom Atzma'ut, Israel's Independence Day, is less commonly observed by the Messianic community as a whole than within the wider Jewish community. Nevertheless, personal and congregational support of Israel and the Zionist movement is almost universal. Some congregations take note of *Yom Atzama'ut*, the Sabbath before the day of observance, and a few even mention *Yom Yerushalayim* (celebrating the reunification of Jerusalem). As is the case of the Jewish community as a whole, "the nature of its religious observance is yet to evolve" (Donin, *To Be a Jew*, 267).

Among Messianic synagogues the minor fasts, such a the Ninth of Av, the Tenth of Tevet, and the Seventeenth of Tammuz, and the Fast of Gedliah, all of which recall incidents from the Babylonian siege and, in the case of the Ninth of Av the Roman siege as well, are seldom if ever observed.

Shavuot is the festival commemorating the giving of the Ten Commandments at Sinai. Messianic Jews seldom observe the entire *Taryag* (613 Commandments), but confess the Ten Commandments as the fundamental basis of God's moral law. This festival is Pentecost and, as such, it is also the commemoration of the giving of the *Ruach* (the Holy Spirit). For Messianists, the giving of the Spirit seems to overshadow the giving of the Law, and the Messianic synagogues are only beginning to synthesize both aspects of this festival.

Kenneth Warren Rick

132 • NATIONAL BAPTIST CONVENTION, USA

The worship calendar in most congregations of the National Baptist Convention, USA, Inc. combines important days of the Christian year with numerous annual days—memorial observations and celebrations of various functions and organizations in congregational life and the black community. These days were established primarily because of economic and social needs rather than scriptural mandate. The number of annual days has declined in recent years, and a new emphasis on Christian education as the basis for giving is emerging.

Originally black Baptist worship took place in segregated settings controlled by whites. From these origins, two major influences on the development of the worship calendar that churches of the National Baptist Convention, USA, Inc. would follow can be seen. First, during their worship in

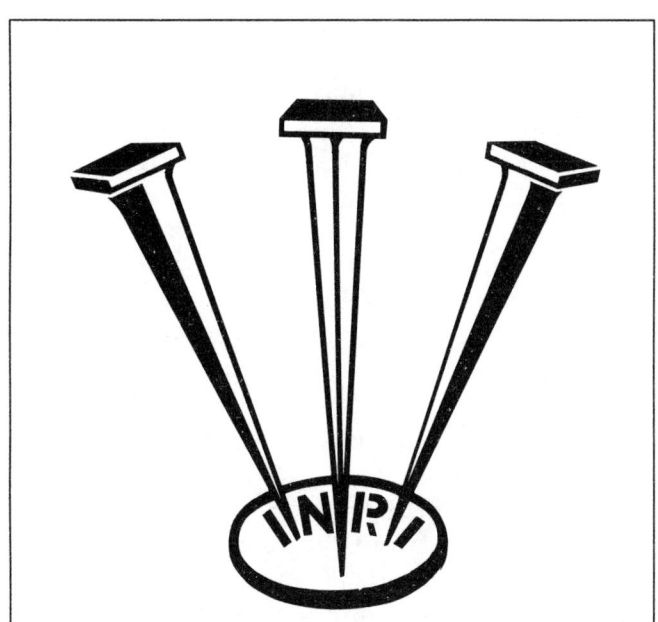

Nails. A widely used symbol of the Crucifixion, the three nails remind us of violent manner of Jesus' death.

the segregated section of the church of the masters, black worshipers absorbed the custom of observing major Christian yearly dates in a manner similar to that of most white Baptist, Methodist, and Presbyterian churches.

Second, in the struggle to build churches independent of white control, an importance was attached to fund raising and establishing the church as an autonomous center for black community life that would later result in the observance of days to honor and sustain these efforts.

The Value of Independent Churches

Before establishing independent churches, black Baptists held their own church or camp meetings in any accommodations available. Segregated from yet still under the control of the main body of the white church, black members began to make plans to purchase property of their own and saved pennies toward that end. This had to be done covertly because of considerable opposition from white slave masters and white preachers who controlled the worship of the pre-liberated and early post-slavery black church. As the black community became more stable after slavery, the importance of maintaining permanent church meeting places became deeply instilled.

Thus, observance of the local church's anniversary and the pastor's anniversary share prominence along with Christmas and Easter among the more important annual days celebrated in most congregations of the National Baptist Convention USA, Inc. Ash Wednesday and Good Friday are two other dates from the Christian year most frequently included among the annual days observed by these congregations.

Adding Annual Days

As churches became more permanent and more affluent, more days were added to celebrate other functions and organizations of the local church fellowship. Among these were Watch Night service, New Year's Day, Auxiliary Anniversaries, Choir Day, Women's Day, Usher Board Day, Men's Day, Sunday School Day, Promotion Day, Nurses Guild Day, Homecoming, Founder's Day, and Thanksgiving Day. Other regular events on the church calendar included revivals, social hours, and General Fellowship Days exchanged between churches. Later, most National Baptist Convention USA, Inc. churches added commemorations of black history and Martin Luther King's birthday, as well as workshops, seminars, dances, and social hours.

Because the church historically was the only institution "owned" by black people, the worship calendar in black churches has revolved around these social and religious activities.

Because of the restricted opportunities in secular areas of employment, the black church has historically attracted many of the most productive minds from the community, and these individuals have produced programs of great ingenuity and imagination for worship and financial participation.

Consolidating Annual Days

The events celebrated by churches in the National Baptist Convention, USA, Inc. has remained relatively constant over the past fifty years. Almost without exception, those events of the Christian year perceived as major, such as Easter and Christmas, continue to be celebrated in all black churches. However, in recent years, the number of afternoon and evening programs to honor auxiliaries or celebrate events to which members are willing to commit their time is showing marked decline in all areas of the country.

Many larger churches, rather than having an annual day for each group or auxiliary such as Choir, Usher's, Nurses', Women's and Men's Days, are combining all "Annual Days" into one fund-raising event. Pastors often introduce this concentrated yearly program of tithing and increased financial conscientiousness to offset the perceived loss of revenue from not having as many annual days.

In the next twenty years, we will probably see an increased emphasis on Christian education, which will mean that the Christian year for the National Baptist Convention, USA, Inc. will focus on reading through the Bible annually with added emphasis on fellowship of spirit rather than afternoon financial programs. Teaching the Bible during the Sunday morning service will help congregations grow spiritually and increase their level of giving. Once people understand giving as taught in the New Testament, they will give more to the support of the church.

Robert E. Davis, Sr.

133 ✦ National Baptist Convention of America

Observance of the Christian year has greatly increased in the National Baptist Convention of America, Inc. during the past twenty years. A growing number of well-trained pastors, educational resources offered by the denomination, and innovative use of art forms have all been instrumental in overcoming the historic Baptist resistance to such observance.

Historically, the traditional church calendar has not been a primary concern of pastors and member churches in the National Baptist Convention of America, Incorporated, even though many of the festivals of the Christian year are now celebrated. The Baptist church has always focused upon freedom, autonomy, and the proclamation of the Word, especially the black Baptist churches. These hallmarks of Baptist heritage have tended to isolate Baptist churches from the mainstream Protestant liturgical churches. Baptists have traditionally regarded the Christian year commemorations as strictures to the indwelling of the Holy Spirit and intense study of the Word.

However, during the first seventy years of the denomination's existence, member churches have systematically observed a large segment of the Christian year—Christmas, Holy Week (especially Palm Sunday, Maundy Thursday and Good Friday), and Easter. They also observe Thanksgiving Day and Thanksgiving Sunday. These days are not among the festive days of the traditional Christian year, but Baptists have always considered them appropriate expressions of gratitude to God for all his benefits. Moreover, New Year's Day or New Year's Sunday are also observed in acts of worship to express gratitude to God and to invoke his blessings for the new calendar year.

Expanded Observance

Within the last twenty years, member churches of the National Baptist Convention of America, Incorporated, have embraced Advent, Epiphany, Ascension Day, Pentecost Sunday, Trinity Sunday, and All Saints' Day. The expansion to include these additional observances can be attributed to improved leadership from better-educated pastors and from directors of Christian education who have raised the teaching ministry of the church to a new level that surpasses by far that of the traditional church school (Sunday school).

Lent, Palm Sunday, and Holy or Passion Week emerged as periods of the Christian year to be celebrated because of their proximity to Easter, and because of an emphasis on Bible study focusing on the events in the life of Christ immediately preceding Easter or Resurrection Day, as it is referred to in the member churches. Intensive Bible study during Holy Week is often supported by the ministry of music when choral groups render cantatas on Maundy Thursday or Good Friday. Also on Good Friday, worship services are conducted from twelve noon to three o'clock in the afternoon and include brief sermons on each of the seven last words of Christ from the cross.

Change through Education

The practical axiom that attitudes can be changed through teaching has been demonstrated in many member churches of the denomination fortunate to have pastors with college and/or seminary training who have successfully communicated the significance of the Christian year.

There are still some member churches of the denomination that have not been convinced that observance of the Christian year is beneficial to the worship experience. Attitudes in the rural churches are particularly difficult to influence, due to lack of education and support from informed pastors. The denomination, through the National Baptist Congress of Christian Workers, has organized the National Convention at Study, which addressed this problem by offering short courses for churches and pastors on church history and Christian worship. The National Convention at Study convenes for a week in June of each year. Leadership skills and general pastoral functions are also included in the curriculum.

In addition to the National Convention at Study focus, seminars and workshops are conducted by curriculum specialists and Christian educators in the denomination throughout the year at the Baptist associations and state convention levels. Participation by pastors and churches in the interdenominational alliances throughout the United States, special workshops and seminars conducted by the Convention's Liaison Office, and the Convention's participation and membership in the professional religious organizations like the Congress of National Black Churches have also promoted use of the festive days of the Christian year, even among the more reluctant rural churches.

Even with all of these efforts, the Christian year is not fully implemented even in the urban and suburban churches. But when congregations, rural and urban/suburban, have had the opportunity to participate in a teaching ministry which explores the meaning and uses of the Christian year, the results have usually been positive.

Drama and dance in worship have in recent years been introduced to the member churches of the denomination. These two art forms have served as highly creative and effective means of exploring the meaning of the Christian year. The response from congregants has been very favorable.

These trends in education and use of drama and dance suggest that member churches of the denomination will continue to incorporate greater use of the Christian year.

134 • PRESBYTERIAN CHURCH (USA)

Presbyterians have been gradually recovering the Christian year and most congregations now observe at least Advent, Christmas, Lent, and Easter. Observance frequently takes the form of family-centered activities, study programs, and a wide variety of artistic and cultural expression.

In the tradition of John Calvin, today's Presbyterians honor the weekly celebration of the resurrection of our Lord as the greatest of Christian festivals. For centuries, on the other hand, they have frowned on Christmas, Easter, and other traditional church festivals because of possible pagan origins. Slowly, we have begun recovering the Christian year. One probably can safely say that every Presbyterian congregation keeps Christmas and Easter. (It remains true, however, that in many congregations the decision to place a Christmas tree in the sanctuary will create controversy.)

Most of Presbyterian congregations further observe Advent and Lent as seasons of intentional spiritual preparation for the major festivals. And every year, more churches put out red paraments and bright banners to celebrate Pentecost or Christ the King. Beyond these special times, the _Presbyterian Planning Calendar_ lists also Epiphany, the Baptism of the Lord, the Transfiguration of the Lord, Passion/Palm Sunday, Trinity Sunday, and All Saints' Day.

The planning calendar is a helpful resource for congregations who are moving into the rhythms of the church year. It provides essays about the church year, a calendar of the liturgical colors, lists of liturgical seasons important to other faiths and suggests ways to make each season meaningful in worship or in study.

Music and the Arts

With our tradition of congregational singing, Presbyterians think first of festivals of song to celebrate high points of the Christian year. What congregation doesn't plan for a special music service at Christmas and at Easter? The greater challenge is to bring integrity of proclamation into these almost mandatory musicfests. At a time when people otherwise inactive in the church gather to hear the "holiday" music, worship leaders strive to make sure the good news of Christ is proclaimed clearly and in fullness.

Consequently, musical services at Christmas and Easter increasingly involve both Word and sacrament. The offering of the Lord's Supper, "the joyful feast of the kingdom," is coming to be regarding as especially appropriate when remembering the Incarnation and Resurrection. Some congregations on Christmas Eve combine passing the elements of the Supper with the traditional sharing of the light, so that the act of candle lighting becomes a renewal of commitment, a further response to the Word proclaimed.

These highest of our holy times invite all the arts to enter the celebration of worship: banners, flowers, greenery, candles, paraments, vestments, pageants, drama, choral readings, and liturgical dance. These traditional expressions of festive faith and awe also give opportunity for people less often involved in worship to bring an offering of talents. Pentecost, celebrating the Creator Spirit, is an especially happy time for a festival of the arts spilling over into a climatic hour of creative worship.

Family Activities

Because seasonal festivals of the church are often family-centered, such celebrations as caroling, the hanging of the greens, and of course Advent workshops invite intergenerational involvement in worship and in activity. During Holy Week, a Seder feast climaxing in a Maundy Thursday celebration or a well-paced Tenebrae service can bring all ages into shared experience.

At least one congregation uses Advent as an occasion to help families learn how to do household worship. After a brief worship time informed by the Advent theme, teaching and role-play give the goals and possible methods for family worship. Then each family or household forms into a small group, using suggested guidelines to rehearse worship together before the closing carol.

Our congregation finds it important to create "extended" families or households through this event, so that single people are not excluded, but rather embraced. Most worship planners, aware that many of the seasons of the church year coincide with secular holidays, use pastoral sensitivity in seeking worship designs that will draw in those living in nontraditional families, or away from home, or who otherwise might feel in some way more isolated by the family-focused expectations of the season.

In celebrating seasons of the church year, we also draw upon the rich diversity of cultural traditions represented in our denomination. Nine days before Christmas, Hispanic Presbyterians invite the infant Jesus to find a place in their home in the fiesta of Las Posadas. African-American Presbyterians frequently deepen their Christmas celebrations with an observance of Kwanza, with its focus on heritage and on family unity in the context of faith. *The Presbyterian Hymnal*, arranged to follow the church year, celebrates our diversity by including seasonal hymns and carols from Native American, Chinese, Japanese, Puerto Rican, Hispanic, and African-American sources.

Worship and Education

Being "people of the Word," Presbyterians tend to bring study into any celebration of the church year. Advent and Lent, as seasons of preparation, find many congregations sponsoring events that combine worship and education. Sometimes these take the form of lecture/worship series built around topics illuminating historical or theological understandings of the seasonal celebration. Sometimes the themes involve spirituality and devotional disciplines.

It is traditional for confirmation/commissioning classes or Communion preparation classes to choose Lent as a time for the spiritual discipline of study. But an increasing number of congregations call adults to learn about the worship dimensions of marriage, baptism or funerals by studying Supplementary Liturgical Resources appropriate for Advent or for Lent. The study guides for *The Directory of Worship* also lend themselves to this sort of worship/learning experience.

As our public worship is more and more shaped by the seasons of the church year, Presbyterians are also drawn into that same pattern in household worship as well as in personal disciplines of prayer and meditation. In fact, it is through these shared rhythms of worship that thoughtful believers are discovering a crucial insight about the meaning of communal worship. Bound together into one community of faith as we are, Presbyterians are coming to see that our personal and our household times of worship are not separate from, but rather join with, the worship of our particular congregation, our denomination, and the church throughout the world as all together move in rhythm of a share sense of ordinary and of sacred time.

Melicent Honeycutt Vergeer

135 ✦ PRESBYTERIAN CHURCH IN AMERICA

The sermon remains central to worship in the Presbyterian Church in America, and selection of texts is determined by the minister's choice rather than a church year lectionary. While it is customary to preach on seasonal topics at Christmas and Easter, freedom from mandatory observance of the Christian year continues to be stressed and no churches are known to follow it.

Ministers in the Presbyterian Church in America (PCA) hold the preaching of God's Word in the highest possible regard. Given their denomination's creedal stance, this outlook is understandable! The Westminster Confession of Faith declares: "The whole counsel of God concerning all things necessary for His own glory, man's salvation, faith and life, is either expressly set down in Scripture, or by good and necessary consequence may be deduced from Scripture" (I:6). Since in part it is the nature of Scripture to convey the eternal purposes of God and his gracious plan for redemption, it is only logical that the confession emphasize the importance of preaching the Scriptures: "The reading of the Scriptures with godly fear, the sound preaching and considerable hearing of the Word...are all parts of the ordinary worship of God" (XXI:5).

"The Directory for Worship," in the _Book of Church Order (BCO)_, which makes practical application of the doctrinal statements of the PCA to specific aspects of corporate worship, underscores the importance of preaching the Word: "The preaching of the Word is an ordinance of God for the salvation of men. Serious attention should be paid to the manner in which it is done. Preaching requires much study, meditation, and prayer, and ministers should prepare their sermons with care, and not indulge themselves in loose, extemporary harangues, nor serve God with that which costs them naught" (_BCO_, 531-1).

Free Selection of Texts

While stressing the prominence of preaching faithfully the Word of God, the _Book of Church Order_ allows latitude in the choice of which portion of that Word is to be expounded. The only instruction given on that point reads: "The subject of the sermon should be some verse or verses of Scripture, and its object, to explain, defend and apply some part of the system of divine truth. . . .

It is proper also that large portions of Scripture be sometimes expounded, and particularly improved, for the instruction of the people in the meaning and use of the Sacred Scriptures" (_BCO_, 53-2).

This means that appointed texts for the church year (lectionary) need not be followed. In fact, no congregations in the PCA are known to utilize a lectionary.

Sola Scriptura. Several reasons account for the rejection of a lectionary approach. First, the denomination holds dearly to the principle of _sola scriptura_. Scripture, and only Scripture, determines what must be preached. Strict adherence to a lectionary is regarded as infringing on this principle. True, only Scripture is given by a lectionary as the proper text for any sermon, but the choice of the text is denied the preacher who is guided by the lectionary. The minister must be sensitive to the Holy Spirit speaking through the Word. He or she selects those portions of God's Word to expound for their encouragement and edification.

Lectio Continua. Second, the practice of _lectio continua_ prevails in the denomination as opposed to _lectio selectia_. Expository preaching is the norm in the PCA—often in the form of systematic expositions of books and lengthy passages (e.g., the Sermon on the Mount, the Upper Room discourse, the parables). In an effort to lay precept upon precept and line upon line and so enhance the biblical knowledge of the congregation, ministers are instructed to preach in sequence through portions of Scripture rather than choose at random unrelated texts.

Traditio Accepto. Finally, the denomination has adopted the pattern of _traditio accepto_, and in particular the accepted tradition of holding no day above another. While it is true that most PCA pastors preach on Incarnation themes at Christmas and resurrection themes at Easter, this practice is not required. In fact, a few teaching elders avoid these themes at these seasons just to make the point that such "holy days" (holidays) are of human origin and are not signaled out by Scripture for special attention.

However, Dr. Brian Chapell, Professor of Homiletics at Covenant Theological Seminary, the PCA's only seminary, writes: "Distance from the battles of the Reformation, and a growing sense of the need to reach our culture, have made reformed churches more sensitive to the cultural calendar, but not more willing to mandate a liturgical calendar." He expresses well the sentiment of the PCA regarding the Christian year.

Wilson Benton, Jr.

136 ◆ PROGRESSIVE NATIONAL BAPTIST CONVENTION

Churches in the Progressive National Baptist Convention follow a worship calendar reflecting the African-American experience of God as liberator and sustainer, rather than the conventional Christian year. Annual observances include Christmas and Easter, but most Sundays are designated for focus on aspects of the church's ministry and role in society.

The Progressive National Baptist Convention is a part of the free-church tradition. Its congregations modify the Christian year followed in the denominations that use the Common Lectionary in order to address the spiritual and social needs of African-American worshipers.

Progressive Baptist congregations generally do not observe many of the traditional days such as Epiphany, Pentecost, Trinity Sunday, All Saints' Day, and Reformation Sunday. But they include on their calendar many observances which are not part of worship in mainline Protestant churches. These special days originate from a variety of sources, including cultural traditions, liberation theology, and the educational background of individual pastors. Which days a congregation includes in its church year varies according to its traditions and the influence of its pastors. And, the calendar of each church will vary from year to year, based on the program priorities.

—————— A Typical Calendar ——————

The following calendar, used by the Allen Temple Baptist Church of Oakland, California, is illustrative of the yearly cycle in Progressive National Baptist churches:

December 31	Watch Meeting Service
January	1	New Year's Day Fasting and Prayer
	5	Communion Sunday
	12	Martin Luther King, Jr.'s Birthday
	26	Baptismal Celebration
February	2	Communion
	4	Annual Meeting
	10	Black History
	16	Black History
	23	Black History and Boy Scout Emphasis
March	1	New Members Fellowship
	8	Annual Youth Day
	15	Pew Captain—Evangelism
	22	Black Male Redemption
	29	World Mission Sunday
April	5	Communion
	12	Music Department Sunday
	12	Palm Sunday
	17	Seven Last Words Preached by Seven Women
	19	Easter
	26	Baptism and New Member Discipleship Sunday
May	3	Communion
	10	Mother's Day
	17	Evangelism
	24	Baptism and Sunday School
	31	World Mission and Memorial Day Sunday
June	7	Communion
	14	Scholarship Awards and Graduation Recognition
	21	Father's Day
	28	Annual Urban Ministry Promotion
July	5	Freedom Sunday
	12	Hispanic Ministry Sunday
	19	Ecumenical Fellowship
	26	Ministers in Training Sunday
August	2	Communion
	9	Progressive
	16	
	23	Credit Union Sunday
	30	World Mission Sunday
September	6	Communion
	13	Deacons' Day
	14	Music Education
	20	Ushers' Day
	27	Annual Revival
October	4	Communion and New Members' Day
	11	Youth and Children's Day
	18	Loyalty Day
	25	Baptismal Emphasis
November	1	Communion
	8	Youth Day
	15	Young Adults
	22	Evangelism

November 26   Thanksgiving Worship
        29   Annual Women's Day
December 6   Advent Sunday
        13   Annual Minister's and Lay
               Minister's Day
        20   Christmas Sunday
        25   Ecumenical Christmas Worship
        27   College Students Emphasis
        28   Kwanza Observance

Special High Days

1. Ordination
2. Installation of Church Officers
3. Christian Education Week
4. Volunteers Appreciation
5. Public Safety Observance
6. Baby Dedication Sunday (on third Sunday of each month)
7. Children's Week
8. Athletic Day Observance
9. Library Sunday
10. Senior Citizen's Day

The scheduling of these services varies from year to year, and the calendar is flexible enough to meet changing needs. For example, in response to crises like the Oakland earthquake and Oakland Hills fire, special services were called to address the anxieties of the community.

Lay members take a prominent role in planning and leading special observances. Prior to revival, Loyalty Day, and New Year's worship observances, the laity are present for prayer, anointing, and twenty-four-hour seasons of fasting and introspection.

——— Worship and Social Concerns ———

Progressive National Baptist churches also stress social concerns in their worship calendars. In addition to NAACP Sunday and Voter Registration Sunday, days may be designated for focus on such programs as prison ministry and AIDS hospice ministry. Allen Temple Baptist Church designates a day of worship for the promotion of its job information ministry and drug and alcohol recovery ministry. These worship services have the same priority as the observance of Christmas, Mother's Day, and Easter.

More and more churches are promoting Rites of Passage Sunday for children and youth, usually in connection with Saturday and Sunday church school promotion.

Worship in the Progressive National Baptist tradition does not emphasize the liturgy of historic and Reformation churches as much as response to the activity of God as liberator and sustainer in the hostile and unfriendly environment of the African-American pilgrimage in American culture. Cornel West of Princeton University describes the African-American religious experience as a "kind of Good Friday state or existence in which one is seemingly forever on the cross, perennially crucified, continuously abused, and incessantly devalued—yet sustained and empowered by hope against hope for a potential and possible triumphant state of affairs" (Cornel West, _Prophetic Fragments_ [Grand Rapids: Eerdmans, 1988], 5).

This religion is neither worldly or an idealistic earthly quest for paradise in the political sense, but a Christ-centered emphasis of survival and struggle in an absurd and insane world. The church year in the Progressive National Baptist Convention reflects this religious and social reality.

J. Alfred Smith, Sr.

137 ◆ REFORMED CHURCH IN AMERICA

Though heir to the Calvinist Reformation which eliminated worship practices not specified in Scripture, the Reformed Church in America has in recent decades turned toward fuller usage of the Christian year. Increasingly, congregations are discovering that the liturgy, music, symbols, and education connected with the church year do not threaten the primacy of Scripture but dramatize the biblical story and help connect faith to all aspects of human experience.

The extent to which congregations in the Reformed Church in America (RCA) practice the church year varies widely. A few churches observe only Christmas, Easter, and Palm Sunday. More than 80 percent keep Advent, Lent, Maundy Thursday, and Pentecost. About three-quarters observe Good Friday, around 40 percent celebrate Epiphany, Ascension, and Ash Wednesday, and almost a quarter mark Trinity Sunday. (Survey data from _Worship: A Newsletter for Congregations in the Reformed Church in America_ [March 1987]: 3).

Modes of Observance

The mode of observance similarly varies. Some churches pattern all of congregational life on the church year. For others, the most noticeable variation is changed paraments.

Using liturgical colors is in fact the most common way to mark the seasons. Varying paraments and vestments visibly affects worship space. Banners reinforcing seasonal color and symbol are especially popular during Advent, Christmas, Easter, and Pentecost. They may be fixed or used in procession, especially with children waving palms on Palm Sunday. Color drapes are used on crosses or as dossal cloths.

Some congregations schedule the sacrament of the Lord's Supper at the beginnings of seasons, most often Advent, Christmas, Lent, Easter, and All Saints' Day.

Music helps set the seasonal tone. Brass instruments and bells give a celebrative mood to Easter and Pentecost. The "Hallelujah Chorus" may be sung on Easter or Ascension. Hymn festivals are used on Trinity, All Saints', and Christ the King Sundays. Services of lessons and carols find a place at Christmas.

Candles, flowers, and other accouterments enrich worship at various points in the year. Advent wreaths use candles. Some churches light a Christmas Christ candle, have services of Tenebrae (darkening) on Maundy Thursday, and use a Paschal candle. One congregation lights its candelabra chandelier annually on Pentecost.

A profusion of lilies is common on Easter and poinsettias at Christmastide. The absence of flowers during Lent provides contrast. A bare, gnarled tree might be used during Lent. A rough-hewn cross for Holy Week turns around filled with lilies for Easter.

One congregation has a chancel-height, airy fabric sculpture for Ascension Sunday. Chrismons are widely used, appearing at the beginning of Advent or just before Christmas. On Pentecost in some congregations, worshipers wear red and children receive wind gifts—balloons, windsocks, pinwheels. One congregation has a Pentecost fair to recruit folks for mission tasks.

Special services mark the church year. On Christmas Eve early services are held for families as well as eleven o'clock services. Other special services include Ash Wednesday (with imposition of ashes), Maundy Thursday, Good Friday (often ecumenical), and Easter sunrise.

Liturgy reflects the church year. For example, some churches omit confession of sin during Christmas and Easter celebration. Multiple languages may be used for Pentecost readings. The year's necrology is read on All Saints' Day.

Beyond worship, some congregations schedule all-church events. Wreath-making and activities with fellowship suppers accent Advent. Lent offers intergenerational learning opportunities. New member classes take place during Lent in preparation for reception at Easter, or during Easter for Pentecost.

The Reformed Heritage

Such a wide variety in practice is remarkable for congregations originating in the Calvinist Reformation. Historically, this tradition sought to recover the primitive simplicity of the early church by patterning worship in "only what is ordained by God in the Scriptures." (Horton Davies, *The Worship of the English Puritans* [Westminster, U. K.: Dacre Press, 1948],16). Distracting or presumptuous innovations are avoided. Reformed worship was often bare in comparison with other forms (M. Eugene Osterhaven, *The Spirit of the Reformed Tradition* [Grand Rapids: Eerdmans, 1972], 58). Most accretions to the church calendar were eliminated.

Some shape and pattern to the year was preserved, however. The 1907 revision of *Liturgy and Psalms* (RCA constitutional liturgy) contained the year's Scripture lessons divided into three seasons: the Advent of our Lord, the Death and Resurrection of our Lord, and the Mission of the Holy Comforter. "Certain occasions" had appointed prayers and Psalms: Advent, Christmas day, Epiphany, Good Friday, Easter Day, Whitsunday, and All Saints' Day. In 1953, Reformed liturgical scholar Howard Hageman stated that the seasons of the Christian year "have always been observed by our Reformed church." (Howard G. Hageman, *Lily Among the Thorns* [New York: Reformed Church Press, 1953], 115).

Movement toward the Whole Church Year

Several factors contributed to a gradual, but logical, movement from observing days—Christmas, Good Friday, Easter—to keeping the church year as a whole. One influence has been the liturgical renewal movement. Increased availability of resources encourages enrichment of worship through symbol, sense, color, and season.

The RCA Commission on Worship also encouraged this movement. Significantly, the 1968 revision of _Liturgy and Psalms_ introduced a fuller version of the Christian year. It contained a "church-year calendar" with the three seasons further defined: Advent (Advent, Christmas, Epiphany), Death and Resurrection (Ash Wednesday, Lent, Palm Sunday, Good Friday, Easter, Ascension), and Mission of the Holy Spirit (Pentecost and Sundays after). It provided prayers and canticles for the Christian year. It used terminology common to the wider church, such as Ash Wednesday, Lent, Ascension, and Pentecost. These changes in language and amount of material gave the church year new prominence.

Perhaps the most important development encouraging this shift was the addition of Common Lectionary texts and naming of liturgical days and colors on the RCA plan calendar in the early 1980s. A tradition of lectionary use, historically based on _lectio continua_—continuous readings—made introduction of the church year-based Common Lectionary logical. A 1988 resource, _Pray to the Lord_, offered corporate prayers organized by liturgical day and season.

Wide adoption of "Children and Worship" a church year-based program, encourages churches to reinforce children's experiences by following the church year in congregational life.

Why is the RCA observing more of the Christian year? There is a growing appreciation that the church year provides a dynamic annual curriculum that dramatizes the biblical story. As it unfolds, we celebrate historic events that form our faith foundation. These themes also embrace our experiences of longing, waiting, fulfillment, joy, doubt, and growth, so familiar texts are fresh each cycle. Following the church year enables Christians to understand all experience in the light of Christian faith.

What is the future of the church year in the RCA? Surely wide variation will continue among congregations. However, more probably will observe the church year in deeper ways. Doing so will form congregational life and ensure a full presentation of the Christian story. The role of the arts is apt to expand. Traditional liturgical objects like Advent wreaths and Paschal candles will find increasing use. More congregations will develop distinctive practices.

Understanding of seasons may deepen. When change is new, sometimes only outward trappings change. As experience of the church year in the RCA lengthens, understanding will deepen. Lectionary texts will increasingly inform season understandings. For example, a tradition of living more than half a century with "The Season for the Death and Resurrection of our Lord" makes it difficult to see that Lent is really about discipleship, priorities, and growing in faith and that Holy Week is the time to meditate on Christ's passion. Maybe the prevalent confusion between Advent and Christmas will abate and more churches will celebrate two distinct seasons.

Increasing observance of the church year has enriched worship in the RCA, complementing the Reformation understanding of the primacy of Scripture.

Carol Peterkin Meyers

138 • REFORMED EPISCOPAL CHURCHES

The Reformed Episcopal Church has always used The Book of Common Prayer _to guide worship life. However, the extent to which congregations have observed the church year outlined in the prayer book has varied. In recent years there has been a resurgence of interest in fuller observance of the church year, motivated by commitment to following scriptural insight concerning worship._

The Reformed Episcopal Church (REC) embraces the English liturgical tradition as expressed in _The Book of Common Prayer_. The denomination has retained the Christian year primarily because of its commitment to the Word of God, first and foremost. REC worship leaders take the Pauline injunction to "redeem the time" (Eph. 5:16) to mean that the daily, weekly, and seasonal cycles of time created by God should all be sanctified through worship.

The Redemption of Time

The Book of Common Prayer guides the church in the redemption of time. It calls for worship on a daily, weekly, and seasonal routine. Daily, there is Morning and Evening Prayer. Weekly, the Lord's Supper can and should be observed.

Seasonally, the church year recapitulates the life of Christ. Each natural season comes under an event in Christ's life, starting before his birth and continuing after his Ascension when the church begins to grow: Fall is the season of Advent, preparation for the coming of Christ. In winter comes Christmas, marking the birth of Christ, and Epiphany, the first appearing of our Lord in his ministry to the Gentiles. In early spring, Lent focuses on the temptations, trials, suffering, and death of Christ. Then comes the spring celebrations of the Resurrection at Easter and of the Ascension, the enthronement of the Lord in heaven to establish his kingdom. Finally, in later spring and summer, Pentecost (sometimes called the Trinity season) directs attention to the growth of the church through the Holy Spirit.

At the beginning of these church seasons, there are special days on the church calendar. The lectionary prescribes worship and there are even lessons for the Eucharist to be observed on those days. In the Reformed Episcopal Church, most churches observe the special days such as Christmas, Ash Wednesday, Lent, and Easter. Many churches are beginning also to hold services on other days in the church year such as All Souls' Day (November 1), Epiphany, Holy Week, Easter Vigil (Saturday evening before Easter), Ascension Day, and Transfiguration Day, to name the main ones.

Seasonal Services and Evangelism

REC churches are discovering that these services are not only good for the faithful, but they are excellent times to bring others into the life of the church. After all, it is easier to work with someone on a seasonal basis to try to establish church routines. How better to draw someone into the life of the church than by gradual introduction to the church's worship?

Thus, the Reformed Episcopal Church is enjoying a resurgence of interest in all of the aspects of the church calendar. Some parishes observe more days than others. By and large, however, the trend is in the direction to which the REC, on the basis of Scripture, has always been committed— the redemption of time for our glorious Lord and Savior, Jesus Christ.

Ray Sutton

139 • ROMAN CATHOLIC CHURCHES

Practice of the church year, which has developed over centuries in the Roman Catholic tradition, underwent major revision as a result of the Second Vatican Council. The changes were designed to recover the primacy of the "paschal mystery" of Christ's death and resurrection in both of the major cycles, the Christological and the sanctoral.

> Christ's saving work is celebrated in sacred memory by the church on fixed days throughout the year. Each week on the day called the Lord's Day the church commemorates the Lord's resurrection. Once a year at Easter the church honors this resurrection and passion with the utmost solemnity. In fact through the yearly cycle the church unfolds the entire mystery of Christ and keeps the anniversaries of the saints.

This statement from the opening of the *General Norms for the Liturgical Year and the Calendar*, which became effective in 1970 under Pope Paul VI, reveals the two primary cycles of the liturgical year in the Roman Catholic tradition: the cycle of feasts and commemorations, which remember the life and actions of Jesus Christ, and the cycle of anniversaries commemorating holy people or those Christians whose lives and actions best exemplify what it is to follow Christ. Both of the cycles, Christological and sanctoral, have their foundation in the building block of Sunday, the weekly celebration of the Resurrection.

Christological and Sanctoral Cycles

Observance of Sunday, the first feast, underlay the development of the annual feast of Easter. And it is Easter, that annual commemoration of Jesus' passing over from death to life, which gives rise to the structure of the liturgical year, first in the extension of Easter for fifty days (the Pentecost), then in the time of preparation for Easter, known as Lent. This first part of the Christological cycle, known as the paschal cycle, extends from Ash Wednesday to the Sunday of Pentecost in the current calendar.

The other part of the Christological cycle is the Incarnation cycle, centered on the celebration of God become human and the consequent sanctification of humanity. Christmas is at the center of the cycle, surrounded by that feast's extension of twelve days until January 6, and the period of preparation, known in the contemporary church as Advent. This cycle, from the first Sunday of Advent until Epiphany, and including the Baptism of the Lord beyond that, makes up the other anchor of the liturgical year.

The sanctoral cycle that commemorates the saints also has its theological basis in the weekly celebration of the Resurrection. It is in and through Christ that the martyrs suffered and died, filled with hope and confident of the Resurrection, and it is in and through Christ that the saints lived and died, modeling a life lived in close communion with Christ. The structure of commemorations in the contemporary church follows the ancient tradition of commemorating a martyr (or a saint) on their death date, which was their birthday into eternal life.

The New Calendar and the Centrality of Easter

The new calendar promulgated in 1970 retained as its basis the Christological and sanctoral cycles form the historic Roman Catholic liturgical calendar, but also instituted major revisions. The changes that the Second Vatican Council set in motion and which took shape in the 1970 calendar were based first of all on a concern that the primacy of the life and death of Jesus Christ were becoming obscured behind the avalanche of prepatory celebrations and saints' feasts. The primary focus of the liturgical year is the "paschal mystery," the dying and rising and Christ and its implications for each Christian life. Thus, new emphasis was placed on the centrality of Easter. Measures taken toward that end included restorations to the liturgy, particularly the three holy days from Holy Thursday evening to Easter Sunday evening, and the returning of Lent to its earlier focus as a time of preparation for Easter, especially for those preparing to be baptized at Easter. Moreover, other commemorations, especially those of saints and particular parish celebrations, were moved out of the time of Lent and Easter so as not to distract from the primary focus. The Incarnation cycle was likewise restored so that Advent moves towards Christmas, and Christmas celebrated in all its fullness in the time between December 25 and January 6.

The new calendar also implemented changes in the sanctoral cycle. Vatican II clearly ranked the two cycles by explaining that the "Proper of Seasons," or the Christological cycle, took precedence over the "Proper of Saints" or sanctoral cycle. Because of that, many saints were removed from the calendar, particularly those for whom no historical foundation could be found. In some cases, even saints with historical precedence were deleted from the universal calendar in an effort to "clean house" and relieve the clutter of nineteen hundred years of accumulation. Conversely, the 1970 calendar also added saints, primarily from geographical areas which had been previously underrepresented in the calendar, specifically those countries to which Christianity had come in recent times.

Coping with Change

Twenty-two years after the promulgation of the new calendar, some Roman Catholic communities are still wrestling with the changes, some have forgotten what it was like before Vatican II, and many have moved forward, prophetically revealing what future directions may look like.

One of the most difficult changes for many Catholics to cope with was the "loss" of their favorite saint, a classic example being St. Christopher. Also, many perceive an imbalance among honored saints in the sanctoral cycle. They believe a calendar of celibate Italian men does not represent the diversity which has always characterized the church.

Within the Christological calendar an issue still being dealt with is the difficulty of ritualizing the alternation of preparation and fulfillment. The season of Lent, the period of preparation for Easter, is given far more emphasis than the period of fulfillment, namely the fifty days of Easter. To overemphasize one and de-emphasize the other is to lose the balance in and the truth of the death and resurrection of Christ. Many Catholic communities seem still to prefer penance to celebration, reflection on sin over hope in salvation.

Conflicting Calendars

Another contemporary issue with which many churches grapple is the interaction of the church calendar and the many other calendars to which people owe allegiance. The liturgical year is but one sequence of fast and feast to which most people are called. Many families live their lives based on the academic calendar. The calendar of

Ladder and Reed. *The ladder and reed appear frequently as symbols of our Lord's suffering on the cross. It recalls the cruel act of giving him vinegar to drink when he called for water and accents the suffering he bore.*

solution to a lack of diversity in the representative saints in this two-tiered system. Each community would have their own sanctoral cycle in addition to the universal calendar.

Another profound influence on the marking of the liturgical year has been the adoption of the R.C.I.A. (Rite of Christian Initiation of Adults). In parishes where this restored process of initiation has been followed for several years, parishioners report a renewed (or new) understanding of what Lent really is, how the year unfolds, and most particularly, the centrality of Easter, with its celebration of baptism at the core. More than any treatise on the importance of the church calendar, the experience of accompanying new Christians through the richness of the liturgical year has restored Easter as "the culmination of the entire liturgical year: dying he destroyed our death and rising he restored our life" (*General Norms for the Liturgical Year and the Calendar*, 18).

Lizette Larson-Miller

the civil religion can conflict with the liturgical calendar. The Feast of Pentecost, for example, lands on Mother's Day in May.

Probably the most prominent and the most frustrating clash is between the Incarnation cycle and the retail industry calendar. The Catholic church tries to honor the season of Advent as a season of preparation for Christmas, and Christmas as a twelve-day celebration beginning December 25. The retail industry, on the other hand, insists that Christmas begins in mid-October and ends on the evening of December 24. All of these conflicts pull Christians in two different directions, either towards an integration of the calendars marking their lives or towards a countercultural movement which makes a choice against the prevailing norms of society.

The influence of individual churches and groups of churches on the future of the calendar is also a factor in the living of the church year. Many communities see two liturgical calendars as a just solution: the universal calendar, in which the primary feasts are celebrated in conjunction with the whole church, and the local calendar, in which the "saints" of a parish, the anniversary of the church's dedication, and the commemoration of special events may be celebrated. Some see the

140 • SALVATION ARMY

Worship in the Salvation Army does not include sacraments or observance of the traditional church year. Salvationists regard these practices as unnecessary to the life of consecration to God, experienced through the inward power of the Holy Spirit. They do, however, believe in the importance of ceremonies such as child dedication, enrollment of soldiers (members), and commissioning of officers (clergy), events which recognize and celebrate decisive moments in an individual's spiritual life.

The Salvation Army is nonsacramental, practicing neither water baptism nor the rite of Communion in its corporate worship. Like the Quakers, Salvationist believe that sacraments and ordinances are symbols of spiritual truths and seek to experience the realities these symbols represent.

A Spiritual Approach

General Frederick Coutts explains The Salvation Army's position on sacraments in his book *In Good Company*: "Our witness is simply that the presence of Christ may be realized, and His grace freely received, without the aid of any material elements. Our testimony is not against the sacraments—and never has been—but to the truth that the unsearchable riches of grace can be communicated by the Holy Spirit and received directly by the believer who comes to the throne of grace in faith. (Allan Satterlee, _Notable Quotables: A Compendium of Gems from Salvation Army Literature_ [Atlanta: The Salvation Army, 1985], 177).

For Salvation Army founder William Booth, the one true sign of the church and of conversion was participating in the work of redemption. (Roger Green, _War on Two Fronts: The Redemptive Theology of William Booth_ [Atlanta: The Salvation Army, 1989], 56). In an 1889 address, he declared, "Neither water, sacraments, church services not Salvation Army methods will save you without a living, inward change of heart and a living active faith and communion with God...and an active, positive, personal consecration of yourself and all you have got to help Him who hung upon the cross to fill the world with salvation and bring lost sinners to His feet." Periodic observances of the sacraments were not to be criticized, but simply deemed unnecessary for experiencing and demonstrating holiness of heart. For Booth, as for Salvationist today, the scriptural essentials were baptism by the Holy Spirit and constant communion with God.

General Albert Orsborn portrays the Army's spiritual approach to the sacraments in his song, "My Life Must Be Christ's Broken Bread":

My life must be Christ's broken bread,
My love his outpoured wine,
A cup o'erfilled, a table spread
Beneath his name and sign,
That other souls refreshed and red,
May share his life through mine.

———— Sacramental Ceremonies ————

The Salvation Army's spiritual approach does not exclude all ceremony, however. Salvationists recognize that ceremonies help individuals and congregations mark spiritual milestones. For that reason, the Army practices the dedication of children, the enrollment of soldiers, and the commissioning of officers (clergy) and local officers (lay leaders).

With the flag of the Salvation Army as backdrop, each of these ceremonies marks a solemn covenant and a joyous celebration. In the dedication ceremony, parents affirm their desire for the child

to live entirely for God and serve wherever God leads. They promise that they will not keep their child from "hardship, suffering, poverty or sacrifice in the service of Jesus Christ and the Salvation Army" and that they will be to the child true examples of salvationism. The congregation is asked to participate by declaring their intention to pray for parents and child and to help them carry out the promises made in the dedication ceremony.

The enrollment of soldiers (members) begins with the signing of "The Articles of War" (a soldier's covenant), which affirms agreement with Salvation Army doctrine and principles. Soldiers (members) promise, among other things, to abstain from alcohol and tobacco and to pursue a life of holiness.

Officers (clergy) are ordained and commissioned after signing a covenant promising to love and serve God, to make soul-winning the first purpose of their life, and to uphold the doctrines and principles of the Salvation Army. Local officers (lay leaders) are commissioned by their corps officer for specific tasks at the local corps (church) level.

While they are not intended as replacements or substitutes for traditional sacraments, each of these Salvation Army ceremonies is, in some measure, sacramental because they are external symbols of inexpressible inward works of grace.

Lesa Salyer

141 ✦ Southern Baptist Convention Churches

Observance of the Christian year has been on the increase in the Southern Baptist Convention since the 1960s. Civic and denominational calendars have greatly influenced Southern Baptist worship in the past, but many congregations are turning toward the Christian year because of the vivid way it involves the worshiper in the biblical narrative and deepens spiritual life. It also provides an especially meaningful context for the ordinance of believer's baptism.

Historically, Southern Baptists have observed parts of the Christian calendar, including Sunday as the Lord's Day—the Christian Sabbath set aside for worship of the risen Lord, and Easter Sunday.

Special seasonal services, mostly of a musical character, have been customary at Christmas time, but there was no set liturgy for Christmas services or for a season of Advent. Another annual tradition was the spring revival—preaching services with evangelistic intent.

Gradual Advances

Interest in the Christian year has surged during the past few decades among a significant number of Southern Baptist congregations. In the 1960s many congregations enlarged the scope of their observance to include Holy Week. Palm Sunday, Maundy Thursday, and Good Friday services were established. In some churches the spring revival gave way to a series of preaching services during Holy Week.

In the 1970s new interest emerged in the observance of Advent, with four Sundays devoted to preparation for the birth of Christ. Advent banners, wreaths, and family devotional books came into use. Crescent Hill Baptist Church became a leader in Advent observance. The congregation prepared an Advent book of devotions. Visually and liturgically the Sunday worship services took on a new look. Evening services began on the first Sunday in Advent with a Hanging of the Greens service, and each Sunday evening service afterward took on a special character, such as a Moravian Love Feast, a Christmas choral service, a drama, or a Lessons and Carols service.

Increased observance of other seasons of the Christian year has come about in the past two decades, roughly in this order of introduction: the full Lenten season, Pentecost Sunday, Epiphany as the manifestation of Jesus' glory in his earthly ministry, and Eastertide as a season rather than Easter Sunday alone. Other dates such as World Communion Sunday and Reformation Sunday have also come to be observed.

Also during the 1970s through 1990s, use of the Common Lectionary has been introduced in Baptist worship. The regular reading of two or three texts and sermons based on the prescribed texts has encouraged emphasis on the Christian year in preaching.

Benefits for Baptists

About a third of Southern Baptist churches now observe all the aspects of the Christian year referred to above. They have experienced worship renewal through such practice for several reasons.

(1) The Christian year invites the congregation to enter more fully into the narrative world of the Bible and the life of Christ. The year revolves around Christ's entrance into the world, his ministry, death, resurrection, and presence in the church through the Holy Spirit. The life of the people of God called Israel is integrated into Advent and Lent and through regular lections in the Common Lectionary.

This narrative world of the Bible is a much more spiritually powerful way of structuring the year than other calendars that tend to dominate in its absence: the civic calendar with July 4th, Memorial Day, Mother's and Father's Days, Labor Day, Thanksgiving, etc.; and the denominational calendar of program promotion.

A vigorously promoted calendar from denominational headquarters in Nashville became dominant in Southern Baptist life during the twentieth century. Nearly every Sunday was designated for emphasis on some program or offering. The calendar included, for example, Lottie Moon Christmas Offering for Foreign Missions, Annie Armstrong Easter Offering for Home Mission, Cooperative Program Sunday, Race Relations Sunday, Baptist Men's Day, World Hunger Sunday, Senior Adult Sunday, Women's Missionary Union Focus Week, and Thanksgiving Offering for Children's Homes. The denominational calendar had a remarkable effect in building programs and raising offerings, but worshipers often lost sight of their yearly pilgrimage within the story of the Bible and life of Christ. Churches introducing the Christian year had to use sensitivity in negotiating competition with the denominational calendar.

(2) The Christian calendar emphasizes our human role in preparation for the birth of Christ and then his death and resurrection. Advent and Lent encourages intense spiritual focus and preparation.

(3) Recovery of the Christian year unites Southern Baptists more closely with the larger ecumenical fellowship of Christians and involves them in learning from that larger fellowship.

(4) The Christian year gives vivid visual, narrative, and experiential context for teaching of major Christian doctrines like Incarnation, Atonement, Resurrection, and the Holy Spirit.

(5) Spiritual disciplines at home which correspond to what is going on at church can be devel-

oped. The use of family Advent wreaths and devotions is a prime example of this benefit.

(6) At Crescent Hill, the Christian year provides the context for the ordinance of believer's baptism by immersion. We always baptize persons on Christmas Eve and Easter Sunday. The meaning of the seasons interacts in a powerful way with the personal decision to follow Christ and be baptized. Sometimes we also have Pentecost Sunday baptism. The Lenten season has become for us a season of baptismal renewal culminating in the renewal of baptismal vows on Easter Sunday morning following the baptism of new Christians.

(7) The seasons of the Christian year have awakened Southern Baptist churches to the full use of all their senses in worship. Symbols and visual arts, drama and pageantry are now used to greater effect and were introduced first as parts of the Christian year.

Response and Prospects

Pastors, ministers of music, and lay worship committees are increasingly making use of the Christian year. The response has been mostly positive in most Southern Baptist churches who have introduced the church year. There has been some resistance from people who were devoted to the denominational calendar and were afraid it would be displaced, or who were afraid their Baptist church was becoming "too Catholic" or "too Episcopalian." Overall, introduction of the Christian year has been greeted with acceptance and joy.

I see an increased use of the Christian year in a certain segment of the Southern Baptist Convention, particularly among congregations which are ecumenically oriented and open to the use of arts and liturgy in worship.

In an increasingly secular society, the Christian year is a substantial help in creating a narrative world that can inform and shape that lives of Christians.

H. Stephen Shoemaker

142 ✦ UNITED CHURCH OF CHRIST

The Christian year structures worship in the United Church of Christ. Because its themes mirror a full range of human experience, practice of the Christian year enables worshipers to unite more fully with Christ and the community of faith.

The United Church of Christ stands in the tradition of the apostolic church and the Protestant Reformation. Drawing on these deep historic roots, its congregations practice the Christian year in public worship.

Christmas and Easter are basic to the rhythm of Christian worship each year. But the Christian year is more than these two events—it comprehends the entire calendar year. Each portion of the year, in varying ways, leads us to enter fully the life of Christ and the community of the faithful.

The Half Year of the Lord

The Christian year is divided into two halves. The time from Advent until Pentecost is the half year of the Lord. The time from Pentecost until Advent is the half year of the church.

The Christian year begins at Advent, the four-week season which precedes Christmas. Readings that speak that hope and expectation are used in worship. We recall the lives of John the Baptist and Mary, the mother of Jesus. An Advent wreath with four candles is commonly used. Each week the appropriate number of candles are lighted in order to designate how close Christmas has come.

Following Advent the twelve-day season of Christmas, during which we celebrate the nativity of our Lord, extends from December 25 until January 6. Worship once again includes familiar readings and the singing of Christmas music. It is a time of joy for promises kept and hopes fulfilled.

The season of Epiphany begins on January 6th and runs until the beginning of Lent at Ash Wednesday. The day of Easter, fixed by a lunar formula, determines when Ash Wednesday appears in the calendar. Thus, Epiphany varies in length from year to year but its meaning remains the same—the unfolding to the world of the nature and power of the Christ just born. We hear stories of Simeon and Anna perceiving the true nature of the Christ and affirming the testimony of the birth. The season also points to the development of Jesus' self-awareness, marked by his baptism. Correspondingly, it is a time of reflection on commitment to Jesus as the one offered to fulfill human needs and longings.

Lent begins on Ash Wednesday and lasts for forty days, excluding Sundays, until Easter Day. The season begins with the imposition of ashes, a practice reclaimed from the historic church by many in contemporary worship. Lent is marked by additional times of devotion and personal reflection. It is a season to come to terms with ourselves, on the heels of being asked to come to terms with Jesus. It is a time to recognize our culpability in the shortcomings of the world that can deny the one whom Simeon and Anna acknowledged. Lent turns the tables on us.

Holy Week concludes Lent and is marked by the use of palm branches, Maundy Thursday Communion that recalls the Last Supper and the offering of the great commandment, and a Good Friday vigil of penitence.

The season of Easter begins with the celebration of the resurrection of Jesus. This can begin on Saturday evening with a service of light or on Easter morning. The theme is always the theme of new life and renewal. The celebration of Holy Communion at Easter commonly takes place as an experience shared with those first disciples for whom the risen Christ was made known in the breaking of the bread and the pouring of the wine. The season lasts for fifty days until the day of Pentecost. The entire season is one of joy and belief in the possibilities of overcoming the barriers imposed by the powers of destruction in our world.

The Half Year of the Church

The day of Pentecost is a celebration of the birth of the church and the coming of the Holy Spirit to our community. It begins the half year of the church. We call the days of Pentecost "ordinary days"—routine days during which we experience growth and development. These are days of nurturing in the church, the family of God's people.

The power and presence of the Holy Spirit becomes the source of faith, comfort, and strength to move forward and engage the world around us in efforts to advance the realm of God. This is a long season as befits a time of pilgrimage and nurturing.

A Mirror of Human Experience

Practice of the Christian year is spiritually powerful because its themes mirror our human experience so completely that we are able to link ourselves with Jesus Christ and the community of faith in ways that endure. As normal human beings we live our lives with the same dynamics that the Christian year acknowledged. We approach life with hope and expectation (Advent). It is hope that allows us to set goals, plan, and move forward. It is hope that enables us to envision new days and make things happen for the good. Life without expectation—Advent—is an empty life.

Personal strength is built upon hopes being realized and promises fulfilled—Christmas. To know that promises can be kept is the basis for trust in all our lives. Christmas assures us that we can live with trust in our world.

Human life is also marked by the process of unfolding wisdom. Epiphany mirrors this human dynamic and helps us make truth our own and formulate our beliefs.

As human beings we also need to come to terms with our shortcomings. We need to see the part that we contribute to the barriers that exist in human relationships in our world. We need to come to terms with failure. Lent is our time of being honest with ourselves—the spiritual parallel to the watershed experience in human life.

To be alive is to find new direction and resolve in the aftermath of falling short. To live full lives we need to go forward. Trouble cannot be the final word in our human experience. Easter is the spiritual word for the human experience of new beginnings and opportunities.

Most of life is spent in routine. We do what we have to do. We develop relationships and find moments of peace and joy. Pentecost is the spiritual parallel of this process—the time of growth and maturity in the routine of life.

The Christian year in worship is the portrayal and the ceremonial of what living a full human existence is all about. It combines the realities of human living with the message of Holy Scripture for personal wholeness.

Dennis F. Frederickson

143 ✦ UNITED METHODIST CHURCHES

In the late eighteenth and nineteenth centuries, observance of the Christian year by American Methodists was mainly limited to "great festivals" such as Christmas, Easter, and Whitsunday (Pentecost). A movement toward recovery of the entire Christian year gained momentum in the mid-twentieth century, and in 1984 United Methodists adopted the ecumenical Common Lectionary and calendar.

Methodism began as a movement led by John Wesley (1703–1791), a priest of the Church of England who followed the Christian year as set forth in *The Book of Common Prayer*. When the Methodists in America set up the Methodist Episcopal Church in 1784, Wesley sent them an adaptation of *The Book of Common Prayer*, entitled *Sunday Service of the Methodists in North America*. In this work he simplified the Anglican version of the Christian year to include: Sundays of Advent (four), Nativity of Christ (Christmas), Sundays after Christmas (up to fifteen), Sunday before Easter, Good Friday, Easter Day, Sundays after Easter (five), Ascension Day, Sunday after Ascension Day, Whitsunday (Pentecost), Trinity Sunday, and Sundays after Trinity Sunday (up to twenty-six). Every Sunday was, of course, the Lord's Day and all the Fridays in the year (except if one fell on Christmas Day) were "days of fasting or abstinence."

A Combined Calendar

In 1792 the American Methodists officially abandoned large section of Wesley's *Sunday Service*, including the table of the Christian year, but they did not by any means abandon the entire Christian year. First, they continued strongly to emphasize the weekly Lord's Day, the most basic observance of the Christian year. Second, the *Discipline* (official book of church law) from 1784 until the middle of the nineteenth century advised preachers, "Everywhere avail yourself of the great festivals by preaching on the occasion." However, what these "great festivals" were was not specified. Third, evidence from denominational hymnals and *Discipline* indicates that in the years following 1792 Methodists were encouraged to observe at least Christmas, New Year, Good Friday, Easter, and Whitsunday.

During the nineteenth and early twentieth centuries, a form of Christian year observance gradually developed that combined the traditional Christian year with civil holidays and promotional days. In the mid-nineteenth century Methodists, like most American Protestants, began to re-emphasize Christmas and Easter. Soon much of December became in effect a Christmas season, and Palm Sunday became a popular prelude to Easter. In the late nineteenth and early twentieth centuries a few Methodists were observing—or at least advocating the observance of—the Lenten season (including Ash Wednesday and Holy Week), a forty-day Eastertide, Ascension, Pentecost, and Trinity Sunday. Civil celebrations such as Independence Day, Thanksgiving Day, and Memorial Day (or the previous Sundays) were prominent in the calendars of Methodist churches. So were camp meetings and revivals, anniversary celebrations, homecomings, and observances such as Rally Day, Children's Day, and later Mother's Day.

Recovery of the Entire Christian Year

The recovery of the traditional Christian year accelerated in the middle third of the twentieth century. The official hymnal of 1935 contained a calendar that included the four Sundays in Advent, Christmas and the Sunday following, Epiphany, Ash Wednesday, the Sundays in Lent, Thursday before Easter, Good Friday, Easter Sunday, Ascension day and the Sunday after Ascension, Whitsunday, and Trinity Sunday.

The first edition of *The Book of Worship* (1945) contained a calendar and lectionary for the entire Christian year: the Sundays in Advent, Christmas and the Sundays after Christmas, the New Year, Epiphany and the Sundays after Epiphany, Ash Wednesday, the Sundays in Lent, each day in Holy Week, Easter and the Sundays after Pentecost (beginning with Trinity Sunday), Festival of Christ the King (first Sunday in August), the Sundays in Kingdomtide, All Saints' Day (November 1), and Thanksgiving.

The 1965 edition of *The Book of Worship* and the official hymnal of 1966 continued this calendar with minor changes and expanded the lectionary to include Old Testament, Epistle, and Gospel readings, a Psalm, and another act of praise for each Sunday. A color was suggested for each day or season, since colored chancel paraments and clergy stoles have become popular.

In 1968 the Methodist Church united with the much smaller Evangelical United Brethren Church, which likewise had a growing interest in recovering the Christian year, to form the United Methodist Church. The new denomination joined with other Christian denominations in the development of an ecumenical Christian calendar and lectionary.

In 1982 an ecumenical Common Lectionary, based on a common calendar of the Christian year, was published for trial use, and a Revised Common Lectionary was published in 1992. For each Sunday and other appointed days in the Christian year there are first and second lessons (from the Old and New Testaments), a Psalm, and a Gospel. The Common Lectionary and the calendar on which it was based were officially adopted by the United Methodist Church in 1984, and the Revised Common Lectionary was included with the following calendar (and suggested colors) in *The United Methodist Book of Worship*, published in 1992.

ADVENT (purple or blue)

First Sunday to the Fourth Sunday of Advent

CHRISTMAS SEASON (white or gold)

Nativity of the Lord (Christmas Eve, Christmas Day); First Sunday after Christmas Day; New Year's Eve or New Year's Day; Epiphany of the Lord

SEASON AFTER THE EPIPHANY (ORDINARY TIME)

First Sunday after the Epiphany (Baptism of the Lord) (white); Second Sunday to the Eighth Sunday after the Epiphany (green); Last Sunday after the Epiphany (Transfiguration Sunday) (white)

LENT (purple; red as an alternative for Holy Week)

Ash Wednesday; First Sunday to the Fifth Sunday in Lent; Sixth Sunday in Lent (Passion/ Palm Sunday); Monday to Wednesday of Holy Week; Holy Thursday*; Good Friday* (no color); Holy Saturday* (no color)

EASTER SEASON (white or gold)

Resurrection of the Lord (Easter Eve, Easter Day, Easter Evenings)*; Second to the Sixth Sunday of Easter; Ascension of the Lord; Seventh Sunday of Easter; Day of Pentecost (red)

SEASON AFTER PENTECOST (ORDINARY TIME, OR KINGDOMTIME)

First Sunday after Pentecost (Trinity Sunday) (white); Second to the Twenty-sixth Sunday after Pentecost (green); All Saints (white); Thanksgiving (red or white); Last Sunday after Pentecost (Christ the King/Reign of Christ) (white)

The Great Three days from sunset Holy Thursday to sunset Easter Day are a unity—the climax of the Christian year.

Hoyt L. Hickman

144 ✦ VINEYARD

Vineyard Fellowships usually celebrate Christmas and Easter in worship, but do not otherwise follow the Christian year.

The Christian year for the most part is not observed in the Vineyard movement. This nontraditional stance is typical of the movement, which is only fifteen years old.

In Langley, the only parts of the Christian year we do observe are Christmas and Easter, which seems to be standard for most of the Vineyard Fellowships.

At Easter, a large multicongregational celebration is held on Sunday morning. Some elements include a large wooden cross at the stage front which is progressively covered with fresh flowers brought by the congregation. The worship band then leads in a time of celebration consisting of upbeat songs of praise, which is followed by an informal message about the Easter story. The morning is concluded with a time of prayer ministry for all who respond, inviting the presence of the risen Christ to fill his people.

Our observance of Christmas takes several forms. We usually put on a Christmas banquet, not for our own congregation, but for the poor in the community. We also deliver hampers of food—

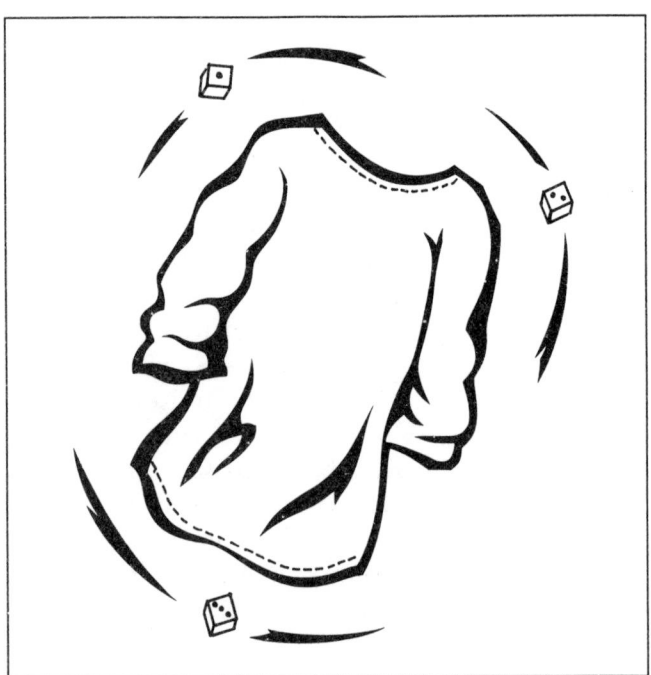

Seamless Coat. This common symbol of the seamless tunic and dice refers to the soldiers who sat beneath the cross casting lots for Jesus' seamless coat.

about 120 of them valued at $100 each during the most recent Christmas. These actions indicated our desire that our Christmas expression be focused outward, giving to the community.

We have begun holding a candlelight service on Christmas Eve, singing Christmas music and listening to an evangelistic message centered on the first Christmas and why Jesus came to earth.

At this point, I do not see a trend towards further recovery of the Christian year in the Vineyard movement.

Brian Doerksen

145 ✦ WESLEYAN CHURCHES

A part of the Holiness movement, the Wesleyan Church has never followed the full church calendar. However, aspects of the Christian year have been introduced incrementally in many congregations, enabling them to enjoy some of its benefits without abandoning their nonliturgical worship tradition.

For churches in the Holiness movement, the day of Pentecost has special relevance. Yet year after year, and in church after church, Pentecost Sunday would come and go with little or no notice. In the past, only Christmas and Easter were observed with regularity in most Holiness churches. The rest of the Christian year belonged to the mainline denominations, and in its place was an annual calendar of special days more cultural than biblical, such as Mother's Day, Father's Day, Independence Day/Dominion Day, Thanksgiving Day, Homecoming, and, of course, Rally Day.

In the Wesleyan Church, that calendar still stands. It probably always will. But an increasing number of congregations are broadening their horizons by incorporating elements of the Christian year. The historical steps toward recovery of the Christian year in this denomination are easily discernible and may provide a model for churches unfamiliar with the Christian year but interested in fostering a more biblical calendar.

Preparing the Way: Commercial Christmas

First, Christmas was a "season" when nothing else from the Christian year was. Long before Advent was recognized or observed, the weeks before Christmas were devoted to carols and Christmas preparations. The reasons for this tradition were distinctly nonliturgical: an abundance of carols, especially when secular songs of the holiday were omnipresent; a social calendar full of Christmas parties and events; and elaborate preparations for the special days (decorating the sanctuary, bagging Christmas "treats" for the children, etc.).

All this required time. The force behind the scenes, of course, was the merchant. Christmas became a liturgical season in most nonliturgical churches because it was first a commercial season.

Discovery of Advent

Advent slipped into Wesleyan calendars without much fanfare in the 1960s and 1970s. The days were already set aside for Christmas preparation, and the "discovery" of the Advent wreath not only made the idea of Advent popular but also made the name more familiar and therefore less threatening. Family wreaths, family calendars, and family Advent calendars were the key to its acceptance; it was to be a family celebration.

About this same time, the popularity of the Chrismon tree, hung with symbols of the Christian faith, rather than decorative ornaments, led to programs for the Hanging of the Greens, though that term may not have been used. Because Advent entered Wesleyan church life by this route, it does not have the sober, serious tone associated with it in more liturgical churches.

Preparation for Easter

Observance of Holy Week was a logical next step. Some churches already observed Palm Sunday and were open to a Maundy Thursday Communion service and/or a midday meditation on Good Friday. If preparing our hearts for Christmas was spiritually beneficial, preparing our hearts for Easter now seemed important too.

What, then, of Lent? Full participation in a penitential season is not a reasonable expectation for a traditionally nonliturgical church, but a great stride was taken when a denominational department promoted "Forty Days of Fasting and Prayer," which has since become a new tradition in many parishes. Local churches in which Lent may never be specifically mentioned still focus on the disciplines of the Christian life, and pastors sensitive to the benefits of observing the Christian year are eager to incorporate Lenten values into their programs, with or without liturgical labels.

Further Increments

More selected holy days were added to the calendar of local churches as the Christian year was introduced incrementally. Pentecost Sunday now enjoys more visibility across the church. Homecoming has become a modified All Saints' Day in some parishes, in tone if not in terminology, and Reformation Sunday is popular in some areas as well. As the educational level of the Wesleyan ministry continues to rise, a greater use of the Christian year can be expected.

The Wesleyan Church will never be "high church," nor should it be. It will never adopt the Christian year in its entirety; the fear of regimented spirituality is too strong. Yet the limited calendar now in place in many congregations will "season" the soul of the church, and more Wesleyans will experience the blessings of the Christian year without the fear of "going formal."

Bob Black

146 • WISCONSIN EVANGELICAL LUTHERAN SYNOD

Growing interest in liturgical renewal and the Christian year in the Wisconsin Evangelical Lutheran Synod is reflected in the recent publication of a new hymnal and companion volume. These publications follow, with some adaptations, the lectionary and calendar proposed by the Inter-Lutheran Commission on Worship in 1973.

Much has changed in the understanding and practice of the Christian year in the Wisconsin Synod (WELS) since the publication of its *Book of Hymns* in 1917. That pocket-sized book provided the text (but no music) for two forms of the "Order of Morning Service." Form I was an outline of the service; Form II printed the text in some detail. Both of these forms provided for only one Scripture lesson. The following year one of the hymnal's editors expressed the belief in the official magazine of the synod that "the average church-goer will thank us for not putting in more than one Scripture lesson."

A survey taken in 1987 in preparation for the publication of a new hymnal reflects the extent to which attitudes had changed since 1917. Of the total of nearly 70,000 persons who responded to the survey, 83.6 percent judged "adding a reading from the Old Testament in addition to the New Testament Epistle and Gospel" to be desirable. Many WELS congregations regularly include three Scripture readings as part of their worship.

The ILCW and the New WELS Hymnal

The same 1987 survey showed that of the 761 pastors who responded, 78 percent were following the three-year lectionary prepared by the Inter-Lutheran Commission on Worship (ILCW). The three-year lectionary included in *Christian Worship: a Lutheran Hymnal*, the book for worship published by the WELS, is based on the ILCW readings.

The WELS was not a participant in the work of the ILCW but did thoroughly study the proposed lectionary when it was published in 1973. This study was carried out by various pastoral conferences with the findings submitted to a specially appointed Lectionary Committee. The findings of this Committee, reported to the synod in 1977, declared that "no doctrinal, pastoral, or liturgical reasons were found to stand in the way of the use of this series of texts" and that "no consideration would preclude the use of this series for worship." The synod in turn resolved that "the use of this series of texts be left to the discretion of the individual congregations of the synod." Not only were the ILCW readings in fact used extensively in the congregations of the synod, but several volumes of sermon studies based on these texts were published in the WELS.

In preparing the three-year lectionary for the new hymnal only certain minor revisions in the suggested readings were made. The desire was to continue to make use of the many worship helps that have become available from various publishers.

WELS Variations on the Christian Year

Christian Worship: A Lutheran Hymnal divides the Christian year into three major seasons: the Time of Christmas, the Time of Easter, the Time of Pentecost. The variations from the ILCW lectionary are primarily the result of a few changes in the calendar. The readings selected for the Sixth Sunday in Lent reflected an emphasis on Palm Sunday rather than on Passion Sunday found in ILCW. The last four Sundays of the year are named the "End Time." Reformation Sunday is the First Sunday of the End Time, followed by the Sunday of the Last Judgment and the Sunday of the Saints Triumphant. The Last Sunday of End Time retains the name used in the ILCW calendar: Christ the King. As much as possible readings chosen for these Sundays were taken from the ILCW series. The calendar lists thirty-two minor festivals and eighteen occasions with propers provided for each of them.

The new hymnal has a table listing the readings for Years A, B, and C, but does not include the complete set of propers for the Sundays, festivals, and occasions of the year. The propers are published in a companion volume to the hymnal. Included there are the suggested Psalm of the day, prayer of the day, verse of the day, and hymn of the day. The decision was made to publish the propers in a separate volume to allow for the inclusion of additional orders of worship and more hymns in the people's book.

Along with the three-year lectionary a slightly revised version of the one-year historic series is included in the hymnal. Only a few of the standard Epistles and Gospels were changed. A set of Old Testament readings were selected so that three lessons might be read in the service when the one-year series is used.

Use of the Three-Year Lectionary

Even though the three-year lectionary is receiving extensive use in the WELS, there are some who fault the selections for their lack of a central theme on some Sundays. This is especially true when on a number of consecutive Sundays in the Epiphany and Pentecost seasons the second lesson is read from one of the Epistles in a more or less continuous fashion. Careful study of the selected texts for a given Sunday will, however, often yield helpful insights which can be put to good use in preaching.

Strong encouragement is given at the synod's Wisconsin Lutheran Seminary to use one of the lectionary selections as the text for the sermon. Following this practice will mean that all of the biblical doctrine is adequately presented by the preacher in a given year, and the danger of dwelling on certain pet subjects will be lessened. It is also emphasized that the Gospel is the main lesson for the day and should suggest the basic theme for worship planning.

The present emphasis on the Christian year and the lectionary is the result of several factors: the publication of _The Lutheran Hymnal_ in 1941 in which the WELS was an active participant; the general emphasis on liturgical renewal found among other Lutheran church bodies and in the church at large; and the efforts of several individuals within the WELS who urged a greater appreciation of the Christian year. All of this has had a most salutary effect on the work of the WELS and helped to bring about the publication of a new hymnal.

147 • WOMEN'S AGLOW FELLOWSHIP

While they do not follow the church calendar in a formal way, Women's Aglow groups do observe many of the seasons of the Christian year. They also enrich their worship with observance of the annual Jewish feasts described in the Old Testament.

Aglow is a charismatic organization which draws together women of many denominations, races, classes, and cultures. Our appreciation for the Christian year has been influenced by a variety of historical traditions, including Catholic, Lutheran, Methodist, Baptist, and Pentecostal.

Easter, Pentecost, and Christmas are among the seasons held in high esteem by Aglow women around the world. These seasons are enthusiastically celebrated in remembrance of the fulfillment of the plans and purposes of God. Local, area, and national Aglow groups often incorporate special worship into their meetings, which help to focus the participants on the significance of the particular event being recognized.

Along with these more traditional celebrations, we also have come to appreciate the seven Jewish feasts, which are a part of the roots of the Christian faith. Our worship has been enhanced by an understanding of the significance of the feasts of Passover, Unleavened Bread, First Fruits, and Pentecost conveyed through our Messianic Jewish friends. And we look forward with them to the fulfillment of the yet remaining feasts of Trumpets, Day of Atonement, and Tabernacles.

Some Aglow groups have invited Messianic Jews to lead them in celebration of the Jewish Passover. Seeing God's plan of salvation through the *seder* (Passover ceremony) has set many free to worship God in a new way as well as bringing a clearer understanding of the parables and teachings of Jesus. Many of us have found our Western way of thinking expanded and enlightened as we have learned to view the Scriptures from a Jewish as well as a Gentile perspective.

Thus, our celebrations of events and seasons during the church year have been greatly enriched by this better understanding of the Jewish culture and customs. And, the various practices of Jewish worship referred to in Scripture, such as praising, shouting, dancing, raising of hands, laughing, bowing, kneeling, and psalm-singing, have also become accepted as part of the Aglow worship culture.

We view all of our worship as part of a powerful, interdenominational movement for revival through prayer and intercession in the final era before the return of Christ.

Lorene Carlson and Ruth Collingridge

148 • ALTERNATIVE PRACTICE OF THE CHRISTIAN YEAR IN LITURGICAL CHURCHES

St. Gregory Nyssen Episcopal Church in San Francisco draws on ancient traditions of both the Eastern and Western church, as illuminated by modern scholarship, in its innovative practice of the Christian year. In contrast to many modern churches, St. Gregory's makes Holy Week and Easter, rather than Christmas, the high point of the year.

Working creatively with the Christian year requires grasping its fundamental spirit. Put simply, the Christian year is a lectionary—a plan for reading the Bible in church. It does not commemorate times when scriptural events actually happened (except for the Passion these are unknown) but instead schedules readings in thematic clusters, which we call "seasons."

Though the lectionary grew by fits in overlapping segments, historical research finds that all parts center on the death and resurrection of Jesus. This point is plain in the Passion reading cycle, but the readings for the festal round com-

memorating his birth and ministry were also anciently chosen for Passion associations and synchronized with other Passion readings months away. By no accident, our calendar's primitive unity mirrors the gospels themselves, which constantly present Jesus' ministry and teaching in the light of his cross and his risen life with his church.

An "Easter Church" and the Lenten Season

St. Gregory Nyssen Episcopal Church in San Francisco shapes the year to promote this basic New Testament focus, drawing on ecumenical tradition and modern learning. Every Sunday service begins with the ancient universal greeting, "Christ is risen! *He is risen indeed*!" and, as in Eastern churches, Lent never suppresses Alleluias or other joyful Sunday chants. Above all, Holy Week (Passion Week) centers our community life. As one lay member puts it, "This is an Easter church; other churches I've known are Christmas churches." Another has observed, "There are two seasons at St. Gregory's—Easter and Easter's Coming."

Soon after Epiphany, members organize to clean the church, write and rehearse music, plan worship, publicize, send invitations, cook, and create art work and vestments. A festive Mardi Gras supper-Eucharist, with a parish talent show and children's piñata party, starts Lent, followed by the traditional Ash Wednesday morning rites. Thereafter, clergy prepare candidates for baptism and—in years when the bishop will visit us—for confirmation at the Maundy service (see below).

Creating a traditional *and* popular Holy Week today demands innovation. Ancient Holy Week services filled each day with scriptural devotions for people with leisure to follow them. Modern liturgists who crop and compress these, while keeping the familiar calendar, are still finding working people must skip important services. At St. Gregory's we instead reschedule these devotions so that busy people can take full part. A weekly Lenten series of scripture meditations, venerating the cross in Taizé format, concludes on the Friday evening before Holy Week with a Byzantine-style reading of all four Passion stories. Thus, traditional Good Friday devotions from East and West spread through Lent, preparing for our chief Passion commemoration.

Palm Sunday Procession

On Palm Sunday most Western liturgies re-enact Jesus' entering Jerusalem, and then read one of the synoptic Passions, doubling up from two ancient lectionaries to underscore the Passion focus of the week ahead. But modern scriptural criticism shows the entry story is itself a Passion meditation rather than a historical account. So without doubling up, we devote this and every Holy Week service to one Passion scripture.

Our Palm Sunday opens the week with a congregational procession around the block, flourishing a forest of local palm fronds and singing psalm-refrain Hosannas to the rhythm of drums, sistrum rattles, noisy thuribles, and other instruments—all in Ethiopian and other African liturgical use today. Along the way, we gather neighbors and bystanders to join us for the sermon and Eucharist and for more services through the week.

Maundy Tuesday Baptism

On Maundy Tuesday evening (not the traditional Thursday), we read John's version of the Last Supper. G. Diekmann and others have argued that this timing, which suits John's passion story, is the likeliest actual date for the event, but we adopted it for pastoral reasons. Even after we scheduled all our services at convenient evening hours, our lay people found it hard to devote three nights in a row to church, and Good Friday attendance particularly suffered. Since Tuesday was already our regular night for parish suppers and meetings, we took Diekmann's suggestion, and attendance at all Holy Week services increased. The Last Supper service in Holy Week became to model for all our weekly Tuesday gatherings.

Maundy Tuesday features another calendar innovation, again meeting a pastoral need in the light of research: it is our chief night of the year for baptism. Until recently, in concert with mainline liturgical renewal, we baptized at the Easter Vigil, dismissing the complaints of parents who found the late hour hard for children, and candidates who found the Easter congregation, thronged with strangers, a strange context for this intimate action. Increasingly our people opted for baptism at other times, when they could gather family and friends to meet St. Gregory's regular community. Then research by T. Talley and P. Bradshaw discovered that baptism was *not* anciently part of the Easter Vigil, but happened in more intimate services before Easter, suggesting we seek a similar alternative.

John's story of the Last Supper and the footwashing provided the answer. Footwashing, the one ritual action John describes Jesus performing that night, is John's closest connection of Jesus with baptism. After three years we have agreed, moreover, that the Easter Vigil flows smoother and swifter without the added baptismal rites.

We fill our flexible worship space with dinner tables, under a tent/like array of African folk fabrics that soften the acoustics and lend an air of intimate splendor. On this night, as at all Tuesday suppers, we follow the second-century Didache rite, sharing the eucharistic bread and cup in the course of a meal. (Several usable versions of this supper rite are published; we call ours the "Feast of Friends," from its Jewish title, *chaburah*.) The congregation arrives bearing potluck dishes and sets them on sideboards. After lighting lamps, singing a Passion carol, and sharing hors d'oeuvres with a glass of wine, we bless the eucharistic loaf to start the meal and serve courses one by one.

Readings from John's account of the Last Supper accompany each course, with silences and guided conversation at each table. All take turns serving each other, as John's gospel emphasizes. Hymns of the Last Supper and the Passion fill the evening. Supper concludes with John's story of the footwashing.

At that point we baptize our candidates, the bishop confirms them, and the whole church sings a Russian chant assuring them they have put on Christ. Those baptized take candles specially decorated with their baptismal names and join the clergy carrying bowls of water to each table to start the footwashing there, where each washes the feet of another in turn. Such a mixture of baptism and footwashing occurred anciently at Milan, but here we enroll the whole congregation. At last we bless the eucharistic cup and share it to complete the meal. The service ends with the *missa*, and ancient blessing of intimate warmth and joy, rediscovered by A. Kavanagh. The congregation crowds around the bishop singing the traditional Russian chant "God grant him many years!" as the bishop lays hands on everyone in rapid succession, blessing us all.

Good Friday Triumphal Vespers

We keep Good Friday with a triumphal vesper service celebrating Christ's universal victory on the cross, and its promise of resurrection—the authentic biblical context for the Passion, particularly emphasized in Eastern church worship. Our worship space and ministers are decked in black and red cloths from folk weavers in the wide ecumenical world outside the Christian church. After lighting lamps and reading appointed lessons from the Old and New Testaments, we sing John's Passion to the remarkably modern-sounding medieval chant of Sarum. The congregation take the part of Christ, while choir and soloists sing the rest. This arrangement, invented by R. Carskadden, causes newcomers to tell us every year what an overwhelming experience they had singing Christ's part.

Following the sermon, all process to the altar table in a simple dance-step, singing of the triumph of the cross. There the clergy cense the table and the people, and all place flowers in profusion around the icon of Jesus' burial, while chants and prayers from East and West recall the burial story and Jesus' presence today with all the departed awaiting resurrection. At last we hand out hot-cross buns to end the Good Friday fast, and leave the church quietly. It is a hushed and intimate conclusion to what many of our people find the most moving service of the year.

Easter Vigil

Early Christians kept Easter at night, like the Jewish Passover. Starting with a special form of the homely evening lamplighting, they read, sang, prayed, and feasted until dawn. Modern Christians keeping vigil on a smaller scale normally celebrate one of these moments of light and sleep through the other. We choose the lamplighting and begin Easter at nightfall when all ages can attend, for this is our *one* Easter service, bringing the whole congregation together. It is also our most ecumenical service, as clergy from other churches and parish alumni return year after year to celebrate with us, and newcomers swell our attendance to over two hundred worshipers.

We deck the church with special artwork, vest all clergy and lay ministers in bright Indian and African folk fabrics, and load side tables with food for the feast. As darkness falls in the unlighted church, the choir chant and lead arriving worshipers in simple folk carols until the clergy enter to welcome the people and explain the service for first-timers, enrolling their full participation.

As the choir begins a Bulgarian-Russian chant depicting angels hymning the Resurrection, the clergy leave to fetch the Paschal Candle. (This is not the cryptic vestigial symbol church suppliers sell, but a tall, stout, plain candle our people have gorgeously painted all over in colored waxes.) We light no magical "new fire" but carry in the Paschal Candle already lighted—the earlier and homlier custom—to the traditional Western *Exsultet* chant. Meanwhile the candlelight spreads to people's hand-candles throughout the church, and then a vigil of readings, silences, and hymns begins.

In fiery semidarkness we read four Old Testament passages of promise and salvation, ending with the Creation story in Genesis 1 (one of the latest passages written in Hebrew scripture, and richly eschatological), a Pauline letter, and a sermon. Then all stand to hear the original conclusion to Mark's gospel, the story of the empty tomb. Now, for the first of many times on this night, we sing the *Easter Troparion* from ancient Jerusalem: "Christ is risen from the dead, trampling down death by death, and upon those in the tombs bestowing life." This first time we sing it in the original Greek, to a Greek tune; soon we will sing it in English to the tunes of many nations, while "tramping death" with dances, as Christians anciently did.

But first the congregation process out to the courtyard, singing a *litany* that calls departed saints and heroes of every age to "Come rejoice with us!" Throughout Lent church members have nominated this list, and many of the names now draw delight and laughter from the crowd. There the preaching professor from our local Baptist seminary mightily delivers a joyous ancient Easter sermon, attributed both to Hippolytus of Rome and John Chrysostom, inviting everyone to feast at the Easter banquet whether they have fasted or not. Then all re-enter the church—now brightly lit—singing the troparion and moving in step around the altar table.

Here for the next half hour the whole congregation of two hundred sing and dance classic Western and Eastern carols to the rhythm of drums and sistrums, and chant the Eastern troparion, now to Slavic, now to Arabic or early American melodies. Between hymns clergy of all denominations cense and greet the people—"Christ is risen! _He is risen indeed!"_—and blessing them, renew the dance. The kiss of peace concludes the dances, the bread and wine come to the table for the eucharistic thanksgiving and Communion. A final dance carol ends with the clergy blessing the people. Then tables of food and drink are carried in, and we feast past midnight. At last the worshipers team up to straighten the church, go home to sleep, and return for our Easter picnic at noon.

——— Easter Season and Pentecost ———

Easter continues in a festive spirit until Pentecost. Easter is the season of our annual stewardship pledge drive, a season we choose because the Resurrection inspires all Christian community living, planning and service. Moving the drive to this season even strengthened our pledges.

At Pentecost we fill the church with tongues, first singing the Acts story in the original Greek, then in a rush of church members reading at once in all the languages they know—a surprising variety!—and finally in English before the sermon. All these celebrations, newly combining music and customs from many ages and churches, revive the popular spirit that once characterized traditional forms. After one Easter service, a Jesuit professor told his students, "You have just had the closest possible experience to worship in the fourth century."

——— Christmas Innovations ———

In Western churches the Advent/Christmas/Epiphany seasonal cycle has entered long-needed revision. Christmas and Epiphany, originally two dates for the same feast, later acquired distinctive readings from the Nativity cycle, rather accidentally following a season of eschatological readings labeled "Advent"—the name for the Roman imperial judgment review. Rationalizing this arrangement is difficult—and superfluous now—because the medieval Western four-week Advent and twelve-day Christmas has vanished in all but name. Popular custom and scholarly reform now extend both seasons months earlier into the year. Unlike Easter, Christmas has become a folk festival, which popular culture celebrates during the weeks _before_ not after, December 25.

Christian evangelistic priorities press official worship to follow suit, and our traditional church year's history gives no grounds to resist such a popular choice. Indeed, official reform has already set the new course. Virtually all revised lectionaries start the traditional Advent readings on justice and eschatological hope in October; and because the lectionary creates our "season," Advent now begins there. (Some Eastern lectionaries traditionally provide an earlier Advent; in the West, Church of England reformers have led in this direction with innovative reading schemes, such as the modular _Lectionary 2._) Although colorful printed church calendars may still suggest the bygone seasonal schedule, parish worship planners now have every reason to embrace liturgical and evangelistic reality creatively.

At St. Gregory's we have tried out various revised lectionaries during this season—most recently the English _Lectionary 2,_ which offers innovations beyond calendar reform. Now and throughout the year our children follow the plan in a simpler way, with a simpler service, before joining the adults for Communion. Thus, parents and children can share the Bible readings together.

We choose hymns and prayers to match the Scripture, and sing and dance Christmas carols through most of December along with popular culture. And as at Easter, we celebrate Christmas with a single evening Eucharist for the whole congregation at the lamplighting hour so children can take an active part. On this night we present the Nativity reading in the form of a folk play composed from several English medieval mystery plays, enrolling both adults and children, and enlivened with congregational carol-singing. Because Christmas is conventionally a family occasion (indeed, many of our single people are away visiting relatives) we conclude with a simple collation of eggnog and sweets before families and friends go home to exchange gifts together.

Our last gathering of the year is a Feast of Friends on New Year's Eve, when our community shares naturally and informally throughout the eucharistic meal, and the final eucharistic cup leads into a night of charades.

Richard Fabian

149 ✦ ALTERNATIVE PRACTICE OF THE CHRISTIAN YEAR IN THE FREE-CHURCH TRADITION

The Christian year has been instrumental in shaping congregational identity as the people of God in contrast *with the surrounding culture. The church has placed emphasis on the symbol of light. Ceremonies throughout the extraordinary time of the Christian year point to God's light shining in a dark world and his people as bearers of that light.*

From the beginning of our time together, our congregation had a deep conviction that we were a part of what God has already been doing for centuries in and through his people. As a newly formed community, we were also trying to discover what God intended the role of this particular congregation to be in today's culture in the city of San Francisco. We sought to discover what it would mean for us to be a people who reflect God's heart and character in our life together, a people whose values and attitudes are shaped by God, and not by the political and cultural climate of San Francisco.

Shortly after our congregation was formed, we spent three weeks learning about the Christian year and its significance in helping to shape the life and identity of our congregation. Many of our people had some exposure to Advent and Lent, but no knowledge of the Christian year as the larger context of those seasons. The Christian year served to reinforce our identity as God's people and remind us of our connection with God's people down through the ages and the richness of our Christian heritage. It also provided the alternative of celebrating God and his action in our world, as opposed to celebrating holidays which are culturally oriented or dictated to us by the greeting card industry.

Advent as Alternative Celebration

During Advent, the lighting of the Advent wreath is incorporated into our Sunday worship and weeknight worship. A litany based on Isaiah 11 is used during the lighting ceremony. With each worship service, a new leader-reader portion is added to the end of the litany previously read. This creates a building effect from service to service and week to week that enhances the mood of expectation and longing during Advent. In addition, banners depicting the Advent wreath and the Isaiah 11 passage provide visual focus.

The majority of our people have Advent wreaths set up in their homes and daily devotional material for use throughout the season. Our intent is to slow down and reflect on God's coming during this time and not be distracted by the hustle and busyness that usually characterizes the Christmas season. It requires real discipline and focus on celebration of Advent as an *alternative*, not as an addition, to the world's busy celebrations.

We have a large number of families with young children in our congregation. Our Sunday school teachers have provided materials and activities such as the Jesus tree, Advent calendar, and Advent chain to help the children celebrate at home and to help parents begin to establish their own family traditions which are rooted in Christ and our identity as his people. Our congregation also participates in "alternative gift-giving." Instead of giving each other gifts, the money is redirected towards a ministry that helps those in need.

Because the world has "stolen" Christmas from the church, much thought and attention have been given to the celebration of Advent and Christmas in our congregation. At each and every turn, our celebration of Advent and Christmas is an attempt to reject the world's values and focus on the meaning of the incarnation of God for a broken and needy world.

Light at Epiphany

Beginning with Advent, light becomes a symbol we use in our celebration of the extraordinary time of the Christian year (the seasons based on the life of Christ—Advent, Christmas, Epiphany, Lent, Easter). Our celebration of Epiphany continues the theme of God's light coming into a dark world. Epiphany reminds us that God has come and manifested himself not just to the Jewish nation, but to Gentiles—to us—as well. As God's light has come into our lives to make us his church, God sends us forth to be the light of Christ in our world.

At the end of our worship on Epiphany Sunday, we act these beliefs out symbolically. Our pastor walks up to the front of the sanctuary and lights a candle from the Christ candle, which has already been lit on Christmas. He then lights the candles of several of our church leaders and charges them, saying, "You are the light of the world." They, in turn, walk down the center aisle and light the candles of the people sitting by the aisle, giving each of them the same charge. The people sitting by the aisle then turn to the persons next to them and repeat this act. The process continues until all the people's candles are lit, a stirring vision of Christ's presence, his light, in our midst and in our world.

Lent: Christ's Cross and God's Grace

The fullness of God's light shining in our world during Epiphany is starkly contrasted by the darkness of Lent. The mood is both somber, because of the depth of our sinfulness, and joyful, because of God's great grace and mercy extended to us. The cross on the altar is draped by a sheer purple cloth to draw attention to it during the forty days of Lent.

During our weeknight service, in addition to the draped cross, seven candles are set on the table. All the candles are lit on the beginning of the season. But each week as we come to worship and reflect on Christ's journey to Jerusalem and the cross, the light grows dim as one additional candle is extinguished. As Christ draws nearer to the cross, the fullness of his light diminishes. Finally, during our Good Friday service (which is conducted in darkness), the seventh and final candles is extinguished. Jesus Christ, the Light of the world, is killed on the cross and the world is left in darkness!

Our emphasis during the Lenten season is not just on our sin and our need for repentance, but also on God's grace, without which we would not be able to see our sinful condition and turn back to God. We also see that the journey Christ took to the cross is our journey and destination as well. Just as Christ was our Suffering Servant, we are called to a life of self-denial and to walk in the way of the cross.

Easter and Pentecost

Easter is a celebration of the victory of God over death and breaking of Satan's grip on the world. On Easter morning we are called to worship this victorious God with our choir singing the Hallelujah chorus from Handel's _Messiah_. God's victory over death empowers God's people to follow their Lord in the way of the cross, as they look forward in hope to that glorious day when all peoples and nations will bow their knees to the risen Lord.

Pentecost is the celebration of the birth of the church. So it is fitting that on Pentecost Sunday we receive new members into our church after a nine-session class that begins in September. At this time, we are reminded again of what it means to be the church in this world, to be a people who reflect God's heart and a passion for God's world.

Regular celebration of these seasons of the Christian year has been tremendously helpful for our congregation. In the midst of busy schedules and scattered events, the Christian year provides a predictability and rhythm to our lives. It brings a cohesiveness to all the different facets of our lives and reminds us over and over again that God is at the center of our lives and this world. We can never tire of hearing this message rehearsed with each new season of the Christian year, because all the voices in our culture around us tell us that we are "number one" and we ought to live for ourselves. Hearing the truth of the gospel told through the Christian year gives us perspective to know what is really crucial and essential to our lives and exposes the lies and deceptions of this world.

Each time we go through the seasons of the Christian year, our lives—both individually and corporately—become more oriented to the truth of the gospel and our calling as God's people is made clearer. Although the stories of Christ's birth and death are familiar to our ears, our hearts receive God's truth in a fresh and new way each time. Not only are we building traditions in our life together, but God is building a corporate identity in us through our experience of the Christian year together.

150 • ALTERNATIVE PRACTICE OF THE CHRISTIAN YEAR IN PENTECOSTAL/ CHARISMATIC CHURCHES

Many Pentecostal assemblies have begun to discover in recent years that the stability, organization, and connection with historic Christian roots that comes with following the lectionary and church year supports rather than conflicts with spontaneity and enthusiasm in worship.

Pentecostals have not traditionally kept the church year. They have been more likely to observe secular holidays, such as New Year's Day, Fourth of July, and Mother's Day. It is not that Pentecostals have been hostile to the observance of Christian holidays—most assemblies have special programs of some kind for Christmas and

Easter, for example. Rather, the idea of organizing church life around the Christian year has simply been alien to them.

Quiet Adoption of the Lectionary

Many Pentecostals, though, are beginning to adopt the church year. One influential assembly, Christ Church in Nashville, Tennessee, quietly made the change eight years ago. They began by using the lectionary for sermon preparation. The senior and associate pastors, who rotate their preaching schedules, decided to take several days each fall to plan their sermons for the following year. By using the lectionary, they felt that they would not fall as easily in the rut of preaching on their own favorite subjects, or what might be some trend at the time, but would be stretched to deal with passages they might not otherwise use.

Most of the congregation is not aware that the pastors are using the lectionary, because they have been careful to maintain the Pentecostal style of preaching. Even so, several members of the church are involved in gathering relevant material for the message, which is placed in large envelopes and given to the ministers several weeks in advance. The pastors then read the material and develop an interesting and relevant message from it. Two passages are publicly read in the Sunday morning service. One becomes a responsive reading printed on the back of the church bulletin to be read by the entire congregation, the other read by a selected reader.

As the preaching became seasonal in nature, the music and decoration of the church began to follow suit. The minister of music was given a copy of the preaching schedule, and he used this to plan what material to introduce at what times to the choir. Little by little the use of the lectionary has become the centerpiece around which the worship schedule of the church is planned.

Christ Church leans very heavily on the lectionary from Advent to Pentecost, but uses the time between Pentecost and Advent to develop instructional series. For example, the church has a very active Bethel program, an intensive two-year study of the scripture developed by Lutherans. So one year the preaching between Pentecost and Advent dealt with the highlights of the Bethel series. (Many of the larger Pentecostal churches use the Bethel series, available through Adult Christian Education, P.O. Box 8398, Madison, WI 53708.) The next year the church dealt with the major doctrines contained in the Apostles' Creed. The sermons are always developed to be interesting, even entertaining, and applicable to life. The rest of the service points to the theme.

An Irresistible Mix

There are many advantages for a church that follows the church year. It tends to consecrate time to the rhythm of faith rather than to the transitory values of secular society. It serves the practical purpose of allowing a large church to organize and plan around central themes. It gives a sense of continuity with the ages and with other communities of Christians. It adds an element of stability to an otherwise very mobile and aggressive church environment. Christ Church is filled with entertainers, and it can put on a very impressive show. The church year and the lectionary connects the excitement to Christian roots. Many people find the mix irresistible.

The recovery of the church year is going on throughout numerous Pentecostal assemblies. In most it becomes the invisible support for the more visible and active spontaneity for which Pentecostals are known. Many have found that far from being incompatible, the rhythm of the church year and lectionary provides a platform on which spontaneous praise and testimony can find meaning and effectiveness in the lives of worshipers.

Dan Scott

151 ✦ ALTERNATIVE PRACTICE OF THE CHRISTIAN YEAR IN SEEKERS' SERVICE/ BELIEVERS' WORSHIP

In endeavoring to reach unchurched seekers, Willow Creek Community Church incorporates into its worship recognition of the holidays of the general calendar followed in society rather than rigidly adhering to the Christian year. Thus the church has sponsored special presentations and outreach efforts in connection with Thanksgiving and the Fourth of July as well as Easter and Christmas.

Since Willow Creek Community Church is nondenominational and only seventeen years old, there are no real traditions for following the Christian year. Christmas and Easter are the only two Christian holidays the church celebrates with special programs. The church has also given services for some holidays not part of the Christian year: Thanksgiving, New Year's Day and the Fourth of July.

Willow Creek concentrates on preaching and living the gospel for seekers and the unchurched. By recognizing the rhythms of the surrounding communities more than denominational traditions, the church wants to remove any possible hindrances to people attending services. This position is the result of a conscious decision by the leadership. Naturally, such an approach does not disparage the validity of another tradition. Willow Creek simply stands in line with many other nonconformist or evangelical churches.

——— Continuing Experimentation ———

Rather than start a lot of traditions that, through time, may become hidebound, Willow Creek grants itself the freedom to experiment and maintain its freshness. For many who attend after growing up in more structured communities, this approach may take some getting used to. The effect is one of unexpectedness and anticipation, as attenders look forward to each holiday to see what will happen next. Many may feel that there is too much dependence on "entertainment," but each new presentation is meant to represent the gospel in an original fashion.

There have been, in past years, celebrations of Christmas and Easter through drama and music. For instance, volunteer writers and musicians have produced a dramatic musical for Easter entitled "The Choice." It chronicles the last week of Christ's life, including his death and resurrection, using contemporary music styles and modes of speech. Seating was packed out at all seven shows in April 1992. The musical's effect was powerful and gave members an excellent opportunity to bring unbelievers to see and hear the gospel.

Christmas programs have been produced, but not on a regular basis. Many Christmas Eve services are held, however—some on December 23 as well as December 24.

As with everything it attempts, Willow Creek works hard to present itself and its services and programs as professionally as possible. Twice the church organized a massive Fourth of July celebration, complete with fireworks and food, for members and seekers. During Thanksgiving, it conducts an extensive food drive and distributes these freewill offerings to the needy in Chicago and the suburbs. At Christmas time, many get involved in community outreach. Other special days on the American calendar, such as Mother's and Father's Days and Memorial Day, are alluded to in worship.

Steve Burden

PART TWO

Introduction to the Christian Year

The Christian year is a guide to spirituality and a textbook of theology. The Christian year is a journey that follows the life of Christ and invites the worshiper to remember and sense the significance of dozens of scriptural events, persons, and images. The Christian year has developed through centuries of practice. At times, it has been changed or abbreviated in order to focus even more clearly on the person and work of Christ. But it always has challenged Christian worshipers to deepen their understanding of their faith, to marvel at the great power and love of God as shown in Jesus Christ, and to celebrate their place in the body of Christ. This section describes the history, theology, and spirituality of the Christian year and serves as a foundation for the sections that will follow.

✌ **TWO** ✌

The History and Theology of the Christian Year

Regulating the life of the church today by the Christian calendar is no easy task. Life-long habits need to be reoriented to this way of marking time. If churches are to accomplish this task, worship leaders and planners must learn a great deal about the history and theology that have shaped the Christian calendar. The great benefit of the Christian year is that the worshiping church is able to follow a rich and meaningful way of orienting its life around the work of Jesus Christ. Studying the history and theology of the Christian year can only help the church do justice to the profound implications of each aspect of Jesus' life.

152 • WHAT IS THE CHRISTIAN YEAR?

The Christian celebrates the saving events of God in Jesus Christ by marking those particular events in which God's saving purposes were made known.

The most common term for the yearly celebration of time in worship is the Christian year. The Christian year, developed in antiquity, was a vital part of worship until the Reformation, when Protestants abandoned much of it because of the abuses attached to it in the late medieval period. Protestants claimed that nearly every day of the year had been named after a saint. The emphasis on these saints and the feasts connected with their lives overshadowed the celebration of the Christ-event in the more evangelical pattern of Advent, Christmas, Epiphany, Lent, Holy Week, Easter, and Pentecost celebrations. Consequently Protestants discontinued observing the Christian year and lost its positive aspects as they attempted to remove Roman excesses. The current return to the Christian year among Protestants advocates a very simple and unadorned year that accents the major events of Christ, a Christian year similar to that of the early church.

Contemporary liturgical scholarship has pointed out that the focal point and source of the Christian year is the death and resurrection of Christ. Even the earliest Christians recognized that the death and resurrection of Jesus began the "new time." The fact that two major events of the church took place during Jewish celebrations— Passover and Pentecost—helped the early Christians to associate themselves with the Jewish reckoning of time and yet dissociate themselves by recognizing that a new time had begun. Thus, like the Jews, the early Christians marked time but, unlike the Jews, they marked their time now by the events of the new age.

The unique feature of the Christian conception of time is the major moment (kairos) through which all other kairoi and chronoi find their meaning. This unique moment is the incarnation, death, and resurrection of Christ. Thus, in Christianity, all time has a center. Paul developed this notion in his epistle to the Colossians declaring that Christ is the creator of all things (1:16), the one in whom all things hold together (1:17), and the one through whom all things are reconciled (1:20). Christ is the cosmic center of all history. Everything before Christ finds fulfillment in Christ. Everything since Christ finds its meaning by pointing back to Christ.

From Christ the center, three kinds of time are

discerned. First, there is fulfilled time. The incarnation of God in Christ represented the fulfillment of the Old Testament messianic longings. Here, in this event, all the Hebraic hopes rooted in the sequence of significant historical moments of the Old Testament were completed. For in Christ the new time (kairos) had arrived as Jesus himself announced: "'The time has come,' he said. 'The Kingdom of God is near. Repent and believe the good news!'" (Mark 1:15).

Second, the coming of Christ is the time of salvation. The death of Christ came at the appointed time as Paul wrote to the Romans: "You see, at just the right time, when we were still powerless, Christ died for the ungodly" (Rom. 5:6; see also Matt. 26:18; John 7:6). Jesus' death was the moment of victory over sin: "Having disarmed the powers and authorities, he made a public spectacle of them, triumphing over them by the cross" (Col. 2:15). Consequently, the death of Christ introduced the time of salvation: "I tell you, now is the time of God's favor, now is the day of salvation" (2 Chron. 6:2).

Third, the Christ-event introduces the Christian anticipatory time. This aspect of time is based on the Resurrection, the Ascension, and the promise of Christ's coming again. Consequently, the church, like the Old Testament people of God, lives in anticipation of the future. Now, however, it is understood Christologically as the time of Christ's glory (1 Tim. 6:14) and as the time of the final judgment (John 5:28-30; 1 Cor. 4:5; 1 Pet. 4:17; Rev. 11:18).

This Christian conception of time is important because it plays a significant role in the worship of the church. The historic and unrepeatable Christ-event is the content which informs and gives meaning to all time. Therefore, in worship we sanctify present time by enacting the past event of Jesus in time which transforms the present and gives shape to the future. The oldest evidence of a primitive church year is found in Paul's first letter to the Corinthian Christians in A.D. 57. Here Paul refers to "Christ our Passover lamb" and urges the people to "keep the festival" (1 Cor. 5:7-8). This reference seems to suggest that the early Christians celebrated the death and resurrection of Christ during the Jewish Passover.

There is considerable information from the second and third centuries to describe the significance of Easter. It became the major day of the year for baptism, which was preceded by a time of prayer and fasting. However, we do not have evidence of a fully developed church year until the fourth century. Because space does not permit a full treatment of the origins and development of the church year, the following summary will do no more than outline the church year and touch on the origin and meaning of each part.

Advent. The word *advent* means "coming." It signifies the period preceding the birth of Christ when the church anticipates the coming of the Messiah. Although it signals the beginning of the church year, it appears that Advent was established after other parts of the year as a means of completing the cycle. Its purpose was to prepare worshipers for the birth of our Lord. The Roman church adopted a four-week season before Christmas, a practice that became universally accepted.

Epiphany. The word *epiphany* means "manifestation." It was first used to refer to the manifestation of God's glory in Jesus Christ (see John 2:11) in his birth, his baptism, and his first miracle. Although the origins of the Epiphany are obscure, it is generally thought to have originated among the Christians in Egypt as a way of counteracting a pagan winter festival held on January 6. Originally it probably included Christmas (celebrated on December 25 to replace the pagan festival of the sun). In the fourth century Christmas became part of Advent, and the beginning of Epiphany on January 6 became associated with the manifestation of Jesus to the wise men (i.e., the Gentile world). The celebration of Epiphany is older than that of Christmas and testifies to the whole purpose of the Incarnation. Therefore the emphasis in worship during Epiphany is on the various ways Jesus was manifested to the world as the incarnate Son of God. This period ends with attention to the Transfiguration.

Lent. Lent signifies a period of preparation before Easter. The origins of Lent lie in the preparation of the catechumen before baptism. The setting aside of a time of preparation for baptism goes back as early as the Didache and is attested to in Justin Martyr and detailed in the Apostolic Tradition of Hippolytus. Gradually the time of preparation was associated with the number forty:

Moses spent forty years preparing for his mission; the Israelites wandered in the wilderness for forty years; Jesus spent forty days in the wilderness. In addition, the congregation joined the catechumenate in preparation, making it a special time for the whole church.

Scriptural readings and sermons during this period highlight the ministry of Jesus, especially his teaching in parables and his miracles. Special emphasis is given to the growing conflict of Jesus with his opposition and the preparation he himself made for his death. The church joins Jesus in the recalling of this significant period of his life.

The period of Lent was gradually marked off by Ash Wednesday at its beginning and Holy Week at its ending. The beginnings of Ash Wednesday lie in obscurity. It was in use by the fifth century, and the meaning of it was derived from the use of ashes, a penitential symbol originating in the Old Testament and used in the church as early as the second century to symbolize repentance. The formula used for the imposition of ashes is based on Genesis 3:19: "Remember man, that you are dust and into dust you shall return." These words signal the beginning of a time dedicated to prayer, repentance, self-examination, and renewal. It ends in the celebration of the Easter resurrection when the minister cries, "Christ is risen!"

Before Easter, however, the church enacts the final week of Jesus. Although traces of a special emphasis during this week can be found in the third century, Holy Week was developed in the fourth century by the Christians of Jerusalem. The essential feature of Holy Week was to link the final events of Jesus' life with the days and the places where they occurred. Jerusalem, of course, was the one place in the world where this could actually happen. For here were the very sites of his last days. As pilgrims poured into Jerusalem, the church of Jerusalem evolved this structure to provide them with a meaningful cycle of worship. The worship services that were developed during this time are still used today in some churches. The use of the ancient Maundy Thursday service, the Good Friday veneration of the cross, and the Saturday night vigil make Holy Week the most special time of worship in the entire Christian calendar.

Easter. The Easter season stands out as the time of joy and celebration. Unlike Lent, which is somber in tone, Easter is the time to focus on resurrection joy. Augustine said:

> These days after the Lord's Resurrection form a period, not of labor, but of peace and joy. That is why there is no fasting and we pray standing, which is a sign of resurrection. This practice is observed at the altar on all Sundays, and the Alleluia is sung, to indicate that our future occupation is to be no other than the praise of God.

The preaching of this period calls attention to the post-resurrection appearance of Jesus and the preparation of his disciples to witness to the kingdom. It is fifty days in length.

Pentecost. The term _pentecost_ means "fifty," referring now to the fifty days after Passover when the Jews celebrated the Feast of Weeks, the agricultural festival that celebrated the end of the barley harvest and the beginning of the wheat harvest. In the Christian calendar the term is associated with the coming of the Holy Spirit and the beginning of the early church. Possible evidence of Pentecost in the Christian church goes back to Tertullian and Eusebius in the beginning of the third century. More dateable, however, are the references made by Egeria to the celebration of Pentecost in Jerusalem during the latter part of the fourth century. Liturgist A. A. McArthur describes the event in these words:

> Just after midday the people gathered at the sanctuary on the traditional site of the ascension, and the passages about the ascension from the gospel and Acts were read. A great candlelight procession came to the city in the darkness, and it was eventually about midnight when the people returned to their homes.

Pentecost is the longest season in the church, having twenty-seven or twenty-eight Sundays, lasting until Advent. Preaching during this time should concentrate on the development of the early church with an emphasis on the power of the Holy Spirit in the ministry of the apostles and the writing of the New Testament literature.

In sum, the following excerpt from the _Constitution on the Sacred Liturgy_ captures the importance of celebrating the church year.

The church is conscious that it must celebrate the saving work of the divine Bridegroom by devoutly recalling it on certain days throughout the course of the year. Every week, on the day which the Church has called the Lord's Day, it keeps the memory of the Lord's resurrection, which it also celebrates once in the year, together with his blessed passion, in the most solemn festival of Easter.

Within the cycle of a year, moreover, the Church unfolds the whole mystery of Christ, from his incarnation and birth until his ascension, the day of Pentecost, and the expectation of blessed hope and of the Lord's return.

Recalling thus the mysteries of redemption, the Church opens to the faithful the riches of the Lord's powers and merits, so that these are in some way made present in every age in order that the faithful may lay hold on them and be filled with saving grace. (par. 102)

Robert Webber

153 ♦ THE PROBLEM OF THE CIVIL YEAR IN WORSHIP

Many churches that have rejected the practice of the Christian year follow the secular way of marking time. This article describes some of the "calendars" that churches use to mark time and points out some of the problems with the observance of civil occasions in particular. It is written from a Reformed perspective but will be useful to churches in any tradition.

As any liturgist knows, we have to take more than one "church year" into account as we plan our worship services. The last time I counted, I came up with *six* distinguishable "years."

First is the *lectionary year,* used by congregations from many denominations to organize their worship planning. Next, and familiar especially to churches within the Reformed tradition, is the *catechism year,* patterned after the "Lord's Days" of the Heidelberg Catechism. Third is the *hallmark year*—Mother's Day, Father's Day, Valentine's Day—a list of special occasions that many churches recognize in one fashion or another. Fourth and fifth are the *denominational programs year* (Missions Sunday, World Hunger Sunday, and the like) and a *local congregation activities year* (Stewardship Sunday, Boys' or Girls' Club Sunday, the service for commissioning of church school teachers). And, last but not least, is the *civic holiday year.*

Most of the "years" are not very problematic on a theological level. They are, to be sure, often difficult to juggle—what do you do, for example, when Mother's Day and Pentecost occur on the same Sunday? But a creative mind and a willingness to do some compromising are often adequate for dealing with such challenges.

The civic holiday year, though, presents some special theological problems. And it also raises some emotionally laden issues. In the World War I era, for example, a well-known Reformed pastor in the Midwest refused to allow the American flag to be displayed in his sanctuary. This caused such uproar in his Dutch Calvinist community that he was physically attacked one night as he walked home from the church.

Is it appropriate to integrate civic themes and symbols into our Christian worshiping life? As worship planners, how do we deal with a Dominion Day or an Independence Day?

The Relevance of Context

One possible solution is simply to ignore our civic life altogether. Some Christians have argued for this option. They believe that a Christian worship service should in no way reflect the national setting in which it takes place. If a Christian family from Ireland should happen to attend a service in Minneapolis, they insist, the Irish visitors should be able to identify with everything that is going on in the worship event.

But this requirement is defective for both practical and theological reasons. On the practical level it is simply unreasonable to expect that foreign visitors will feel completely at home in our services. Our language and accents and modes of cultural expression will inevitably reflect our specific surroundings.

Furthermore, from a theological point of view it is good that this is so. God has placed us in specific cultural and national contexts. We shouldn't ask black worshipers in South Africa or a peasant congregation in El Salvador to make no mention of their particular political circumstances as they worship the divine Ruler. Nor should we ask it of ourselves. Applying the gospel to our actual circumstances is one of the exciting challenges of the Christian life. Our worship experience provides us with one important opportunity to take up that challenge.

Remembering Our Loyalties

It is one matter to incorporate our national context into our worship. It is another to foster non-Christian loyalties as we worship. And there can be no question that the danger of alien loyalties is a real one in dealing with the relationship between Christian worship and civic symbols.

Take the flag question. Strictly speaking, there is nothing wrong with having a national flag in a place of worship. As a reminder of our national "place" and as a stimulus to reflect seriously on what it means to be Christian citizens, a flag can be a rather innocent symbol.

But it is difficult to assess this issue properly without also reckoning with the constant danger of nationalistic pride. We are often asked to offer to our nations the kind of allegiance that we should direct only to God. A national flag seldom serves as a mere reminder of the fact that we are citizens of a specific nation. It is a powerful symbol—even a seductive one—that can evoke feelings of loyalty and pride that are not proper for Christians. And when a national flag stands alongside the so-called Christian flag, we can easily be led to think that God and Caesar have equal importance in our lives.

When we come together for Christian worship, we are acknowledging our identify as members of "a chosen race, a royal priesthood, a holy nation" (1 Pet. 2:9, RSV). And we need to be reminded that other racial and priestly and national loyalties are constantly competing for our allegiance. Our worship services are gatherings in the divine throne-room, where we acknowledge that our true loyalties belong to God alone. Nothing in our liturgical content or setting should detract from this expression of fidelity.

Political Heresy

The relationship between Christian commitment and political citizenship is subject to considerable confusion. Much preaching on this subject is downright silly, full of shallow sentimentality and naive interpretations of such passages as the "render unto Caesar" saying and Romans 13. This is certainly inexcusable in the Reformed/Presbyterian tradition, where John Calvin and John Knox and Abraham Kuyper and Allan Boesak

and other Calvinists have provided us with such a rich store of Christian reflection on the basic issues of civil life.

Reformed theological wisdom is desperately needed on such matters today, given the heresies that are so prominent in popular political piety. How, for example, can Christians who believe that only Christ's sacrifice can truly atone for sin refer to deaths of soldiers who have died in the service of their country—however courageous their actions—as "the supreme sacrifice"?

Patriotic songs also contain many dangerous teachings. Take, for example, the "eschatological" verse of "America the Beautiful." Themes that in the book of Revelation are used to describe the Holy City are here applied to the United States: "alabaster cities," "undimmed by human tears," the "shining sea." As if the United States will become the promised New Jerusalem! And yet Reformed Christians—even the kind who sometimes boast of their commitment to "sound theology"—often sing these words without a thought to the heresies they are mouthing.

This is not mere nitpicking. Given the sinfulness of the human condition, idolatry is a very real threat. Political life has certainly not been immune to the general danger of forming idolatrous allegiances. And when nations and governments have exceeded their God-ordained boundaries by asking citizens for the ultimate loyalties, they have often borrowed the language of religion. The Roman emperors demanded that they be addressed as "Lord." And Hitler deceived the German people into thinking that they were a "holy nation" and a "chosen race." We must be very diligent in warning the people of God against applying the themes of Zion to the nations in whose midst we are called to serve our only true and righteous Sovereign.

A Multinational People

It is one thing, though, to acknowledge the dangers that we must guard against; it is another to put these concerns into practice. How can we sensitize God's people to these important concerns, knowing full well that we are dealing with issues that carry much emotional freight?

We can promote a general awareness in our worship of the multinational character of the body of Jesus Christ. Our worship here below is a preparation for the worship of the Lamb, who has ransomed us "from every tribe and tongue and people and nation" (Rev. 5:9, RSV), thereby giving us a new kind of communal identity. "No other blood will do"—not Canadian blood, or Scottish blood, or Dutch blood, or Brazilian blood.

We can regularly give expression to this new sense of identity in our worship by praying for Christians in other national settings, by reminding ourselves of the dangers of national pride, by remembering the ways in which Christians have had to oppose existing political regimes in order to be faithful to the gospel.

Healthy Patriotism

There is a legitimate place for patriotic sentiments in the Christian life. Some Christians deny this, but they are usually focusing on patriotic excesses when they issue their condemnations.

To be a "patriot" is to have affection for the "fatherland." The explicit analogy to the parent-child relationship is a helpful one. It is a good and natural thing to love our parents. But our love has gotten out of bounds if we think our parents are literally the best parents in the whole world—so wonderful that everyone else also ought to value them as the world's greatest parents.

That's the kind of out-of-bounds thinking that takes hold when nationalistic feelings get to be excessive. People start to think that their country—which they quite naturally have very affirmative feelings toward—is the best country in the world.

Christians need to work hard at keeping patriotic feelings within proper bounds. There is nothing wrong with loving my country simply because it is *my* country—just as I love my parents simply because they are *my* parents. But this does not put my country beyond criticism.

To honor our nation in a godly manner is to want it to contribute to the cause of Christ's kingdom. To love our country with a Christian love is to want our nation to do justice and love mercy and walk in humility before the face of the Lord.

Citizens in Church

We don't leave our citizen roles and our patriotic affections at the door when we enter the church building for worship. It is not reasonable or good to expect that we will do so. God has given each of us a national setting in which to live. Christian citizenship is a good and important calling.

Our worship services provide us with opportunities to become more aware of who we are as the elect people of God. Worship must speak to the actual dilemmas and trials and joys and challenges that we experience as we attempt to serve the Lord in the broad and complex patterns of our lives. Liturgy and citizenship, then, must intersect.

But seductive patriotic symbols and nationalistic boastings have no proper place in Christian worship. Nor is the church a place where superficial sentimentality and dangerous political heresies can be tolerated. Our worship services are opportunities to come as the blood-bought people of the Lamb—a people who are presently scattered among the nations—into the presence of the one Ruler whose authority knows no rivals.

Richard J. Mouw[1]

154 ✦ THE ORIGINS OF THE CHRISTIAN YEAR

In the first centuries A.D. the cycle of Christian time grew out of the conviction that all time finds its meaning in the death and resurrection of Christ. Thus the early Christians, beginning with the paschal event, extended the Christian calendar forward to Pentecost and backward to Lent and Holy Week. Later, in the fourth century, Advent, Christmas, and Epiphany were developed to complete the cycle.

The Easter Cycle

In the first days of the life of the church following Pentecost, there is no indication of any observance of special times. However, it is clear that by the time of Paul's ministry it had become customary for local communities to gather for the breaking of bread on the first day of the week, and it has been suggested that occurred after sundown ending the Sabbath (see Acts 20:7-12). By the end of the first century the observance of the first day by common worship seems established, as was the observance of the fourth and sixth days of the week with fasting (see Didache, chaps. 1 and 14.) For most of the church, this shaping of the week sufficed, and one week was like every other. The Gentile church had no reason to adopt the major annual festivals of Judaism. However, it seems likely that the community in Jerusalem continued to observe Passover, with its day of preparation a memorial of the death of Jesus. This community was largely dispersed following the destruction of the city by Titus, and our earliest evidence for the annual observance of Passover by Christians comes from Asia Minor. For example in the _Epistula Apostolorum_, 15, a document assigned to Asia Minor in the second century (perhaps the first half of the century), the risen Christ is presented as addressing the apostles in the following words:

> And you therefore celebrate the remembrance of my death, i.e., the Passover; then will one of you be thrown into prison for my name's sake, and he will be very grieved and sorrowful, for while you celebrate the Passover, he who is in custody did not celebrate it with you. And I will send my power in the form of my angel, and the door of the prison will open, and he will come out and come to you to watch with you and to rest. And when you complete my Agape and my remembrance at the crowing of the cock, he will again be taken and thrown in prison for a testimony, until he comes out to preach, as I have commanded you.

In Asia Minor the preparation of the Passover (the fourteenth day of the first spring month, Nisan) was observed with fasting, and a vigil was kept through the night of Jewish feasting until cockcrow, when the observance was ended with a simple Eucharist. When it became difficult to observe the day according to the Jewish calendar, which was adjusted as needed by rabbinical authorities, some Christians in Asia Minor adopted the local version of the Julian calendar and kept their Passover on the fourteenth day of its first spring month, Artemisios. When the capital of the empire moved to Constantinople in the fourth century, the Roman calendar was adopted in Asia Minor, and we encounter its designation of 14 Artemisios, April 6, as a fixed date associated with _Pascha_ (the Aramaic word for Passover adopted by Christians). By the third century in the West, on the other hand, the historical date of the Lord's death had been computed to have been March 25.

The emperor Hadrian rebuilt Jerusalem in 132, and all the circumcised, including Christians, were forbidden to enter the new city, Aelia, built upon the rubble of the old. With the expulsion of Jewish Christians, Gentile bishops came to assume leadership of the Jerusalem church. It is believed that it was this mixing of Gentile leadership with local Jewish Christian custom that led to the observance of the paschal fast on Sabbath and the vigil through the night from Sabbath to the Lord's Day, with the concluding Eucharist in the early hours of Sunday morning, in accordance with prevailing Gentile custom. So the annual Passover became Easter Sunday. For many in the second century the annual paschal fast on Sabbath was joined to the weekly fast on Friday to yield a two-day fast, and in the following century, both Syria and Egypt yield evidence of the further extension of the paschal fast to six days, the "Holy Week" still known to us.

In the second century we encounter significant evidence that the celebration of our Lord's triumph, begun with the Eucharist that terminated the paschal fast, was extended for fifty days, called the Pentecost. This was probably derivative from the counting of fifty days to the Feast of Weeks in Judaism, but it took on a distinctive Christian character as a period of rejoicing during which fasting and kneeling in prayer were considered inappropriate. During the third century this period, but especially Pascha itself, came to be considered the most appropriate time for baptism, and in some churches the immediately preceding weeks were devoted to the preparation of candidates for that rite. After the Council of Nicea (A.D. 325) that period was extended to the forty days we know as Lent.

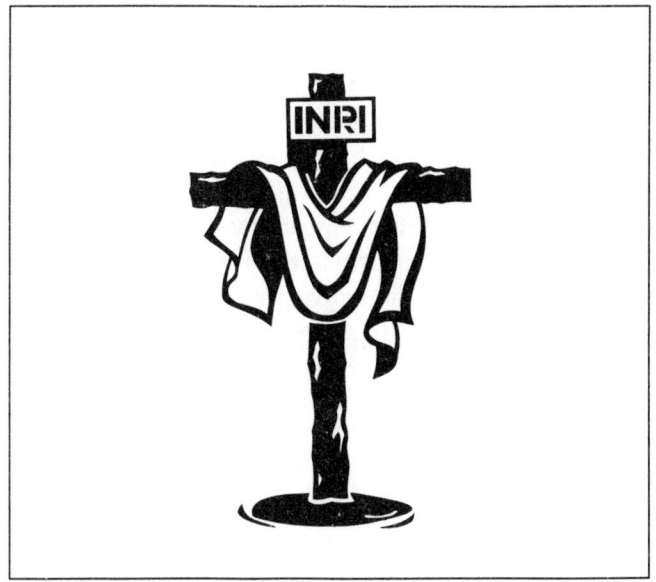

Cross and Winding Sheet. _This symbol speaks of the completion of Jesus' work on the cross and of his descent into death._

The Christmas Cycle

The date of our Lord's birth is not known, and the Gospels are clearly indifferent to the question. Mark, indeed, does not mention the Nativity and is content to present the baptism in Jordan as the beginning of the gospel. Around the turn of the second to the third century, Clement of Alexandria reports that some Basilideans celebrated the baptism on January 6, and there is reason to believe that he associated this same date with the birth of Jesus. This would be just nine months after the paschal date of April 6, and some of the early paschal homilies in Asia Minor speak not only of the Lord's passion and resurrection, but also of the Incarnation and so of the conception in the womb of the virgin. By the fourth century we know that the date of the Lord's death had been taken to be that of the conception as well, allowing the setting of the Nativity date nine months later. As January 6 appeared in the East as that nativity date, so by the early fourth century (or earlier) December 25 was recognized as the nativity date in the West. That was also the date of a pagan festival, the Birthday of the Invincible Sun, instituted by the emperor Aurelian in A.D. 274. The relationship between the new Roman festival and the Christian association of the birth of the Lord with the same date remains disputed. Some believe that Christians chose the date already celebrated and recast it as the birthday of the Sun of Righteousness. Others suppose the Christian date to have been arrived at independently by computation from March 25, established as date of the Lord's death (and conception?) long before Aurelian's festival.

In the course of the fourth century, the two festivals of the Nativity of Christ (December 25) and the Epiphany (January 6) were mutually adopted in East and West. In the East, Epiphany celebrated both Christ's birth and baptism in the Jordan. In the West, however, the Matthean nativity narrative was divided, and the January 6 festival celebrated the visit of the Magi, leading to the restricted understanding of Epiphany as "the manifestation of Christ to the Gentiles."

Not until the sixth century did there appear the fast before Christmas, a fast of forty days progressively shortened at Rome to the four Sundays of Advent, which we now know as the opening season of the Christian year.

Thomas J. Talley

155 • A Theology of the Christian Year

The resurrection of the crucified Christ is the point on which the weekly and annual cycles of the Christian calendar turn. In fact, it supplies the clue to the whole history of salvation and indeed the cosmos. Every Sunday and every Easter day is a commemoration and celebration of the resurrection of Jesus and an anticipation of the day when the same Lord will come again in glory to judge the living and the dead and finally establish God's universal kingdom.

Sunday

Let us begin by looking at Sunday. It was "on the first day of the week" that the tomb of Jesus was found empty (Matt. 28:1; Mark 16:2; Luke 24:1; John 20:1) and the risen Lord interpreted the Scriptures to the two on the road to Emmaus and revealed himself to them, and later to his other disciples, at table (Luke 24:13-32, 33-49). In Paul's time, the Christians at Ephesus gathered on "the first day of the week" to hear the apostle preach and to break bread (Acts 20:7-11). A century later, Justin Martyr reports that Christians from town and country gathered together in one place "on the day of the sun" in order to hear the Scriptures read and expounded and to take Eucharist: "We assemble on Sunday because it is the first day, that on which God transformed the darkness and matter to create the world, and also because Jesus Christ our Savior rose from the dead on the same day" (*First Apology*, 67). The contemporary Epistle of Barnabas, taking the recurrent first day as also the eighth, speaks of "celebrating with gladness the eighth day, in which Jesus rose from the dead," "the beginning of a new world" (15:8-9) or, as Basil of Caesarea put it in the fourth century, "the image of the age to come" (*On the Holy Spirit*, 27). All these themes are resumed in Charles Wesley's hymn "For the Lord's Day":

Come, let us with our Lord arise,
Our Lord, who made both earth and skies;
Who died to save the world he made,
And rose triumphant from the dead;
He rose, the Prince of life and peace,
And stamped the day for ever his . . .

Then let us render him his own,
With solemn prayer approach the throne,
With meekness hear the gospel word,

With thanks his dying love record;
Our joyful hearts and voices raise,
And fill his courts with songs of praise.

When the followers of Jesus assemble "in his name," they find the risen Lord present "in their midst" (cf. Matt 18:20). For the preacher in particular, this is the ground and realization of the promise that, when the gospel is proclaimed, "whoever hears you, hears me" (Luke 10:16). All faithful preaching of "Christ crucified" (1 Cor. 1:23) is the gift of Christ's enabling presence and a means by which the living Lord continues to speak to his people and to the world. Even when the Resurrection is not specially emphasized (and we shall see later that it is quite appropriate for the preacher to focus on other events in the Lord's career over the course of the year), every sermon is implicitly a testimony to the Resurrection and an offer of eternal life to those who through Christ come to God in repentance, trust, and obedience. That the Christian assembly, and the preaching which is a constitutive element in it, regularly take place on a Sunday is an expression, in the symbolism of cosmic and historical time, of the foundational, continuing, and yet-to-be-fulfilled importance of the resurrection of the crucified Christ to the gospel, the history of salvation, and the destiny of the world.

The Eastern Orthodox think of every Sunday as "a little Easter." Conversely, Athanasius of Alexandria had already called the fifty days of the Easter season "one great Sunday." Let us look for a moment at Easter as the church's yearly focus on Christ's death and resurrection.

Easter: The Christian Passover

"Christ our Passover has been sacrificed for us" (1 Cor. 5:7; cf. 13:1, 19:36). The earliest Christian Pascha appears to have been a unitary commemoration and celebration of Christ's death and resurrection. In the Asian churches the feast was kept each year on 14 Nisan; in Rome, on the following Sunday. The Roman practice won out by the third or fourth century. The Easter night of Saturday to Sunday, during which the Paschal Vigil was held, remained in that time of keen eschatological expectation the favored moment for the Lord's final advent. The Old Testament prophecies, whose reading formed the scriptural core of the vigil service, had found their first fulfillment in the death

and resurrection of Christ, and now their universal consummation was awaited. Good Friday, which emerged into prominence with the more chronologically, geographically, and even dramatically oriented liturgical events of Holy Week around the sites of Jerusalem in the latter fourth century, had some earlier grounding in the weekly observance of Fridays as fast days. Palm Sunday, and then Maundy Thursday, became purely annual occasions in which the historical commemoration of the detailed events of Jesus' entry into Jerusalem and the Last Supper was the dominant content.

Eastertide

From Tertullian we know also that, as early as the second century, Easter extended forward into a "most joyous season" of fifty days. During the entire seven weeks of Eastertide, Christians did not kneel for prayer but rather stood in order to mark the heavenly location of believers in the risen and exalted Christ, in anticipation of the general resurrection; nor did they fast, for they were enjoying a foretaste of the heavenly banquet with the messianic bridegroom. Easter was the season of the Alleluia, a hopeful sign of the time when "we shall do nothing but praise God" (Augustine). The oldest practice of the church draws heavily on the Fourth Gospel, the Acts of the Apostles, and the Apocalypse for scriptural readings during "the great fifty days": the followers of Christ, rejoicing in the gift of the other Paraclete, the Spirit of truth, spread the good news of salvation and tasted the life of heaven.

Pentecost

The fiftieth day of Easter retained the name that could also designate the whole period: Pentecost. The first evidence we have of a special feast to "seal" the Pentecostal period comes from the fourth century. In dependence on Acts 2:1ff., the gift of the Holy Spirit to the 120 is commemorated and the Spirit's abiding presence in the life and witness of the church is celebrated. Our oldest testimony to the feast links the descent of the Spirit to the ascent of Christ, and preachers continued to make the connection. A separate observance of the Ascension on the fortieth day (cf. Acts 1:3) is, however, attested only a little later than the evidence for the feast of Pentecost of the

***The Empty Cross.** The symbol of the empty cross with the rising sun speaks of the resurrection of Jesus. Often, as is the case with this cross, the INRI (Jesus of Nazareth, the King of the Jews) is displayed at the head of the cross, as are the nails.*

fiftieth. It may be that first Pentecost, and then Ascension as a distinct feast, together with the development of Holy Week, all mark a growing tendency to historicism in the church's liturgical sense, where the church of the earliest centuries had held the death, resurrection, and exaltation of Christ closer together in a single mystery whose evangelistic and eschatological import was brought home to the assembled believers by the Holy Spirit.

The permanent contribution of the Easter/Pentecost season to the method and message of the preacher resides in its insistence on the theological inseparability of Christ and the Spirit. The Spirit of truth, the other Paraclete, brings to remembrance all that Jesus has said (John 14:26), takes the things of Christ and declares them (16:14), vivifies the flesh which even in the case of the Incarnate Word is of no avail on its own (6:63). When Peter preaches under the Holy Spirit's inspiration, it is Christ crucified and risen that he proclaims, and baptism in the name of Jesus Christ is promised to bring the gift of the Holy Spirit (Acts 2:14ff., 38). It is only by the Holy

Spirit that one can confess "Jesus is Lord" (1 Cor.12:3), and when the Spirit is given to believers, it is to transform them into the likeness of their Lord (2 Cor. 3:18, cf. Gal. 5:5-6, 13-25). The Spirit enables Christ's fellow-heirs to call God "Abba" (Rom. 8:14ff.; Gal. 4:6). It is through Christ that we have heard the gospel, become believers, and been sealed with the Holy Spirit as the pledge of our inheritance unto a day of redemption (Eph. 1:13-14, 4:30). "If the Spirit of him who raised Jesus from the dead dwells in us, he who raised Christ Jesus from the dead will give life to your mortal bodies also through his Spirit which dwells in you" (Rom. 8:11). What is thematically celebrated in "the Great Fifty Days" governs the message and method of all faithful preaching.

Beginning locally before the year 1000, the Western church has kept the first Sunday after Pentecost as Trinity Sunday. This more "dogmatic" feast can serve at least two purposes: it is a reminder that the work of our salvation—the self-giving incarnation and passion of the Son, his exaltation and continuing intercession, and the mission of the Spirit—is grounded in the eternal mystery of God; and it also allows us to rejoice in the fact that Christian worship is no less than a creaturely sharing in the life and communion of the Triune God.

Lent

The calendrical influence of Easter extends also backwards through Lent. In the patristic church, the Paschal Vigil was the high moment for the administration of baptism into the death and resurrection of Christ. The climactic rites of Christian initiation described in the so-called Apostolic Tradition of Hippolytus belong to the great service of Easter eve. After a preparatory catechumenate of several years, the learners finally emerged as "the elect," and in the weeks immediately preceding Easter they underwent decisive instruction in the faith, summarized at last in the creed and in the Lord's Prayer, and the candidates were solemnly exorcised in order to "make room" for the Holy Spirit who would henceforth fill their lives. Our season of Lent originated in the final weeks of preparation for baptism. It became also the season when penitents were made ready to have their baptismal privileges restored to them. Because we never outgrow our baptism, and indeed all of us continue throughout this life to struggle in grace to master the remnants of sin, it eventually came to be regarded as a salutary practice for all believers to "remake" their own baptismal preparations each year during Lent. In our own time, the Roman Catholic church, in a widely imitated step, has introduced into its paschal liturgy a "renewal of baptismal vows." Traditional Scripture readings for Lent relate the story of redemption and include Old Testament types of baptism as well as Gospel episodes which have baptismal resonances. The preacher has the opportunity to recall Christians to their baptismal foundations, somewhat in the way the apostle Paul grounded his exhortations and ethical instructions in the decisive act of grace which baptism signifies (e.g., Rom. 6; 1 Cor. 6:11; 12:12-13; Col. 2:11–3:17).

There is, however, a secondary pivot in what may perhaps be thought of as the irregular ellipse of the church year, namely the incarnation of the Word. It is to Christmas as a focal celebration that we now look.

Christmas: The Savior's Birth

When Jesus saw the light of day, it was in fact rather the world that was being illuminated by the incarnation of the divine Word. The birth of the eternal Son of God from a human mother was the early dawn of a new day, the drawing near of "the Sun of righteousness" (Mal. 4:2). Although Scripture does not help us to fix Christ's nativity on December 25 (Rome) or January 6 (Egypt), it was doubtless influenced along one track or another by the natural practice of observing the winter solstice as the point at which "the sun begins again to grow." Eventually the Roman date won out. That the present-day Slavonic Orthodox celebrate Christmas on a different date (thirteen days after what the rest of the world calls December 25) is only due to their refusal to make the "secular" transition from the Julian to the Gregorian calendar.

Epiphany

Some other aspects of Christ's "manifestation" to the world were left to a January season of Epiphany (Greek _epiphaneia_; Latin _manifestatio_): his showing to the Gentiles (the Western church placed the visit of the Magi on January 6, whereas the East associates it directly with Christ-

mas), his public appearance as the divine Son (the Eastern church places Christ's baptism on January 6, and the Western church traditionally kept January 13), and the shining forth of his glory at the wedding feast of Cana (the second Sunday after Epiphany in the West). An ancient Latin Epiphany antiphon weaves these themes together beautifully:

> Today the heavenly Bridegroom weds his Church,
> since Christ has washed away her sins in the Jordan;
> the wise men hasten with their gifts to the royal wedding,
> and the guests are made glad by the water turned to wine.

A hymn by Christopher Wordsworth prolongs this threefold manifestation into Christ's ultimate epiphany:

> Sun and moon shall darkened be,
> Stars shall fall, the heavens shall flee;
> Christ will then like lightning shine.
> All will see his glorious sign;
> All will then the trumpet hear,
> All will see the Judge appear:
> Thou by all wilt be confest,
> God in Man made manifest.
>
> Grant us grace to see thee, Lord,
> Mirrored in thy holy word;
> May we imitate thee now,
> And be pure, as pure art thou;
> That we like to thee may be
> At thy great Epiphany;
> And may praise thee, ever blest,
> God in Man made manifest.

The preacher's task is to allow the glory of God to be seen in the face of Christ Jesus (2 Cor. 4:6), so that, being by that beholding changed from glory into glory (3:18), the righteous by faith may at the last shine like the sun (Matt. 13:43).

Advent

Epiphany became, after Easter and Pentecost, the next most favored moment for Christian baptism; and the preceding season of Advent, which is confined to Western Christianity, may in that respect have had origins similar to Lent. The liturgical themes of Advent, however, offer only a few hints of preparation for individual baptism and seem rather to envisage more directly the first and final comings of Christ. They encourage Christians to relive the Old Testament expectations that they believe were fulfilled at Bethlehem and, simultaneously, to prepare themselves for the Lord's return at the consummation. Isaiah is a favored source of Scripture lessons, since the book lends itself to a "stereoscopic" reading that sees the prophecies as both realized in Christ and yet still outstanding until the End.

The preacher will use the season of Advent not only to build up to the celebration of Christmas but also, following medieval practice, to confront the "four last things" of death and judgment, heaven and hell. This is the existential application to each individual of Christ's awaited coming again in glory to judge the quick and the dead (cf. 2 Cor. 5:10).

Two traditional feasts related to the date of Christmas are the Annunciation (March 25, nine months before December 25; cf. Luke 1:26-38) and the Presentation of Christ in the temple (February 2, forty days after Christmas; cf. Luke 2:22-40).

The Rest of the Year

If we were to draw the "irregular ellipse" of the church's year, we should find the line fading into brokenness shortly after the feast of the Epiphany (January 6) until just before Lent (for many centuries the West had the pre-Lenten Sundays of Septuagesima, Sexagesima, and Quinquagesima), and then again from Pentecost or Trinity Sunday until just before Advent (the twentieth-century Roman feast of Christ the King, now placed on the Sunday immediately preceding Advent, is but the most recent instance of anticipating the season). For long the "green" Sundays—the most "neutral" color for liturgical vestments—were numbered "after Epiphany" and "after Pentecost" or "after Trinity." Beyond the first week or two, these scarcely constituted coherent season, although there may still be continuing tendencies to thematize the earthly life and ministry of Jesus (particularly the former) and the ongoing life and mission of the church in the second. The current Roman Catholic bluntly designates these periods as "ordinary time" (*per annum*).

"Ordinary Sundays" remain, however, precisely Sundays. That fact calls the preacher to bring the Scripture readings and the sermon into relation to the pivotal event and mystery of Christ's death and resurrection.

Lectionaries

Lectionaries do not fall directly from heaven. Rather they codify and promote patterns in the liturgical reading of Scripture that have commended themselves to the church over a greater or lesser extent of time, space, and confessional tradition. They are necessary because it is impossible to read the whole of the Bible in a particular service of worship; they are valuable insofar as they allow the broad range of the biblical witness to be heard. Lectionaries perpetually exhibit a certain tension between the reading of entire biblical books in course (*lectio continua*) and the eclectic selection of passages from the canon that are appropriate to particular times and occasions. The more definite the theological or Christological content of a feast or season, the more likely are the lessons from the Old Testament and the New (Epistle and Gospel) to be arranged for their typological and thematic point and counterpoint; this is a strong testimony to belief in the unity of the Scripture, although there is a danger that the Old Testament in particular will be used for snippets to match the New. On the other hand, the individual books of the Bible have a greater chance of communicating their characteristic message when they are read more continuously. Mixed cases are found in, say, the semicontinuous reading of Isaiah in Advent, or of St. John, the Acts, and the Revelation in Eastertide.

The many coincidences of lectionary patterns over time, space, and confessional boundaries bear witness to a remarkably common sense among Christians as to what Scriptures belong when, if the full range of redemptive history is to be commemorated, celebrated, and anticipated over a regularly recurring period (hitherto usually a year). In recent decades, various ecumenical efforts have been made to bring the various confessional practices into even greater harmony. In Britain, *The Calendar and Lectionary* (1967) of the semi-official Joint Liturgical Group, which spreads the readings over a two-year period, has exercised great influence on the official revisions of Anglican and Protestant churches. Unfortunately, this pioneering work has tended to isolate the British, since churches in other areas, particularly of the English-speaking world, have preferred to base themselves on the three-year Sunday and festive lectionary of the postconciliar Roman Catholic church (_Lectionary for Mass_, 1969). In particular, the pattern of "naming" the three years after the gospels of Matthew, Mark, and Luke has proved popular. In some respects, however, the Roman lectionary has undergone adaptation in its reception by others. Thus the American Consultation on Common Texts, in order to avoid the sometimes strained typologies of the Roman Old Testament snippets, has attempted a more continuous reading of the Old Testament in each of the three years in the Sundays after Pentecost, with only a rough typological correspondence between the Pentateuch and Matthew, the Davidic narrative and Mark, and the prophets and Luke.

Protestant preachers in many regions and denominations are increasingly finding it a boon to have the scriptural matter of their sermons "provided" for them through the use of a lectionary. If, as Karl Barth almost implied on a couple of occasions, one should preach with the Bible in one hand and the newspaper in the other, the use of a lectionary offers a better chance for the Scriptures to relate to our current perceptions of the world and human affairs, rather than the other way around. This is not to say that a particular event may not sometimes impel the preacher to turn to another Scripture for the sermon, but the congregation ought not to be robbed of the steady and consistent reading of the Scriptures in the worship assembly.

We thereby come to one final theme that has tentatively surfaced at a number of points in our discussion and now needs to be dug out: the theme of history and mystery, of time and eschatology.

History and Eschatology

It is sometimes argued that the fourth century marked a dramatically new phase in the Christian understanding of history and of this temporal world. Certainly it is no accident that this century—that of Constantine's conversion—provides our first evidence for the practice of an annual Holy Week (Palm Sunday, Maundy Thursday, Good Friday), a feast on the day of Pentecost (and soon a separate Ascension day), and a celebration of the Savior's birthday and public appearance (with Christmas and Epiphany becoming distinct feasts).

Yet it may be a mistake to discern a drastic change rather than a more subtle and gradual shift of emphasis. There was no sudden decline from _kairos_ into _chronos_ (to use a distinction beloved of an older biblical theology). The church's Constantinian "settlement into the world" was foreshadowed, if H. Conzelmann's exegesis of Luke-Acts in _Die Mitte der Zeit_ has value at all, in the Lucan accommodation to the delay of the Parousia.

There was probably from the first a touch of historical commemoration in the early designations, as we saw of Wednesday and Friday as weekly fast days. The weekly Sunday and the yearly Easter, both inferable from the New Testament writings, commemorate the raising of Jesus from the dead, which was considered as _at least_ an historical event. The resurrection was, of course, _more_. That is why Christian worship is always also a celebration of Christ's presence and an anticipation of the Lord's return. With Christ, the final kingdom began its irruption into this world, and all our created time has become, as the Orthodox theologian Olivier Clement puts it, "porous" to God. Every Sunday, in particular, is a declaration of the eschatological qualification brought to time and history by the resurrection of the crucified Christ from the dead.

Over time, though so qualified, is not abolished. The Savior himself "needed"—we can infer after the event—the years of his earthly life, from the moment of his conception to the day of his ascension, for the multifaceted work of redemption. Moreover, the mystery of God's design for the world apparently includes the centuries that have since passed. And still the Parousia has not taken place. What is worked out in time and history will belong, we conclude, to the final kingdom of God, however marvelous the transformation it will undergo in the general resurrection which Christ's presaged. If the Creator's saving purpose accommodates itself to time and history in these ways, it is entirely appropriate to commemorate, celebrate, and anticipate it in the temporal symbolism that the church's calendar represents. That is in no way to deny the openness of all Christian worship and the whole of Christian existence to the entire mystery of God.

Geoffrey Wainwright[2]

156 ✦ HOW THE PRACTICE OF THE CHRISTIAN YEAR AFFECTS CONGREGATIONAL LIFE

The way Christians keep time is a way of remembering. In communal worship we remember and celebrate the events that make us who we are. Consequently the celebration of the Christian year forms us into Christ's body in the world.

Among the most remarkable aspects of the twentieth-century reform and renewal of Christian worship is the rediscovery of the church year. Twenty years ago no one could have predicted the extraordinary impact that the scholarship and the theology and practice of the church year would have on our preaching and worship. Every Christian tradition, except for the most narrowly sectarian Protestant churches, has established or proposed a version of the ecumenical new calendar and lectionary. The liturgical churches, of course, have always used calendar and lectionary to order the worship life of the people. What prompts our reflection here, however, is an unprecedented convergence across denominational lines—including "free churches" and "liturgical churches"—on a basic theology of time represented in the new three-year lectionary.

Protestants are in the process of rediscovering the church year, not as an imposition from "outside," but as a fundamental feature of authentic Christian worship that was part of Christian and Jewish experience from the beginning. For Judaism and for Christianity, time—and how we keep it—is crucial to faith itself. Why is this so? Because God's self-revelation is historical and temporal. The events in and through which the living God has chosen to communicate with humankind are historical events. Even more to the point, remembering and proclaiming those events are the heartbeat of all preaching and worship. The community gathered about the Scriptures, the baptismal font, and the Table of the Lord is a community of memory. It keeps time with God by retelling and entering into the meaning and power of those "past" events again and again.

There is a considerable lack of understanding of how the laity enters into the formative and expressive range of the cycles of the church year. How a local congregation appropriates such faith and theological meaning into its ongoing worship and spirituality in common life and ministry is the point at issue.

Keeping Time as Part of Our Human Experience

In one sense time is so obvious but so hidden from us. Our temporality is itself a feature of all human experience. We know that a family gains identity and deepens its life by keeping anniversaries and by knowing how to celebrate well the significant events which mark that family's history. Birthdays are kept with special rituals and celebrations; but so, too, in healthy families, are memories of deaths, transitions, and the characters and events of family history. At a family reunion the foods are brought and ordered, the stories of our grandparents, aunts, and uncles are told, the songs and entertainments are performed, and the memories recited and made real.

Eating and drinking together in a family takes time. In everyday life we come to understand certain matters only after we have had meals on birthdays, after funerals, with all the children home and with them all gone, and during the subtly changing seasons of our lives. How much more, then, is our eating and drinking at the Lord's Table and our singing and hearing the Word of God this way. The meaning of our eucharistic meal deepens as we mature in the times and places of such gathering.

The way Christians keep time—or fail to keep time—is a theological expression of what is remembered and lived. "Why do they keep coming, Sunday upon Sunday, year upon year, just to hear me preach, to sing the same songs, and to pray together?" This startling question from a beleaguered pastor opens up our subject to the real issue of congregational faith and life. Why, indeed, do Christians continue, over time, to gather with such regularity? Obligation? Custom? Or could they be searching for a way of opening their temporal lives to God—a search, perhaps, for genuine transformation? The answer is: all of the above.

Honest reflection upon the connections between worship and our deeper hungers for God raises a series of theological issues about temporality and the cycles of time that give Christian memory and proclamation its distinctive character. Whatever else our motives may be, human beings come to worship because there is a restlessness for God and a sense, however obscured, that time and place and life need somehow to be sanctified. The search for holy times and places is itself an expression of a deeper hunger we have for the transformation of our transitory lives. Worship, no matter how dull and routine, holds out some hidden promise of sanctification in the very midst of life with all its changes, confusions, suffering, joy, and mystery.

Keeping Time as a Christian Community

The Christian community gathers to remember and to enact its particular identity as those called out by God in Christ. Because all ministries are rooted in the redemptive presence and activity of Christ in the world, the church's sense of time and place is oriented toward God's self-giving in the whole person and work of Jesus Christ. Christian worship involves the gathering of a baptized people who are commissioned and empowered to serve the world. Such servanthood does not take place unless the church remembers with the whole sweep of Scripture and is enabled to hope for a real future in light of God's promises.

How may we speak in our local churches of Christian worship as forming and expressing ordinary people in the mystery of God's unfolding relationship with us? How can pastors and musicians, and the other liturgical ministries of the laity, enable a congregation to enter more deeply into the rhythms of the church year, the week, and the shape of each day's prayer and work? Consider a short definition and then let us draw some concrete pastoral applications from this in light of what has already been said.

Christian worship is the ongoing liturgy of Jesus Christ in and through his body in the world. It is the ongoing relationship of love and service between God and the people of God formed in the story of Creation, covenant, prophecy, and the incarnation, death, resurrection, and reign of Christ. Worship is, therefore, something communal because it is our distinctive way of remembering and celebrating who and whose we are. The adequacy of how we sing and pray and are shaped by Word and sacrament requires living with the whole reality of what God has done, in Creation and redemption, and the whole promise of the reign of God in the whole Creation.

Such an account of Christian liturgy shows the mutuality of divine and human dialogue. Christian life together is thus patterned in accordance with the humanity shown in God's history with us. The faith of the church from its beginnings manifests in its pattern of worship over time an implicitly Trinitarian structure—God the Father made manifest in history and prophecy, and supremely in the events of Jesus Christ—suffering, dying and rising—and in the Holy Spirit indwelling and making alive the community of those who believe. The early church remembered Jesus especially with the keeping of Sunday, the day of creation and of resurrection. The very term "Lord's Day" had become a Christian term for the first day for the week by the early second century. Sunday was, and is in essence, a weekly anniversary of the Resurrection. But it takes time for all such a claim means to be unfolded. This is the domain of the church year.

The temporal pattern of the year and the reading, preaching, singing, and hearing of God's Word over time itself witnesses to the holy history of God's act focused in the unfolding story of Christ's redeeming life, teachings, dying, and rising. The center point for the church was and is the Christian Passover—the Easter Pasch—which we celebrate as the three days at the climax of Holy Week. This, in turn, is approached by remembering our mortality and by preparing ourselves for the renewal of baptismal covenant at Easter. The two other great feasts in the early church were Epiphany and Pentecost. The new ecumenical lectionary and calendar recover the relationship between Easter and Pentecost in the "Great Fifty Days" as a time of the outpouring of the Spirit.

Entering into the rhythms of the church year thus implies that our musical experiences sensitively unfold this. By working carefully together, pastors and musicians can provide an extraordinary opportunity for the congregation to "live into" the unfathomable riches of the cycles of Christian time. This implies that entering into the cycles of the liturgical year is a way of unfolding and exploring the gospel itself: opening the treasury of who Jesus is and what he does in and through human community called forth to conversion and transformation. So we enter Advent/Christmas/Epiphany precisely as a way of expectation, reception, and manifestation of the love of God in human form. But in so doing, the Scripture itself opens new dimensions of reality to us. The same is true of Lent/Easter/Pentecost. In this case, the central mystery of participation in the death and resurrection of Christ is at the heart of the journey.

Far from "playing church," a genuine entry into these two focal cycles of the Christian year, with the interconnection of Old and New Testament and the treasury of the church's prayer and song, provides the very pattern of the Christian life itself. This is why the pastor's understanding of the cycles of time and the ability to guide the church's worship through such feasts and seasons is itself a spiritual discovery. Because the community of faith and each faithful person continue to experience the changes of life—growth, suffering, joy, passages of various kinds, and death—the liturgical year is never the same. For our lives are constantly being reinterpreted into the story of God with us. In this manner, "Keeping time with Jesus" may never fall into habitual routine or empty cycles of ceremony. Rather, in and through such remembrance and retelling, our very lives are given significance and a deeper sense of time and place.

Keeping Time
"Between the Times"

But this leads us to a further aspect of the spirituality of the cycles of time. There is a tension that is part of the intrinsic nature of the Gospel claim itself. Christianity claims that the Messiah has come, ushering in the new age and opening up a way into the Kingdom of God. At the same time, the world and our human existence go on. Empires still rise and fall; there is birth and suffering and human passage and death. There is the *already* of death and resurrection and the salvation from sin and death; but there is unmistakably the *not yet*. The rule and reign of God has not fully come in human history. So we live between the times. This tension is the permanent feature of Christian worship and of the Christian life. The ongoing liturgy of Christ in the world still calls us to journey and to serve a broken, suffering world. The sanctification of time and place and human life cannot be possessed apart from the concrete world of human experience. Yet authentic Christian worship is a time and a place of remembering and rehearsing and proclaiming what is yet to be, while all the time being about the work of redemptive love, mercy, and justice among the human family.

Not only the year as the arena of sanctification, but the week and the day as well, are part of the discipline and discovery of the spiritual life. The early church took the week, with the Lord's Day at its beginning and end, as the most significant liturgical cycle. For Sunday—the day of Creation and of resurrection from the dead, the "first day" and the "eighth day"—was the paradigm of the gathering in the Spirit. Christians celebrated the Eucharist every Lord's Day as the pattern for orienting all other time, including the liturgy of the hours for the sanctification of the day and the feasts and seasons in which Word and Eucharist reflected the unfolding of the larger story of salvation.

The pastor and musicians must therefore offer the treasury of this tradition to contemporary Christians. To be a community of living memory is thus to desire to live in light of who God in Christ is: his advent and birth, his appearance and death, and his resurrection, ascension, and lifegiving Spirit given to the community of faith. Within this discipline of time we live with the symbols, the sign-actions of God in baptism and Eucharist, and the works of love and mercy.

Don E. Saliers[3]

157 • AN OVERVIEW OF THE CHRISTIAN YEAR

Throughout the past generation, worship leaders and planners from many traditions have been working toward a consensus or ecumenical approach to the Christian year, resulting in the following outline of the year-long calendar.

ADVENT SEASON
    First Sunday of Advent to fourth Sunday of Advent
CHRISTMAS SEASON
    Christmas Eve/Day
    First Sunday after Christmas
    New Year's Eve/Holy Name of Jesus
    Second Sunday after Christmas
    Epiphany
SEASON AFTER EPIPHANY
    First Sunday after Epiphany (Baptism of the Lord)
    Second Sunday after Epiphany to Eighty Sunday after Epiphany
    Last Sunday after Epiphany (Transfiguration Sunday)

LENTEN SEASON
    Ash Wednesday
    First Sunday of Lent to fifth Sunday of Lent
    Holy Week
        Passion/Palm Sunday
        Monday in Holy Week
        Tuesday in Holy Week
        Wednesday in Holy Week
        Holy Thursday
        Good Friday
        Holy Saturday
PASCHAL (EASTER) SEASON
    The Great Paschal Vigil
    Pascha Day
    Pascha Evening
    Second Sunday of Pascha to sixth Sunday of
      Pascha
    Ascension (Sixth Thursday)
    Seventh Sunday of Pascha
    Pentecost
AFTER PENTECOST
    Trinity Sunday (First Sunday after Pentecost)
    Sundays after Pentecost
    Christ the King (Last Sunday after Pentecost)

158 • COLORS OF THE CHRISTIAN YEAR

Colors of the various seasons of the Christian year express the mood or feeling of the season. The following outline presents the colors most often associated with Christian seasons.

Advent. Blue or violet express the penitential nature of the season as well as the royalty of Christ.

Christmas. White expresses the celebrative nature of the season.

After Epiphany. Green expresses the ongoing eternal nature of growth. Use white for Baptism of the Lord Sunday and for the last Sunday which celebrates the transfiguration of our Lord.

Lent. Black, violet, grays, and/or muted blues express the solemnity of Lenten time.

Holy Week. Red is used as the color of the blood of Christ and of the martyrs. Black is also used to express the somber nature of Holy Week. For Holy Communion on Maundy Thursday, use white or red. For Good Friday and Holy Saturday, red, black, or no color.

Easter. Gold or white expresses the joy of the season. Use red on Pentecost Sunday. Red symbolizes fire and the coming of the Holy Spirit.

After Pentecost. Green expresses the ongoing work of God. Use white on Trinity Sunday, All Saints' Day, and Christ the King Sunday. White expresses the celebratory nature of these days.

Other Uses of Color

White: wedding, funeral, Thanksgiving, dedication, baptism
Red or Scarlet: church anniversary, ordination/installation, confirmation, reception into the church, revival, preaching, missions, work of the Holy Spirit

During weekday services, use the color of season (after Epiphany, Passiontide, after Pentecost), or color of preceding Sunday (in Advent, Christmas, Lent, and Easter), unless a color is specified in the calendar for the day (Good Friday, etc.).

Denominational promotions and thematic events (Day/Week of Prayer for Christian Unity, World Communion Sunday, etc.) may be worked in with the Christian calendar emphasis for a given day without overshadowing that emphasis. Laity (women's, men's, children's) days, church vocations, missions, etc., may be honored without supplanting the calendared day or season.

Civil and commercial holidays and observances NEVER supersede the Christian use for the main services on _any_ Sunday, nor mix with them, if it can be helped. Civil days include national, state, and local holidays (Presidents' birthdays, Memorial, Flag, Independence days, etc.). Commercial observances include Valentine's, St. Patrick's, Grandparents', Mothers' and Fathers' days, etc. If possible, observe these in Sunday evening or midweek services, or with a church school or fellowship event.

159 • INTRODUCTION TO THE ANTHOLOGY OF CONGREGATIONAL SONG

The anthology of songs for each season of the Christian year is a compilation of traditional hymns, gospel songs, popular hymns, and Scripture choruses chosen for their suitability for the seven major celebrations of the church year: Advent, Christmas, Epiphany, Lent, Holy Week, Easter, and Pentecost. (You will find a listing of songs under each particular season in Volume 5. See chapters 5, 9, 14, 17, and 26 in particular.) The selections represent an interdenominational spread, and the purpose of the anthology is to help music leaders in choices of seasonal materials where presence of scriptural allusion is also at hand.

The church calendar traditionally centers around two primary events in Christ's earthly ministry: his resurrection and his nativity. Since the apostle Paul emphasizes that without the Savior's resurrection from the dead the believer's faith is logically futile (1 Cor. 15:17), value of the Nativity naturally hinges on the validity of the Resurrection and thereby parallels the earlier historical emphasis that the church placed on Easter (the older of the celebrations), compared to Christmas. The Vatican II–based reforms of the church calendar in 1969 have also brought three features into focus, harking back to early church practices:

(1) The calendar is regulated by a two-event sequence (A: Beginning of Lent to the day of Pentecost; and B: the opening of Advent to the day of Epiphany). Here Sundays are arranged in two groups: each side of Easter, and each side of Christmas. The period of Sundays after Epiphany and the long period of Sundays after Pentecost (up to 27, plus Sunday of the Fulfillment) are now termed "Sundays of the Year"—that is, ordinary Sundays—by Roman/ecumenical definition.

In the 1970s studies in Frankish (Gregorian) chant revealed the early medieval custom of baptizing Christian converts (neophytes) at the conclusion of the Easter Vigil, where they also offered these converts a chalice of milk and honey. This ceremony had followed at least forty days of biblical training and catechetical practice, and was likely less penitential in character than the later traditions/accretions known as Lent. Accordingly, much of the music in this anthology affirms church calendar reforms that have, in fact, returned to earlier historical viewpoints or practices. It clarifies why, for instance, a number of the selections for Lent exemplify faith, promise, dedication, obedience, service, praise of God's grace, or spiritual growth in addition to traditional themes of sober contemplation or denial of self.

(2) The three-day period of Maundy Thursday, Good Friday, and Holy Saturday is currently revisualized as a single, integrated spectrum of Christ's love for the believer (John 13:1) and the unsaved (John 12:32), seen in tandem with his struggle between personal wish and divine obedience in Gethsemane (Luke 22:42) and his absence from his beloved ones in death (John 16:16, 32). In this context the *triduum* is not "three events" (Passion, Crucifixion, Death) but a "single focus" that celebrates the destruction of the works of the devil and the sinner's redemption (1 John 3:8; John 1:12). As practical assistance, each citation for Holy Week in this article is accompanied by a caption that assigns the song to the day most appropriate; this facilitates any wish to emphasize the integrated focus of the *triduum* period and makes Passion (Palm) Sunday materials immediately identifiable.

(3) The forty days before Easter and the fifty days after Easter are more properly intended to celebrate the Lord's resurrection: a: either in terms of the cost paid at Calvary, or b: in terms of his glory ascribed by the Father through his resurrection (Heb. 12:2). This aspect of calendar reinterpretation has been helpful for bridging worship-style differences between liturgical and nonliturgical believers; it is a biblical basis for including songs of adoration, testimony, praise, anticipation, and gratitude throughout the year, and for bringing such songs into the "forty-plus-fifty" time period as well. It is the reality of Christ's resurrection and the Holy Spirit's presence in the life of the individual believer and the corporate body of believers that drives all logic of the church calendar, thus coloring all the varied nuances of the separate seasons.

The anthology here presents a simple format for guiding song-choice. Information is read from left to right by: a: citation-title; b: scriptural quotation or allusion; c: author(s)/composer(s); d: tune-name (if extant); e: an available published source in siglum listing, with page/number; and f: occasional captioned description of usage or proper context—ceremonial or historical. Because of the large flowering of hymn-writing in the United States and Britain between the late 1960s and the middle 1980s, identity of compositional, copyright, or publication date is listed for pieces appearing within the last thirty years.

The hymns and songs in the anthology represent a wide survey of Christian denominations, providing wide stylistic variation within the repertory itself. Denominations include Anglican, Baptist, Congregational, Christian Reformed, Evangelical Covenant, independent free church, Lutheran, Mennonite, Methodist, Moravian, Pentecostal (Assemblies of God), Presbyterian, Roman Catholic, and Seventh-day Adventist. Some material from the Taizé community is also included. This section allows music leaders to select congregational songs appropriate to their own worship tradition that may, in fact, be shared with one or more of the other traditions. At best, numerous opportunities for fresh choice are available.

Another musical issue congruent to congregational song is the format for singing Alleluias. It is a practice ranging from formal choral works and praise-choruses to Roman-based liturgies. Absorbed into Latin from Hebrew ("Praise Ye the Lord"), the Alleluia was introduced as a praise-formula in fourth-century Western chant under Damasus I as a part of the Easter liturgy. Ultimately it was extended throughout the church year by Gregory I (except during Lent, where it was replaced by the tract). By the time of Charlemagne's unification of Frankish (Gregorian) chant-usage, the Alleluia had developed a format for singing that has changed relatively little to the present, even in post–Vatican II rites. Occurring in the Synaxis of the Mass, the Alleluia is normally given three consecutive statements and then followed by brief verses of Scripture, prior to being recapitulated at the conclusion. Traditionally the first Alleluia was sung by a cantor and then repeated by the choir. Contemporary practice allows the congregation to sing the Alleluia. In medieval examples (and in certain contemporary settings) the final Alleluia of a sequence of statements often contains a notational extension on a single syllable (the final vowel of "Alleluia"). This is known as a *Jubilus*, and there are references to the Jubilus as far back as Augustine's time, where he speaks of ululation in the Ambrosian rite and of his reactions (*Confessions*, Bk. X).

As a matter of history the Jubilus itself became a basis for polyphonic composition in the early thirteenth century—particularly at the Notre Dame school of Paris. Here Jubili were extracted from context to become supportive substructures for texted upper parts in rhythmic modes (formulae): sources of organa and motets.

Alleluias traditionally are added to all antiphons during the Easter season. They also occur during other major celebrations, as well as throughout ordinary time, where they are linked to the reading of the Gospel. Alleluias also form colorful refrains to certain hymns and are the main text to several praise-choruses (e.g., by Ray Repp or Jerry Sinclair); they have been the subject of classical-era contrapuntal work (e.g., Mozart: *Canon*, K. 533); and most recently in works such as Randall Thompson's SATB a cappella *Alleluia* of 1940, which has become a fixture in musical Americana.

Finally, as the reader studies this anthology , it will become apparent that a good number of well-known hymns and gospel songs that enjoy frequent use were not included. Here the main goal has been to broaden scope and representative variety; while it is true that many well-employed Christmas citations appear, on the whole the options for each season will be wider rather than merely familiar. This is particularly visible in the distinction between the selections for Lent and Holy Week. These songs and hymns are purposefully kept separate and thereby tend to enrich the entire choice-spectrum for the weeks between Ash Wednesday and Easter Sunday. Accompanying commentaries, while very short, will help to narrow choices for particular seasons.

The following list of abbreviations will lead the reader to the resources for songs for each of the seasons of the Christian year.

The Sources

AHB
Anglican Hymn Book. London: Church Book Room Press, Ltd., 1965.

AHON
American Hymns, Old and New. Compiled by Albert Christ-Janer, Charles Hughes, and Carleton Smith. New York: Columbia University Press, 1980.

ALYA 1
Aleluya: The Music of Lausanne II. Charlotte, N.C.: Lausanne Committee for World Evangelization, 1989.

ALYA 2
Aleluya: The Songs of Renewal. Valley Forge, Pa.: National Ministries, 1992.

BPH
The Baptist Hymnal. Nashville: Convention Press, 1975.

CHRE
The Church Hymnary, rev. ed. London: Oxford University Press, 1927.

CPH
The Christian Praise Hymnal. Nashville: Broadman, 1972.

CVH
Hymnal of the Evangelical Covenant Church of America. Chicago: Covenant Press, 1950.

DVS
The Dove Songbook: Songs of the Spirit for Today's Christian Community. Carol Stream, Ill.: Hope Publishing Co., 1975.

FHEA
Favorite Hymns of Early America. Edited by Leonard Van Camp. Macomb, Ill.: Roger Dean Publishing Co., 1975.

GLP
Glory and Praise. Phoenix: Epoch Universal Publications, 1987.

H–III
Church Hymnal Series III. New York: Church Hymnal Corporation, 1981.

HB
The Hymn Book. Richmond, Va.: Presbyterian Church in the United States, United Presbyterian Church in the USA, and the Reformed Church in America, 1955.

HCS
Hymnal for Colleges and Schools. Edited by E. Harold Geer. New Haven, Conn.: Yale University Press, 1956.

HFG
Hymns for the Family of God. Special Edition. Nashville: Paragon Associates Inc., 1976.

HMOC
Hymnal of the Moravian Church. Elk Grove, Ill.: Walter M. Carqueville, 1969.

HWB
Hymnal: A Worship Book. Elgin, Ill.: Brethren Press, 1992.

LBW
The Lutheran Book of Worship. Minneapolis: Augsburg Publishing House, 1982.

LH
The Lutheran Hymnal. St. Louis: Concordia Publishing House, 1941.

LW
Lutheran Worship. St. Louis: Concordia Publishing House, 1982.

MCB
Master Chorus Book. Compiled by Ken Bible. Kansas City, Mo.: Lillenas, 1987.

MH
The Methodist Hymnal. Nashville: Whitmore and Smith, 1939.

MH-66
The Methodist Hymnal. Nashville: The Methodist Publishing House, 1966.

MMH
The Mount Mary Hymnal. Boston: McLaughlin and Reilly, 1937.

MMP
Maranatha! Music Praise Chorus Book. Nashville: The Benson Co., 1983.

MNH
The Mennonite Hymnal. Scottdale, Pa.: Herald Press, 1969.

NEPT
Ye Olde New England Psalm Tunes, 1620–1820. Bryn Mawr, Pa.: Presser, 1930.

NJSS
New Jesus-Style Songs, I. Minneapolis: Augsburg Publishing House, 1972.

OXBC
The Oxford Bood of Carols. London: Oxford University Press, 1964.

P:1, 2
Praises. Edited by Frank Garlock and Ron Hamilton. Greenville, S.C.: Musical Ministries, 1991. Three volumes in two.

PH
Pilgrim Hymnal. Philadelphia: Pilgrim Press, 1974.

PSH
Psalter Hymnal, Doctrinal Standards and Liturgy of the Christian Reformed Church. Grand Rapids: Publication Committee of the Christian Reformed Church, 1934.

SBAH
Service Book and Hymnal of the Lutheran Church in America. Minneapolis: Augsburg Publishing House, 1958.

SC
The Singing Church. Carol Stream, Ill.: Hope Publishing House, 1958.

SDAH
The Seventh Day Adventist Hymnal. Washington D.C.: Review and Herald Publishing Association, 1987.

SHP
The B.F. White Sacred Harp. Troy, Ala.: Sacred Harp Book Co., 1949.

TAIZÉ
Music from Taizé. Chicago: GIA Publications, Inc., 1981.

WB
The Worshipbook. Philadelphia: The Westminster Press, 1972.

W-II
Worship II: A Hymnal for Roman Catholic Parishes. Chicago: GIA Publications, 1975.

WH
We Have Come into this House to Worship Him. Compiled by Jesse Peterson and Mark Hayes. Leawood, Kans.: Tempo Music, 1976 (vol. 1), and 1989 (vol. 2).

H1982
The Hymnal 1982. New York: Church Hymnal Corporation, 1982.

Secondary References

Horace T. Allen, "A Hymn Lectionary," in *Reformed Liturgy and Music* 16 (Fall 1982): 159–164.

Lesley A. Davies, "Prepare the Way of the Lord: An Anthology of Hymns for the Season of Advent," in *Reformed Liturgy and Music* 22 (Summer 1988): 130–133.

Joan Halmo, "Hymns for the Pascal Triduum," in *Worship* 25 (March 1981): 137–159.

Marion J. Hatchett: *A Manual for Clergy and Church Musicians*. New York: Church Hymnal Corporation, 1980.

160 ♦ BIBLIOGRAPHY ON THE HISTORY AND THEOLOGY OF THE CHRISTIAN YEAR

Adam, Adolf. *The Liturgical Year*. New York: Pueblo Publishing, 1981. Adam's volume accounts for the history and theological/spiritual meaning of the liturgical year after Vatican II reforms. The volume is comprehensive, paying attention to the paschal mystery as central and Sunday worship as the kernel of celebration. The book encompasses all seasons and celebrations, including daily prayer, and is both readable and scholarly—a good primary source. There are explanatory notes for each subject. Ecumenical/Catholic.

Belisle, Augustin. *The Wheel of Becoming*. Petersham, Mass.: St. Bede's Publications, 1987. Belisle writes concerning the correlation of the church year cycle and the cycle of human life rhythms. His "wheel of becoming" is divided into times for Watching (Advent), Birthing (Christmas/Epiphany), Giving (Lent), Dying (Holy Week), Rising (Easter), Believing (Ascension/Pentecost), and Living (ordinary time). Those who experience and draw significance from the wheel lead "inspirable" lives that evidence the Kingdom of God within. Devotional. Ecumenical/Roman Catholic.

Bosch, Paul. *Church Year Guide*. Minneapolis: Augsburg, 1987. This volume includes descriptions of the each season of the Christian year, along with helpful suggestions and resources for worship planning.

Buckland, Patricia. *Advent to Pentecost.* Wilton, Conn.: Morehouse-Barlow, 1979. Buckland has authored a basic introduction to the history of the church year with many practical helps to church leaders and congregations regarding traditions and services for the seasons and special days. The volume may be used with the Anglican *Book of Common Prayer* and contains many illustrations. Ecumenical/Anglican.

Carroll, Thomas, and Thomas Halton. *Liturgical Practice in the Fathers.* Collegeville, Minn.: Glazier/Liturgical Press, 1988. Quotations from the early church fathers that shed light on the history and meaning of the liturgical seasons.

Days of the Lord: The Liturgical Year. 7 vols. Collegeville, Minn.: Liturgical Press, 1990. A comprehensive guide to the seasons of the Christian year, with reference to the readings and special services of each season. Roman Catholic/Ecumenical.

Every, George, Richard Harries, and Kallistos Ware. *The Time of the Spirit.* Crestwood, N.Y.: St. Vladimir's Seminary Press, 1984. An anthology of readings for the church year, with selections centered on monthly or seasonal themes or on saints celebrated within time periods noted. Editors are from Roman, Orthodox, and Anglo-Catholic backgrounds. Topics include Creation, the human person, death and the communion of saints, Advent, prayer, the church, the gifts of the Spirit, and others. Orthodox/Ecumenical.

Forell, George W. *The Christian Year: Sermons of the Fathers.* 2 vols. New York: Nelson, 1965. An fascinating collection of sermons from the early, medieval, and Reformation churches that correspond with the main feasts in the Christian year. Ecumenical.

Hamerton-Kelly, Robert. *Spring Time: Seasons of the Christian Year.* Nashville: The Upper Room, 1980. The author's contribution is a pastor's experience of the church year as a rehearsal of the stages of life, an imitation of Christ and discipleship in progress. It is insightfully reflective and devotional as it ponders appropriate Scripture passages, and its contents offer a unique vision of time and event helpful for personal piety or public presentation. Ecumenical/United Methodist.

Hickman, Hoyt L., Don E. Saliers, Laurence Hull Stookey, and James F. White. *The New Handbook of the Christian Year.* Nashville: Abingdon, 1992. A comprehensive guide to the Christian year, including insightful introductions to each season of the year, sample services, and helpful suggestions for planning in the local parish. One of the best introductions available. Ecumenical.

Jarrell, Stephen T. *Guide to the Sacramentary.* Chicago: Liturgy Training Publications, 1983. The volume is intended to be used in conjunction with the Sacramentary and to prepare presiders with a one-page overview of each Sunday in the church year. It gives a "feel" and some guidelines for the unity of the liturgy. Ecumenical/Roman Catholic.

Johnson, Lawrence, ed. *The Church Gives Thanks and Remembers.* Collegeville, Minn., Liturgical Press, 1984. The volume contains four essays on the liturgical year. Searle addresses Sunday as its "heart." Guzie speaks of the significance of "remembrance" through the period. Regan considers the year as a source of spirituality, and Hughes sees both conflict and challenge in our celebration of it. All articles are concise and thought-provoking. Ecumenical/Roman Catholic.

The Liturgical Year: Celebrating the Mystery of Christ and His Saints. Washington, D.C.: Bishop's Committee on the Liturgy, United States Catholic Conference, 1985. A brief teaching on the nature of liturgical time and the Christian year.

Martimort, A.-G., I. H. Dalmais, P. Jounel, et al. *The Liturgy and Time.* London: Geoffrey Chapman, 1985. The authors offer historical context and theological analysis for understanding Sunday and the week, the liturgical year, and Liturgy of the Hours in the post–Vatican II church. Each act of celebrating begins with introductions and/or instructions with doctrinal, spiritual, pastoral, and innovative guidelines. Bibliographies with each chapter. Roman Catholic.

McArthur, A. Allan. *The Evolution of the Christian Year.* London: SCM, 1953. An account of the historical development of the Christian year. Now somewhat dated, but still useful as a general overview.

Metford, J. C. J. *The Christian Year.* New York: Crossroad, 1991. An overview of the Christian year in light of its historical development and modern practice. An accessible overview, valuable for parish libraries and group study. Ecumenical.

Nardone, Richard M. *The Story of the Christian Year*. New York: Paulist, 1991. Nardone tracks the history of the Christian year from its simple beginnings to its complex development before Vatican II, demonstrating how the liturgical year was almost lost to accommodate the sanctoral calendar. His work is concise and detailed and points appreciatively to the present and unfinished work of the council. Roman Catholic.

Norms Governing Liturgical Calendars. Washington, D.C.: United States Catholic Congress, 1984. Both temporal and sanctoral cycles are represented in this volume specifically related to the New General Roman Calendar. General norms for the liturgical year and the calendar, particular calendars, and a commentary comprise the three main divisions. The book also provides the most important documents in postconciliar reform of the liturgical year and Roman calendar, including norms and directives for local parishes. Roman Catholic.

Pfatteicher, Philip H. *Festivals and Commemorations*. Minneapolis: Augsburg, 1980. The volume is a Christian calendar combining temporal (celebrations—feasts, fasts, special observances), and sanctoral cycles (individuals—representing outstanding examples of Christian faith). The author's purpose is to impart a fuller vision of the "everydayness" of faith to modern Christians. Short historical and biographical sketches accompany each commemoration in a "genealogical exploration" of spirituality and spiritual ancestors. All traditions represented. Ecumenical/Lutheran.

Porter, H. Boone. *Keeping the Church Year*. New York: Crossroad, 1977. Porter has authored a readable, concise, practical guide to the church year for clergy, lay readers, altar guild members, musicians, and sacristans—in fact, anyone responsible for "creative role[s] in stimulating and developing the life of [congregational] worship." The book is divided into seven major areas, six corresponding to the seasons (feasts, fasts, and special occasions), and a final chapter addressed to worship leaders. Ecumenical/Anglican.

Power, David, ed. *The Times of Celebration*. Concilium no. 142. New York: Seabury, 1981. Ten essays on the liturgical year, addressing the issue of how the liturgical year can shape faith in modern culture. Roman Catholic/Ecumenical.

Reformed Liturgy and Music 25:1 (Winter 1991). Theme issue on the liturgical calendar. Includes articles on both the theology of the Christian year and on worship planning for the various seasons.

The Roman Calendar: Text and Commentary. Washington, D.C.: U.S. Catholic Conference, 1975. A translation of the official calendar and commentary of the Roman Catholic church.

Supplemental Liturgical Resource 7: Liturgical Year: The Worship of God. Louisville: Westminster/John Knox , 1992. A volume that includes liturgical texts for every season of the Christian year, along with commentary and suggestions for worship planning.

Talley, Thomas J. *The Origins of the Liturgical Year*. Rev. ed. Collegeville, Minn.: Liturgical Press, 1990. This volume is perhaps the current definitive history of the Christian year, relying on the most recent liturgical scholarship. Ecumencial.

Westerhoff, John H., III. *A Pilgrim People: Learning through the Christian Year*. Minneapolis: Seabury, 1984. An insightful essay on the power of the Christian year to form Christians according to the gospel narrative, with attention to how the Christian year speaks to persons of all ages. Ecumenical.

Whalen, Michael D. *Seasons and Feasts of the Church Year: An Introduction*. New York: Paulist, 1993. A very readable and comprehensive introduction to the Christian year. This volume outlines the entire year, giving the theological rationale for its structure and guidelines for worship planning. A good volume to begin with. Roman Catholic/Ecumenical.

Wilde, James A., ed. *At That Time*. Chicago: Liturgy Training Publications, 1989. Ten authors offer pastoral perspectives on "Christian time." Their writing covers subjects such as : "chronos and kairos"; Christian day, week, and year; festival and fast days; initiation in the church year; the sanctoral cycle and the Christian life span. Easily read. Primarily intended for catechumens. Ecumenical/Roman Catholic.

The Year of the Grace of Our Lord. Crestwood, N.Y.: St. Vladimir's Seminary Press, 1980. The volume is a scriptural and liturgical commentary on the calendar of the Orthodox church from the pen of an unnamed monk. The book begins with an explanation of the liturgical year (which begins in September) and proceeds through Sundays and feasts of the Byzantine Rite. It is a devotional and pastoral (rather than technical), guide to Scripture readings, prayers, and spiritual growth with Eastern distinctives. Ecumenical/Eastern Orthodox.

161 ✦ BIBLIOGRAPHY OF GENERAL WORSHIP RESOURCES FOR THE CHRISTIAN YEAR

Denominational Worship Books and Handbooks

For basic worship resources that follow the shape of the Christian year, see the following representative resources:

Roman Catholic: *The Roman Missal: The Sacramentary.* New York: Catholic Book Publishing Co., 1974. *The Roman Missal: Lectionary for Mass.* New York: Catholic Book Publishing Co., 1970.

Episcopal: *Book of Common Prayer.* New York: Church Hymnal Corporation, 1979. *Book of Occasional Services.* New York: Church Hymnal Corporation, 1979. *The Proper for Lesser Feasts and Fasts.* New York: Church Hymnal Corporation, 1990.

Lutheran: *Lutheran Book of Worship.* Minneapolis: Augsburg, and Philadelphia: Board of Publication, Lutheran Church in America, 1978. Philip H. Pfatteicher and Carlos R. Messerli, *Manual on the Liturgy: LBW.* Minneapolis: Augsburg, 1980. *Occasional Services.* Minneapolis: Augsburg, and Philadelphia: Board of Publication, Lutheran Church in America, 1982. Philip H. Pfatteicher, *Commentary on the Occasional Services.* Philadelphia: Fortress, 1983. Philip H. Pfatteicher, *Festivals and Commemorations.* Minneapolis: Augsburg, 1980; *Commentary on the Lutheran Book of Worship: Lutheran Liturgy in its Ecumenical Context.* Minneapolis: Augsburg Fortress, 1990. Missouri Synod Lutherans have published similar volumes, such as *Lutheran Worship* (St. Louis: Concordia, 1982). The Wisconsin Evangelical Lutheran Synod has published *The Pastor's Agenda* (Milwaukee: Northwestern Publishing House, 1983).

Presbyterian/Reformed: *Book of Common Worship.* Louisville: Westminster/John Knox, 1993. *Supplemental Liturgical Resource 7: Liturgical Year: The Worship of God.* Louisville: Westminster/John Knox, 1992. See also *Reformed Liturgy and Music,* which regularly features lectionary-based resources. The Reformed Church in America has issued *Pray to the Lord* (New York: Reformed Church Press, 1988). The Christian Reformed Church publishes *Reformed Worship*, which regularly features services for the Christian year.

Methodist: *The United Methodist Book of Worship* (Nashville: United Methodist Publishing House, 1992), which includes materials earlier presented in *The Book of Services* (Nashville: United Methodist Publishing House, 1984) and *Seasons of the Gospel: Resources for the Christian Year* (Nashville: Abingdon, 1979). See also David L. Bone and Mary J. Scrifes, *The United Methodist Music and Worship Planner* (Nashville: Abingdon, 1992), which contains worship planning suggestions for each Sunday in the Christian year. See also Hoyt L. Hickman, Don E. Saliers, Laurence Hull Stookey, and James F. White, *The New Handbook of the Christian Year* (Nashville: Abingdon, 1992).

Christian Church (Disciples of Christ): *Thankful Praise: A Resource for Christian Worship.* St. Louis: CBP Press, 1987.

Mennonite: *Worship Resources*, Worship Series No. 12. Newton, Kans.: Faith and Life Press; Scottdale, Pa.: Mennonite Publishing House, 1978.

U.C.C.: *Book of Worship: United Church of Christ.* New York: United Church of Christ, 1986.

Lectionary and Preaching Themes

Many lectionary-based preaching guides are currently available, representing every worship tradition. The following are the representative works, published for ecumenical audiences. Not every one of these volumes corresponds with the Common Lectionary; some follow the Roman or Episcopal lectionaries. But all seek to present guidelines for preaching in a larger liturgical context.

The Revised Common Lectionary. Consultation on Common Texts. Nashville: Abingdon, 1992. A list of the complete revision to the Common

Lectionary along with a helpful introduction on its development.

Proclamation 3. 28 vols. Philadelphia: Fortress, 1984.

Proclamation 4. 24 vols. Minneapolis: Fortress, 1988.

Craddock, Fred B., John H. Hayes, Carl R. Holladay, and Gene M. Tucker. *Preaching through the Christian Year*. 3 vols. Philadelphia: Trinity Press International, 1992.

Dozeman, Thomas, Kendall McCabe, and Marion Soards. *Preaching the Revised Common Lectionary*. Nashville: Abingdon, 1992–. A 12-volume series of commentaries based on the lectionary.

Duckworth, Robin. *This the Word of the Lord*. 3 vols. London: Bible Reading Fellowship and New York: Oxford University Press, 1982.

Fuller, Reginald. *Preaching the Lectionary: The Word of God for the Church Today*. Collegeville, Minn.: Liturgical Press, 1984.

Hessel, Dieter T. *Social Themes of the Christian Year*. Philadelphia: Geneva Press, 1983.

Lowry, Eugene. *Living with the Lectionary*. Nashville: Abingdon, 1992.

Maly, Eugene H. *The Word Alive: Commentaries and Reflections on the Scripture Readings for all Sundays, Solemnities of the Lord, Holy Days, and Major Feasts of the Three Year Cycle*. New York: Alba House, 1982.

Ramshaw, Gail. *Richer Fare: Reflections on the Sunday Readings*. New York: Pueblo Publishing, 1990.

Ramshaw, Gail, ed. *Homilies for Christian People: Cycles A, B, C*. New York: Pueblo Publishing, 1989.

The Year of Grace of the Lord: A Scriptural and Liturgical Commentary on the Calendar of the Orthodox Church. Trans. Deborah Cowen. Crestwood, N.Y.: St. Vladimir's Seminary Press, 1980.

Walker, Michael. *From Glory to Glory: Biblical Reflections from Advent to the Feast of Christ the King*. London: Collins Liturgical Press, 1978.

Prayers, Liturgical Texts, and Other Resources

The following resources include supplemental texts for Christian worship, representing many worship traditions.

Bowe, Barbara, ed. *Silent Voices, Sacred Lives: Women's Readings for the Liturgical Year*. New York: Paulist, 1992.

Brown, Carolyn. *Forbid Them Not*. Nashville: Abingdon, 1992–. Volumes with ideas for lectionary-based planning for children. Based on the Revised Common Lectionary.

Companion to the Lectionary. 4 vols. London: Epworth Press, 1987. The volumes are entitled, "Prefaces to the Lessons," "Hymns and Anthems," "A New Collection of Prayers," and "Prayers of Intercession." Taken together, they form complete set of worship planning resources based on the (Anglican) lectionary. Anglican/Ecumenical.

Crouch, Timothy J., Nancy B. Parks, Chris E. Visminas, and Mark R. Babb. *And Also with You*. Cleveland (v. 1&2); Akron (v. 3): OSL Publications 1992–4. Three volumes of lectionary-based worship resources. Based on the Revised Common Lectionary

Deiss, Lucien. *Come, Lord Jesus: Biblical Prayers with Psalms and Scripture Readings*. Chicago: World Library Publications, 1981. Contains hymns, canticles, readings, and prayers for each season in the Christian year. Roman Catholic/Ecumenical.

Duck, Ruth C. *Bread for the Journey: Resources for Worship* (1981); *Flames of the Spirit* (1987); *Touch Holiness* (1990). New York: Pilgrim Press. Worship resources in the U.C.C. tradition written with a concern for inclusive language.

Hostetter, B. David. *Psalms and Prayers for Congregational Participation*. 3 vols. Lima, Ohio: C.S.S. Publishing, 1985. Based on the Common Lectionary but still useful for worship planning.

Karay, Diane. *All Seasons of Mercy*. Westminster: Philadelphia, 1987. Karay's work is a collection of original prayers for congregational worship during the seasons of the church year that are coordinated with the three-year cycle. Each seasonal section contains prayers of four types: calls to worship, prayers of praise, prayers of confession or affirmation, and pastoral prayers. Ecumenical/Presbyterian.

Kirk, James G. *When We Gather: A Book of Prayers for Worship*. 3 vols. Philadelphia: Geneva Press, 1985. Based on the Common Lectionary.

Konstant, David, and Paul Burns. *The Bidding Prayer for the Church's Year*. Mayhew-McCrimmon: Great Wakering Press, 1976, 1982. Contains bidding prayers for each Sunday in the Christian year.

Ideas for the Church Year. San Jose: Resource Publications, 1989. Supplemental liturgical texts for every season of the Christian year.

O'Donnell, Michael J. *Lift Up Your Hearts.* Cleveland: OSL Publications, 1989–1991. Three volumes of Communion resources based on the Revised Common Lectionary.

Perham, Michael. *Enriching the Christian Year.* Collegeville, Minn.: Liturgical Press, 1993. Prayers and other liturgical texts from Lent through ordinary time, with additional resources for important themes in Christian worship, such as Creation, justice and peace, reconciliation, and others. Anglican/Ecumenical.

Ramshaw, Gail. *Intercessions for the Christian People: Prayers of the People for Cycles A, B, C of the Roman, Episcopal, and Lutheran Lectionaries.* New York: Pueblo Publishing, 1988.

Sourcebook for Sundays and Seasons. Chicago: Liturgy Training Publications. An annual publication that includes prayers, readings, and suggestions for art and music for each season of the Christian year.

Shepherd, Massey H. *A Liturgical Psalter for the Christian Year.* Minneapolis: Augsburg, 1976.

Tilson, Everett, and Phyllis Cole. *Liturgies and Other Prayers for the Revised Common Lectionary.* 3 vols. Nashville: Abingdon, 1992–1994. Supplemental worship resources that correspond with the themes of the lectionary readings for each Sunday.

Music and the Arts

Almost every recently published hymnal has an extensive section of resources for the Christian year. Many of the liturgical handbooks already described also contain information on the environment for worship and the arts based on the Christian year. In addition, see these resources.

Erspamer, Steve. *Clip Art for Year A.* Chicago: Liturgy Training Publications, 1992. Brief introductions to each liturgical observance in the Christian year, along with a number of the examples of clip art for use in church bulletins.

Schimdt, Clemens. *Clip Art for the Christian Year.* Collegeville, Minn.: Liturgical Press, 1988.

Troeger, Thomas, and Carol Doran. *New Hymns for the Lectionary: To Glorify the Maker's Name.* New York: Oxford University Press, 1986. A small, supplemental hymnal that introduces several hymns that correspond to lectionary readings, especially for occasions often lacking in appropriate hymns.

Wetzler, Robert, and Helen Huntington. *Seasons and Symbols: A Handbook on the Church Year.* Minneapolis: Augsburg, 1962. The volume is a compendium of symbols related to the church year. Each of the seasons is introduced with a short bit of prose, and more than seventy graphic illustrations are combined with explanatory text to provide an excellent resource for worship. Ecumenical.

PART THREE

The Season of Advent

⊛ THREE ⊛

Introduction to Advent Worship

Advent is the time of preparation for the birth of Christ. Historically, however, Advent was not the beginning of the Christian year, but the end. The original themes of Advent focused on the second coming of Jesus. Gradually Advent also came to mean preparing for the coming of Christ. Today we inherit both themes: the end of the Christian year and the expectation of the second coming of Christ as well as the beginning of the Christian year and the expectancy of the birth of Christ, the Redeemer. These themes are developed in the articles that follow.

162 ✦ THE ORIGINS OF ADVENT WORSHIP

The history of Advent teaches us a great deal about its meaning and prepares us to observe this time with reverence and understanding. This history reveals the simultaneous importance of both penitence and hope, of both remorse and rejoicing.

Preliminary Considerations

To be serious about the Christian faith is to be serious about its history. To be sensitive to the history of God's people is to be responsive to the movement of time. The God "in whom we live, and move, and have our being" is made known to us and interacts with us in history. In certain dynamic moments, God invades our time and our history, and affords us a divine-human encounter, a glimpse, a momentary revelation. The ultimate act of God's invasion into history is Jesus Christ—incarnate, crucified, dead, risen, ascended, and coming again.

It is commonplace to suggest that the essence of existence is the ability to remember; we are because we remember. As people of God, we are who we are—indeed, we recognize whose we are—precisely because we remember and celebrate those decisive times when God acted in history for us. This remembering, however, is not a simple recalling of past events. It means to capture at once the mighty acts of God in the past, to recognize what God is doing among us in the

present movement, and to anticipate the continuing activity of God in the future. Liturgical, ritual remembering, therefore, looks back, looks around, and looks forward.

The early history of the liturgical year has been an area of intense investigation by scholars of Scripture, liturgy, and early Christian history. Jewish worship, still undergoing its own development in the first centuries of the common era, was anchored in the weekly rhythm of the Sabbath, but made provision for daily prayer and an annual commemorative cycle. In like manner, the early Christian community seems to have moored its worship in the weekly celebration of the Resurrection on the first day of the week, intensified by a discipline of daily prayer and enriched by the gradual development of a yearly cycle of feasts and fasts. The shape of this annual cycle developed slowly over several centuries, with many variations according to local custom. In the course of time, the variety of local traditions were combined to create the annual cycle we know today, but with continuing variants to honor local needs.

It should be noted that the liturgical feasts and seasons did not develop in the order in which they now occur in the annual cycle. Advent, for example, was one of the last seasons to take its place and has not always been considered the beginning of the liturgical year. This article will present each feast and festival in the annual cyclical order, not in order of origin and development. This procedure will be somewhat problematic at points because the roots of one liturgical feast are often closely interwoven with another feast of more ancient origin. Some degree of movement between the days and seasons is inevitable, but we shall endeavor to present the materials as clearly as possible.

Advent: Fast or Festival?

Searching the origins of Advent leads us to two principal locales: the missionary region of the church's expansion, northern and western Europe and the city of Rome itself. The beginnings of Advent in the missionary territory first appear near the end of the fourth century. Being influenced by the Eastern church as a result of maritime commerce along the Mediterranean, a period of penitential preparation was established in connection with the baptismal festival taking place on Epiphany, January 6, as a time of spiritual discipline for all of the faithful and of intensive catechesis for those being initiated on Epiphany. This pre-Epiphany period of fasting eventually took on the forty-day (less Saturdays and Sundays) length of Lent. This extended Advent back to November 11, St. Martin's Day. It was not until the sixth century that Advent in the region became less focused on preparation for Epiphany baptism and more on preparation for the Nativity celebration. The Councils of Tours (565) and Macon (581) document a period of preparation for the Nativity lasting from November 11 to Christmas Eve. It must be noted, however, that the shift from baptismal preparation to Nativity preparation did not diminish the penitential character of Advent.

In Rome, the development of Advent was totally different. There is no trace of Advent until the sixth century. Epiphany was not a baptismal day at Rome, and therefore, Advent understood as a penitential season for baptismal preparation was unnecessary. Consequently, from its beginnings at Rome, Advent was preparation for Christmas, not Epiphany. The Roman Advent undoubtedly had roots in the December Ember Days. Gregory the Great (590–604) established four Sunday Advent masses and three Ember Day masses that utilized Advent themes. The sober nature of the Ember Days, however, never managed to stifle the spirit of the Roman Advent, which was characterized by festive and joyful preparation for the celebration of the nativity of

Jesus. The divergence between the European mission territory and the city of Rome can also be noted in the dominant themes that pervade their respective Advent periods. In Rome, the focus was on joyful preparation for the historical incarnation of Christ—the point in time that marks the beginning of God's salvatory action in Christ. In the hinterlands, the emphasis was decidedly eschatological: Advent focused not on the coming of the Christ in flesh at Bethlehem but on the final coming of the exalted Christ, the Parousia. The eschatological themes concerning the last judgment, being prepared for the second advent of the Redeemer, fit easily into the earlier missionary scheme of penitential preparation. The Advent traditions of these two regions began to converge in the eighth century, but final solutions to the divergent origins and themologies were not found until the thirteenth century. Even then, the solutions were little more than conflated compromises. In the early twelfth century, Roman custom was prevalent. The liturgy was festive and adorned in white and gold. The Gloria in Excelsis, the church's great song of praise, was being sung, and the joyful Alleluia, often suppressed during periods of penitence, remained in place. By the end of the century, however, the pendulum had shifted. The liturgy was stripped of its festal elements, the Gloria was silenced, the color was penitential black or one of its derivatives, and the mood was decidedly more somber.

In contemporary practice, even with the immense amount of liturgical scholarship and renewal in the last century, we still have an Advent of difficult dimensions. Richard C. Hoefler calls Advent a "season under stress" and writes, "In the orderly parade of Sundays and Seasons of the Church year, Advent seems somehow always to be out-of-step.... Even the most cursory study of this schismatic season will quickly reveal the reason. Advent is caught in the collision of conflicting interpretations and practices."

The three-year ecumenical lectionary, adopted in one of several revisions by many churches in the United States and Canada, including several churches that historically have not been liturgical in their orientation, has dealt with the Advent problem in a helpful manner. The readings from the Bible, particularly those from the Hebrew Scriptures and the Gospels for the final Sundays after Pentecost, emphasize eschatological themes and come to a powerful climax on the last Sunday after Pentecost, observed by many churches as the festival of Christ the king. This focus brings the liturgical cycle to a grand climax as the church anticipates Christ's second coming. The readings from the Gospels for the first Sunday of Advent create a bridge that continues the eschatological emphasis. The Gospels for the second and third Sundays present the preparatory ministry of John the Baptizer, while the fourth Sunday's Gospel presents the Annunciation. Thus we have two themes—our anticipation of Christ's Second Advent yet to be and his First Advent in Bethlehem— coming together.

Theologically and pastorally, Advent has its foundation in Christian hope. The basis of our hope is God's coming among us in Jesus Christ. As Hoefler writes, "We are saved and redeemed not because we have successfully made the effort to come to him, but because he has made the surprising effort to come to us." For centuries, the people of Israel awaited their Anointed One, the Messiah. That he would come and release them from the bondage of displacement and initiate a new beginning in their lives was only a small part of the complex of hope that laid heavily on their whole being as God's people. It was their hope, for all that his coming could mean, that gave meaning to their existence.

For the church, the coming of Christ means still more. In the coming of Christ as "the Word made flesh," our hope is not diminished, but it is intensified. We do not feel relaxed because of this presence, but instead, we experience a holy joy, a peaceful excitement about God's presence in our lives and in the world. The intensification of our hope expresses itself in the daily, thankful experience of Christ's presence in our lives and in our continual desire for the day on which Christ will come again to us in glory. This sense of expectation is well expressed in this passage from the litany of the Moravian Church:

Lord, for Thy coming us prepare;
May we, to meet Thee without fear,
At all times ready be:
In faith and love preserve us sound;
O let us day and night be found
Waiting with joy to welcome Thee.

Our lives are shaped by Advent hope. "Christ has come and his coming prepares us for his coming in glory and his continual coming to us in Word and Sacrament. God gives us in Advent the story of his coming, and that story prepares us to receive him whenever he confronts our lives."

Advent will continue to be a difficult season to manage. The conflicts that emerge will continue to plague pastors, musicians, and parish liturgy committees. But the difficulties that are present may instead be opportunities pregnant with possibility. It should not be our intention to allow Advent to be overcome by Christmas. Regardless of where a congregation enters into Advent in a given year, there is entirely too much in it, biblically, theologically, historically, pastorally, and musically, to give it up before its time. Yet there is little use in breaking our backs, let alone our spirits, to make Advent a little Lent in December. Everyone needs a pause from the frenzy of December to reflect and pray. Everyone also needs to rejoice for "our redemption draweth nigh!"

163 ✦ The Spiritual Journey of Advent Worship

Advent is a corporate spiritual journey that calls for expectant waiting and readiness for the coming of Christ. When the church travels this journey and treats it as a discipline of life and prayer, the joy of Christmas is immeasurably intensified.

What we do during Advent finds its meaning in the _Pasch_, the death and resurrection of Christ. Christ was born to die and to be raised to new life for the sake of the world's redemption. Therefore Advent is never celebrated as a season to itself, but the season in which the one who has died for the restoration of the world is awaited. The Light for which we wait in Advent is the Light that dispels the darkness at Easter. Incarnation and atonement must always be brought together as two vital parts of the redemption tapestry.

The word _advent_ means "coming." During Advent, we celebrate the coming of Christ at Bethlehem, his coming into our hearts, and his Second Coming. For four weeks before Christmas, our worship calls us into a time to wait for the coming of the Lord. We begin at what may seem a distance from the coming of Christ in Bethlehem and proceed closer each week to the birth. Thus worship during the first two weeks emphasizes the second coming of Christ and the need to prepare for his return.

The preparations we make for the second coming of Christ are similar to the preparations Israel was making for the coming of the Messiah. Terms such as *hope*, *eager anticipation*, *longing*, and *looking toward the day* all express the kind of inner feeling Israel had as it waited for the Messiah. Those descriptive terms likewise capture the feelings we Christians have as we await the consummation of history and the redemption of all things.

But readiness is more than a feeling. It includes moral and spiritual preparation, the kind alluded to by Peter when he wrote, "What manner of persons ought you to be in holy conduct and godliness?" (2 Pet. 3:11, NKJV). Consequently, a life of godly conduct is emphasized in the Scripture readings of the first two weeks of Advent.

Starting with the third week of Advent, the emphasis shifts to the feeling of joy. Since the day of his appearing is coming closer, the accent falls on what Christ will do in his coming. Both his first and second comings are related to salvation, redemption, the renewal of Creation, the restoration of all things to the Father, and the sure destruction of evil. Since the putting down of the devil and his kingdom of darkness makes way for joy, the sense of that emotion is captured in the Scriptures, antiphons, hymns, prayers, and instruction of the third week.

In the fourth week of Advent, we are brought closer to the event of Jesus' birth. Consequently, the accent or our worship falls on the Incarnation: God with us. In this service, we are drawn up into the rejoicing of those immediately involved in the events surrounding the miraculous conception of Jesus Christ. We listen or sing together the Annunciation to Mary and Mary's great response, the Magnificat. These readings, together with the prayers and antiphons, bring us closer to Christ and increase our anticipation for his birth.

Advent is the season that breaks into the long Pentecost season with the dramatic announcement of the second coming of Jesus. This radically new message with its call to repentance and its high sense of expectancy demands high drama. An Advent full of color and bursting with drama and appropriate symbols will serve the meaning of Advent and ready the people for the second coming of Christ and for the birth of the Son, which historically comes first. Below are ways to convey the spirit of joyous anticipation:

- Consider the worship environment for Advent. Traditionally churches are "greened" during Advent. Some churches green the sanctuary at the beginning of Advent, while other churches wait until the third week of Advent (the traditional date for greening the church in December 17). December 17 is called O Sapentia because of the tradition of singing the "O" Antiphons before and after the Magnificat. The use of the "O" Antiphon texts and the greening of the church express the growing anticipation for the coming of the Lord. For a service of greening see chapter 6.

- Plan special services that feature the readings appropriate to Advent as well as music written specifically for this season. See the service of Nine Lessons and Carols in chapter 6.

- Do not neglect the penitential character of Advent. The entrance rites during Advent may express the sobriety of repentance. Do not use an act of praise such as the Gloria in Excelsis Deo or upbeat praise songs. Instead sing or say the canticle Benedictus (Luke 1:68-79), or sing praise and worship music that fits the theme of repentance.

- Prior to the entrance rites, use the service for the lighting of the Advent wreath. The lighting of the first candle the first week, the first and second the second week, and so on until the climax of lighting the Christ candle (the fifth and middle candle) on Christmas Eve. The Advent candles express a sense of drama and expectancy. See the texts included in chapter 4.

- Observe *Gaudite* Sunday, the Sunday of joy. The third Sunday of Advent is known as Gaudite Sunday in the Roman Catholic and Lutheran traditions. The term comes from the antiphon of the introit psalm "rejoice in the Lord always" (Eph. 4:4). Gaudite Sunday is the most festive of the four Sundays of Advent. It is also the Sunday that proclaims the Virgin Mary as the bearer of God's Son. A rose may be placed in an obvious place as the symbol of Gaudite.

- Use Advent colors. The colors of Advent are royal purple or sarum blue. Rose colors may be used on Gaudite Sunday. These deep colors express the penitential theme of Advent.

- Use drama to bring to life narrative portions of Scripture, such as John the Baptist's announcement of the coming Christ.

- Sing Advent hymns, preserving Christmas hymns for the Christmas season.

Robert Webber

164 • THE PENITENTIAL CHARACTER OF ADVENT WORSHIP

Advent is a penitential season, calling us to both personal and corporate repentance. Acts of confession and lament are appropriate not only for personal wrongdoing but also for the evil principalities and powers that pervade our culture.

Today in the United States, we live in a culture so profoundly pagan that Advent is no longer really noticed, much less observed. The commercial acceleration of seasons, whereby the promotion of Christmas begins even before there is opportunity to enjoy Halloween, is superficially a reason for the vanishing of Advent. But a more significant cause is that the churches have become so utterly secularized that they no longer remember the topic of Advent. This situation cannot be blamed merely upon the electronic preachers and talkers, or the other assorted peddlers of religion that so clutter the ethos of this society, any more than it can be said simplistically to be mainly the fault of American merchandising and consumerism.

Thus, if I remark about the disappearance of Advent, I am not particularly complaining about the vulgarities of the marketplace prior to Christmas, and I am certainly not talking about getting "back to God" or "putting Christ back into Christmas" (phrases that betray skepticism toward the Incarnation). Instead, I am concerned with a single, straightforward question: In biblical context, what is the subject of Advent?

Tradition has rendered John the Baptist an Advent figure, and if that is an appropriate connection, then clues to the meaning of the first coming of Christ may be found in the Baptist's preaching. Listen to John the Baptist:

"Repent, for the kingdom of heaven is at hand" (Matt. 3:2, RSV). In the gospel according to Mark, the report is, _"John the baptizer appeared in the wilderness, preaching a baptism of repentance for the forgiveness of sins"_ (Mark 1:4). Luke contains a parallel reference (Luke 3:3). It should not be overlooked, furthermore, that when John the Baptist is imprisoned, Matthew states, _"From that time Jesus began to preach, saying, 'Repent, for the kingdom of heaven is at hand' "_ (Matt. 4:17). And later, when Jesus charges his disciples, he tells them: _"And preach as you go, saying, 'The kingdom of heaven is at hand' "_ (Matt. 10:7).

For all the greeting-card and sermonic rhetoric, much rejoicing does not seem to happen around Christmastime, least of all about the coming of the Lord. There is a lot of holiday frolicking, but that is not the same as rejoicing. Outbursts of either frolicking or rejoicing are premature if John the Baptist has credibility. He identifies _repentance_ as the message and the sentiment of Advent. And in the texts just cited, that seems to be ratified by Jesus himself.

In the context of the biblical accounts, the repentance that John the Baptist preaches is no private or individualist effort, but the disposition of a person as related to the reconciliation of the whole of Creation. _"Repent, for the kingdom of heaven is at hand."_

The eschatological reference is quite concrete. John the Baptist is warning the world, the principalities and powers as well as common people, of the impending judgment of the world in the Word of God signaled in the coming of Christ.

There seems to be evidence in the Lukan account about John the Baptist that indicates that some of the people and, notably, the ecclesiastical officials did not comprehend his preaching, or if they did, they did not heed it, or they did not heed it promptly. Yet it is equally edifying that the political authorities, represented by Herod the tetrarch, did understand the political scope of John's admonition of the judgment enough to imprison John and, subsequently, subject him to terrible interrogation, torture, and decapitation—a typical fate for political prisoners now, as then. When Jesus made John's preaching his own and instructed his disciples accordingly, he foreshadowed his own arrest, trial, humiliation, crucifixion and, for that matter, the history of the early church found in the book of Acts.

The depletion of a contemporary recognition of the radically political character of Advent is in large measure occasioned by the illiteracy of church folk about the Second Advent, and in the mainline churches, the persistent quietism of pastors, preachers, and teachers about the Second Coming. That topic has been allowed to be preempted and usurped by astrologers, sectarian quacks, and multifarious hucksters. Yet it is impossible to apprehend either Advent except through the relationship of both Advents. The pioneer Christians, beleaguered as they were because of their insight, knew that the message of both Advents *is* political. That message is that in the coming of Jesus Christ, the nations and the principalities and the rulers of the world are judged in the Word of God. In the Lordship of Christ, they are rendered accountable to human life and, indeed, to all created life. Hence, the response of John the Baptist, when he is pressed to who the meaning of the repentance he preaches, is *"Bear fruits that befit repentance."*

In another part of the biblical literature traditionally invoked during Advent, the politics of both Advents is emphasized in attributing the recitation of the Magnificat to Mary:

He has put down the mighty from their thrones,
and exalted those of low degree;
He has filled the hungry with good things,
and the rich He has sent empty away.
(Luke 1:52-54, RSV)

In the first Advent, Christ the Lord comes into the world; in the next Advent, Christ the Lord comes as Judge of the world and of all the world's thrones and pretenders, sovereignties and dominions, principalities and authorities, presidencies and regimes, in vindication of his Lordship and the reign of the Word of God in history. This is the truth, which the world hates, which biblical people—repentant people—bear, and by which they live as the church in the world in the time between the two Advents.

William Stringfellow[4]

❧ FOUR ❧

Resources for Planning Advent Worship

Planning Advent worship is a great challenge, given its short duration and the rich and varied resources that are available. The following chapter presents a collection of such resources, ranging from texts appropriate for reading and praying to artistic contributions to Advent worship. These range from centuries-old hymns and symbols to prayers written especially for this volume. Worship planners of local congregations are encouraged to study the resources presented below and to use them as may be appropriate and meaningful. In every case, congregations are encouraged to maintain a distinction between Advent and Christmas themes, saving the latter for the celebration of Christ's birth on Christmas day and throughout the season that follows.

165 ◆ LECTIONARY TEXTS FOR ADVENT

The following are the texts suggested for the Sundays of Advent in the Revised Common Lectionary. Brief descriptions of each lesson are provided to aid in recalling the basic theme of each passage.

—— Year A (1995, 1998, etc.) ——

SUNDAY	OLD TESTAMENT	PSALM/ CANTICLE	EPISTLE	GOSPEL
First	Isaiah 2:1-5, God will teach us what to do. Swords to plows.	122	Romans 13:11-14, Wake up! The day is almost here.	Matthew 24:36-44, no one knows the day or the hour.
Second	Isaiah 11:1-10, the peaceful kingdom.	72:1-7, 18-19	Romans 15:4-13, Christ, root of Jesse, hope of the Gentiles.	Matthew 3:1-12, the preaching of John the Baptist.
Third	Isaiah 35:1-10, the road of holiness, the desert will rejoice.	Luke 1:46-55	James 5:7-10, How do you live while you wait for the day? Patience.	Matthew 11:2-11, John's messengers: "Are you the one?"
Fourth	Isaiah 7:10-16, The sign of Emmanuel. God hasn't given up.	80:1-7, 17-19	Romans 1:1-7, promise to David for all through Good News in Jesus.	Matthew 1:18-25, the birth of Jesus, Emmanuel.

—————— **Year B (1996, 1999, etc.)** ——————

SUNDAY	OLD TESTAMENT	PSALM/ CANTICLE	EPISTLE	GOSPEL
First	Isaiah 64:1-9, a prayer for mercy and help. God like a potter.	80:1-7, 17-19	1 Corinthians 1:3-9, Christ will keep us faultless on that day.	Mark 13:24-37, coming of the Son of Man. No one knows when.
Second	Isaiah 40:1-11, comfort people. A voice in the desert.	85:1-2, 8-13	2 Peter 3:8-15a, the day will come like a thief. Be holy.	Mark 1:1-8, the preaching of John the Baptist.
Third	Isaiah 61:1-4, 8-11, good news to the poor, captives, love justice.	126	1 Thessalonians 5:16-24, may God keep you until the coming of Christ.	John 1:6-8, 19-28, God sent John as messenger. John's message.
Fourth	2 Samuel 7:1-11, 16, God's words of hope to David and descendants.	Luke 1:46-55	Romans 16:25-27, God will help you stand firm.	Luke 1:26-38, birth of Jesus announced to Mary.

—————— **Year C (1994, 1997, etc.)** ——————

SUNDAY	OLD TESTAMENT	PSALM/ CANTICLE	EPISTLE	GOSPEL
First	Jeremiah 33:14-16, time is coming when I will choose a King.	25:1-10	1 Thessalonians 3:9-13, thank God for you. May you be ready when he comes.	Luke 21:25-36, coming of Son of Man. Fig tree; watch out.
Second	Malachi 3:1-4, I will send my messenger.	Luke 1:68-79	Philippians 1: 3-11, I pray your love will keep growing until that day.	Luke 3:1-6, John the Baptist, "Get ready."
Third	Zephaniah 3:14-20, Rejoice Jerusalem! Punishment over.	Isaiah 12:2-6	Philippians 4:4-7, Rejoice, be gentle, do all good. The Lord is coming soon.	Luke 3:7-18, the preaching of John the Baptist.
Fourth	Micah 5:2-5a, God promises a ruler from Bethlehem.	Luke 1:46-55	Hebrews 10:5-10, Why did Christ come? To be a sacrifice for us.	Luke 1:39-45, Mary visits Elizabeth. Magnificat.

Revised Common Lectionary, descriptions by H. A. Tillinghast

169 ♦ LIGHTING THE ADVENT CANDLE

The custom of lighting Advent candles in expectation of the coming of Christ is perhaps the most prevalent symbol in Advent worship. An Advent wreath containing five candles is hung at the front of the church. The four corner candles correspond to the four Sundays of Advent; the center candle represents Christ. Each Sunday one of the candles is lit until the Christmas Eve service when the Christ candle is lit. Normally the candles are lit during the opening acts of worship. The following are two sample texts that can appropriately accompany the lighting of the Advent candles. (Another text is included in the traditional service for Advent that is found in the next chapter.)

Traditional Example

The minister and choir may gather at the back of the church. As a family lights the Advent candle the following words acclaiming the Advent hanging may be said. Then follows the opening hymn.

LEADER: Come and save us, O Lord God of Hosts. [read from the back by the minister or some other reader]

PEOPLE: **Come and save us, O Lord God of Hosts.**

LEADER: Show the light of your countenance, and we shall be saved.

PEOPLE: **Come and save us, O Lord God of Hosts.**

LEADER: Glory to the Father, and to the Son, and to the Holy Spirit.

PEOPLE: **Come and save us, O Lord God of Hosts.**

Ralph E. Dessem[5]

Contemporary Example

Congregations may develop their own ceremony for the lighting of the candle drawn from themes of Advent such as hope, peace, joy, and love. The following litany is an example of a call to worship with the lighting of the candle developed from "a common account of Hope" written by the Faith and Order Commission of the World Council of Churches.

LEADER 1: Advent is a time of hope as we await the birth of Jesus and the coming of the risen Christ. But the risen one is also the one who was crucified. This reminds us that our life of hope is not a guarantee of safety, but an invitation to risk. To live in hope is never to have reached our goal, but always to be on a risk-laden journey.

PEOPLE: **To live in hope is to risk affirming the new and reaffirming the old.**

LEADER 2: Hope sends us on untried paths. When we lock ourselves to the past, we may grow deaf to the promptings of the Spirit. Yet the Spirit will ever reaffirm the truth of Christ, who is the same yesterday, today, and forever. Hope embraces the risk of new departures and of faithfulness to the past.

PEOPLE: **To live in hope is to risk self-criticism as the channel of renewal.**

LEADER 1: Renewal arises as we are judged by God and led to a repentance that bears worthy fruit. Only those who can smile at themselves and their faults can be ultimately serious about their selves. Hope embraces the risk of self-criticism as the way to renewal.

PEOPLE: **To live in hope is to risk dialogue.**

LEADER 2: Genuine encounter with others demands vulnerability. It requires a willingness to explore new ways of stating God's truth. Because in dialogue we can receive a fuller understanding of our own faith and a deeper understanding of our neighbor, hope embraces the risk of dialogue.

PEOPLE: **To live in hope is to risk struggle.**

LEADER 1: Christians are denied the privilege of being "neither hot nor cold." We are called to confess our faith boldly, even when this means saying no to parts of the society in which we live. Hope embraces the risk of struggle.

PEOPLE: **To live in hope is to risk scorn.**

LEADER 2: To many of our contemporaries, our hope appears vain. To live in hope is nevertheless to continue to give witness to the saving power of Jesus—"to give account of the hope that is in us"—whether we are ignored or attacked. Hope embraces the risk of ridicule.

PEOPLE: **To live in hope is to risk death for the sake of that hope.**

LEADER 1: Today Christians seldom face death for the sake of their faith, but genuine witness should still be costly. The Christian hope is not that death can be avoided, but that it can be overcome. Those who truly live in hope have come to terms with death and can risk dying with their Lord.

Keith Watkins[6]

167 ◆ THE "O" ANTIPHONS

The seven "O" Antiphons are ancient texts developed for use during the last seven days of Advent (December 17–23). Eventually these antiphons were gathered into the well-known hymn "O Come, O Come, Emmanuel." Today these ancient prayers can be used in a variety of ways during the season of Advent, as the following examples suggest.

The Traditional Texts

First antiphon, December 17
O Wisdom, O holy Word of God (Sir. 24:3), you govern all creation with your strong yet tender care (Wisd. of Sol. 8:1). Come and show your people the way to salvation (Isa. 40:3-5a).

Second antiphon, December 18
O sacred Lord of ancient Israel (Exod. 6:2-3), who showed yourself to Moses in the burning bush (Exod. 3:2), who gave him the holy law on Sinai mountain: come, stretch out your mighty hand to set us free (Exod. 6:6).

Third antiphon, December 19
O Flower of Jesse's stem, you have been raised up as a sign for all peoples (Isa. 11:10; Rom. 15:12); kings stand silent in your presence (Isa. 5:15); the nations bow down in worship before you. Come, let nothing keep you from coming to our aid (Hab. 2:3; Heb. 10:37).

Fourth antiphon, December 20
O Key of David, O royal Power of Israel, controlling at your will the gate of heaven (Isa. 22:22; Rev. 3:7): come, break down the prison walls of death for those who dwell in darkness and the shadow of death; and lead your captive people into freedom (Isa. 42:7; Ps. 107:14; Luke 1:79).

Fifth antiphon, December 21
O Radiant Dawn (Isa. 58:8), splendor of eternal light (Heb. 1:3), sun of justice (Mal. 4:2): come, shine on those who dwell in darkness and the shadow of death (Luke 1:78-79; Isa. 9:2).

Sixth antiphon, December 22
O King of all the nations, the only joy of every human heart (Hag. 2:8); O Keystone (Isa. 28:16) of the mighty arch of man (Eph. 2:14): come and save the creature you fashioned from the dust (Gen. 2:7).

Seventh antiphon, December 23
O Emmanuel (Isa. 7:14, 8:8), king and lawgiver (Isa. 33:22), desire of the nations (Gen. 49:10), Savior of all people, come and set us free, Lord our God.

A Traditional Form of the "O" Antiphons for Use as a Call to Worship

O Wisdom proceeding from the mouth of the highest,
reaching from eternity to eternity
and disposing all things with strength and sweetness:
   Come, teach us the way of knowledge.
O Lord and Leader of Israel,
you appeared to Moses in the burning bush
and delivered the law to him on Sinai:
   Come, redeem us by your outstretched arm.
O Root of Jesse,
you stand as a sign of the people;
before you rulers do not open their mouths;
to you all nations shall pray:
   Come and deliver us, do not delay.
O Key of David and Scepter of Israel,
you open and no one shuts;
you shut and no one opens:
   Come and release from prison those who sit in darkness and in the shadow of death.
O Dayspring, Splendor of Eternal Light and Sun of Righteousness:

Come and enlighten those who sit in darkness and in the shadow of death.
O King of nations,
Come and save those whom you formed of clay.
O Emmanuel, our King and Lawgiver,
the Expectation and Savior of the nations:
Come and save us, O Lord our God.

An Expanded Form of the "O" Antiphons with Spoken Reflections or Homilies

ANTIPHON ONE: O WISDOM

LEADER: O Wisdom,

ALL: You come forth from the mouth of the Most High. You create the universe and hold all things together in a strong yet gentle manner. O come to teach us the way of truth.

A reading from the book of Sirach (24:1-3):
Wisdom will praise herself, and will glory in the midst of her people. In the assembly of the Most High she will open her mouth, and in the presence of his host she will glory (saying): "I came forth from the mouth of the Most High, and covered the earth like a mist."

Meditation: From at least the time of Solomon, the Hebrew people saw God's wisdom personified as a woman whose house is set in order. Her every word is a gem of insight meant to lead all Creation on the path back to the Creator. St. John the Divine says that Jesus Christ is God's ultimate Word of Wisdom. And though given birth by a woman, it is he who becomes the very womb of God from which we receive birth into a new realm. He would gather us as a hen gathers her chicks. He would celebrate our distinctiveness as male and female, old and young, Anglo and people of other color. Yet he would set our world in order by destroying any attempt to use difference to support attitudes of indifference or destruction. For in Christ Jesus, as Paul reminds us, all are indeed one (Gal. 3:28) even as all creation cries out in expectation for the final day of unity in him (Rom. 8:22).

LEADER: Behold, the Name of the Lord comes from afar.

ALL: Let the whole earth be filled with his glory.

ALL SING:

O Come, O Wisdom from high,
Who orders all things mightily,
To us the path of knowledge show;
And teach us in her ways to go,
Rejoice! Rejoice! Emmanuel
Shall come to you, O Israel.

ANTIPHON TWO: O ADONAI

LEADER: O Adonai and leader of Israel,

ALL: You appeared to Moses in a burning bush and you gave him the law on Sinai. O come and save us with your mighty power.

A reading from the book of Exodus (19:18-19):
Mount Sinai was covered with smoke, because the Lord descended on it like fire. The smoke billowed up from it like smoke from a furnace, the whole mountain trembled violently, and the sound of the trumpet grew louder and louder. Then Moses spoke and the voice of God answered him.

Meditation: Adonai, it is the Hebrew word for Lord. The personal name of God was far too holy to be uttered by the Israelites as they remembered the events at Mt. Sinai and Moses' returning with the Law on tablets of stone. They would simply call God Adonai and not risk tampering with the name of one who creates out of nothing by the passing of his breath across the emptiness of space—one who could so utterly destroy with the same breath that not even a fine powdery residue would testify to the former presence of a transgressor. Trembling before the God who burns in bushes which are left unconsumed, parts waters, and shakes mountains, they would simply call him Adonai.

The first creed of the church was simply this: "Jesus Christ is Adonai." In him the fullest glory of heaven is revealed as the babe trembles in its mother's arms, the boy craves knowledge in the presence of the temple's scribes, and the fire of compassion burns in the heart of the man—even as he mounts the hill of Golgotha and the requirements of Moses' Commandments are fulfilled on this second mountain in the fiery glory of Love's sacrifice.

We pray that Adonai might teach us the law of love.

LEADER: Prepare the way of the Lord, Alleluia!
ALL: **Make his paths straight, Alleluia!**
ALL SING:

> O come, O come, thou Lord of might,
> Who to your tribes on Sinai's height
> In ancient times once gave the law,
> In cloud and majesty and awe.
> Rejoice! Rejoice! Emmanuel
> Shall come to you, O Israel.

ANTIPHON THREE: O STOCK OF JESSE
LEADER: O Stock of Jesse,
ALL: **You stand as a sign for the nations; kings fall silent before you whom the people acclaim. O come to deliver us and do not delay.**

A reading from the book of Isaiah (11:1, 10):
A shoot will come up from the stump of Jesse; from his roots a Branch will bear fruit. . . . In that day the Root of Jesse will stand as a banner for the peoples; the nations will rally to him, and his place of rest will be glorious.

Meditation: Jesse is the father of King David and, therefore, the progenitor of Israel's monarchy—a monarchy cut to the stump during Isaiah's prophetic years. Isaiah is specific: The hopes and dreams of Israel lie in the loins of one long dead. Yet the imagery is confusing. Will it be a new branch and flower from ancient Jesse's line, or will it be the very root that once gave him life that will stand as a sign for the nations? Which will it be?

The answer is, of course, one of paradox: both—root and fruit. The Lord who once worked in and through his instrument Jesse will take on his very flesh and be born a distant grandchild.

The sign for the nations will be one who is at once human and divine, servant and monarch, taproot of grace and flower of holiness. Thus, his bare-branched cross becomes for his followers the sign and bud of life.

Here we pray that we may be so rooted in his gifts of absolute forgiveness, love, and life that we may be delivered from eternal death and, paradoxically, bear abundantly the fruit of righteousness.

LEADER: Rejoice greatly, O Jerusalem.
ALL: **Behold, your king comes.**
ALL SING:

> O come, O Rod of Jesse's stem,
> From every foe deliver them
> That trust thy mighty power to save,
> And give them vict'ry o'er the grave.
> Rejoice! Rejoice! Emmanuel
> Shall come to you, O Israel.

ANTIPHON FOUR: O KEY OF DAVID
LEADER: Key of David and Scepter of Israel,
ALL: **What you open no one else can close again; what you close no one can open. O come to lead the captive from prison; free those who sit in darkness and in the shadow of death.**

A reading from the book of Isaiah (22:22) and the Revelation (3:7):
I will place on his shoulder the key to the house of David....What he opens no one can shut, and what he shuts no one can open.

Meditation: Isaiah's prophecy finds fulfillment in the words of St. John's revelation; only one man can truly be entrusted with the Key to the Kingdom of God—the realm of which Israel is yet a sign anticipating a fuller revelation. Others had been tried and had failed—even the most recommended. For they quickly forgot their role as servant of God and became consumed by how they might open treasures for themselves while shutting others out. Only one could bear the key of David.

Jesus Christ shoulders the cross and thus bears the key of David. He is, in fact, that very key. His life opens to us the gates of eternal life and his triumph over death's sting slams forever shut the doors to perdition.

No man but one is worthy to bear the key of David. Yet again, God exceeds himself in generosity. To us, to you and me, his church, our Lord says, "I will give you the keys of the kingdom of heaven; whatever you bind on earth will be bound in heaven, and whatever you loose on earth will be loosed in heaven" (Matt. 16:19).

Here we pray that the Lord may so unfetter our souls that we may rejoice to apply the key of the gospel to others imprisoned in dungeons of guilt and despair.

LEADER: Come, Lord, and make no delay.
ALL: **Loosen the bonds of your people Israel.**
ALL SING:

> O come, O Key of David, come

And open wide our heavenly home.
Make safe the way that leads on high
And close the path to misery.
Rejoice! Rejoice! Emmanuel
shall come to you, O Israel.

ANTIPHON FIVE: O DAYSPRING

LEADER: O Rising Sun,

ALL: **You are the splendor of eternal light and the sun of justice. O come and enlighten those who sit in darkness and in the shadow of death.**

A reading from the book of Isaiah (9:2) and the letter to the Hebrews (1:3):
The people walking in darkness have seen a great light; on those living in the land of the shadow of death a light has dawned....The Son is the radiance of God's glory and the exact representation of his being, sustaining all things by his powerful word.

Meditation: As Advent draws to its conclusion and we long for the candlelit splendor of Christmas, we recall the promise of the prophet Malachi, "For those who revere my name, the sun of righteousness will rise with healing in its wings." It is no coincidence that the church has chosen to celebrate the birth of her Lord at the time of year when darkness is longest and light is shortest. In so doing, we make known our belief that even in a world darkened by personal sin and institutional oppression, there is reason to hope. When the wings of the most high overshadow us, it is not darkness that is brought, but light. And the gray coldness of human isolation is strangely warmed into a community that reflects his radiant love.

Here we pray that our eyes may sparkle anew in holy amazement as we behold the one who is the very Word of God become a lamp for our feet and a light to our path.

LEADER: Out of Zion, the perfection of beauty, God has shined.

ALL: **Our God shall come, Alleluia!**

ALL SING:

O come, O Dayspring from on High,
And cheer us by your drawing nigh;
Disperse the gloomy clouds of night,
And death's dark shadow put to flight.

Rejoice! Rejoice! Emmanuel
Shall come to you, O Israel.

ANTIPHON SIX: O KING OF NATIONS

LEADER: O King whom all the peoples desire,

ALL: **You are the cornerstone which makes all one. O come and save man whom you made from clay.**

A reading from the book of Isaiah (28:16) and the letter to the Ephesians (2:21-22):
So this is what the Sovereign Lord says: "See, I lay a stone in Zion, a tested stone, a precious cornerstone for a sure foundation; the one who trusts in him will never be dismayed." . . . In him the whole building is joined together and rises to become a holy temple in the Lord. And in him you too are being built together to become a dwelling in which God lives by his Spirit.

Meditation: It is true that many decaying monuments stand in memory of monarchs and prelates long ago deceased. And even the most glorious ones seem cold and pulseless apart from the human activity echoing in marble chambers. It was this sense that caused one Roman cleric to remark, "The Vatican seems to be little more than a cemetery for dead popes." Nevertheless, we humans seem to believe that great movements and magnificent edifices are the substance of any real kingdom.

The testimony of Scripture is quite to the contrary. The armies of God are angels unseen and the temple of God is not made of brick and mortar but of human souls cemented together by divine love. Jesus Christ is both the cornerstone, which makes our spiritual foundation secure, and the capstone, which is our pinnacle of glory.

Here we pray that his unseen kingdom, which is not of this world, may be manifest in and through our spiritual community, that the prayer of Jesus to the Father may find its answer in our midst, "Father . . . may they be brought to complete unity to let the world know that you sent me and have loved them even as you have loved me."

LEADER: Behold, the Lord shall come with all his saints with him. Alleluia!

ALL: **And in that day the light shall be great. Alleluia!**

ALL SING:

O come, Desire of nations, bind

In one the hearts of all mankind;
O bid our sad divisions cease,
And be for us our King of peace.
Rejoice! Rejoice! Emmanuel
Shall come to you, O Israel.

ANTIPHON SEVEN: O EMMANUEL

LEADER: O Emmanuel,
ALL: **You are our king and judge, the one whom the peoples await and their Savior. O come and save us, Lord, our God.**

A reading from the book of Isaiah (7:14):
Therefore the Lord himself will give you a sign: The virgin will be with child and will give birth to a son, and will call him Immanuel.

Meditation: Immanuel. The name is a compound of two Hebrew words—*immanu*, meaning "with us" and *El*, meaning "God." God with us. Immanuel is but one appellation for God's Son. It is, however, the premier title. For in the person of Jesus of Nazareth, the covenant promise made so long ago to Moses and Israel is most radically realized. "My presence will go with you, and I will give you rest." "Immanu-el," Immanuel, it is a word of comfort for those whose hearts are on a pilgrimage. Immanuel, it is the name for the God who leads us on that pilgrimage. Immanuel, this is the name for the one who is at one and the same time provision for the journey and the journey's destination.

Here we pray that Immanuel will continue to sustain the church terrestrial until the day we complete our sojourn and, leaving behind the exile of temptation and sin, join the church celestial.

LEADER: Drop down, O heavens, from above and let the skies pour down righteousness.
ALL: **Let the earth open and bring forth salvation.**
ALL SING:

O come, O come, Emmanuel,
And ransom captive Israel,
That mourns in lonely exile here
Until the Son of God appear.
Rejoice! Rejoice! Emmanuel
Shall come to you, O Israel.

Brian Hooper[7]

The "O" Antiphons as a Form of Prayer

LEADER: O wisdom, O holy word of God, you watch over all creation with a strong and tender eye.
PEOPLE: **Come and lead your people into the way to salvation.**
LEADER: O sacred Lord of the Hebrew people, who revealed yourself to Moses in the burning bush and delivered the holy law to him on Mount Sinai.
PEOPLE: **Come, stretch forth your mighty arm and set us free.**
LEADER: O flower of Jesse's stem, you have grown up as a sign for all peoples; kings stand silent in your presence and all the nations bow down to worship you.
PEOPLE: **Come, let nothing keep you from coming quickly to our aid.**
LEADER: O key of David, O royal power of Israel, you who control the gate of heaven, come, destroy the prison of death and release those who dwell in darkness and the shadow of death.
PEOPLE: **Come, release your captive people into freedom.**
LEADER: O radiant dawn, you who are the Splendor of eternal light and the son of justice.
PEOPLE: **Come, let your light shine on those who dwell in darkness and the shadow of death.**
LEADER: O king of all people, the one who is the only joy of every human heart, O cornerstone who binds all people together.
PEOPLE: **Come and save the people you fashioned from dust.**
LEADER: O Emmanuel, the King and lawgiver, the desire of all the nations, the Savior of all people.
PEOPLE: **Come and set us free, O Lord our God.**

168 • TRADITIONAL OPENING PRAYERS FOR ADVENT

The following prayers, which are used at the opening of worship in many liturgical traditions, are based on centuries-old texts.

First Sunday of Advent (Sunday between Nov. 27–Dec. 3, inclusive)
Almighty God, give us grace to cast away the works of darkness, and put on the armor of light, now in the time of this mortal life in which your Son, Jesus Christ, came to visit us in great humility; that in the last day, when he shall come again in his glorious majesty to judge both the living and the dead, we may rise to the life immortal; through him who lives and reigns with you and the Holy Spirit, one God, now and for ever. Amen.

Second Sunday of Advent (Dec. 4–10)
Merciful God, who sent your messengers the prophets to preach repentance and prepare the way for our salvation: Give us grace to heed their warnings and forsake our sins, that we may greet with joy the coming of Jesus Christ our Redeemer; who lives and reigns with you and the Holy Spirit, one God, now and for ever. Amen.

Third Sunday of Advent (Dec. 11–17)
Stir up your power, O Lord, and with great might come among us; and, because we are sorely hindered by our sins, let your bountiful grace and mercy speedily help and deliver us; through Jesus Christ our Lord, to whom, with you and the Holy Spirit, be honor and glory, now and for ever. Amen.

Fourth Sunday of Advent (Dec. 18–24)
Purify our conscience, Almighty God, by your daily visitation, that your Son, Jesus Christ, at his coming, may find in us a mansion prepared for himself; who lives and reigns with you, in the unity of the Holy Spirit, one God, now and for ever. Amen.

Book of Common Prayer

169 ♦ PRAYERS FOR ADVENT WORSHIP

Christian prayer takes its inspiration from the Bible. The following prayers for the Advent season are based on images found in Scripture. Brief commentaries follow each prayer, directing worship planners to Scripture passages that can be used in conjunction with each prayer.

Prayers for the Opening of Worship

Lord God, we hunger and thirst after many things. Come and create a deep longing within us that we might delight to be in your presence. Sound the alarm within our soul that we might wake from our spiritual drowsiness and watch and wait for Christ's coming. This we pray in Jesus' wonderful name. Amen!_

Commentary: The imagery for this prayer is drawn from the first stanza of the Advent hymn "O Lord How Shall I Meet You?" which, in turn, is based on Psalm 63:1. The additional theme of watching and waiting refers to Matthew 25:1-13.

Redeemer God, come, as we seek to open our hearts, creating a welcome space for you to abide. Startle us from our sloth and rescue us from that which distracts us from knowing your grace and love. Inspire our preparation and guide our worship that our Advent waiting might lead us to Bethlehem's manger. In Jesus' name. Amen!

Commentary: The third stanza of the hymn "Lift Up Your Hearts" paints the picture of the worshipers inviting God to draw near and dwell within their hearts. The desire is to feel in a very profound sense the living presence of God's grace and love. This echoes the request from the apostle Paul's prayer in Ephesians 3:17.

Gracious and Ever Faithful God, over the centuries your people have prayed Maranatha. Come, Lord Jesus! Come! As we begin [or continue] our journey through this Advent season be among us with your guiding Spirit. Open our eyes that we might see, open our ears that we might hear, and open our hearts that we might truly worship in spirit and truth your Son who is coming again. In anticipation we pray this in Jesus' mighty name. Amen!

Commentary: The scriptural prayer Maranatha of 1 Corinthians 16:22b forms the foundation for this prayer. This is only one example how the prayers or words of Scripture can be used to give shape to our prayers today.

Prayers of Confession

CONFESSION
Merciful God, we are grateful for the promise of your forgiveness. We desparately need it! So many things have crowded thoughts of you out of our minds this past week. We have been so

busy shopping, cooking, decorating, mailing, and entertaining that at times we have forgotten your nearness. Sadly we confess that our anxieties have been more real to us than your peace. While not our intention, we have had a tendency to focus more on our wants than on our worship of you. The prospects of exchanging gifts with our family and friends create more excitement within us than welcoming the priceless Gift of your Son. Lord, we know these practices must grieve your loving heart, for when we pause long enough to catch our breath, we realize something is missing. Forgive us, cleanse us, restore us, strengthen us—not because our faith is so great or our prayers so fervent, but because you love us so radically. [The prayer may include a period of silence for personal confession or reflection on the individual's relationship with God.] In Jesus' amazing name. Amen!

ASSURANCE

LEADER:	(reads John 3:16)
PEOPLE:	**(read Matthew 1:21)**
ALL:	**(read Romans 8:1)**

Commentary: The disturbing truth that there was no room for Jesus in the overcrowded inn (Luke 2:7) which was mirrored by Martha's hyperactive efforts to entertain Christ (Luke 10:38-42) remind us how powerful distractions can be even when Christ is before us. The words of assurance could be printed in the bulletin responsively as noted above or pronounced only by the worship leader. It is crucial, however, to sound clearly the word of grace that God is always ready to forgive and restore us.

CONFESSION

Almighty God of the prophets, you have called us to glorify your name through our love for you and for one another. We confess that our praise is more on our lips than with our lives.

We profess repentance while we resist change;

We talk of peace while we prepare for war;

We sing of love but we curse our enemies;

We pray your will be done but insist on our way.

Have mercy upon us, tender God, and cleanse and forgive our selfish ways. May Jesus Christ,

who came long ago, come once more into our lives. Help us to be at peace with you, ourselves, and one another as members of your kingdom, which now is at hand. [Opportunity for silent confession.] Through Jesus Christ our Lord. Amen!

Commentary: The fourth stanza of "O Come, O Come, Immanuel" (O come, O Branch of Jesse's stem / Unto your own and rescue them!) could be inserted between the above prayer and the words of assurance. Please note: It is wise to always use the actual words of Scripture to pronounce God's pardon rather than those of a hymn or poem. This captures more faithfully and first-hand God's good news of forgiveness to us.

ASSURANCE

This prayer should be followed by words of assurance, as follows:

LEADER:	(reads Romans 5:8)
PEOPLE:	**(read Romans 5:11)**
ALL:	**(read Romans 5:1)**

Commentary: This prayer is based on Jesus' summary of the Law of God (Matt. 22:37-39) that we are to love God and one another. It further echoes the realistic struggle that Paul confesses regarding his own inconsistency of faithfully living out the faith (Rom. 7:14-25).

CONFESSION

Almighty and Gracious God, as we journey through this season of Advent, we are confronted once again with the good news of Christ's coming. We pause amidst all our words and singing to be quiet before you. (The worship leader then directs the congregation with a suggested example, e.g.):

Dear people of God, use this silence to reflect upon and review your relationship with God. Perhaps today you sense God very closely. If so, celebrate and praise God for this friendship. Or perhaps today you realize that you are quite distant from God. If so, consider with the Holy Spirit's help what has caused this separation and what steps you can take to renew your communion with God. Then again some of us today may be confused and not have any idea where we are with God. If so, invite God to enlighten you and help you know how much God truly delights in you. [Silent reflection.]

ASSURANCE

To be followed by words of assurance: 1 John 1:9 and 1 Timothy 1:15 (spoken in unison).

Commentary: A disadvantage of any spoken prayer of confession is that people are forced to confess that for which they may not have any involvement. Surveys have discovered that worshipers find silent opportunities for confession to be most meaningful for realizing God's presence and considering their relationship with God.

A Prayer for the Illumination of God's Word

Creator God, you remind us that the darkness of ignorance and doubt cannot overcome your life-giving Word. May your Holy Spirit, who first inspired these words of Scripture, shine your light and once again awaken us to the hearing and living of this radiant truth. In Jesus' name. Amen!

Commentary: The opening words of John's Gospel (vv. 1-5) provide the imagery of light, darkness, and the supremacy of the eternal Word, Jesus Christ.

Offertory Prayers

Most High God, we marvel at the willingness of Mary to offer herself so completely to you. Yet in truth we realize that you ask the same of each of us. Refresh our memories with the abundance of our blessings so that we too might say with glad and generous hearts, "Lord, we are your servants, may we gratefully respond as you invite us to give." Accept the gifts we humbly present to you that your Son and our Savior, Jesus Christ, might be glorified. Amen!

Commentary: Mary's surrendering act of dedication from Luke 1:38 patterns this prayer. Further, the imagery of God as being Most High comes from Luke 1:32.

Lord God, you loved us so fully that you gave your only Son, Jesus, to be born and live among us. As we offer our gifts and expressions of love to you, guide us not only in the presentation of these resources, but inspire us as well in the proper use of all that we possess. During these days of Advent waiting, may we dedicate ourselves to rightly celebrate and share Christ's life and love with others. In Jesus' name. Amen!

Commentary: The intertwining imagery of God's gift of Christ and our giving is built around John 3:16 and the stewardship principles of 1 Corinthians 9:6-15.

Pastoral or Intercessory Prayers

Almighty and Everlasting God, we praise and bless your holy name. Our hearts are filled with gratitude because you did not allow us to suffocate in our sins but provided the way of redemption through your Son, Jesus Christ. You are ever faithful, remembering your covenant promises made first to our father in the faith, Abraham, and then renewed through David. All these prophecies, which people longed for, have come to fulfillment in Jesus. For all these expressions of your tender mercy we are thankful and praise you. [The leader may wish to pause and provide a period of silence for the worshiper to offer God additional words of praise.]

Grant us, loving Lord, your guidance so that we might walk before you. May we follow the way proclaimed by John the Baptist when he shattered the centuries of silence in declaring, "Prepare the way for the Lord, make straight paths for him." Since we know your salvation and have tasted the forgiveness of our sins, may we be your representatives of mercy to others in need.

Grant your sustaining Spirit to those who face times of trouble and doubt.

Be near to those who are weak in health or mind or for those who await the slowness of the healing process to restore them.

For those amongst us who have faced the darkness of separation, defeat, or loss of a loved one, surround and walk with them, awakening them to your tender presence amidst their sorrow and pain.

Encourage those who challenge the injustices of our day as they seek to confront and dismantle those systems and structures of evil that imprison the poor, homeless, the disadvantaged, the young, the old.

Gracious Lord, as we gather today we realize there are many other concerns that weigh down our soul. We pause now in this silence to bring any further prayers before you or to simply quiet our soul and listen to you speak to us.

Reveal yourself afresh to us that we might be your people. Create in us open hearts so that we might grow in spirit and truth, and thereby prepare us for the coming of our Lord Jesus Christ. In his name we pray. Amen!

Commentary: The groundwork for this prayer is Zechariah's song (Luke 1:68-79). Verses 69-75 provide a model for praise and thanksgiving while verses 76-79 offer a pattern for petition. Once again we see how Scripture furnishes us with a rich collection of imagery and examples of prayer and how we can pray.

Eternal Lord and God, we are grateful that you have called us to be your children and friends. While in times past we have stumbled in the darkness, you have kindled and set ablaze the glorious light of Jesus Christ. We thank you that Christ, who came once, is always coming again so we need not fear that we have missed him. Lord, grant us the proper spiritual vision that we too with the prophet Isaiah might stand on the tip of our toes and know this Christ who comes to us.

Gracious God, we thank you that Christ is our Wonderful Counselor. Life is filled with both decisions and temptations. Provide us with your wisdom and discerning spirit so we might choose well to live well. Grant your special guidance on us as a congregation as we seek your direction in being your representatives in this community.

Gracious God, we thank you that Christ is our Mighty God. Many within our world are consumed by power, and sadly many are harmed by the selfish and misguided use and abuse of power. But the power of Christ is gentle yet strong. Release this mighty strength through your Spirit so we might live faithful lives for Christ. Overcome the resistance in our lives that Christ might deeply dwell within our lives. Grant us the courage this week to be bold and yet tender as we seek to encourage those who are struggling.

Gracious God, we thank you that Christ is our Everlasting Father. In a world where many hunger for meaning and purpose, we can rejoice that we belong to you. We are not nameless creatures but people bearing your very name. In your fatherly love, we ask that you would be near to those who face the surgery this week.... Remember your promises to those who are lonely or widowed or separated by whatever causes. Grant us the wholeness of Christ that we might care for our souls as well as our bodies.

Gracious God, we thank you that Christ is our Prince of Peace. While tension, conflict, and crime seem to rule our streets and as broken relationships are all too common in many of our families, we know this is not your purpose. Only Christ can adequately heal and restore that which is twisted and torn. Lord, may each of us be receptive to receive Christ's peace and seek your courage to ask forgiveness of those we have wronged or hurt. We remember those places of tension around our land and throughout our world.... Grant us the resources that we might be your faithful peacemakers to participate through prayer and action in expanding your kingdom.

Gracious God, we are bold to lift these prayers to you because you have called us to come before the throne of Christ's amazing grace. Help us and hear us as we pray with expectation in Jesus' name. Amen!

Commentary: The powerful words of Isaiah's prophecy (Isa. 9:2, 6) have created the pattern and development of this prayer. Once again this sample illustrates how Scripture can model and inspire us in our own prayers.

Tom Schwanda

170 • ADVENT CANTICLES

The song of Zechariah (Luke 1:68-79), also known as the Benedictus Dominus Deus, is the canticle of Advent. It may be used as a call to worship, as an act of praise, or as a response between Scripture readings. Another appropriate canticle for the season of Advent is the Song of Mary (the Magnificat) from Luke 1:46-55.

Blessed be the Lord, the God of Israel;
 he has come to his people and set them free.
He has raised up for us a mighty savior,
 born of the house of his servant David.
Through his holy prophets he promised of old,
 that he would save us from our enemies,
 from the hands of all who hate us.
He promised to show mercy to our fathers
 and to remember his holy covenant.
This was the oath he swore to our father
 Abraham,
 to set us free from the hands of our enemies,
Free to worship him without fear,
 holy and righteous in his sight
 all the days of our life.

You, my child, shall be called the prophet of the
 Most High,
 for you will go before the Lord to prepare
 his way,
To give his people knowledge of salvation
 by the forgiveness of their sins.
In the tender compassion of our God
 the dawn from on high shall break upon us,
To shine on those who dwell in darkness and the
 shadow of death,
 and to guide our feet into the way of peace.
Glory to the Father, and to the Son, and to the
 Holy Spirit:
 as it was in the beginning, is now, and will
 be for ever. Amen.

171 ✦ AN ADVENT AFFIRMATION OF FAITH

Use the Nicene Creed, Apostles' Creed, or the following biblical creed for Advent.

LEADER: I hear a voice in the wilderness:
  "Prepare the way of the Lord,
  Make straight in the desert
  a highway for our God."
PEOPLE: **I believe every valley shall be lifted
  up and every
  mountain and hill be made low;
  I believe the uneven ground shall
  become level,
  and the rough places a plain,
  I believe the glory of the Lord shall
  be revealed,
  and all flesh shall see it together
  For the mouth of the Lord has spoken.**

Adapted from Isaiah 40:3-5

Tall Cross. The two arms of the tall cross are regarded as a symbol of the staff of Moses (see Numbers 21:9) and of the prophecy of the coming of Christ (see John 3:14): "As Moses lifted up the serpent in the wilderness, so must the Son of Man be lifted up." Consequently, it is a popular symbol of Advent.

172 ✦ PRAYER OF THANKSGIVING FOR ADVENT EUCHARIST

The following liturgy for the Lord's Supper features images appropriate to the season of Advent. Other texts are included in the sample services in the next chapter.

LEADER: The Lord be with you.
PEOPLE: **And also with you.**
LEADER: Lift up your hearts.
PEOPLE: **We lift them up to the Lord**
LEADER: Let us give thanks to the Lord our God.
PEOPLE: **It is right to give our thanks and praise.**
LEADER: It is truly right and our greatest joy to give you thanks and praise, O Lord our God, creator and ruler of the universe. You formed us in your image and breathed into us the breath of life. You set us in this world to love and serve you, and to live in peace with all that you have made.
  When we turned from you, you did

not turn from us. When we were captives in slavery, you delivered us to freedom, and made covenant to be our sovereign God. When we were stubborn and stiff-necked, you spoke to us through prophets who looked for that day when justice shall triumph and peace shall reign over all the earth.

Therefore we praise you, joining our voices with the celestial choirs and with all the faithful of every time and place, who forever sing to the glory of your name:

PEOPLE: **Holy, holy, holy Lord, God of power and might,**

heaven and earth are full of your glory.

Hosanna in the highest.

Blessed is he who comes in the name of the Lord.

Hosanna in the highest.

LEADER: You are holy, O God of majesty, and blessed is Jesus Christ, your Son, our Lord. You sent him into this world to satisfy the longings of your people for a Savior, to bring freedom to the captives of sin, and to establish justice for the oppressed. He came among us as one of us, taking the lot of the poor, sharing human suffering. We rejoice that in his death and rising again, you set before us the sure promise of new life, the certain hope of a heavenly home where we will sit at table with Christ our host.

We give you thanks that the Lord Jesus, on the night before he died, took bread, and after giving thanks to you, he broke it, and gave it to his disciples, saying: Take, eat, this is my body, given for you. Do this in remembrance of me. In the same way he took the cup after supper, saying: This cup is the new covenant sealed in my blood, shed for you for the forgiveness of sins. Whenever you drink it, do this in remembrance of me.

Remembering your gracious acts in Jesus Christ, we take from your creation this bread and wine and joyfully celebrate his dying and rising, as we await the day of his coming. With thanksgiving we offer our very selves to you to be a living and holy sacrifice, dedicated to your service. According to his commandment.

PEOPLE: **We remember his death, we proclaim his resurrection, we await his coming in glory.**

LEADER: Gracious God, pour out your Holy Spirit upon us and upon these your gifts of bread and wine, that the bread we break and the cup we bless may be the communion of the body and blood of Christ. By your Spirit make us one with Christ, that we may be one with all who share this feast, united in ministry in every place. As this bread is Christ's body for us, send us out to be the body of Christ in the world.

Strengthen us, O God, in the power of your Spirit to bring good news to the poor and lift blind eyes to sight, to loose the chains that bind and claim your blessing for all people. Keep us faithful in your service until Christ comes in final victory, and we shall feast with all your saints in the joy of your eternal realm through Christ, with Christ, in Christ in the unity of the Holy Spirit, all glory and honor are yours, almighty God, now and forever.

PEOPLE: **Amen.**

Book of Common Worship[8]

173 ♦ ADVENT BLESSINGS

The following blessings are based on traditional texts used in Advent worship. The images they convey are appropriate to the sense of waiting and expectation that is central to Advent worship.

May Almighty God, by whose providence our Savior Jesus Christ came among us in great humility, sanctify you with the light of his blessing and set you free from all sin. Amen.

May he, whose Second Coming in power and great glory we await, make you steadfast in faith, joyful in hope, and constant in love. Amen.

May you, who rejoice in the first Advent of our Redeemer, at his second Advent be rewarded with unending life. Amen.

And the blessing of God Almighty, the Father, the Son, and the Holy Spirit, be upon you and remain with you for ever. Amen.

May the Sun of Righteousness shine upon you and scatter the darkness from before your path; and the blessing of God Almighty, the Father, the Son, and the Holy Spirit, be among you, and remain with you always. Amen.

Book of Occasional Services[9]

The Arts in Advent Worship

Advent is a season for seeing, hearing, touching, imagining. Advent Scripture readings are filled with evocative images and Advent anticipation has inspired some of the most cherished music in the Christian church. Every tradition of Christian worship has developed meaningful ways of leading Advent worship through the arts. This chapter presents several ideas for incorporating the arts into Advent worship.

174 ✦ Perspectives on the Environment for Advent Worship

Advent worship involves both penitence and joy, moods that can be conveyed by the visual environment of the worship space. Adapt the following suggestions to local custom.

Passing into Winter

How does one decorate for Advent in a manner that respects the sobriety of the season—that brings about a feeling of "not yet," a sense of waiting and longing? Begin by stripping away the harvest bounty of November. Simplify and clean the worship place and its entryways. Take a long walk out-of-doors, and look at how the world moves into winter.

Advent is the church's winter, a season with a heightened risk of starvation, of disease, of isolation. Winter is exile, a time of pregnancy and anxiety, a passing into death and judgment. The cooperation and self-sacrifice needed if we all are to survive the season can become for us a holy sign. The Advent worship environment should bring reminders of winter—not as cute decorations but as a *memento mori*, a reminder of death.

In contrast, Christmastime is the church's "second spring." No sooner does the sun turn its course back toward the light, than we Christians banish winter with flowers and lights and green branches held high. The Messiah comes to comfort our fear, to warm what is cold, to turn winter into everlasting spring.

Use natural wintry materials for Advent that are transformed with lights, greens, and ornaments for Christmastime. Near the font, images of John the Baptist and Isaiah can be used throughout the two seasons. The genealogy of Jesus is properly part of the days of Christmastime, flowing back a bit into the final seven days of Advent—the week of the "O" Antiphons. A "Jesse tree" can be the parish's Christmas tree, set up on December 17 in the vestibule or gathering place. Ornaments are prepared throughout Advent and put on the tree on Christmas Eve.

The Wheel of Time, the Crown of Heaven

Advent wreaths may be suspended. Putting the wreath in a fixed position, such as on a table, defeats its function as a turning wheel. The wreath does not need to be decorated with ribbons or small banners or oddly colored candles. Nor should the image of the suspended wreath be forsaken in favor of four candles set in a row. The circle is the primary symbol; the candles are secondary.

An old wagon wheel makes a sturdy frame—a prerequisite for a suspended wreath. Large, professionally made beeswax candles are more reliable than the colored paraffin pillar candles, which often drown their own wicks. The right combination of plumbing fixtures can be turned into candle holders. Hung with garland, the slowly rotating wheel is an enormously powerful symbol.

If we stand underneath one, we have a gateway into timelessness, a hole to peek into heaven. it is the perfect vantage point to shout the words of Isaiah: "Oh, that you would rend the heavens and come down!"

Midnight Blue and Deep Purple

Historically speaking, the shade of purple one used for vestments had more to do with the dyestuffs available than with any particular significance among the various shades of purple. Vesture for penitential seasons came in every shade from blood red to blue-black. Somberness and sobriety seemed to be the primary aim of the colors. That is why festive purples or light blues are, traditionally speaking, inappropriate to Advent or Lent.

Using distinct vesture colors for these two penitential seasons makes a necessary, if subtle, distinction between them. It is difficult to sustain much of an argument for the relative merits of either deep blue or deep purple. The two colors signify much the same things. They are the color of the dawn, the mythological color of royal blood, the color of ardor, of passion, of longing—and, in great contrast, of coldness, of frostbite, of midnight.

An Antidote to the Shopping Season

We need to learn the art of balancing liturgical touchstones—the elements returned year after year with the unexpected, jarring "voices in the wilderness"—elements that keep us from growing too comfortable or complacent. Although fine preaching is needed to distinguish for the assembly the images of gift giving, generosity, and the sanctity of material things (images that are more a part of Christmastime than Advent), there is really nothing good about greed, conspicuous consumption, or self-indulgence—nothing holy in a celebration that glorifies those who have and mocks those who have not.

A countercultural December affects environment ministers most directly. For example, the weekend after Thanksgiving there are always a number of parishioners who want to know where the crèche is. People are more and more mimicking the early decorations of the shopping malls in their homes. Most people regard *Advent* as merely the ecclesiastical word for "holiday season."

Even if the church holds off on the poinsettias until December 25, there is often pressure to decorate the worship space with evergreens throughout Advent, if only to get the most value from the dollars spent on them. Please resist this temptation. Just because the church may have an Advent wreath—a foretaste of Christmastime's greenery—there is no reason to hang wreaths on the front door of church. Besides, if the wreath is large and well constructed, and the church simplified and cleaned, you will not need much more to create a suitable environment for the parish to keep its Advent.

Peter Mazar[10]

175 • A SAMPLE ADVENT BANNER

Since the Scripture readings for Advent are filled with so many images, Advent banners are helpful in portraying their message in a colorful and powerful symbolic way. Always begin preparations for Advent by considering the Scripture lessons that will be read. The following description is one example of a visual image that is based on an appropriate Scripture reading.

Several Advent lessons talk about preparing the way of the Lord. The path should be made straight, level, and smooth. This suggests a banner that shows a road beginning from a dark, rocky place that forces it through a torturous route. Gradually, the way becomes straighter and smoother until it is upgraded to the status of a highway for our Lord. This idea of progression can be presented in an especially effective way if the banner is made so that it moves each Sunday to reveal the next part of the road. Think of mounting the whole banner like a huge roller towel. Of course, a banner fixed in this way is stationary and can not be used as a processional banner. The same design of a road can be adapted to fit on an ordinary flat banner.

The road, at the beginning, twists and turns, doubles back on itself, and seems to make much little progress. The roughness of the terrain is suggested by stuffed, irregular shapes made of coarse, dark fabric in a variety of sizes. The shapes can be sewn and stuffed separately, then attached to the banner. These very dimensional elements gradually give way, in turn, to a quilted area with stitched furrows and ridges. Along the way, the road had become straighter and now has gentle curves. Finally, at the end of the journey, the road is straight, and the earth is flat and smooth.

The progression of the colors and textures is important in this banner. Begin with dark browns and grays, then change to middle-value browns, grays, and gray-greens. Continue with slightly more intense greens, and finally, use a light, clear yellow-green in a smooth, soft fabric like velour. If making a smooth color-and-value transition from grays and browns to greens is difficult, imagine that the whole road goes through a desert, and make the value transition from dark to light using only browns and grays. The suggestion of a village at the end of the road marks the arrival point and the end of the journey.

Jill Knuth[11]

176 ✦ THE ADVENT WREATH

The Advent wreath, which hangs at the front of the church with its five candles, symbolizes the coming of Christ. Sample texts that can accompany the lighting of the candles are printed ealier in this chapter.

In the past two decades, the ancient custom of the Advent wreath has enjoyed an immense recovery throughout the world as a symbol that does

The Advent Wreath. The Advent wreath has become a widely used symbol of Advent waiting. The four candles represent the four Sundays of Advent, while the fifth (middle) candle represents the arrival of Jesus. It is lit on Christmas Eve or Christmas day.

for Advent what the manger scene and the Christmas tree do for Christmas.

While the specific origins of the Advent wreath are not known, we do know that it began centuries ago in what is now eastern Germany and was then associated with the Yule tradition of burning lights. By the sixteenth century these lights became Advent symbols in Christian homes. From that tradition, the custom of a different candle to represent each of the four weeks of Advent developed.

Originally, the Advent wreath was a wreath of evergreens placed in a circle containing four candles. Each Sunday a different candle was lighted until all four candles shed their light together. The gradual increase of light symbolized the growing anticipation of the birth of Jesus.

While a ready-made Advent wreath can be purchased at a Christian bookstore (also available in many department stores), you may prefer to make your own. Make a circle as small or as large as you wish from coat hangers or other sturdy wire. Then purchase a bunch of evergreens and attach them to the circle with fine wire. Finally, place the four Advent candles around the outer rim, and the Christ candle in the midst.

Note that the service of each week has a different emphasis. This emphasis is articulated throughout each week through the designated Scripture readings. Each successive candle represents a step toward the realization of Jesus' birth:

First Week—Vigilant waiting for the birth of Christ;
Second Week—Personal preparation for the birth of Christ;
Third Week—The joy of our waiting;
Fourth Week—The Incarnation of the Word in the womb of the Virgin Mary;
Christmas Day—The Christ candle represents the birth.

Finally, by the colors of the candles you will want to symbolize the twin themes of Advent—preparation and joy. Since preparation is solemn and even penitential, the first, second, and fourth candles should be dark blue or purple. The third candle, which symbolizes the joy of anticipation, is always rose-colored. And the Christ candle is white, the symbol of festivity.

You can place the Advent wreath on a stand, hang it from the ceiling, or place it in another central location. It enhances the Advent worship to have the wreath in a place visible to the entire congregation.

Robert Webber

177 ✦ AN ANTHOLOGY OF HYMNS AND SONGS FOR ADVENT

Advent symbolizes three distinct historical events of Scripture:

(1) Christ's second coming;
(2) The prophetic ministry of John the Baptist and his forbearers of the Old Testament; and
(3) The angelic annunciations, both to Joseph and to Mary, of the coming birth of the Savior.

Advent begins with the broadest scope in prophetic time and narrows the time span to the specific point of the annunciation of the Lord's coming birth. The spirit of worship is consequently one of hope, of expectancy, and of certitude in the prophetic statements concerning the Messiah's arrival. It is both the historical affirmation of Christ's first coming and expectation of his second Advent, a reality-to-come, that is the true hope of the believer (Titus 2:13-14).

Advent consists of four Sundays. The first immediately follows the last Sunday after Pentecost (that is, the Sunday of the Fulfillment), while the final one is the Sunday nearest Christmas Eve (the Nativity season itself being Christmas Eve, Christmas dawn and day, together with the first and second Sundays prior to January 6). Congregational selections for Advent in this anthology reflect the three themes described above. In a number of instances, the most appropriate Sunday for specific hymns will be suggested. (Note: please refer to article #159 for a key to the hymnals and songbooks abbreviated below.)

A Message Came to a Maiden Young
Luke 1:26-29 [Dutch: P. Dearmer; arr. D. McK. Williams] ANNUNCIATION TUNE; see W-II:1

Advent Canticle
John 1:1-3,14; [Mark Hayes (1976)] see WH:97

Advent of Our God
Philippians 2:5-7 [C. Coffin/W. Walter] FESTAL SONG; see SDAH:117

Ah, Think Not the Lord Delayeth
2 Peter 3:9 [P. Dearmer/arr. J. Konig] ALLIES IST AN GOTTEST SEGEN; see PH:112; Chorale

Angel Gabriel from Heaven Came, The
Luke 1:26-27 [S. Baring-Gould/Basque Carol] GABRIEL'S MESSAGE; see H-III:

Arise, Sons of the Kingdom
Luke 19:38 [J.Rist/Hamburg, (1598)] AUS MEINES HERZENS GRUNDE; see LH:69; Chorale

Behold, He Cometh
Luke 21:28 [Jerry Kirk (1967)] see WH:109

Blessed Be the God of Israel
Isaiah 7:13; Isaiah 9:2; Matthew 1:1 [M. Perry/ B. Harwood (1987)] THORNBURY; see HS-II:20; Unison melody; chordal underlay

Blest Be the God of Israel
Luke 1:68-79 [J. Quinn/New Version, (1708)] ST. MATTHEW; see H-III:193

Blest Be the God of Israel
Luke 1:68-79 [J. Quinn/English Traditional] FOREST GREEN; see CPH: 79; Chorale

Bridegroom Soon Will Call Us, The
Matthew 25:4,6 [J. Walter/Praetorius] ACH GOTT VON HIMMEL-REICHE; see LW:176; Chorale

Canticle of the Blessed Virgin
Luke 1:46-55 [Grail (1955)/J. Gelineau] MAGNIFICAT; see W-II:40; Gelineau Chant example

Christ Is Coming
Revelation 22:20 [F. Kahn/J. Beck, McDuff/W. Owen] Preparation Judgment, BRYN CALFARIA; see HS:58, HMOC:35, HFG:303

Christ Returneth!
Matthew 24:44 [Turner/McGranahan] CHRIST RETURNETH; see HFG:304

Christ, Whom Earth and Sea and Sky, The
Psalm 19:1-4; Luke 1:26 [V. Fortunatus/Swiss melody] Solothurn; see H-III:156a,b

Come, Thou Long-Expected Jesus
Isaiah 61:1-2, Matthew 21:5 [C. Wesley, C. Wesley/ R. Prichard, C. Wesley/J. Thommen] SAINT HILARY, HYFRYDOL, CASSEL; see SBAH:5, BPH:79, HMOC:58

Come, Thou Long-Expected Jesus
Matthew 21:5 [Shelley Hamilton (1985)] see P-II:70; Scripture Song

Come, Thou Precious Ransom, Come
Matthew 21:5 [Olearius (1664)] MEINEN JESUM LASS ICH NICHT; see LH:55; Chorale

Come to Us, Mighty King
John 1:14 [Anon./Giardini] TRINITY; see WB:343

Comfort, Comfort Ye My People
Isaiah 40:1 [Olearius/Bourgeois] PSALM 42; see BPH:77

Coming Again
Matthew 24:30; 1 John 3:2 [M. Lister (1987)] see MCB:118; Scripture Chorus

Countdown Song
John 14:2-3 [Anon.] see NJSS:69

Creator of the Stars of Night
Philippians 2:10 [Latin (9th C.)/Plainsong, Mode 4] CONDITOR ALME SIDERUM; see LW:17, Ambrosian

Dawn of Day, The
Revelation 21:1-5; 22:20 [L. Deiss (1982)] see GLP:62; compound meter

Emmanuel, Emmanuel
Isaiah 7:14 [B. McGee (1987)] see MCB:31; Scripture Chorus

Even So, Come
Revelation 22:17 [G. Johnson (1987)] see MCB:91; Scripture Chorus

Every Valley
Isaiah 40 [B. Dufford (1970)] see GLP:66

Hail Him, the King of Glory
Matthew 25:31 [de Fluiter] see SDAH:202

Hail to the Lord's Anointed
Psalm 72; Isaiah 61:1-2 [J. Montgomery/Gesius] see HCS:36

Hail to the Lord's Anointed
Psalm 72; Isaiah 61:1-2 [J. Montgomery/T. Noble] ROCKPORT; see HB:146

Hail to the Lord's Anointed
Psalm 72; Isaiah 61:1-2 [J. Montgomery/J. Farmer] FARMER; see HWB:185

Hail to the Lord's Anointed
Psalm 72; Isaiah 61:1-2 [J. Montgomery/B. Tours] TOURS; see HB:186

Hail to the Lord's Anointed
Psalm 72; Isaiah 61:1-2 [J. Montgomery/G. Webb] WEBB; see HB:99

Hark! A Thrilling Voice
Matthew 25:31 [Latin (16th C.)/W. Monk] MERTON; see H-1982:59

Hark! The Glad Sound! The Savior Comes
Isaiah 61:1-2; Luke 4:18 [P. Doddridge/T. Haweis; P. Doddridge/Folk Hymn] CHESTERFIELD COMMUNION; see LH:66, MNH:112; Early American

Hark! 'Tis the Watchman's Cry
1 Thessalonians 5:6 [Anon./D. Grundy (1965)] COLLEGE CROSS; see AHB:85

He's Still the King of Kings
Luke 1:33 [Gaither/Moultrie (1971)] KING OF KINGS; see HFG:242; Southern Gospel

Hills of the North, Rejoice
Revelation 7:9-10 [C. Oakley/M. Shaw] LITTLE CORNARD; see HB:478

His Name Is Life
Revelation 5:5; Isaiah 9:8 [C. Licciardello/ W. Gaither] see MCB:2; Scripture Chorus

How Long, Dear Savior?
John 13:33 [J. Ingalls] NORTHFIELD; see FHEA:9; Early American

I Long for You
Psalm 84:2 [Balhoff, Ducote and Daigle (1981)] see GLP:105; Psalmodic

Is It the Crowning Day?
1 John 3:12 [Whitcomb] Glad Day; see HFG:310; Traditional Gospel Song; 2nd Coming

Jesus Came, the Heavens Adoring
Zechariah 9:9 [G. Thring] SEIH, HIER BIN ICH; see LH:56

Jesus Is Coming Again
Matthew 25:13 [J. Peterson] COMING AGAIN; see HFG:305; Traditional Gospel Song; 2nd Coming

Jesus, Name above All Names
Ephesians 1:20-21 [N. Hearn (1987)] see MCB:1; Scripture Chorus

Judge Eternal, Throned in Splendor
Psalm 89:14-15 [H. Holland/Traditional Welsh] RHUDDLAN; see HB:517; Psalmodic

King Is Coming, The
Jude 1:14 [Gaither/Millhuff (1970)] KING IS COMING; see HFG:313; Southern Gospel

King of Glory, The
Psalm 24:7-10 [W. Jabusch/Israeli Folk/ arr. J. Ferguson (1973)] PROMISED ONE; see HUC:75

King Shall Come, The
1 John 3:2 [J. Brownlie/A. Davisson] CONSOLATION; see LBW:33; Early American

Let All Mortal Flesh Keep Silence
Habakkuk 2:20 [Moultrie/French Carol] PICARDY; see HFG:166

Lift Up Your Heads
Psalm 24:7 [G. Weissel/J. Freylinghausen] MACHT HOCH DIE TUR; see H-III:105; Chorale

Lift Up Your Heads
Psalm 24:7 [G. Weissel/A. Lemke] MILWAUKEE; see LBW:32

Lo, He Comes with Clouds Ascending
Acts 1:11 [C. Wesley/H. Smart/M. Maden/based on J. Cennick] REGENT SQUARE STORL; see HFG:306, SBAH:13; 2nd Coming

Lo, What a Glorious Light Appears
Revelation 21:1-4 [I. Watts/attr. A. Merrill] NEW JERUSALEM; see SDAH:446; Fulfillment

Long Ago, Prophets Knew
Luke 1:29-30, 38 [F. Green/arr. G. Holst] THEODORIC; see HS:68

Maranatha
Revelation 22:20 [B. Marlowe (1972)] see NJSS:92; 2nd Coming; Youth Oriented

Maranatha— Alleluia II
Revelation 22:20 [Br. Robert/J. Berthier (1981)] see TAIZ:78; Cantor with Mixed Voices

Maranatha— Come Soon
Revelation 22:20 [Anon. (1989)] see WH-II:329; 2nd Coming

My Lord, What a Morning
Matthew 24:29-30 [Traditional] STARS FALL; see HFG:316; 2nd Coming

My Soul Doth Magnify the Lord
Luke 1:46-49 [Anon. (1976)] see WH:106; Annunciation; Magnificat

My Soul Magnifies the Lord
Luke 1:46-49 [Anon.] see GLP:165; Annunciation; Magnificat

My Soul Proclaims with Wonder
Luke 1:46-55 [C. Daw, Jr. (1986)/J. Moyer (1990)] Walnut; see HWB:181; Paraphrase of Magnificat; a Carol

O Bride of Christ, Rejoice!
Revelation 21:2-4 [J. Wallin/Traditional German] AUF MEINEN LIEBEN GOTT; see CFH:104; 2nd Coming

O Bride of Christ, Rejoice!
Revelation 21:2-4 [V. Peterson/K. Stieler] WO SOLL ICH FLIEHEN HIN; see LW:20; 2nd Coming

O Come, Divine Messiah
Romans 8:22-23 [Fr. Pellegrin/French (16th C.)] VENEZ, DIVIN MESSIE; see W-II:194; French Noel

O Come, O Come Emmanuel
Isaiah 7:14 [A: Latin, Mode I/ B: Setting, J. Minchin (1964)] VENI IMMANUEL; see HFG:169, WB:490

O Day of God, Draw Nigh
Psalm 9:19 [L. Bourgeois/W. Crotch] ST. MICHAEL; see WB:491; Psalmodic

O How Shall I Receive Thee?
John 12:13; James 5:9 [P. Gerhardt/Teschner] ST. THEODULPH; see SBAH:11; Chorale

O Lord, How Shall I Meet You?
John 12:13; James 5:9 [P. Gerhardt/J. Crueger] WIE SOLL ICH DICK EMPFANGEN?; see LW:19; Chorale; 4th Sunday

O Savior, Rend the Heavens Wide
Matthew 25:31-34 [Von Spee/Traditional German] O HEILAND, REISS DIE HIMMEL AUF; see LW:32; Chorale; 4th Sunday

O Zion, Acclaim Your Redeemer
Matthew 21:5 [M. Servoss/J. McGranahan] GA SION; see CVH:106; Gospel Song Traditional

Of the Father's Love Begotten
Revelation 1:8 [A. Prudentius/13th C. Mode 5] DIVINUM MYSTERIUM; see HFG:176; Plainsong

On Jordan's Bank the Baptist's Cry
Matthew 3:3; Isaiah 40:3 [C. Coffin/Praetorius] PUER NOBIS NASCITUR; see LH:63; 2nd or 3rd Sunday

Once He Came in Blessing
Philippians 2:7, 8 [Roh, tr. Winkworth/J. Wolle] Advent; see HMOC:64; General Choice

Our Hope an Expectation, O Jesus, Now Appear!
1 Peter 1:3-4 [L. Laurenti/J. Freylinghauser] REJOICE; see HMOC:37; 1st Sunday

Peace, My Friends
John 14:27-28 [R. Repp (1972)] see NJSS:10; Scripture Chorus

Praise We the Lord This Day
Luke 1:28-38 [Anon./H. Gauntlett] ST. GEORGE; see H-1982:267; Annunciation

Prepare the Way, O Zion
Matthew 21:5 [F. Franzen/Swedish] MESSIAH; see SBAH:9; 1st Sunday

Rejoice All Ye Believers
Matthew 25:1-6 [L. Laurenti/Swedish] VIGIL; see SBAH:14; 1st Sunday

Rejoice, Rejoice Believers
Matthew 25:1-6 [L. Laurenti/Welsh] LLANGLOFFAN; see H-1982:68; 1st Sunday

Tell Out, My Soul
Luke 1:46-55 [T. Dudley-Smith/W. Greatorex] WOODLANDS; see HS-II:56; 4th Sunday

There's a Voice in the Wilderness
Isaiah 40:3-11 [J. L. Milligan/H. Bancroft] ASCENSION; see HUC:80; 2nd or 3rd Sunday

This Could Be the Dawning of That Day
2 Peter 1:19 [W. and G. Gaither (1971)] DAWNING; see HFG:307; 2nd or 3rd Sunday

This Is the Threefold Truth
1 Corinthians 15:3-4; Acts 1:11 [F.P. Green/ A. Foster (1984)] CHALLENGE; see SDAH:203

To a Maid Engaged to Joseph
Luke 1:26-33 [G. Grindal/H. Edwards III (1984)] ANNUNCIATION; see HS-I:55; 4th Sunday

Veiled in Darkness, Judah Lay
Isaiah 9:2; Luke 2:8 [D. Rights/R. Leich (1972)] PITTSBURGH; see WB:613

Voice of God, The
Isaiah 42:3 [L. Connaughton/G. Dyson (1970)]
WINTON; see HS-II:63; English Cathedral Style

Wake, Awake for Night is Flying
1 Thessalonians 5:6; Matthew 25:6,7 [P. Nicholai/
P. Nicholai, arr. J. S. Bach] WACHET AUF; see
SDAH:210; Chorale; 1st Sunday

Watchman, Tell Us of the Night
Isaiah 21:11 [J. Bowring/G. Elvey] WINDSOR; see
HB:149; 1st Sunday

Watchman, Tell Us of the Night
Isaiah 21:11 [J. Bowring/J. Parry] ABERYSTWTH;
see HB:216; 1st Sunday

We are Watching, We Are Waiting
1 Peter 1:13; 2 Peter 3:13 [Cushing/Root] THE
BEAUTEOUS DAY; see AHON: 391; 2nd Sunday

What a Day That Will Be
Revelation 21:4 [J. Hill] WHAT A DAY; see
HFG:314; 1st Sunday

What If It Were Today?
Acts 1:11b [L. Morris] WHAT IF IT WERE TODAY; see
HFG:311; 1st Sunday

When Came in Flesh the Incarnate Word
Galatians 4:4 [J. Anstice/Scottish Psalter (1615)]
DUNDEE; see AHB:75B; 4th Sunday

When He Comes
1 Thessalonians 4:14-17 [T. Dudley-Smith/D.
Wilson (1984)] DAVID; see SDAH:220; 1st Sunday

When He Shall Come
John 14:3 [A. Pearce] PEARCE; see HFG: 309; 1st
Sunday

When the Lord in Glory Comes
Matthew 24:30 [T. Dudley/D. Wilson (1984)]
GLORIOUS COMING; see HS-I:60; 1st Sunday

You Will See Your Lord A-Coming
Matthew 24:30 [a.: Anon (1843)/b.: Millenial
Harp, arr. Hooper (1984)] a: OLD CHURCHYARD,
b: early Advent hymn; see AHON:377, SDAH:438

178 ◆ AN ADVENT DANCE

_The dance below is an Entrance dance that may be used
with the prayers centering around the Advent wreath.
It is based on the well-known hymn "O Come, O Come
Emmanuel."_

_O Come, O Come, Emmanuel, and ransom cap-
tive Israel_ . . . On the words "O Come, O Come . . ."
the procession moves down the aisle, arms
stretched in front, palms facing up. (Practice hold-

ing the arms out in such a way as to really feel
them as an extension of the self seeking God.)

. . . that mourns in lowly exile here . . . Leader
with the wreath stops, and all the rest bow from
the waist, lowering arms. (At this point in the third
verse, the sequence is changed. See later directions.)

. . . until the son of God appear. All raise their
bodies and lift up arms as before.

(Chorus) _Rejoice! Rejoice! Emmanuel_ . . . A double
line separates as everyone turns to face his or her
partner while taking a big step backward, opening arms wide to the sides in a joyful manner. A
pathway is thus formed through which the leader
dances with the wreath. (It is easy to improvise
with a wreath in one's hands. Show it off, turning
from side to side in a spirit of delight.) The leader
must be at the head of the line again in time for
the next words.

. . . shall come to thee, O Israel. The leader continues dancing in front as the rest link right el-
bows with their partners, raise their free arms, and
swing around one time in the center of the aisle.
They end with their arms down by their sides, in
original lines.

Repeat the entire sequence described so far, pro-
gressing toward the altar while the assembly sings
the second verse and chorus. By the beginning of
the third verse, the leader places the wreath on a
table and the double line separates to the left and
right and encircles the table, leaving out the bowing. By the beginning of the third chorus, all are
standing still, facing the table.

(Chorus—third time). _Rejoice! Rejoice! Em-
manuel_ . . . On "Rejoice, rejoice," all take a step
toward the altar, holding hands and lifting arms
up. On "Emmanuel" all back away, lowering arms,
releasing hands, and then lifting arms back out to
the side.

. . . shall come to thee, O Israel. All turn in place,
arms lifted. Pause. The minister lights the first
candle (on second week he or she lights the second candle, etc.) and says a prayer for Advent. The
minister then joins the group, and they all circle

around the table, hands joined, as the next verse is sung or simply hummed. The chorus movements are repeated as before (stepping toward the altar, arms raised, etc.), and all then slowly file off to their places in the assembly as a final verse and chorus is sung.

Ronald Gagne[12]

SIX

Sample Advent Services

This chapter features three sample services for the Sundays of Advent and two occasional services that may be held during Advent. The full texts of the Sunday services are presented along with commentary that articulates the theological and liturgical rationale for the various acts of worship and describes the non-textual dimensions of the services. Planners may adapt the entire service or parts of the service into a form suitable for their congregation. These texts and commentaries may also be used for study by liturgical planners or educational ministries in local congregations.

179 • A TRADITIONAL SERVICE FOR ADVENT

The following service is a creative adaptation of the traditional pattern and texts for worship in the season of Advent. It will be of particular help for those who plan more formal Advent worship. For others, the commentary included with this service will provide a guide to thoughtful planning for the Advent season.

PREPARING FOR WORSHIP WITH GOD'S PEOPLE

Commentary: The setting for Advent worship is very important in conveying the nature of the season. Banners, paraments (cloths that cover the Communion table and pulpit), bulletins, printed liturgies, or worship-folder covers may be designed to reflect the colors, symbols, and primary characters of the season. The colors of the season are blue, which suggests hope, and purple, which suggests penitence. Traditional Advent symbols include the stump or root of Jesse (Isa. 11), a blooming desert (Isa. 35), and the shepherd of Israel (Isa. 40:9-11; Ps. 80). Biblical characters associated with the narratives of Advent include John the Baptist, Zechariah and Elizabeth, and Isaiah. It can be very effective to coordinate the symbols, colors, and texts used on banners, paraments, and bulletin covers, especially when these reflect the sermon topic of a given Sunday. Whatever choices are made, great care should be given to avoid any of the secular symbols of the Christmas season.

Gathering of the Congregation, with organ, piano, or instrumental prelude

Commentary: Pre-service music should also be chosen to reflect the appropriate mood of the season. The excited joy of Christmas carols should be saved for Christmas day. Instead, music should reflect a deep sense of yearning or expectation. Arrangements of the most familiar Advent, not Christmas, hymns will serve to set this mood, while allowing worshipers to focus on the texts of hymns as they prepare for worship. The texts of unfamiliar hymns should be printed in the printed liturgy for this purpose.

Entrance Prayer

LEADER OR PEOPLE:

Almighty God, our hearts yearn for your presence. Be with us now as we listen to your Word and offer the prayers and praises of our hearts. Teach us to rely on your promise of salvation. Prepare our hearts for the glorious coming of our Lord and Savior, Jesus Christ. Amen.

Commentary: Advent is a penitential season, during which time worshipers prepare for the coming of Christ. Like the preservice music, the opening of the service should be meditative. The entrance prayer may be preceded or followed by a period of silent reflection. The spoken prayer may be followed by a brief prayer or by an introit sung by a choir or vocal soloist.

All texts in this series of services are appropriated to either leader, pastor, or people. The texts assigned to the leader may be spoken by the pastor, but do provide an opportunity for lay leadership in worship. Texts assigned to the pastor are those that are most appropriately spoken by ordained clergy, including the opening greeting, the declaration of pardon, the prayer of consecration at Communion, and the benediction. Texts assigned to the people may be spoken by the entire congregation or by a chorus of voices rehearsed for speaking these texts, but may also be spoken by the leader or pastor, depending on the practice of a given congregation. Only the texts spoken by the congregation need to be printed for their use, although the entire text of the service may be printed if resources allow. In general, lay leadership and congregational participation foster dynamic and meaningful worship services and should be a high priority for worship planners.

Lighting of the Advent candles

Commentary: An Advent wreath may be placed in a prominent position in the front of the sanctuary. The wreath traditionally features four purple or blue candles imbedded in a wreath of greens, surrounding a large white candle in the middle. On the first Sunday of Advent, the first purple candle is lit; on the second Sunday of Advent, the two purples candles are lit; and so on, until all the candles, including the large, white candle, are lit on Christmas day.

These candles are symbolic of the light of Christ. The increasing number of candles lit over the span of the Advent season points to the growing anticipation of Christ's imminent coming.

In many congregations, the various candles are said to represent various aspects of the Advent celebration, representing, for example, the characteristics of Advent faith (candle 1 representing hope; candle 2, peace; 3, joy; 4, love; and 5, Jesus Christ, Light of the world) or several Advent-related events (candle 1 representing the prophets; candle 2, the Annunciation; 3, the visitation; 4, the journey to Bethlehem; 5, the birth of Jesus). According to traditional practice, worship on the third Sunday of Advent focuses on the theme of joy. This is reflected in the traditional readings for this Sunday as well as in the use of a rose or pink (instead of purple) candle in the Advent wreath. Each of these alternatives is to be preferred to association with explicitly Christmas-related events (e.g., the visits of the shepherds or magi). But often, any explicit association is arbitrary and unconnected to the rest of the service. Unless each candle can be said to represent some theme that will be prominently featured throughout a given Advent service, it is preferable to simply associate them with the general theme of the coming Light of the world, as is reflected in the choice of texts below.

LEADER: Jesus said, "I am the light of the world;
the one who follows me will not walk in darkness
but have the light of life.

PEOPLE: **We light this candle as a sign of the coming light of Christ**:

LEADER: (reads Old Testament Lesson)
First Sunday of Advent: Isaiah 9:2
Second Sunday of Advent: Isaiah 42:16
Third Sunday of Advent: Isaiah 49:6
Fourth Sunday of Advent: Isaiah 58:8
Christmas: Isaiah 60:1-3

PEOPLE: **Come, Lord Jesus, our light and life.**

LEADER: Until that day, let us walk in the light of the Lord.

Commentary: Various members of the congregation may read the lessons and light the candles used in this part of the service. All ages should be represented in the choice of these leaders.

BRINGING PRAISE TO GOD
Call to Worship

LEADER: "The hour has come for you to wake up from your slumber, because our salvation is nearer now than when we first believed. The night is nearly over; the day is almost here. So let us put aside the deeds of darkness and put on the armor of light." (Rom. 13:11-12). People of God, with the assurance of these promises, let us bring our praise and prayers to God.

Commentary: The call to worship should both challenge and invite the people to bring their worship and reflect the themes of the service. This passage from Romans 13 is especially appropriate because of its use of the image of light, which was used in the previous section of the service, and because of its call to renewal, which is essential to the nature of Advent.

Entrance Hymn
"Savior of the Nations, Come"

Commentary: Other appropriate hymns include "O Come, O Come Emmanuel"; "Come, Thou Long Expected Jesus"; "On Jordan's Bank the Baptist's Cry"; "O Lord, How Shall I Meet You?"; "Hark! A Thrilling Voice Is Sounding"; "Hark! the Glad Sound!"; and "The Savior Comes." Most hymnals now include a substantial number of hymns focusing exclusively on Advent themes, in addition to Christmas carols and hymns. The latter should be saved for Christmas.

Greeting

PASTOR:	The Lord be with you.
PEOPLE:	**And also with you.**
PASTOR:	(reads Revelation 1:4-5)

Commentary: Use of this text as a greeting is especially appropriate because of the reference to the Christ as the one "who is, who was, and who is to come." In Advent, we remember Israel's anticipation of Christ's first coming and renew our anticipation for his second coming.

Passing of the Peace

PASTOR:	And now, even as we have received our Lord's greeting, let us greet one another.
PEOPLE:	(saying to each other) **The Lord be with you.**

Commentary: The passing of the peace, or mutual greeting, traditionally precedes the sacrament, reminding us of how we join in one fellowship at our Lord's Table. This act is also appropriate at this point in the opening of the service, as a way of acknowledging the horizontal dimension of our gathering in Jesus' name—that is, our relationship with each other in Christ's body—even as the greeting reminds us of the vertical dimension of our worship—our relationship to God. Other services in this series place this act at other points in the liturgy.

OFFERING CONFESSION OF SINS

Call to Advent Penitence

Commentary: On the first Sunday of Advent, the worship leader may wish to briefly explain the nature of Advent worship, including reference to any visual symbols used by the congregation, sermon topics for the four weeks of Advent, and any other related local practice. This description should include reference to the penitential nature of Advent, calling the congregation to penitence, which would thus appropriately precede the act of confession. Any description given should strive to avoid a strongly didactic character.

Invitation to Confession

LEADER:	"So let us put aside the deeds of darkness and put on the armor of light" (Rom. 13:12). Sisters and brothers in Christ, in obedience to God, we confess our sins now before him.

Commentary: The general call to Advent penitence can be followed by a specific call to confession of sins. This verse from Romans 13 recalls the call to worship used earlier in the service.

Prayer of Confession
[silence]

LEADER:	O God, we live in darkness, ignoring the power of the Light of the world.
PEOPLE:	**Lord, have mercy.**
LEADER:	We live in ignorance, failing to acknowledge the Wisdom of your Word.
PEOPLE:	**Christ, have mercy.**
LEADER:	We live in turmoil, shunning the peace that passes all understanding.
PEOPLE:	**Lord, have mercy.**
LEADER:	May Christ, who came long ago, come to enlighten our hearts and to grant us true wisdom and peace.

Commentary: The prayer of confession should be preceded by a moment of silence. This allows for the people to read the text of the prayer of confession and to focus their attention on this significant liturgical act. This is especially important if the prayer of confession is being used for the first time by a congregation.

The responses of the people may be sung. Many denominational hymnals include settings of the

Alpha and Omega. *This symbol reminds us that Advent is a time of preparation for both the beginning (Jesus' birth) and the end (the Second Coming). Often the alpha and the omega are connected with other symbols, such as the* chi rho *above.*

Kyrie Eleison (Lord, have mercy). See listing of the service music in various hymnals in the commentary on the Communion service below.

The metaphors used in this prayer recall some of the images found in the readings used at the lighting of the Advent candles and anticipated images used later in the Prayers of the People, providing textual unity to the service.

Prayer of Petition for Salvation

People: (singing) "Come, Thou Long Expected Jesus"....

Commentary: This Advent hymn is a petition for Christ to come as our Savior, functioning at this point in the liturgy as a continuation of the prayer of confession. Any announcement of this hymn that may be necessary should be made prior to the prayer of confession. Alternate hymns or solo or choral anthems may be appropriate, provided that the text is either a continuation of the prayer of confession or a prayer for deliverance from sin.

Declaration of Pardon

LEADER: The gospel of Advent and Christmas is this:
(Isaiah 40:1-2 *or* Isaiah 44:21-22)
In the name of Jesus Christ,

PEOPLE: **We are forgiven. Thanks be to God.**

Commentary: The use of an Old Testament text as a Declaration of Pardon is especially appropriate for Advent.

Thanksgiving

Commentary: The thanksgiving may consist of a acclamation of praise sung by the congregation. This may include the singing of a psalm or hymn of thanksgiving, Scripture songs of praise, or a metrical setting of a psalm or canticle. This is also a very appropriate time for a choir or solo anthem, provided that the text is an acclamation of praise for God's promised salvation. In some congregations, the traditional canticle "Glory to the God in the Highest" is not sung during Advent, reflecting the penitential nature of the season.

Invitation to Discipleship

LEADER: (reads 1 Timothy 6:11-16)

Commentary: Our service to God flows out of our experience of his salvation. Thus it is appropriate for the declaration of pardon, during which worshipers experience again God's word of grace, to be followed by a challenge to Christian service and an opportunity to commit themselves to that service. In Advent, this challenge can appropriately call worshipers to renew both their anticipation of Christ's coming and their obedience to God's law. These acts of invitation and dedication may also appropriately follow either the sermon or the sacrament of the Lord's Supper

This sample service features these acts following both the declaration of pardon and Communion, serving to emphasize the theme of renewal and call to service that is important to the Advent season.

Prayer or Hymn of Commitment

"May the Mind of Christ, My Savior"
[or]
"O Jesus, I Have Promised"

Commentary: Or another hymn of promise or commitment.

LISTENING TO GOD'S WORD

Prayer for Illumination

PEOPLE: **God of love and power, you are revealed to us in your Word, in accounts of prophecy and fulfillment** that direct our attention to Jesus Christ. Illumine us now as we hear your Word proclaimed that we may open our hearts to him, yearn for his coming in glory, and serve him with joy. Amen.

Commentary: The following Scripture lessons are based on the suggestions of one lectionary for the first Sunday of Advent. Lessons should be chosen by worship planners based on the text of the sermon of the day and the lectionary that may be used in a given congregation.

Old Testament Reading: Isaiah 2:1-5

Psalm: Psalm 122

Commentary: The psalm may be sung by the choir or congregation. Musical resources for singing the Psalms are included in the commentary with the Pentecost service in this series.

New Testament Readings: Matthew 24:36-44; Romans 13:11-14,

Commentary: Many traditions set apart the reading of the Gospel by having it read from a different location than the other readings, such as in the middle of the congregation. This practice highlights that God's Word is present in our midst as the people of God and therefore may be appropriate for each lesson.

Sermon

Commentary: Sermons during the Advent season should especially address scriptural themes unique to the season of Advent, including our expectation of Christ's second coming and the penitence appropriate in preparation for that coming.

RESPONDING TO GOD'S WORD

Statements of Faith
    Nicene Creed
    Hymn: "On Jordan's Bank the Baptist's Cry."

Commentary: It is often appropriate to follow the sermon with a hymn that either uniquely captures its message or provides worshipers with an opportunity for an appropriate response to its message. Whatever hymn is chosen should be carefully labeled and introduced so as to suggest its purpose. The hymn "On Jordan's Bank the Baptist's Cry," for example, may be used as a declaration of faith following a sermon on the preaching of John that calls us to announce the news of Christ's coming. In contrast, the hymn "O Lord, How Shall I Meet You," may be used as prayer of humility following a sermon that calls the worshiper to penitent humility in preparation for Christ's coming.

Concerns of the Congregation

Commentary: At this point, members of the congregation may make known to each other concerns for mutual prayer. These may be announced by the pastor or lay worship leader, by church members assigned to monitor the prayer needs of the congregation, or by individual worshipers in a time of sharing reasons for thanksgiving and intercession.

Prayers of the People

Commentary: The following prayer is ordered after verses from the well-known advent hymn "O Come, O Come, Emmanuel." Each section of the prayer follows a pattern: a spoken petition concerning individual needs, a time of silence for reflection upon these personal needs, a second spoken petition concerning world needs, and one verse of the Advent hymn. The verses of the hymn may be sung by a soloist, choral ensemble, or the entire congregation. Any instrumental accompaniment should be subdued and prayerlike.

The prayer may be extended to use each verse of the hymn, thereby roughly emulating the practice of the ancient church in using the "O" Antiphons for the days immediately preceding Christmas. These antiphons were each prayers of petition for the coming Christ that are now loosely reflected in each verse of the hymn "O Come, O Come, Emmanuel" (i.e. O Wisdom, O Branch of Jesse, O Key of David, etc.).

The following prayer is but one example of how to incorporate hymn and anthem texts that are themselves a prayer into the spoken congregational prayer. This is a very helpful way of integrating the musical contributions of a choir, soloists, or of congregational hymnody into the structure of the liturgy, avoiding any impression that these important contributions are nonessential accretions to the liturgy or mere musical performances.

Petition for Freedom from Evil

LEADER 1: Almighty God, we are bound by shackles of sin. Deliver us, we pray, through the power of Christ, from the bonds of our own evil patterns of life, that we may live in his joy. Convict us, in these quiet moments, of our need for this deliverer.

[silence]

LEADER 2: Almighty God, lover of justice and mercy, enter also our world with power, we pray, that all captives to evil in mind, body, and soul, may be freed through the radical and radiant power of our Lord Jesus Christ.

PEOPLE SING:

O come, O come Emmanuel / and ransom captive Israel / that mourns in lowly exile here / until the Son of God appear / Rejoice, rejoice, Emmanuel / shall come to you, O Israel.

Petition for Knowledge

LEADER 1: Lord God, usher us into the knowledge of true wisdom. In the quietness of this moment, help us to ponder our own often misguided pursuit of knowledge and challenge us to rely only on knowledge of you as the source of true Wisdom.

[silence]

LEADER 2: Almighty God, fountain of all wisdom, enlighten also our world by your Wisdom, that all people may rejoice in the knowledge of your truth, and may worship you from generation to generation.

PEOPLE SING:

O come, O Wisdom from on high / who ordered all things mightily / to us the path of knowledge show / and teach us in its ways to go. / Rejoice, rejoice, Emmanuel / shall come to you, O Israel.

Petition for Salvation

LEADER 1: Lord God, bring us your salvation, we pray. We know our own sin and trust in only you to save us. In this quiet moment, we offer ourselves to you, trusting in you alone to provide each individual gathered here with the knowledge and joy of knowing you.

[silence]

LEADER 2: Lord God, bring also your salvation to our world. Extend the bounds of your kingdom, we pray. Use us, your people, to tell the world of the promise of salvation and to point them to Jesus Christ, our Lord.

PEOPLE SING:

O come, O Branch of Jesse's stem / unto your own and rescue them! / From depths of hell your people save / and give them victory o'er the grave. / Rejoice, rejoice, Emmanuel / shall come to you, O Israel.

Petition for Peace

LEADER 1: Lord God, work your peace in our world, we pray. Quiet even our troubled hearts, even now as we bring our personal concerns to you.

[silence]

LEADER 2: Almighty God, whose will it is to hold both heaven and earth in the peace of your kingdom, give peace to your church, peace among nations, peace in our homes, and peace in our hearts; through your Son, Jesus Christ, our Lord. Amen.

PEOPLE SING:

O come, O King of Nations bind / all peoples in one heart and mind / Bid all our sad divisions cease / and be yourself our King of Peace / Rejoice, rejoice, Emmanuel / shall come to you, O Israel.

CELEBRATING THE SACRAMENT OF THE LORD

Commentary: The following liturgy for Communion is presented according to traditional rubrics: the invitation, the prayer of thanksgiving, the institution, etc. Other rubrics or divisions of the

Communion liturgy are suggested in other services for the Christian year printed in this volume. The basic pattern of the liturgy remains the same, but the rubrics chosen to label a section of the liturgy may highlight different aspects or emphases of that liturgy. These traditional rubrics highlight the continuity of this liturgy with that of the church of all ages.

Offertory

LEADER 1: Offer to God a sacrifice of thanksgiving, and make good your vows to the Most High (Ps. 50:14).

PEOPLE: **We now present the offering of our lives to our Lord.**

Presentation of Gifts

PEOPLE [SINGING]:
(The Doxology)

Commentary: At this point, the elements for Communion and the gifts that have been received may be brought forward. The doxology may be sung using either a traditional text, such as "Praise God from Whom All Blessings Flow," or a doxological stanza of an Advent hymn, such as the final stanza of the hymn "Hark! A Thrilling Voice Is Sounding."

Invitation to the Table

LEADER 1: "Comfort, comfort my people, says your God. Speak tenderly to Jerusalem and proclaim to her that her hard service has been paid for, that she has received from the Lord's hand double for all her sins" (Isa. 40:12). Sisters and brothers in Christ, the Lord's promise gives us comfort and one who has and is fulfilling this promise brings us joy. His table is spread before us. Come now to the joyful feast of our Lord.

Prayer of Thanksgiving

LEADER 1: Lift up your heart.
PEOPLE: **Lift them up to the Lord.**
LEADER 1: Let us give thanks to the Lord our God.
PEOPLE: **It is right of us to give thanks, it is our joy and our peace, at all times and in all places to give thanks to you, holy Father, almighty and**

everlasting God, through Christ, our Lord.

LEADER 1: We praise you, O God, for creating this world and for creating us in your image. We bless you for your promises to crush the head of the serpent, our tempter, with the one who will rule on David's throne. We worship you for your promise to wipe away all the darkness of sin and terror of injustice by the one who is the Light of the world and the Prince of Peace. Since the time is at hand when the promised one shall come, since the day of our deliverance has begun to dawn, with full confidence in your promises we live in joy and we sing your praise.

Commentary: This section of the prayer of thanksgiving is a prayer to God, the Father, in praise of the acts of creation and redemption. This particular prayer is comprised of phrases that recall Old Testament messianic promises. These phrases may be exchanged for others that are more central to the worship of a local congregation on a given Advent Sunday, perhaps recalling the text of the sermon of the day or of the readings associated with the lighting of the Advent candles.

PEOPLE: **Holy, holy, holy Lord, God of power and might,**
heaven and earth are full of your glory.
Hosanna in the highest.
Blessed is he who comes in the name of the Lord.
Hosanna in the highest.

Commentary: The text "holy, holy, holy . . . ," which is often referred to by its Latin name, *Sanctus*, and the text, "Blessed is he . . . ," which is often referred to by its Latin name, *Benedictus*, have been set to music countless times throughout the history of the church. Worship planners will likely want these texts to be sung by a choir or the congregation. Occasionally, an alternate acclamation of praise may be chosen to reflect the specific theme of a given service, such as the final doxological stanza from the Advent hymn, "Hark! A Thrilling Voice Is Sounding."

Most hymnals include musical settings for many portions of the Communion liturgy, including "Holy, Holy, Holy" (Sanctus); "Blessed Is He Who Comes" (Benedictus); "Christ Has Died, Christ Is Risen" (the Memorial); "O Lamb of God" (hymn at the breaking of bread). These may be appropriately sung anytime the sacrament is celebrated. Examples of these musical settings can be found in *The Worshiping Church* (Carol Stream, Ill.: Hope Publishing, 1990),795–845; *The Hymnal 1982* (New York: Church Hymnal Corporation, 1982), S76–176; *The Presbyterian Hymnal* (Louisville: Westminster/John Knox, 1990), 565–605; *United Methodist Hymnal* (Nashville: UMC Publishing, 1979), 17–31; *Rejoice in the Lord* (Grand Rapids: Eerdmans, 1985), 564–67;*Lutheran Book of Worship* (Minneapolis: Augsburg, 1978), 56–119; and many other hymnals.

LEADER 1: We praise you for Jesus Christ, our Lord, who came in the fullness of time to dwell among us: Emmanuel, God with us. He became our Wonderful Counselor, our Prince of Peace, healing the sick and befriending the outcast. He gave of himself freely, as a servant, even to death on a cross. He rose on the third day, and now reigns as Lord of creation. He will come again in power and strength to establish his kingdom forever. We bring our praise to you, Lord Christ, and we offer our thanksgiving for the gift of this feast.

Commentary: This paragraph, which traces the history of Christ's life on earth, may be replaced by a hymn that does the same, such as "Savior of the Nations, Come." Making this change may require that the "Holy, holy, holy," which precedes it, be spoken to allow for a smooth transition. If such a change were made, the congregation should be informed how the hymn functions as an integral part of the Communion liturgy.

Institution

LEADER 1: For the Lord Jesus, on the night when he was betrayed, took bread, and when he had given thanks, he broke it and said, "This is my body, which is for you; do this in remembrance of me." In the same way, he took the cup after supper, saying, "This cup is the new covenant in my blood; do this, whenever you drink it, in remembrance of me." For whenever you eat this bread and drink this cup, you proclaim the Lord's death until he comes.

Memorial

LEADER 1: We join in obeying our Lord's command. People of God, as you come to the table, what do you proclaim?

PEOPLE: **Christ has died. Christ has risen. Christ will come again.**

Commentary: The memorial is a direct response to the institution, allowing the people to express the nature of their testimony in coming to the Table. The text printed here for the people's response is traditional and may be found in many musical settings in the sources listed above. If the text is spoken, it may be altered to reflect the nature of the season. An appropriate response for Advent would be: "We proclaim the death and resurrection of our Lord. We long for his coming in glory."

Prayer of Consecration

PASTOR: Lord God, send your Holy Spirit to us we pray, that in this feast we may meet our Lord. May we come ever more to know him by faith, to minister to each other in love, and to yearn for the coming heavenly feast in hope. Amen.

Breaking of the Bread and the Pouring of the Cup

Commentary: At this point, the pastor prepares the bread and cup for the people. This will most often include breaking the common loaf of bread and pouring the wine or juice from a large pitcher into the common cup. These gestures should be rehearsed so as to convey both a spirit of reverence and of joyful welcome to the Table. Words appropriate to this action are found in the Maundy Thursday service in this series of services, if desired.

Invitation

PASTOR: Friends in Christ, the Lord has prepared his Table for his church. All who love him and trust in him alone for their salvation are now invited to come to the Table of the Lord.

PEOPLE: **We come with gladness. Thanks be to God!**

PASTOR: The gifts of God for the people of God.

Sacrament

PASTOR: (as the people take the bread) The bread of heaven, the body of Jesus Christ, hope of the world, for you.

PASTOR: (as the people take the cup) The cup of salvation, the blood of Jesus Christ, hope of the world, for you.

Commentary: During the sacrament, appropriate instrumental, choral, or solo music may be played or sung, or the congregation may sing a series of Communion hymns. Preference should be given to texts that focus on the coming of Christ, the participation in the heavenly banquet that will follow his second coming, and the subject of the sermon of the particular Sunday.

Canticle: "The Song of Mary" (Luke 1:46-55)

Commentary: Though traditionally sung by the church during service of evening prayer, the song of Mary (often named by the first word of its Latin text—Magnificat) also provides a fitting response to the Sacrament, especially during Advent and Christmastide. This may be spoken from Luke 1:46-55, either by a single voice or by a chorus of voices, or sung by choir, soloist, or the congregation. Settings of this canticle can be found in nearly every hymnal. (One very effective metrical setting of this canticle that is printed in many recent hymnals is "Tell Out, My Soul, the Greatness of the Lord.")

PREPARING FOR SERVICE IN THE WORLD

Charge to the People

LEADER: The Law of God (reads from Exod. 20; Deut. 5; or Matt. 22:37-40) Go now into the world, full of expectation for the coming of our Lord and full of joy in his service.

Commentary: This charge may be appropriately given from near a doorway leading out of the worship space. It is most often appropriate to use a text that summarizes the call of the Gospel that was the basis for the sermon of the day.

Hymn of Dedication (Recessional)
"Hark! the Glad Sound! The Savior Comes"

Commentary: The final hymn of the service should reflect the essential theme of service of the particular Sunday and should direct the attention of the worshipers to their mission in the world. During this hymn, worship leaders may recess from the front of the worship space toward the exits as a symbol of their movement into the world.

Benediction

PASTOR: May the God of peace make you holy in every way and keep your whole being—spirit, soul, and body—free from every fault at the coming of our Lord Jesus Christ (1 Thess. 5:23).

PEOPLE: **Amen.**

OR

PASTOR: May Jesus Christ, whose second Advent you await, make you steadfast in faith, joyful in hope, and constant in love, through the power of the the Holy Spirit.

PEOPLE: **Amen.**

Commentary: The first option points to the nature of Advent as a season of penitence and renewal; the second, to Advent as a time of waiting for Christ's second coming. Selection should be based on the unique focus of the individual service.

Dispersal of the Congregation
(organ, piano, or instrumental postlude)

Commentary: The music that is played as the congregation exits the worship space should reflect the nature of the service. If the service presented a call to penitence in preparation for Christ's coming, the music should be meditative. If the service presented a bold challenge to proclaim God's promise of salvation, the music should be more assertive.

John D. Witvliet

180 ◆ A CREATIVE SERVICE FOR ADVENT

This service draws on the historical Advent service to model an Advent worship for the free-church tradition. Adapt this service in a way suitable to the local congregation.

—————— Service ——————

Preparation and Reflection

Taped Music [Monks of Weston Priory]: "The Goodness of God" (or some other suitable music)

Opening Prayer

LEADER: Our loving God, we thank you for this blessed season wherein we are called to prepare anew to receive your gift of love to us.

As we begin, we confess before you that while we long, deep within, to know Jesus more intimately, we come as weary children, feeling unable to stretch out our hand to receive him. We pray that your Holy Spirit would mediate mercy and grace to us this hour, and would lift us up. Help our eyes to see, our ears to hear, and our hearts to prepare for Jesus to be born anew in us this Advent season.

Introduction to Advent

LEADER: Advent is a time of preparation and waiting. Advent, like birthdays and anniversaries, provides a time to reflect upon a relationship and to enrich it. But as we approach such events with friends or family members, often we are painfully reminded of all that our relationships are not. And we are unsure how to celebrate with integrity, not wanting our actions toward people to be a sham, an untrue expression of how we really feel.

For similar reasons, Advent can arouse a similar disease within us. How do I celebrate the coming of one who seems a stranger to me, or to whom I am presently estranged? God desires our honest reflection and action. During Advent, as we prepare to celebrate the birth of Christ, we can freely ask, "Who are you, Jesus?" and "Who do you want to become . . . to me?"

LEADER: Let us now pray together as we prepare to listen to the Scriptures.

PEOPLE: **Our loving Father, we come to this Advent worship desiring to pay attention, to listen to your word to us. We pray that as we listen to the Scriptures that you will make clear to each one of us what your particular calling to us is: What is the grace, the gift, that you long to give to each of us in order that we might grow in our intimacy with Jesus? Amen.**

Each text should be read slowly, with pauses for silent responses between readings.

FIRST READER: (Isaiah 11:1-10)
A shoot shall come out from the stump of Jesse,
   and a branch shall grow out of his roots.
The spirit of the Lord shall rest on him,
    the spirit of wisdom and understanding,
    the spirit of counsel and might,
    the spirit of knowledge and the fear of the Lord.
His delight shall be in the fear of the Lord.
He shall not judge by what his eyes see,
   or decide by what his ears hear;
but with righteousness he shall judge the poor,
   and decide with equity for the meek of the earth;
he shall strike the earth with the
   rod of his mouth,
   and with the breath of his lips
   he shall kill the wicked.
Righteousness shall be the belt around his waist,
   and faithfulness the belt around his loins.
The wolf shall live with the lamb,
    the leopard shall lie down with the kid,
    the calf and the lion and the fatling together,
    and a little child shall lead them.
The cow and the bear shall graze,
   their young shall lie down together;
   and the lion shall eat straw like the ox.
The nursing child shall play over the hold of the asp,

and the weaned child shall put its hand
on the adder's den.
They will not hurt or destroy
on all my holy mountain;
for the earth will be full of the
knowledge of the Lord
as the waters cover the sea.
On that day the root of Jesse shall stand as a
signal to the peoples;
the nations shall inquire of him, and his
dwelling shall be glorious.

This is the word of the Lord.
PEOPLE: **Thanks be to God.**

[pause]

SECOND READER: (Psalm 25:4-12, 14)

Make me to know your ways, O Lord;
teach me your paths.
Lead me in your truth, and teach me,
for you are the God of my salvation;
for you I wait all day long.
Be mindful of your mercy,
O Lord, and of your steadfast love,
for they have been from of old.
Do not remember the sins of my youth
or my transgressions;
according to your steadfast love
remember me,
for your goodness' sake,
O Lord!
Good and upright is the Lord;
therefore he instructs sinners in the way.
He leads the humble in what is right,
and teaches the humble his way.
All the paths of the Lord are
steadfast love and faithfulness,
for those who keep his covenant and his
decrees.
For your name's sake, O Lord,
pardon my guilt, for it is great.
Who are they that fear the
Lord?
He will teach them the way
that they should choose.
The friendship of the Lord is for those who fear
him,
and he makes his covenant known to them.

This is the word of the Lord.
PEOPLE: **Thanks be to God.**

[pause]

THIRD READER: (1 Corinthians 1:2b-9)
To those who are sanctified in Christ
Jesus, called to be saints, together
with all those who in every place call
on the name of our Lord Jesus Christ,
both their Lord and ours; grace to you
and peace from God our Father and
the Lord Jesus Christ.

I give thanks to my God always for
you because of the grace of God that
has been given you in Christ Jesus,
for in every way you have been
enriched in him, in speech and
knowledge of every kind—just as
the testimony of Christ has been
strengthened among you—so that
you are not lacking in any spiritual
gift as you wait for the revealing of
our Lord Jesus Christ. He will also
strengthen you to the end, so that
you may be blameless on the day of
our Lord Jesus Christ. God is faithful;
by him you were called into the fellowship of his Son, Jesus Christ our
Lord.

This is the word of the Lord.
PEOPLE: **Thanks be to God.**

[pause]

FOURTH READER: (Matthew 11:25-30)
At that time Jesus said, "I thank you,
Father, Lord of heaven and earth, because you have hidden these things
from the wise and the intelligent and
have revealed them to infants; yes,
Father, for such was your gracious
will. All things have been handed over
to me by my Father; and no one
knows the Son except the Father, and
no one knows the Father except the
Son and anyone to whom the Son
chooses to reveal him.

"Come to me, all you that are weary
and are carrying heavy burdens, and
I will give you rest. Take my yoke
upon you, and learn from me; for I
am gentle and humble in heart, and
you will find rest for your souls. For my
yoke is easy, and my burden is light."

This is the word of the Lord.

PEOPLE: **Thanks be to God.**

[pause]

LEADER: Advent prepares us for an encounter with Jesus of Nazareth. Let us now pause, collect our thoughts, and silently reflect on the following:

- When I think of Jesus, in what form or manner does his character come to mind?
- When I pray—apart from the times that I am praying in company with children—do I ever pray to Jesus? Why or why not?
- How does my relationship with Jesus compare with my relationships with the other members of the Trinity?

Allow God's Spirit to cause your present *general* actions, relationship, and thoughts toward Jesus to surface.

[silence]

Prayer: Holy Father, we thank you that from our beginning you have known us and loved us. You know our fears and hesitations, our vision that is askew. I thank you that your work of redemption weaves through and around our limited perceptions of you, and I pray that you will both expose the flaws and mend, or create anew, a tapestry of relationship between us and your Son. A work that will bespeak both the truth and beauty for which you have created us. Amen.

[silence]

LEADER: In a few moments I will ask you to quietly reflect on the specific picture or symbol that you most naturally associate with Jesus. I will slowly list a variety of names and images that are often associated with Jesus.

- With which are you comfortable?
- With which are you uncomfortable?
- To which do you find yourself drawn toward?
- From which do you find yourself shrinking?

Offer your private responses as silent prayer to God at this time. Close your eyes, and listen as I slowly read:

- Son of God
- Exalted One
- Teacher
- Judge
- Master
- Brother
- Servant
- Friend
- Husband
- Lover

[silence]

PRAYER: Blessed Jesus, I pray you will enlarge, in our mind, heart, and spirit, the picture you desire for us at this time. Help us to see you, to hear you, to touch you, to know you in a more all-encompassing way—in the world around us as well as in our inner world. We pray in your name, for the sake of your kingdom—within and without. Amen.

Celebration of the Eucharist

LEADER: During Eucharist, we receive from Jesus, the one who has already come and the one to whom we open ourselves again, saying, "Come again!"

We each come at this time with different longings and different perceptions of Jesus and with differing levels of relationships.

Those of you who are presently living in a graced time of joy and hope can easily come to the Table. Your gratitude is your prayer, and as you receive the bread and wine, you are saying, "Thank you; feed me more, enliven me yet more."

Today I want particularly to encourage those of us who are struggling; who are feeling apathy, numbness regarding our lives of faith in God; for the many who are weighted with stress, pain, or confusion; for those who feel unworthy to receive.

I invite you to come to the Table, and as you come, know that

1. your decision to come forward expresses the prayer of faith;

2. your kneeling position before the Table expresses your prayer of

loving submission; and

   3. your receiving of the bread and wine expresses a prayer of hope. Your gestures can speak what your words and feelings cannot.

Prayer for the Bread and Wine
(directed to Jesus)

Invitation to Eucharist

Music: "Eat This Bread," "Prepare the Way," "Gloria, Gloria" (Music from the Taizé community by Jacques Berthier, available in North America from GIA Publications)

Hymn of Response: "Come, Thou Long Expected Jesus"

Benediction

Leader: Go with the blessing of God and the expectation of meeting Jesus in a new way this Advent season.

—————— Commentary ——————

Preamble. The attached Advent chapel is roughly equivalent to the service that was offered at Canadian Theological Seminary in November 1991. The chapel calendar for the year allowed one service to be devoted to Advent. I had to decide whether I would instruct the students and faculty or would simply lead them in worship. I was tempted to teach (given that the church year is a new concept for many), but felt that the timing of the service (coming one week before the end of the term) meant that I would be addressing a weary and discouraged student, faculty, and staff congregation, one that needed as few words as possible. My goal for the chapel was that it become for the participants a time of "peace-filled beckoning."

Entrance. The chapel was dimmed, with the lighting emphasizing the Table/altar, which held candles and the bread and wine. (The wine was on this occasion in separate Communion cups, on several small trays.) The dim lights were for the benefit of the students, who usually come to the chapel for lectures. I needed to communicate that this time was for a different purpose. Having the quiet music of the Monks of Weston Priory helped focus on my purpose of worship; it was cheerful and hopeful, yet soothing.

The introduction to Advent was minimal. I wanted to anticipate some personal or theological barriers that the participants might have come with in order to help them be placed in a position to enter the worship time and receive a grace during it. During this introduction, I was assuming the stereotype of seminarians (and seminary faculty), namely that objective study of the Scriptures and theology often seems to result in a subjective sense of displacement regarding one's relationship to God.

Word. The Scriptures were chosen from typical lectionary readings for the season, but I did overrule the lectionary in that I did not remain with readings for the first day of Advent but decided instead to choose from these readings those that I felt would be especially encouraging to this congregation at this time.

Rather than a homily or sermon, I chose to allow that time to be used for guided reflection and silent prayer. I wanted the students to be free to sit in the presence of God with no expectation placed upon them other than to trust that God wanted to receive them as they were and to give himself to them anew this season. (In the conservative evangelical tradition, much stress is often placed on what should we be doing for God. In this service, I wanted to err on the side of grace.)

Eucharist. The participants were invited to come and, if they chose, to take the elements and kneel around the Table as they partook of them. They were encouraged to take as much time at the Table (or at their seats) as they desired.

The liturgy is quite self-explanatory at this point. They were a weary group, faculty, staff and students alike, and I felt the physical prayer of kneeling could bring a freedom from the need to cognitively pray at this time. (The service at this point went far beyond what I had expected. The congregation responded in an overwhelming way as people remained around the Table for some length of time. Particularly moving for me was to see an elderly retired faculty member kneeling alongside his very young students, receiving together.)

The songs selected for this time were chosen for the progression they brought. "Eat This Bread" was a promise (though somber in tone) that if we eat this bread we will never be hungry; "Prepare the Way" was also a promise, focusing on the God who will come and in his coming will make his salvation known to all his creation; and "Gloria, Gloria" was pure celebration. Having received God's promises and having eaten at his table, we have something to celebrate.

Dismissal. Having been nourished and fed by God, we can with a new confidence sing "Come Thou Long Expected Jesus" and leave the chapel with a refreshed sense of hope and expectation as we enter the preparation and waiting time to come.

Diane S. George Ayer

181 ✦ A Convergence Service for Advent

The service below draws on the traditional Advent service, but incorporates elements of the praise-and-worship and the charismatic traditions to provide a guideline for contemporary churches. The reader should adapt the service as needed to his or her local church.

The Setting. The sanctuary can be festively decorated for this season. While more secular ornamentation should be kept to a minimum, many symbols of Christ's coming and subsequent life are helpful in setting the tone. Particularly, the use of evergreens brings the concept of everlasting life to the forefront. Wreathes, branches, and even small trees can help. One custom used widely in the church is the "Chrismon tree." The tree is placed near the front of the auditorium and decorated with symbols, or chrismons, of Christ and his church. These symbols can be placed on the tree at the beginning of Advent, or added each week during the service with an explanation of the meaning of each. This could take place during the offering. Many bookstores carry books showing the various symbols of Christianity.

An Advent wreath may be prominently displayed in the front of the church to be used as a point of special significance during worship. Most Advent wreaths have three purple candles and one rose-colored candle with a white paschal candle in the center.

ACTS OF ENTRANCE

Processional

Commentary: Advent processionals introduce the congregation to the theme for that particular Sunday. These themes can be derived from the Advent wreath ceremony, the sermon series, etc. Special Advent banners are especially helpful. A great fall project could involve different groups from the church (including the children) in making an Advent banner. Usually the processional is accompanied by a traditional Christmas hymn or carol rather than a worship chorus.

ACTS OF PRAISE AND WORSHIP

Commentary: The time of praise and worship can be a blending of Christmas carols, hymns, and contemporary worship choruses. Several special Advent choruses have recently been written, and they give the church a special opportunity for a different feel to this part of the service. In addition to worship books, many cantatas contain wonderful choruses and hymns that can be used. Other hymns and choruses that announce Christ's second coming are also very appropriate. This allows for a blending of remembrance and anticipation. Special litanies or readings for the Advent season can be found or written.

MINISTRY OF THE WORD

Lighting of the Advent Candle

Commentary: During Advent, an additional part of the service is the lighting of the Advent wreath. This can proceed directly out of the time of praise and worship that has focused us on the coming of Christ.

A small group of people proceed to the front of the church (a kinship group, church fellowship group, family, etc.). As one person lights a candle, another (or others) read a Scripture and/or an appropriate text that describes what the candle represents. Each week an additional candle is lit, culminating with the Christ candle on Christmas Eve or Christmas day.

Themes for the various candles vary and can be determined by the worship leaders. The most common themes are

First Sunday: Expectation
Second Sunday: Proclamation
Third Sunday: Joy (rose candle)
Fourth Sunday: Purity
Resources for Advent candle ceremonies are available at many Christian bookstores.

After the Scripture or text, a chorus or hymn is sung. Sometimes a different verse of "O Come, O Come Emmanuel" is used for each Sunday.

Collect for the Day

Commentary: The Advent ceremony leads us to a focus on the Word, beginning with a collect from the Book of Common Prayer or other resource.

Readings

Commentary: The Old Testament, New Testament, and Gospel readings, as well as the Psalms, are taken from the lectionary for each of the Sundays in Advent. Most lectionaries are on a three-year cycle, beginning with Advent.

Creed

Commentary: In addition to the Apostles' and Nicene Creed, Christmas creeds (compilations of specific Scriptures, etc.) can be used.

MINISTRY OF THE TABLE

Commentary: As the church celebrates Holy Communion during Advent, the major themes of the season should come forth in this more liturgical section.

Eucharistic Prayer

Commentary: Follow one of the prayers of thanksgiving or prepare your own. As people come forward to receive the bread and wine, sing familiar hymns, songs, and choruses that are appropriate. Provide opportunity for the laying on of hands with anointing and prayer.

Prayer after Communion

Sending Hymn

Commentary: A traditional hymn or carol of Christmas can be used.

Randolph W. Sly

182 ✦ THE SERVICE OF NINE LESSONS AND CAROLS

The Service of Lessons and Carols was first developed in the late nineteenth century by Archbishop Benson for use in King's College Chapel, Cambridge. The service, which has as its focal point the coming of Christ, is characterized by a very simple pattern. It is ordered around Scripture readings that pertain to Christ's coming, followed by songs (both choral and congregational) and prayers. Since its first use and subsequent spread throughout the world, the service has been adapted in many ways, ranging from a very simple service of readings and congregational songs to an elaborate production. Though usually a Christmas Eve service, this service may be used on any Advent Sunday. Some churches hold the service a second time on Epiphany evening (using Epiphany hymns) as a way of bringing Christmastime to a dramatic closing. Worship committees should exercise a great deal of flexibility and imagination in planning this service.

Organ Prelude or Preservice Instrumental Music

Processional Hymn: "Once in Royal David's City"

The Bidding Prayer

LEADER: Beloved in Christ, we come by this service to prepare ourselves to hear again the message of the angels, and to go in heart and mind to Bethlehem, and to see the loving-kindness of our God, and the Babe lying in a manger.

Let us therefore open the Holy Scriptures and read the earliest tale of that disobedience to God's holy will, which is common to us all; and then the story of the birth of Jesus Christ our Lord, to save us from our sins and make us pure and happy; and let us thanks him with our carols of praise.

But first let us pray for the needs of this whole world, and especially for peace and goodwill among all people, that they may learn to love one another, as children of one God and Father of all.

And because this would most rejoice his heart, let us remember before him the poor and helpless, the cold, the hungry, and the oppressed; the sick and they that mourn; the lonely and the unloved; the aged and the little children; and all who know not the Lord Jesus, or who love him not, or who by sins have grieved his heart.

Lastly let us remember before God all those who rejoice with us, but upon another shore and in a greater light, that multitude no one can number, with whom, in this Lord Jesus, we evermore are one.

These prayers and praises let us humbly offer up to the throne of heaven, in the words that Christ himself has taught us.

The Lord's Prayer

Blessing

The almighty God bless us with divine grace, Christ give us the joys of everlasting life, and unto the fellowship of the citizens above may the King of angels bring us all. Amen.

Hymn: "Of the Father's Love Begotten"

First Lesson:

Genesis 3:8-15—God announces in the Garden of Eden that the seed of woman shall bruise the serpent's head.

Carol: "Adam Lay Ybounden"; text: fifteenth century, anon.; music by Boris Ord or Benjamin Britten

Second Lesson:

Genesis 22:15-18—God promises to faithful Abraham that his seed shall the nations of the earth call blessed.

Hymn: "O Come, O Come, Emmanuel"

Third Lesson:

Isaiah 9:2, 6-7—Christ's birth and kingdom are foretold by Isaiah.

Carol: "Lo, How a Rose E'er Blooming"; music by Michael Praetorius

Fourth Lesson:

Isaiah 11:1-9—The peace that Christ will bring us is foreshown; *or* Micah 5:2-4—The prophet Micah foretells the glory of little Bethlehem.

Carol: "O Little Town of Bethlehem"

Fifth Lesson:

Luke 1:26-35, 38—The angel Gabriel salutes the blessed Virgin Mary.

Carol: "There Is No Rose"; text: XV English; music by Benjamin Britten

Sixth Lesson:

Matthew 1:18-25—Saint Matthew tells of the birth of Jesus.

Carol: "The First Noel"

Seventh Lesson:

Luke 2:8-20—The shepherds go to the manger.

Carol: "Infant Holy, Infant Lowly" (traditional Polish carol) *and/or*

Carol: "Lullay, My Liking"; text: fifteenth-century English; music by Gustav Holst

Eighth Lesson:

Matthew 2:1-11—The wise men are led by the star to Jesus.

Carol: "In the Bleak Midwinter" *and/or*

Carol: "On This Day Earth Shall Ring" (Personent Hodie)

Ninth Lesson:

John 1:1-14—Saint John unfolds the great mystery of the Incarnation.

Carol: "Silent Night, Holy Night"

The Collect (*or suitable free prayer, or other prayers for the season*)

LEADER: The Lord be with you.
PEOPLE: **And with your spirit.**
LEADER: Let us pray: Lord Jesus, Child of Bethlehem, who in love made humankind, create in us love so pure and perfect that whosoever our heart loves may be after thy will, in thy name, and for thy sake. Amen.

The Christmas Blessing (*if appropriate*)

Hymn: "O Come, All Ye Faithful"

Dismissal (*if a silent recessional is not preferred*)

LEADER: May the One, who by his Incarnation

gathered into one things earthly and heavenly, fill you with the sweetness of inward peace and goodwill; and the blessing of God, the love of Christ, and the fellowship of the Holy Spirit remain with you always.

Go forth in peace and joy.

PEOPLE: **Thanks be to God! Alleluia!**

Closing Voluntary _(optional)_

183 ✦ A SERVICE FOR THE HANGING OF THE GREENS

The hanging of the greens, or the greening of the church, is the act of decorating the church in the spirit of Advent and Christmas. In recent years it has been recognized that the work of hanging the greens should be done in the context of worship. Therefore it is recommended that the church be brought together in a special time of worship (perhaps on the weekend before the first Sunday of Advent) to green the church and hang the Advent wreath. Acts of worship may include Scriptures, prayers, explanation, and blessings of the bells, candles, crèche, boughs, holly, ivy, poinsettias, the Christmas tree, and the Advent wreath.

ENTRANCE

The Entrance Hymn
During the Entrance Hymn, a procession may occur in which a sample of each of the greens to be hung is brought to a table in the front of the church.

The Greeting and Call to Worship

An Act of Praise

An Opening Prayer

THE SERVICE OF THE WORD

Let us walk in the light of the Lord.
Scripture Reading: Isaiah 2:1-5
*Blessing of candles, bells, and Advent wreath
Hymn

Let us prepare a highway for the Lord.
Scripture Reading: Isaiah 40:1-5
Blessing of boughs, holly, ivy, poinsettias, and Christmas tree
Hymn

Let us prepare to meet our Lord.
Scripture Reading: Isaiah 62:6-7, 10-12
Blessing of the crèche
Hymn

RESPONSE TO THE WORD
The various groups are now charged to decorate the church as an act of worship. They disperse to their various tasks. After the completion of the greening of the church, the people return for the Dismissal.

THE DISMISSAL
After the greening of the church, the people assemble in the worship space.

Hymn

Passing of the Peace

Benediction

Words of Dismissal

*When the various greens are blessed, each one is carried by a different person to the front of the worshiping community where the green is set apart in prayer to symbolize the message of Advent and Christmas.

Ralph E. Dessem and Thomas J. Tozer[13]

PART FOUR

The Seasons of Christmas and Epiphany

The waiting of Advent soon turns to the celebration of Christmas and Epiphany: Christ is born, the Word is made flesh. The communities of worshiping believers can be heard singing the angels' song: "Glory to God in the Highest." This is a season of celebration; it is also a season of mystery. For it is during Christmas and Epiphany that Christians marvel at the amazing love of Jesus, who became human for our sake. Although the commercial lights and hype ends on Christmas Day, Christians are only then beginning their celebration of Christ's birth.

SEVEN

Introduction to Christmas and Epiphany Worship

The secular world ends Christmas on December 25. However, in the ancient church Christmas began on December 25 and ended on January 6, Epiphany. This chapter introduces the reader to the origins and theological themes of the Christmas season and urges a recovery of this season in the contemporary church.

184 ♦ AN INTRODUCTION TO THE WORSHIP OF THE CHRISTMAS SEASON

The Christmas season extends from December 25 to January 5 and includes at least one Sunday and sometimes two. Christmas day is the most widely celebrated day of the Christian year. Customarily more people attend the midnight Christmas Eve service than any other celebration of the church.

The shape of worship during the Christmas season will follow the general order of worship (Entrance, Word, Table, Dismissal). However each of these parts will be filled with the words, symbols, sounds, and sights of Christmas joy. It is in these parts of worship, carefully planned and played out by the congregation, that worship will form within the people the true spirit of Christmas joy.

In Christmas worship the Entrance sets the tone of worship. Because Christmas is a joyous and festive occasion, use music, processions, dance, choirs, and instruments to lead the people in a joyous entrance. Many churches drop the confession from the Entrance because Christmas is not a time for penitence.

In the service of the Word, use a dialogic reading or a drama as well as a special reference to Christmas themes in the creed and prayers. Follow the lectionary reading to maintain a biblical integrity with the event being celebrated.

In the service of the Table use a special Christ-

mas prayer of thanksgiving, and for the dismissal prepare a benediction and words of dismissal that bless people in the Christmas spirit of giving.

From the very beginnings of the Christmas celebration in the early fourth century, the theme of the Christmas season has always been the arrival of the light, the light that has come to dispel darkness.

Historically, three services are celebrated on Christmas day: the midnight service, a service on Christmas morning, and another on Christmas night. The texts of these services stress the birth of Christ, but in such a way that the birth is not isolated from the death of Christ and his coming again. These themes are present in the Christmas preface prayer which states, "Grant that as we joyfully receive him for our redeemer, so may we with sure confidence behold him when he shall come to be our judge." What is at the heart of Christmas is the gospel—the overthrow of evil and the establishment of God's reign in our lives and over a restored Creation.

What we are called to remember as we construct Christmas services is that Christmas is clearly a celebration of redemption. The prayers, antiphons, Scripture readings, and hymns for Christmas point us to the source of our redemption, namely the paschal mystery in which the Incarnation finds its ultimate meaning. This is clearly announced in the Epistle reading for Christmas Eve: "Jesus Christ . . . gave himself for us to redeem us from all iniquity and to purify himself a peoples of his own who are zealous for good deeds" (Titus 2:13-14, RSV).

Christmas worship is not confined to a single day but extends for twelve days. The origin for these twelve days of festivity lies in the early church.

The early Christians of the East celebrated the birth of Christ on January 6 (they converted a pagan celebration of the birth of a god on this date into the birth of Jesus since the birth date of Jesus is not known). In the West, Christians began to celebrate Christmas on December 25 (they converted the pagan festival of the Invincible Sun into the birth of Jesus). Eventually these two dates became the boundaries of the Christmas season with the celebration of the birth of Jesus on December 25 representing the beginning of the festival and the celebration of the manifestation of Christ to the world through the visit of the magi on January 6 (Epiphany) representing the end of the Christmas festival.

Robert E. Webber

185 • THE ORIGINS OF CHRISTMAS AND EPIPHANY WORSHIP

Following the lead of secular culture, many Christians place Christmas as the most important day in the Christian year. This article suggests that a more profound understanding of Christmas arises out of an awareness of the history of the Christian year. Christmas should be understood in light of the events which follow—Epiphany and, eventually, Easter.

The proclamation of Christ's resurrection is the central focus of the Christian message. Yet for many churches, and not a few Christians, the annual festival of the birth of Christ has come to take a place of equal or greater significance. We might fill the church for an Easter morning service of resurrection, but we often multiply the services and special events at Christmas. The musicians may have their skills in refined condition at Easter, but often more time, rehearsal, and money is spent for the Christmas cantata and pageant. Writing of the special Christmas service, H. Boone Porter has noted:

No doubt many people will be moved by it, even if the music is ill-chosen or the sermon poorly

prepared or the decorations in poor taste. Those who are responsible for leading worship should not be seduced by such tolerance. Great feasts should be the occasion for raising the standard of quality, not lowering it. People may say (and will say) that they want the service just like last year and the year before that and the year before that. Yet people are not likely to return year after year if no new insight, no new vision, no new sense of spiritual reality is communicated to them. The larger crowd on Christmas Eve presents a challenging opportunity to communicate the Good News of the Incarnation as effectively as possible. (*Keeping the Christian Year* [New York: Seabury, 1977], 15)

The faith of the early church was grounded in the proclamation of the resurrection of Christ. So central was it to the church's life that Paul was able to write, "Now if Christ is preached as raised from the dead, how can come of you say that there is no resurrection of the dead? But if there is no resurrection of the dead, then Christ has not been raised; if Christ has not been raised, then our preaching is in vain and your faith is in vain. But in fact Christ has been raised from the dead" (1 Cor. 15:12-14, 20, RSV).

The fervor of the early Christians for the proclamation of the Resurrection meant that it would be the fourth century before the church would celebrate the birth of Jesus in a regularized fashion. With the Nativity festival originating as late as it does, one would hope that it would be easy to piece together an accurate picture of its genesis and subsequent development. Unfortunately, such is not the case.

The scholarly opinion concerning the origin of the date of Christmas falls basically into two camps. The first and most widely held viewpoint understands the celebration of Christ's nativity on December 25 to be an intentional Christianization of an earlier pagan fest. In 274, the Roman emperor Aurelian established the date as a commemoration of Emesa, the Syrian god of the sun. A temple to Sol Invictus was constructed in Rome on the Campus Martius, and a conclave of priests was established to administer its affairs and officiate at its rites. By establishing the annual festival of Christ's nativity to coincide with the pagan festival of the sun, the church could draw upon the ripe sun imagery already present in the prophetic announcements of the Hebrew Scriptures and the New Testament's evangelical tradition. As Adolf Adam has noted, "Christians could now make the triumphant claim to their pagan fellow citizens that they, the Christians, were celebrating the feast of the true Sun which alone can give light and salvation to the world" (*The Liturgical Year* [New York: Pueblo Publishing, 1992], 123).

A second hypothesis was originally proposed by Louis Duchesne in his comprehensive work entitled *Christian Worship: Its Origin and Evolution*. Duchesne held that the date of December 25 for the annual Nativity celebration was determined by a series of computations. Important witnesses in the early church, notably Tertullian and Hippolytus, recognized that March 25 was the date of Christ's death. A symbolic number system, allowing for no imperfections (fractions) would take March 25 also as the date of Jesus' conception. A perfect nine months later would result in the birth of Jesus on December 25. Such a symbolic number system seems strange to our twentieth century point of view, but it was not at all peculiar to the thought modes of the late third century.

As noted earlier, the most popular and widely held viewpoint concerning the date of Christmas is that the early Christians intentionally Christianized the pagan sun festival. However, it is impossible to completely discard the computation hypothesis. It is difficult to believe that the church would intentionally set themselves openly against the pagan feast of the emperor until after the legalization of Christianity under Constantine in 313. Augustine's Sermon 202 suggests that the Donatists were celebrating the Nativity on December 25, which would imply that the festival was known to Rome prior to the Donatist schism of 312. If Augustine's witness is accepted, then a nativity feast on December 25 was established in North Africa sometime before 312 and arising out of some other locus than the transformation of an established pagan feast.

In any event, the feast was firmly established by 336 and documented in the calendar of the Greek artist and calligrapher Philocalus, and usually referred to as the Chronograph of 354. In a portion of the work dating from 336, a list of martyrs, is found the words, "on the eighth of the kalends of January, Christ, born in Bethlehem of Judea."

Quite apart of the thematic differences between Christmas and Epiphany, the search for the origin of January 6 as the date of the latter takes us through a similar series of possibilities as we noticed with Christmas. Scholars have appealed again to the possibility that Epiphany was the intentional Christianization of a pagan festival. In Alexandria on the night of January 5–6, the pagans would celebrate the birth of the god, Aion, and in the course of the festivities water would be drawn from the Nile, water that on the night of January 6 would turn into wine. The baptism of Jesus and the miracle of the wedding feast at Cana were early associated with this feast. Again, it is easy to jump to the conclusion that the church responded to this thematically coincidental paganism by urging the substitution of their own tradition; but the story may not be that simple. Even the suggestion that January 6 was arrived at by a series of computations, based on April 6 as the death-date of Christ, has not been without its proponents.

Managing the multitude of lessons, theological themes, Christmas hymns and manger carols, decorations, vestments, and paraments, service times, and liturgical options for a festival as important to the Christian faith as the nativity of Jesus—in as little time as we have to devote to it—is no easy task. Even when we wisely and rightly extend and complete the proclamation of the coming of the Christ through the feast of Epiphany, we are still faced with the problem of what parts of the story to emphasize and what to leave out. At the very least, it demands that we read the story of our Lord's coming among us, ask ourselves how this coming speaks to us and to the world, and plan our worship and liturgical life so that we address the needs of the people with no uncertainty.

The first major conflict that immediately presents itself is that between the story of our Lord's birth, recorded in its familiar form in Luke 2, and the powerful proclamation in the first chapter of John's gospel that boldly asserts the incarnation of the Savior. This is not an either/or proposition. For those churches that make use of a lectionary, this need not be a problem. Most revisions of the lectionary provide three sets of lessons for Christmas to be distributed through the services of Christmas Eve and Christmas day. In many churches the major service of lessons, carols, and candles will be based around the story of the Nativity recorded in Luke. The later service, at midnight or the next morning will focus on the incarnation of the Word of God. The message of Christmas is more than the historical birth of a baby; it is also the incarnation of the Savior. It is more than cattle and kings kneeling in a stable, it is the entire world on its knees before the Lord of life and death. It is more than angels singing glory, it is beholding the glory that is full of grace and truth for us. No one can argue about the fact that the story of our Lord's birth is meaningful, even stimulating, but the gospel that the world needs to hear now is the vigorous, earthy, dynamic, demanding, if at times offensive gospel of the Word made flesh. Adrian Nocent has captured it so wonderfully.

> Incarnation means not only that God is with us but also that we are redeemed and with God. . . . In the truly traditional thinking of the Church, there is nothing poetic about the incarnation. In fact, the emphasis is, if anything, on a rather brutal fact: The Word came to do God's will, event to the point of dying on a Cross. . . . We are thus not passive bystanders of the incarnation. The incarnation radically transforms the history of the world and the personal history of each of us. (*The Liturgical Year*, vol. 1 [Collegeville, Minn.: Liturgical Press, 1977], 192).

The feast of the Epiphany, remembering the appearance or manifestation of God in Christ, is generally held to be the older of the feasts connected with the historical coming of Jesus. The traditional history of the feast day held that Epiphany was the birth festival of the Eastern church on January 6, roughly analogous to the Western church's Christmas on December 25. As the tradition goes, in the middle of the fourth century, after the peace of the church, an interchange of the two festivals took place with the church, East and West, celebrating both. While this explanation is conveniently satisfying, it is a gross oversimplification of the details. But the real difficulty in unraveling the feast of the Epiphany has to do with the multiplicity of themes that have from very early been associated with it. From Clement of Alexandria in the early third century, we find out that the baptism of Jesus played a significant role in the development of Epiphany. The wedding feast at Cana, Jesus' first miracle, was early associated with Epiphany as well. Popular thought today associates Epiphany with the arrival of the magi to offer their gifts. Of this tradition, Adolf Adam wrote:

Epiphany is also known as the feast of the Three Holy Kings or as Three Kings' Day. This emphasis obscures the fact that the feast is not a saint's feast, but a feast of the Lord. Moreover, as everyone knows, the gospel account says nothing about kings or about Magi being three in number. Origen is the first to speak of three Magi; he probably gets the number from the three gifts. The designation "kings" first occurs in Caesarius of Arles in the sixth century. The names Caspar, Melchior, and Balthasar have been used since the ninth century. (*The Liturgical Year* [New York: Pueblo Publishing, 1992], 146)

It is interesting to note that these three miraculous events—the visit of the magi, the baptism, and the miracle at Cana's wedding feast—are preserved for us still in the lectionary for the day of Epiphany and the first two Sundays following. This convergence of stories probably results from the fact that these three stories, these three miraculous events, stand near the beginning of three of the Gospels, Matthew, Mark, and John, respectively. These Gospels, being the favorite texts of important early Christian communities, may well have given local shape to the liturgical year, and the combination of these local customs has given us our present tripartite emphasis for Epiphany. The one whose light we have followed, of whom it was said, "thou art my beloved Son," and whose glory was manifested in the water made wine, is the one who was flesh among us for our salvation.

The entire complex of biblical and theological material—from incarnation, to manifestation, to transfiguration, all seen in the light of redemption, provides the church with an unlimited gospel tradition from which may flow our prayer and proclamation of worship and life.

Neil Alexander

186 • RECOVERING THE TWELVE-DAY CHRISTMAS TO EPIPHANY CELEBRATION

The commercialization of Christmas may be combated by following the suggestions below to recover a full twelve-day celebration that begins at Christmas and ends at Epiphany.

The word *epiphany* means "manifestation" and refers in particular to the manifestation of Jesus as Savior not only of the Jews, but of all the peoples of the world.

The merchants of our land are calling the shots on Christmas, at least as to when our parishioners _feel_ it is Christmas time. The commercialization of Christmas has overpowered the church's 1,500-year-old tradition of Advent. Christmas is popularly understood to _end_, not _begin_, on December 25. Consequently, Epiphany has been relegated to utter obscurity, an afterthought that appears as a curious inscription on the pastor's program planning calendar.

Epiphany: Its Context

The elevation or rehabilitation of Epiphany will be effected less by straining to discover its uniqueness than by recovering its proper context, i.e., by treating the systemic problem of Advent and Christmas.

The essential antidote is the straightforward, unabashed, and unwavering recognition of Christmas as a twelve-day celebration from December 25 to January 6. Perseverance here will work slowly to transform the context of Epiphany and thereby its identity and place in the life of the church. There are many gestures that will work in this direction, for example:

(1) Schedule your church Christmas decorating party _late_ in Advent. Plan this months in advance and secure commitments from parishioners for specific responsibilities (so they won't later tell you how busy they are on the afternoon or evening of the 21st). Invite families to attend. Sing carols!—the children no longer learn them in public schools.

(2) Designate the "Sundays _after_ Christmas" as the "Sundays _of_ Christmas (tide)." The new consensus (CCT) lectionary, by labeling them "Sundays _after_," unwittingly reinforces the cultural tendency to view Christmas as the one day climax of the Christmas shopping season.

(3) Hymnal editors, in the subject designations that appear in the indices and under each hymn, should forgo nomenclature such as "Jesus Christ: His birth" in favor of "Christmastide" or even "December 25–January 6." Moreover, hymnal commissions should note the lectionary readings for Advent and begin to include those hymns traditionally found in the "Jesus Christ: His Second Coming" section along with the Advent hymns. An

expanded Advent section will encourage the pastor who otherwise would exhaust the Advent selections and grasp prematurely for Christmas carols. (The Episcopal _Hymnal 1982_ provides a larger Advent section.)

(4) Encourage the scheduling of church and family Christmas events during the twelve days of Christmas. Publicize these according to the Day of Christmas, Fourth Night Concert, Twelfth Night Party, and so forth. Our local ministerial association traditionally has a Christmas gathering with spouses. One year, our Advent schedules were so packed that we could not find an open date before the 24th. We broke with tradition and met instead "after Christmas," on the 28th. The party was a real success—everyone attended for a change and the mood was much more relaxed, each of us having behind us the pressures unique to pastors prior to the 25th. Christmas concerts, Sunday school programs, caroling, etc., within the twelve days may not "feel right" initially, but give this practice time to take hold.

(5) Schedule an annual Service of Nine Lessons and Carols during the twelve days. For solo pastors without pulpit relief, the First Sunday of Christmas is an opportune time; it "changes the pace" on what is usually a "low" Sunday and is a highly participatory service that is always well-received. Moreover, the singing of so many Christmas carols in one service reinforces the twelve days' tradition. A drawback is that such a service may overlay the themes proper to those days (Holy Family, Innocents, Holy Name, etc.). This can be remedied by selecting Scripture passages that expand these lectionary themes.

(6) Include on the church calendar (local and national) the minor festival days that are related to Christmas:

> December 26 as St. Stephen, Deacon and Martyr
> December 27 as St. John, Apostle and Evangelist
> December 28 as Holy Innocents
> The First Sunday of Christmas also as Holy Family
> January 1 as The Holy Name of Our Lord Jesus Christ
> The First Sunday after Epiphany as The Baptism of the Lord
> February 2 (the 40th day counting from

Christmas) as The Presentation of Our Lord Jesus Christ in the Temple

Appropriate lectionary texts for these days may be found in *The Book of Common Prayer.*

Epiphany: Christmas Finale

Attention to the context of Epiphany will go a long way toward giving it the esteem that is properly its due. When such a favorable climate is created, the desire for a liturgical gimmick to elevate the day will subside.

The identity and character of the day ought to be centered in the liturgy for Epiphany, which is properly a eucharistic one. Whatever else is planned for the occasion should not detract from this central focus. Because Epiphany usually falls on a weekday, the parish celebration is likely to be an evening one. (When Epiphany falls on a Lord's Day, the Eucharist may be celebrated at the morning service and the annual evening Epiphany events centered around Epiphany vespers or evening prayer.)

The Epiphany service of Word and sacrament may be colored in ways complementary to the lections and themes proper to the day. Congregations that are otherwise ambivalent to the use of incense in worship may be open to the use of frankincense on this night. Children present may be invited to add the magi to the crèche scene. At the offertory, persons attired as the three kings may present the eucharistic gifts while the congregation sings "We Three Kings."

Without in any way detracting from the eucharistic liturgy that is the center and focus of Epiphany, other customs may evolve. The Episcopal church with whom a previous Presbyterian congregation of mine shared its worship space observes an Epiphany pattern that we came to appreciate. A potluck supper is followed by a short eucharistic service.

The Christmas decorations are then taken down. At the conclusion of the evening, all gather for Epiphany cake. Baked inside are "gifts" that obligate the person in whose piece they are found to certain privileges and responsibilities:

3 beans—persons are crowned kings or queens for the season

1 ring—person must make next year's cake

1 thimble—a test of patience and diligence; some creative talent of craftsmanship must be displayed at next year's Epiphany

1 dime—a test of stewardship; at next year's Epiphany the person must show how it grew

To the degree that a congregation respects the integrity of Advent and celebrates Christmas as a twelve-day festival of the Incarnation, Epiphany, centered around the Lord's Table, will be less a *postscriptum* and more the Christmas finale that is rightly its glory.

O star of wonder, star of night,
Star with royal beauty bright,
Westward leading, still proceeding,
Guide us to thy perfect light.

Robert E. Webber

❧ EIGHT ❧

Resources for Planning Christmas and Epiphany Worship

Christmas worship should be festive and joyous, expressing the themes of Incarnation and birth, themes which inaugurate the special announcement that salvation has come, that God is with us, that the time has been fulfilled. The resources of this chapter help the church capture these themes and the joy they bring to the people of God.

187 ♦ LECTIONARY TEXTS FROM CHRISTMAS TO EPIPHANY

The following are the texts suggested for the Sundays of Advent in the Revised Common Lectionary. Brief descriptions of each lesson are provided to aid in recalling the basic theme of each passage. Descriptions of each lesson are provided to aid in recalling the basic theme of each passage.

——— **Year A (1996, 1999)** ———

SUNDAY	OLD TESTAMENT	PSALM	EPISTLE	GOSPEL
Christmas Eve	Isaiah 9:2-7, for to us a child is born; Prince of Peace.	96	Titus 2:11-14, God shows grace; control self as we wait for the day.	Luke 2:1-20, birth of Jesus; shepherds and angels.
Christmas Day	Isaiah 52:7-10, the beauty of the messenger of peace.	98	Hebrews 1:1-4 (5-12), God who spoke now speaks through Son.	John 1:1-4, Word from beginning has become flesh.
First Sunday after Christmas	Isaiah 63:7-9, the Lord's unfailing love to God's people.	148	Hebrews 2:10-18, Jesus became human to set us free.	Matthew 2:13-23, escape to Egypt; death of innocents.
New Year's Eve/Day	Ecclesiastes 3:1-13, there is a time for everything.	8	Revelation 3:1-12, the New Heaven and the New Earth; Good News in Jesus.	Matthew 25:31-46, final judgment: the sheep and the goats.
Second Sunday after Christmas	Jeremiah 31:7-14, the joyful return of the exiles.	147:12-20	Ephesians 1:3-14, spiritual blessings in Christ.	John 1:1-9, 10-18, the Word became flesh.
Epiphany	Isaiah 60:1-6, glory of God's people; all will come to them.	72:1-7, 10-14	Ephesians 3:1-12, God's plan for Gentiles shown to Paul.	Matthew 2:1-12, the visitors from the East.

———— Year B (1997, 2000) ————

SUNDAY	OLD TESTAMENT	PSALM	EPISTLE	GOSPEL
Christmas Eve	Isaiah 9:2-7, for to us a child is born; Prince of Peace.	96	Titus 2:11-14, God shows grace; control self as we wait for the day.	Luke 2:1-20, birth of Jesus, shepherds and angels.
Christmas Day	Isaiah 52:7-10, the beauty of the messenger of peace.	98	Hebrews 1:1-4 (5-12), God who spoke now speaks through Son.	John 1:1-4, Word from beginning has become flesh.
First Sunday after Christmas	Isaiah 61:10-62:3, rejoice Jerusalem, you will be victorious.	148	Galatians 4:4-7, God sent Christ at right time; we are God's heirs.	Luke 2:22-40, Jesus presented in the temple.
New Year's Eve/Day	Ecclesiastes 3:1-13, there is a time for everything.	8	Revelation 3:1-12, the New Heaven and the New Earth; Good News in Jesus.	Matthew 25:31-46, final judgment: the sheep and the goats.
Second Sunday after Christmas	Jeremiah 31:7-14, the joyful return of the exiles.	147:12-20	Ephesians 1:3-14, spiritual blessings in Christ.	John 1:1-9, 10-18, the Word became flesh.
Epiphany	Isaiah 60:1-6, glory of God's people; all will come to them.	72:1-7, 10-14	Ephesians 3:1-12, God's plan for Gentiles shown to Paul.	Matthew 2:1-12, the visitors from the East

———— Year C (1995, 1998, 2001) ————

SUNDAY	OLD TESTAMENT	PSALM	EPISTLE	GOSPEL
Christmas Eve	Isaiah 9:2-7, for to us a child is born; Prince of Peace.	96	Titus 2:11-14, God shows grace; control self as we wait for the day.	Luke 2:1-20, birth of Jesus, shepherds and angels.
Christmas Day	Isaiah 52:7-10, the beauty of the messenger of peace.	98	Hebrews 1:1-4 (5-12), God who spoke now speaks through Son.	John 1:1-4, Word from beginning has become flesh.
First Sunday after Christmas	1 Samuel 2:18-20, 26, the child Samuel lives in temple.	148	Colossians 3:12-17, the life of virtue.	Luke 2:41-52, the boy Jesus in the temple.
New Year's Eve/Day	Ecclesiastes 3:1-13, there is a time for everything.	8	Revelation 3:1-12, the New Heaven and the New Earth; Good News in Jesus.	Matthew 25:31-46, final judgment: the sheep and the goats.
Second Sunday after Christmas	Jeremiah 31:7-14, the joyful return of the exiles.	147:12-20	Ephesians 1:3-14, spiritual blessings in Christ.	John 1:1-9, 10-18, the Word became flesh.
Epiphany	Isaiah 60:1-6, glory of God's people; all will come to them.	72:1-7, 10-14	Ephesians 3:1-12, God's plan for Gentiles shown to Paul.	Matthew 2:1-12, the visitors from the East.

Revised Common Lectionary, descriptions by H. A. Tillinghast

188 • TRADITIONAL OPENING PRAYERS FOR CHRISTMAS WORSHIP

Many of the following texts date to the earliest recorded years of the history of the church. Each of the prayers express the basic themes of Christmas worship. Adapt the prayers below to local style and custom.

The Nativity of our Lord: Christmas Eve or Day (Dec. 24–25)

O God, you make us glad by the yearly festival of the birth of your only Son Jesus Christ: Grant that we, who joyfully receive him as our Redeemer, may with sure confidence behold him when he comes to be our Judge; who lives and reigns with you and the Holy Spirit, one God, now and forever. Amen.

or

O God, you have caused this holy night to shine with the brightness of the true Light: Grant that we, who have known the mystery of that Light on earth, may also enjoy him perfectly in heaven; where with you and the Holy Spirit he lives and reigns, one God, in glory everlasting. Amen.

or this

Almighty God, you have given your only-begotten Son to take our nature upon him, and to be born [this day] of a pure virgin: Grant that we, who have been born again and made your children by adoption and grace, may daily be renewed by your Holy Spirit; through our Lord Jesus Christ, to whom with you and the same Spirit be honor and glory, now and forever. Amen.

First Sunday after Christmas Day (Dec. 26–30)

Almighty God, you have poured upon us the new light of your incarnate Word: Grant that this light, enkindled in our hearts, may shine forth in our lives; through Jesus Christ our Lord, who lives and reigns with you, in the unity of the Holy Spirit, one God, now and forever. Amen.

Second Sunday after Christmas Day (Dec. 31–Jan. 5, if not celebrated as Epiphany)

O God, who wonderfully created, and yet more wonderfully restored, the dignity of human nature: Grant that we may share the divine life of him who humbled himself to share our humanity, your Son Jesus Christ; who lives and reigns with

Crib or Crèche. The symbol of the simple crib with the chi rho *(abbreviation for Christ) is a popular symbol of Christmas.*

you, in the unity of the Holy Spirit, one God, for ever and ever. Amen.

Epiphany (Jan. 6 or the last Sunday preceding Jan. 6)
(The Last Day of the Christmas cycle/season)

O God, by the leading of a star you manifested your only Son to the peoples of the earth: Lead us, who know you now by faith, to your presence, where we may see your glory face to face; though Jesus Christ our Lord, who lives and reigns with you and the Holy Spirit, one God, now and for ever. Amen.

Selections from *The Book of Common Prayer*

Each of these prayers follow the same pattern. This is called a "collect" prayer. Originally, these brief, pointed prayers were used to end a time of common prayer. Thus, they "collected" the prayers of the people together in a single unified prayer before the time of prayer would end. Throughout the history of the church, this form has been used in a variety of places in liturgical celebration. Observe the following form for the preparation of your own "collect" prayer:

a. Ascription of Praise

b. Description of a Characteristic of God
c. The Petition
d. A Closing Ascription of Praise

See the example below:

FORM	PRAYER
Ascription to God	O God of light;
Description of a Characteristic of God	You who dispel the darkness in the birth of your Son
The Invocation	May the light of your Son who has been birthed into history, be poured forth in our hearts and may the darkness of the world be pierced by the glory of his birth.
The Closing Ascription of Praise	That we may glorify and praise you through your Son Jesus Christ who lives and reigns with you and the Holy Spirit. Amen.

Robert Webber

189 • PRAYERS FOR CHRISTMAS WORSHIP

The following prayers are based on the language of appropriate Scripture readings for the Christmas season. They can be used as printed or can serve as models for other prayers. Consult the commentary after each prayer for specific Scripture references and related information.

—— Invocations or Opening Prayers ——

Be near us Lord Jesus we ask you to stay, close by us forever and love us we pray. Immanuel, we invite you to draw near and dwell with us. Surround and sustain us with your tender caring presence that what we say and do in worship might prepare us to live forever with you in heaven. In Jesus' powerful name we pray. Amen!

Commentary: The first sentence is directly taken from the third stanza of the popular carol, "Away in the Manger." The remainder of this prayer is a paraphrase of the rest of the third stanza. The bib-

lical foundation for these ideas are in Matthew 1:21-23. This prayer illustrates the great value of reading and reflecting on hymns as a source for enriching and expanding our language for worship.

Come Eternal Lord, and open our eyes to Jesus, your Bright Morning Star, that together with your Holy Spirit the lingering shadows of darkness might be transformed into your renewing Light. Awaken us to your presence and ever faithful nearness. In Jesus' name. Amen!

Commentary: Revelation 22:16 refers to Christ as the Bright Morning Star. This aspect of Jesus' ministry is further pictured in the sixth stanza of the hymn "O Come, O Come, Emmanuel."

—— Prayer of Confession and —— Words of Assurance

PRAYER OF CONFESSION

Dear Heavenly Father, we sing with great enthusiasm, "Joy to the world, the Lord has come, let earth receive her King." Yet as we review the true desires of our hearts we would confess that we are more prone to seek the gifts and benefits that Christ can grant than actually receive him deep within our lives. There are times when we are frightened by what might happen if we truly took Jesus seriously and resolved to invite him into all the diverse dimensions of our lives. Lord, have mercy upon us and cleanse us. Forgive the distorted images we hold of Christ which prevent us from living with him with the same trust and obedience as Joseph and Mary. Renew your sustaining Spirit within us that we might truly know and live in your joy... [opportunity for silent confession] ...through Jesus' redeeming name. Amen!

WORDS OF ASSURANCE

LEADER:	(reads Luke 2:10)
PEOPLE:	**(read Luke 2:11)**
ALL:	**(read Romans 10:9)**

RESPONSE

As an act of praise and gratitude for God's redeeming gift of Jesus the singing of stanza three of "Good Christian Friends, Rejoice" (Jesus Christ was born to save!) is most appropriate here.

Commentary: The unifying theme of this prayer has been taken from the popular carol "Joy to the World," which in turn has been inspired by Psalm 98. Also at work within this prayer is the often subtle distinction between wanting to receive Jesus' benefits on our own terms and not the actual gift of Christ. This awareness reflects Jesus' rebuke of the Pharisees who were more interested in externals (see Mark 7:6-7; cf. Isa. 29:13).

Prayer for Illumination

Mighty God, the shepherds of old were full of your praises that all they had heard and seen was mirrored by what they had been told. Move amongst us now with your Holy Spirit that we too might hear and experience the wonder and joy of the living Word as we seek to welcome the written Word into our lives. In Jesus' name. Amen!

Commentary: The shepherd's response of meeting Jesus (Luke 2:20) is repeated and elaborated to become our request to see and know Christ through the reading and preaching of the Scriptures.

Offertory Prayer

Gracious Lord, in this season of abundance may we not lose sight of your perfect Gift amidst all our many gifts. Correct our vision that we might not only receive your Good News, but respond with gratitude in sharing Christ with others. Accept the gifts we now offer. May your Spirit enlarge and multiply their use to those both near and far. In Jesus' precious name. Amen!

Commentary: This prayer borrows its images from both 2 Corinthians 9:15 and Luke 2:20. It further captures the evangelistic theme that the shepherds were the first human messengers to share the Good News with others. It reminds us that our offering to God includes not only what we place in the collection plate, but also how we live our daily lives.

Pastoral Prayer

Most Gracious and Loving God, our hearts are bursting with the good news of great joy that has come to us. We too join the saints of old in participating in the drama of Christ's birth. May we come to know his name and taste his joy more fully. Therefore, with Mary we sing out the praise of our soul. While we are only one small group of people amidst the huge cosmos of Creation you have remembered us. We are grateful for the blessings that you have poured into our souls. Truly you delight in us. We pause in silence as we speak from the depth of our hearts recounting the great things you have done for us.

Great God, the very act of praising you enlarges our perception. Our remembrance of your mighty acts reminds us that you often surprise us by your ways. We tend to be impressed with the prominent and powerful. Yet you tumble the proud and arrogant and lift up the humble. You fill the hungry with the needed resources to sustain them while chasing away the self-sufficient empty handed. May we remember how you have displayed your special favor upon the poor and needy. May we not close our hearts to those who are despised, rejected, and left without the proper trappings of society. Jesus calls to mind the same truth when he reminds us that as we serve, care, bind up, and love the least of our society we are actually ministering unto him.

Faithful God, you have kept your promises to us over the many centuries of time. In your calling of us to be your people you challenge us to proclaim by our lips and lives the same truths that each succeeding generation may also drink from the wells of your abundant grace and truth. In caring and providing for the children and youth of this congregation and community may we not shut our hearts to those who are older in years. Awaken the timeless truth of Christ within us that we might be aware of peoples of all ages and places. This we ask humbly ask in the strong and tender name of Jesus Christ our Lord. Amen!

Commentary: Mary's song, recorded in Luke 1:46-55, establishes the design for this prayer. This prayer has not exhausted all the images present in the Magnificat but illustrates how verses 46-50 pertain to the element of praise and verses 51-55 relate to the petitions and concerns for others.

Tom Schwanda

190 • A CREED FOR CHRISTMAS WORSHIP

During the Christmas season, use the Nicene Creed, the Apostles' Creed, or the following creed, adapted from Philippians 2:5-11.

I believe the Word was in the form of God
   and did not count equality with God
   a thing to be grasped.
He emptied himself,
   took the form of a servant,
   and was born in our own likeness.
I believe he humbled himself
   and became obedient unto death.
I believe God has highly exalted him
   and bestowed on him the name
   which is above every name.
I believe that at the name of Jesus
   every knee shall bow, every knee
   in heaven and on earth and under the
      earth.
I believe that every tongue will confess
   that Jesus Christ is Lord
   to the glory of God the Father. Amen!

191 ✦ A DRAMATIC READING FOR CHRISTMAS

The following reading is based on various Scripture readings for the Christmas season.

READER 1: The world was filled with the darkness of sin and desperately needed a savior. God promised such a deliverer through the prophets.

READER 2: Isaiah wrote: "The people walking in darkness have seen a great light; on those living in the land of the shadow of death a light has dawned" (Isa. 9:2).

READER 3: This light came to us through Jesus Christ. He was born to be the light for our darkness.

READER 4: Concerning Jesus, the apostle John said: "In Him was life, and that life was the light of men" (John 1:4).

READER 2: For the most part, people did not recognize this light. Often Jesus spoke of His mission.

READER 4: At one point He said, "I am the light of the world. Whoever follows me will never walk in darkness, but will have the light of life" (John 8:12).

READER 1: God does not desire that humans stay in the darkness that they created for themself. At Christmas we can remember this marvelous gift of deliverance.

READER 3: Jesus said, "I have come into the world as a light, so that no one who believes in me should stay in darkness" (John 12:46).

READER 4: The light brought to the world through Christ continues to shine. His Spirit dwells in us, sending light to the world.

READER 3: For God, who said, "Let light shine out of darkness," made his light shine in our heart to give us the light of the knowledge of the glory of God in the face of Christ (2 Cor. 4:6).

READER 2: His light shines through His church, each part of the body can be a beacon of love to a world that still does not know the light has come.

READER 1: Jesus spoke these words: "You are the light of the world . . . let your light so shine before men, that they may see your good works and glorify your Father who is in heaven" (Matt. 5:14a, 16, RSV).

READER 5: The light of Christ will shine for eternity. We carry His light now and will live forever in its warmth. The apostle John records this vision: "Then I saw a new heaven and a new earth. . . . I saw the Holy City, the new Jerusalem, coming down out of heaven from God. . . . I did not see a temple in the city, because the Lord God Almighty and the Lamb are its temple. The city does not need the sun or the moon to shine on it, for the glory of God gives it light, and the Lamb is its lamp. The nations will walk by its light, and the kings of the earth will bring their splendor into it" (Rev. 21:1-2a, 22-24).

Randolph W. Sly

192 ✦ LITANY FOR CHRISTMAS SUNDAY

The reading below may be read at the beginning of worship after the gathering and before the Hymn of Entrance.

LEADER: Christmas, a day of celebration . . . a day of remembrance. God the Son became flesh and came to dwell among humans.

PEOPLE: **Help me, Lord, to remember him this coming Christmas Day. Amidst the presents and people, let me see Him.**

LEADER: His coming was prophesied in the Old Testament. For centuries humankind had been eagerly awaiting the Messiah's arrival. They prayed for it and talked about it endlessly. They anticipated this glorious day as the beginning of their deliverance.

PEOPLE: **Keep us from being disillusioned this Christmas. We sing carols, decorate trees, shop for gifts, and eagerly await for the day to arrive. It finally comes, only to be over too soon. Open our eyes, Lord, to a deeper understanding of the Advent. May we remember that the coming of the Christ child was not the end but the beginning. To celebrate his coming is to look forward to his work in the world.**

LEADER: His birth took place in a stable, yet he was born a King. He was wrapped in common cloth, yet acclaimed as one uncommonly born. He was fragile, weak, a typically dependent baby; yet he was the Son of God.

PEOPLE: **Jesus is the Christ of Christmas and the cross. His greatest gift was his own life, which he willingly laid down on the cross. With each bow and box, ribbon and wrapping, may we think of this greatest gift and be thankful. His common birth is a sign of our common heritage in him. For there is no one too great or too lowly that they cannot be touched by the love of God found in him. He has become the meeting point for all humankind.**

LEADER: Heaven touched earth in one great angelic chorus. The rejoicing of the heavenly host was displayed before some shepherds near the city. The Lord himself sent forth the word that His Son had been born.

PEOPLE: **Those who cared for the temple sheep were the first to see the true Lamb of God. They came and found**

him just as they were told. Heavenly Father, thank You that we have found Him, too, just as you said we would. That is why we are here together as Christ's church.

LEADER: Let us make a place for him this Christmas. He is not to be a casual observer of the festivities. He is the guest of honor! Let us give him the highest place! Let us ascribe all glory due his name!

PEOPLE: **For He, who was born of a virgin, is truly God the Son. He became fully human that his death might fully pay for sin. He rose from the dead and today we declare that the Christ of Christmas ascended to the right hand of God. He rules over his church. He sent the Spirit to baptize our hearts, and one day every knee shall bow and every tongue confess that he is Lord! To each other we say "Merry Christmas!" To him we say, "Glory to God in the highest! For you have come and set us free."**

Randolph W. Sly

193 ✦ THE BLESSING OF THE CRÈCHE

In many churches it is a tradition to bless the crèche during the opening of the Christmas service. A person in the processional may carry a figure representing the Christ child to the crèche and lay the child in the crèche as a symbol of the birth of Christ. Then, the following may be said:

The minister and others standing before the crèche may say:

MINISTER: The Virgin will be with child, and will give birth to a son.

PEOPLE: **And they will call him Immanuel, God with us.**

MINISTER: The Word became flesh and lived for a while among us.

PEOPLE: **And we have seen his glory.**

MINISTER: The Lord be with you.

PEOPLE: **And also with you.**

MINISTER: Almighty God, you have created and brought into being all that is; and when we your creatures fell away from you, you became one of us, born in a manger in the city of Bethlehem. Grant that as he humbled himself and was made in the likeness of man that we may find mercy in him, be clothed with his divinity and share in his kingdom; to the glory of his name, who lives and reigns forever and ever.

PEOPLE: **Amen.**

Robert E. Webber

194 ◆ AN ENTRANCE RITE FOR EPIPHANY

Emphasize the importance of Epiphany by elaborating the opening of worship with a special dialogue. The litany below will help the congregation realize the significance of the day and will underscore their own need to be a light to the world.

The minister, choir, banner bearer, and others (i.e., children dressed as the three wise men bearing gifts) gather in the back of the sanctuary. The service begins as a leader from the congregation leads the people in the first question of the Litany for Epiphany.

PEOPLE: **Why do we celebrate Epiphany today?**

LEADER: We celebrate the visit of the wise men who symbolize that God's salvation is available to all persons, not just the Jews.

PEOPLE: **Why is Epiphany known as the season of light?**

LEADER: Remember the words of the prophet: "The people who walked in darkness have seen a great light; those who dwelt in a land of deep darkness, on them light has shined" (Isa. 9:2, RSV).

PEOPLE: **We have heard that Jesus said, "I am the light of the world; he who follows me will not walk in darkness, but will have the light of life" (John 8:12, RSV).**

LEADER: "This is the message we have heard from him and proclaim to you, that God is light and in him is no darkness at all" (1 John 1:5, RSV).

PEOPLE: **"Come let us walk in the light of the Lord" (Isa. 2:5, RSV).**

LEADER: "You are the light of the world...let your light so shine before men, that they may see your good works, and give glory to your Father, who is in heaven" (Matt. 5:14-16, RSV).

PEOPLE: **May our lives lead people to God the way the star led the wise men to Jesus.**

LEADER: "Arise, shine; for your light has come, and the glory of the Lord has risen upon you (Isa. 60:1, RSV).

Christ Memorial Church, Holland, Michigan

195 ◆ PRAYERS FOR EPIPHANY

The following scripturally based prayers capture the power images associated with worship on Epiphany. Adapt to local need or custom.

Prayers of Invocation or Opening Prayers

Eternal Lord, as we gather in worship may we focus more fully on your presence. Help us to listen to your Spirit so we too can hear your gracious words of welcome, "Come, follow me, the kingdom of God is near." Open our hearts and enliven our faith that we might follow you in our worship and witness now and every day this week. In Jesus' strong and tender name. Amen!

Commentary: Epiphany is the season that reveals the fullness of Jesus Christ who comes to make known God. The words of Mark 1:15, 17 provide the language which invites us in our worship to become receptive to this divine manifestation.

Mighty God, open once more the heavens and send forth your renewing Holy Spirit. Speak to us this day so that we might hear and respond in joy as we worship your Son Jesus Christ. Baptize us with your delight that we might know that we belong to you. In Jesus' precious name. Amen.

Commentary: This prayer's imagery is drawn from Jesus' baptism (Matt. 3:16-17), a common theme for Epiphany. Further, this prayer acknowledges at the beginning of worship the crucial truth that God delights and loves us as sons and daughters.

Prayers of Confession

CONFESSION

Mighty King of Glory, we come before you in the good name of Jesus. Gather us in your grace and mercy so that we might speak with integrity and truth. We humbly confess that we are not the people we desire to be. Nor are we the people you desire to make us. Forgive us when we limit you by our narrow and distorted vision. Too often we are prone to become fascinated with the spectacular and lose sight of the commitments that fill each day. In our efforts to produce and prolong mountain top thrills we are often quick to dismiss the ordinary responsibilities that summon our faithfulness. O God, cleanse our hearts, forgive our sins, and transfigure our perceptions that we might see and follow Jesus wherever he leads. Through Christ alone we are restored and made right with you and others . . . [opportunity for silent confession] . . . This we pray in Jesus Christ, who is your Son and our Savior. Amen.

WORDS OF ASSURANCE

LEADER:	(reads Luke 9:35b; 5:20b)
PEOPLE:	**(read John 1:29b)**
ALL:	**(read 1 John 1:7)**

The stirring story of Jesus' transfiguration (Luke 9:28-36, cf. Matt. 17:1-13; Mark 9:2-13) invites us to join the early disciples to locate ourselves amidst similar distorted perceptions. The initial Scripture from the words of assurance (taken from the Transfiguration narrative) indicates how one portion of Scripture can provide a connection between the various components of the order of worship.

CONFESSION

Almighty and Gracious God, on this Epiphany we are confronted once again with the Jesus Christ, the light of the world. We pause amidst all our words and singing to be quiet before you.

(The worship leader then directs the congregation with an example, such as the one provided here.)

Dear people of God, use this silence to reflect upon and review your relationship with God. Perhaps today you sense God very closely, if so cel-ebrate and praise God for this friendship. Or perhaps today you realize that you are quite distant from God, if so, consider with the Holy Spirit's help, what has caused this separation and what steps you can take to renew your communion with God. Then again some of us today may be confused and not have any idea where we are with God, if so invite God to enlighten you and help you know how much God truly delights in you: (silent reflection)

Words of Assurance (unison): Romans 6:5, 11; 8:1

Words of Assurance (unison): Isaiah 44:21-22; 43:25

Prayer for Illumination

Holy Father, fling open the shutters of our souls with your Holy Spirit so the radiance of your Scriptures may shine into our hearts with the illuminating knowledge of your glory and Christ's presence. Hear us and guide us as we pray in Jesus' powerful name. Amen!

Commentary: The words of 2 Corinthians 4:6 provide rich pictorial language for seeking God's guidance as the Scriptures are read and expounded.

Offertory Prayer

Loving God, you have blessed us with the eternal gift of your Son Jesus Christ. Like the wise men of old, create within us the joy of giving, as we humbly offer the treasures of our lives so Christ might be truly honored and we might know his delight deep within our souls. In Jesus' name. Amen!

Commentary: The inspiration for this prayer is drawn from the example of the magi (Matt. 2:11). Further this passage illustrates that the wise men offered their gifts after they had met Jesus. If it is not your regular practice to receive the offering after the sermon, then perhaps you may wish to alter the sequence in keeping with this Scripture. Matthew's passage reminds us that our giving is a response of gratitude for being in Christ's presence not an appeal or effort to bargain our way to God.

Most gracious and generous God, you manifested your great love in the coming of Jesus Christ. As his life revealed your grace and truth may the presentation of our tithes and offerings display our best to you, ever faithful Lord. Expand our hearts and enlarge our giving that others may discover the fullness of your abundance. For the sake of Christ and his kingdom we pray. Amen

Commentary: The self-offering of God in Christ which encourages our responsive giving is built around the imagery of John 1:14, 16-18.

─────── Pastoral Prayers ───────

Eternal Lord and God, it is our joyful privilege to join with you in prayer. Scripture reminds us that Jesus Christ was no stranger to celebration. He accepted the invitation to be part of the wedding feast of Cana in Galilee. Accept also our prayers of praise and adoration which we offer to you, gracious and loving God. We are grateful that you are a God who takes interest in the daily delight and distress of our lives. We rejoice that the same transforming power that changed water into wine is present to work wonders in our lives and those of the world. We marvel at the mystery of Christ's presence and power which reveals what has been hidden from those who are too busy to observe your promises.

Where hardness of heart or dullness of spirit lingers, soften us with your Holy Spirit. Awaken our memories that we might recall the mighty acts of Christ on our behalf. May the reminder of his glory encourage our faith and dependence upon you, mighty God. Stretch our imaginations that we might see with the eyes of Jesus those who are in need.

Tender and compassionate Lord, be pleased to be present with those who are sick or recovering from illness. In particular we ask that you refresh . . . with the awareness of your presence and promises.

We also name . . . as shut ins or those unable to be with us in worship today.

Come alongside any who have tasted the grief or loss of family or friends. . . . Be near also to those who have lost jobs or whose marriages are unraveling or for those struggling in troubled relationships with their partners, children, or parents. May we further recall the needs of our community and country. We remember those who serve in positions of leadership and power. May they exercise their responsibilities with wisdom and compas-

sion that reflects that of Christ. Amidst the global community in which we live, make us sensitive to the needs of people harmed by famine, tension, war, and disputes that occupy the headlines of our media. Melt any residual resistance lingering within us which causes us to neglect these and other needs that would occupy the compassion and concern of Christ.

Lord, beyond these spoken prayers, be attentive to hear us in this silence as we offer any praises and petitions to you from our hearts . . . [opportunity for silent prayer]

Lord God, we submit and release all these prayers to you in the powerful and transforming name of Christ our Lord. Amen!

Commentary: Jesus' participation in the wedding of Cana (John 2:1-11) furnishes us with a rich collection of imagery and themes that can inspire our praying. A common thread which laces this prayer is that Epiphany is a season in which Jesus Christ comes to reveal that which is hidden and manifest the power and character of God.

God of splendor and majesty, you surprise us again and again with your goodness and grace. Into the deep shadows and suffocating darkness of our world you have sent Jesus Christ as the light of the world. His liberating light redeems and frees us from that which imprisons us. Most excellent Lord, shine again on us with this radiance of Christ. Set us ablaze with your glory that others might know that we have been in your renewing presence. We pause in silence to acknowledge and speak the praises of our hearts for your promises and provisions to us. . . .

Guiding Lord, our Scripture reminds us of our need to follow Christ so we might daily be in his light rather than lost in the temptations of the darkness. Create a yearning within us as individuals and as a church so that we might delight in your will and desire to follow your ways. Grant us this awareness whether we are at school, at work, at home, or in the community. Increase our consistency that our light might not flicker or fade but burn brightly for others to see.

Merciful God, we seek your healing light to shine upon those who are facing surgery . . . or awaiting test results . . . or whose healing process is slower than expected. . . . Overcome any fears of darkness with the laser light of Christ's presence and promises. Dispel the darkness for those who may doubt and wrestle with the hard questions of life.

Gracious Lord, we cannot escape the responsibilities that are ours because we know your liberating light. Each day we are surrounded by many people who struggle and stumble in the darkness. May we not selfishly hoard the light but to willingly reflect it to others. May our speech and actions mirror your glory as we repeat Christ's wonderful story. Arouse our courage and revive our boldness that our efforts of ministry might be multiplied to spread the good name of Jesus to others. We also remember our missionaries scattered about the globe who serve as an extension of this congregation. Grant them the encouragement and support they need for the challenges that they face. We especially remember . . . at this time. Radiant Lord, we lift also the colleges, Bible schools, training programs, and seminaries which prepare future leaders for the church. May the various means of media be harnessed for your glory to faithfully communicate this redeeming light. Hear us, O God, as we listen in silence for your voice or present any additional concerns. . . . We offer these prayers only in the strong and compassionate name of Jesus, the light of the world. Amen!

Commentary: This prayer weaves together a number of passages that collect the common image of light. The major themes are derived from John 8:12; 2 Corinthians 4:6; and Ephesians 5:8. There are also echoes of Graham Kendrick's song, "Lord, the Light of Your Love" ("Shine, Jesus, Shine") that enhance and add color to this prayer.

Tom Schwanda

196 ✦ PRAYERS OF THANKSGIVING FOR CHRISTMAS AND EPIPHANY EUCHARIST

———— Prayer of Thanksgiving for ———— Christmas Eucharist

Prayer of Thanksgiving for Epiphany Eucharist

MINISTER: The Lord be with you.
PEOPLE: **And also with you.**
MINISTER: Lift up your hearts.

PEOPLE: **We lift them to the Lord.**
MINISTER: Let us give thanks to the Lord our God.
PEOPLE: **It is right to give our thanks and praise.**
MINISTER: It is truly right and our greatest joy
to give you thanks and praise,
O holy God, creator and ruler of the universe.
You created light out of darkness
and brought forth life on the earth.
You formed us in your image
and called us to love and serve you.
When we were unfaithful
and turned from your ways,
you did not forsake us,
your love remained steadfast.
You delivered us from captivity,
made covenant to be our sovereign God,
and sent prophets to call us back to your way.

In the fullness of time
you sent your only Son Jesus Christ
to be our Savior.
In him, your Word, dwelling with you
from all eternity,
became flesh and dwelt among us,
full of grace and truth,
and we beheld your glory,
Immanuel!

Therefore we praise you,
joining our voices with the celestial choirs
and with all the faithful of every time and place,
who forever sing to the glory of your name:

(The people may sing or say:)

Holy, holy, holy Lord, God of power and might,
heaven and earth are full of your glory.
Hosanna in the highest.

Blessed is he who comes in the name of the Lord.
Hosanna in the highest.

(The minister continues:)

You are holy, O God of majesty,

and blessed is Jesus Christ, your Son,
    our Lord.
Born in humility,
he came to rule over all.
Helpless as an infant,
he showed the power of your love.
Poor in things of the world,
he brought the wealth of your grace.
Rejected by many,
he welcomed all who sought him.
In his dying and rising,
you gave birth to your church,
delivered us from slavery to sin and
    death,
and made with us a new covenant by
    water and the Spirit.

(If they have not already been said, the words
of institution may be said here, or in relation
to the breaking of the bread.)

MINISTER: We give you thanks that the Lord
    Jesus,
on the night before he died,
took bread,
and after giving thanks to you,
he broke it, and gave it to his disciples,
    saying:
Take, eat.
This is my body, given for you.
Do this in remembrance of me.

In the same way he took the cup,
    saying:
This cup is the new covenant sealed
    in my blood,
shed for you for the forgiveness of
    sins.
Whenever you drink it,
do this in remembrance of me.

Remembering your gracious acts in
    Jesus Christ,
we take from your Creation this bread
    and this wine
and joyfully celebrate his dying and
    rising
as we await the day of his coming.
With thanksgiving we offer our very
    selves to you
to be a living and holy sacrifice,
dedicated to your service.

(The people may sing or say one of the following:)

1

MINISTER: Great is the mystery of faith:
PEOPLE: **Christ has died,**
    Christ is risen,
    Christ will come again.

2

MINISTER: Praise to you, Lord Jesus:
PEOPLE: **Dying you destroyed our death,**
    rising you restored our life.
    Lord Jesus, come in glory.

3

MINISTER: According to his commandment:
PEOPLE: **We remember his death,**
    we proclaim his resurrection
    we await his coming in glory.

4

MINISTER: Christ is the bread of life:
PEOPLE: **When we eat this bread and drink**
    this cup,
    we proclaim your death, Lord Jesus,
    until you come in glory.

(The minister continues:)

Gracious God,
pour out your Holy Spirit upon us
and upon these your gifts of bread
    and wine,
that the bread we break
and the cup we bless
may be the communion of the body
    and blood of Christ.
By your Spirit make us one with
    Christ,
that we may be one with all who share
    this feast,
united in ministry in every place.
As this bread is Christ's body for us,
send us out to be the body of Christ
    in the world.

(Intercessions for the church and the world may
be included here.)

Empower us by your Spirit, O God,
to be Christ's presence in the world
even as Jesus was God-with-us.
Give us courage
to speak his truth,

to seek his justice,
and to love with his love.
Keep us faithful in your service
until Christ comes in final victory
and we shall feast with all your saints
in the joy of your eternal realm.

Through Christ, with Christ, in Christ,
in the unity of the Holy Spirit,
all glory and honor are yours, almighty
    God,
now and forever.

PEOPLE: **Amen.**

Prayer of Thanksgiving for Epiphany Eucharist

MINISTER: The Lord be with you.
PEOPLE: **And also with you.**
MINISTER: Lift up your hearts.
PEOPLE: **We lift them to the Lord.**
MINISTER: Let us give thanks to the Lord our
    God.
PEOPLE: **It is right to give our thanks and
    praise.**
MINISTER: It is truly right and our greatest joy
    to give you thanks and praise,
    God of majesty and splendor.
    By your power you created all that is,
    making a universe out of chaos,
    and ruling over all things in love.
    Throughout the ages you called your
        people
    to love and serve you,
    and to be your light among the nations.
    When we failed you,
    you did not fail us
    and sent prophets to call us back to
        your ways.

    We praise you that in the fullness of
        time,
    you revealed your love
    by sending your Son Jesus
    to be the Light of the world.
    He came to heal our brokenness
    and to set before us the ways of
        justice and peace.

    Therefore we praise you,
    joining our voices with angels and
        archangels

    and with all the faithful of every time
        and place,
    who forever sing to the glory of your
        name:

(The people may sing or say:)

**Holy, holy, holy Lord, God of power
    and might,
heaven and earth are full of your
    glory.
Hosanna in the highest.
Blessed is he who comes in the
    name of the Lord.
Hosanna in the highest.**

(The minister continues:)

You are holy, O God of majesty,
and blessed is Jesus Christ your Son,
    our Lord.
He was born to dwell among us,
full of grace and truth;
in him we have seen your glory.
Baptized by John in the Jordan,
he lived for you,
spoke your truth,
showed your love,
and gave himself for others.
In his death on the cross, he over-
    came death.
Rising from the tomb, he raised us to
    eternal life,
and made with us a new covenant
by water and the Spirit.

(If they have not already been said, the words
of institution may be said here, or in relation
to the breaking of the bread.)

MINISTER: We give you thanks that the Lord
    Jesus,
    on the night before he died,
    took bread,
    and after giving thanks to you,
    he broke it, and gave it to his dis-
        ciples, saying:
    Take, eat.
    This is my body, given for you.
    Do this in remembrance of me.

    In the same way he took the cup,
        saying:
    This cup is the new covenant sealed

in my blood,
shed for you for the forgiveness of sins.
Whenever you drink it,
do this in remembrance of me.

Remembering your gracious acts in
Jesus Christ,
we take from your creation this bread
and this wine
and joyfully celebrate his dying and
rising
as we await the day of his coming.
With thanksgiving we offer our very
selves to you
to be a living and holy sacrifice,
dedicated to your service.

(The people may sing or say one of the following:)

1

MINISTER: Great is the mystery of faith:
PEOPLE: **Christ has died,**
Christ is risen,
Christ will come again.

2

MINISTER: Praise to you, Lord Jesus:
PEOPLE: **Dying you destroyed our death,**
rising you restored our life.
Lord Jesus, come in glory.

3

MINISTER: According to his commandment:
PEOPLE: **We remember his death,**
we proclaim his resurrection,
we await his coming in glory.

4

MINISTER: Christ is the bread of life:
PEOPLE: **When we eat this bread and drink**
this cup,
we proclaim your death, Lord Jesus,
until you come in glory.

(The minister continues:)

Gracious God,
pour out your Holy Spirit on us
and upon these your gifts of bread
and wine,
that the bread we break
and the cup we bless
may be the communion of the body
and blood of Christ.

By your Spirit make us one with
Christ,
that we may be one with all who share
this feast,
united in ministry in every place.
As this bread is Christ's body for us,
send us out to be the body of Christ
in the world.

(Intercessions for the church and the world may
be included here.)

Illumine our hearts, O God,
with the radiance of Christ's presence,
that our lives may show forth his love
in this weary world.
Teach us to befriend the lost,
to serve the poor,
to reconcile our enemies,
and to love our neighbors.
Keep us faithful in your service
until Christ comes in final victory
and we shall feast with all your saints
in the joy of your eternal realm.

Through Christ, with Christ, in Christ,
in the unity of the Holy Spirit,
all glory and honor are yours, almighty
God,
now and forever.
PEOPLE: **Amen.**

Book of Common Worship[14]

197 ✦ BLESSINGS FOR CHRISTMAS AND EPIPHANY WORSHIP

The following blessings are appropriate for use during the season of Christmas and Epiphany.

May Almighty God, who sent his Son to take our nature upon him, bless you in this holy season, scatter the darkness of sin, and brighten your heart with the light of his holiness. Amen.

May God, who sent his angels to proclaim the glad news of the Savior's birth, fill you with joy, and make you heralds of the gospel. Amen.

May God, who in the Word made flesh joined heaven to earth and earth to heaven, give you his peace and favor. Amen.

May Christ, who by his incarnation gathered into one things earthly and heavenly, fill you with his joy and peace; and the blessing of God Almighty, the Father, the Son, and the Holy Spirit, be among you, and remain with you always. Amen.

May Almighty God, who led the magi by the shining of a star to find the Christ, the Light from Light, lead you also, in your pilgrimage, to find the Lord. Amen.

Book of Occasional Services[15]

NINE

The Arts from Christmas to Epiphany

Christmas is a time pageantry, for drama, musicals, special dramatic services, and joyous festivity. Consequently there is more worship material available for the Christmas season than any other season of the church year.

The arts may be used effectively as servants of the Christmas text in the music of the Entrance, in dramatic readings and presentations of Scripture, in sermons, in processions and recessions, and in special services such as Christmas Eve or Epiphany. Some practical suggestions are made in this chapter.

198 ✦ THE USE OF THE ARTS IN CHRISTMAS WORSHIP

The arts during Christmas may symbolize the Incarnation and thus speaks in a profound way to the meaning of "God with us." Adapt the suggestions below to local customs.

1. The greening of the church done for Advent remains through the Christmas season.

2. The Advent wreath remains hung during Christmas with all five candles lit. Adorn the wreath with a Christmas bow and change all the candles to white.

3. Dramatize the lighting of the five candles as a symbol of the presence of Christ at the beginning of the service by using the Service of the Light for the Acts of Entrance.

4. Make both the processional and the recessional expressions of great joy with persons bearing banners, crosses, incense, and with dancers who express the great joy of Christmas.

5. Proclaim one of the Scripture readings with drama, storytelling, or creative antiphonal reading.

6. For Christmas Eve, incorporate the blessing of the crèche.

199 ✦ THE WORSHIP ENVIRONMENT AT CHRISTMAS

Will the parish Christmas decorations show good liturgical sense? Here are some guidelines for planning the worship environment for the Christmas season.

Decorations should not be limited to the area around the altar, ambo (pulpit), and chair. To do so creates a stage setting. Keep this area free from distraction by limiting the floral arrangements around the altar and by placing crèche figures elsewhere. Hackneyed decorations, such as masses of poinsettias or wreaths hung on every pillar, though beautiful in themselves, can have a numbing effect. Such overkill also obscures what these decorations signify.

First determine how you will embellish the assembly area, especially in the space over everyone's heads. Then determine where more "intimate," deeply traditional elements will be put—an apple-hung fir tree, a large suspended globe of intersecting wreaths, a place for the icons of the Christmastime feasts, the Bethlehem scene. These things are best located where they can be visited and contemplated before or after worship—near the baptistery or the gathering area or a shrine.

The most serious problem facing all parish ministers in preparing the Christmas season is the schizophrenia of the parish in early January when its church building is clad in red, white, and green but the homes of the parishioners (and the parish school) have already been stripped of their finery. Under such circumstances, worship is a sham. Liturgical ministers can't begin to do their jobs unless they also help the parish live the Christian calendar at home as well as in church.

Wasting money and resources on decorations is certainly offensive. However, equally offensive is the notion that miserliness in worship somehow reflects the gospel. The gospel doesn't demand that we pretend to be poor, but that we break down the barriers between rich and poor. If ethnic customs are any gauge, the poor know the value of flamboyant festival excess. Communal celebration means the pooling of resources to enable those who live in everyday simplicity to share in festival abundance. Fasting begets feasting. Perhaps we shouldn't judge celebrations by the money spent but by the efforts invested by rich and poor alike, all made able to contribute their gifts and talents to one another.

The whole notion of decorating for Christmastime creates unique problems with few easy solutions. For example, at this season, any exceptional effort in liturgy, such as fine music or decorations, has the potential for coming off as just another holiday extravaganza. Yet Christmastime, especially in its full flowering at Epiphany, calls forth the "brightest and best" the parish can muster (although that should never turn into something pompous or triumphalistic).

The evergreens, flowers, or lights—anything you might use to grace Christmas worship—runs the risk of reminding people of a shopping mall, of appearing to glorify money and power. Ironically, the more beautiful and well-executed the Christmas worship environment is, the more it is likely to remind some parishioners of commercial displays. This is an unsolvable dilemma, exacerbated by many Christians' lack of appreciation for their own symbols.

—————— Opening Up Our Images ——————

Environment ministers—those folks entrusted with the care and keeping of the material things of the liturgy—have a responsibility to open up for parishioners the meaning of the images of Christmas. While trees, wreaths, lights, and holiday foods we see everywhere in December have various meanings to many people, we often forget that Christians have found specifically Christian meanings in theses symbols and held them dear for centuries.

If we ask ourselves what a tinseled tree or an evergreen wreath or even a plum pudding has to do with the birth of Jesus in Bethlehem, we're likely to be stymied. But if we ask what these things have to do with the union of heaven and earth, with time dissolving into timelessness, with the everlasting presence of Emmanuel, God with us, then perhaps we will find our answers.

The bright tree is our return to paradise. With greenery and flowers, winter melts into Eden's endless spring. Fruit cakes represent the harvest of justice. Eggnog is the milk and honey of the promised land. Sending cards hastens the ingathering of all people. Mistletoe heralds the coming of the Prince of Peace. Lights strung around our doors welcome all the world to the homecoming of heaven.

Each of these holy signs can offer comfort and joy, and they can also offer tremendous challenge. Like the prophets, like John raging in the wilderness, our Christmas symbols can threaten us to open our doors to those who have no feast, to restore this good earth to the freshness of Eden, to labor long to bring about the reign of justice and compassion. Holy signs are always a two-edged sword.

Even the crèche is not so much a representation of a birth long ago and far away, but the birth that is to be, of the "hopes and fears of all the years," when the poor and the rich will stand side by side with animals and angels, offering themselves each to the other, lost in wonder and praise, the circle of the saints surrounding the Lamb.

Peter Mazar[16]

200 ◆ An Anthology of Songs and Hymns for Christmas and Epiphany

There are more songs and hymns available for Christmas than for any other time in the Christian year. The following are representative selections appropriate for worship. Care should be taken to avoid hymns and songs that do not center on the coming of Christ at Christmas, such as is the case in many secular songs of the season. Article #159 provides a key to the hymnal abbreviations used below.

A Great and Mighty Wonder
John 1:14 [St. Germanus/H. Gauntlet] St. Alphege; see SBAH:18

Ah, Dearest Jesus, Holy Child
Luke 2:14 [M. Luther] Von Himmel Hoch; see HB:173, Chorale

All My Heart Today Rejoices
Matthew 2:10 [P. Gerhardt/J. Ebeling] Warum Sollt Ich; see HFG:203, Chorale

All Praise to Thee, Eternal Lord
Philippians 2:6-7 [M. Luther/T. Tallis] Tallis' Canon; see SBAH:21, one of the great 16th century tunes

Angels From the Realms of Glory
Matthew 2:2 [J. Montgomery/H. Smart] Regent Square; see HFG:190

Angels We Have Heard on High
Luke 2:14 [French Carol] Gloria; see HFG:192

Away in a Manger
Luke 2:7,12 [Anon./J. Murray] Mueller; see HB:157

Away in a Manger
Luke 2:7,12 [Anon./J. Murray] Away in a Manger, see HFG:185

Away in a Manger
Luke 2:7,12 [Anon./W. Kirkpatrick] Cradle Song; see HFG:187

Before the Marvel of This Night
1 John 4:9; Luke 2:14 [J.Vajda/C. Schlak] Marvel; see HS-II:276, includes descant; good choral piece

Behold the Babe
Luke 2:14, 39-40 [R./ Hamilton (1980)] see P-II:62, contemporary

Born in a Manger
Luke 2:7 [R. Hamilton (1980)]see P-II:65; contemporary

Born in the Night, Mary's Child
Luke 2:7 [G. Ainger (1964)] Mary's Child; see WB:312

Born to Die
Matthew 20:28 [R. Hamilton (1980)] see P-II:66, contemporary

Break Forth, O Beauteous Heavenly Light
Ephesians 2:14 [J. Rist/J. Schop] Ermuntre Dich; see HFG:207, chorale

Child in the Manger
Luke 2:12 [M. MacDonald/Gaelic, arr. F. Bock] Bunessan; see HFG:198

Christmas, Awake!
Luke 2:10-11 [J. Byrom/Wainwright] Yorkshire; see SBAH:19

Christmas Bell
Matthew 2:11, Philippians 2:10, Revelation 1:18 [N. Chavers (1979)] see P-II:68

Christmas Brings Joy to Every Heart
Luke 2:13-14 [Ingemann/Weyse] Christmas Brings Joy; see SBAH:46

Christmas Carol, A
Luke 2:4, 8 [M. Joncas (1983)] see GLP:3

Cold December Flies Away
Isaiah 11:1, 10; Luke 2:11-12 [Catalonian, tr. H. Hawhee/Catalonian Carol (1982)] Lo Desembre Congelat; see LBW:53, tune is a variant of a French Noel

Dawning Fair, Morning Wonderful
Luke 2:17 [Traditional] Que Preciosas Manaitas; see AHON:440

First Noel, The
Luke 2:14 [English] The First Noel; see HFG:179

From East to West
Philippians 2:6-7 [Sedullius/Plainsong] A Solis Ortus Cardine; see SBAH:20

From Shepherding of Stars
Luke 2:10 [S. Janzow/R. Hillert (1969)] Shepherding; see LW:71

Gentle Mary Laid Her Child
Luke 2:7 [J. Cook/Carol] Tempus Adest Floridum; see HB:167

Gloria I
Luke 2:14 [Br Robert/J. Berthier (1981)] see TAIZ:7, 3-voices; in Latin

Gloria III
Luke 2:14 [Br Robert/J. Berthier (1969)] see TAIZ:97, Canon a 2, with bassline

Glorious the Day
Matthew 2:6, 24, 29, 31 [F. Green/J. Gardner (1969)] Ilfracombe; see HS-I:77

Glory to God in the Highest
Luke 2:14 [T. Dudley-Smith/R. Proulx] Russwin; see HS-I:72, contemporary, Cathedral style

Go, Tell it on the Mountain
Luke 2:17 [Traditional American] Go Tell it on the Mountain; see HFG:205

God Rest You Merry, Gentlemen
Luke 2:10 [Traditional English] God Rest You Merry; see HB:166

Good Christian Men Rejoice
Matthew 2:10 [Latin/German] IN DULCI JUBILO; see HFG:177

Happy Christmas Comes Once More
Luke 2:14 [N. Grundvig/C. Balle] EMMANUEL; see SBAH:28

Hark! The Herald Angels Sing
Luke 2:13 [C. Wesley/F. Mendelssohn] MENDELSSOHN; see HFG:184

He Whom Shepherds Once Came Praising
Luke 2:8-9; Matthew 2:11 [German, 14th C.] QUEM PASTORES; see LW:54

Hills are Bare at Bethlehem, The
Isaiah 53:2 [R. Scherf/W. Walker] PROSPECT; see LBW:61

I Am So Glad Each Christmas Eve!
Luke 2:9, 13-14 [M. Wexelsen/P. Knudsen] CHRISTMAS EVE; see SBAH:45

I Heard the Bells on Christmas Day
Luke 2:14 [H. Longfellow/J.T., 1910] CHRISTMAS BELLS; see AHON:347

I Heard the Bells on Christmas Day
Luke 2:14 [H. Longfellow/J. Calkin] WALTHAM; see CVH:117

I Know Not How that Bethlehem's Babe
John 14:11 [H. Farrington/E. Harper] SHIRLEYN; see MH:112

I Think of That Star
Isaiah 9:6 [A. Skoog] BETHLEHEM'S STJARNA; see CVH:115

I Wonder as I Wander
Matthew 2:2 [Appalachian Folksong] I WONDER; see HFG:183

In Bethlehem, 'Neath Starlit Skies
Luke 2:7 [G. Stutsman] WAIT'S CAROL; see MH:103

In Bethlehem of Judah
Luke 2:8 [T. Calvin/Traditional Malawi (1976)] TAMKWIMBA KWA JESU; see HS-I:124, based on a Tumbuka Hymn

In the Bleak Mid-Winter
Revelation 20:11 [C. Rosetti/G. Holst] CRANHAM; see MH:104

Infant Holy, Infant Holy
Luke 2:7-9, 13 [Polish] W. ZLOBIE LEZY; see HFG:194

It Came Upon the Midnight Clear
Luke 2:14 [L. Sears/R. Willis] Carol; see HFG:197

Jesus, Rose of Sharon
Song of Solomon 2:1 [R. Gollner (1989)] see WH-II:397; Scripture Chorus

Joy to the World
Psalm 98 [I. Watts/G. Handel] ANTIOCH; see HFG:171

Joy Bells Are Ringing
Luke 2:32 [N. Frykman/W. Soderberg] JULEN AR INNE; see CVH:114

Joyful News
Psalm 98 [I. Watts/arr. N. Cheshire] see SHP:244

Listen to the Christmas Bell
Luke 2:11 [R. Hamilton (1980)] see P-II:64, contemporary praise hymn

Lo, How a Rose E'er Blooming
Isaiah 11:1 [German/M. Praetorius] ES IST EIN ROS'; see HFG:174

Long Ago
John 1:14; Mark 4:39; Luke 7:22; [R. Hamilton (1982)] see P-II:55; contemporary praise hymn

Long Ago and Far Away
Luke 2:13 [E. Horn 3rd/R. Vaughan-Williams] RESONET IN LAUDIBUS; see SBAH:44

Lord, Who Left the Highest Heaven
Philippians 2:6-7 [T. Dudley-Smith/German, arr. W. Monk] ALL SAINTS; see HS-I:45; traditional, cathedral style

Love Came Down at Christmas
Luke 2:9; Matthew 2:2 [C. Rossetti/Irish] GARTAN; see SBAH:37

Mary, Mary
Luke 1:31 [Avery and March (1967)] ROSECHESTER; see SC:106; contemporary praise hymn

Nino Lindo (Child So Lovely)
Matthew 2:11 [Venezuelan Text and Tune] CARACAS; see HWB:207; Personified paraphrase of text; Spanish/English

Now Is Born the Divine Christ Child
Luke 2:15-16 [French Traditional] IL EST NE; see SDAH:133, numerous settings

O Come, All Ye Faithful
Luke 2:15 [Latin/J. Wade] ADESTE FIDELES; see HFG:193

On Christmas Night All Christians Sing
Isaiah 9:2; Luke 2:13 [Traditional English] SUSSEX CAROL; see LW:65

O Jesus Sweet
Philippians 2:6-7 [attr. Thilo/arr. J. S. Bach] O JESULEIN SUSS; see SDAH:134, Chorale

O Little Town of Bethlehem
Micah 5:2 [P. Brooks/L. Redner] ST. LOUIS; see HFG:178

O Sleep Now, Holy Baby
Luke 2:35 [Spanish Folk, tr. Robb; Spanish

Folktune] A La Ru; see H1982;113

O Thou Joyful, O Thou Wonderful
Isaiah 9:2 [J. Falk/Sicilian] Sicilian Mariner's Hymn; see CVH:122

On a Bethlehem Hill
Luke 2:8,12 [P. Scholtes/White spiritual, arr. R. Wetzel] see WB:536, Early American

On This Day Earth Shall Ring
Luke 2:7; Matthew 2:11 [J. Joseph, transl./*Piae Cantiones*, 1582, arr. 1956] Personent Hodie; see WB:538

Once in Royal David's City
Luke 2:5,7 [C. Alexander/H. Gauntlett] Irby; see SBAH:41

Our Day of Joy is Here Again
John 1:4-5; Luke 1:52 [A.Skoog] Nu Gladjens Timme; see CVH:123

Prince of Peace
Isaiah 9:6; Luke 1:31 [L. Mink (1982)] see WH-I:19; contemporary praise hymn

Puer Natus in Bethlehem
Luke 2:11 [Latin, 14th C./Plainsong; Mode 1; harm. by R. Proulx (1975)] see W-II:233; plainsong context

Race That Long in Darkness Pines, The
Isaiah 9:2 [J. Morrison/Traditional] Covenanters; see HB:153

Redeeming Love
Isaiah 53:4 [G. and W. Gaither] Redeeming Love; see HFG:199, Southern Gospel

Rejoice, Rejoice This Happy Morn
Luke 2:13 [B. Boye/P. Nicholai] Wie Schon Leuchtet; see SBAH:32, Chorale: many important settings

Rise Up Shepherd and Follow
Luke 2:15-16 [Black Spiritual/arr. A. Blackman (1984)] see SDAH:138

Silent Night, Holy Night
Luke 2:16 [J. Mohr/F. Gruber] Stille Nacht; see HFG:195

Some Children See Him
Matthew 5:8 [W. Hutson/A. Burt] Some Children; see HFG:181

Songs of Praise the Angels Sang
Luke 2:13 [J. Montgomery/Moravian] Monkland; see SBAH:432

Stable Lamp is Lighted, A
Matthew 3:9 [R. Wilbur/P. Tollefson (1982)] Tollefson; see H1982:104; contemporary

Stable Lamp is Lighted, A
John 12:13 [R. Wilbur/D. Hurd (1984)] Andujar;

see HS-II:24; spiritual song

That Boy Child of Mary
Luke 1:31b [T. Colvin/Traditional Malawi/arr. Colvin (1969)] Blantyre; see HS:114, 9/8 meter and imitative voicing

There's a Song in the Air!
Luke 2:13; Matthew 2:9 [J. Holland/K. Harrington] Christmas Song; see HB:155

This Is Christmas
Isaiah 7:14; Philippians 2:6-7; John 3:16 [R. Hamilton (1980)] see P-II:61; contemporary spiritual song

Thy Little Ones, Dear Lord, Are We
Luke 2:16 [H. Brorson/J. Schultz] Paedia; see SBAH:49

To Abraham the Promise Came
Genesis 22:15-18; John 1:14 [American Folk, arr. by J. Powell] Babe of Bethlehem; see WB:608, early American

To Thee With Joy I Sing
Luke 2:7,14 [Appalachian Carol, arr. D. Johnson (1968)] see WB:610; Early American

To Us a Child of Hope is Born
Isaiah 9:6-7 [J. Morrison/L. Mason] Zerah; see HWB:189, text-paraphrase, music suggests polonaise

'Twas in the Moon of Wintertime
Luke 2:13,16; Matthew 2:11 [St. J. de Brefeuf/French tune] Jesous Ahatonia; see HWB:19, Native American text and imagery

Under the Feeble Stable Lamp
Matthew 2:1-2; Luke 2:11,14 [A. Keller] Holy Manger; see SBAH:43

What Child Is This?
Luke 1:66 [W. Dix/English tune] Greensleeves; see HFG:180, Renaissance context

When Christmas Morn is Dawning
Luke 2:16 [E. Posse/German tune] Christmas Dawn; see SBAH:35

Where is This Stupendous Stranger?
Matthew 11:28-29 [C. Smart/A. Wyton (1977)] Kit Smart; see HS-I:25, Unison, contemporary Lydian mode

Where is This Stupendous Stranger?
[C. Smart/J. Fyock (1948)] Mcrae; see HWB:200

While Shepherds Watched Their Flocks by Night
Luke 2:10 [N. Tate/Handel] Christmas; see HFG:175

Wonderful Counselor
Isaiah 9:6 [N. Lupo (1989)] see WH-II:417; Scripture chorus

Wonderful Counselor

    Isaiah 9:6 [B. Yarger (1983)] see MMP:129, Scripture chorus

Steve Cushman

201 ♦ CHRISTMAS MUSICALS

Many congregations include in their worship life during the Christmas season a musical drama in which many of the children of the congregation participate. The following article describes some recently published musicals for consideration.

Planning music for the Christmas season and devising ways to involve children in Christmas worship is always a challenge. Year after year we search for new ways to tell the old story. What many weary children's choir directors and harried church school coordinators aren't aware of is that good, complete programs are readily available. While altogether too many mediocre cantatas have given the genre a bad name, some musical programs do offer quality music suitable for children's voices. These programs are easily produced and flexible enough to accommodate large or small groups and, most important, they tell the Christmas story in a fresh but faithful way. Of the three described below, two would be appropriate as preludes or postludes to a worship service; the third would better serve as the first part of a church school program or a children's choir carol concert.

A Night for Dancing by Hal Hopson. Dallas: Choristers Guild, 1974. No. CGCA-155. Performance time: 20 minutes.

This little cantata relates the story of Christ's birth through the eyes of Matthew the shepherd boy and all the animals that accompany him as he meets Mary, Joseph, and Jesus.

The opening "Procession of Joy" is a spirited piece in which all participants move joyfully toward the stable. Next, in "The Adoration of the Animals," Joseph greets the visitors and leads them to Mary and the baby Jesus. All the animals kneel and listen carefully to "Mary's Lullaby." Matthew and his friends respond with a prayerful "Carol of the Animals" that concludes with the audience joining their voices in the final "Gloria." The cantata ends with a benediction, "Go Now in Peace," leading into the "Dance of the Nativity," during which the animals and Matthew leave as joyfully as they came, spreading the good news to others on their way.

A Night for Dancing is appropriate for a wide range of children's voices. While the animals' parts can and should be sung by five- to eight-year-olds, the parts for Matthew, Joseph, and Mary require older elementary children or even junior high- or high-school-aged young people. Although the program includes no speaking parts, the solos demand a few strong singers—"Mary's Lullaby" in particular needs a clear soprano voice.

Hopson has included simple yet effective suggestions for dramatization. Directors can easily increase the number of participants by adding one or more shepherds to Matthew's part, using pairs or even groups of animals to sing the animal solos, or adding a choir of angels to strengthen the singing throughout. Costumes can be kept simple: robes for Mary and Joseph, pillowcase togas for Matthew and the shepherds, choir robes for the angels, and tagboard masks for the animals. One very effective performance tip is this: be sure to use the whole sanctuary or room. If the stable consists of a manger placed near the front, the procession should come from the rear of the room so that the congregation feels they are part of the story.

With its straightforward retelling of Christ's birth, its concluding benediction, and its joyful recessional, *A Night for Dancing* would make a fitting conclusion to a service of worship.

A Gift for Him by Terry Kirkland. Nashville: Triune Music, 1982. Lorenz Music, No. TU 147. Performance time: 15 minutes.

Although all the melodies in this brief Christmas musical are new, they are not difficult to learn. As composer Kirkland says in his introduction to the cantata, his intention was to write simply so that young children could learn the songs quickly and perform them well.

A Gift for Him is written for unison or two-part singing with piano and optional handbell accompaniment. The handbell parts are also relatively simple, requiring only two octaves of bells (although additional notes are scored for those groups that desire three octaves). The piece is well within the grasp of kindergarten through third graders; if the performing group includes older children, several selections lend themselves well to short solos with dramatic interpretation.

The musical tells the Bethlehem story, beginning with the introductory "It's a Quiet Night" and continuing with songs telling of the arrival of Jesus, the worship of the shepherds, and finally the angels' alleluias. The joyful conclusion reveals how the children can return "gifts" to Jesus by showing patience like that of Joseph and Mary, spreading the good news as the shepherds did, and singing praises as the angels sang them long ago.

Because this cantata is brief and carries a clear and simple message, churches may want to use it as a prelude or postlude to a worship service. The program's emphasis on returning gifts to Jesus makes it a suitable "musical offering" for a liturgical setting.

The composer suggests using visual art to illustrate the various scenes as the children sing. With simple costuming and a minimum of dramatic interpretation, several children could easily act out the story as it is sung. No matter how elaborate or simple the visual effects become, the eloquent simplicity of the melodies coupled with the lovely addition of handbells will convey the Christmas message in a new and memorable way.

Silent Night by Hal Hopson. New Berlin, Wis.: Jenson, 1980. No. 43319021. Performance time: 15 minutes.

This children's musical is so full of dramatic possibilities, musical integrity, and just plain fun that it is worth devising a setting in which to perform it. "Silent Night" is not suited for performance during a worship service, but it would make a delightful beginning for a church or school Christmas celebration. Although written for children's chorus, it could be performed by a wide range of singers—young children to sing the chorus parts and older children, or even adults, to sing and act the parts of Herr Gruber, Pastor Mohr, Hilda, and Karl, the organ repairman.

The musical tells the familiar story of how Franz Gruber composed "Silent Night" one Christmas Eve long ago. Hopson's lighthearted addition of three church mice—Hickory, Dickory, and Dock (who feast on the organ bellows, making the instrument horribly out of tune and unplayable)—may be more fantasy than fact, but it makes for some delightfully humorous moments.

The musical concludes with Herr Gruber singing his carol accompanied by his guitar and all the village children. The final words, "All together now," invite the audience to join in singing the beloved old carol.

Suggestions for simple costumes and staging are included in the score. Although the speaking parts are brief enough to be handled by younger children, a production featuring adults in these roles would be especially fun for all involved. (For example, your minister playing Pastor Mohr and the church organist acting the part of Herr Gruber could turn an ordinary program into a memorable event!) Any number of children may be added to the group of carolers so that all members of the youth choir or church school can participate in the performance. The chorus parts are not complicated and convey the happiness and joy of the season.

The three programs described on these pages by no means exhaust the possibilities available for Advent and Christmas. Many excellent children's musicals, cantatas, and programs are published; all it takes is a bit of ingenuity and imagination to tailor one of them to fit the needs of your children and your church. One word of caution, however, before you begin planning your performance: once you produce a successful musical involving the children and the congregation in worship, you will have committed yourself to coming up with another one—and another one—and another one! But the joy and pride on the children's faces as they participate in a worship service should make it all worthwhile.

Criss VanHof[17]

TEN

Sample Services for Christmas and Epiphany

The entries in this chapter demonstrate the richness of the Christmas season. All congregations interested in worship renewal should examine the following services, which combine innovative and traditional ideas for Christmas, New Year, and Epiphany celebration.

202 ◆ A CHRISTMAS EVE SERVICE

Below is the bare outline of a Christmas Eve service that can be adapted and suited to fit the character of any church. Because Christmas is an occasion of great rejoicing, the Christmas Eve service should bear all the marks of a great festive occasion.

THE MUSIC OF CHRISTMAS

(The service may begin with a 30 minute festive carol sing)

THE FESTIVE ENTRANCE

(Choir, dancers, banner carriers, and ministers assemble at the back of the church)

MINISTER: Rejoicing in the birth of Christ child, let us go forth in peace, Alleluia, Alleluia.

PEOPLE: **In the name of Christ, Amen, Alleluia, Alleluia.**

Entrance Hymns: "O Come All Ye Faithful" and "Of the Father's Love Begotten"

Commentary: Make the procession festive. Use liturgical dance, banners, incense, musical instruments. Express festivity and joy. Process around the church. Sing from all corners of the church. Make it alive. After all are in their place, continue to sing "Of the Father's Love Begotten" as a way of expressing the mystery of the event being celebrated.

The Christmas Acclamation

MINISTER: Christ is born, Alleluia, Alleluia.

PEOPLE: **He is born indeed, Alleluia, Alleluia.**

The Gloria in Excelsis Deo
(or some other suitable Act of Praise)

The Opening Prayer

THE SERVICE OF THE WORD

The Old Testament Lesson: Isaiah 9:2-4, 6-7
The Responsorial Psalm (say or sing): Psalm 96
The Epistle Lesson: Titus 2:11-14
The Alleluia Verse

Commentary: There are a number of joyful Alleluia verses that can be sung by choir and or choir and people alternatively. Use one of these with the people standing ready to hear the gospel reading.

The Gospel: Luke 2:1-10

Commentary: Read the gospel from the middle of the church to symbolize incarnation—God among us. Festoon the procession to the reading with dance, incense, or pageantry that will highlight the importance of this reading.

The Sermon

The Creed
(or some other response of faith)

The Prayer of the People

The Passing of the Peace

THE COMMUNION

For a Christmas Eve Communion see *Holy Communion* (Nashville: Abingdon Press, 1987), 18ff. For Communion song, sing the joyous carols of Christmas.

THE DISMISSAL

The Christmas Blessing

May God, who sent his angels to proclaim the glad news of the Savior's birth, fill you with joy, and make you heralds of the gospel. Amen.

or

May Almighty God, who lent his Son to take our nature upon him, bless you in this holy season, scatter the darkness of sin, and brighten your heart with the light of his holiness. Amen.

Dismissal Hymn

"God Rest Ye Merry Gentlemen"
"Joy to the World"
"Go Tell It on the Mountain"

The Words of Dismissal

MINISTER: Go in Christmas joy to love and serve the world
PEOPLE: **Thanks be to God.**

203 • A CHRISTMAS COMMUNION SERVICE

Christmas marks the culmination of the Advent season. The time of waiting is past, and God's people celebrate the arrival of their Messiah, who has visited and redeemed his people.

The Opening

LEADER: Glory to God in highest heaven and on earth peace for those on whom his favor rests.
PEOPLE: **In the tender compassion of our God, the morning sun has risen upon us who lived in darkness.**
LEADER: The Word has become flesh, has come to dwell among us, and we have seen his glory.
PEOPLE: **Glory as of the only Son from the Father, full of grace and truth.**

LEADER: To us a child is born, to us a son is given.
PEOPLE: **Alleluia.**
LEADER: All the ends of the earth have seen the salvation of our God.
PEOPLE: **Alleluia.**

Hymn: "Go, Tell It on the Mountain"

CONFESSION AND ASSURANCE

The Call to Confession

Brothers and sisters in Christ, draw near to God and he will draw near to you; humble yourself before him and he will lift you up. The sacrifice acceptable to God is a broken spirit. The Lord will not despise a broken and contrite heart.

The Confession

Almighty God and Father in heaven, who also makes his home with those of a humble and contrite spirit: Before you and our Lord Jesus Christ we confess the sin of ignoring your presence in the Spirit, of failing to look for the return of our Savior and Judge. We also confess our blindness to your coming in those who are lonely, hungry, cold, poor, and sick. In your great goodness, put away our offenses and cleanse us from our sins, for Jesus' sake. Amen.

Declaration of Pardon

Here is a trustworthy saying that deserves full acceptance: Christ Jesus came into the world to save sinners (1 Tim. 1:15). For God so loved the world that he gave his only Son, that whoever believes in him should not perish but have eternal life (John 3:16).

Hymn: "On Jordan's Bank," stanza 5

The Dedication

Now let us dedicate ourselves to live in obedience to the will of God. (Here follows Phil. 2:1-7)

Hymn: "Hark! The Herald Angels Sing"

THE PROCLAMATION OF THE WORD

Prayer for Illumination

O God, whose glory fills the skies, O Christ, the true and only Light, shine on us with your light and truth through the Word that gives light to all people. Empower us by your Spirit to walk in that light and to reflect your glory. Amen.

Scripture Reading

Sermon

Prayer for Blessing on the Word

THE RESPONSE

Hymn

The Creed (Say or sing the Apostles' Creed or the Nicene Creed.)

The Intercessory Prayer

The Offertory

Hymn: "As with Gladness Men of Old"

THE LORD'S SUPPER

LEADER: Brothers and sisters in Christ, the Gospels tell us that on the first day of the week, the day on which our Lord rose from the dead, he appeared to his disciples in the place where they were gathered and was made known to them in the breaking of the bread. Come, then, to the joyful feast of the Lord.

(If the Communion elements are not already on the table, they may be brought forward at this point.)

The Thanksgiving

LEADER: Lift up your hearts.
PEOPLE: **We lift them up unto the Lord.**
LEADER: Let us give thanks to the Lord our God.
PEOPLE: **It is right for us to give thanks.**
LEADER: It is our joy and our salvation
at all times and in all places
to give thanks to you,
O Lord, holy Father,
almighty, everlasting God,
through Christ, our Lord.
Because the light of your glory
has shone with splendor in our world.
For you gave Jesus Christ, your only Son,
to be born for us of Mary
that we might have power to become
your children through Him:
who existed before the world was
called into being,
but came down to save us

by being born of a humble virgin,
lying in a crib,
walking on earth as a man;
who became poor that by his poverty
we might become rich;
who was humbled that we might be
exalted;
who gave us peace and joy
when we were without hope and
without God.
Therefore with the whole company of
saints
in heaven and on earth
we proclaim and celebrate the birth
of our Savior
and we sing with joy.

Hymn: "Joy to the World"

The Institution

LEADER: We give thanks to God the Father that our Savior, Jesus Christ, before he suffered, gave us this memorial of his sacrifice, until his coming again. For on the night of his arrest he took bread and, after giving thanks to God, broke it and said, "This is my body which is for you; do this as a memorial of me." In the same way, he took the cup after supper and said, "This cup is the new covenant sealed by my blood. Whenever you drink it, do this in remembrance of me."

The Memorial

PEOPLE: **His death, O God, we proclaim.**
His resurrection we declare.
His coming we await.
Glory be to you, O Lord.

Prayer of Consecration

LEADER: Heavenly Father, be present with your life-giving Word and Holy Spirit, that we may be nourished and strengthened through this supper. Grant that all who share the communion of the body and blood of your Son may be united in him. And may we remain faithful in love and hope until we feast joyfully with him in his eternal kingdom. Now, as our Savior Christ has taught us, we pray: Our Father who art in heaven, hallowed be . . .

Preparation of the Elements

(as the minister breaks the bread and pours the cup)
The bread which we break
is a sharing in the body of Christ.
We who are many are one body
for we all share in the same loaf.
The cup for which we give thanks
is a sharing in the blood of Christ.
The cup which we drink
is our participation in the blood of Christ.

The Invitation

Come, all you who are thirsty,
come to the water;
and you who have no money,
come, buy, and eat!
Come, buy wine and milk
without money and without cost.
Why spend money on what
is not bread,
and your labor on what
does not satisfy?
Listen, listen to me,
and eat what is good,
and your soul will delight
in the richest of fare." (Isa. 55:1-2)

The Dedication

LEADER: We praise you, Lord,
for these your gifts of bread and wine.
PEOPLE: **We offer you ourselves
as your people in your service.**
LEADER: Blessed is he who comes in the name
of the Lord.
PEOPLE: **We will receive the bread of heaven.
We will drink the cup of salvation.**
LEADER: The gifts of God for the people of
God.

The Communion

(when the people are ready to eat the bread)
Take, eat, remember, and believe that the
body of our Lord Jesus Christ was given for a
complete remission of all our sins.

(when the people are ready to drink the cup)
Take, drink, remember, and believe that the
precious blood of our Lord Jesus Christ was
shed for a complete remission of all our sins.

(During the distribution of the elements the
people may sing some of the following hymns:
"Deck Thyself, My Soul, with Gladness"; "Let All

Mortal Flesh Keep Silence"; "Of the Father's Love
Begotten"; "I Come with Joy to Meet My Lord.")

The Thanksgiving

LEADER: Congregation in Christ, since the
Lord has fed us at his table, let us
praise his holy name with thanksgiving.

Hymn: "O Morning Star"/"How Bright Appears the
Morning Star"

THE DISMISSAL

May the God of hope fill you with all joy and peace
in believing, so that by the power of the Holy Spirit
you may abound in hope (Rom. 15:13). Amen.

Reformed Worship[18]

204 ✦ A HOLY FAMILY SERVICE

In many liturgical traditions, the Sunday after Christmas is the celebration of the Holy Family. The emphasis on the Holy Family is a recent one, having originated in Canada in the nineteenth century and spreading since around the world. Given the breakdown of the family in the twentieth century, a day emphasizing the Christian family seems quite prudent.

The emphasis of the Holy Family service is on the example Jesus' family has left us, asking for grace that our families may follow their good example. An opening prayer may petition that our families "may live as the Holy Family united in respect and love" and the concluding prayer ask that "we may constantly imitate the examples of the Holy Family and so attain to their eternal company after the trials of this life."

The Old Testament reading from the Apocrypha (Sir. 3:2-6, 12-14) refers to the attitude children should have toward their parents. (A good alternative reading is 2 Samuel 2:13-15, 19-23.) The Epistle reading from Colossians 3:12-21 calls all families to the Christian way of life. The Gospel readings for each year are as follows:

Year A: Matthew 2:13-15, 19-23 (Flight of the Holy Family to Egypt and their return to Nazareth)

Year B: Luke 2:22-40 (Presentation of Christ in the temple)

Year C: Luke 2:41-52 (Pilgrimage of Mary and

Joseph with Jesus to the Feast of the Passover in Jerusalem)

These texts can be expressed in creative ways with drama or storytelling.

O.T., Epistles, and Psalm texts that can be used with every year are:

> 2 Samuel 2:18-20, 25
> Psalm 128:1-5
> Colossians 3:12-17

Music

"Once in David's Holy City" or use Christmas carols

Other Possibilities

Have parts of the service led by families and use reading from secular sources that call attention to the plight of contemporary families. Adapt these materials to local custom and usage.

Robert E. Webber

205 • A Children's Christmas Service

The service below is designed to allow young people to participate. It may be used on a Sunday night or another appropriate time when the congregation gathers to celebrate Christmas.

——— Introductory Instructions ———

Environment. For the candlelight service, lower the lights and place a glowing candle in each window. Place a large, unlit twenty-foot tree front right, the manger front center, and the pulpit and Advent wreath front left.

The tree should be prepared carefully before the service as follows: Place a double-framed cross, formed from stiff wire (coat-hanger wire is ideal) in the front part of the tree. The cross should be proportioned to the tree (about eight by four feet for a twenty-foot tree).

Decorate the tree with five sets of lights, each on a separate switch so that it is possible to control one set at a time as directed in the service. One set of lights should be arranged on the cross with electrical tape. Someone in the congregation with knowledge of electrical circuits can be enlisted to build a simple control box.

The lights on the first four strands should have a variety of colors; the lights on the cross strand, one color. Lights should be turned on at the specified points in the program.

Prelude. The prelude is longer than usual and provides an opportunity for participation by high school and college students. Use flute, oboe, harp, violin, marimba, piano, and organ. The music is quiet and reflective and provides opportunity for prayer.

Processional. As soloist and choir sing "O Come, Little Children, O Come, One and All," candle-bearers process up the center and side aisles to take their positions. When they are in place, the Sunday school children and staff slowly enter, led by additional candle-bearers, and take their seats in the front part of the sanctuary. The processional concludes with the hymn "Once in Royal David's City."

Drama. Young people who will act out the nativity story during the narration should enter with the processional. A church may decide on many roles (e.g., numerous shepherds, angels, wise men) or few roles (e.g., only Mary and Joseph), depending on time and number of students available.

The seventh and eighth graders serve as actors. Clothed in simple costumes made from sheets, robes, and shawls, the actors should remain seated until their part of the drama. This part of the service may require several rehearsals to ensure a smooth performance. Students should pantomime their character's actions as the younger children read the narration.

——— The Service ———

Prelude: "O Little Town of Bethlehem" _Manz_
"Sinfonia" (Christmas Oratorio) _J. S. Bach_
"In Dulci Jubilo" _Dupre_

Choral Invitation and Processional:
"O Come, Little Children" _Schultz_
"Once in Royal David's City" (The congregation shall rise and join on stanzas 5 and 6.)

Greeting

Litany

READER:	I am like a green pine tree; your fruitfulness comes from me.
PEOPLE:	**Thanks be to God for his inexpressible gift.**
READER:	I have loved you with an everlasting love; I have drawn you with loving-kindness.

PEOPLE: **Thanks be to God for his inexpressible gift.**

READER: Turn to me and be saved, all you ends of the earth,
for I am God, and there is no other.

PEOPLE: **Thanks be to God for his inexpressible gift.**

READER: But when the time had fully come, God sent his
Son, born of a woman, born under law, to
redeem those under law, that we might
receive the full rights of sons and daughters.

PEOPLE: **Thanks be to God for his inexpressible gift.**

Hymn: "Beautiful Savior"

Preschool—Kindergarten:
"Christmas News"
"Glory to God in the Highest"
"Rock-a-bye Jesus"

Poem: "A Baby Jesus"

Hymn: "Come, Thou Long Expected Jesus"

Offertory Prayer

Offertory: "When Lights Are Lit on Christmas Eve" *Held*

Grades 1–6: "Light One Candle" *Sleeth*
(Children take their places on the platform and remain there.)

Choir: "The Star Carol" *Burt*
(The sanctuary lights are dimmed.)

THE MEANING OF THE CHRISTMAS TREE—Grade 6

(Some sections are spoken by individuals, others by the group.)
The Christmas tree means many things
to people everywhere;
to some it means a festive time,
to some a Christmas prayer.

It is our wish on this blest night
to tell you people here
the purpose of the Christmas tree,
and why it brings good cheer.

(Illuminate first set of lights in the Christmas tree)

As we behold the Christmas tree,
we think of many things—
of toys—and games—and Christmas treats,
and all the joys they bring.

These lights should tell us more than this
as we their radiance view;
they tell us of the coming Lord,
which men of old foreknew.

Through God's own inspiration
Isaiah did foretell:
A virgin shall bring forth a Son,
his name—Emmanuel."

Hymn: "O Come, O Come, Emmanuel"

THE PROPHETS TELL OF GOD'S SALVATION—Grade 5

"The virgin will be with child and will give birth to a son, and will call him Emmanuel."

Isaiah told his people more
about this virgin's Son:
he shall be called the "Prince of Peace,"
for he's the Mighty One.

"For to us a child is born, to us a son is given, and the government will be on his shoulders. And he will be called Wonderful Counselor, Mighty God, Everlasting Father, Prince of Peace."

It was the prophet Micah
who told where he'd be born—
in Bethlehem of Ephrathah
so early in the morn.

"But you, Bethlehem Ephrathah, though you are small among the clans of Judah, out of you will come for me one who will be ruler over Israel."

These lights upon the Christmas tree
should speak to everyone
the prophecies of men of old
as they foretold God's Son.

Hymn: "O Little Town of Bethlehem"
(Illuminate second set of lights)

JESUS IS BORN—Grade 4

Another group of lights, reminds us one and all,
how God gave his own Son, born in a lowly stall.

The listing of the people, the trip to David's

town, the inn so overcrowded; a stable then was found.

"In those days Caesar Augustus issued a decree that a census should be taken of the entire Roman world. (This was the first census that took place while Quirinius was governor of Syria.)

"So Joseph also went up from the town of Nazareth in Galilee to Judea, to Bethlehem the town of David, because he belonged to the house and line of David. He went there to register with Mary, who was pledged to be married to him and was expecting a child.

"While they were there, the time came for the baby to be born, and she gave birth to her firstborn, a son. She wrapped him in cloths and placed him in a manger, because there was no room for them in the inn."

Grades 1–6: "Were You There" *Sleeth*
(Illuminate third set of lights)

THE ANNOUNCEMENT OF JESUS' BIRTH—Grade 3

> We place more lights upon our tree,
> but they are all in vain
> unless the Savior's birth we see
> in every shining strain.
>
> Attending Jesus' wondrous birth
> were miracles divine;
> the shepherds in the fields did quake
> as angel voices chimed.
>
> And there were shepherds nearby, keeping
> watch over their flocks at night."

Hymn: "While Shepherds Watched Their Flocks by Night"
(Illuminate fourth and fifth sets of lights simultaneously)

A SIGN IS GIVEN—Grade 3

> As we add still more gleaming lights
> to our large Christmas tree,
> the message of the Savior's birth
> the eyes of all must see.

" 'This will be a sign to you: You will find a baby wrapped in cloths and lying in a manger.' Suddenly a great company of the heavenly host appeared with the angel, praising God and saying:

" 'Glory to God in the highest, and on earth peace to men on whom his favor rests.' "

Hymn: "Angels We Have Heard on High"

Grades 1–6: "The Birthday of a King" *Neidlenger* "You Are the King of Glory" *Ford*

THE SHEPHERDS SEE GOD'S SALVATION—Grades 1 and 2

"When the angels had left them and gone into heaven, the shepherds said to one another, 'Let's go to Bethlehem and see this thing that has happened, which the Lord has told us about.'

"So they hurried off and found Mary and Joseph, and the baby, who was lying in the manger. When they had seen him, they spread the word concerning what had been told them about this child."

Hymn: "That Boy-Child of Mary"—Grades 1 and 2

THE KINGS FOLLOW THE STAR—Grades 5 and 6

"After Jesus was born in Bethlehem in Judea, during the time of King Herod, Magi from the

Angel. *The angel is a common symbol of Christmas because of the central role angels played in proclaiming the birth of the Savior.*

east came to Jerusalem and asked, 'Where is the one who has been born king of the Jews? We saw his star in the east and have come to worship him'

"When King Herod heard this he was disturbed, and all Jerusalem with him. When he had called together all the people's chief priests and teachers of the law, he asked them where the Christ was to be born.

" 'In Bethlehem, in Judea,' they replied, 'for this is what the prophet has written:

" 'But you, Bethlehem, in the land of Judah, are by no means least among the rulers of Judah; for our of you will come a ruler who will be the shepherd of my people Israel.'

"Then Herod called the magi secretly and found out from them the exact time the star had appeared. He sent them to Bethlehem and said, 'God and make a careful search for the child. As soon as you find him, report to me, so that I too may go and worship him.'

"After they heard the king, they went on their way, and the star they had seen in the east went ahead of them until it stopped over the place where the child was.

"When they saw the star, they were overjoyed. On coming to the house, they saw the child with his mother Mary, and they bowed down and worshiped him. Then they opened their treasures and presented him with gifts of gold and of incense and of myrrh."

Hymn: "As with Gladness Men of Old"

Grades 1–6: "Born Today" *Eilers*

CHRISTMAS WISHES—Grades 1–4

The message of the Savior's birth
To you we did repeat;
The lights upon our tree are lit,
Our program is complete.

A parting hymn we'll sing for you,
In closing prayer we'll bow;
And as you leave we bid to you,
A Merry Christmas now.

THE REASON FOR HIS COMING—Junior High

I beg your pardon, please—

We cannot leave this evening,
for there are some of us
who'd spend our Christmas grieving.
We told of Jesus' birth
and praised his holy name,
but one thing we forgot—
The reason why he came.

Look at the lights again
upon our Christmas tree.
There's something hidden there,
it's form you cannot see.
It's been there all the time,
not visible to you;
the other lights upon the tree
have hidden it from view.

Choir: "What is This I See?" *Johnson*

The lights upon this tree
are like our cares external,
that rob each Christmastide
from all things that are eternal.
Our Christmases would be
much more beautiful
if we could only see
the Gift that's spiritual!

The decorating of the tree
with the lights and tinsel bright,
greeting cards and gifts to buy
before that Christmas night;
cooking, baking, planning meals
for friends and relatives—
these are the cares that hide the Lord;
we hardly know he lives!

These things that occupy our hearts
are all important, too,
but like the lights upon the tree
they hide our Lord from view.
Look! And behold what we forgot
and to you have denied:
the reason why our Lord was born
was to be crucified!

(Turn off sets 1–4 so that only cross is illuminated.)

Look well upon this lighted cross
and fix it in your mind,
that in the midst of Christmas joys
the cross of Christ you find.
For all our celebration
at Christmastime this year,

unless it centers in the cross,
will give no lasting cheer!

Solo: "I Wonder As I Wander" *Appalachian folksong, adapted by John Jacob Niles*

A CROSSLESS CHRISTMAS MEANS NOTHING— Grades 3–6

When the cross by itself
is lit on the tree,
its form and its beauty are easy to see.
But when all the lights around it are on,
its beauty is lost—its image is gone.

This tree is your heart on this holy night;
the lights are the joys that make our hearts bright.
There should from this service a lesson remain:
without Jesus' cross our Christmas is vain!

Now join us in song
as our voices we raise;
to him we belong,
to him we give praise.

Hymn: "The First Noel"

CHRISTMAS PRAYER

God, you have gladdened us this night by fulfilling your promise of redemption. For this we have come to offer our thanks. We confess that too often we have let our own thoughts and plans become so important that we have not given time or attention to your will. For this we beg your forgiveness. Sweep out of our hearts, we pray, all selfishness, anxiety, and concern for earthly pleasure so that we may joyfully make room to receive your only begotten Son as our Savior.

Help us to understand more fully how great, how unending is your love for us. Send your Holy Spirit to help us demonstrate your love in our lives so that those around us may earn to know you and Jesus Christ, whom you have sent. Bless us as we receive him into our hearts and homes. Bless us as we look ahead with hope to the day when he will come to us in glory. Amen.

Grades 1–6: "Be Near Me, Lord Jesus" *Kirkpatrick*

BENEDICTION—Grades 1–8
(Bring up sanctuary lights.)

We have seen God's salvation. Let us leave in peace.

Go now to your house and honor his birth. May the cross of our Lord be the cause for your mirth.
May Jesus, the Savior, who fills us with light, grant a Christ-blessed Christmas to you on this night!

Quiet Recessional
The congregation is invited to join the choir in singing carols. Please remain seated at the close of the service until your row is released by the candle-bearers.

Richard P. Musser,
William De Vries,
Charlotte Larson[19]

206 ✦ LAS POSADAS (A HISPANIC CHRISTMAS SERVICE)

Hispanic Christians often celebrate Christmas with this Las Posadas service. This service dramatizes Mary and Joseph's search for a place to stay. It is normally celebrated during the Advent season. In its focus on the events immediately preceding Jesus' birth, it can be most appropriately used near or on the celebration of Christmas.

In the Hispanic experience *Las Posadas* follows a historical tradition of *fiesta,* a feast. In the religious sense, fiesta is the conjunction of sacred *time* and *space* to portray a sacred *event.* Fiesta then becomes a ritual—a ritual of celebration which through collective expression justifies and sanctions a special order. Accordingly, in the Hispanic expression, fiesta has a certain carnival character. This carnival character is one of rejoicing, a popular participation by putting aside all pretensions and being a part of a regenerative moment. Further, fiesta is a religious drama where human participation rehearses the revelation of God, the strength and grace of God in sacred imitation.

To understand this concept of fiesta is to appreciate Las Posadas, a Hispanic celebration of Advent preparation ordinarily held nine days before Christmas. All too often, this fiesta is viewed by non-Hispanics as a quaint cultural expression of popular religiosity. In reality, Las Posadas in the Hispanic tradition is a celebration of devotion to the child Jesus, honoring the infant by giving him a place in their home. The name accentuates the importance of the child Jesus in the home, for *posada* means a lodging house, an inn, a place where one can *posar*, rest and be at home.

The celebration of Las Posadas, while practiced in several Latin American countries, is more at home in the Mexican culture. The theme is relatively simple but preparations may be elaborate at times. The essence of Las Posadas is that Mary and Joseph go about the community seeking lodging. They are refused lodging at several homes until they are finally accepted. The enactment of Las Posadas is a community event. The persons who represent Mary and Joseph are selected by the community and are usually active members in a local parish. Particular homes are volunteered as the places where the plea for lodging is sung and the home where lodging is granted. Children usually lead the procession, carrying figures of Mary and Joseph on a donkey. As the procession arrives at each home, they knock on the door while singing *"Para Pedir Posadas"* ("Requesting Lodging"). This song is a request from the processing party to the homeowner and a reply by the homeowner to the processing party.

Para Pedir Posadas
(Requesting Lodging)
(outside petition)

En nombre del cielo	In the name of heaven
Os pido posa	I request lodging
Pues no puede andar,	Since she can no longer walk,
Ya mi esposa amada.	My beloved wife.

(inside reply)

Aqui no es meson.	This is not an inn.
Sigan adelante	Go farther on
Pues no puedo abrir.	Since I cannot open.
No sea algun tunante.	You might be a rogue.

(outside petition)

Venimos rendidos.	We are very tired.
Desde nazaret.	We come from Nazareth.
Yo soy carpinter.	I am a carpenter.
De nombre Jose.	My name is Joseph.

(inside reply)

No me importa el nombre,	The name does not matter,
Dejenme dormir.	Let me sleep.
Pues que yo les digo	And I tell you again
Que no hemos de abrir.	We will not open for you.

(outside petition)

Posada te pide,	Lodging is requested,
Amada casero,	Beloved innkeeper,
Por solo una noche	For only one night
La Reina del Cielo.	By the Queen of Heaven.

(inside reply)

Pues si es una Reina	If it is a Queen
Quien la soliticita,	Who makes the request,
¿Como es que de noche	How is it that at night
Anda tan solita?	She travels alone?

(outside petition)

Mi esposa es Maria.	My wife is Mary.
Es la Reina del Cielo	She is the Queen of Heaven
Y madre va a ser	And she will be the mother
Del Divino verbo.	of the Divine word.

The processional party, after suffering rejection at several homes, is finally admitted. The following refrain is sung by all.

Entren, Santos Peregrinos
(Enter, Holy Pilgrims)

Entren, Santos Peregrinos,	Enter, holy pilgrims,
Reciban este rincon	Receive this corner
No de esta pobre morada	Not from this humble house
Sino de mi corazón.	But in my heart.

While each home visited is supposed to turn away the pilgrims until the procession reaches the designated "inn," every house visited usually gives treats and the celebration increases with each visit. When all have been accepted at the designated inn (home), the leader, usually a priest or minister, reads Scripture and offers prayer and a short homily. It is customary for the homeowner to prepare a short welcome to all the guests that reflects the spirit of the celebration and encourages hospitality. Then the party begins in a lively carnival spirit. During the evening, it is customary to sing traditional Advent hymns: "Noche De Paz" ("Silent Night"); "Venid Fieles Todos" ("O Come All Ye Faithful"); "En El Taller De Nazareth" ("In the Shop at Nazareth"); "Hoy A La Tierra" ("Today, to Earth").

In some Hispanic communities throughout the United States, Las Posadas has become an opportunity to dramatize community issues. Issues such as immigration and discrimination become a focus of this fiesta. The themes expressed in Las Posadas relate to the contextual experience of

Hispanics as an immigrant people. Many still see the United States as the land of opportunity and the symbol of liberty expressed in the now famous words written by philanthropist Emma Lazarus in 1883 and inscribed on the Statue of Liberty in 1903:

> Give me your tired, your poor,
> Your huddled masses, yearning to breathe free,
> The wretched refuse of your teeming shore.
> Send these, the homeless, tempest tossed, to me:
> I lift my lamp beside the golden door.

While the hand is extended to immigrants, the tragic reality is that for many Hispanics the doors are never fully opened. The season of Advent, when the story of Mary and Joseph seeking refuge is vividly enacted, becomes a living reality for Hispanics. It is not surprising that this drama is also a way to express a reality.

Theologically and pastorally, the question of welcoming rest was considered in a temporary way. The reworked Posadas retained the element of processing Mary and Joseph in costume. But a new theme song was added in which a key question repeats each time Mary and Joseph and the other singers reach a new place in the neighborhood. "We ask you, we ask you, where can we rest? Where can we welcome the poor and oppressed?" With these words, Sr. Carol Frances Jegen, BVM, Mundelein College, Chicago, has described the contemporary meaning of Las Posadas. She further describes the contemporary fiesta: "The procession began with an opening prayer. At the end of the journeyings, when the final door opened in true Posadas fashion, the entire group spent time reflecting on two scripture passages (Luke 2:17, Mary and Joseph's journey to Bethlehem) and (Matthew 25:31-40, 'Lord when did we see you hungry and feed you, etc.'). Prayers of petition for all the refugees of today's world, and for church and government leaders, conclude the service."

Las Posadas is celebrated primarily by Roman Catholic Christians. Protestant Hispanics are only now beginning to appreciate this tradition as their heritage. Perhaps Las Posadas will become more meaningful to Protestant Hispanics when contemporary Christian celebrations aid them in both sharing their traditional faith and living this reality.

Rubén R. Armendáriz[20]

207 ✦ THE NAME OF JESUS SERVICE

The traditional New Year's watchnight service can take on a new character if it is combined with the ancient Name of Jesus service. The historical beginnings of this service go back to the eighth century. The biblical motif celebrated is the naming of Jesus at the rite of circumcision, a ritual performed in Jewish tradition on the eighth day after birth.

Texts
Numbers 6:22-27
Psalm 67
Galatians 4:4-7
Philippians 2:9-13
Luke 2:15-21

Hymns
[Traditionally the hymns attributed to Bernard of Clairvaux are sung on this day.]

"Jesus, the Very Thought of You"
"O Jesus, King Most Wonderful"

Other hymns and songs:
"Jesus Is All the World to Me"
"Jesus Shall Reign"
"Jesus, Jesus, There's Something about that Name"

Additional
- Communicate the gospel reading through drama or storytelling.
- Use the John Wesley covenant, which was designed for watchnight services by Wesley. (See following article.) The covenant best occurs after the sermon.

208 ✦ THE COVENANT RENEWAL SERVICE FOR THE NEW YEAR

The covenant of renewal originated with Charles Wesley in 1755. The purpose of the service was to effect a renewal of faith through a renewal of the covenant with God. Forgotten for generations, the service has been recovered in the twentieth century. Below is the covenant which may be used in a New Year's watchnight service or in the service of the First Sunday of Epiphany (Baptism of our Lord).

The service given here borrows heavily from the British Methodist covenant service. It is designed for use as the main service of worship on the first Sunday after Epiphany (Baptism of the Lord). You may wish to use the following introduction in John Wesley's own words either printed on the bulletin cover or in place of the greeting.

Dearly beloved, the Christian life, to which we are called, is a life in Christ, redeemed from sin, and through Him consecrated to God. Upon this life we have entered, having been admitted into that New covenant of which our Lord Jesus Christ is mediator, and which he sealed with His own blood, that it might stand for ever.

On one side the Covenant is God's promise that He will fulfill in and through us all that He declared in Christ Jesus, who is the author and Perfecter of our faith. That His promise still stands we are sure, for we have known His goodness, and proved His grace in our lives day by day. On the other side we stand pledged to live no more unto ourselves, but to Him who loved us and gave Himself for us, and has called us to serve Him that the purpose of His coming might be fulfilled.

From time to time, we renew our vows of consecration, especially when we gather at the Lord's Table: but on this day we meet expressly, as generations of our fathers have met, that we may joyfully and solemnly renew the covenant which bound them and binds us to God.

Let us then, remembering the mercies of God, and the hope of His calling, examine ourselves by the light of His Spirit, that we may see wherein we have failed or fallen short in faith and practice, and, considering all that this Covenant means, may give ourselves anew to God.

ORDER OF WORSHIP

Gathering (suitable music may be offered)

Greeting

LEADER: Grace and peace from God our Father and the Lord Jesus Christ.

PEOPLE: **Amen.**

LEADER: Come let us worship the Lord who established a new covenant through his Son Jesus Christ.

PEOPLE: **We come in spirit and in truth.**

Hymn: "O for a Thousand Tongues to Sing"

Prayer of Adoration

LEADER: Let us pray:

Let us worship our creator, the God of love;

God continually preserves and sustains us;

we have been loved with an everlasting love; through Jesus Christ

we have been given complete knowledge of God's glory.

PEOPLE: **You are God; we praise you; we acknowledge you to be the Lord.**

LEADER: Let us glory in the grace of our Lord Jesus Christ.

Though he was rich, for our sakes he became poor;

he was tempted in all points as we are,

but he was without sin;

he went about doing good

and preaching the gospel of the kingdom;

he accepted death, death on the cross;

he was dead and is alive forever;

he has opened the kingdom of heaven

to all who trust in him;

he sits in glory at the right hand of God;

he will come again to be our Judge.

PEOPLE: **You, Christ, are the King of Glory.**

Let us rejoice in the fellowship of the Holy Spirit,

the Lord, the Giver of Life.

Through the Spirit we are born into the family of God,

and made members of the body of Christ;

the witness of the Spirit confirms us;

the wisdom teaches us;

the power enables us;

the Spirit will do far more for us than we ask or think.

PEOPLE: **All praise to you, Holy Spirit.**

Silent Prayer

The Lord's Prayer

First Lesson
Ecclesiastes 3:1-13 (All Years)

Psalm or Anthem
Psalm 8 (All Years)

Second Lesson
Revelation 21:1-61a (All Years)

Hymn

Commentary: Appropriate hymns include "Come, Let Us Use the Grace Divine," "God of the Ages," and "O God, Our Help in Ages Past"

Gospel
Matthew 25:31-46 (All years)

Sermon

Hymn: "Come, Let us See the Grace Divine"

Confession of Sin

LEADER: Let us humbly confess our sins to God.

O God, you have shown us the way of life
through your Son, Jesus Christ.
We confess with shame our slowness to learn of him,
our failure to follow him, and our reluctance to bear the cross.

PEOPLE: **Have mercy on us, Lord, and forgive us.**

LEADER: We confess the poverty of our worship,
our neglect of fellowship and of the means of grace,
our hesitating witness for Christ,
our evasion of responsibilities in our service,
our imperfect stewardship of your gifts.

PEOPLE: **Have mercy on us, Lord, and forgive us.**

Let each of us in silence make confession to God.

(Silence)

LEADER: Have mercy on us, Lord, and forgive us.

PEOPLE: **Have mercy on me, O God, according to your steadfast love;**
In your abundant mercy blot out my transgressions.
Wash me thoroughly from my iniquity, and cleanse me from my sin.
Create in me a clean heart, O God, and put a new and right spirit within me.

LEADER: Now the message that we have heard from God's Son
and now announce is this: God is light,
and there is no darkness at all in him.
If we live in the light—just as he is in the light—
then we have fellowship with one another,
and the blood of Jesus, his Son,
purifies us from every sin.
If we say that we have no sin, we deceive ourselves,
and there is no truth in us.
But if we confess our sins to God,
he will keep his promise and do what is right;
he will forgive us all our wrongdoing.

PEOPLE: **Amen. Thanks be to God.**

Collect

LEADER: Let us pray:

PEOPLE: **Father, you have appointed our Lord Jesus Christ**
as Mediator of a new covenant;
give us grace to draw near with fullness of faith
and join ourselves in a perpetual covenant with you,
through Jesus Christ our Lord. Amen.

The Covenant

LEADER: In the old covenant,
God chose Israel to be a special people and to obey the law.
Our Lord Jesus Christ, by his death and resurrection,
has made a new covenant with all who trust in him.
We stand within this covenant and we bear his name.
On the one side, God promises in this covenant
to give us new life in Christ.
On the other side, we are pledged
to live not for ourselves but for God.
Today, therefore, we meet
to renew the covenant which binds us to God.

(The people stand.)

Friends, let us claim the covenant God has made with his people,
and accept the yoke of Christ.
To accept the yoke of Christ means that we
allow Christ to guide all that we do and are,
and that Christ himself is our only reward.
Christ has many services to be done;
some are easy, others are difficult;
some make others applaud us, others bring only reproach;
some we desire to do because of our own interests;
others seem unnatural.
Sometimes we please Christ and meet our own needs,
at other times we cannot please Christ
unless we deny ourselves.
Yet Christ strengthens us and gives us the power to do all these things.
Therefore let us make this covenant of God our own.
Let us give ourselves completely to God,
trusting in his promises and relying on his grace.

PEOPLE: **I give myself completely to you, God.**
Assign me to my place in your creation.
Let me suffer for you.
Give me the work you would have me do.
Give me many tasks
or have me step aside while you call others.
Put me forward or humble me.
Give me riches or let me live in poverty.
I freely give all that I am and all that I have to you.
And now, holy God, Father, Son, and Holy Spirit,
you are mine and I am yours. So be it.
May this covenant made on earth continue for all eternity.
Amen.

Concerns and Prayers

The Peace

Offering

Great Thanksgiving

Breaking of Bread and Taking of the Cup

Giving of the Bread and the Cup

Prayer After Communion
LEADER: Let us give thanks to the Lord.
PEOPLE: **Lord, we give thanks for the gift of this holy meal.**
We praise you that you sent your Son,
that through him we might be reconciled completely to you.
Christ sacrificed himself for us;
grant that all we are and all we do be a response to him,
in whose strong name we pray. Amen.

Hymn: "A Charge to Keep I Have"

Dismissal with Blessing
LEADER: May the God who established a covenant with those who seek to enter the kingdom be always present with you.
PEOPLE: **Amen.**
LEADER: May Jesus Christ who sealed the new covenant with his sacrifice on the cross bring you peace.
PEOPLE: **Amen.**
LEADER: May the Holy Spirit of God guide your life, now and for ever.
PEOPLE: **Amen.**
LEADER: Go in peace to serve God and your neighbor in all that you do.
PEOPLE: **Amen. Thanks be to God!**

————— **Commentary** —————

This covenant service may be celebrated on various days at the beginning of the calendar year. If used as a Watch Night (New Year's Eve) service, the lessons given in the order of worship are appropriate. It may be the main service on the first Sunday after Epiphany—Baptism of the Lord. If so, the lessons for that day should be used. The first Sunday of the year is also appropriate. When celebrated on the first Sunday after Epiphany, it marks a natural culmination of the Advent and Christmas/Epiphany experience.

During the year, a covenant service could mark a special anniversary, such as the founding of a congregation. If it is celebrated at another time, the following lessons may be read: Jeremiah 31:31-35; Hebrews 12:22-29; John 15:1-8; or Matthew 11:27-30.

If a service of baptism and/or reaffirmation is to be incorporated, it may follow at the place indicated "Responses and Offerings." In this case the renunciation of sin and profession of faith can replace the confession of sin in the text of the order of worship just given.

In most situations it is impossible to follow Wesley's practice of having long periods of instruction precede the service. But authentically celebrated Advent and Christmas seasons naturally prepare a congregation for the renewal of baptismal covenant. Announcements of the service should be sensitively planned to contribute to more mature and eager participation.

Although at times the Lord's Supper has been omitted from the service, the covenant service is in reality a special form of the celebration of Holy Communion which renews our personal commitment to Christ in the light of all that our baptism into Christ means.

Hoyt Hickman, et al.[21]

209 ♦ A TRADITIONAL PROTESTANT EPIPHANY SERVICE

The following service is a creative adaptation of the traditional pattern and texts for worship on Epiphany. It will be of particular help for those who plan more formal Epiphany worship. For others, the commentary included with this service will provide a guide to thoughtful planning for the Advent season.

The principal theme of an Epiphany service of worship is rooted in the paschal mystery and the redemption which it brings to the world. The coming of the magi to pay homage to Jesus (the theme of the Epiphany gospel reading of Matt. 2:1-12) is no mere interesting tale with a moral, but a story that speaks to the very essence of the gospel and its redemptive motif. For it has to do with the extension of salvation to the Gentiles and is pro-

claimed in the Epiphany service as the fulfillment of the Old Testament reading for the day: "Arise, shine; for your light has come, and the glory of the Lord has risen upon you. . . . Nations shall come to your light, and kings to the brightness of your rising" (Isa. 50:1-6). Likewise, the epistle reading carries a salvific message (Eph. 3:2-3a, 5-6) proclaiming that "the Gentiles are fellow heirs, members of the same body, and partakers of the promise of Christ Jesus through the gospel." It is no wonder that the Epiphany in the early church was a major celebration, standing second in rank to Easter. For through Epiphany the manifestation of God's salvation is indeed made clear.

But the point of this feast goes beyond the manifestation of God in history and demands the manifestation of Christ in our own experience and then from us to others. Each of us is one for whom Christ is manifested as Savior of the world and King of the universe. And unless the Epiphany takes root in us and is born within, and unless we express it to others, the purpose of God's appearance has been stifled and thwarted.

The Service

God's Word of Greeting

Commentary: The worship setting for Epiphany should reflect the festive nature of the celebration. Colors appropriate for use include vibrant shades of gold, white, yellow, and green. Images traditionally associated with Epiphany include the gifts of the magi. Events associated with the Epiphany season include not only the coming of the magi, but also the baptism of Jesus, the wedding at Cana, and—at the end of the Epiphany season—the transfiguration of Jesus. Banners, paraments, and printed liturgy covers may feature these colors, images, and events for the day of Sunday of Epiphany only or for the entire season of Epiphany, which a congregation may choose to observe until the beginning of Lent. If the latter choice is made, perhaps a collage of symbols related to each of the above events in the life of Christ could be featured.

Commentary: The headings used in this order of service highlight the nature of our worship as a response to God. Each heading points to an element in the worship service in which we hear God's word to us: the greeting, the declaration of pardon, the sermon, the Communion, and the benediction. Within each heading, each action of worship either leads up to or responds to these words. These headings may be used for any service in the Christian year.

Gathering of the Congregation (with organ, piano, or instrumental prelude)

Commentary: Pre-service music for Epiphany can appropriately be very celebrative. If selections are based on Epiphany hymn tunes, then the hymn texts may be printed in the order of service as a guide to the pre-service meditation of the people.

Declaration of Trust

LEADER: Our help is in the name of the Lord, the maker of heaven and earth. (Ps. 124:8).

PEOPLE: **Amen.**

Commentary: Many congregations begin each service with this declaration of trust, which is appropriate to any service in the Christian year. It functions as a way of expressing the congregation's solidarity in their trust in God as worship begins.

Call to Worship: Isaiah 60:1-3

Commentary: This passage is taken from the Old Testament lesson for Epiphany. It announces the nature of the service as a celebration of God's grace and uses the central epiphanic image of light.

Processional Hymn: "As With Gladness Men of Old"

Commentary: Other appropriate hymns include "How Bright Appears the Morning Star," "Songs of Thankfulness and Praise," and "Hail to the Lord's Anointed" (a metrical setting of Ps. 72).

Greeting

PASTOR: The grace of God has dawned upon the world with healing for all humankind. (Titus 2:11)

PEOPLE: **And also with you.**

PASTOR: Grace, mercy, and peace from God the Father and Christ Jesus our Lord. (1 Tim. 1:2)

PEOPLE: **Amen.**

God's Word of Pardon

Invitation to Confession

LEADER: God is light; in him there is no darkness at all. If we claim to have fellowship with him yet walk in darkness, we lie and do not live by the truth. But if we walk in the light, as he is in the light, we have fellowship with one another, and the blood of Jesus, his Son, purifies us from all sin. If we claim to be without sin, we deceive ourselves and the truth is not in us (1 John 1:5b-8). Aware of God's presence with us, let us now humble ourselves, confess our sin, and seek his grace.

Prayer of Confession

PEOPLE: **Almighty God, we enter your presence humbly, aware that we approach you from a world that chooses to walk in darkness, apart from you. Each one of us has ignored and even denied the enlightening power of Jesus Christ. We confess now our sins to you, God of power and might. Penetrate our darkness by the power of Christ's light, that we may live in the joy of knowing and loving you and each other.**

Declaration of Pardon

LEADER: The good news of the gospel is this: If we confess our sins, he is faithful and just and will forgive our sins and purify us from all unrighteousness. (1 John 1:9)

PEOPLE: **In Christ, we are forgiven. Thanks be to God!**

Commentary: The use of 1 John 1 for both the call to confession and the declaration of pardon provides unity to this section of the service. This passage is especially appropriate for use on Epiphany because of its use of the image of God as light.

Thanksgiving of the People

Canticle, all singing: "Glory to God in the Highest" or "How Bright Appears the Morning Star"

Commentary: Most hymnals include a setting of this traditional canticle. For a list of service music found in a representative group of hymnals, consult the commentary to the Communion liturgy of the Advent service in this series. Other acclamations of praise are also appropriate for use at this time, including choral and solo anthems and several hymns for Epiphany.

Act of Fellowship

LEADER: Brothers and sisters in Christ, in this spirit of thanksgiving, let us greet each other as members of the body of Christ, reflecting our union with him and with each other.

PEOPLE: [to each other] **God's peace be with you.**

Commentary: The passing of the peace is often placed at the beginning of the service (see the Advent service in this series) or just prior to the Communion liturgy (see the Lenten service in this series). Yet since it is our reconciliation with God that leads to our reconciliation with others in the body of Christ, it is also appropriate to greet fellow worshipers at this point, following the celebration of reconciliation with God.

God's Word of Life

THE WORD IS READ AND PREACHED

Prayer for Illumination

O God, out of the depths of eternity you moved in our history in the birth of Jesus Christ, our Lord. In him was life and the life was our light. The light shines in the darkness, and the darkness has not overcome it. Cause that light to shine ever brighter as the ancient word of promise and the gospel word of fulfillment are now read. Enable us to hear it afresh that it may bring new life and joy to our lives. Through Jesus Christ, our Lord. Amen.

Scripture Readings

Old Testament Reading: Isaiah 60:1-6
Psalm: Psalm 72:1-14
New Testament Reading: Ephesians 3:1-12; Matthew 2:1-12

Commentary: If a portion of this passage was used at the beginning of the service, an alternate lesson may be chosen. The Psalm may be sung by the choir or congregation. Musical resources for singing the Psalms are included in the commentary with the Pentecost service in this series.

Response

LEADER: The Word of the Lord, the Light of the world.

PEOPLE: **Thanks be to God.**

Sermon

Commentary: The sermon for Epiphany can appropriately focus on the account of the magi as well as on the general theme of Christ as the Light of the world.

RESPONSE TO THE WORD

Statement of Faith: The Apostles' Creed
Testimonies or Pledges of Faith

Commentary: The Epiphany observance celebrates the manifestation of Christ, the Light of the world, and hence provides a natural opportunity for the church to focus on the nature and extent of its ministry to the local community and to the world as the body of Christ. The sermon for Epiphany will likely challenge worshipers to reflect the light of Christ in the world. An appropriate response to the sermon could then include brief reports of the church's mission, testimonies of the Spirit's work through the local church, or specific challenges to the congregation regarding opportunities for service.

Concerns of the Congregation

Commentary: At this point, members of the congregation may make known to each other concerns for mutual prayer. These may be announced by the pastor or lay worship leader, by church members assigned to monitor the prayer needs of the congregation, or by individual worshipers during a time of sharing reasons for thanksgiving and intercession.

Prayers of the People

Prayers of Adoration

Prayers of Petition

Prayers of Dedication

Commentary: These three aspects of the prayer may be led by three different members of the congregation. Each section of the prayer may close with the words, "All this we pray. . . ," to which the congregation would respond, "through Jesus Christ our Lord. Amen." This method for the prayers of the people, which would be appropriate for any Sunday in the liturgical year, allows for "the priesthood of all believers" to be represented by various leaders for prayer. It also allows the prayer to focus on a variety of occasions for prayer or petition, given the unique interests, gifts, and perspectives of each prayer leader.

The prayers of both petition and dedication should make specific reference to any testimonies or challenges to commitment that may have immediately preceded the prayer.

Offering

LEADER: People of God, having heard the call of the gospel, we now offer our gifts to God, as a token of our thanksgiving for the gifts of Jesus Christ, and pledge of our commitment to his service.

PEOPLE: **Amen.**

[The gifts are received.]

People sing: "Praise God from whom all blessings flow . . . "

Commentary: This offertory sentence may be used for any service in the Christian year. During the singing of the doxology, the gifts of money as well as the gifts of bread and wine (or juice) for the sacrament may be brought forward. An alternate doxology for use during Epiphany is the final stanza of the hymn "O Love, How Deep, How Broad, How High."

God's Gift of the Sacrament

Commentary: The following Communion liturgy is organized so as to point to the "geography" of the worship space. The first part of the Communion liturgy is the approach to the Table, which features many images of approaching the light of Christ. During the second part of the liturgy we are at the Table, communing with the Lord. The third part of the Communion liturgy is our dispersal into the world for the purpose of reflecting Christ's light. The text of this liturgy does not vary significantly from a traditional Communion liturgy and may be presented using traditional headings. But picturing the liturgy as an approach to and dispersal from the Table may helpfully reinforce the message of Epiphany.

This structure may be reinforced by having each section of the liturgy led from a different place in the worship space. The approach to the Table may be led, for example, from within the congregation, while the final section of dispersal may be led by various leaders stationed near the doorways which exit from the worship space.

APPROACH TO THE TABLE

Invitation

LEADER: Friends, this is the joyful feast of the people of God. Hear the declaration of our Savior Jesus Christ: "I am the Light of the world. Whoever follows me will never walk in darkness but will have the light of life." Come, let us approach together the table of our Lord.

Prayer of Thanksgiving

LEADER: Lift up your hearts.

PEOPLE: **We lift them up to the Lord, our Light and Life.**

LEADER: Let us bring our praise to God.
We praise you, O God, for in Jesus Christ—the mystery of the Word made flesh—you sent a light to shine upon the world, that he might bring us out of darkness into your marvelous light. Therefore with all Christians we praise your name and sing with joy:

PEOPLE: **Holy, holy, holy Lord, God of power and might, heaven and earth are full of your glory. Hosanna in the highest. Blessed is he who comes in the name of the Lord. Hosanna in the highest.**

Commentary: Most hymnals include a setting of this traditional canticle. For a list of service music found in a representative group of hymnals, consult the commentary to the Communion liturgy of the Advent service in this series.

LEADER: We remember with joy the grace by which you created all things and made us in your image. We rejoice that you called a people in covenant to be a light to the nations. Yet we rebelled against your will. In spite of prophets and pastors sent forth to us, we continued to break your covenant. In the fullness of time, you sent your only Son to save us. Incarnate by the Holy Spirit, born of your servant Mary, sharing our life, he reconciled us to your love. At the Jordan your Spirit descended upon him, anointing him to preach to good news of your reign. He healed the sick and fed the hungry, manifesting the power of your compassion. He sought out the lost and broke bread with sinners, witnessing the fullness of your grace. We beheld his glory and await seeing his glory extended to the ends of the earth. For joy of knowing him our Lord and Savior, we bring our praise and thanksgiving. Amen.

Commentary: Note the several references to Christ as light, to the baptism of Christ, to the manifestation of Christ's presence to the world—all of which make this prayer uniquely suited to use during Epiphany.

Institution

LEADER: The Lord Jesus, on the night when he was betrayed, took bread, and when he had given thanks, he broke it and said, "This is my body, which is for you; do this in remembrance of me." In the same way, he took the cup, after supper, saying, "This cup is the new covenant in my blood; do this, whenever you drink it, in remembrance of me." For whenever you eat this bread and drink this cup, you proclaim the Lord's death until he comes."

Memorial

PEOPLE: **By sharing in this feast, we proclaim that Jesus Christ, who once was dead, but now is risen, is the Light of the world!**

THE SACRAMENT

Prayer of Consecration

LEADER: Let us pray.

PEOPLE: **Gracious God, in your light we see light. So pour out now your Holy Spirit upon these gifts, we pray, sanctifying them and showing them to be good gifts for your holy people, the body and blood of your Son Jesus Christ, the Light of the world. Amen.**

Invitation

PASTOR: Friends in Christ, the Lord has prepared his table for his church. All who love him and trust in him alone for their salvation are now invited to come to the table of the Lord.

PEOPLE: **We come with gladness. Thanks be to God!**

PASTOR: The gifts of God for the people of God.

Communion

PASTOR: (as the people take the bread): The body of Jesus Christ, broken for you.

PASTOR: (as the people take the cup): The blood of Jesus Christ, shed for you.

Commentary: During the sacrament, appropriate instrumental, choral, or solo music may be played or sung, or the congregation may sing a series of Communion hymns. Preference should be given to texts that focus on Christ as the Light of the world, the sacrament as a means for proclaiming Christ's love to the world, and the subject of the sermon of that particular Sunday.

DISPERSAL INTO THE WORLD

Thanksgiving

LEADER: Jesus Christ is the Light of the world!

PEOPLE: **Thanks be to God!**

LEADER: Lord, now let your servants depart in peace.

PEOPLE: **For our eyes have seen your salvation, which you have prepared in the sight of all peoples.**

LEADER: A light to reveal you to the Gentiles.

PEOPLE: **The glory of your people Israel.**

LEADER: Glory to the Father, the Son, and the Holy Spirit.

PEOPLE: **Amen and Amen!**

Commentary: This thanksgiving is based on the Song of Simeon (Nunc Dimittis) from Luke 2:28-31. While appropriate for use in every service in the Christian year, its reference to Christ as the Light of the world makes it especially appropriate for use on Epiphany.

God's Word of Blessing

Charge to the People

LEADER: People of God, go now in the power of Christ and extend the radiance of Christ's light into our dark world. Live as children of light, for the fruit of light consists in all goodness, righteousness, and truth. Have nothing to do with the fruitless deeds of darkness, but rather expose them. And in all things, give thanks to God the Father, in the name of Jesus Christ. (based on portions of Eph. 5:8ff)

Hymn of Dedication (Recessional): "Lord of the Universe"

Commentary: The text of the final hymn may be chosen to focus on the church's mission in reflecting Christ's light to the world. This type of text also highlights the symbolic quality of the recessional, which dramatizes the church's going out into the world in Christ's name. This theme can be emphasized on Epiphany by having white and gold banners or streamers that may have been used to prepare the worship space carried out by those leading the procession, perhaps by liturgical dancers.

Benediction

PASTOR: May Christ be manifested in you, that you may be a light to the world. And may the blessing of God Almighty, Father, Son, and Holy Spirit, be among you and remain with you always. Amen.

Dispersal of the Congregation (with organ, piano, or instrumental postlude)

Commentary: Post-service music should be festive on Epiphany Sunday, in the manner of the recessional hymn.

John D. Witvliet

210 ✦ A CONVERGENCE EPIPHANY SERVICE

The service outlined below is designed for January 6. Since many churches celebrate Epiphany on the first Sunday of January, much of the following material could be adapted or incorporated into a standard Sunday morning service in an evangelical or charismatic church. Adapt to local custom and style.

ACTS OF ENTRANCE

Processional

Commentary: As Epiphany marks a special pilgrimage for the magi to the Christ child, the church could, at this service, become the processional. Have the people gather in the foyer or another part of the church and process together into an empty sanctuary to a hymn or contemporary worship choruses that are upbeat and victorious.

The processional is led by a crucifer, followed by banner carriers, singers, dancers, and the congregation. Three men dressed as wise men could also help lead the processional. Each person coming that night should bring something to present to the Christ child, based on a theme announced earlier. Ideas included food for the poor, new toys for the nursery, or some other special offering.

Opening Sentences

I will make you a light for the Gentiles,
That you may bring my salvation to the ends of the earth (Is. 49:6b).

Acts of Praise and Worship

Commentary: The songs should be focused on the power of the gospel to change lives. Just as the Wise Men were led to Jesus by the light of a star, so the light of Jesus' in us guides those around us to him. He is continually "manifested" to the world through his church. Litanies, responsive readings, poetry, etc., can all be utilized during this time of worship.

MINISTRY OF THE WORD

Collect

Heavenly Father, you used the light of a star to tell the world of Your Son; through the church and by Your Holy Spirit send your light again that all the peoples of this world will learn of His love; through Jesus Christ our Lord, who lives and reigns with you and the Holy Spirit, one God, world without end. Amen.

Readings

First Reading: Isaiah 60:1-6
Psalm 72
Second Reading: Ephesians 3:1-12
Third Reading: Matthew 2:1-12

OR

See Lectionary Texts

Message

Commentary: The theme of Epiphany holds a great deal of breadth and depth for preaching. However, a drama concerning the magi, a reading, etc., could be used instead. If you have someone creative in your church, have them write a short contemporary play based on the story of the discovery of Christ (Matt. 2).

Testimonies are also very useful after the readings. Choose members from the congregation to talk about their own personal epiphanies.

Creed

Commentary: The Apostles' Creed, which is the baptismal creed of the church, should be said. It reminds us that Epiphany is a time to celebrate Christ's reality in our own lives, which was sealed in baptismal waters.

MINISTRY OF THE TABLE

Offertory

Commentary: Epiphany is a day of giving. The Wise Men came bearing gifts. If the processional involved the giving of gifts, these should now be consecrated. Tithes and other offerings should also be collected, and then a prayer of dedication said over them all.

If the church is interested in designating a special season of sacrificial giving, Epiphany is a good day to begin. At the end of the offertory, a time of dedication for such special emphases can be added.

Great Thanksgiving

Commentary: Communion, if celebrated, focuses on Christ's manifestation; thus, Communion becomes a time of celebration as we remember that he has revealed himself to us as our Savior and Lord. If Communion is not celebrated, the service should end with more time in musical praise and worship. This could be followed by a prayer of dedication, sending the people out as light to the world, the manifest presence of Christ to those who know them.

✎ ELEVEN ✎

The Season after Epiphany

The time after Epiphany may be as short as four weeks and as long as eight weeks, depending on the date of Easter. The best way to calculate the Sundays of this time is to use a Christian calendar available in any local Christian bookstore.

The time after Epiphany is marked by two special events, one on the first Sunday, the other on the last. The first Sunday celebrates the baptism of the Lord and the last his transfiguration, a clear example of an epiphany. Although August 6th is the traditional date for the celebration of the Transfiguration, the Common Lectionary allows for both options. The arrangement of lectionary texts for the season after Epiphany is laid out well for those who like to preach a series of sermons on a particular book. It is also a good season for evangelism and missions, since the theme of the texts continue to express various ways in which Christ is manifested as the one who has come to save the world.

211 ◆ LECTIONARY TEXTS FOR THE SEASON AFTER EPIPHANY

The following are the texts suggested for the season after Epiphany in the Revised Common Lectionary. Brief descriptions of each lesson are provided to aid in recalling the basic theme of each passage. The calendar during many years may not have eight Sundays after Epiphany. The readings for the Transfiguration are traditionally read on the Sunday preceding Ash Wednesday.

———— Year A (1996, 1999) ————

SUNDAY	OLD TESTAMENT	PSALM	EPISTLE	GOSPEL
Baptism of the Lord	Isaiah 42:1-9, Lord's servant; bring justice to nations.	29	Acts 10:34-43, Peter's speech before Cornelius is baptized.	Matthew 3:13-17, the baptism of Jesus.
Second Sunday after Epiphany	Isaiah 49:1-7, servant chosen to bring light to the nations.	40:1-11	1 Corinthians 1:1-9, blessings in Christ will keep you firm.	John 1:29-42, John: "behold the Lamb of God."
Third Sunday after Epiphany	Isaiah 9:1-4, those in darkness have seen a great light.	27:1, 4-9	1 Corinthians 1:10-18, divisions in the church. Is Christ divided?	Matthew 4:12-23, Jesus' ministry begins, calls the four
Fourth Sunday after Epiphany	Micah 6:1-8, what does the Lord require: justice, mercy, piety.	15	1 Corinthians 1:18-31, God chose 'foolish' to shame the 'wise.'	Matthew 5:1-12, sermon on the mount; the Beatitudes.
Fifth Sunday after Epiphany	Isaiah 58:1-9a (9b-12), true piety: care for the oppressed and poor.	112:1-10	1 Corinthians 2:1-12, (13-16), God's wisdom hidden to world but clear to us.	Matthew 5:13-20, you are salt and light; the law.

Continued…

————— **Year A (1996, 1999) cont.** —————

SUNDAY	OLD TESTAMENT	PSALM	EPISTLE	GOSPEL
Sixth Sunday after Epiphany	Deuteronomy 30:15-20, "I give you a choice between life and death."	119:1-8	1 Corinthians 3:1-9, we are partners working together for God.	Matthew 5:21-37, teaching about law, anger, adultery.
Seventh Sunday after Epiphany	Leviticus 19:1-2, 9-18; "you are to be holy; love neighbor as self"	119:33-40	1 Corinthians 3:10-11, 16-23, our foundation is Christ; you are his temple.	Matthew 5:27-37, teaching about adultery, divorce, and vows.
Eighth Sunday after Epiphany	Isaiah 49:8-16a, the Lord will again come and comfort him	131	1 Corinthians 4:1-5; don't judge anyone until you receive the light.	Matthew 6:24-34, Jesus' teachings about God and our possessions.
Transfiguration	Exodus 24:12-18, God appears to Moses	99	2 Peter 1:16-21, gospel is not a made up story; we are eyewitnesses.	Matthew 17:1-9, the Transfiguration.

————— **Year B (1997, 2000)** —————

SUNDAY	OLD TESTAMENT	PSALM	EPISTLE	GOSPEL
Baptism of the Lord	Genesis 1:1-5, the days of Creation.	29	Acts 19:1-7, Paul baptizes in the name of Jesus.	Mark 14:4-11, John and baptism.
Second Sunday after Epiphany	1 Samuel 3:1-10 (or 20), the Lord calls Samuel.	139:1-6, 13-18	1 Corinthians 6:12-20, your body is Christ's.	John 1:43-51, disciples called: Philip and Nathanael.
Third Sunday after Epiphany	Jonah 3:1-5, 10, Jonah to Ninevah; the people repent.	62:5-12	1 Corinthians 7:29-31, world passing away; not much time.	Mark 1:14-20, Jesus preaches good news, calls disciples.
Fourth Sunday after Epiphany	Deuteronomy 18:15-20, Lord will raise up a prophet among you.	111	1 Corinthians 8:1-13, concerning food offered to idols.	Mark 1:21-28, Jesus in Capernaum; man with evil spirit.
Fifth Sunday after Epiphany	Isaiah 40:21-31, God creator of universe, with whom to compare?	147:1-11, 20c	1 Corinthians 9:16-23, compulsion to preach: "I'm free and a slave."	Mark 1:29-39, Jesus heals and preaches in Galilee.
Sixth Sunday after Epiphany	2 Kings 5:1-14, Elisha cures Naaman, the foreign commander.	30	1 Corinthians 9:24-27, image of the race and need for self-control.	Mark 1:40-45, Jesus heals a leper and becomes known.
Seventh Sunday after Epiphany	Isaiah 43:18-25, God is doing a new thing, forgives disobedient people.	41	2 Corinthians 1:18-22, Jesus the Christ is Yes to God's promises.	Mark 2:1-12, Jesus heals; scribes object to his presumption.

Continued...

──────── **Year B (1997, 2000) cont.** ────────

SUNDAY	OLD TESTAMENT	PSALM	EPISTLE	GOSPEL
Eighth Sunday after Epiphany	Hosea 2:14-20 the Lord will show love and mercy.	103:1-13	2 Corinthians 3:1-6, the law kills but the Spirit gives life.	Mark 2:13-22; new and the old; cloth and wineskins.
Transfiguration	Exodus 24:12-18, God appears to Moses.	50:1-6	2 Corinthians 4:3-6, Gospel: hid to the lost, shines in our hearts.	Mark 9:2-9, the Transfiguration.

──────── **Year C (1995, 1998, 2001)** ────────

SUNDAY	OLD TESTAMENT	PSALM	EPISTLE	GOSPEL
Baptism of the Lord	Isaiah 43:1-7, God's promise to rescue the people; don't fear.	29	Acts 8:14-17, Apostles send Peter and John to Samaria.	Luke 3:15-17, 21-22, John the Baptist and the baptism of Jesus.
Second Sunday after Epiphany	Isaiah 62:1-5, Jerusalem no longer forsaken. Lord pleased.	36:5-10	1 Corinthians 12:1-11, spiritual gifts.	John 2:1-11, the wedding in Cana.
Third Sunday after Epiphany	Nehemiah 8:1-3, 5-6, 8-10, Ezra reads law to people.	19	1 Corinthians 12:12-31a, body of Christ.	Luke 4:14-21, Jesus begins his work; preaches in Nazareth.
Fourth Sunday after Epiphany	Jeremiah 4:1-10, call to repentence; threat of invasion	71:1-6	1 Corinthians 13:1-13, the nature of Christian love.	Luke 4:21-30, Jesus is rejected in Nazareth.
Fifth Sunday after Epiphany	Isaiah 6:1-8, 9-13	138	1 Corinthians 15:1-11	Luke 5:1-11
Sixth Sunday after Epiphany	Jeremiah 17:5-10, blessings for those who trust God.	1	1 Corinthians 15:12-20, we are foolish if Christ has not been raised.	Luke 6:17-26, beatitudes and curses.
Seventh Sunday after Epiphany	Genesis 45:3-11, 15, Joseph: God sent me ahead to save you.	37:1-11	1 Corinthians 15:35-38, 42-50, first and second Adams: living being; life giving Spirit.	Luke 6:27-38, love and non-judgment toward enemies.
Eighth Sunday after Epiphany	Isaiah 55:10-13, "my word shall not be empty."	92:1-4, 12-15	1 Corinthians 15:51-58 "Where, O death, is your sting?"	Luke 6:39-49, good fruit, bad fruit; house on rock.
Transfiguration	Exodus 34:29-35	99	2 Corinthians 3:12-4:2	Luke 9:28-36 (37-43), the Transfiguration.

Revised Common Lectionary, descriptions by H. A. Tillinghast

212 ✦ RESOURCES FOR THE BAPTISM OF OUR LORD SUNDAY

The first Sunday after Epiphany is the celebration of the baptism of Jesus. This article provides an introduction to worship on this day and some resources for worship planning.

The baptism of Jesus was a major event celebrated in the worship of the early church. The early Fathers saw this even as significant in the saving action of Christ. Here the divine Sonship of Christ is first announced: "This is my beloved Son in whom I am well pleased" (Matt. 3:17). Furthermore, the ascent of the Spirit on Jesus was seen then and now as the anointing of Jesus for public ministry. And the baptism by John was evidence of the substitutionary character of that ministry, suggesting that Jesus was baptized for those for whom he would die. These themes are all captured in the appointed lessons for the day. Perhaps it is time for the Western church to make more of the Epiphany service as follow-up to the experience of Incarnation and a beginning to our own personal experience of the Christ who not only has been born within, but is the one who must be declared to others. In one sense Epiphany is evangelism Sunday.

(1) Make this day a baptism day. Baptisms on this day are highly appropriate. Emphasize the meaning of baptism. Create a special "Baptism of the Lord" banner. Also, make this a day for the renewal of baptismal vows (see volume 6, chapter 20).

(2) Use special resources in worship. Use the Taizé litany below in the Entrance; tell the Gospel reading as a story; develop special prayers and blessings that relate to the themes of Christ's baptism and of our baptism into Christ (see resources below).

An Entrance Rite for the Baptism of the Lord Sunday

A festive Entrance rite emphasizes the special nature of this day and helps people to make connections between the baptism of the Lord and their own baptism. Adapt the material below to local usage.

The minister, choir, others, and the banner carrier gather at the back of the church. The service begins with the litany of the baptism of our Lord said from the back of the church and proceeds in the fashion normal to your community.

THE LITANY OF "THE BAPTISM OF OUR LORD"

O Christ, by your epiphany, light has shone on us to assure us of the fullness of salvation: grant your light to all whom we shall encounter today: **Kyrie eleison. (Lord, have mercy.)**

O Christ, you humbled yourself and received baptism at your servant's hands, showing us the way of humility: grant us to serve humbly all the days of our life: **Kyrie eleison.**

O Christ, by your baptism you washed away every impurity, making us children of the Father: grant the grace of adoption as God's children to all who are searching for him: **Kyrie eleison.**

O Christ, by your baptism you sanctified the creation and opened the way of repentance and new life to all who are baptized: make us instruments of your gospel in the world: **Kyrie eleison.**

O Christ, by your baptism you revealed the Trinity, your Father calling you his beloved Son, through the Spirit descending upon you: renew a spirit of true worship in the royal priesthood of all the baptized. **Kyrie eleison.**

O Christ, made manifest as the true light of God: **gladden our hearts on the joyful morning of your glory, call us by our name on the great Day of your coming, and give us grace to offer unending praise with all the hosts of heaven to** the Father in whom all things find their ending, **now and ever. Amen.** (from *Praise God: Common Prayer at Taizé*)

Entrance Hymn

Traditional: "The Sinless One to Jordan Came"; "When Jesus Went to Jordan's Stream" Contemporary: "Majesty"; "All Hail King Jesus"

Greeting and Call to Worship

MINISTER: Beloved Son upon whom the Spirit came

PEOPLE: Come and be present to us in our
worship

The *Gloria in Excelsis Deo,* or some other song
of praise such as "Thou Art Worthy" or "Be Exalted, O God" or a cluster of praise songs that extol Christ.

THE OPENING PRAYER

Lord Jesus Christ, You humbled yourself and became baptized for us sinful people and God declared you to be his beloved Son. May those of us
who have been baptized into you live in our baptism by rejoicing in you and caring for others; we
pray in your name, for you dwell with the Father
and the Holy Spirit and live as one God forever,
world without end. Amen.

The Interrogatory Creed
for Baptism Sunday

In the early church the creed at baptism was
recited in the form of question and response,
known as the interrogatory creed. Today this practice has been restored. Use this form of the creed
on Baptism Sunday.

CELEBRANT: Do you believe in God the Father?
PEOPLE: **I believe in God, the Father al-
mighty, creator of heaven and
earth.**
CELEBRANT: Do you believe in Jesus Christ, the
Son of God?
PEOPLE: **I believe in Jesus Christ, his only
Son, our Lord.**
**He was conceived by the power of
the Holy Spirit**
and born of the Virgin Mary.
**He suffered under Pontius Pilate,
was crucified, died, and was bur-
ied.**
He descended to the dead.
On the third day he rose again.
He ascended into heaven,
**and is seated at the right hand of
the Father.**
**He will come again to judge the
living and the dead.**
CELEBRANT: Do you believe in God the Holy
Spirit?
PEOPLE: **I believe in the Holy Spirit**
the holy catholic church,

the communion of saints,
the forgiveness of sins,
the resurrection of the body,
and the life everlasting.

A Benediction for
Baptism Sunday

The benediction below draws on the theme of
baptism Sunday. Adapt and use according to local
custom.

May God the Father, who sent His Spirit upon
His Son,
bless you with the presence of His Spirit.
May Jesus who received the Spirit and mani-
fested the Father
abide in you and make you a manifestation of
His life,
And may the Spirit who came upon Christ in
the fullness of power
empower you to live a life of faith.
To the glory of God, Father, Son, and Holy
Spirit.

213 ✦ RESOURCES FOR THE OTHER SUNDAYS IN THE SEASON AFTER EPIPHANY

*The following are supplemental liturgical resources for
the season after Epiphany. Adapt to local need and custom, taking these examples as models.*

Traditional Opening Prayers

Adapt these opening prayers to local style.
These prayers contain the general themes of
Epiphany and of the services in the season after
Epiphany.

**First Sunday after the Epiphany: The Baptism
of our Lord** (Sunday between Jan. 7–13)
Father in heaven, who at the baptism of Jesus in
the River Jordan proclaimed him your beloved Son
and anointed him with the Holy Spirit: Grant that
all who are baptized into his name may keep the
covenant they have made, and boldly confess him
as Lord and Savior; who with you and the Holy
Spirit lives and reigns, one God, in glory everlasting. Amen.

Second Sunday after the Epiphany (Jan. 14–20)
Almighty God, whose Son our Savior Jesus Christ

is the light of the world: Grant that your people, illumined by your Word and Sacraments, may shine with the radiance of Christ's glory, that he may be known, worshiped, and obeyed to the ends of the earth; through Jesus Christ our Lord, who with you and the Holy Spirit lives and reigns, one God, now and forever. Amen.

Third Sunday after the Epiphany (Jan. 21–27)
Give us grace, O Lord, to answer readily the call of our Savior Jesus Christ and proclaim to all people the good news of his salvation, that we and the whole world may perceive the glory of his marvelous works; who lives and reigns with you and the Holy Spirit, one God, for ever and ever. Amen.

Fourth Sunday after the Epiphany (Jan. 28–Feb. 3)
Almighty and everlasting God, you govern all things both in heaven and on earth: Mercifully hear the supplication of your people, and in our time grant us your peace; through Jesus Christ our Lord, who lives and reigns with you and the Holy Spirit, one God, for ever and ever. Amen.

Fifth Sunday after the Epiphany (Feb. 4–10, if not the last)
Set us free, O God, from the bondage of our sins, and give us the liberty of that abundant life which you have made known to us in your Son our Savior Jesus Christ; who lives and reigns with you, in the unity of the Holy Spirit, one God, now and for ever. Amen.

Sixth Sunday after the Epiphany (Feb. 11–17, if not the last)
O God, the strength of all who put their trust in you: Mercifully accept our prayers; and because in our weakness we can do nothing good without you, give us the help of your grace, that in keeping your commandments we may please you both in will and deed; through Jesus Christ our Lord, who lives and reigns with you and the Holy Spirit, one God, for ever and ever. Amen.

Seventh Sunday after the Epiphany (Feb. 18–24, if not the last)
O Lord, you have taught us that without love whatever we do is worth nothing: Send your Holy Spirit and pour into our hearts your greatest gift, which is love, the true bond of peace and of all virtue, without which whoever lives is accounted dead before you. Grant this for the sake of your only

Son Jesus Christ, who lives and reigns with you and the Holy Spirit, one God, now and for ever. Amen.

Eighth Sunday after the Epiphany (Feb. 25–Mar. 3, if not the last)
Most loving Father, whose will it is for us to give thanks for all things, to fear nothing but the loss of you, and to cast all our care on you who care for us; preserve us from faithless fears and worldly anxieties, that no clouds of this mortal life may hide from us the light of that love which is immortal, and which you have manifested to us in your Son Jesus Christ our Lord; who lives and reigns with you, in the unity of the Holy Spirit, one God, now and for ever. Amen.

Last Sunday after the Epiphany (The transfiguration of our Lord)
(This Proper is always used on the Sunday before Ash Wednesday.)
O God, who before the passion of your only begotten Son revealed his glory upon the holy mountain: Grant to us that we, beholding by faith the light of his countenance, may be strengthened to bear our cross, and be changed into his likeness from glory to glory; through Jesus Christ our Lord, who lives and reigns with you and the Holy Spirit, one God, for ever and ever. Amen.

Book of Common Prayer

A Biblical Creed for Sundays after Epiphany

The creed below, adapted from Mark 8:39, 1 Corinthians 12:3, Romans 10:9, and Acts 2:36, may be used in any of the Sundays of Epiphany.

LEADER: Who do you say that Jesus is?
PEOPLE: **He is the Christ.**
LEADER: I want you to understand that no one speaking by the Spirit of God ever says "Jesus be cursed!" and no one can say "Jesus is Lord" except by the Holy Spirit.
PEOPLE: **We confess with our lips that Jesus is Lord and we believe in our heart that God has raised him from the dead.**
LEADER: Let the whole world know that God has made him both Lord and Christ!
PEOPLE: **Amen!**

A Benediction for the Sundays after Epiphany

The benediction below may be used in any or all of the Sundays of Epiphany.

O Jesus Christ, who is the Light of lights and whose manifestation as the light of the world we celebrate on this day.

Bless us with the Light of your life in the week that lies ahead and cause us to be witnesses of your light in our lives, in our relationships, in our homes, and in our places of work and play.

In the name and by the power of the Father, the Son, and the Holy Spirit. Amen.

214 ✦ AN ANTHOLOGY OF HYMNS AND SONGS FOR THE SUNDAYS OF EPIPHANY

The music listed in this article covers a broad range of Epiphany themes.

The season of Epiphany can contain four to nine Sundays. It begins January 6 and continues to (but does not include) Ash Wednesday. The season represents Christ's public exposure to the world as light to the Gentiles, as God with us, as Messiah in revealed person. Primary biblical references to the symbolism of this season are (apart from the angelic announcement of his birth) the visit of the magi (Matt. 2:1-3), the infant Christ's presentation at the temple (Luke 2:22), the twelve-year-old Christ among the temple elders (Luke 2:41, 46-47), his baptism at the Jordan (Matt. 3:13-17), his first acts of ministry, and his transfiguration (Mark 9:2-8).

Epiphany has a world-directed focus and emphasizes outward commitment, presentation of the gospel, and missions. Churches following the three-year lectionary cycle normally observe three major Epiphany themes in the following order: his baptism, his presentation at the temple, and (the final Sunday after Epiphany) his transfiguration.

Seven of the nine compositions below penned by modern composers are based on the Psalms. This feature is a reasonable indication of a larger (and measurable) penchant among Scripture chorus writers to treat the Psalms with special affection. There is some justification in considering the vast body of Christian contemporary praise and worship choruses as a type of American Urban Psalter, a practice that has deep historical roots and precedence.

All Praise to You, O Lord
John 2:1-2,11 [H. Beadon/C. Lockheart] CARLISLE; see H1982:138; wedding at Cana

All the Earth Shall Worship
Psalm 66:4 [Dave Moody (1989)] see WH-II:333; His authority to the world

Arise and Shine in Splendor
Isaiah 60:1-6 [Opitz/H. Isaac] INSBRUCK; see LH:126

As With Gladness Men of Old
Matthew 2:1-11 [W. Dix/K. Kocher] DIX; see LH:127, Magi: Visit

Behold His Glory
Matthew 17:2 [D. Harris (1989)] see WH-II:289; the Transfiguration

Brightest and Best of the Stars of Morning
Job 38:7, Matthew 2:9 [R. Reber/Leipzig, 1675] LIEBSTER IMMANUEL; see SBAH:53, the Magi

Brightest and Best of the Stars of the Morning
Job 38:7, Matthew 2:9 [R.Reber/J. Harding] MORNING STAR; see LH:128; the Magi

Christ is the World's Light
John 8:12 [F. Green/French, 17th C.] Christe Sanctorum; see HS-I:127; Light to the world

Christ Upon the Mountain Peak
Matthew 17:2 [B. Wren/C. Taylor (1985) B. Wren/ P. Cutts (1977)] MOWSLEY SHILLINGFORD; see HS-I:12; the Transfiguration

Come, Pure Hearts
[Latin Sequence Hymn/Ned Rorem] PURE HEARTS; see H-III:158; the Evangelist's testimony of Christ

From the Eastern Mountains
Matthew 2:1-11 [G. Thring/W. Pitts] PRINCE-THORPE; see MNH:140; Magi:visit

Hail the Blessed Morn
Matthew 2:2 [R. Heber/Southern Harmony (1835)] STAR IN THE EAST; see HWB:221; early American

Hail, Thou Source of Every Blessing
Matthew 2:11 [B. Wood/Halle, (1704)] O DURCHBRECHER; see LH:129; Light to the Gentiles

How Beautiful are Their Feet
Romans 10:15 [A. Wood, (1790)] WOCESTER; see NEPT:nn

In His Temple Now Behold Him
Luke 2:22 [H. Pye/H. Purcell, arr. Gieseke,

(1981)] Westminster Abbey; see LW:186; presentation in the temple

Jesus Has come and Brings Pleasure

[J. Allendorf/Cothen, 1733] Jesus ist Kommen, Grund Ewige Freude; see LW:78

Jesus, Life of All the World

John 8:12, 14:6 [M. Clarkson/J. Cruger] Jesu Meine Zuversicht; see HS-I:129; Light to the world

Kingdom of God, the

Matthew 13:31-32 [G. Grindal/A. Lovelace] Mustard Seed; see HWB:224

Lift High the Cross

John 12:32 [G. Kitchin/S. Nicholson (1974)] Crucifer; see CPH:594; Proclaiming Christ

Light Our Way

John 8:12 [Tom Coomes (1983)] see MMP:13; light to the world

Lord is My Light, The

Psalm 27:1 [P. Mills (1989)] see WH-II:79; his presence to believers

Lord, Who Throughout These 40 Days

Matthew 4:1-2 [C. Hernaman/Day's Psalter] St. Flavian; see WB:470: The Temptation

March of the Wisemen

Matthew 2:1-2 [R. Hamilton (1985)] see P-II:63; magi: visit

Now May Thy Servant

Luke 2:28-32 [D. Westra/L. Bourgeois] Nunc Dimittis; see PSH:345; presentation in the temple, Simeon's Canticle

Nunc Dimittis

Luke 2:28-32 [Br. Robert/J. Berthier (1981)] see Taiz:22; mixed-voice and equal-voice options with guitar acct.

O God of God; O Light of Light

Psalm 43:3 [J. Julian/Stuttgart, 1744] O Grosser Gott; see LH:132; light to the world

O God of Light, Your Word a Lamp Unfailing

Psalm 119:105 [S. Taylor/D. Evans] Charterhouse; see WB:499

O Jesus, King of Glory

Matthew 2:1-12 [M. Behm/M. Teschner] Valet Will Ich Dir Geben; see LH:130; Chorale; numerous organ settings also

O Love How Deep, How Broad, How High

Ephesians 3:18-19 [T. a Kempis/J. Bingham (1984)] Infinite Love; see SDAH:148; His love to the world

O Thou, Who by a Star Didst Guide

Matthew 2:2 [J. Neale/H. Hiles] St. Leonard; see SBAH:54; magi: visit

O Zion, Haste

Isaiah 40:9 [M. Thomson/J. Walch] Tidings; see MH:475; light to the world

Proclaim the Power of our God

Psalm 68:2,4; 32-34 [D. Holsinger (1989)] WH-II:394; Kingdoms of the earth praise him

Send Forth Your Word, O God

Psalm 72:8 [M. Price (1991)] Proclamation; see CPH:588; witness to the world

Send Me, Lord (Thuma Mina)

Isaiah 6:8c [Traditional South African (1989)] see ALYA-I:44; witness to the world

Share His Love

Matthew 28:18-19 [W. J. Reynolds (1973)] Sullivan; see CPH:567; witness to the world

Shine, Jesus, Shine

John 1:9; 8:12 [G. Kendrick (1980)] Shine; see CPH:579; light of the world

Sing to the Lord

Psalm 33:3; Psalm 72:18-19 [M. Chapman (1983)] see MMP:106; witness to the world

Sinless One to Jordan Came, the

Matthew 3:13 [G. Timms/arr. G. Hancock (1978)] Solemnis Haec Festivitas; see H-III:118b; 1st Sunday after Epiphany

Songs of Thankfulness and Praise

John 2:1; Matthew 3:13-17 [W. Wordsworth/J. Richardson] Tichfield, Salzburg; see SBAH:55; at the Jordan, at Cana

Spirit of the Lord, the

Luke 4:18 [E. Stacey (1976)] see WH-I:185; his initial reading at Nazareth

Star Carol, the

Matthew 2:10 [W. Hutson/A. Burt] Star Carol; see HFG:201

Star Proclaims the King is Here

Matthew 2:9 [C. Sedulius/Wittemberg (1535)] Wo Gott Zum Haus; see LH:131; Magi:Visit

Stay, Master

Matthew 17:4 [S. Greg/J. Wainwright] Yorkshire; see MH:122; the Transfiguration

Thou Light of Gentile Nations

Luke 2:32 [J. Franck/M. Teschner] Valet Will Ich Dir Geben; see LH:138

Tis Good, Lord, to be Here

Matthew 17:4 [J. Robinson/J. S. Bach] Potsdam; see LH:135; the transfiguration

To the Glory of Jesus Christ

Psalm 119:11 [R. Hamilton (1978)] see P-I:21; Testimony to the world

Tu has Venido a la Orilla
   Matthew 4:19-20 [C. Gabarain/Same (1979)]
   PESCADOR DE HOMBRES; HWB:229; Spanish and
   English texts
We've a Story to Tell the Nations
   Matthew 24:14 [H. Nichol] MESSAGE; see CPH:
   586; testimony to the world
With the Father's House
   Luke 2:41-52 [J. Woodford/J. Konig] FRANCONIA;
   see LH:133; the youth Christ at Jerusalem
Worship the Lord
   Psalm 96:9 [Monselle, Steele and Fettke (1985)]
   JANICE; see CPH:115; Magi:Visit; (indirect allu-
   sion)

Stephen Cushman

215 ◆ RESOURCES FOR TRANSFIGURATION SUNDAY

The last Sunday before Ash Wednesday is traditionally a season in which the church remembers the transfiguration of Jesus as recorded in the gospels. This article introduces you to this day and provides resources for worship planning.

Aureole. The Latin word aurum _means gold. Hence the word_ aureole _is often used to describe a halo of radiance encircling the body or head of one of the three persons of the Trinity. As a Christmas symbol, it speaks of the divinity and power of Jesus._

The Eastern church has always regarded the Transfiguration with higher respect than has the Western. This may be because of their theology of "divination," which promises that human persons will become full of the glory of God. It is here, in the Transfiguration, where the greater glory of God in the man Jesus is manifest to Peter, James, and John. Here we see a more full expression of the deity of Christ and the glory he has with his Father. And we gain a glimpse of the glory he will share with us as his children!

The Transfiguration is well situated in the last Sunday after Epiphany, for it is a final Epiphany of Christ and it is also well suited to the pilgrimage we are about to take during Lent, for during Lent we prepare to suffer with him so that we might also be raised with him into the newness of life he brings. So the Epiphany of our Lord is a significant link from his manifestation as the Savior of the world at the end of the Christmas season to his manifestation as the Savior of the world at his resurrection.

Ideas for Transfiguration Sunday

(1) Farewell to the Alleluias. Transfiguration Sunday is the last Sunday before the beginning of Lent. Traditionally during Lent the Alleluias are not sung because of the season's penitential nature. Some churches festoon Transfiguration Sunday with a plethora of Alleluias as a way of extolling the transfiguration of Christ and as a way of saying good-bye to the Alleluias for the Lenten season (Alleluias not to be sung until the Easter announcement "He is risen from the dead"). Lace various Alleluias into the service (at the Entrance hymn, Psalms, reading of New Testament, Communion song), and at the end of the service have the choir sing a number of Alleluias and designate these as the "good-bye to Alleluia" songs.

(2) In worship use some or all of the ideas for services that appear in the following paragraphs.

An Entrance Rite for Transfiguration Sunday

The minister, choir, banner carriers, and other participants gather in the back of the sanctuary. After a period of silence the minister or other reader begins with the words of the opening Transfiguration litany.

Loving Father, you transfigured your beloved Son and revealed the Holy Spirit in the bright cloud: Enable us to hear the Word of Christ with faithful hearts.
Kyrie eleison.

Loving Father, you made light to rise in the darkness, and you have shone in our hearts, to make known your glory in the face of Jesus Christ: Revive in us the spirit of contemplation.
Kyrie eleison.

O Christ, you took your friends with you and led them to a high mountain: May your church stay close to you, in the peace and hope of your glory.
Kyrie eleison.

O Christ, by your Transfiguration you revealed the Resurrection to your disciples before your Passion began; we pray for the church in all the difficulties of this world; in our trials may we be transfigured by the joy of your victory.
Kyrie eleison.

O Christ, you led Peter, James, and John down from the mountain and into the suffering world; when our hearts crave permanence, may we know the permanence of your love as you take us with you on your way.
Kyrie eleison.

O Christ, you will transfigure our poor bodies and conform them to your glorious body; we pray to you for our brothers and sisters who are dying; may they be changed into your likeness, from glory to glory.
Kyrie eleison.

The Lord be with you,
And also with you.
Let us pray.

Silence

O God, whose face we cannot see, you have made known your love by the lives of faithful witnesses. We give you thanks for the revelation of your glory in the face of our Lord Jesus Christ, for your confirmation of his disciples and for the promise of his victory. May the light of your presence shine on your people, that all may see the fulfillment of their hopes in the coming of our Savior, Jesus Christ.
Amen.

Lord Jesus Christ, light shining in our darkness, have mercy on our tired and doubting hearts. Renew in us the courage we need,
that we may bring to completion the work your calling has begun in us.
Freely you gave your life on the Cross,
freely you took it again in your Resurrection,
for you live and reign now and for ever.
Amen.
(from *Praise God: Common Prayer at Taizé*)

Greeting and Call to Worship

LEADER: The Lord be with you.
PEOPLE: **And also with you.**
LEADER: O Christ, you who were transfigured on Mt. Tabor, come and transfigure us into your glory as we sing to you.
PEOPLE: **Alleluia.**

Entrance Hymn

Traditional
   "Alleluia! Sing to Jesus"
   "Christ Whose Glory Fills The Skies"
   "O Wondrous Type! O Vision Fair"

Contemporary
   "Let There Be Glory and Honor and Praise"
   "O The Glory of Your Presence"
   "May the Fragrance of Jesus Fill This Place"

The Confession of Sin

Commentary: On Transfiguration Sunday it is appropriate to use a confession of sin in the Entrance.

The Gloria/Act of Praise

Commentary: Sing the "Gloria in Excelsis Deo" or some other suitable song of praise.

The Opening Prayer

LEADER: The Lord be with you.
PEOPLE: **And also with you.**
LEADER: Let us pray.
ALL: Almighty God,
         Today the whole of human nature glitters in the divine
         Transfiguration. May we your servants receive the Holy Light
         and be transfigured by the power of your Holy Spirit, through
         Jesus Christ who lives with you and the Holy Spirit forever. Amen.

Prayer of Thanksgiving for Transfiguration Sunday

MINISTER: The Lord be with you.
PEOPLE: **And also with you.**
MINISTER: Lift up your hearts.
PEOPLE: **We lift them to the Lord.**
MINISTER: Let us give thanks to the Lord our God.
PEOPLE: **It is right to give our thanks and praise.**
MINISTER: It is truly right and our greatest joy
to give you thanks and praise,
eternal God our Creator.
You brought light out of darkness
and set the sun to brighten the day
and the moon and stars to illumine
the night.
Your glory blinds the eyes of our sin,
while your radiance warms our needy
hearts.
You lead us by the light of your truth
into the way of righteousness and
peace.

Therefore we praise you,
joining our voices with the heavenly
choirs
and with all the faithful of every time
and place,
who forever sing to the glory of your
name:

(The people may sing or say:)

**Holy, holy, holy Lord, God of power
and might,
heaven and earth are full of your
glory.
Hosanna in the highest.**

**Blessed is he who comes in the
name of the Lord.
Hosanna in the highest.**

(The minister continues:)

You are holy, O God of majesty,
and blessed is Jesus Christ, your Son,
our Lord.
On a lonely mountain
his body was transfigured by your divine splendor.
In his face, we have glimpsed your
glory.

In his life, we see your love.
For your image is untarnished in him,
and the burden of human sorrow and
suffering
could not diminish his reflection of
your holiness.
The world was dark at his death,
but the light of his life could not be
extinguished.
From the grave he rose like the sun,
with blinding power and radiant
peace.

(If they have not already been said, the words
of institution may be said here, or in relation
to the breaking of the bread.)

MINISTER: We give you thanks that the Lord
Jesus,
on the night before he died,
took bread,
and after giving thanks to you,
he broke it, and gave it to his disciples, saying:
Take, eat.
This is my body, given for you.
Do this in remembrance of me.

In the same way he took the cup, saying:
This cup is the new covenant sealed
in my blood,
shed for you for the forgiveness of
sins.
Whenever you drink it,
do this in remembrance of me.

Remembering your gracious acts in
Jesus Christ,
we take from your creation this bread
and this wine
and joyfully celebrate his dying and
rising
as we await the day of his coming.
With thanksgiving we offer our very
selves to you
to be a living and holy sacrifice,
dedicated to your service.

(The people may sing or say one of the following:)
1
MINISTER: Great is the mystery of faith:
PEOPLE: **Christ has died,**

**Christ is risen,
Christ will come again.**

2

MINISTER: Praise to you, Lord Jesus:

PEOPLE: **Dying you destroyed our death,
rising you restored our life.
Lord Jesus, come in glory.**

3

MINISTER: According to his commandment:

PEOPLE: **We remember his death,
we proclaim his resurrection
we await his coming in glory.**

4

MINISTER: Christ is the bread of life:

PEOPLE: **When we eat this bread and drink
this cup,
we proclaim your death, Lord Jesus,
until you come in glory.**

(The minister continues:)

Gracious God,
pour out your Holy Spirit upon us
and upon these your gifts of bread
and wine,
that the bread we break
and the cup we bless
may be the communion of the body
and blood of Christ.
By your Spirit make us one with
Christ,
that we may be one with all who share
this feast,
united in ministry in every place.
As this bread is Christ's body for us,
send us out to be the body of Christ
in the world.

(Intercessions for the church and the world may
be included here.)

Gracious God,
pour out your Holy Spirit upon us
and upon these your gifts of bread
and wine,
that the bread we break
and the cup we bless
may be the communion of the body
and blood of Christ.
By your Spirit make us one with
Christ,

that we may be one with all who share
this feast,
united in ministry in every place.
As this bread is Christ's body for us,
send us out to be the body of Christ
in the world.

(Intercessions for the church and the world may
be included here.)

Illumine our lives, O God,
with the radiance of Christ's love,
and inspire us to shine in faith and
witness
as his holy disciples.
Transform us into his likeness
that we may live for you, as he lived,
and love others, as he loved them.
Give us strength to serve you faithfully
until the promised day of resurrection,
when with the redeemed of all ages
we will feast with you at your table in
glory.
Through Christ, with Christ, in Christ,
in the unity of the Holy Spirit,
all glory an honor are yours, almighty
God,
now and forever.

PEOPLE: **Amen.**

Book of Common Worship[22]

216 ◆ BIBLIOGRAPHY FOR ADVENT, CHRISTMAS, AND EPIPHANY WORSHIP

Brown, Raymond E. *A Coming Christ in Advent* (1988) and *An Adult Christ for Christmas* (1977). Collegeville, Minn.: Liturgical Press. Essays on the Gospel narratives of the birth of Jesus by a noted New Testament scholar. Ecumenical.

Brokhoff, John R. *Advent and Event*. Lima, Ohio: C.S.S., 1980. A study guide to Scripture readings for Advent and Christmas, in light of the liturgical services of these seasons. Ecumenical.

Days of the Lord. Vol. 1: Advent, Christmas, Epiphany. Collegeville, Minn.: Liturgical Press, 1991. This useful volume and its companions are liturgical commentaries, guides for examining and understanding the structure of the post-conciliar reforms of Vatican II. Two- to three-page commentaries for each Sunday in each of the three church years (A, B, and C), are presented with exegetical, pastoral, and liturgical notes. The book commences with a valuable chapter on the Sacrament of the Liturgical Year and concludes with an extensive section of notes. Ecumenical/Roman Catholic.

Griffen, Elton, ed. _Celebrating the Season of Advent_. Collegeville, Minn.: Liturigcal Press, 1986. Essays on almost every aspect of Advent worship: theology, Scripture readings, art, symbols, music, children, and more. Ecumenical.

Groh, Dennis E. _In Between Advents_. Philadelphia: Fortress, 1986. Groh's unique perspective of "Advent as an arrival in search of hospitality" is born out of his convictions that (1) this season is a good time to consider the work of Christ that must yet be worked out in us and our world, and (2) Advent emphasizes our welcoming of both love's object and love's ruler who will help us achieve that purpose. The author includes a great deal of exegesis relating to ancient near-Eastern hospitality tradition from biblical and archaeological sources. Ecumenical.

Hopko, Thomas. _The Winter Pascha_. Crestwood, N.Y.: St. Vladimir's Seminary Press, 1984. Hopko has authored forty meditations covering the period from Christmas to Epiphany. Original material has been augmented with biblical readings, liturgical hymns, verses of the season, references to saints and church fathers, and contemporary Christian teachers and spiritual guides. Ecumenical/Roman Catholic.

Irwin, Kevin W. _Advent-Christmas: A Guide to the Eucharist and the Hours_. New York: Pueblo Publishing, 1986. A handbook to each service in the Advent and Christmas season, including eucharistic and daily prayer services. Roman Catholic/ecumenical.

Kirk, James G. _Meditations for Advent and Christmas_. Louisville: Westminster/John Knox, 1989. The work is a collection of short, original commentaries on Scripture texts appropriate to the Sundays and weekdays from Advent to Epiphany. Each two- to three-page selection ends with a prayer, and the volume may be used either devotionally or as a resource for preparation of homilies or sermons. Ecumenical/Presbyterian.

L'Engle, Madeleine. _The Irrational Season_. New York: Harper & Row, 1977. L'Engle's work is an original collection of Advent to Advent musings, the uniqueness of which may be explored with great delight. Her vision of each subject/theme manifests creativity and sensitivity, especially to numerous pieces of poetry, prose, Scripture, and hymn texts found therein. The work's twelve chapters could be read both privately and publicly. Ecumenical.

Nocent, Adrian. _The Liturgical Year_. Vol. 1. Collegeville, Minn.: Liturgical Press, 1977. This volume covers the period of Advent, Christmas, Epiphany, and Sundays two to eight in ordinary time. Each section is divided into three parts: biblico-liturgical reflections on the church year, structure and themes of the season, and suggestions from the past (the "O" antiphons). The elements of Scripture exegesis, historical/cultural context, and liturgical/pastoral commentary are valuable. Ecumenical/Roman Catholic.

National Conference of Catholic Bishops. _Prayers of the Advent and Christmas Seasons_. Washington, D. C.: U.S. Catholic Conference, 1987. Texts of appropriate prayers for the Advent season. Roman Catholic/ecumenical.

O'Driscoll, Herbert. _A Year of the Lord_. Wilton, Conn.: Morehouse-Barlow, 1986. O'Driscoll provides twenty-three topical commentaries on Scriptures related to the Common Lectionary from the Advent to the reign of Christ as King in the church year. The seasoned pastor's original insights are creative and thought-provoking, and the volume may be used as a resource for sermon preparation, group study, or personal meditation. Ecumenical/Anglican.

O'Gorman, Thomas J. _An Advent Sourcebook_. Chicago: Liturgy Training Publications, 1988. This volume and its companions are sourcebooks of prayers, poems, hymns, homilies, Scripture, sacramentary texts, and ancient and contemporary writing gleaned from Roman, Eastern, and Anglican rites, and other sources which have been compiled to assist in Christmastime liturgy. Material covers the period of from Chrismas Eve to Jesus' baptism. Book folds flat for ease of the user. See the other volumes in this series listed in the other bibliographies in this volume. Ecumenical.

Perham, Michael, and Kenneth Stevenson. _Welcoming the Light of Christ_. Collegeville, Minn.: Liturgical Press, 1991. This collection of services and prayers for the season from All Saints to Candlemas is a commentary on *The Promise of His Glory*, (see next entry). Academic and pastoral insights are offered by inclusion of both background and history as well as specific detail (hymns, readings, and so on) and appropriate ways in which services may be used in the local setting. Ecumenical/Anglican.

The Promise of His Glory. Collegeville, Minn.: Liturgical Press, 1991. The volume exists as a collection of new services for All Saints to Candlemas. It preserves the distinctiveness of the Evangelists' messages, uses resources from Eastern and Western Catholic and Reformed traditions, distinguishes Christian from secular Christmas, and takes advantage of more than one liturgical shape for the season. Services for all events are provided, and there are special sections for canticles and responsories, prayers and appendices with an alternative calendar, table of collects, and notes on lectionaries. Ecumenical/Anglican.

Rest, Friedrich. *Our Christian Worship*. Lima, Ohio: C.S.S. Publishing, 1985. Rest's small volume provides original resources for the seven Sundays and worship days of Advent and Christmastide, which include all of the elements of a Protestant service (excepting the homily/sermon and the Eucharist). Other resources and notes are offered at the end of the volume. Ecumenical/Protestant.

Simcoe, Mary Ann, ed. *A Christmas Sourcebook*. Chicago: Liturgy Training Publications, 1984. This volume and its companions are sourcebooks of prayers, poems, hymns, homilies, Scripture, sacramental texts, and ancient and contemporary writing gleaned from Roman, Eastern, Anglican rites, as well as other sources which have been compiled to assist in Christmastime liturgy. Material covers the period of from Chrismas Eve to Jesus' baptism. Book folds flat for ease of the user. Ecumenical.

Stuhlmueller, Carroll. *Biblical Meditations for Advent and the Christmas Season*. New York: Paulist, 1980. Fr. Stuhmueller's strategy is to get his anxious audience to slow down and experience hopeful anticipation through a reflective encounter with the Advent and Christmas seasons via a study of appropriate Scriptures, for which he provides original commentary and prayer. Weekdays and Sundays for both seasons are included. Meditations may be used privately or may provide the foundation for public presentation. Ecumenical/Roman Catholic.

See also article #161, the bibliography of general resources for the Christian year. All of the resources listed there include resources for Advent, Christmas, and Epiphany worship.

PART FIVE

The Season of Lent

On Ash Wednesday, the church marks an important transition, beginning the great cycle of Easter that extends from Ash Wednesday to Pentecost. The season of Lent is not primarily a meditation on the suffering and cross of Christ; this is saved for Holy Week. Rather, it is a season of penitence and prayer, reflection and renewal, all designed to prepare the worshiping community for the remembrance of Christ's death and celebration of his resurrection during Holy Week. More specifically, Lent is preparation for baptism. For new Christians who are baptized on Easter, Lent is a time to prepare for their new identity in Christ. For those who have been baptized, it is a time of self-examination so that they might reclaim their identity as those who have been buried with Christ in baptism and raised with him to new life.

TWELVE

Introduction to Lenten Worship

Lenten worship is a season for personal and corporate spiritual renewal. It is a time for intense study of God's Word, for meditation, for prayer, and for self-examination. It begins quietly with ashes and builds in intensity as the observance of Christ's death and resurrection grow closer. The following articles explore this season, introducing the reader to the meaning of Lent and showing how the Lenten pilgrimage puts the gospel in motion in a convicting and empowering way.

217 • AN INTRODUCTION TO LENT

The history of Lent reveals traditions rich with meaning. Lent deepened the experience of early Christian community as new believers were baptized and as the events of Christ's death and resurrection were celebrated.

In the liturgical rites of most churches, there is a pastoral exhortation to the people at the beginning of the Ash Wednesday liturgy that expresses well the focus of Lent. One such elocution is the following from the *Book of Common Prayer* (1979) of the Episcopal Church:

Dear People of God: The first Christians observed with great devotion the days of our Lord's passion and resurrection, and it became the custom of the Church to prepare for them by a season of penitence and fasting. This season of Lent provided a time in which converts to the faith were prepared for Holy Baptism. It was also a time for those who, because of notorious sins, had been separated from the body of the faithful and were reconciled by penitence and forgiveness, and restored to the fellowship of the church. Thereby, the whole congregation was put in mind of the message of pardon and absolution set forth in the Gospel of our Savior, and of the need which all Christians continually have to renew their repentance and faith. I invite you, therefore, in the name of the Church, to the observance of a holy Lent, by self-examination and repentance; by prayer, fasting and self-denial; and by reading and meditating on God's holy Word. And, to make a right beginning of repentance, and as a mark of

our mortal nature, let us now kneel before the Lord, our maker and redeemer.

The current experience of Lent in many churches begins with the Ash Wednesday liturgy that often includes the imposition of ashes as a sign of our mortality, and moves slowly and methodically through five weeks of preparation coming to a climax in the liturgy for Palm Sunday. The blessing and procession of palms, the singing of the great Hosanna, and the Gospel proclamation of the triumphal entry of Jesus into Jerusalem, combine to create a brief festal interlude in the discipline of Lent. This same rite, however, intensifies our focus upon the sufferings and death of our Lord in the days of Holy Week. Toward the end of our paschal fast, we experience the quiet tragedy of the acts of Friday, the solitude of the Great Sabbath, the quiet joy of the Paschal Vigil, and the blasting ecstasy of the first Eucharist of Easter. It should come as no surprise that this progression of our Lent-to-Easter season, with due allowance for details, is the reverse of the actual pattern of development. The early Christians placed the resurrection of the Lord at the very center of their religious observance.

The Passover was deeply ingrained in the lives and traditions of the early Jewish-Christian community. Such a significant event in the life of a community of faith is not easily dismissed, even in the face of another event of redemptive significance. While the resurrection of our Lord had immediate and far-reaching impact upon the Jewish-Christian community, there is no reason to assume that it immediately supplanted the annual observance of Passover. The great and mighty act accomplished by God in the death and resurrection of Jesus in no way detracted from the earlier act of God that brought their ancestors out of bondage into freedom. Indeed, the blending of the two traditions in the Jewish-Christian community added richness to the meaning of both.

The celebration of the Passover in customary fashion was preceded in some places by fasting on the day of preparation for the Passover, the day, according to the chronology of John's gospel, that Jesus was crucified. The rich content of Passover was certainly in the mind of Paul when he wrote, "Christ, our paschal lamb, has been sacrificed. Therefore let us celebrate the festival" (1 Cor. 5:7-8). The early Christian communities of Jewish background did not quickly or easily give up the annual Passover observance. As late as the end of the second century, the paschal controversy was being waged with vigor. The controversy was centered on a dispute between the Christians in Asia and those in Rome (and the other major Western centers of the church) over the date of Easter. The Asians, led in their position by Polycarp of Smyrna and Polycrates of Ephesus, pleaded for an annual celebration of Pascha on the fourteenth day of Nisan, the anniversary of the Crucifixion, regardless of the day of the week upon which it would fall. Rome, as the center of the Western churches, led by Anicetus and Victor I, supported the view that Easter should always fall on the Sunday next after the fourteenth of Nisan. Each side of the controversy claimed to be preserving the practice and understanding of the apostles, but it is worthy to point out that each group appealed to different apostles. In the fourth century, the Council of Nicea settled the issue, declaring that Easter would be celebrated on the Sunday after the first full moon of spring. That declaration, while making it impossible for Christians to celebrate Easter on the same day as the Jewish community would celebrate Passover, in no way succeeded in eliminating from the Christian celebration the rich imagery of Passover.

It is not unreasonable to assume, then, that in the earliest years the Christian community celebrated the unitive commemoration of the death and Resurrection on one day. The power and impact of that salvific event, however, could not be contained in one day. By the fourth century, the annual commemoration took on a more programmatic, historically oriented nature. The one day was expanded into three holy days, the paschal triduum. The original triduum was, as the word suggests, three days: Friday, a remembrance of the Crucifixion; Saturday, a sabbath of rest in commemoration of the Lord's rest in the grave; and Sunday, the festal celebration of Resurrection.

The practice of the earliest years of the church varied widely. In some places, due to the understanding that the liturgical day began at sundown of the previous calenderical day, the Eucharist of Holy Thursday was soon considered part of the paschal triduum. In other locales, the Eucharist was celebrated several times on Holy Thursday, while in Rome the day took the reconciliation of penitents as its content and did not include Eucharist as a regular part of its liturgical observance until the seventh century.

The expansion of the paschal fast behind the "three holy days" can be noted in the third-century document Didascalia Apostolorum. Here we find that the fast has been extended to a full week with provisions for water, bread, and salt for the first four days. The expansion of the one-week fast into the six-week fast has normally been explained by the suggestion that it was to parallel the expansion of the one-day fast into the six-day fast. While there is some evidence of truth to that, it is not universally that simple. The notable exception to this pattern is the Byzantine tradition, which keeps its Lenten fast for six weeks before Holy Week, making seven in all. At the end of the liturgy of the six weeks is sung: "Now that we have fulfilled the forty-day Lent which is profitable to our souls, we beseech Thee to behold the Holy Week of Thy Passion." It is clear from this that the "keeping of the fast" did not have identical dimensions in every place.

What does appear to be constant was the desire that the Lenten fast be forty days. The number of weeks before Pascha varied depending upon whether Holy Week was included and upon the number of days in a week that were reckoned to be fast days. Sunday, for example, was not a fast day because it is always the Lord's Day, the day of resurrection. In some places, Saturday was also not a fast day, except for the fast of Holy Saturday. The reason for the desirability of a forty-day fast is scriptural: Moses, Elijah, and particularly Jesus fasted for periods of forty days. This tradition continues to be preserved today in the pericopes for the first Sunday in Lent. In all three lectionary years, the gospel reading is a synoptic account of Jesus' forty-day fast and temptation in the wilderness.

The character of Lent is twofold. The forty days give us the opportunity to make preparation for the celebration of the major event of the liturgical year and for the central event of our lives: the death and resurrection of Jesus Christ. At the same time, Lent has an integrity all its own. It can be argued, of course, that everything the Christian is or does should be approached in light of the paschal event. While this may be true, the searching examination of one's life, one's prayerful "in-reach" and one's struggling with the demands of discipleship need not always be focused toward "getting ready" for Easter. Christ is risen and the power of his Risen Spirit will make himself known to us whether or not we are prepared. The powerful promise of resurrection is not dependent upon our readiness to receive. We can keep Lent for its own sake. We are freed to interact with God and with each other for spiritual examination and growth in our daily pilgrimage in life, not just in our annual pilgrimage to the cross.

Many churches are finding new meaning in the keeping of Lent. Even those churches that are historically nonliturgical in their orientation are finding that a renewed sense of the Lenten journey in preparation for the great celebration of Easter is a welcome enrichment to the late winter/early spring months. In planning for Lent, it is well to consider any number of possibilities give intensity to the meaning of this liturgical season. The traditional Shrove Tuesday celebration, carried on in some congregations by a pancake supper and in others by their own version of the Mardi Gras, commends itself as a final opportunity for celebratory fun and feasting as the people of God before solitude is imposed on Ash Wednesday. Congregations that are unable to gather for festivities on Tuesday might consider a "farewell to Alleluia" as part of the liturgy for the last Sunday after the Epiphany or a Sunday night parish activity built on a Shrove Tuesday theme.

The arrival of Ash Wednesday should be blatantly noticeable. The entire church facility should reflect the nature of Lent. Visually, a drastic change should be apparent in the worship space. The imposition of ashes is a vivid reminder of our personal and corporate need for God. Clergy and other worship leaders insecure about introducing what appears to be a conflict between the imposition of ashes and the Gospel for the day might look upon that struggle positively. There are few liturgical assemblies in the year at which the real crux of discipleship can be so powerfully addressed.

The Sundays in Lent present the next problem and opportunity. Noting that the Sundays are in Lent and not of Lent, the question must be raised concerning how they should be handled liturgically. One could, no doubt, argue that since every Sunday is the Lord's Day, the weekly Sunday gathering for Word and Sacrament should proceed ahead unimpeded, celebrated as usual, in all its fullness. There is much that commends this position. But such a stance is not wise because it does not take into account the needs of the people to express liturgically their Lenten disciplines. If every congregation had a full cycle of daily prayer and other liturgical expressions during the weekdays of Lent, then the normal eucharistic liturgy would be fine. But given the fact that for the most part such conditions do not exist, the major time the people gather for worship is still Sunday morning. Therefore, Sundays in Lent should reflect that reality. Trimming down the liturgy, cutting back on the flamboyance of the music, even changing the style of the preaching can aid in making the Sunday liturgy reflective of the more ascetical focus of Lent.

On Ash Wednesday we are invited to begin our journey toward Easter and to live disciplined paschal life. Thomas J. Talley has written,

> To do this is to enter for the time upon a different sense of who I am, a more profound sense of who I am, achieved by disengagement from preoccupation with the structure which normally defines me. It is a matter of rediscovering ourselves by forgetting who we are and this forgetting, this turning in a new direction, is metanoia, conversion, repentance. Repentance is not preoccupation with an unsavory past, but the very opposite of that. It is the positive embrace of our helplessness as a moment of transcendent truth. It is the exciting discovery of humility, of poverty, of nakedness, and of the utter seriousness of our life in God.

Neil Alexander

218 ✦ THE SPIRITUAL DISCIPLINE OF LENT

The following article describes the Lenten spiritual journey and suggests practical means for personal and corporate renewal.

Nearly everyone knows the clichés concerning Lent: we are to "give up" something as a kind of obscure penance. Protestants of a more austere piety have made much of the need for a season of self-denial as a test of pious discipline. Whereas Roman Catholics undergo (or used to undergo) a Lenten period of obligatory abstinence, Protestants of a more Reformed sensibility have focused upon moral introspection, perhaps with fewer chocolates. Such practices are not without merit, especially for those of us in economic conditions of abundance. Ash Wednesday and the season of Lent, however, call for something else.

Rather than a season for giving up something, let us consider Lent a season of taking on something. At the very heart of the Christian faith is our common participation in the life, suffering, death, resurrection, and Spirit-giving of Jesus Christ. Such participation is sometimes referred to as sharing in the paschal mystery of Christ. St. Paul exclaims, "Christ our Passover is sacrificed for us: Therefore let us keep the feast" (1 Cor. 5:7-8). The church is thus called to remember and live out in communal form this graced power of new life. In speaking of the paschal mystery we refer to an inexhaustibly rich set of meanings. Lent points us toward the narrative of passion-death-resurrection, celebrated in the three days which climax Holy Week and, hence, the whole season. At the same time the paschal mystery is encountered each Lord's day in Word and the Supper. Furthermore, the paschal mystery also refers to our continuing experience of living in the presence of the Lord in daily use of the means of grace: prayer, the reading and meditating on Scripture, fasting as well as works of mercy. To such the journey of Lent invites us afresh every year.

Let us say, then, that Lent is a double journey—a journey together (and alone) toward the mystery of God's redemptive embrace in the death and resurrection of Christ. At the same time, it is a journey into the depths of our humanity. Without a shared, living memory of who Jesus Christ was, there would be no faith community with a distinctive Christian identity. Without a living encounter over time with who Christ is in our midst, there would be no unfolding of Christian life and ministry. The double journey of Lent, then, is a baptismal journey.

Historically considered, Lent developed as a season of preparation and formation for initiation into the church at Easter. The forty days of preparation involved the whole church, not only those preparing to be baptized. The journey of discipline, prayer, and instruction, which was known in the early church as the "catechumenate," provided those already baptized with a yearly reentry into the meaning and deepening range of commitment entailed by baptism. This was also a period when any people who had lapsed from the church could be reconciled and restored to fellowship. Ash Wednesday emerged in early medieval times as a day of penitence to mark the beginning of Lent's forty days (excluding the Sundays) of preparation for the paschal celebration at Easter, beginning with Maundy Thursday evening through Sunday morning. The great theme of Ash Wednesday is "return to the Lord." This day emphasizes our mortality and humanity. It is time for putting aside the sins and failures of the past in order to journey toward who we are yet to become by the grace of Christ in baptism.

In our own time nearly every major Christian tradition has begun to recover the significance of Lent as a time of common preparation and mutuality. The practical suggestions which follow are all rooted in the hope of this recovery for the entire local congregation: how to best "take on" forms of devotion and common life which flow from and prepare for the realities made present at Easter.

Searching the Scriptures Together

Lent provides an especially appropriate time for common Bible study, especially if this is directly related to the texts that will be read, sung, and proclaimed in the Sunday assembly. For those congregations using the Common Lectionary, this may take the form of reading the texts through the week, at table as families or in specific study or prayer gatherings, or in the context of simple common meals as a congregation on a week night. Each of the three yearly cycles permits a different gospel focus. So, for example, in Year A, we may journey from the temptations following Jesus' baptism (Matt. 4:1-11) through Nicodemus and the Samaritan woman at the well through Matthew's account of the Passion on Palm Sunday. Such a common biblical study, enriched greatly if all three readings and the Psalm appointed for each Sunday are touched upon, will take us into the central images (water, rebirth, the raising of Lazarus, and so on) as well as the implications of being baptized into Christ. A careful study of each year's sequence of Sunday lections will also prepare the congregation to hear the sermon and to participate more fully in the readings, the Psalter, and the hymns, if well chosen. On the basis of such a common discipline, each person will be drawn more deeply into the possibility of personal reflection in solitude.

The Lenten practice of searching the Scriptures could follow the classical pattern of reading-reflection-(meditation)-prayer, undertaken both as a group and in solitude. We need both time together and time alone in reading and prayer. This movement through the biblical accounts, which enable us to journey with Jesus toward Jerusalem in light of the whole witness of Scripture, will deepen the range of prayer, both liturgical and devotional. Moreover, such study should sharpen our appreciation of what the Lord's Supper signifies as well as increase awareness of the biblical content of the hymns we sing during the Lent and its culmination in Holy Week and Easter.

Prayer and Fasting

Many persons in our society find it immensely helpful for personal discipline to have a season intentionally dedicated to "simplify" the way they live. So Lent can indeed be a significant period in learning to eat in less costly and indulgent ways. But merely giving up food in the name of self-improvement is hardly the essential motivation here. Rather, the point is to learn the connections between learning to live more simply for the sake of solidarity with the poor as well as for the sake of uncluttering our senses. We might then take on the discipline of relating prayer and restraint to our need to wait upon God. The image of the desert way is one of the classical expressions of the Lenten journey—clearly derived from the way of Jesus in the desert. Only by intentionally entering the desert way can we be kept from idolatry and perhaps from spiritual self-indulgence.

Each congregation might hold a series of simple common meals of soup and bread which can be marked by readings, simple prayers, and the giving of money (perhaps the equivalent of the normal cost of a meal) to a designated ministry. In some cases these meals might take the form of a simple "love-feast" consisting of hymn singing, shared experiences of faith, and intercessory prayer in the context of rolls and tea or other appropriate simple foods. Such meals could be held in a fellowship hall or with smaller groupings of families in individual homes. The rhythm of such a common discipline at table and with specifically focused common prayer has been, in my own experience, very powerful in forming an awareness appropriate to the essential baptized life.

Many congregations also produce Lenten booklets of prayer and meditations written by members of the congregation. This can provide a remarkable opening for shared spiritual experience as well as for sensing the range of gifts in the community. Such prayers and meditations may focus on the central images of Lent—from the ashes of repentance and mortality through the desert way to the unforgettable images of Holy Week itself: the Upper Room, a kiss of betrayal, words of denial, prayers of agony, sleeping friends, the arrest and trial, Pilate's question, the procession to Golgotha, on through the Crucifixion.

The way of prayer is also a way of discipline. Fasting, almsgiving, and solidarity with all who hunger and thirst are the esssence of Lent. These are means of confronting both the mystery of God and Christ and the human struggle within us against spiritual self-deception. This is precisely what the ancient church emphasized in its catechumenate each year early in preparation for Easter. Our point is not, however, to "play early church." Rather, the journey of Lent is to deepen our participation in Christ by following him in disciplines of the soul and body.

The disciplines of Bible study, prayer, and fasting, and the practice of simple "sacrificial meals" or love feasts together are already related to the Lord's Day. But it is especially important to note that the Sundays in Lent are themselves both receiving and shaping occasions for the Lenten experience of the people. Those persons responsible for planning ought to pay particular attention to the environment of the sanctuary and the other gathering places for the congregation. Appropriate art work—from weaving to photography—

can create an environment that portrays the Lenten journey itself. I have been especially impressed with the creation of "prayer images" created by painting or by photographs that lead us to contemplate a particular baptismal symbol— water in all its moods and ranges, for example. We can invite a prayerful consideration of solidarity with the poor by a careful display of images in our gathering places. It is quite possible to create a litany of images which could be used in worship, whether brought in by children or by appropriately restrained dance movements.

Crucial to the whole environment is simplicity and sobriety without sullen or heavy effects. The music selected, the textures of vestments or paraments or banners, the use of storytelling and, above all, the prayer forms used in common worship, should reflect the Lenten journey. At base we are to bear in mind that this journey is one of deepening conversion to the central mystery of God's self-giving in Christ.

Worship planning may itself be a spiritual discipline for those called to participation. The pastor cannot and should not do everything required. Therefore, Lent also provides a particularly appropriate season for training the laity for various responsibilities in worship: reading, leading prayer, musical offerings, and serving. It is especially effective if the team of persons who will be assisting to plan and lead the Holy Week and Easter services could find special time for a planning retreat in the first week of Lent. Their own planning, as any conscientious choir already knows, will itself deepen their ownership. More important, it will deepen their participation in the rhythm of the Lenten journey toward Easter.

———— Theology of Lent in Practice ————

Essential to living through the double journey of Lent is an understanding of the unfolding meaning of the church as a baptized community. This requires a more intentional process of prayer, searching the Scriptures, and sharing questions and problems of faith and life and of new disciplines oriented to the simplification of our lifestyles (as individuals, household units, and as congregations). Thus, the Sundays of Lent ought to be receiving points for the renewal of discipleship.

For all the intensity of Lent we seek in our time and society a whole new pace. Church activities during Lent should not exhaust us with mere busyness, especially if it is guilt-induced. My point here is not to sprint through Lent in a series of events, classes, liturgical services, and devotional self-preoccupation, only to collapse on Easter Sunday. No, the point of these suggestions is to give us an understanding from the "inside out," so to speak. The prayer and discipline of Lent should sustain and refresh us so that we may give full expression to the reality of having been baptized in Christ. In this way, those who seek baptism or its renewal in confirmation will be supported by the whole congregation's eager yearning for reaffirmation and renewal of the baptismal covenant. Lent serves the glory and the saving faith born at Easter. Thus, it invites the possibility of a new approach to exploring with the whole of the congregation what it means to belong to one another in Christ. The rhythms and the profound contrasts awakened in us by the Lenten Scriptures and by the journey toward Jerusalem with its paradox of death and resurrection are, we shall find, absolutely essential to living faith as the people of God.

Don E. Saliers[23]

219 ‧ Some Questions and Answers About Lent

Below is an educational piece on the meaning of Lent that may be reprinted in the church bulletin or other local publication. Adapt it to meet the needs of your congregation.

What is the Lenten season, and why is it set apart?
  It is a period of six weeks preceding the anniversary of the Savior's death, and is set apart as a special season of fasting, penitence, and prayer.
Why is it called Lent?
  Because it always comes in the spring of the year, and the old Saxon word *lent* means "spring."
With what remarkable event in Jesus' life does the Lenten season correspond?
  The forty days which He spent fasting in the wilderness.
Why is the first day of Lent called Ash Wednesday?

It is called so from the custom that prevailed in the early church of sprinkling ashes on the heads of penitents the first day of Lent in token of humiliation and sorrow for sin.

Are there any examples of this custom mentioned in the Bible?

Yes, the example of Daniel and of David and the people of Nineveh, to which our Lord himself refers in Matthew 11:21.

If Lent is only of forty days' duration, why does it begin forty-six days before Easter?

There are six Sundays in Lent, and as all Sundays are feast days in honor of the Resurrection, they are taken out. To make up for these, six days are added to the beginning of the season.

How should the Lenten season be observed by Christians?

As a special season for drawing near to God by extraordinary acts of penitence, charity, and religious devotion, and by fasting and abstinence from all things that tend to draw the heart from God.

What is the object of keeping Lent?

To deepen the religious life, to purify the heart from sin, and to unite us more closely to the Savior.

Why does the church require us to observe the Lenten fast?

1. Because repentance and humiliation are essential to growth in grace.
2. Because these duties are apt to be neglected and forgotten unless some special time is set apart for their observance.

What objection do people sometimes raise against the observance of the Lenten fast?

They say that it is a useless and superstitious custom, and that Christ nowhere commanded his disciples to fast.

How do we answer this objection?

1. Fasting was a common practice not only among God's chosen people (Exod. 34:38; 2 Sam. 12:16;1 Kings 19:8; Ps. 35:13; Joel 1:14; Jon. 3:5).
2. Jesus fasted and so did his disciples. He did not command his followers to fast; he assumed that they would and gave directions on how to fast (Matt. 6:17). Fasting has the highest divine authority.
3. A few persons who accept the principle of Lent complain that the season is so long that people weary of its observance relax its discipline. But it is intentionally made long so that it must be kept by ordered rule and rational self-control, instead of impulsive actions and emotional devotions.

Richard Lobs III

❧ 𝕿𝕳𝕴𝕽𝕿𝕰𝕰𝕹 ❧

Resources for Planning Lenten Worship

The special nature of Lent as a time of preparation for the death and resurrection of Jesus is expressed in the resources of this chapter. All the Scripture texts and the preaching of this season as well as the environment, singing, and resources for spiritual discipline shape the personal and corporate spiritual experience of the congregation.

220 ◆ LECTIONARY TEXTS FOR THE LENTEN SEASON

The following are the texts suggested for the Sundays of Lent in the Revised Common Lectionary. Brief descriptions of each lesson are provided to aid in recalling the basic theme of each passage. The readings for the sixth Sunday of Lent (Psalm or Passion Sunday) are included in the next chapter.

———— Year A (1995, 1998, 2001, 2004) ————

SUNDAY	OLD TESTAMENT	PSALM	EPISTLE	GOSPEL
Ash Wednesday	Joel 2:1-2, 12-17 or Isaiah 58:1-12, warning about the Day, call to repentance.	51:1-17	2 Corinthians 5:20b–6:10, let God turn you from enemy to friend. Now!	Matthew 6:1-6; 16-21, teachings: charity, prayer, fasting.
First Sunday in Lent	Genesis 2:15-17; 3:1-7, creation of humans; disobedience.	32	Romans 5:12-19, sin came with Adam, grace came with Christ.	Matthew 4:1-11, the temptation of Jesus.
Second Sunday in Lent	Genesis 12:1-4a, God calls Abram.	121	Romans 4:1-5, 13-17, example of Abraham, promise through faith.	John 3:1-17, Nicodemus, God so loved the world, or Matthew 17:1-9, the Transfiguration.
Third Sunday in Lent	Exodus 17:1-7, complaining of Israel, water from the rock.	95	Romans 5:1-11, we have been put right with God through Christ.	John 4:5-42, Jesus and the Samaritan woman.
Fourth Sunday in Lent	1 Samuel 16:1-13, covenant with David, who is anointed king.	23	Ephesians 5:8-14, You were in dark, have been brought to light.	John 9:1-41, Jesus heals the man born blind.
Fifth Sunday in Lent	Ezekiel 37:1-14, valley of dry bones, can these bones live?	130	Romans 8:6-11, life by nature and life in the Spirit.	John 11:1-45, the raising of Lazarus.

—— Year B (1996, 1999, 2002, 2005) ——

SUNDAY	OLD TESTAMENT	PSALM	EPISTLE	GOSPEL
Ash Wednesday	Joel 2:1-2, 12-17 or Isaiah 58:1-12, warning about the Day, call to repentance.	51:1-17	2 Corinthians 5:20b–6:10, let God turn you from enemy to friend. Now!	Matthew 6:1-6; 16-21, teachings: charity, prayer, fasting.
First Sunday in Lent	Genesis 9:8-17, covenant with Noah, deliverance through water.	25:1-10	1 Peter 3:18-22, Flood prefigures our baptism.	Mark 1:9-15, Jesus tempted and preaches repentance.
Second Sunday in Lent	Genesis 17:1-7, 15-16, promise given to Abraham, sign is circumcision.	22:23-31	Romans 4:13-25, Abraham: God's promise received through faith.	Mark 8:31-38 or Mark 9:2-9, deny self and take up the cross.
Third Sunday in Lent	Exodus 20:1-17, Ten Commandments.	19	1 Corinthians 1:18-25, Christ's death as nonsense and offense.	John 2:13-22, cleansing of temple foretells Passion.
Fourth Sunday in Lent	Numbers 21:4-9, the snake of bronze could heal.	107:1-3, 17-22	Ephesians 2:1-10, in past we were dead; now, made alive in Christ.	John 3:14-21, God sent Son not to condemn but to save.
Fifth Sunday in Lent	Jeremiah 31:31-34, new covenant, written on human hearts.	51:1-12 or 119:9-16	Hebrews 5:5-10, Jesus prayed to be spared, but was faithful.	John 12:20-33, "final hour" Son of Man to be glorified.

—— Year C (1994, 1997, 2000, 2003) ——

SUNDAY	OLD TESTAMENT	PSALM	EPISTLE	GOSPEL
Ash Wednesday	Joel 2:1-2, 12-17 or Isaiah 58:1-12, warning about the Day, call to repentance.	51:1-17	2 Corinthians 5:20b–6:10, let God turn you from enemy to friend. Now!	Matthew 6:1-6; 16-21, teachings: charity, prayer, fasting.
First Sunday in Lent	Deuteronomy 26:1-11, my ancestor was a wandering Aramean.	91:1-2, 9-16	Romans 10:8b-13, this is our faith; it is open to all equally.	Luke 4:1-13, the temptation of Jesus.
Second Sunday in Lent	Genesis 15:1-12, 17-18, God makes a covenant with Abram.	27	Philippians 3:17–4:1, imitate me and others who set right example.	Luke 13:31-35 or Luke 9:28-36, Jesus' love for Jerusalem.
Third Sunday in Lent	Isaiah 55:1-9, God's offer of mercy, a lasting covenant.	63:1-8	1 Corinthians 10:1-13, don't worship idols, stand firm in test of faith.	Luke 13:1-9, turn from your sins, parable of fig tree.
Fourth Sunday in Lent	Joshua 5:9-12, observing Passover.	32	2 Corinthians 5:16-21, God through Christ changes enemies to friends.	Luke 15:1-3, 11b-32, parable of lost son.
Fifth Sunday in Lent	Isaiah 43:16-21, escape from Babylon, road through wilderness.	126	Philippians 3:4b-14, judging worth by Christ, running for the prize.	John 12:1-8, Jesus is anointed in Bethany.

Revised Common Lectionary, descriptions by H. A. Tillinghast

221 ◆ TRADITIONAL OPENING PRAYERS FOR LENT

The prayers below, many of which are based on centuries-old texts, express the basic themes of a worship that prepares the people to journey into the death of Jesus. Adapt to local style.

Ash Wednesday (Seventh Wednesday before Easter—First Day of the Lent-Easter Cycle)

Almighty and everlasting God, you hate nothing you have made and forgive the sins of all who are penitent: Create and make in us new and contrite hearts, that we, worthily lamenting our sins and acknowledging our wretchedness, may obtain of you, the God of all mercy, perfect remission and forgiveness; through Jesus Christ our Lord, who lives and reigns with you and the Holy Spirit, one God, for ever and ever. Amen.

First Sunday in Lent

Almighty God, whose blessed Son was led by the Spirit to be tempted by Satan: Come quickly to help us who are assaulted by many temptations; and, as you know the weaknesses of each of us, let each one find you mighty to save; through Jesus Christ your Son our Lord, who lives and reigns with you and the Holy Spirit, one God, now and forever. Amen.

Second Sunday in Lent

O God, whose glory it is always to have mercy, be gracious to all who have gone astray from your ways, and bring them again with penitent hearts and steadfast faith to embrace and hold fast the unchangeable truth of your Word, Jesus Christ your Son; who with you and the Holy Spirit lives and reigns, one God, for ever and ever. Amen.

Third Sunday in Lent

Almighty God, you know that we have no power in ourselves to help ourselves: Keep us both outwardly in our bodies and inwardly in our souls, that we may be defended from all adversities which may happen to the body, and from all evil thoughts which may assault and hurt the soul; through Jesus Christ our Lord, who lives and reigns with you and the Holy Spirit, one God, for ever and ever. Amen.

Fourth Sunday in Lent

Gracious Father, whose blessed Son Jesus Christ came down from heaven to be the true bread which gives life to the world: Evermore give us this bread, that he may live in us, and we in him; who lives and reigns with you and the Holy Spirit, one God, now and for ever. Amen.

Fifth Sunday in Lent

Almighty God, you alone can bring into order the unruly wills and affections of sinners: Grant your people grace to love what you command and desire what you promise; that, among the swift and varied changes of the world, our hearts may surely there be fixed where the true joys are to be found; through Jesus Christ our Lord, who lives and reigns with you and the Holy Spirit, one God, now and for ever. Amen.

Book of Common Prayer

222 ◆ PRAYERS FOR LENT

The following prayers, written in a contemporary style, draw on images from Scripture. Use these and the commentary provided for each prayer as a guide to the writing of prayers for worship. Note how each prayer is tailored to a specific liturgical function.

Opening Prayers or Prayers of Invocation

Journey with us, O holy God, as we begin (or continue) our way to the cross. Sharpen our focus that our attention may center more on you than ourselves. Lead us through the shadows of darkness and prepare our hearts that we might be a people of prayer, ready to receive and respond to your Son and our Savior, Jesus Christ. In his name we pray. Amen.

Commentary: The reference for this prayer originates in Mark 11:15-17. Here Jesus cleanses the temple, restoring it for its proper use. Likewise, this prayer at the beginning of worship seeks to prepare us both for the service and season of Lent.

All-knowing and all-caring God, we gather this day drained by another week. We are like a parched desert, empty and in need of replenishment. Visit us with your presence, saturate us with your Spirit, and bathe us in the streams of living water that our lives might acknowledge and worship you to the praise and honor of Jesus Christ. Amen!

Commentary: Too often our worship begins where people are not. This prayer seeks to address the emptiness that is legion in so many worshipers on a Sunday. The imagery is drawn from John 7:37-38 while echoes of John 4:13-14 can also be heard.

Prayer of Confession

O God, our great shepherd, you tenderly gather us as lambs, carrying us with your all-embracing love. Yet, like sheep, we wander from you: following our own ways, ignoring your voice, distrusting your provisions. Forgive our stubborn rebellion, our hardened hearts, our lack of trust. Refresh us once again by your quiet waters of mercy and restore our souls by your redeeming love. Guide our paths that we might follow you more closely . . . [opportunity for silent confession] . . . Through Jesus Christ, our good shepherd, we pray. Amen!

RESPONSE

Commentary: An appropriate response that could be sung here before the words of assurance is, "Lord, Who Throughout These Forty Days." The first two stanzas in particular encourage both the act of confession and the assurance that Christ has conquered sin and provides the means for our forgiveness.

WORDS OF ASSURANCE

LEADER:	(reads 1 Peter 2:25)
PEOPLE:	**(read John 10:11, 9)**
ALL:	**(read 1 Peter 2:24)**

Commentary: Psalm 23 is the model for this prayer. All too frequently this popular psalm seems the exclusive domain of the terminally ill and funerals. This prayer seeks to liberate the dynamic message for everyday living. The words of assurance continue the same image of Jesus as the good shepherd. This further illustrates the beauty of how the Old and New Testaments can interact and reinforce common themes for worship.

Prayer of Illumination

Lord God, we approach your Scriptures with reverence and gratitude that you have preserved for us your lifegiving revelation. Be present with us through your Holy Spirit and lift high the cross so that Christ's amazing love might be proclaimed in the reading and doing of your inspired Word. In Jesus' powerful name. Amen!

Commentary: This prayer unites the motifs of the refrain from the popular hymn, "Lift High the Cross" with James 1:22. The theme could be expanded by linking it with the imagery of 2 Timothy 3:16-17. The crucial dimension this prayer seeks to underscore is that Scripture is best understood and most faithfully proclaimed when it is lived out by each worshiper throughout the week.

Offertory Prayers

Mighty God and Father, you overwhelm us with your great mercy. At the time of our greatest need you surprised us with your wondrous love. Jesus offered his life for us to remove our dreadful curse. As you draw us into this renewing relationship of love, may we respond with gratitude as we offer the substance of our souls to continue the ministry of Christ. For his name and glory we pray and present our gifts. Amen!

Commentary: The familiar Lenten hymn, "What Wondrous Love," is foundational to this prayer. The reinforcing themes of Romans 5:6, 8 integrate to encourage our response to God's generous self-giving in Christ.

Lord God, may we never allow our offering of gifts to become a source of pride or boasting. Fix our gaze upon Calvary and correct our motivation. Christ's amazing and divine love demands that we hold back nothing, offering our souls and our lives. Faithfully we seek to continually present our sacrifice of praise in what we give and how we live. To the glory and honor of Christ. Amen!

Commentary: The stirring words of "When I Survey the Wondrous Cross" are woven together with Hebrews 13:15 to invite our participation in the ministry of giving.

Pastoral Prayer

Gracious God and heavenly Father, we praise and honor your great and powerful name. Your name is above every name for you alone are Lord and God. Our hearts are alive with worship as we hallow and bless you. Receive the silent expressions of our praise . . .

Lord, you hear our prayer (refrain spoken by the entire congregation after each section)

Ever faithful God, you have called us to belong to you. Come then with the fullness of your kingdom and let your will be done in us even as it is done in heaven. Lengthen our souls that we might live more by faith than fear as we prepare to live in your unfolding kingdom. Enlarge our trust as we speak to you in silence. . . .

Lord, you hear our prayer

Abundant Lord, you have supplied our daily provisions that we might work, eat, and clothe ourselves. Yet we are painfully aware of others, even within our own community, who lack these basic resources. May we never take our blessings for granted and foolishly believe they are the result of only our own labors. Grant us compassionate hearts that we might act on behalf of Christ and assist those in need. Create this same loving concern for those who are ill, shut in, or facing the darkness of loss and grief. Listen to the petitions of our heart, O gracious God. . . .

Lord, you hear our prayer

Merciful God, we acknowledge that often our tongues speak faster than we are able to think. Frequently we wish we could retract and erase hastily spoken words. Even this past week our tempers have worn thin with those whom we love. Forgive our slowness to apologize and grant us courage in participating in your ministry of reconciliation. May we not proudly wait for the other person to act but humbly seek to make those first awkward steps. Remove the resistance that lingers in these cold and broken relationships. . . .

Lord, you hear our prayer

Holy God, we are grateful for your protection amidst the temptations and evil of our day. Be our strength and shield and increase our awareness to always be alert. Guard us from foolish activities and attitudes and increase our ability to confront our personal weaknesses. Disarm the powers of darkness and slash the tentacles of anger and hatred that are at war within and around us. We pray especially for those who seek to be your peacemakers in places of conflict and turmoil. From our own wounded hearts listen to our cries for peace and security. . . .

Lord, you hear our prayer

Eternal Lord and God, may our hearts not despair, even amidst seemingly hopeless odds. Etch deeply into our memories that you are a mighty God of power and compassion. Direct our paths that we might grow in your kingdom of power and glory both now and forever. . . .

Lord, you hear our prayer

Commentary: The early disciples of Jesus asked him how to pray (Luke 11:1). Christ responded by offering what we usually call the Lord's Prayer (Matt. 6:9-15). This prayer models once again how Scripture offers us a format for praying. Each petition focuses on a separate theme. Obviously there is great flexibility and opportunity for tailoring this to individual settings. A further feature of this prayer is the congregational refrain, **Lord, you hear our prayer**. Many litanies use a different version inviting the worshiper to state: Lord, hear our prayer. However, that approach conveys more of an attitude of begging than confidence. Since Jesus introduces this prayer with the encouraging statement, "This is how you should pray" (Matt. 6:9a, NIV), it is appropriate to acknowledge that truth with this response.

Lord God, giver of eternal life and hope, we praise you for your goodness and mercy. Moved by our brokenness and rebellion, you sent your Son, Jesus the Messiah, to restore us to peace with you, ourselves, and others. We are grateful for Christ and his obedience to face the cross and suffer on our behalf. Startle us, for we are often slow in spirit, that your passion was not just to forgive us and have us continue on our own ways. Rather, it is your consuming desire for us to follow you and enjoy your friendship whether we are in good times or bad. Christ, your Son and our Savior, sounds the call when he shakes our souls with the reminder: "If any want to become my followers, let them deny themselves and take up their cross daily and follow me" (Luke 9:23, NRSV).

Lord, these are difficult words for us amid our maze of activities and responsibilities. Yet, Jesus calls us not as tourists to visit a religious display but as pilgrims to follow in his way. Plant within us a growing awareness of what it means to be your servants and representatives in our contemporary world.

Grant us wisdom and courage to discover what following you means as we study at school, work at the office and factory, play at home, spend in the marketplace, participate in the community, and grow in Christ in the church. Sharpen our focus to realize that every dimension of life is your concern and needs to be placed before Christ for transformation.

Remold our hearts that we might be servants to others in need. Whether these people be family, friends, or strangers, may our lives reflect the love of Christ. May we never use our wealth and influence as a means of reducing our actual participation in the pain and problems of others. The spectrum of service is vast and no one or any single church can do all. But help us to see what we can do, guided and encouraged by your Holy Spirit. Sanctify our motivation, that our service is inspired by gratitude and not guilt. May we never be ashamed of speaking or acting on the good name of Jesus Christ but willingly do what his love commands. Hear us and help us Lord, as we pause in silence to receive your direction for our lives or offer other petitions to you. . . .Through the cross of Christ our Savior and Lord, we pray. Amen!

Commentary: The difficult words of Jesus' call to discipleship in Luke 9:23 form the inspiration and basic image of this prayer. An important element of this is while it challenges the congregation to action in Christ, the motivation is not one of guilt but gratitude. Frequently, pastors and worship leaders resort to guilt to manipulate the people of God to action. This is a contradiction of the gospel and an insult to God.

Tom Schwanda

223 ✦ THE GREAT LITANY

Worship planners can learn valuable lessons from traditional liturgical texts. Notice how this text expresses reverence for God, trust in God's power to act in a vast variety of circumstances, and an attitude of humility. Use this prayer during the season of Lent or adapt as needed, keeping in mind its reverent and humble spirit.

The Great Litany below is a penitential prayer that may be used as the Entrance Rite during one or more Sundays of Lent. Traditionally it is used on the First Sunday of Lent, at least to express the penitential character of the season. The ministers may process to their places in silence as the congregation stands. The ministers may prostrate themselves on the floor for a short time. Then the entire congregation kneels as together the litany is said or sung. This litany may replace all the usual acts of Entrance, and the Service of the Word may commence after the litany has been completed. The bold text is spoken by all.

O God the Father, Creator of heaven and earth,
Have mercy upon us.

O God the Son, Redeemer of the world,
Have mercy upon us.

O God the Holy Ghost, Sanctifier of the faithful,
Have mercy upon us.

O holy, blessed, and glorious Trinity, one God,
Have mercy upon us.

Remember not, Lord Christ, our offenses, nor the offenses of our forefathers; neither reward us according to our sins. Spare us, good Lord, spare thy people, whom thou hast redeemed with thy most precious blood, and by thy mercy preserve us for ever.
Spare us, good Lord.

From all evil and wickedness; from sin, from the crafts and assaults of the devil; and from everlasting damnation,
Good Lord, deliver us.

From all blindness of heart; from pride, vainglory, and hypocrisy; from envy, hatred, and malice; and from all want of charity,
Good Lord, deliver us.

From all inordinate and sinful affections; and from all the deceits of the world, the flesh, and the devil,
Good Lord, deliver us.

From all false doctrine, heresy, and schism; from hardness of heart, and contempt of thy Word and commandment,
Good Lord, deliver us.

From lightning and tempest; from earthquake, fire, and flood; from plague, pestilence, and famine,
Good Lord, deliver us.

From all oppression, conspiracy, and rebellion; from violence, battle, and murder; and from dying suddenly and unprepared,
Good Lord, deliver us.

By the mystery of thy holy Incarnation; by thy holy Nativity and submission to the Law; by thy Baptism, Fasting, and Temptation,
Good Lord, deliver us.

By thine Agony and Bloody Sweat; by thy Cross and Passion; by thy precious Death and Burial; by thy glorious Resurrection and Ascension; and by the Coming of the Holy Ghost.
Good Lord, deliver us.

In all time of our tribulation; in all time of our prosperity; in the hour of death, and in the day of judgment,
Good Lord, deliver us.

We sinners do beseech thee to hear us, O Lord God; and that it may please thee to rule and govern thy holy Church Universal in the right way,
We beseech thee to hear us, good Lord.

That it may please thee to illumine all bishops, priests, and deacons, with true knowledge and understanding of thy Word; and that both by their preaching and living, they may set it forth and show it accordingly,
We beseech thee to hear us, good Lord.

That it may please thee to bless and keep all thy people,
We beseech thee to hear us, good Lord.

That it may please thee to send forth laborers into thy harvest, and to draw all mankind into thy kingdom,
We beseech thee to hear us, good Lord.

That it may please thee to give to all people increase of grace to hear and receive thy Word, and to bring forth the fruits of the Spirit;
We beseech thee to hear us, good Lord.

That it may please thee to bring into the way of truth all such as have erred, and are deceived,
We beseech thee to hear us, good Lord.

That it may please thee to give us a heart to love and fear thee, and diligently to live after thy commandments,
We beseech thee to hear us, good Lord.

That it may please thee so to rule the hearts of thy servants, the President of the United States (or of this nation), and all others in authority, that they may do justice, and love mercy, and walk in the ways of truth.
We beseech thee to hear us, good Lord.

That it may please thee to make wars to cease in all the world; to give to all nations unity, peace and concord; and to bestow freedom upon all peoples,
We beseech thee to hear us, good Lord.

That it may please thee to show thy pity upon all prisoners and captives, the homeless and the hungry, and all who are desolate and oppressed,
We beseech thee to hear us, good Lord.

That it may please thee to give and preserve to our use the bountiful fruits of the earth, so that in due time all may enjoy them,
We beseech thee to hear us, good Lord.

That it may please thee to inspire us, in our several callings, to do the work which thou givest us to do with singleness of heart as thy servants, and for the common good,
We beseech thee to hear us, good Lord.

That it may please thee to preserve all who are in danger by reason of their labor or their travel,
We beseech thee to hear us, good Lord.

That it may please thee to preserve, and provide for, all women in childbirth, young children and orphans, the widowed, and all whose homes are broken or torn by strife,
We beseech thee to hear us, good Lord.

That it may please thee to visit the lonely; to strengthen all who suffer in mind, body, and spirit; and to comfort with thy presence those who are failing and infirm;
We beseech thee to hear us, good Lord.

That it may please thee to support, help and comfort all who are in danger, necessity, and tribulation.
We beseech thee to hear us, good Lord.

That it may please thee to have mercy upon all mankind,
We beseech thee to hear us, good Lord.

That it may please thee to give us true repentance; to forgive us all our sins, negligences, and ignorances; and to endue us with the grace of thy Holy Spirit to amend our lives according to thy Holy Word,
We beseech thee to hear us, good Lord.

That it may please thee to forgive our enemies, persecutors, and slanderers, and to turn their hearts,
We beseech thee to hear us, good Lord.

That it may please thee to strengthen such as do stand; to comfort and help the weakhearted; to raise up those who fall; and finally to beat down Satan under our feet,
We beseech thee to hear us, good Lord.

That it may please thee to grant to all the faithful departed eternal life and peace,
We beseech thee to hear us, good Lord.

That it may please thee to grant that, in the fellowship of [_____ and] all the saints, we may attain to thy heavenly kingdom,
We beseech thee to hear us, good Lord.

Son of God, we beseech thee to hear us.
Son of God, we beseech thee to hear us.

O Lamb of God, that takest away the sins of the world,
Have mercy upon us.

O Lamb of God, that takest away the sins of the world,
Have mercy upon us.

O Lamb of God, that takes away the sins of the world,
Grant us peace.

O Christ, hear us.
O Christ, hear us.
Lord, have mercy upon us. (or Kyrie eleison)
Christ, have mercy upon us. (or Christ eleison)
Lord, have mercy upon us. (or Kyrie eleison)

When the Litany is sung or said immediately before the Eucharist, the Litany concludes here, and the Eucharist begins with the Salutation and the Collect of the Day.

On all other occasions, the Officiant and People say together:
Our Father, who art in heaven,
hallowed be thy Name,
thy kingdom come,
thy will be done,
on earth as it is in heaven.
Give us this day our daily bread.
And forgive us our trespasses,
as we forgive those who trespass against us.
And lead us not into temptation,
but deliver us from evil. Amen.

V. O Lord, let thy mercy be showed upon us;
R. As we do put our trust in thee.

The Officiant concludes with the following or some other Collect.

Let us pray.
Almighty God, who hast promised to hear the petitions of those who ask in thy Son's Name: We beseech thee mercifully to incline thine ear to us who have now made our prayers and supplications unto thee; and grant that those things which we have asked faithfully according to thy will, may be obtained effectually, to the relief of our necessity, and to the setting forth of thy glory; through Jesus Christ our Lord.
Amen.

The Officiant may add other Prayers, and end the Litany, saying

The grace of our Lord Jesus Christ, and the love of God, and the fellowship of the Holy Ghost, be with us all evermore.
Amen.

Book of Common Prayer

224 ◆ PRAYER OF THANKSGIVING FOR LENTEN EUCHARIST

The following prayer of thanksgiving is appropriate for use in Lenten liturgies of the Lord's Supper. Notice how the images suggested in the prayer complement the Scripture readings for Lent and the idea of Lent as a spiritual pilgrimage and time of repentance and renewal.

MINISTER: The Lord be with you.
PEOPLE: **And also with you.**
MINISTER: Lift up your hearts.
PEOPLE: **We lift them to the Lord.**
MINISTER: Let us give thanks to the Lord our God.
PEOPLE: **It is right to give our thanks and praise.**
MINISTER: It is truly right and our greatest joy to give you thanks and praise, O God our creator and redeemer. In your wisdom, you made all things and sustain them by your power. You formed us in your image to love and serve you, but we forgot your promises and abandoned your commandments.

In your mercy, you did not reject us
but still claimed us as your own.

When we were slaves in Egypt you
freed us
and led us through the waters of the
sea.
You fed us with heavenly food in the
wilderness,
and satisfied our thirst from desert
springs.
On the holy mountain you gave us
your law
to guide us in your way.
Through the waters of Jordan
you led us into the land of your
promise,
and you sustained us in times of trial.
You spoke through prophets
calling us to turn from our willful
ways
to new obedience and righteousness.
You sent your only Son
to be the way to eternal life.

Therefore we praise you,
joining our voices with choirs of angels
and with all the faithful of every time
and place,
who forever sing to the glory of your
name:

(The people may sing or say:)

**Holy, holy, holy Lord, God of power
and might,
heaven and earth are full of your
glory.
Hosanna in the highest.
Blessed is he who comes in the
name of the Lord.
Hosanna in the highest.**

(The minister continues:)

You are holy, O God of majesty,
and blessed is Jesus Christ, your son,
our Lord.
He took upon himself the weight of
our sin
and carried the burden of our guilt.
He shared our life in every way,
and though tempted, was sinless to
the end.

Baptized as your own, he went willingly to his death
and by your power was raised to new
life.
In his dying and rising,
you gave birth to your church,
delivered us from slavery to sin and
death,
and made with us a new covenant by
water and the Spirit.

(If they have not already been said, the words
of institution may be said here, or in relation
to the breaking of the bread.)

MINISTER: We give you thanks that the Lord
Jesus,
on the night before he died,
took bread,
and after giving thanks to you,
he broke it, and gave it to his disciples, saying:
Take, eat.
This is my body, given for you.
Do this in remembrance of me.

In the same way he took the cup, saying:
This cup is the new covenant sealed
in my blood,
shed for you for the forgiveness of
sins.
Whenever you drink it,
do this in remembrance of me.

Remembering all your mighty and
merciful acts,
we take this bread and this wine
from the gifts you have given us,
and celebrate with joy
the redemption won for us in Jesus
Christ.
Accept this our sacrifice of praise and
thanksgiving
as a living and holy offering of ourselves,
that our lives may proclaim the One
crucified and risen.

(The people may sing or say one of the following:)

1

MINISTER: Great is the mystery of faith:

PEOPLE: **Christ has died,**
Christ is risen,
Christ will come again.

2
MINISTER: Praise to you, Lord Jesus:
PEOPLE: **Dying you destroyed our death,**
rising you restored our life.
Lord Jesus, come in glory.

3
MINISTER: According to his commandment:
PEOPLE: **We remember his death,**
we proclaim his resurrection,
we await his coming in glory.

4
MINISTER: Christ is the bread of life:
PEOPLE: **When we eat this bread and drink**
this cup,
we proclaim your death, Lord Jesus,
until you come in glory.

(The minister continues:)

Gracious God,
pour out your Holy Spirit upon us
and upon these your gifts of bread
and wine,
that the bread we break
and the cup we bless
may be the communion of the body
and blood of Christ.
By your Spirit unite us with the living
Christ,
and with all who are baptized in his
name,
that we may be one in ministry in
every place.
As this bread is Christ's body for us,
send us out to be the body of Christ
in the world.

(Intercessions for the church and the world may
be included here.)

Help us, O God, to be obedient to
your call
to love all your children,
to do justice and show mercy,
and to live in peace with your whole
creation.
Guide us through the desert of life,
quench our thirst with the living waters,

satisfy our hunger with the bread of
heaven.
Give us strength to serve you faithfully
until the promised day of resurrection,
when the redeemed of all the ages
we will feast with you at your table in
glory.

Through Christ,
all glory and honor are yours, almighty Father,
with the Holy Spirit in the holy church,
now and forever.
PEOPLE: **Amen.**

Book of Common Worship[24]

225 ✦ LENTEN BLESSINGS

During the season of Lent, the blessing is often spoken
as a prayer for the people instead of as a proclamation
of God's blessing. The following are traditional texts
for Lenten blessings.

Grant, most merciful Lord, to your faithful people
pardon and peace, that they may be cleansed from
all their sins, and serve you with a quiet mind;
through Christ our Lord. Amen.

Grant, almighty God, that your people may recognize their weakness and put their whole trust
in your strength, so that they may rejoice forever
in the protection of your loving providence;
through Christ our Lord. Amen.

Keep this your family, Lord, with your never-fail-
ing mercy, that relying solely on the help of your
heavenly grace, they may be upheld by your divine protection; through Christ our Lord. Amen.

Look mercifully on this your family, Almighty God,
that by your great goodness they may be governed
and preserved evermore; through Christ our Lord.
Amen.

Look down in your mercy, Lord, on your people
who kneel before you; and grant that those whom
you have nourished by your Word and sacraments
may bring forth fruit worthy of repentance;
through Christ our Lord. Amen.

Look with compassion, O Lord, upon this your people; that, rightly observing this holy season, they may learn to know you more fully, and to serve you with a more perfect will; through Christ, our Lord. Amen

Book of Occasional Services[25]

226 ♦ RESOURCES FOR LENTEN RETREATS AND DISCIPLINES

The following resources may be helpful in developing a Lenten retreat or a program for the devotional life of members in your denomination.

A Lenten Form for Self-Examination

Below is a form for directed prayer either during a Lenten retreat or for personal self-examination. Adapt as needed.

Pride
Putting self in the place of God as the center and objective of our life. Pride is the refusal to recognize our status as creatures, dependent upon God.

Irreverence
Deliberate neglect of God's worship, or contentment with a perfunctory participation in it. It is manifested in cynicism toward the holy or use of Christianity for personal advantage.

Sentimentality
Satisfaction with pious feelings and beautiful ceremony without striving for personal holiness.

Distrust
Refusal to recognize God's wisdom and love. Undue worry, undue anxiety, scrupulosity, or perfectionism. Attempts to gain or keep control of our life by spiritualism, astrology, undue timidity, or cowardice.

Disobedience
Rejection of God's known will. The refusal to learn God's nature as revealed in Holy Scripture. Breaking confidence by irresponsibility, treachery, and the unnecessary disappointment of others. Breaking legal or moral contracts.

Impenitence
Refusal to search out and face up to our sins, or to confess them before God. Self-justification by believing our sins to be insignificant, natural, or inevitable; by refusing to apologize; by being unwilling to forgive ourselves.

Vanity
Failure to credit God and others for their part in our lives. Boasting, exaggeration, ostentatious behavior, undue concern over "things."

Arrogance
Being overbearing, argumentative, opinionated, obstinate.

Resentment
Rejection of talents, abilities, or opportunities God and man give us. Rebellion, hatred of God or man. Cynicism.

Envy
Dissatisfaction with our place in God's order of creation. Manifests itself in jealousy, malice, and contempt for others or others' "things."

Covetousness
The refusal to respect the integrity of other creatures, expressed in the accumulation of material things to prove self-worth, the use of others to personal advantage, or in the quest for status and power at the expense of others.

Avarice
Manifested in inordinate ambition or domination of others. The waste of natural resources or personal possessions. Extravagance or living beyond our means. It is also manifested in undue protection of our "things." Stinginess.

Gluttony
Overindulgence of natural appetites for food and drink, and by extension the inordinate quest for pleasure or comfort. Manifests itself in intemperance and lack of discipline.

Lust
Misuse of sex. It includes unchastity, immodesty, prudery, and cruelty. Lust does not recognize marriage as the God-ordained relationship for sexual intercourse.

Sloth
The refusal to respond to our opportunities for growth, service, or sacrifice. It includes laziness in spiritual, mental, or physical duties. Neglect of family. Indifference to injustice or the world's

suffering ones. Neglecting the needy, lonely, or unpopular.

Sloth also involves spiritual failure. It fails to give attention to the maturing of one's family and/or self. It fails to grasp and live out the missionary enterprise of the Christian life.

A Worksheet for the Development of a Lenten Rule of Discipline

Below is a rule of discipline that may be altered to suit the needs of your congregation. This discipline orders the spiritual experience of Lent and provides a disciplined order for congregants to follow. It is based on *The Book of Common Prayer*. Other books of prayer or devotion may be substituted for *The Book of Common Prayer*.

A Word about Lent

Lent is a time to do spiritual inventory. Below are many time-honored disciplines to help you in this season of growth.

Sundays are not counted as part of the Lenten season. Sundays are feast days and never fast days. Sundays at any time of the year, including Lent, celebrate the Resurrection of our Lord Jesus.

Prayer in Public

I _____ will _____ will not worship God on the Lord's Days of Lent.

I plan to worship in public on one or more weekdays of Lent: _____ yes _____ no.

If "yes," please know that at St. Mark's we worship with the Daily Office of Morning Prayer on Mondays, Tuesdays, Thursdays, and Fridays, at 8:30 a.m. We celebrate the Holy Eucharist each Wednesday at 7:00 a.m.

Prayer in Private

I plan to pray daily: _____ yes _____ no.
If "yes" here is the time I commit myself to be at prayer _____.
Here is the place I will pray _____.

I plan to pray one or more of the Daily Offices from *The Book of Common Prayer*:
_____ yes _____ no.
I know how to use *The Book of Common Prayer* for praying the Daily Offices:
_____ yes _____ no.

If "no," I will ask _____ for instruction. I will do that _____ (time) _____ (day).

Here are the Daily Offices I am committed to pray:
_____ Morning Prayer, p. 75
_____ Noon Office, p. 103
_____ Evening Prayer, p. 115
_____ Compline, p. 127

Fasting

Definition of fasting: to eat or drink no calories or diet beverages. Definition of abstinence: To not eat or drink specific types of food or beverage; for example, meat. Fasting and abstinence are good disciplines which may be used in combination. Some days are good for one discipline and other days for the other.

Here is a food or food group I will not eat during Lent _____ (except on Sundays). On __ M __ T __ W __ Th __ F __ Sat. I will not eat solid food until sundown.

I will eat vegetarian all through Lent:
_____ yes _____ no.

Here is another aspect of my food intake I wish to discipline this Lent: _____
_____.

Study

Here are books I want to read this Lent:
_____.

I need to ask _____
for suggestions.
I will do that (date/time) _____
_____.

I plan to devote _____ minutes per day to study.

Mercy

In Scripture, mercy, almsgiving, fasting, and prayer are sometimes tied together. Lent is a time to inventory our generosity. I plan to pray, and ask God to show me a person toward whom I can show mercy: _____ yes _____ no.
I plan to give $_____ to _____
_____ (list persons or organizations).

Exercise

I plan to pay attention to my body this Lent:
_____ yes _____ no.

Here is how: _____.
I need a physical: _____ yes _____ no.

Scripture

I plan to read the Lenten readings from _The Book of Common Prayer:_ _____ yes _____ no. Turn to page 951 in the Prayer Book, and find the words "Ash Wednesday." There you will find the readings for the next Wednesday, Ash Wednesday. Each day during Lent move down the page one day. If you do not understand these instructions, whom will you ask for clarification? _____

Solitude

Definition: A time spent in silence away from the demands of people and events. I will dedicate myself to solitude on the following schedule _____.
Here is where I will seek the solitude: _____.

Thanks, but no thanks

Frankly, good rector, I am so exhausted, so weary, so depressed, that I need to be free from discipline. My gift to myself is to do just that. For me, that will free me for a Holy Lent:
_____ yes _____ no.
I will call another Christian to discuss this:
_____ yes _____ no.
I will call _____
on _____.

Three Kinds of Fast for Lent

The material below may be reproduced in a Lenten bulletin to provide direction for the kind of fast congregants may want to experience.

The Normal Fast. Involves abstaining from all forms of food, but not from water, and must be distinguished from the absolute and partial fast. It seems clear that this is the type of fast Jesus did most often. In Luke 4:2 we are told Jesus "ate nothing" but not that he drank nothing. After that fast we are told he "was hungry" but not that he was thirsty. The normal fast may also include fasting from sleep, called "a watching" (2 Cor. 6:5; 11:27).

The Absolute Fast. Abstaining from eating and drinking (Ezra 10:6; Acts 9:9). It must not be longer than two days and caution must be exercised. This is usually an exceptional form of fasting for exceptional situations.

The Partial Fast. (See Daniel 10:3.) Here the emphasis is upon restriction of diet rather than complete abstention. One may abstain from eating certain meals; for example, dinner. One may abstain from eating certain foods and drinking certain drinks; for example, meat and coffee.

Richard Lobs III

✍ 𝐅𝐎𝐔𝐑𝐓𝐄𝐄𝐍 ✍

The Arts in Lenten Worship

On first thought, it may seem that the arts would not have a role in the quiet, reflective, prepara-tory season of Lent. But, in fact, it is the quietness and reflection of Lent which gives the arts a role as important as in any other season. For the arts are often able to express and call forth the self-examination, meditation, and reflection appropriate to this season. The following chapter provides guidelines for the use of the arts during Lent.

227 • THE ENVIRONMENT FOR LENTEN WORSHIP

Thinking about the environment for worship requires delving into the meaning of Lent. The following article explains the meaning of Lent and draws out implications for how the visual arts may be used to complement Lenten worship.

Lent is a season of simplicity, a time to strip away the false and to expose the truth. Things need to be torn apart and turned inside out. How else can the wind and sun cleanse a winter's worth of rot?

Throughout the year hospitality demands that a church be clean and free from clutter—including the mess that sometimes surrounds the bulletin boards, music racks, lost-and-found cabinets, and crying rooms. But Lent requires something more than tidiness. There should be a genuine austerity, a plainness that communicates a season when we get back to basics. We try to make more evident what is important about these forty days: the assembly, the penitents, the elect, the candidates.

Simplifying

There are many ways to simplify the worship environment: Use vesture that is textured, un-adorned, in dark violets, grays, and earth tones. Cover the lectionary or book of the gospels with this material. Don't add appliqué such as passion symbols: These turn vestments into billboards.

Candles can be lit and a cloth put on the altar only from the preparation of the altar until Communion. Use unbleached candles and unbleached cloth.

Remove statues, crosses, and other art from the building. Opaque fabric panels can cover unre-movable art and possibly even some windows. Use plain earthenware instead of metals or glass. Remove plants and flowers. Remove last year's paschal candle from the baptistery.

A simplified worship place may be able to sustain a few elements—as decoration—to bring out the unique character of Lent. Here's a brief overview of certain Lenten images, with possibilities for translating this imagery into the worship place.

Holy Spring

The paschal season—Lent, triduum, and Easter-time—is the springtime of the church. And spring takes many forms, from an orchard full of blossoms and butterflies to a flooding river engorged with mud and drowned animals. If Easter is the church's Maytime, Lent is its mudtime, a season of blizzards in the north and tornadoes in the south. Lent may mean "spring," but it's a threatening, blustery, life-and-death sort of season. There's good reason March was named after the god of war.

Be judicious about using signs of spring during Lent. Bear in mind spring's dangerous—and muddy—alter ego. It's almost in deference to this deadly side of spring that the church traditionally forbids the use of flowers during Lent. Maybe let just a single daffodil each week or a sprig of pussywillow or a bowl of crocus offer a small foretaste of Eastertime's abundance.

Lent, triduum, and Eastertime are planned as a whole. The worship environments of these seasons relate to and complement each other. If Eastertime is like an orchard, a garden, or a pasture, Lent is like a wasteland or a barren desert. If Eastertime is a homecoming banquet, Lent is the fasting of a long journey home. If Eastertime is a honeymoon, Lent is an anxious courtship.

During the triduum the holy font is filled with water, and chrism is welcomed as one of the "Easter gifts" of the bishop. It makes sense to keep the font dry during Lent and the ambry emptied of chrism. During Eastertime, let the font babble with water and chrism impart its fragrance throughout the room—with perhaps the punch of an added oil-based scent. During the triduum the wood of the holy cross is planted in the midst of the assembly as a tree of life. During Eastertime that cross might be surrounded by flowers and lights.

Psalm 137, "By the rivers of Babylon we sat and wept," is a Lenten song of exile. We hang our alleluias—our harps—on the willows. "For how can we sing the Lord's song in a foreign land?" Weeping willows set up in the worship space, hung with simple harps, are an emblem of Lent worth returning to year after year. Willows and poplars are found in just about every nation and climate. Like the catechumens, they are thirsty for water. It is no mystery why willows are a favorite Palm Sunday branch: They are one of the first plants to bud in the spring. The custom of veiling statues—certainly the most ambitious alteration of the worship environment in years past—is a strong symbol of exile. After all, the word *sin* means "separation," and it is sin that drove us from paradise. In this land of our exile, death denies us the company of our ancestors, the saints. A veil separates us from the vision of heaven, a vision that sacred images are meant to anticipate.

Prayer, fasting and almsgiving. Lent is a *memento mori*, a reminder of death. That is the meaning of "mortification." The three pillars of Lenten mortification are the disciplines of prayer, fasting, and almsgiving, and these disciplines need both practical and symbolic attention.

In the vestibule or gathering area, make avail-

Peter's Sword. The sword, scabbard, and the severed ear pictured here recall Peter's defense of Jesus in the Garden of Gethsemane (see Luke 22:38, 49-50).

able any parish take-home materials. Advertise special Lenten prayer services here. The well-stocked church library or bookstands deserve prominence at this season. Set up a hamper for receiving donations to charity. Include literature or signs that describe whatever was agreed upon as the focus of parishwide fasting, prayer, and almsgiving.

This takes an eye for attractiveness of both design and function. The whole area is to express how the parish keeps Lent and is to draw thoughtful attention before and after worship. This area is a good place to display a clay bowl of ashes, or perhaps images of the desert, or of journeys, or other small-scale Lenten images that would not be as appropriate in the worship area itself.

As a final suggestion, advertise the season to the neighborhood by hanging something outside the church building. Even more effective than within the building, strips of fabrics outside, perhaps in a monochromatic arrangement of purples, would be a simple way to announce that this community is preparing the Passover.

Peter Mazar[26]

228 • THE ENVIRONMENT FOR THE SERVICES OF LENT

Planning the visual environment for worship requires understanding the liturgical needs of each individual service of the season. This article examines each service and presents particular ways to express the themes of Lent through the visual elements of worship and space.

Environment for liturgy during the Lenten season should enhance the liturgical worship of the community. It is important to keep the environment in proportion to the space used. Too large a banner for a small chapel will detract, and too small a nosegay floral arrangement in a large basilica will lose its impact.

Plan your service and then reflect on how best you can use the space to enhance the prayer experience of the community. The liturgy should always flow; so don't plan or create situations in which the action must be stopped or interrupted to prepare for the next part of the service. If at all possible, a theme should be used to keep the Lenten season unified. Variations on the environment help to add variety and yet cohesiveness in the overall design and experience of prayer.

John Foley, S.J., has written a song entitled "Wood Hath Hope." And certainly the wood of the cross is our reminder of salvation and our personal invitation to transformation.

> Wood hath hope
> When it's cut, it grows green again
> and its boughs sprout green again
> Wood hath hope.

As a unifying theme for Lent, this image is helpful to recall when to planning the environment.

For Ash Wednesday, the environment should be forceful, yet simple and striking, while not overstated. Ask a carpenter in the community to fashion a large wooden cross out of four-inch by four-inch pieces of redwood or similar wood. The cross should be about five feet tall. In the sanctuary suspend the cross above the altar; it may be kept there for the entire Lenten season or placed in a stand off to the side for subsequent Sundays. Or, it can be used in the procession each Sunday, or as a focal point for the Scripture readings during each Sunday of Lent. From the suspended cross, drape a piece of purple cloth (about thirty-six inches wide and eight yards long). Drape the cloth over the left arm of the cross, allowing it to hang and cascade down to the right hand corner of the altar, and then to the floor and out toward the congregation, providing there is enough material. The altar should be covered with a floor length off-white material. The lectionary may be placed on a stand on the altar where the purple drape meets the altar. In front of the altar (or close to it) place a rectangular flower box—about six inches in height and almost the length of the altar. In this, place twelve to eighteen dark blue irises, to form a single row, each should be equally spaced allowing the leaves to form a cross-work pattern. This will achieve an effect of simplicity and reverence. The choice and arrangement of flowers help to set a mood. It is also important to create a place for the ashes and not just have them appear out of nowhere.

In the space in front of and to the left side of the altar, place a three-foot square cube and cover it with a deep purple cloth. The ashes for distribution can be stored behind the cube. On top of the cube place a brazier filled with glowing coals. During the Liturgy, incense may be added to the charcoal fire, thus bringing the senses of sight and smell into the prayer experience. In front of this set a small wicker basket filled with six white irises or a bunch of white fuschias in contrast with the purple cloth. The celebrant and ministers of ashes should be dressed in suitable vestments of purple or shades of purple to contrast and/or complement the other purple used.

The first Sunday of Lent in Cycle A uses the account of creation of our first parents and their fall to sin. Thus the use of the image of verdant green wood, cut down, is appropriate for this Sunday and the following ones. A large piece of driftwood with a central cavity will be instrumental in creating the effect of the transformation the Lenten season brings about. If not driftwood, another substantially shaped tree root will do as well. This should be cleaned up and placed in front of the altar, a focal point for each Sunday in Lent.

On the second Sunday of Lent plant a small amount of greenery in it. Gradually, our transformation is beginning to take effect as symbolized by this seemingly lifeless piece of wood. The Gospel reading (Matt. 17:1-13) reinforces this idea.

On the third Sunday of Lent add more greenery—perhaps a potted plant in front of or behind the dry wood. This Sunday the predominant image is water and the life it gives. Hopefully our growth continues, as does the dry wood's.

The fourth Sunday of Lent is traditionally known as Laetare Sunday. Around the driftwood add more greenery and some flowers—blue irises to represent the Passion time and calla lilies to look forward to the Easter event. The flowers and greenery may be arranged behind and in front of the driftwood to vaguely suggest a cross. This Sunday might be an appropriate time to use the song "Wood Hath Hope" in the liturgy—to renew our hope in the wood of the cross just as Jesus renewed the faith of the man born blind in today's readings (John 9:1-41).

Each Sunday the large wooden cross may be used either in the procession or placed in a stand off to the side and draped in purple.

On the fifth Sunday of Lent introduce a simple purple banner of a solid color and a simple pattern of gold leaves in a swirling pattern. These banners will help to give height to the sanctuary area. Gradually each Sunday builds upon the preceding one to lead up to the great Easter event.

In planning liturgies, remember to pray also with the eyes. Use texture, variations on color schemes, heights and depth. These aspects can only enhance an already prayerful experience.

Thomas S. Rambert, S.J.[27]

229 ◆ AN ANTHOLOGY OF HYMNS AND SONGS FOR LENT

The following article presents representative hymns and songs for the season of Lent. Note how the hymns that relate to the events of Christ's passion and death are saved for Holy Week.

The season of Lent begins on Ash Wednesday and continues through the Saturday immediately preceding the Sunday of the Passion (Palm Sunday). Both Lent and Holy Week are now recognized as part of the time of Easter. Holy Week begins on Palm Sunday, and also includes lesser celebrations on Monday, Tuesday, and Wednesday of that week, prior to the climatic commemorations of the triduum.

In this article several citations either declare in the versification Christ's ultimate victory in resurrection—the outcome of his sacrifice for sin—or affirm his eternal person and authority as God the Son. We recall that Lent is a conscious recognition of God's total plan in redemption, and its bearing on the believer's relationship to him in gratitude, the discipline of personal discipleship, personal walk, and witness. There is also emphasis on Christ's love, his purity as the Lamb of God, his grace. The penitential attitude of the worshiper is likewise appropriate, but has been placed in tandem with the broader—and historically earlier—contexts of Christian self-discipline, dedication, cultural mandate, and courage in Christ.

TITLE	AUTHOR/COMPOSER	TUNE	STYLE	SCRIPTURE REFERENCE
And When the Battle's Over	H. Waters/A. Lind		Scripture chorus	2 Timothy 4:7-8
Are Ye Able, Said the Master	E. Marlatte/H. Mason	BEACON HILL	gospel song	Matthew 20:22
Be Thou My Vision	Irish tune/D. Evans	SLANE	traditional	Philippians 3:7
Behold, What Manner of Love	P. Van Tine (1978)		Scripture chorus	1 John 3:1
Because He Lives	W. Gaither (1971)		Southern gospel song	John 14:19
Blessed Are the Persecuted	E. Bergen/Tonga tune (Zambia)		African	Matthew 5:6, 8, 11-12
Blessed Jesus, At Your Word	T. Clausnitzer/J. Ahle	LIEBSTER JESU	Chorale	Romans 8:28; Hebrews 13:21

TITLE	AUTHOR/COMPOSER	TUNE	STYLE	SCRIPTURE REFERENCE
Christ Is the World's True Light	G. Briggs/P. Coller	ST. JOAN	traditional	John 8:12
The God of Abraham Praise	D. Dayyan/M. Lyon	YIGDAL	traditional	Exodus 3:14-15
He Is My Everything	Anon./arr. L. Leatherman (1987)		Scripture chorus	Philippians 3:7-8
Help Us to Help Each Other, Lord	C. Wesley/Scottish Psalter, 1635	DUNFERMLINE	traditional	Ephesians 4:15-16
How Can We Name a Love	B. Wren/M. Williamson (1975)	TRADITIONAL/ CONTEMPORARY		Ephesians 3:19
I Will Come and Bow Down	M. Nystrom (1989)		Scripture chorus	Psalm 95:6
If Asked Whereon I Rest My Claim	S. Wallgren/Swedish folk	MIN SALIGHETGRUND	traditional	Galatians 6:14
Jesu, Jesu, Fill Us with Your Love	Ghanaian/tr. T. Colvin (1981)	GHANA FOLKSONG	African styling	John 13:5, 14-15
Lord, Look upon Our Working Days	I. Frasee/D. Kettrig (1972)	AUDREY	contemporary	Isaiah 64:8-9
Lord of All Nations, Grant Me Grace	O. Spannaus/Slovak/ arr. R. Hillert (1967)	BEATUS VIR	traditional	Galatians 3:26-28
Lord, Thou Hast Searched Me	American Folk/arr. A. Cassells-Brown (1978)	TENDER THOUGHT	Early American	Psalm 139
Master, No Offering	E. Parker	LOVE'S OFFERING		John 12:3; Matthew 26:7
My Hands Belong to You	A. Weber/F. Hernandez (1978)		Scripture chorus	Romans 12:1
Precious Lord, Take My Hand	T. A. Dorsey	PRECIOUS LORD	black spiritual	Psalm 5:11
Teach Me Thy Way, O Lord	H. Loland (1980)		Scripture chorus	Psalm 86:11-12
What More Can I Tell about God?	Sam (Kmher) (1989)		Khmer hymn	1 Corinthians 13:12
What Wondrous Love Is This	from J. Mercer/ Hesperian Harp, 1848	WONDROUS LOVE	Early American	John 3:16; Isaiah 53:6
Whatever It Takes	L. and M. Wolfe/L. Wolfe (1975)	SCRIPTURE CHORUS		Philippians 3:8

Continued...

TITLE	AUTHOR/COMPOSER	TUNE	STYLE	SCRIPTURE REFERENCE
Wheresoe'er I Roam	C. Rosenius/Danish	Var Jag Gar		John 10:11; Revelation 7:14
Wilt Thou Forgive That Sin	J. Donne/arr. E. Posten (1967)	Donne	traditional contemporary	1 John 1:9
Worthy Is the Lamb	D. Wyrtzen (1973)	Scripture Chorus		Revelation 5:12
Your Cause Be Mine	B. Leech/A.R. Eckhardt (1973)	Richmond Beach	traditional English style	John 18:37

Steve Cushman

Sample Services for Lent

The services of this chapter are presented for worship planners in both the traditional and free-church tradition of worship. These services, when celebrated with strong spiritual emphasis, order and organize personal and corporate spiritual experience. A congregation may choose to worship during Lent following these services. Primarily, however, they are presented as models from which a church may draw for the development of their own worship. Adapt these services to the custom and style of your congregation.

230 • A TRADITIONAL ASH WEDNESDAY SERVICE

The service below draws on many traditional Ash Wednesday texts and is designed for use in liturgical and traditional churches that do not already have a prescribed liturgy for Ash Wednesday. It also provides a model for planning worship in other styles and traditions.

ENTRANCE

Commentary: The visual setting for Ash Wednesday should be stark and solemn. As the first day of Lent, this occasion is an appropriate time for the introduction of the colors and symbols that will be used throughout the season by a congregation. The color purple is most commonly used, suggesting the penitential nature of the season. Common Lenten symbols include the cross, a person on a journey, or images of the desert. Use of dark gray and various earth tones is also appropriate for Ash Wednesday, recalling the ashes as an image of human mortality.

Gathering in Silence

Commentary: Silence is essential to capturing the solemn nature of the occasion and may be interspersed at appropriate places throughout the service.

Greeting

PASTOR: The grace of our Lord Jesus Christ be with you.

PEOPLE: And also with you.

Opening Prayer

PEOPLE: **Almighty and everlasting God, you breathed into dust the breath of life, creating us for fellowship with you. You brought about our redemption through Jesus Christ to restore us to fellowship with you. Today we acknowledge you as our Creator and Redeemer. We acknowledge the frailty of our lives, the pain of our sinfulness, and even the weakness of our faith. Work in us, we pray, a spirit of true humility and fervor, as we join now to offer our prayers to you. Amen.**

Commentary: This prayer could also be spoken by a single voice from the back of the worship space, perhaps quite slowly and reflectively.

Silence

Hymn: "Lord, Who throughout These Forty Days"

Commentary: Many churches choose to avoid any instrumental (including organ and piano) accompaniment to hymns and service music used at this service. This contributes to the stark ambiance of this service. Rehearsing any congregational music with a few strong singers or a choir prior to the service can allow for the singing to remain strong.

The Torch. This symbol recalls the betrayal of our Lord (see John 18:3).

WORD OF GOD

Old Testament Readings: Joel 2:1-2, 12-17a
New Testament Readings: Matthew 6:1-6, 16-21;
2 Corinthians 5:20b–6:2

Response

LEADER: The Word of the Lord.
PEOPLE: **Thanks be to God.**

Commentary: This response to the reading of Scripture is appropriate for every service in the Christian year.

Sermon

RESPONSE OF PENITENCE AND DEDICATION

Bidding to Lenten Penitence and Dedication

LEADER: People of God, each year we remember and celebrate the death and resurrection of our Lord Jesus Christ, by which he overcame death and provided for us redemption from sin. Lent is a season of preparation for this celebration, a time for personal and communal renewal and penitence. I invite you then to self-examination, prayer, meditation upon God's Word, giving of alms, and fast-

ing during this season of Lent. May God bless us as we strive to walk in the way our Lord.

Commentary: The imposition of ashes is certainly an optional part of worship on Ash Wednesday for nonliturgical Protestant churches. For some worshipers it may create an unnecessary barrier to the penitence appropriate for the day. Yet there is no more powerful symbol of our mortality than ashes, and no more powerful way to remind the worshiper of his or her need for renewal, reasons which commend the continuation of this tradition.

Imposition of Ashes

LEADER: We begin our Lenten observance by using the centuries-old symbol of ashes. By this we are reminded of our own frailty and mortality and called to humility and penitence.

PEOPLE: **Almighty God, you have created us out of the dust of the earth. May these ashes be to us a sign of our mortality, that we may remember that it is only by your gracious gift that we are given everlasting life. Amen.**

LEADER: (to the People, as the ashes are placed on the forehead of each worshiper) Remember that you are dust, and to dust you shall return.

Commentary: The imposition of ashes reminds the worshiper of his or her own mortality and need for repentance. After the printed prayer, worshipers should be invited to the front of the worship space, where the officiating clergy and other assistants will places the ashes on the forehead of each worshiper. They may be imposed in the shape of a cross.

The ashes are traditionally created by the burning of the palm branches that were used by the local parish during the previous year.

Prayer of Confession

(Leader and people read *Psalm 51* responsively.)

Commentary: The psalm should be read by the entire congregation as a prayer of confession. The psalm may be broken into several sections, each of which could be followed by a refrain or antiphon sung by a solo voice or choir. An appropriate refrain text would be, "Create in me a clean heart, O God, and renew a right spirit within me." Music for the refrain and other antiphons may be found in _The Presbyterian Hymnal_ (Louisville: Westminster/John Knox, 1990), _The Celebration Psalter_ (St. Louis: Cathedral Music Press, 1991), _Psalm Refrains and Tones_ (Carol Stream, Ill.: Hope Publishing, 1988), _Lead Me, Guide Me_ (Chicago: GIA Publications, 1987), _Psalms for the Church Year_, vols. 1–4 (GIA Publications), _United Methodist Hymnal_ (Nashville: UMC Publishing House, 1979), and several other hymnals and church music collections.

Silence

LEADER: Almighty and everlasting God,

PEOPLE: **We enter this season of Lent in penitence and humility, aware of our own mortality and sinfulness. Encourage us with your presence, we pray, that we may empty ourselves of whatever separates us from you and one another. Teach us to rely on no strength but yours, as we journey with your Son toward your kingdom through Jesus Christ, our Lord. Amen.**

Commentary: In some traditions, any declaration of pardon is omitted throughout the Lenten season. This reinforces the penitential nature of the season, but unnecessarily separates the worshiper from the announcement of the gospel, which never fails to accompany God's people. A helpful balance can be achieved by including a declaration of pardon that acknowledges the significance of Christ's sacrifice on our behalf.

Declaration of Pardon

PASTOR: (reads Psalm 103:8-12)

Prayer of Dedication

LEADER: (reads Psalm 116)

Commentary: This may be read by a single voice from the back of the worship space. It should be read slowly and reflectively.

Silence

LEADER: Lord, our God,

PEOPLE: **Make of us pilgrims throughout these forty days. We pledge to walk in the light of your Word and by the power of your Spirit. Strengthen us in our commitment, we pray, that we may serve you and each other in the love of Christ, our Lord. Amen.**

Offertory

LEADER: We present now our gifts to God.

Offertory Hymn: "May the Mind of Christ, My Savior"

Commentary: This or another hymn of dedication may be sung as the gifts are received and as the table is prepared for the sacrament.

HOLY COMMUNION

Commentary: The following liturgy for the Lord's Supper is intentionally simple and stark. Each of the essential components of the liturgy are present, but only with the fewest possible words. Worship leaders may wish to reinforce this solemnity by leaving a time of silence after each component of the liturgy. The somber tone of the service should remain constant throughout, but should not obscure the message of God's grace which is proclaimed each time the sacrament is observed. The invitation to the Table and the concluding benediction are points where the tone of the worship leader should noticeably reflect the joy of the gospel, even in the context of the starkness of this service.

Prayer of Thanksgiving

LEADER: Let us lift our hearts to God.

PEOPLE: **We praise you, O God, for creating this world,**
for creating us in your image,
for remaking us after the image of Jesus.
We acknowledge our sin before you, trusting in your gracious love toward us.
Accept now our praise to you:

PEOPLE: **Holy, Holy, holy Lord, God of power and might,**
heaven and earth are full of your glory.
Hosanna in the highest.
Blessed is he who comes in the name of the Lord.
Hosanna in the highest.

Commentary: While this text is most often sung, it is appropriate for Ash Wednesday to speak the text.

LEADER: We praise you, Lord Christ,
for your pilgrimage on this earth
for your obedience even to death,
and for your victory over death.
Teach us, we pray, to walk in your ways.

Institution

PASTOR: The Lord Jesus, on the night when he was betrayed, took bread, and when he had given thanks, he broke it and said, "This is my body, which is for you; do this in remembrance of me." In the same way, he took the cup, after supper, saying, "This cup is the new covenant in my blood; do this, whenever you drink it, in remembrance of me." For whenever you eat this bread and drink this cup, you proclaim the Lord's death until he comes."

Memorial

PASTOR: What is your proclamation in this feast?

PEOPLE: **Our Lord has died, is risen, and will reign forever.**

Prayer of Consecration

PASTOR: Holy Spirit of God,
come upon us now, we pray,
teach us true penitence in the way of Jesus.
By this feast, remind us of our union with him.
Amen.

Invitation to the Table

PASTOR: Come now, the Lord offers this feast for you, his people.

The Sacrament

PASTOR: (as the people take the bread) The body of Christ for you.

PASTOR: (as the people take the cup) The blood of Christ for you.

Thanksgiving

PEOPLE: **We bless you, O God, for shower-**
ing upon us these gifts of your love. May your presence go with us from this feast as we walk in the way of our Lord.

Benediction

PASTOR: The grace of our Lord Jesus Christ be with you all. Amen.

or

PASTOR: Almighty God, give to your people pardon and peace. Go with them as they walk in the way of Christ in this season, that they may come to know you more fully. Amen.

Commentary: The first option is appropriate as a very simple, direct statement of God's blessing. The second is presented as an option for churches who replace the benediction during Lent with a prayer for God's guidance. This latter option may be chosen as gesture of humility appropriate for the season, but should not reflect any lack of confidence of God's continuing presence with his people.

Dispersal of the Congregation
[in silence]

John D. Witvliet

231 ✦ A CREATIVE ASH WEDNESDAY SERVICE

The service below is intended for us in the free-church tradition, particularly among evangelical churches. It reflects a traditional pattern for worship and a wide range of musical and textual resources.

─────── The Basic Pattern ───────

Preparation and Reflection: Confitemeni Domino ("Let Us Confess to the Lord" [Taizé])
(As you begin this service, take a few moments to bring yourself before the Lord—your present state of mind and preoccupation, as well as a simple confession of your desire to meet God during this time.)

Opening Prayer

Introduction to the Lenten Season

Scripture Readings: Isaiah 58, Luke 9:23-25

(For the Scripture readings, please listen to the Word rather than read along in your own Bible.)

Receiving of the Ashes

Music: "Healer of My Soul;" "Father Make Us Holy"

Scripture Readings: Isaiah 43:1-3a; 1 Peter 2:9-10

Celebration of the Eucharist
Prayer for the Bread
Prayer for the Wine

Music: "Our Blessing Cup;" "Holy, Holy, Holy;" "I Am the Bread of Life"
Congregation: "I Am the Bread of Life"

Benediction

Postlude

--------- **Commentary** ---------

Order of the Service. If this particular liturgical service is new to a number of people in your congregation, an order of service can help alleviate fear of the unknown and prepare participants for the rhythm of the service.

A preparation and reflection suggestion gently communicates to the congregation that they have gathered for a specific purpose, and leads them toward the posture of inner quiet and expectation, and away from socializing.

Even the most well-thought-through content can become lost if the space in which it is to be communicated is serving to contrast rather than complement the service. If your worship space is already rich with symbolism, you can alter the lighting to highlight the area or symbols that best enrich the service at hand. If the worship space is plain, consider adding a Lenten banner, a cross, or simply use a table, adorned with the necessary elements: goblets of wine, bread, pottery bowls for the ashes, and candles. Candles always help to visually highlight the focus for worship and symbolize the light of the Christ who presents himself among us during worship.

Opening Prayer. At the beginning of any worship service we must seek the grace of God's enabling. Although many congregations in the nonliturgical tradition have begun to include Advent and Lent in their Sunday worship cycle, not all will include an Ash Wednesday service as the introductory service to Lent. Because so many participants are unfamiliar with the Ash Wednesday

service, leaders must be sensitive to pray that God will beckon each participant by his grace. In planning their prayer, leaders will therefore need to be aware of both their congregation's need and the direction in which the Spirit is desiring to lead.

The Ash Wednesday worship should link our participation with that of our biblical and historic predecessors in faith, and then should extend that orthodoxy to include the participant's present spirituality. Participants in an unfamiliar service can be freed to worship by enriching the basic liturgy and by introducing or accompanying the symbols with a minimum of teaching.

Scripture Readings. A lectionary is a helpful tool for choosing appropriate Scripture readings, but you need not be limited to the specific choices given for Ash Wednesday. A glance through various other Lenten readings might draw your attention to an appropriate theme for the congregation's entrance into Lent. Because of the contemporary interest and emphasis on worship renewal, Isaiah 58, which focuses on false and true worship, was chosen for the congregation and service at hand. While not among the readings for Ash Wednesday, Isaiah 58 does, however, appear in the lectionary as an authorized reading for Lent. As far as the present source is concerned, Isaiah 58 was chosen to give a broad picture of worship as God desires it.

Luke 9:23-25, or other Scriptures that affirm the centrality of the cross for Christian discipleship, are both appropriate and necessary.

Pause of Silence. The Ash Wednesday service comprises many elements. Nevertheless, the leader should desire simply that the participants experience an oasis, or a time of stillness in which they encounter God, and that they consequently leave the service with a desire to follow Christ into the ensuing holy season.

Prayer of Confession. Christians past and present have considered the confession of sin to be necessary for spiritual growth, but not all church traditions have included times of confession in their public worship. Therefore, leaders need to consider their congregations and ask how these historic liturgical elements could be consistent with their church's present theology and practice (spirituality). Depending on the results of this analysis, leaders can determine an appropriate approach to confession. This creative liturgy presupposes a congregation that experiences God as a vindictive judge who communicates his expectations of his servants vaguely at best. This service therefore stressed that confession is a grace, a gift from God to us.

Service of Ashes. One's teaching will again depend upon the needs of the congregation, although regardless of the congregation's experience and ease with the service, some level of communication can eliminate superstition and enrich worship.

The ashes used in the traditional Ash Wednesday liturgy come from the palm crosses of Palm Sunday. Hence the primary purpose of Ash Wednesday: to remind us of our mortality. Whatever their origin in the context of your congregation, the ashes offer a point of departure for reflection on mortality in all its aspects.

If "worm theology" is part of the popular spirituality of your tradition, you will want to introduce this emphasis on human mortality with care so as not to unwittingly lead the congregation into an experience of guilt or despair. The point of the exercise is rather to lead them to Jesus, and to an experience of bonding with the host of other disciples that have attempted to follow him throughout the church's history.

If it is appropriate in your tradition for a lay person to lead the service of the ashes, the experience can provide the leader with a heretofore unparalleled experience of compassion for and identification with the human limitation of the church. You can make the service more meaningful for the participants by addressing them by name, "Joan, remember that you are dust, and to dust you shall return." Even if you do not know a person's name, you can quietly ask for it and then include the name in the liturgy.

Music. This service used taped, contemplative vocal music for the preparation time as well as for the service of the ashes and the Eucharist. This music served in effect as prayer on behalf of the congregation. Whether the music is chosen to be listened to or to be sung, it should emphasize that in our mortality and human frailty we need God's grace. This present service focused on the grace of healing, but as you pray about your congregation's needs you might choose to emphasize a different grace.

In addition, you will want to select music that affirms our hope in Christ and emphasizes God's victory over evil.

Scripture Readings/Eucharist. Following the service of the ashes, the service moves toward the most powerful aspect of Ash Wednesday: the juxtaposition of the ashes with the Eucharist. This juxtaposition symbolically emphasizes the fact that human mortality is inextricably linked with God's promise of life. The Eucharist comes as a welcome, hope-filled surprise to the soberness of the earlier portion of the service, thereby serving as a microcosm of the whole Lenten season.

As far as the Scripture readings are concerned, feel free to select any of the numerous passages that focus upon the faithfulness of God, who has called us and who is committed to leading us to the completion of what he has called us to be in Christ. After the humility and confession of the service of ashes, it is time to look up to the God who has called us and who promises to accompany us.

Though the liturgy takes us back to the time when Jesus set his face toward Jerusalem, we participate as those who know the outcome, i.e., the process of Lent brings us out of the darkness of sin and into the light of grace.

Prayers for Bread and Wine. Those whom you have selected to read Scripture or pray can come forward or remain within the congregation depending on what you intend the service to communicate to the congregation. For example, when readings and prayers come from the front of the worship center, at a pulpit or lectern, God's transcendence can be pictured, stressing God's holiness and separateness from us. Conversely, when readings and prayers come from within the congregation, God's imminence is symbolized, stressing God's identification with his people, that God has come among us.

Participation in Eucharist. In some liturgical traditions, communicants come forward to receive the elements, while in others, they remain in their seats and the bread and wine is passed to them. However the congregation may have received the elements, you, as leader, should be sensitive to their contrite hearts (they have just humbly received the ashes), and be careful to express that at this time Christ now comes to us in the bread and wine (also to those who did not feel free to come forward to receive the ashes).

If participants are coming forward to receive the elements, whoever is serving might want to take a more personal approach than usual. For example, rather than simply saying, "the body of Christ," he or she might say, "Ken, the body of Christ, broken that you might have life." If the elements are passed down the rows from person to person, the people can be encouraged to serve each other by name, saying something similar to the preceding example.

Benediction and Postlude. The service is a rich mixture of many elements, so the benediction should be a simple word to go in the confidence and presence of the Lord, and the postlude should affirm the omnipresence of the Creator God who continues to create and redeem life.

Diane S. George Ayer

232 ✦ A CONVERGENCE ASH WEDNESDAY SERVICE

The service below is intended for use by those communities that bring together traditional and contemporary worship styles.

The church should be stripped of extra decorations, leaving a very stark and solemn place of assembly. Except for standard linens, paraments, and frontals, the front of the sanctuary should look quite colorless. Banners may be removed or replaced by ones conveying the seriousness of the event.

Each person must be given a blank piece of paper and a pencil as they enter the sanctuary.

ACTS OF ENTRANCE

Preparation

Commentary: People should enter the sanctuary in silence. If necessary, you can post a sign in the foyer indicating that this is a time of solemn and silent examination. No background music should be used.

Processional

Commentary: The processional, if any, should also be in silence. The ministers enter and either kneel

at the railing or are seated for a time of personal reflection and prayer.

Summary of the Law

Hear the words of our Lord Jesus Christ: "You shall love the Lord your God with all your heart, and with all your soul, and will all your mind. This is the first and great commandment. And the second is like it: you shall love your neighbor as yourself. On these two commandments hang all the law and the prophets."

MINISTRY OF THE WORD

Collect

Let us pray: Almighty and Everliving God, who, through your Son Jesus Christ, provided a way of redemption for all who repent and turn from sin: Create in us a clean heart and renew a steadfast and willing spirit, that we, acknowledging our sinfulness, may live an upright and holy life by the power of your Holy Spirit; through Jesus Christ our Lord, who, with you and the Holy Spirit, lives and reigns, one God, world without end. Amen.

Readings

Commentary: Immediately after the collect, the readings are offered:

FIRST READING:	Joel 2:1-2; 12-17a
	Psalm 103
SECOND READING:	2 Corinthians 5:20–6:10
GOSPEL READING:	Matthew 6:1-6, 16-21

Message

Commentary: A short message of challenge may be given, emphasizing our need to examine our lives for sin and sloppy living, and to repent and turn to Christ.

MINISTRY OF RECONCILIATION

Invitation to Observance

Dear Brothers and Sisters in Christ: Since the beginning of the church, Christians have always observed the days of our Lord's passion and resurrection with great devotion. It became one of the great traditions of the church to prepare for these events through serious examination of our spiritual lives through prayer, repentance, and fasting. Converts to the faith were prepared for baptism during Lent. Those who were separated from the church through serious sin were reconciled and restored to fellowship. The body of Christ was challenged to seek pardon and absolution for those areas where sin had found a place, to find reconciliation with God and with each other and to renew their repentance and faith.

I invite you, therefore, in the name of the Lord and His church, to observe a holy Lent, by self-examination, penitence, prayer, fasting, and sacrificial giving; to further your discipline of reading and meditating on the Word of God, and to make a right beginning to walk in newness of life. Therefore, I invite you to kneel (bow) before the Lord, our Creator and Redeemer.

Rite of Confession

Commentary: Using 1 John 1:9 as a text, invite the people to pray and ask God to reveal areas of sin and weakness. You instruct the people to write on the blank sheet of paper what God reveals. The papers are folded and placed in a receptacle in the front of the church and burned. Ashes from palm branches of the previous year's Palm Sunday are then mixed in with the ashes of the paper. As the papers burn, the minister can explain that just as the list of sins has been consumed never to return, so the Lord has forgiven us and removed our sins from us according to 1 John 1:9.

Prayer of Thanksgiving

Almighty God, you created us out of the dust of the earth. Grant that these ashes may be to us a sign of our mortality and penitence, that we may remember that it is only by your gracious gift that we are given everlasting life, through Jesus Christ our Lord. (From the *Book of Common Prayer*)

Imposition of Ashes

Commentary: This can be optional. While the imposition of ashes dates back to the eleventh century, more recent liturgies make this optional, referencing Jesus' words in Matthew 6:16-18 concerning penitence.

Should the imposition of ashes be done, the following words can be used.

(Name), Remember that you are dust and to dust you shall return. Repent and believe the gospel of our Lord Jesus Christ.

The minister may want to explain that the ashes are seen as a symbol of sorrow and repentance for sin. They are a sign of intention to die to the old ways and live a new life for Christ.

Psalm of Repentance

Commentary: The text of Psalm 51 is then read corporately. Additional prayers and litanies may be offered (for example, the Litany of Penitence in the *Book of Common Prayer,* p. 267).

If there are those who are being reconciled to the church or to other persons, they can be brought forward at this time for special prayer. Also, those who have committed their lives to Jesus Christ in recent months and have not made a public profession of faith may come forward for prayer.

Absolution

Commentary: At this point, the minister addresses the people and says, with joy: "In the name of Jesus Christ, you are forgiven!" The people respond in kind by saying the same words to the minister: "In the name of Jesus Christ, you are forgiven!" Then the people turn to one another and greet each other saying: *"In the name of Jesus Christ, you are forgiven!"*

The minister concludes by saving, "Rejoicing in the fellowship of all the saints, let us commend ourselves, one another, and our whole life to Christ our Lord. To you, O Lord."

Prayers of the People

Commentary: This is a special time of ministry of intercession for those who are still walking without Christ, whether friends, loved ones, unreached peoples, etc; those who have chosen to walk away from Christ and his church; and those who need a fresh touch from the Lord. The ministers may want to invite people with special needs to come forward and ministry teams may, during this time, pray for healing, deliverance, restoration, etc. The minister and/or the people then offer prayers of thanksgiving and praise for the grace and mercy of the Lord.

The Peace

Commentary: As ministry ends, the people can exchange signs of peace and love with one another.

Praise and Worship

Commentary: This is the first music of the

service. Usually a short time of worship with a hymn and choruses sung a cappella or with piano, acoustic guitar, etc. One good hymn to use is "Lord, Who throughout These Forty Days."

MINISTRY OF THE TABLE AND/OR DISMISSAL

Holy Communion

Commentary: The service may continue with Holy Communion if so desired, following a standard form. Observe silence during communion to express the sober nature of the memory observed.

Benediction

LEADER: Go in peace to live for Christ, to serve him alone and to walk in holiness and righteousness all your days, through the grace of our Lord and the power of his Holy Spirit.

PEOPLE: **Thanks be to God!**

Randolph W. Sly

233 ✦ A TRADITIONAL SERVICE FOR THE SUNDAYS OF LENT

The following service is a creative adaptation of the traditional pattern and texts for worship in the season of Lent. It will be of particular help for those who plan more formal Lenten worship. For those with nonliturgical backgrounds, the commentary included with this service will provide a guide to thoughtful planning for the Lenten season. This basic service, with variation of Scripture, hymns, and prayers, may be used for all the Sundays of Lent.

ENTRANCE INTO GOD'S PRESENCE

Commentary: The visual environment for Lenten worship should suggest the penitential nature of the season. Purple, suggesting penitence, is most commonly used color, in addition to dark grays and earth tones. Common Lenten symbols include the cross and images of a desert or a pilgrimage. Fabrics used for communion table, paraments, or banner construction can appropriately be of rough, unrefined quality. The presentation of any colors or symbols should be understated, both to reflect the meditative nature of Lent and to set

up a large contrast with the resplendent colors and symbols that can be used during Easter celebrations.

Gathering of the Congregation

(with Organ, Piano, or Instrumental Prelude)

Commentary: The people may gather in silence during the season of Lent, calling attention to the penitential nature of the season.

Call to Worship

LEADER: "Even now," declares the LORD, "return to me with all your heart, with fasting and weeping and mourning." Rend your heart and not your garments. Return to the LORD your God, for he is gracious and compassionate, slow to anger and abounding in love, and he relents from sending calamity (Joel 2:12-13).

PEOPLE: **In this service of worship and penitence, we offer our hearts to God.**

Commentary: This passage from the prophecy of Joel is traditionally read during the Ash Wednesday service. Using it throughout Lent can unify a congregation's focus on the important Lenten themes of renewal and penitence.

Prayer for Purity

LEADER: Let us pray.

PEOPLE: **Almighty God, to you all hearts are open, all desires known, and from you no secrets are hid. Cleanse the thoughts of our hearts by the inspiration of your Holy Spirit, that we may perfectly love you, and worthily magnify your holy name, through Christ our Lord. Amen.**[28]

Commentary: This prayer is used by many churches to begin their worship service each week of the Christian year. The nature of the text as a humble approach to God makes it especially appropriate for use during Lent.

Greeting

PASTOR: Grace to you and peace from God and our Lord Jesus Christ, who gave himself for our sins to deliver us from the present evil age, according to the will of our gracious God, to whom be glory forever and ever.

PEOPLE: **Amen.**

Hymn: "God Himself Is with Us"

Commentary: The opening hymn may feature a text that focuses on the approach of the worshiper to God. It is traditional that Lenten services do not include the acclamation "Alleluia."

ACTS OF PENITENCE

Commentary: If the sermon includes a call to penitence, this section of the service may appropriately follow the sermon and precede Communion.

Invitation to Penitence

LEADER: People of God, in his Word to us, the Lord has given us instruction regarding his will for our lives. Hear now the law of God:
(Read from Exod. 20; Deut. 5; or Matt. 22:37-40)

Commentary: The law of God, as summarized in the Ten Commandments or by Jesus in Matthew 22, is used by some churches for each service in the Christian year. It may be used prior to confession, as a teacher of sin, reminding us of God's standard for living, or it may be used following the declaration of pardon as a guide to Christian discipleship.

LEADER: Having heard again the standard for life in God's world, let us join in a spirit of humility and confess our sins against God and our neighbor.

Prayers of Confession

Commentary: Each of the following three prayers of confession may be concluded with a sung prayer of confession. Settings of a portion of Psalm 51 or other penitential psalms are appropriate for use, as are general hymns of confession. These may be effectively sung by an unaccompanied solo voice or small choral ensemble and then extended to include the entire congregation. This service suggests the use of the three successive stanzas of the hymn, "God Be Merciful to Me," with one stanza to be used after each spoken prayer.

Confession for Sins of the Human Race

Almighty God, whose will it is to hold all your people in peace, we hear your word. We know the importance of confession. In your presence, we confess the sins of our human race: pride that has led to war, neglect that has caused poverty, greed that has polluted your earth, lust that has led to pornography, hatred that has fostered racism. We know that we share in these sins; in moments of meditation we feel now the weight of these sins . . .

[silence]

ending with solo: "God, Be Merciful to Me"

Confession for Sins of the Local Church and Community

Almighty God, whose will it is that we should live in unity. We hear your Word, we know the importance of confession. In your presence, we now confess to each other the sins of our own community and congregation: failing to support each other in community injuring each other with dishonest words failing to acknowledge the gifts of those of another sex, race, ethnic background, or area of special gift or interest failing to thank you for the good gifts which you have given to our community. In moments of silence, we now pray in confession to you . . .

[silence]

ending with solo: "Gracious God, My Heart Renew"

Confession for Individual Sins

Almighty God, whose will it is to love us,
We confess to you our own private sins.
May our honesty before you not lead to guilt,
     but rather to an assurance of your pardon
     through Jesus Christ our Lord.
O God hear our prayers . . .

ending with congregation singing:

Contrite spirit, pleading cries, you, O God, will
     not despise.
Sinful ways I will reprove, and my tongue shall
     sing your love.
Let my righteous sacrifice then delight your
     holy eyes!

Commentary: A shorter prayer of confession may be substituted for this extended prayer, allowing for the reading of a penitential psalm during each week in Lent. The penitential psalms are Psalms 6, 32, 38, 51, 102, 130, and 143. Many of these psalms also appear as suggestions for use in Lent by various lectionaries.

Declaration of Pardon and Thanksgiving

LEADER: O God, gracious God, you are with us. Help us in this silence to sense the power of your presence.

(moment of silence)

LEADER: You are a great God. You are a gracious God. And this is your Word to us:

PEOPLE: **"There is no one who is righteous, not even one; there is no one who has understanding, there is no one who seeks God"**

LEADER: You are a great God. You are a gracious God. And this is your Word to us:

PEOPLE: **"The wages of sin is death, but the free gift of God is eternal life in Christ Jesus, our Lord."**

LEADER: You are a great God. You are a gracious God. And this is your Word to us:

PEOPLE: **"There is therefore now no condemnation for those who are in Christ Jesus."**

LEADER: You are a great God. For your good gift to us, we respond with joy:

PEOPLE: **Thanks be to God!**

LEADER: And we sing your praise:

PEOPLE: **Amazing grace, how sweet the sound
That saved a wretch like me,
I once was lost, but now am found.
Was blind, but now I see.**

Commentary: Alternate expressions of thanksgiving, including choral or solo anthems, may be chosen. The canticle, "Glory to God in the Highest," however, is not traditionally sung during Lent.

PROCLAMATION OF THE WORD

Prayer for Illumination

PEOPLE: **Spirit of God, open our hearts now to your Word, that our Lenten jour-**

The Lantern. The lantern of the Roman guard is a symbol of the betrayal (see John 18:3).

ney may be shaped by your will, that we may walk in the way of Jesus Christ, and bring honor and glory to his name. Amen.

Commentary: The following readings are based on the suggestions of one lectionary for the first Sunday in Lent.

Old Testament Reading: Genesis 2:4–3:7
Psalm: Psalm 130
Commentary: If the congregation uses a penitential psalm earlier in the service and a psalm of dedication later in the service, worship planners may wish to omit the reading of a psalm at this point. The psalm may be sung by the choir or congregation. Musical resources for singing the psalms are included in the commentary with the Pentecost service in this series.

New Testament Reading: Romans 5:12-19

Sermon

Commentary: Sermons during Lent may appropriately be based on scriptural passages and themes that address Christian penitence and discipleship. These themes anticipate the focus upon Christ's passion, which should be left for Holy Week itself.

ACTS OF DEDICATION

Statement of Faith: The Apostles' Creed

Commentary: Alternate statements of faith may be taken from traditional catechisms or denominational affirmations or confessions of belief. Scriptural affirmations may be drawn from several of Paul's epistles, especially from chapters like Romans 8, Colossians 1, and Philippians 2.

Concerns of the Congregation

Commentary: At this point, members of the congregation may make known to each other concerns for mutual prayer. These may be announced by the pastor or lay worship leader, by church members assigned to monitor the prayer needs of the congregation, or by individual worshipers in a time of sharing reasons for thanksgiving and intercession.

Prayers of the People

PASTOR: Let us pray for the church,

LEADER: Almighty and everlasting God, we trust your promise to bring us to the full knowledge of salvation. In this season of penitence, grant us your presence in special measure, restore our vision for your kingdom, inspire us by the gospel of Jesus Christ, our Lord, that we may be a bold witness to the world. Lord, in your mercy,

PEOPLE: **Hear our prayer.**

PASTOR: Let us pray for the concerns of the local community,

LEADER: Almighty and everlasting God, we trust your promise to never leave or forsake us. We ask your blessing to rest upon [names of the sick may be mentioned] and others who suffer from illness; upon [names of those engaged in special ministry may be mentioned] and others who serve this community in your name; upon [names of those who have requested prayers may be mentioned] and others whose anonymous needs are known only to you. Lord, in your mercy,

PEOPLE: **Hear our prayer.**

PASTOR: Let us pray for our Lenten journey,

LEADER: Gracious God, we trust in the promise of the gospel of Jesus Christ. We ask you to sustain this in our Lenten pilgrimage. Continue to teach us by your Word. Give us courage to live out the Word we have just heard read and preached. Prepare our hearts for the remembrance of Christ's death and for the celebration of his coming to life. Lord, in your mercy,

PEOPLE: **Hear our prayer.**

Commentary: Other forms for the prayers of the people are found in other services in this series. This form of prayer may be extended to include as many sections as may be appropriate in local congregations.

Act of Dedication

Commentary: In addition to the theme of humble penitence which is essential to the season, Lent provides an important opportunity for individual recommitment to the faith and to lives fashioned after Christ's will. This would be an appropriate occasion for individuals in the congregation to be commissioned for service in some aspect of the church's ministry.

Psalm of Dedication: Psalm 116

Commentary: The Psalms are replete with expressions of dedication, such "I will fulfill my vows . . ." or "I will sing praise to the Lord . . ." A different psalm of dedication may be used in this place during each week of Lent, chosen for its individual appropriateness to the sermon topic of the day. The psalm may be read or sung.

Offertory

LEADER: 2 Corinthians 8:9
Let us bring the offerings of our lives and the meditations of our heart to the Lord.

Offerings of money are received for . . .
Offerings of music are [name of offertory music that may be played or sung.]
Offerings of personal prayers to God may focus on [the text of the sermon].
Offerings of bread and wine for the feast of the Lord are made by [name of persons presenting the element for the Lord's Supper.]

Commentary: These four sentences call attention to the many-faceted nature of the congregation's giving. It may be especially helpful to print the text of any offertory music that is played or sung, or to print the text of the sermon if it has not already been printed, so as to guide the reflections of the people during this time. Gifts of money may be received from the people where they are seated, or people may be invited to come forward to place their gifts in offertory baskets in the front of the sanctuary.

Doxology: "Praise God from Whom All Blessings Flow"

Commentary: During the doxology, members of the congregation may bring forward the elements for the sacrament and the monetary gifts which have been received.

CELEBRATION OF THE SACRAMENT

Commentary: The following liturgy for the Lord's Supper is presented as a dialogue between God and the worshiper, alternating between the readings of God's Word and the response of the congregation. This structure is common to many Christian liturgies, both for entire services and for the Lord's Supper. Presenting the Lord's Supper liturgy in this way calls the dialogic nature of worship to the attention of the worshiper. While this structure may be used at any time, it is especially appropriate for use in Lent, a season which focuses on the Christian's penitent response to the gospel message.

The dialogic nature of this liturgy may be reinforced by having each of the "Word of God" sections read by a pastor or an elder from the pulpit and having each of the "Response of the People" sections led by a layperson from within the congregation.

ANNOUNCEMENT OF GOD'S GRACE

The Word of God

LEADER: Jesus said, "I am the bread of life. Those who come to me shall not hunger, and those who believe in me shall never thirst." "Happy are those who hunger and thirst for righteousness, for they shall be filled." (John 6:35, Matt. 5:6)

The Response of the People

The Passing of the Peace

PEOPLE [to each other]:
May God give you peace and nourish you in his meal.

The Prayer of Thanksgiving

LEADER: Let us pray.

PEOPLE: **Lord God, we praise you for providing us with nourishment for body and soul in our journey of faith. Accept now the praises of our hearts.**

LEADER: Lift up your hearts.

PEOPLE: **We lift them up to the Lord.**

LEADER: Let us give thanks to the Lord, our God.

PEOPLE: **It is fitting for us at all times and in all places to give thanks to you, O Lord, Holy Father, Almighty, everlasting God.**

LEADER: We bless you for creating us in your image, for remaking us after the image of your Son. With humble and penitent hearts and minds, we acknowledge your greatness and the splendor of your presence. We join, therefore, with all your saints and angels in bringing you praise:

PEOPLE: **Holy, holy, holy Lord, God of power and might, heaven and earth are full of your glory.**
Hosanna in the highest.
Blessed is he who comes in the name of the Lord.
Hosanna in the highest.

Commentary: Most hymnals include a setting of this traditional canticle. For a list of service music found in a representative group of hymnals, consult the commentary to the Communion liturgy of the Advent service in this series.

LEADER: We bring our thanks to you, for the gift of your Son, Jesus Christ our Lord: the Bread of Life, who came to nourish his children; the Lamb of God, who came to take away the sins of the world, the Servant of the Most High, who remained obedient even to death by execution. For this love for us, for the joyous news of the gospel, for the privilege of walking in the way of our Lord, we bring our praise. Amen.

ANNOUNCEMENT OF GOD'S GIFT OF THE SACRAMENT

The Word of God, the Institution

LEADER: The Lord Jesus, on the night when he was betrayed, took bread, and when he had given thanks, he broke it and said, "This is my body, which is for you; do this in remembrance of me." In the same way, he took the cup, after supper, saying, "This cup is the new covenant in my blood; do this, whenever you drink it, in remembrance of me." For whenever you eat this bread and drink this cup, you proclaim the Lord's death until he comes.

The Response of the People, the Memorial

LEADER: People of God, what do you proclaim in this feast?

PEOPLE: **We proclaim that our Lord Jesus Christ, died as payment for our sins, rose again as victor over death, and will come again in glory.**

THE INVITATION TO THE TABLE

The Word of God

LEADER: Come to me, all you who labor and are heavily burdened, and I will give you rest. Take my yoke upon you, and learn from me; for I am gentle and lowly in heart, and you will find rest for your souls (Matt. 11:28-29).

The Response of the People, the Prayer of Consecration

PEOPLE: **Eternal God, we accept our Savior's invitation. We come to his table in search of rest and peace. Send your Holy Spirit to us, that these gifts may be for us the bread of life and that we may be for the world the body of Christ. Amen.**

PASTOR: Friends in Christ, the Lord has prepared his table for his church. All who

love him and trust in him alone for their salvation are now invited to come to the table of the Lord.

PEOPLE: **We come with gladness. Thanks be to God!**

PASTOR: The gifts of God for the people of God.

THE COMMUNION

The Word of God

PASTOR: (as the people take the bread) Take eat, remember and believe that the body of the Lord Jesus Christ was given for the complete remission of all our sins.

PASTOR: (as the people take the cup) Take, drink, remember and believe that the precious blood of our Lord Jesus Christ was shed for the complete forgiveness of all our sins.

Commentary: A very appropriate sacramental hymn for use at this point is "Lamb of God." See the Maundy Thursday service in this series. Other Communion hymns can appropriately focus on the nature of God's grace to us, centered in the person of Jesus Christ.

The Response of the People, the Thanksgiving

Psalm 103
Commentary: The psalm may be read responsively or sung.

DEPARTURE TO SERVE

Commentary: The following texts call attention to themes of personal renewal and obedience which are especially highlighted during the season of Lent.

Charge to the People

PASTOR: Go into the world in peace. Love the Lord, your God, with all your heart, with all your soul, with all your mind. This is the first and greatest commandment. The second is like it: Love your neighbor as yourself (Matt. 22:37-39).

Commentary: An alternate text should be chosen if this summary of the law is read earlier in the service (see the invitation to penitence).

PEOPLE: We promise our devotion to God and love to our neighbors.

Hymn of Dedication (Recessional)

Benediction

PASTOR: May the God of peace make you holy in every way and keep your whole being—spirit, soul, and body—free from every fault at the coming of our Lord Jesus Christ.

PEOPLE: **Amen.**

or

PASTOR: Almighty God, go now with your people, grant them the peace of your presence, and guide them into ways of holiness and truth.

PEOPLE: **Amen.**

Commentary: See benediction for the Ash Wednesday service.

Dispersal of the Congregation
(with Organ, Piano, or Instrumental Postlude)

Commentary: The people may also disperse in silence during Lent, although this use of silence may most effectively be reserved for use during Holy Week.

John D. Witvliet

234 ✦ A CREATIVE SERVICE FOR THE SUNDAYS OF LENT

The service below is intended for use by those from a Protestant evangelical tradition including those who seek to combine the traditional and the contemporary in their worship.

——————— **The Basic Pattern** ———————

Worship Space. You will probably want to display an Ash Wednesday banner; consider also adding a banner for the first Sunday in Lent. This banner could express, representationally or abstractly, the theme of this Sunday's Service of the Word, namely, our prayer and longing "to see:" to see and receive Jesus as our way and our truth. A brief explanation of the symbolism of the banner could be given in the church bulletin. (You might provide banners for each Sunday in Lent, to remind the people and encourage them along their Lenten journey.)

Since the service will stress our creatureliness, you can give this emphasis more visual force by arranging the chairs or pews (if they are moveable) in a circle, symbolizing both the earth and the community in which we are members. The Eucharist table or altar could then be placed in the center, to represent Christ our Creator.

Call to Worship

LEADER: This past Wednesday, which we call Ash Wednesday, was the first day of Lent. Lent is the season during which we focus our desire upon Jesus and his passion. This focus will often lead us to a more acute awareness of our sinfulness and of our tendency to yield to temptation. During Lent we also choose to face our mortality and to walk with the humility that our finiteness forces upon us: we are God's created people, God's human companions.

Our fallenness is, over the course of our journey in faith, often a source of deep discouragement. But as we enter this Lenten season, we want to recall that both our beginning and our goal are, in God's perspective, "very good." What God created and called good is for us a cause for gratitude. So, as we enter into our worship today, we want to begin by celebrating and glorifying God for the depth, the expanse, and the wisdom of all God's creation.

Underlying this desire to express gratitude is our prayer for the Lenten season: Lord, help us to see. Help us to see your grace in creation, help us to see where we are blind, to see our pains and fears, to see where we are in bondage, to see where we—for the sake of our religion—distort your truth. Help us to see Jesus.

Let us stand together, and honor the God of creation.

Opening Hymn of Invocation:
"O Worship the King"

Opening Prayer

LEADER: Let us pray.

Our loving Creator and ever-redeeming God, we bless you and we desire to fittingly worship you this morning.

We desire to offer gratitude to you alone, O God among the gods.

For your greatness is evident in both the vastness and the intricacy of what you have made.

You who have created us, receive back with pleasure our worship we pray.

From us who lack
the endurance of your mountains
the depth of your oceans
the breadth of your heavens.

You who created time, and placed us within it, receive our praise, weakly though it may flow within the constraints of our finitude.

May both your grace and your wisdom accompany us during this holy season. For Christ's sake we pray. Amen.

(Congregation is seated.)

Reading From Psalm 104 (Complementary psalm to "O Worship the King"):

Commentary: The eight designated readers will be prepared in the outer circumference of the sanctuary or worship center. In succession, each one will stand and read, slowly and dramatically, as though they were heralds, announcing to the people the goodness of their creating and sustaining God.

READER 1: Psalm 104:1-4
READER 2: Psalm 104:5-9
READER 3: Psalm 104:10-13
READER 4: Psalm 104:14-17
READER 5: Psalm 104:18-24
READER 6: Psalm 104:25-26
READER 7: Psalm 104:27-30
READER 8: Psalm 104:31-35
LEADER: This is the Word of the Lord.
PEOPLE: **Bless the Lord, O my soul. Praise the Lord.**

[pause of silence]

Response

LEADER: Let's stand together and, in faith,

offer praises to God:
"I Sing the Mighty Power of God,"
"Praise to the Lord, the Almighty"

(Congregation is seated.)

INTRODUCTION TO THE SEASON OF LENT

LEADER: Most of us are familiar with the traditional theme of Lent. Lent is a time of repentance and preparation for the gift of Easter, the celebration of Christ's resurrection. Often we perceive Lent as a time of self-denial, as a time to begin a specific form of imposed self-discipline in order that we might remind ourselves of the depth of our sinfulness and of the frequency of our failings in our journey with God. While such reflection is essential to Lent, it will be most fruitful when it is motivated by faith and driven by trust, that is, faith in the fact that God finds pleasure in his human creation, and sent Jesus in order to bring God's redemptive love to us; and trust in the fact that he has given us repentance as a grace, a personal gift of God to us that comes for the purpose of instilling life. As we listen to the Word of the Lord, let's be attentive to God's Spirit. Is God drawing my attention toward an attitude or specific quality of spirit that he desires to purge or to enlarge in me? Or is God perhaps forming in me a vision or a picture of my journey in faith, a gift of hope to encourage me?

Let us receive the Word of the Lord.

Old Testament Reading

LEADER: (reads Jeremiah 17:7-10, 12-14)
This is the Word of the Lord.
PEOPLE: **Heal me, O Lord, and I shall be healed; save me, and I shall be saved; for you are my praise.**

Responsorial Psalm

(A quiet reflection time with taped or instrumental music of Psalm 62)

Epistle Reading

LEADER: (reads Romans, 7:14-25a.)
This is the Word of the Lord.

PEOPLE: **Thanks be to God through Jesus Christ our Lord!**

(silent pause)

Introduction to the Gospel Reading

LEADER: We want now to allow ourselves a time for confession based upon a reading from the ninth chapter of John's gospel. As we listen, let's pay close attention to our personal responses to the story. We will listen to the narrative in segments. There will be guided times of silent reflection and prayer in between. Try to pay attention to any feelings that arise within you as you listen. Are you aware of anger? If so, to whom? From what source does it arise? Do you feel joy? From what does that joy spring? Do you feel fear, or confusion? Why? And so on. If you are easily able to picture yourself within the narrative, you might notice which person or group of people you most readily identify with. Pay attention to the reasons for this identification and to your response to it.

Prayer

LEADER: Blessed hovering Holy Spirit, we pray that you would alight upon us and enliven us as we listen. For Christ's sake. Amen.

Gospel Reading

READER 1: John 9:13-17, followed by silent reflection
Question for the congregation: At this time in my faith journey, who is Jesus to me? (silent response)

READER 2: John 9:18-23, followed by silent reflection
Question for the congregation: Of what am I afraid? (silent response)

READER 3: John 9:24-25, followed by silent reflection
Question for the congregation: "One thing I do know, that though I was blind, now I see." What grace or healing have I experienced that provides me with a rootedness in faith? (silent response)

READER 4: John 9:26-34, followed by silent reflection
Question for the congregation: In what areas of my life do I lack certainty, but see that I have continued to walk in trust? (silent response)

READER 5: John 9:35-41, followed by silent reflection

Guided Prayer Reflection

LEADER: Let us ask God's Spirit to reveal the ways in which we are blind. Areas where we are confident of seeing God's truth, but where we are in fact, turning our back on the light of the gospel. (silent response)

Our loving God, we confess to you that in thinking we see, we become blind, and that in our blindness we have, both wittingly and unwittingly, blinded others to your truth. We pray that you would forgive us, continue to enlighten us, and heal us from our sin. We also confess that at times our inability to see comes from our sinful desire for the approval and respect of others. We pray that you would forgive us. Continue to enlighten us, and heal us from our sin. And loving God, as we now approach your Eucharist, we pray that you would free our human spirit and send your Holy Spirit. Cause us to see anew, qualities inherent in your gospel that we have, heretofore, neither seen nor tasted. For the sake of your kingdom we pray. Amen.

CELEBRATION OF EUCHARIST

LEADER: (reads John 15:1-11)
Our call during Lent is "to abide." If we abide, and if we listen, we will bring glory to God and we will have joy: the joy that is ours when we can trust that we are growing in faith. Jesus taught in order that "our joy

may be complete." And he gave us the Eucharist, in order that we might have the confidence of his presence and help in our journey. Jesus offered the bread and wine to his disciples, symbolizing both his broken body and his new covenant, given on their and our behalf. Let us partake with gratitude for our creating God who is continually working out our redemption, not through our own unaided efforts but by the power of Christ through the Holy Spirit who lives in us.

Prayer of Consecration for Bread and Wine

Participation in Eucharist

Exchange of Peace

LEADER: God is redeeming each one of us, as individuals, but God is forming us into a community of redeemed people. Let's express our unity and support for one another by extending the peace of Christ toward one another.

Worship Hymn of Response: "All Creatures of Our God and King"

Benediction (Jude 24-25)

LEADER: Now to him who is able to keep you from falling, and to make you stand

without blemish in the presence of his glory with rejoicing, to the only God our Savior, through Jesus Christ our Lord, be glory, majesty, power, and authority, before all time and now and forever. Amen.

<hr>

Commentary

Preparation. Lent is a sober time of reflection, but it is a means toward an experience of grace; the inwardness is not to become an end in itself. This service, therefore, is designed to offer a broader picture of the possibilities for a Lenten focus. This service serves to remind the congregation of God's initiative in Creation. It underscores too the ironic emphasis that the apostle John places on "blindness" and "sight" as he writes the Passion narratives. You might be able to picture your congregation being drawn by a different theme from the gospel narratives.

Worship Space. Since this service follows quickly upon the very full and rich Ash Wednesday worship, you might want to keep the service plain and simple. The symbolism can be of a quieter kind: the use of banners, the arrangement of seating for the congregation, as well as the "heralds," who represent the Word of God as it encompasses and protects God's people during their times of temptation.

Entrance. Although this service closely follows Ash Wednesday, wherein a fuller explanation of Lent might have been given, the leader cannot assume that all of his congregation participated in that service. In fact, this service is offered with the hope that the Sunday attender who has previously, for whatever reason, avoided participating in Lent might be drawn toward it. The creation emphasis in the accompanying service is given not to deny the often painful time of Lent, but to remind the congregation that God's intentions for us are rooted in goodness.

Word. Rather than have a homily, the Service of the Word is given to brief explanations, offered to make Lent accessible to the congregation, and to a guided reflection and prayer time. Because the reflection time is based upon extensive use of Scripture, you need to pay attention to the overall rhythm, being careful not to overload the congregation with verbal input. The responsorial

The Rope. One of the familiar symbols of the Passion is the rope used to bind Jesus when he was led to Annas and Caiaphas (see John 18:12-13).

psalm comes at a place in the service where it would be timely to allow an instrumental rendering of a familiar psalm or a psalm (such as Psalm 62) that is available on a tape recording. Using such an option allows the congregation to be refreshed and center their thoughts midway.

If the congregation is small and informal, you might want to allow people to stand and express some of the fruit of their reflection. The other members of the congregation could join with spontaneous choruses of praise in response, or with a time of bidding prayers, or intercessory or community prayer, depending on the responses that are shared.

If the congregation is more spiritually mature, you might want to eliminate the specific guided question format and simply allow time for personally discerned times of silence.

Celebration of the Eucharist. During this time it would be appropriate to play again an instrumental version of Psalm 62 or of the psalm that was used during the earlier portion of the service. With the Communion table or alter in the center, you could use any number of formats for participation.

The leader/server could initiate the passing of the bread and wine by serving one person, and then the congregation, subsequently, will take on the role of server, passing the bread and wine around and around the circle until everyone has been served.

If the leader wanted the people to come forward to receive, they could come in a traditional way, being prompted by an usher, or they could come as they are ready.

The focus of the Eucharist is that God provides us with what we need for our journey in faith and we are therefore able to participate with grateful joy. We want to extend that joy and that hope to one another through the kiss or hand of peace.

Dismissal. The congregation is dismissed with the reminder that God created the world and all that resides therein. We appropriately offer God's due praise, and sing with hope.

The benediction is most appropriate to this season of the church year. Because this particularly encouraging benediction grounds the believer in Christ, this passage could be used as the closing benediction for each of the services during Lent. At the close of Lent, the congregation could then be asked to give testimony to how they experienced the grace and truth of it for themselves.

Diane S. George Ayer

PART SIX

Resources for Holy Week

Holy Week is the most significant week of the year for Christian worship. During this week the church remembers the events of Christ's passion and death. The attention of the worshiper during this week is directed to the Lamb of God, the Suffering Servant, the Savior of the world. In worship the church traces Jesus' life through the events of the last days before his death. In doing so, it sees again its own sin and failure, but marvels at the love of Christ for the world. This is a week for careful attention, prayer-filled reverence, and profound wonder at the love of God shown in Jesus. The following chapters provide the historical, theological, and liturgical resources for Holy Week so that worship planners and leaders, students, and all worshipers can participate in the mystery of Christ's love in worship.

SIXTEEN

An Introduction to Holy Week

Much of the worship of Holy Week is based on centuries-old tradition. This chapter introduces the reader to the traditional ways in which Holy Week is observed and to the ways ancient traditions may be adapted to worship today. Notice how carefully Holy Week worship follows the scriptural account of Christ's passion and death. Notice how silence and quiet reflection permeate each service. Notice how these services do not so much seek to explain the mystery of Christ's love as to stand in awe of it and to receive it in faith.

235 ◆ INTRODUCTION TO THE SERVICES OF HOLY WEEK

The following article is a rapid tour of the traditional services of Holy Week. Each of the primary services is discussed briefly, with attention to their primary themes and the features that make each service unique. For more detailed explanation, see the chapters that follow.

The sixth Sunday in Lent, the first day of Holy Week, commonly "Passion" or "Palm" Sunday, presents a peculiar set of problems. The celebration of the triumphal entry into Jerusalem brings to a close the first five weeks of our Lenten fast. In the same liturgy, the solemn reading of the Passion narrative initiates for us the beginning of the Holy Week of our Lord's passion and death. It is important that the liturgy for this day encompass both of these emphases, but with a clear distinction between them. Many congregations have found that celebrating the entry into Jerusalem is best done with a massive parade out-of-doors, complete with singing and swaying. The movement from outside in could well signal the movement in the liturgy from Palm to Passion Sunday. Congregations located in neighborhoods near other parishes might gather jointly in a common place for a joint Palm Sunday parade after which the congregational participants move back into their own facilities for the reading of the Passion narrative and the Eucharist. Music for Palm Sun-

day could be an all-stops-out affair, while the music for Passion Sunday should appropriately focus on the events of the week that it begins.

The services for Monday and Tuesday in Holy Week can take any number of shapes. The key is simplicity and appropriateness to the week. The simple gathering for a prayer office, a quiet, focused liturgical drama, a service of Passion music or a gathering for directed meditation could be the order. There is every reason to dispense with all extraneous instrumental music. Gathering in silence and beginning from silence is appropriate. If hymns are to be sung, the organ could accompany them, but only in a manner appropriate to the nature of the day. Unaccompanied singing, led by members of the parish choir, is perhaps the better solution.

The service for Wednesday in Holy Week could appropriately take the form of corporate confession and forgiveness. Such a service could form an interesting parallel to the Ash Wednesday liturgy. Provision for individual absolution makes personal in a ritual action the forgiveness which is ours in Christ, much like the imposition of ashes on Ash Wednesday made personal our need for repentance and reconciliation. Such a rite, set in the context of Holy Week, establishes a meaningful background on which to contribute the pilgrimage through the three holy days.

For many churches, the liturgy of Holy Thursday is among the most significant services of the year. The rich imagery of the night in which Jesus was betrayed is exceeded perhaps only by the glory of the Easter Vigil. Because of its richness, care must be given to the planning of the liturgy so that its impact is not diminished by trying to pack too much in one service. Special care must be given to the planning and execution of the unusual traditions of this day. The washing of feet after the example of Jesus and the stripping of the altar are potentially moving spiritual experiences, but only if they are carried out with planned simplicity and dignity. Holy Thursday is no time for chaotic spontaneity. Also, there is more than enough biblical and theological material for the day without having to give extreme emphasis to the fact that the last supper of our Lord with his disciples may have been a Passover. The connection of our paschal observance with the Jewish Passover is vividly clear in the *Exsultet* in the liturgy of the vigil of Easter.

Striking by its utter simplicity is the liturgy for Good Friday. In the rites of most churches that keep the traditional Good Friday liturgy, its major components are four: the reading of John's account of the Passion, the terse bidding prayer, the veneration of the wood of the cross with quiet meditation on the mystery of redemption, and Holy Communion. Music should be restrained. Preludes, postludes, and "special" music should be avoided unless it is *critical* to the shape of the liturgy. Everything should focus on the stark, saving reality of the crucified Christ.

It is appropriate here to make a pastoral plea to the parish musicians on behalf of the spiritual needs of the choir members. The multiplicity of services and the vast amount of music to be mastered by the choristers for Lent, Holy Week, and Easter necessitates very often the need for additional rehearsals. An easy option, of course, is to commence choir rehearsal immediately following one of the services of Holy Week. While sometimes there may be no other option, this immediacy of movement deprives the choristers of the same opportunity we have worked so hard to provide for other members of the congregation. The choir is robbed of the benefits of having quiet moments to reflect spiritually upon the liturgy in which they have just participated. It is *unfair* to ask the choristers to gear up a choir rehearsal without time to reflect upon the Maundy Thursday or Good Friday liturgy. Everyone else can stay in the worship space and pray or have a quiet drive home

and a couple of hours in the easy chair to think about what they have experienced. The choir deserves that no less than everyone else. Explore ways that the schedule might be adjusted so that these things don't happen to the choristers: start rehearsals earlier in the year, lengthen the rehearsals in the early weeks of Lent, and, if there is no other way, put a break between the service and the rehearsal for the choir to have some reflection time. A quiet period at the beginning of the rehearsal is the very least you can do to feed your choir spiritually as well as musically.

Neil Alexander

236 • HOLY WEEK IN THE EARLY CHURCH

Worship renewalists have revived the ancient customs of Holy Week worship. In particular Holy Week worship centers around the re-enactment of the last days of Christ. This article summarizes worship on those days in the early church.

In the church of the first centuries after Christ, every Sunday was a "little Easter." The Easter season itself was a special event in which the living, dying, and rising of Christ was not only told in words, but acted out in a participatory drama.

The earliest evidence of an Easter celebration in the New Testament is found in the words of Paul written to the Corinthian community about A.D. 55: "Christ our Passover has been sacrificed for us" (1 Cor. 5:7). The clue to how Easter may have been celebrated in the primitive Christian community is found in the word *Passover,* for the earliest Christians were Jews.

Jewish worship passed two emphases on to early Christian worship: First, worship was rooted in an event. The Passover service, for example, celebrated the Exodus, when God brought the Israelites out of Egypt and made them into his people. Second, celebrating that event in worship made it contemporaneous—the original power of that event evoked feelings among contemporary worshipers similar to the response of the original participants in the event. The event was celebrated and made contemporary by telling the story and acting it out.

Perhaps the best insight into Easter worship as story told and acted out comes from the writing of a woman named Egeria. Her *Diary of a Pilgrimage* contains a firsthand account of Easter in Jerusalem in the late fourth century. The diary, together with liturgies from that period, provides us with an inspiring picture of Easter in the early church.

In those days, preparation for Easter began seven weeks before the date. There was an emphasis on personal identification with the suffering of Jesus. These ancient Christians were convinced that the resurrection could not be adequately experienced without traveling the way of death themselves. They desired to fulfill Jesus' admonitions of Mark 10 in a literal way by taking up the cross and going up to Jerusalem with him (v. 33). They wanted to drink of the cup that he drank (v. 39), and to be baptized with his baptism (v. 39). (Our Lord's forty-day fast in the desert suggested the forty days of Lent.)

While this forty-day experience emphasized fasting and prayer, it was not done in the spirit of legalism or ritualism. The intent was to prepare for Easter by reliving the mystery. Fasting and prayer were not ends in themselves—they led the participants into a deeper experiential appreciation of the mystery of salvation through a subjective identification with Christ. By hearing the Word and by acting it out—not just for a day, but over a period of time—the message took hold more firmly.

Holy Week

According to Egeria, what we call Holy Week was known as the "Great Week" in fourth-century Jerusalem. This week of the climactic events of the arrest, conviction, crucifixion, death, burial, and resurrection of Christ is the most extraordinary week in the Christian calendar, the week in which the redemption of the world happened, in which the re-creation of the world began.

Egeria describes the day-to-day events of the Great Week:

On *Palm Sunday*, all the Christians assembled at the top of the Mount of Olives. Grasping palms and branches in their hands, they sang, "Blessed is he who comes in the name of the Lord," as they walked slowly to the church in Jerusalem. The bishop of Jerusalem, symbolizing Christ, was in the midst of the crowd. When night fell, evening prayers were celebrated, concluded by a prayer in front of a cross erected for the occasion.

On *Monday*, they continually sang hymns and antiphons, and read passages from the Scriptures appropriate to that day in Holy Week. Egeria reports that these readings and songs were continually interrupted with prayers.

On *Tuesday*, they did the same except for this: "The Bishop takes up the book of the Gospels, and while standing, reads the words of the Lord which are written in the Gospel according to Matthew at the place where he said, "Take heed that no man deceive you'" (Matt. 24:4).

On *Wednesday*, everything was done as on Monday and Tuesday except that the bishop read the passage where Judas went to the Jews to set the price they would pay him to betray the Lord (Matt. 26:1ff.; Mark 14:10f.; Luke 22:3-6ff.). Egeria reports that "while this good passage is being read, there is such moaning and groaning from among the people that no one can help being moved to tears in that moment." (This, and similar comments throughout her account, suggest the powerful effect that re-enactment can have on the worshipers' feelings.)

On *Thursday evening*, Communion was celebrated. Then all went home to eat their last meal until Easter, and later returned to worship all night as a way of re-enacting the gospel accounts of Thursday night. "They continually sing hymns and antiphons and read the Scripture passages proper to the place and to the day. Between these, prayers are said."

Early on *Friday*, after worshiping all night, the Christians proceeded to Gethsemane, where they read the passage describing the Lord's arrest (Matt. 26:36-56). Egeria reports that "there is such moaning and groaning with weeping from all the people that their moaning can be heard practically as far as the city." They then went to the place of the cross where the words of Pilate were read (Matt. 27:2-26; Mark 15:1-15; Luke 23:1-25; John 18:28; 19:16). Then the bishop sent the crowd home to mediate, instructing them to return about the second hour so that everyone would be "on hand here so that from that hour until the sixth hour you may see the holy wood of the cross, and thus believe that it was offered for the salvation of each and every one of us."

On *Friday night*, they acknowledged the cross as the instrument of salvation. A cross was put on a table and the people passed by "touching the cross and the inscription, first with their foreheads, then with their eyes; and after kissing the cross, they move on."

On *Saturday,* worship was conducted at the third and sixth hours. After nightfall the Easter Vigil was held. Although Egeria says little about this service, we know from other sources that it was a dramatic re-enactment of the Resurrection. It included a service of light that celebrated Christ as the light of the world, and the annual baptismal service in which people were baptized into Christ's dying and rising. (The early church practice of baptism by immersion was a graphic enactment of burial and resurrection.) And the glorious service that occurred on Sunday morning (after the all-night vigil) celebrated the resurrection of Christ through readings, antiphons, preaching, and the Eucharist.

Consider the involvement, the total immersion in the death and resurrection of their Lord that the worshipers must have experienced. For weeks they had prepared for this service. Then, throughout Holy Week, they had been exhausted by the intensity of following after the events in Jesus' life that led to his death. Now, after another night of vigil and anticipation, the moment of Jesus' resurrection came. Because these people had entered the tomb with him, they were able to experience his resurrection—in a way that would never happen apart from the dramatic journey they had taken.

Finally, Egeria tells us that Easter did not end on Easter day. It was followed by eight days of celebration. The worshipers' fast was over. They identified no longer with death, but with resurrection and life. For eight days the Christians gathered in worship. These festive services were in sharp contrast to the sober preparations for the Passion. They extended the Resurrection side of Easter even as fasting had prepared for the Crucifixion.

Robert E. Webber[29]

237 • THE GREAT TRIDUUM

A special practice of early Christian worship was to treat the three days from Thursday night to Sunday morning as an act of one continuous worship. That practice of the "Three Great Days" has been revived in the worship renewal of the twentieth century.

Most congregations are accustomed to service on Holy (Maundy) Thursday and Good Friday. Far fewer will be familiar with the Paschal Vigil on Holy Saturday/Easter day. On both Maundy Thursday and Good Friday the emphasis is likely to fall on the commemoration of the Last Supper and the crucifixion of Jesus as separate events in the distant past. The integral relationship of these events in the distant past. The integral relationship of these events to each other and to the Resurrection is not stressed. Persons may attend one or both as they chose, with no real sense that anything essential to the meaning of Easter has been lost if they choose to attend either.

Not Three but One

But the services of the historic triduum are more than the commemoration of a series of past events. They are *the celebration of one event,* unique and unrepeatable, that is eternally present in and to the community of faith and the lives of believers—namely, the passover of Jesus from death to life which is known as the paschal (Passover) mystery. Because the passion, death, and resurrection of Jesus are not three separate events, but one event, integral and indivisible, the services of Holy Thursday, Good Friday, and Holy Saturday/Easter Day are not three separate services but one service, integral and indivisible, celebrated over three days. The word *triduum* ("three days") was first used by Augustine to express the essential unity of this single, three-day service. According to ancient understanding, the day begins at sundown rather than at midnight. Thus the evening of Holy Thursday is considered the beginning of Good Friday, the first day of the triduum (Good Friday, Holy Saturday, and Easter day).

A Superficial Resemblance

Although each element of the triduum necessarily includes the remembrance of a past event, the emphasis falls not on historical commemoration but on present reality. Instead of a series of separate commemorations, complete in themselves, each element contributes to the integral meaning of the whole. Thus the resemblance between customary Holy Thursday and Good Friday services and the equivalent services of the historic triduum is only superficial. Musicians and worship planners will want to respect the uniqueness of the triduum and the unity of its component parts. They will also want to help congregations understand that, as part of the triduum, the services of Maundy Thursday and Good Friday are not optional extras for the very devout, but essential elements of the entire service, without which the celebration of Easter is incomplete. To experience fully the meaning of the triduum, it is necessary to participate fully in each of its component parts.

Holy Thursday:
The Triduum Begins

The triduum begins on the evening of Holy Thursday with the commemoration of the institution of the Lord's Supper. The celebration opens in light and joy as the community gives thanks for the meal instituted by Jesus to be the abiding memorial of his death and resurrection every Lord's Day. It closes in shadows and darkness as the community prepares to commemorate the Lord's passion and death.

As part of the triduum, Holy Thursday may come as a disappointment to those who have been trying so hard to keep it from becoming just another Communion service. Basic to Holy Thursday of the triduum is a service of Word and Table much like any other. As part of the triduum, the purpose of Holy Thursday is not to re-enact or imitate the Last Supper as an event of the historic past, but to give thanks for the institution of the Lord's Supper as an encounter with the risen Jesus in the living present. What makes Holy Thursday distinctive are the lectionary readings proper to the day, the rite of footwashing, and the stripping of the church—not the addition of historicizing elements such as the seating of people at table in groups of twelve or the substitution of the Passover Seder.

A New Commandment

The most distinctive feature of Holy Thursday is also its least familiar—the washing of feet. The Common Lectionary Gospel for Holy Thursday Year A and for alternative use in Years B and C is not the institution of the Lord's Supper from Matthew, Mark, or Luke, but the institution of footwashing from John 13:1-15. Jesus washes the feet of his disciples on the night of his betrayal to exemplify the meaning of the new commandment (_novum mandatum_) which he is about to give them (John 13:34). An acted parable of loving service, footwashing is the _mandatum_ from which Maundy Thursday gets its name.

As the ordained servant of the community, the pastor washes the feet, not of the entire congregation, but of a small representative group. Members of this group might include youth and adult candidates for baptism or the renewal of baptism during the Paschal Vigil, elders serving on the session, or any other representative selection of men and women. Although twelve persons have been traditionally chosen for symbolic purposes, the exact number is not important.

No introduction is necessary, but a good introductory formula is provided in _The Book of Alternative Services of The Anglican Church of Canada_ (Toronto: Anglican Book Center, 1985). During the actual footwashing, reverent silence is to be preferred. No words are necessary to interpret the meaning of this naturally symbolic act.

Although footwashing on Holy Thursday has been part of the triduum from very early times, there may be some reluctance to restore a practice so alien to contemporary culture and so potentially repugnant to modern congregations. But perhaps this version is the best argument for its restoration—with proper preparation and interpretation, of course. Attempts to soften its offense—to the one who washes and to the ones who are washed—are to be discouraged. Handwashing or wiping shoes with a cloth are not symbolically equivalent to footwashing as an effective demonstration of humble and loving servanthood.

The Shadows Lengthen

The transition from Holy Thursday to Good Friday is provided by stripping the church of its customary ornamentation after the Holy Thursday Communion. During the stripping, all furnishings—vessels, paraments, candles, candlesticks, vases, flags, banners—are removed from the chancel and church. Originally a purely utilitarian act necessary for cleaning the church prior to Easter, the stripping of the church has come to symbolize the stripping of Jesus before the Crucifixion. The stripping may be carried out by designated persons in silence, either before the silent departure of the people, or after—or it may be accompanied by the recitation of Psalm 22. In addition to the stripping, a veil may be draped over the chancel cross. According to one tradition worth preserving, the organ is heard on Holy Thursday for the last time until Holy Saturday/Easter day.

An alternative transition is the Office of Tenebrae (Shadows), which consists of various psalms, readings, and prayers, as candles are progressively extinguished (often twelve in number) and the lights of the church are dimmed, leaving only one candle still burning. At the conclusion of the office, with the church in darkness, the one remaining candle is carried out of the chancel or hidden from view during the final prayer. A loud noise is made to represent the earthquake that accompanied Jesus' death (Matt. 27:51). The lighted candle is then brought back into the church or restored to view.

The return of the lighted candle proclaims that, as part of the triduum, Tenebrae is celebrated in the light of the Resurrection which the shadows cannot overcome. Enough lights are turned on for the people to depart safely in silence, after which the church is stripped.

However Holy Thursday closes, there is no final blessing, but only silent departure or a simple dismissal. The service is not yet over. There is more to come.

Good Friday: The Triduum Continues

Worshipers return to a bare and undecorated church for the continuation of the triduum on Good Friday. The historic commemoration of the passion is in three parts: the Service of the Word, the Solemn Intercessions, and the Adoration of the Cross. (Roman Catholics also receive Holy Communion on Good Friday, from elements consecrated on Holy Thursday, because Good Friday is traditionally the only day of the year on which the Mass may not be celebrated.) Refrains, responses, and hymns may be sung to guitar or piano accompaniment.

The Service of the Word always includes a reading of the Passion according to John (18:1–19:42), preferably arranged for dramatic presentation by three (or more) readers. As the passion of the risen and victorious Christ, who is in charge throughout, John's Passion narrative is aptly chosen. Though quiet and reflective, Good Friday is a day not of mourning but of solemn joy, always celebrated from the perspective of the Resurrection.

To Make Intercession

The historic intercessions of Good Friday pre-

serve the ancient form of the bidding prayer from the old Roman Sunday liturgy. A useful adaptation of this prayer for contemporary use is included in the Good Friday liturgy of *Lutheran Book of Worship Ministers Desk Edition* (Minneapolis: Augsburg; Philadelphia: Board of Publication, Lutheran Church in America, 1978), although forms more familiar to the congregation may also be used. To lead the intercessions, the pastor may stand in the center aisle, face the people for each bidding, and then turn to face the chancel for each silence and collect, praying with, rather than to, the people.

The concluding Adoration at the Cross can be its most obviously dramatic element, but, as a part of the triduum, the theological heart of Good Friday is the Solemn Intercessions. On Good Friday, Christians commemorate the passion and death of the Lord as an act of intercession on behalf of the world by offering their own intercessions in union with those of the high priest, Jesus, who "always lives to make intercession for them" (Heb. 7:25, RSV).

Adoration (Meditation) at the Cross follows the Intercessions. This act becomes especially vivid if, just before the Adoration, a large, plain wooden cross is carried forward in silent procession by representative members of the congregation and placed in the center of the chancel. The cross should be displayed in a prominent place in the narthex after the stripping of the church on Holy Thursday, to become the first thing seen by worshipers as they return for Good Friday.

The act of adoration is accompanied by traditional devotions which include the Reproaches, a moving recitation of God's accusations against God's people. Although the Reproaches have recently been deleted from some service books because of allegedly anti-Semitic connotations, a text acceptable to the Anti-Defamation League of B'nai B'rith is included in *Handbook of the Christian Year* (Nashville: Abingdon, 1986).

At the close of Good Friday, after the Adoration, there is no blessing. Worshipers depart in silence or with a simple dismissal, as on Holy Thursday.

The Paschal Vigil: The Triduum Concludes

The triduum concludes with the Paschal Vigil, or First Service of Easter, which begins late on Holy Saturday (Easter Eve) or before dawn on the morning of Easter day. The Paschal Vigil opens in the darkness that marked the conclusion of Holy Thursday, but the darkness is soon dispelled by the Service of Light. The congregation gathers outdoors, if possible, where the new fire is kindled from which the Paschal candle is lighted. The Paschal candle leads the congregation in procession into the darkened church, where the Resurrection is proclaimed in the glorious hymns known as *Exsultet*. The traditional text of this musical treasure (though not necessarily its long form) deserves to be sung to its original melody—preferable by a solo voice, although other options are available [see *Handbook for the Christian Year*, 202–6]. As the Haggadah of the Passover Seder directs its participants to regard themselves as if they too had come forth out of Egypt, so the singing of *Exsultet* involves Christians in the events of their liberation, and, with its insistent refrain, "This is the night . . . ," marks the Paschal Vigil rather than Holy Thursday as the Christian equivalent of the Seder Haggadah.

During the Service of the Word which follows, the congregation keeps vigil in semi-darkness as it listens to Old Testament readings or prophecies which anticipate the meaning of Christian baptism. Each reading is followed by its own appointed Psalm and prayer. The number and selection of these Old Testament readings may vary—as many as twelve, but not fewer than three, always including the story of the Exodus (Exod. 14:10–15:1).

Because most congregations are not accustomed to listening to a series of readings from the Bible, every effort should be made to keep this part of the vigil from becoming tedious. Capable, well-prepared lay readers should participate. If a reading contains dialogue, congregational interest is heightened if it can be divided among several voices. The psalmody after each reading may be done in a variety of ways, preferably musical. Gifted lay persons may be invited to lead the psalms to simple melodies and refrains of their own composition.

From Darkness to Light

After the final prophecy is read with its Psalm and prayer, all the lights in the church are turned on, the organ sounds for the first time since Holy Thursday, and "Gloria in Excelsis" or a hymn of resurrection is sung. During the singing, the chancel cross is unveiled and representatives of the congregation restore the furnishings removed on Holy Thursday and decorate the chancel with flowers of the season. In this visually dramatic moment of transition, after keeping vigil in semi-darkness in a church devoid of its usual ornamentation, the essential unity of the entire triduum "comes together" as at no other time for all but the most unobservant participants.

As the anticipation of Christian baptism, the Service of the Word naturally leads to the Service of the Water. New Christians who have received final instruction during Lent (and the washing of feet on Holy Thursday) are baptized into the death and resurrection of the Lord (Rom. 6:3-11). The Paschal Vigil restores the original connection between baptism and the paschal mystery of Christ's dying and rising, and the character of Easter as the primary baptismal festival.

The Service of the Water culminates in the Service of the Bread and Cup at the conclusion of the Paschal Vigil. As the entire triduum reaches its joyful climax, the community welcomes its new sister and brothers to the festive Resurrection feast (anticipated by the meal of Holy Thursday) and gathers around the table of the risen Lord, who is known to Easter people in the breaking of the bread (Luke 24:35). This is the meal of the Christian Passover (Pascha)—equivalent to the Seder—which celebrates the Christian Exodus, not on the evening of Holy Thursday, but in the night of Christ's passing over from death to life.

Other Possibilities

Christians originally gathered before midnight on Holy Saturday and kept what was probably a much more leisurely vigil throughout the night until dawn, when new Christians were baptized and the Easter Eucharist was celebrated. Building on the structure of the twenty-four-hour prayer vigil and the three-hour Good Friday service, efforts to duplicate the pace of the primitive Paschal Vigil might appeal to some congregations. Everyone gathers for the Service of the Light late on Holy Saturday. Consistent with the true meaning of vigil, the Service of the Word is planned to last throughout the night, arranged in units of reading, Psalm, and prayer, according to a printed schedule. Between units, ample time is allowed for people to move about, visit with each other, have a cup of coffee or other refreshment. Participants either remain throughout the night or sign up for various units, with everyone gathering at dawn for baptism, Eucharist, and the breaking of the fast.

Churches of the same denomination in a community might wish to cooperate in the Paschal Vigil, all-night or shorter, gathering in one building or in different buildings for each of its parts and moving between buildings in the manner of a progressive dinner.

The Paschal Vigil might also be celebrated ecumenically by congregations of cooperating denominations in the same vicinity. The Service of Light and Service of the Word could be held either progressively or in the same building. Because most churches recognize each other's baptism (at least in principle), the Service of the Water could be celebrated in common, with all the candidates from participating congregations baptized together in a unified witness to the resurrection. The Service of the Bread and Cup could be celebrated in common, or, where confessional differences make intercommunion impossible, participants could disperse to separate buildings for the resurrection meal.

Establishing a Precedent

As the climax of the triduum, the Paschal Vigil deserves the best efforts of both planners and participants, and should employ the full range of musical and other artistic gifts present in the congregation. Unfortunately, of the three parts of the triduum, the Paschal Vigil is the least familiar. While most congregations expect services on Holy Thursday and Good Friday, there is no precedent for a two-hour service late on Easter eve or before dawn on Easter day. But by celebrating the Paschal Vigil annually for a period of several years, a precedent can be established, and support can be built.

With careful promotion and interpretation, and my involving as many participants as possible, most congregations of average size can expect a good response to a late-evening Paschal Vigil the first year. But it would be a mistake to assume a similar response in subsequent years, without exerting the same effort to educate and involve. Success is measured, not by how many can be persuaded to attend the Paschal Vigil for the first time, but by how many are still attending the Paschal Vigil *after* fifteen consecutive years of annual celebration.

Triduum of the Risen Christ

Just as the triduum is not three services, but one service, celebrating one event, so too the triduum is not an exercise in make-believe or a game of let's pretend—as though we could somehow make the final events of Jesus' life happen all over again. When we commemorate the institution of the Lord's Supper on Holy (Maundy) Thursday, it is the risen Jesus who stoops to wash our feet and feed us—not a Jesus who is about to suffer. When we hear the Passion according to John and offer the Solemn Intercessions on Good Friday, it is the risen Jesus who steps forward and takes charge, just as it is the risen Jesus who always lives to make intercession for us (Heb. 7:25, RSV)—not a Jesus who is about to die. When we announce the Resurrection during the Paschal Vigil, it is the Jesus risen once and for all whom we proclaim—not a Jesus who is being raised all over again. "Christ being raised from the dead will never die again; death no longer has dominion over him" (Rom. 6:9, RSV). The triduum is always to be celebrated from the perspective of this irreversible act.

John D. Grabner[30]

238 ✦ HOLY WEEK IN THE EASTERN ORTHODOX TRADITION

Contemporary worship renewalists in the West have become increasingly interested in the worship content and style of the Eastern Orthodox church. The article below suggests what Western Christians may learn from Eastern worship.

Perhaps more than any other Christian church at the present moment, Orthodox Christians celebrate the crown of the liturgical cycle, Pascha, the day of Resurrection, with intensive participation and joy, coupled with an awesome sense of the holiness of God. So it seemed to me when, for the first time, at about thirty years of age, I experienced Holy Week in an Orthodox church. I brought to the service a background of varied Christian experience, both liturgical and non-liturgical as regards the frequent celebration of the Eucharist.

The dean of the cathedral was a mature and

radiant Christian, Fr. Sergei Glagolev, also a conservatory-trained composer and seminary teacher of liturgical music. His singing, combined with that of the talented deacon, had blessed us throughout Lent.

In the morning of the Saturday that starts Holy Week we had celebrated the raising of Lazarus, and that evening we began the experience of Palm Sunday with the blessing and procession with the palms. It was a church of Slavic background, so "palms" meant boughs of willow, gaily tied bundles with pussy-willows that could be kept from year to year. (Willow branches are an ancient and charming adaptation to the unavailability of palm branches in northern climes.) During the course of the service, there was physical congregational participation in the movement of the procession, in the frequent use of the sign of the cross, in different levels of posture, in the singing, and in the reading of the epistle. The small, rounded building radiated coziness, the domed architecture suggesting both universality and intimacy. Frescoed walls were alive with saints and angels.

The theme of Lent for Orthodox Christians is the prayer of St. Ephraim, said communally with prostrations (kneeling and bowing one's head to the ground):

O Lord and Master of my life!
Take from me the spirit of sloth,
despair, lust of power, and idle talk.

(Bow)

Rather, give the spirit of chastity,
humility, patience, and love to Your
servant.

(Bow)

Yes, O Lord and King, grant that I
may see my own transgressions, and
not those of my brother: For You are
Blessed unto ages of ages. Amen.

(Bow)

This had been the daily prayer, the aim of our lives in a special, intense way, for the days of Great Lent. The services, far from being severe and stark, had been rich and personal. The reception of Holy Communion had been more frequent than at other times, with the biweekly use of the Liturgy of the Presanctified Gifts. Conveyed to our understanding was God's tenderness, his mercy, even

in the recognition of his holiness and of our weakness. Special services called "Bridegroom Services" reminded us that it was the eleventh hour: "Behold, the Bridegroom cometh!" Now, standing on the brink of Easter, we were both weary with our Lenten efforts and yet sad that this particular season of personal and corporate reflection and effort Godward was drawing to a close.

The services of Holy Thursday and Good Friday were long, but very moving. Indeed, from Thursday on, the choir (of which I was a member) seemingly lived in church, going home only to sleep. Thursday we commemorated Jesus' Last Supper with his disciples. We spent Good Friday morning at the foot of the cross, recalling once again the victory which began that day with the descent by the Savior into the realms of death. Flowers filled the church and were lovingly arranged about the "shroud of Christ," his icon woven into a large cloth, which was later venerated by all with prostrations and kisses—and by many with tears. But since the day of Resurrection was about to dawn we were filled with joy and anticipation.

In the kitchens at home, special foods were being prepared for the Easter feast. When possible, meat and dairy products had not been used during the fast, and the meals had been a powerful reminder of the solemnity of the season. With the trees outside, our very souls had seemed to bud in the Lenten spring. Now our homes were filled with the good smells of baking, and we filled wooden molds with the special "cheese Pascha" decorated with the words "Jesus Christ is Victor!" Eggs were dyed, some to eat and some *pysanky,* to exchange. Many of Russian or Ukrainian descent prepared the traditional food baskets, to be blessed together after the paschal liturgy, and shared in the potluck breakfast following.

Due to the length of the services and in anticipation of the reception of converts, it is traditional to serve the first Saturday liturgy, with the reception of the catechumens, in the afternoon. Baptisms are traditionally (and ideally) held at this Liturgy of St. Basil, since baptism is the great paschal mystery, proclaiming our dying and rising with Christ. Each baptized, after a triple immersion, is carried or walks with the clergy and sponsors around the font to the singing of St. Paul's hymn: "As many as have been baptized into Christ have put on Christ! Alleluia!" Together with the faithful, the newly baptized receives his or her first taste of the "fountain of immortality." I watched that afternoon as each member received Holy Communion with the words: "The servant of God, N____, receives the Body and Blood of Christ, for the remission of his/her sins, and unto life everlasting." How special it is, I thought, to be called by name to the Lord's Table.

The paschal liturgy began with Matins around 11:30 P.M. in absolute darkness. And then, with all of the drama of its liturgy, the church celebrated the eternal Pascha. Invited to "Come, receive the light!" from the Paschal candle, we processed around the outside of the church three times while solemnly intoning a hymn which seemed to bridge the gap between penitence and jubilation:

> Thy resurrection, O Christ our Savior
> the angels in heaven sing!
> Enable us on earth
> to glorify Thee in purity of heart.

The procession stopped before the church door. There we stood, with the myrrh bearers, at the tomb of Christ, expecting—but longing—for the words "He is not here, He is risen!" With the clergy and choir, we took our places before the throne (as the altar is called) and continued the song of victory. Now we sang loudly and *allegro*:

> Christ is risen front he dead, trampling down
> death by death
> And upon those in the tombs bestowing life!

In the Orthodox liturgy, virtually everything is sung, except for the sermon. But now the orderliness, the solemn integrity of the service with its measured movement toward Holy Communion, was joyously disrupted again and again by the shout of the celebrants, "Christ is risen!" and the roared response of the people, "Indeed He is risen!" in the several languages of those present. The sermon, as always, was simply the reading of the short homily of St. John Chrysostom with its wonderful invitation to the feast extended to all the faithful. The Paschal Canon was sung, with its great theme, "This is the day the Lord has made," taken from Psalm 118, the last Psalm of Passover, believed to be the hymn Jesus last sang with his disciples.

The Orthodox temple is considered the meeting place of heaven and earth, and the icons (holy pictures which are "written" in strict canonical language) are windows of heaven, their perspective reversed so that we might see in whose presence we stand. The faces glowed merrily with candlelight. Now that the light of Christ had again entered the temple, all was alight.

Everyone who could, remained standing. Children made themselves comfortable on the floor, in the arms of whoever picked them up, or on the chairs reserved for the weary or infirm. Some were overcome by sleep; indeed, more than once the procession had to detour around a sleeping boy of about four, but the children's anticipation was keen and their participation, when possible at that hour, was eager. When the faithful approached the chalice for Holy Communion, the babies and little children came first, in accordance with the wishes of the Savior: "Let the children come to me, and forbid them not, for of such is the kingdom of God."

After the community's participation in the Holy Gifts, the bishop stood with the clergy in the front of the church, and all walked by to greet him and one another with three kisses and the words, "Christ is risen!" "Indeed He is risen!" Each received a bright red egg from the bishop, as a sign that Lent is past, the Lord is risen, and together we are about to enjoy the family feast which also proclaims the good things he has won for us by his victory over death.

It was an unforgettable meal. I was won to Orthodoxy by the joy of God's people—by the warmth of their homes, their music, their icons, their liturgical life. Something was given to me that night which cannot be taken away, and I understand it to be a participation in the kingdom of God.

I believe that explains why, when an "official" atheist propagandist of the Soviet state, years ago, was berating a crowd of Russians, he was silenced simply by the cry of one old man, "Christ is risen!" and the unanimous, jubilant reply, "Indeed, He is risen!" For going to an Orthodox paschal service is like visiting a great cathedral in Europe; it is not only rich with the prayers of those present, but its very walls, as it were, are overlaid with the prayers of the centuries. It is an anticipation of that which is to come and, at the same time, a family feast for those living in Christ or "asleep in the Lord" to enjoy together with Him.

As the reckoning of the Orthodox Pascha includes the stipulation that its celebration be after the Jewish Passover, it usually falls on quite a different date than that observed in the Western churches. Consider a second celebration of the same great feast one year!

Sue Lane Talley

239 • THE ENVIRONMENT FOR HOLY WEEK WORSHIP

The following article suggests ways in which the worship environment can be appropriately designed for the services of Holy Week.

On Palm Sunday, the procession of palms may be enlivened with the use of multicolored balloons, yellow and white daisies, and tepi palm branches in addition to the traditional palms that the congregation waves with shouts of Hosannas. Large six-foot palm branches can lead the procession or form an arch through which the people move—fourteen large branches would do fine. These fourteen palm branches can then be placed in two containers on either side of the sanctuary— six branches in one and eight in the other. These containers can be made out of simple wood, about one foot square and three and four feet high respectively. This will allow the branches to bend out, resembling palm trees. The large wooden cross may also be decorated with palms and a variety of flowers: red carnations, yellow pompoms, white starburst mums, deep blue irises, and yellow and white daisies.

Holy Thursday is a festive celebration and a remembrance of the Passover. Remember the Last Supper is a term given because of hindsight; so the original event was joyous, not maudlin. Most probably the disciples sang the joyful Hallel Psalms that evening. What comes to mind for such a celebration are the colors white and yellow. The wooden cross which has been a motif throughout the Lenten Season may be decorated with an assortment of white and yellow flowers. During this time of the year Scotch broom and yellow forsythia are in bloom (depending upon your locale); a large expansive arrangement for the center of the rear altar (if your church has one) would create a nice backdrop for the liturgy. The procession can bring together many symbols. An individual carries in a board with seven candlesticks

of different heights; others process in with seven lit candles to be placed in the stylized menorah. Another individual may process in with an arrangement of grapes with various dried wheat and different colored grains for creating a texture. These are obvious symbols of thanksgiving, harvest, and Eucharist.

For the celebration of Good Friday, the liturgy speaks for itself, so simplicity is really in order here. The altar is covered with a large red cloth to match the vestment of the celebrant. Additional ministers in the liturgy may wear red stoles. A single red rose may be attached to the large wooden cross which will be used for veneration.

For the Easter Vigil and Easter Sunday liturgies, the environment should be tailored to the celebration. Very often many parishes supplement the numerous readings of the Easter Vigil with slide presentations. Then there is the problem: where to place the screen for all to see and what to do with it once the readings are finished. If your community uses this technique, place the screen where all can see it—usually behind the eucharistic table. Make the screen large and use rear projection so that there will be no need to move any equipment and interrupt the flow of the liturgy. After the Liturgy of the Word, a large procession of bells, banners, and flowers and bread and wine will prepare us for the Eucharist. The banners should be colorful and simple in design and similar, using abstract designs of crosses and bars. These banners—four is a good number— may then be placed in front of the screen to form a backdrop behind the eucharistic table. The stands for the banners can already be in place with potted lilies in front of the stands. To one side of the sanctuary an arrangement can be prepared to display the four prominent symbols of the celebration: the Word, the Paschal candle, baptismal water, and incense. Four stands of varying height would be appropriate—about one foot square with heights of two, three, four, and five feet. The Word may be placed on the tallest, the Paschal candle, on the next tallest, the baptismal water on the next level, and the incense on the lowest. Easter lilies should be arranged around this grouping at different heights. Behind this arrangement can be placed the large wooden cross decorated again with many colorful flowers of triumph.

Thomas S. Rambert, S.J.[31]

SEVENTEEN

Resources for Planning Holy Week Worship

Contemporary worship planners have the privilege of working with a rich body of written prayers, hymns, and liturgical texts from every period in the church's history. This chapter presents some of those resources, along with some written specifically for this volume. When using these resources, be sure to keep in mind the shape of worship for each day in Holy Week, which is described in the following chapters. For additional resources, see the bibliography at the end of Part 7.

240 ◆ LECTIONARY TEXTS FOR HOLY WEEK

The following are the texts suggested for the Sundays of Lent in the Revised Common Lectionary. Brief descriptions of each lesson are provided to aid in recalling the basic theme of each passage.

Passion Sunday or Palm Sunday

Those who do not observe the procession with palms and do not wish to use the Passion gospel may substitute the Gospel and Psalm given for the Liturgy of the Passion with the Gospel and Psalm indicated for the Liturgy of the Palms. Whenever possible, the whole Passion narrative should be read.

SUNDAY	PASSION GOSPEL	PSALM	EPISTLE	GOSPEL
Liturgy of the Palms (A)	Matthew 21:1-11, Jesus enters Jerusalem.	Psalm 118:1-2, 19-29		
Liturgy of the Passion (A)	Isaiah 50:4-9a, Servant of the Lord: obedience in suffering.	Psalm 31:9-16	Philippians 2:5-11, Christ emptied self, was raised.	Matthew 26:14–27:66 or Matthew 27:11-54, Passion reading.
Liturgy of the Palms (B)	Mark 11:1-11 or John 12:12-16, Jesus enters Jerusalem.	Psalm 118:1-2; 19-29		
Liturgy of the Passion (B)	Isaiah 50:4-9a, Servant of God insulted; God defends .	Psalm 31:9-16	Philippians 2:5-11, Christ emptied self, was raised.	Mark 14:1–15:47 or Mark 15:1-39 (40-47), Passion reading.
Liturgy of the Palms (C)	Luke 19:28-40, Jesus enters Jerusalem.	Psalm 118:1-2, 19-29		

continued...

SUNDAY	PASSION GOSPEL	PSALM	EPISTLE	GOSPEL
Liturgy of the Passion (C)	Isaiah 50:4-9a, the Servant: suffer disobedience.	31:9-16	Philippians 2:5-11, Christ emptied self, was raised.	Luke 22:14–23:56 or Luke 23:1-49, Passion reading.
Monday of Holy Week (A, B, C)	Isaiah 42:1-9, the Servant is a light to the nations.	36:5-11	Hebrews 9:11-15, Christ came as High Priest.	John 12:1-11, Mary anoints Jesus.
Tuesday of Holy Week (A, B, C)	Isaiah 49:1-7, the Servant mission in the world.	71:1-14	1 Corinthians 1:18-31, cross is foolish to world, wisdom of God.	John 12:20-36, Jesus speaks about his death.
Wednesday of Holy Week (A, B, C)	Isaiah 50:4-9a, the Servant's humiliation and vindication.	70	Hebrews 12:1-3, let us fix our eyes on Jesus.	John 13:21-32, Jesus foretells his betrayal.
Holy Thursday (A, B, C)	Exodus 12:1-4, (5-10), 11-14, instructions for observing Passover.	116:1-2, 12-19	1 Corinthians 11:23-26, "Jesus on the night betrayed took bread...cup...."	John 13:1-17, 21b-35, Jesus eats the Passover with disciples.
Good Friday (A, B, C)	Isaiah 52:13–53:12, the Suffering Servant endured our pain.	22	Hebrews 10:16-25 or Hebrews 4:14-16; 5:7-9, Jesus, our great High Priest gives us confidence.	John 18:1-19:42, Passion account.
Holy Saturday (for services other than the Paschal Vigil— A, B, C)	Job 14:14 or Lamentations 3:1-9, 19-24, affliction, pain, and suffering.	31:1-4, 15-16	1 Peter 4:1-8, live not by desires, but by will of God.	Matthew 27:57-66, or John 19:38-42, the burial of Jesus.

Revised Common Lectionary, descriptions by H. A. Tillinghast

241 ♦ TRADITIONAL OPENING PRAYERS FOR HOLY WEEK SERVICES

Many of the prayers below are based on centuries-old texts. They aptly express the themes of Holy Week worship. Adapt these prayers to local usage and style.

Sunday of the Passion (Palm Sunday)

Almighty and ever-living God, in your tender love for the human race you sent your Son our Savior Jesus Christ to take upon him our nature, and to suffer death upon the cross, giving us the example of his great humility: Mercifully grant that we may walk in the way of his suffering, and also share in his resurrection; through Jesus Christ our Lord, who lives and reigns with you and the Holy Spirit, one God, for ever and ever. *Amen.*

Maundy Thursday (at the Eucharist)

Almighty Father, whose dear Son, on the night before he suffered, instituted the Sacrament of his Body and Blood: Mercifully grant that we may receive it thankfully in remembrance of Jesus Christ our Lord, who in these holy mysteries gives us a pledge of eternal life; and who now lives and reigns with you and the Holy Spirit, one God, for ever and ever. *Amen.*

Good Friday

Almighty God, we pray you graciously to behold

this your family, for whom our Lord Jesus Christ was willing to be betrayed, and given into the hands of sinners, and to suffer death upon the cross; who now lives and reigns with you and the Holy Spirit, one God, for ever and ever. _Amen._

Holy Saturday

O God, Creator of heaven and earth: Grant that, as the crucified body of your dear Son was laid in the tomb and rested on this holy Sabbath, so we may await with him the coming of the third day, and rise with him to newness of life who now lives and reigns with you and the Holy Spirit, one God, for ever and ever. _Amen._

Book of Common Prayer

242 ✦ PRAYERS OF CONFESSION FOR HOLY WEEK

The following prayers are based on the Scripture readings appropriate for Holy Week. Note the commentary after each prayer, which elaborates the scriptural references on which it is based and provides suggestions for appropriate use.

The Sword and Staff. The sword and staff are well-known symbols of the betrayal.

| PEOPLE: | (read Acts 4:12) |
| ALL: | (read Ephesians 1:7) |

PRAISE

The third stanza of "Hosanna, Loud Hosanna" ("Hosanna in the highest!" that ancient song we sing...) is a fitting response to express our praise for Christ's redeeming love.

Commentary: The scriptural account of Jesus' triumphant entry (Mark 11:1-11) invites us to join the early Palm Sunday crowd. This prayer recognizes that if we were present in the first century our actions would probably have been no different than those reported in Scripture.

For Maundy Thursday

PRAYER

O Gracious God, though you overwhelm us with your patience, we come with a heavy heart. We gather this evening to join you in a most painful remembrance. Our throats become dry and our senses dull as we ponder the Scriptures that speak of Jesus' last night. Merciful God, we confess that our stamina is no stronger than that of Peter, James, and John. We find it difficult to watch and pray under the best of conditions, and when stress

Prayers of Confession

For Palm Sunday

PRAYER

Triumphant Lord and God, we have come to welcome and worship your Son this day. Yet as the words of Scripture echo through our souls we realize how our behavior parallels that of the people of Jerusalem: one day we are celebrating Christ's arrival, the next we are criticizing him for the demands he places on us. Gracious God, have mercy on us, for our faith is seldom mature. At times we resist your message. At times, we treat it carelessly, producing a shallow belief. Yet at other times we compromise and shape our faith around convenience. Loving Lord, we confess our involvement in these sins. Cleanse and renew us by the consistent love and life of Jesus, our Savior and Lord.

(opportunity for silent confession)

In Jesus' redeeming name. Amen!

WORDS OF ASSURANCE

LEADER: (reads Mark 11:9b)

mounts we too are prone to fall to a host of temptations. Lord, even though our spirits are often willing and desirous of following Christ, our lives are often weak in faithfully acknowledging him in the deep challenges of life. Lord of life, surround and support us with your mercy and cleanse us from sin.

(opportunity for silent confession)

We pray this in Jesus' strong name. Amen!

WORDS OF ASSURANCE

LEADER: (reads Romans 8:34-35a)
PEOPLE: **(read John 3:16)**
ALL: **(read 2 Corinthians 9:15)**

Commentary: Jesus' visit to Gethsemane (Matt. 26:36-46) forms the focus of this prayer. Other traditional Maundy Thursday passages could be employed to create alternate prayers (i.e., John 13:1-17; 18-30; Matt. 26:69-75; etc.).

For Good Friday

PRAYER

No, God, we were not there when they crucified Jesus. But we are today. As we unite our hearts in worship, we too can imagine and visualize in our own small way the sharp pain and deep suffering of our Lord. We have attempted to view history and dismiss any personal involvement or guilt by boldly asserting we would never have acted that way. Yet, we did and still do! As much as we try, we cannot escape the frightening truth that we have contributed to Christ's death on the cross. It is for our sins and stubborn rebellion that he died on this day. God, forgive our weak and vacillating faith, which is more conditioned and controlled by the pressure of the crowds than the presence of Christ. Replay the Crucifixion within our minds so that we might see your wounded, outstretched hands of love. Lift the shadows of sin and drive home the redeeming goodness of this Friday.

(opportunity for silent confession)

Through Jesus Christ, the great shepherd of our souls. Amen!

WORDS OF ASSURANCE

LEADER: (reads Romans 5:8)
PEOPLE: **(read Romans 10:9-10)**
ALL: **(read John 8:32)**

Commentary: This prayer echoes the refrain of the well known Afro-American spiritual, "Were You There." Worship on Good Friday calls for a sensitivity to the events of this day in the life of our Lord. One possible way of arranging the service would be to read Scripture, preach, and immediately follow that with the singing of "Were You There." The prayer of confession would then flow from the hymn. To further integrate the truths of this day, the singing of "When I Survey the Wondrous Cross" is an appropriate response following the words of assurance. The basic imagery for this prayer is drawn from 1 Peter 2:24-25 and further reflects the Good Friday scriptural themes.

Tom Schwanda

243 ✦ BIBLICAL CANTICLES FOR HOLY WEEK

The servant songs from Old Testament prophecy of Isaiah are fitting texts for Holy Week worship. Many hymnals include settings of these canticles for congregational singing. Consider also having these canticles read very slowly and reflectively by a single reader or a group of readers.

Isaiah 42:1-4

"Here is my servant, whom I uphold,
    my chosen one in whom I delight;
I will put my Spirit on him
    and he will bring justice to the nations.
He will not shout or cry out,
    or raise his voice in the streets.
A bruised reed he will not break,
    and a smoldering wick he will not snuff out.
In faithfulness he will bring forth justice;
    he will not falter or be discouraged
    till he establishes justice on earth.
In his law the islands will put their hope."

Some commentators suggest that this canticle extends to verse 9. Either reading would be appropriate for Holy Week worship.

Isaiah 49:1-6

Listen to me, you islands; hear this, you distant
    nations:
"Before I was born the LORD called me;
    from my birth he has made mention of
    my name.
He made my mouth like a sharpened sword,

in the shadow of his hand he hid me;
he made me into a polished arrow
    and concealed me in his quiver.
He said to me, "You are my servant, Israel,
    in whom I will display my splendor."
But I said, "I have labored for no purpose;
    I have spent by strength in vain and for
    nothing.
Yet what is due me is in the LORD's hands,
    and my reward is with my God.
And now the LORD says—
    he who formed me in the womb to be his
    servant
    to bring Jacob back to him and gather
    Israel to himself,
    for I am honored in the eyes of the LORD
    and my God has been my strength—
he says: "It is too small a thing for you to be my
    servant
    to restore the tribes of Jacob
    and bring back those of Israel I have kept.
I will also make you a light for the Gentiles,
    that you may bring my salvation to the
    ends of the earth."

Some commentators suggest that this canticle extends to verse 13. Either reading would be appropriate for Holy Week worship.

Isaiah 50:4-9

The Sovereign LORD has given me an instructed
    tongue,
    to know the word that sustains the weary.
He wakens me morning by morning,
    wakens my ear to listen like one being
    taught.
The Sovereign LORD has opened my ears,
    and I have not been rebellious;
    I have not drawn back.
I offered my back to those who beat me,
    my cheeks to those who pulled out my
    beard;
I did not hide my face
    from mocking and spitting.
Because the Sovereign LORD helps me,
    I will not be disgraced.
Therefore have I set my face like flint,
    and I know I will not be put to shame.
He who vindicates me is near.
Who then will bring charges against me?
    Let us face each other!
Who is my accuser?
Let him confront me!
It is the Sovereign LORD who helps me.
    Who is he that will condemn me?

They will all wear out like a garment;
    the moths will eat them up.

Some commentators suggest that this canticle extends to verse 11. Either reading would be appropriate for Holy Week worship.

Isaiah 52:13–53:12

See, my servant will act wisely;
    he will be raised and lifted up and
highly exalted.
Just as there were many who were appalled at
    him—
    his appearance was so disfigured
    beyond that of any man
    and his form marred beyond human
    likeness—
so will he sprinkle many nations,
    and kings will shut their mouths
    because of him.
For what they were not told, they will see,
    and what they have not heard, they will
    understand.

Who has believed our message
    and to whom has the arm of the Lord
    been revealed?
He grew up before him like a tender shoot,
    and like a root out of dry ground.
He had no beauty or majesty to attract us to him,
    nothing in his appearance that we
    should desire him.
He was despised and rejected by men,
    a man of sorrows, and familiar with
    suffering.
Like one from whom men hide their faces
    he was despised, and we esteemed him
    not.

Surely he took up our infirmities
    and carried our sorrows,
yet we considered him stricken by God,
    smitten by him, and afflicted.
But he was pierced for our transgressions,
    he was crushed for our iniquities;
the punishment that brought us peace was upon
    him,
    and by his wounds we are healed.
We all, like sheep, have gone astray,
    each of us has turned to his own way;
and the Lord has laid on him
    the iniquity of us all.

He was oppressed and afflicted,
    yet he did not open his mouth;

he was led like a lamb to the slaughter,
    and as a sheep before her shearers is
    silent,
    so he did not open his mouth.
By oppression and judgment he was taken away.
    And who can speak of his descendants?
For he was cut off from the land of the living;
    for the transgression of my people he
    was stricken.
He was assigned a grave with the wicked,
    and with the rich in his death,
though he had done no violence,
    nor was any deceit in his mouth.
Yet it was the Lord's will to crush him and cause
    him to suffer,
    and though the Lord makes his life a
    guilt offering,
he will see his offspring and prolong his days,
    and the will of the Lord will prosper in
    his hand.
After the suffering of his soul,
    he will see the light of life and be
    satisfied;
by his knowledge my righteous servant will justify
many,
    and he will bear their iniquities.

Therefore I will give him a portion among the
    great,
    and he will divide the spoils with the
    strong,
because he poured out his life unto death,
    and was numbered with the
    transgressors.
For he bore the sin of many,
    and made intercession for the
    transgressors.

244 ✦ BLESSING FOR HOLY WEEK

During Holy Week, the blessing is often in the form of a prayer for the gathered congregation rather than as a pronouncement of blessing.

Almighty God, we pray you graciously to behold this your family, for whom our Lord Jesus Christ was willing to be betrayed, and given into the hands of sinners, and to suffer death upon the cross; who lives and reigns for ever and ever. Amen.

Book of Occasional Services[32]

245 ✦ AN ANTHOLOGY OF HYMNS AND SONGS FOR THE SUNDAYS OF EPIPHANY

The following listings are a sampling of hymns and songs for Holy Week.

TITLE	AUTHOR/COMPOSER	TUNE	DAY/STYLE	SCRIPTURE REFERENCE
Ah, Holy Jesus, How Have You Offended?	J. Heerman/J. Cruger	HERZLEIBSTER JESU	Traditional	Isaiah 53:3
Am I My Brother's Keeper	T. Ferguson/J. Lloyd	WHITFORD	Traditional	Genesis 4:9
An Upper Room Did Our Lord Prepare	F. P. Green/English Folk		Thursday/ Hymn Renaissance	Luke 22:12; John 13:1
At That First Eucharist	W. Turton/W. Monk	UNDE ET MEMORIES	Thursday	John 17:1b
Behold the Lamb	D. Rambo (1979)		Friday/ Scripture Chorus	Revelation 5:6; 13:8

TITLE	AUTHOR/COMPOSER	TUNE	DAY/STYLE	SCRIPTURE REFERENCE
Behold the Lamb of God	M. Bridges/S. Wesley	WIGAN	Friday/ Traditional	John 1:29
Beneath the Cross of Jesus	E. Clephane/F. Maker	ST. CHRIST-OPHER	Friday/ Traditional	John 19:25
Christ Jesus Lay in Death's Strong Bands	M. Luther/Plainsong	CHRIST LAG IN TODESBANDEN	Saturday/ Plainsong	Luke 23:53
Come, Celebrate Jesus	C. Cloniger/J. Rosasco (1983)		Thursday	Matthew 26:26-28
Deep Were His Wounds and Red	W. Johnston/L. Sateran	MARLEE	Friday	Ephesians 2:5
Divided Our Pathways	C. Coehlo/E. Routley (1974)	PATHWAYS	Saturday	John 17:11
Fear Not, Thou Faithful Christian Flock	J. Altenburg/German Folksong	KOMMT HER ZU MIR	Saturday	Ephesians 6:10-13
For God So Loved the World	F. Townsend/A. Smith		Friday	John 3:16
God Is Love	Tr. J. Quinn/A. Murray	UBI CARITAS	Thursday	1 John 4:7-8
God So Loved	Traditional Chinese		Friday	John 3:16
I Come with Joy	B. Wren/A. Lovelace	DOVE OF PEACE	Thursday/ Hymn Renaissance	1 Corinthians 11:23-26
If God Is For Us	J. Foley, S.J. (1965)		Saturday	Romans 8:31-39
If That Isn't Love	D. Rambo (1969)	LOVE	Friday/ Contemporary Gospel	Philippians 2:6-7; Luke 24:40-43
In the Cross of Christ I Glory	J. Bowring/J. Conkey	RATHBURN	Saturday/ Traditional	Galatians 6:14
Into Thy Presence	Anon. arr. L. Leatherman		Friday/ Contemporary	Hebrews 10:19-22
It Is Finished	P. Nash/S. Brown (1985)		Friday	John 19:30
Jesus, Remember Me	Br. Robert/J. Berthier	JESUS REMEMBER THEE	Taizé	Luke 23:42
Lift High the Cross	Kitchin and Newbolt, S. Nicholson	CRUCIFER	Traditional	John 3:14

continued...

TITLE	AUTHOR/COMPOSER	TUNE	DAY/STYLE	SCRIPTURE REFERENCE
Lift Jesus Higher	Anon (1989)		Friday/ Contemporary	John 12:32
Lord, From the Depth to You I Cry	*Pry's Welsh Psalter* (1621)	Sonf	All Week	Psalm 130
The Lord Is Lifted Up	K. Woods, B. Crockett (1984)		Friday/ Contemporary	Philippians 2:9
More Love to Thee, O Christ	E. Prentiss/W. Doane	More Love To Thee	Thursday	Philippians 1:9
More Than Conquerers	B. and J. Grein (1978)		Friday/ Scripture Chorus	Romans 8:37
My Song Is Love Unknown	J. Edwards/S. Crossman	Rhosymedre	Friday/ Traditional	John 1:14; Romans 8:3
O Paradise	F. Faber/M. Williamson	Paradise	Saturday	Philippians 1:23
O Sacred Head, Now Wounded	Medieval/Hassler, arr. Bach	Passion Chorale	Friday/ Traditional	Isaiah 53:5; Matthew 27:39
Peace to Soothe Our Bitter Woes	N. Gruntvig/J. Hartmann	Peace of God	Saturday	Hebrews 10:19; Romans 5:1
Print Thine Image, Pure and Holy	T. Kingo/Geneva Psalter, arr. Bach	Psalm 42	Saturday	
The Royal Banners Forward Go	V. Fortunatus/Plainsong		Friday	
Sing, My Tongue, the Glorious Battle	V. Fortunatus/Plainsong		Friday	Galatians 4:4-5
So Lowly Does the Savior Ride	A. Pennewell/V. Copes (1964)	Epworth Church	Palm/ Passion Sunday	John 12:14-15
This Is My Body	J. Hayford (1984)		Thursday/ Scripture Chorus	Matthew 26:26
Throned Upon the Awful Tree	J. Ellerton/Traditional	Arfon	Friday	Matthew 27:45-46
Ubi Caritas	Br. Robert/J.Berthier (1981)	Taizé	Thursday	1 Corinthians 13:13
We Are the Body of the Lord	T. Fettke (1985)		Thursday/ Contemporary	1 Corinthians 12:27
Were You There?	Spiritual	Were You There	Friday/ Saturday	Matthew 27:35, 59-60

TITLE	AUTHOR/COMPOSER	TUNE	DAY/STYLE	SCRIPTURE REFERENCE
When Christ Comes to Die on Calvary	H. Letterman/R. Hillert (1986)		All Week	Matthew 27:45
When Christ Was Lifted From the Earth	B. Wren/Spiritual	BURLEIGH	Friday/ Saturday/Hymn Renaissance	John 12:32
When I Survey the Wondrous Cross	I. Watts/L. Mason	HAMBURG	Friday	Philippians 3:7
When Jesus Wept	W. Billings	WHEN JESUS WEPT	All Week/ Early American Canon	John 11:35

Steve Cushman

EIGHTEEN

Worship on Palm/Passion Sunday

Palm Sunday celebrates the triumphant entry of Jesus into Jerusalem and makes the beginning of his final days toward the Crucifixion and death. This chapter presents resources that may be used in traditional, creative, and convergence settings of worship.

246 ✦ INTRODUCTION TO PALM SUNDAY WORSHIP

The Palm Sunday services rehearse the triumphant entry of Jesus into Jerusalem. Contemporary renewalists draw on the drama and pageantry of the ancient customs as described below.

In contemporary worship, the ancient tradition of worship described by Egeria has been adapted to the use and style of the modern situation. Consequently some of the features described by Egeria such as meeting outside the church, the Gospel reading of the Triumphant Entry, the progession into the church, and the distribution of the palms have been retained.

If possible the service begins *outside* of the church (or, in the basement or vestibule) to symbolize the entrance of Jesus into Jerusalem through the procession.

In the preparation to worship, the people gather around the worship leaders and the choir. The service begins with an appropriate greeting followed by an anthem such as "Blessed Is the King Who Comes in the Name of the Lord" (or another appropriate anthem or song). The minister then offers a prayer that is followed by the reading of the Triumphant Entry. Another prayer, blessing God for the event celebrated this day, is offered. Then, another suitable anthem is sung, followed by the procession of the congregation into the sanctuary, singing such hymns as "All Glory, Laud and Honor." The mood of this part of the service, like that of the people who received Jesus into Jerusalem, is one of great joy and exuberance. This spirit of enthusiasm can be expressed through a procession in which the worship leaders and choir process around the entire sanctuary as the people sing. At the close of the procession a brief prayer concluding this part of the service is given. The people are then seated for the Service of the Word.

Although it is customary to read both an Old Testament lesson and an Epistle, the Scripture emphasis is placed on the Gospel reading of the Passion in this service. The object is to assist the congregation in experiencing the reality of Jesus' reflection. As the original participants in this drama of redemption cried, "Hosanna, blessed is he who comes in the name of the Lord," and later cried, "Crucify him!" so on Palm Sunday the congregation of worshipers will experience their own participation in receiving Jesus gladly and then turning their back on him. And it will be here, in the reading of the Passion, that the door into Holy Week will swing widely open. It is best to read the Passion Gospel using different roles, allowing the congregation to the crowd. It is customary to have the people seated during the reading of the Passion, standing at the mention of Golgotha (Matt. 27:33; Mark 15:22; Luke 23:33). Or, the people may stand for the reading and kneel at the mention of Golgotha. The service then proceeds with the sermon, the creed, the prayers, the kiss of peace, and the Eucharist.

Robert E. Webber

247 ✦ A TRADITIONAL PALM SUNDAY SERVICE

The following service is a creative adaptation of the traditional pattern and texts for worship on Palm Sun-

day. It will be of particular help for those who plan more formal worship. For those in nonliturgical churches, the commentary included with this service will provide a guide to thoughtful planning for Palm Sunday.

SERVICE OF ENTRANCE

Commentary: The Sunday that begins Holy Week has functioned two ways in the history of the church. First, it has been an occasion for the remembrance and celebration of Christ's entry into Jerusalem, that is, Palm Sunday. It is also an occasion for looking ahead to the long and lonely events of Christ's suffering and death. The following service incorporates both aspects, pointing to the grand irony of a narrative that features one who is hailed as king on Sunday but is crucified on Friday.

This irony should be reflected visually in the banners, paraments, bulletin covers, and Communion ware that are used on Palm Sunday. On the one hand, the triumph and celebration of the day may be reflected with the use of palm branches and with the use of bright hues of the color red—perhaps in the vestments. On the other, Christ's suffering may be reflected by the symbols of Holy Week—the cross, thorns, a whip—and the traditional colors of Holy Week, purple and black. As the service moves from one focus to another, the colors may be changed, perhaps prior to the reading of the Passion account, if that option is chosen (see the Service of the Word below.)

Gathering of the Congregation
(with Instrumental Prelude)

Commentary: The congregation may gather for worship outside the worship space. At this time, palm branches and other greens may be distributed to the congregation in preparation for a congregational procession. Pre-service music may be then played by various instruments, perhaps based on the melody of the processional hymn.

Proclamation of Christ's Entry into Jerusalem

LEADER: (reads Matthew 21:1-11; Mark 11:1-10; or Luke 19:28-40)

Commentary: The opening of this service is filled with drama. The service begins with the announcement of the Christ's entry, read from the Gospel lesson for the day. This should be read with fervor,

like a town-crier proclaiming good news to townspeople. Then the congregation joins the celebration, in response to the following call to worship.

Call to Worship

PASTOR: People of God, gathered in Jesus' name, on this day we recall the festive entry of our Lord into Jerusalem. Like the Hebrews of old, we join now in bringing our praise to our Lord.

READER 1: (Zechariah 9:9)
READER 2: (Psalm 118:26)

Commentary: These Old Testament verses should be read and possibly repeated with great excitement. The processional hymn should then begin without pause. If the congregation has gathered outside, the hymn may be lead by the choir. The procession into the sanctuary can be lead by appointed ushers or by children in the congregation. If the congregation has gathered in the worship space, the procession with palms may include not only choirs and worship leaders, but also children and representatives of each age group within the congregation.

Processional: "All Glory, Laud, and Honor"

Commentary: During the processional hymn, the congregation, led by the choir, the children, and/or the worship leaders processes into the worship space. The singing should continue, perhaps repeating the hymn or singing another appropriate Palm Sunday hymn such as "Hosanna, Loud Hosanna," or "Ride On, Ride On in Majesty."

Greeting

LEADER: (reads Revelation 1:4-5)
PEOPLE: **Hosanna in the highest.**

Ascriptions of Praise

Commentary: The greeting can appropriately be followed by an extend time of praise to God. This time may include choral or solo anthems and hymns of praise. Each text that is sung should focus on the person and work of Jesus Christ, emphasizing his lordship over all creation. Hymns that relate to his passion should be left for later portions of the service.

SERVICE OF THE WORD

Prayer for Illumination

LEADER: Gracious God, teach us by your Word, we pray, that we may bring right worship to the King of the Jews, that we may learn the lessons of his kingdom, and that we may offer our service to him, our Lord Jesus Christ. Amen.

or

Lord Jesus, with the echoes of our praise to you ringing in our ears, we come to hear your Word. Help us to avoid the near-sightedness of the people of old, who worshiped you as king on Sunday and chanted insults to you on Good Friday. Rather, strengthen us now by the hearing of your passion, that we may remember your sacrifice and be reconciled anew to the message of your kingdom. Amen.

Commentary: The first option is desirable if the Palm Sunday readings are chosen; the second if Passion Sunday readings are chosen.

Scripture Readings

Old Testament Reading: Isaiah 50:4-9a
Psalm: Psalm 31:9-16

Commentary: The Psalm may be sung by the choir or congregation. Musical resources for singing the Psalms are included in the commentary with the Pentecost service in this series.

New Testament Reading: Philippians 2:5-11

and/or

Gospel Reading: Matthew 26:14–27:66; Mark 14:1–15:47; Luke 22:14–23:56

Commentary: The first set of readings are traditional for Palm Sunday, amplifying the themes announced in the reading of the Gospel lesson at the beginning of the service. The second option presents accounts of the Passion narrative. The choice of Scripture lessons will depend upon the focus of the sermon.

The Passion narrative can very effectively be portrayed in a dramatic reading or chancel or church drama. This can be produced by reading these extended accounts of Christ's passion with several people, each one taking the part of one character in the scriptural text, with the exception of one reader who read all of the narrative or

connective material in the text. Several fine dramatic adaptations of these chapters are also available, such as later in this chapter or in *Handbook for the Christian Year* (Nashville: Abingdon, 1986), 135–51.

Sermon

Statement of Faith: The Apostles' Creed

Commentary: The New Testament reading from Philippians 5 may be used as a statement of faith following the sermon.

Sermon Hymn: "Christ, the Life of All the Living"

Commentary: The hymn should be chosen as an appropriate response to the call of the sermon. The given hymn is a hymn of thanksgiving for Christ's sacrifice.

SERVICE OF RECONCILIATION

This portion of the service may also take place after the Service of Entrance and before the Service of the Word. It is appropriate after a sermon that ends with a call for renewal and penitence in light of Christ's entry and passion.

Invitation to Confession

LEADER: People of God, having heard the proclamation of his Word, let us examine ourselves and approach our Lord with humility and penitence.

Prayer of Confession

[silence]

PEOPLE: **Gracious God, having heard your Word, we thankfully remember the life of our Lord Jesus Christ on this earth. Yet we also acknowledge our failure to respond earnestly and faithfully to his witness. We often mistake Jesus for a mere earthly king, friendly companion, or problem-solver, failing to see him as the ruler of all creation. We do not appreciate the depth of his passion and sacrifice on the cross, failing to acknowledge him as our way of salvation. Even in this Lenten season, we have not walked faithfully in the way of Jesus Christ. Forgive us, we pray, and bring us ever more fully** into the joy of union with Jesus Christ, our Lord. Amen.

Declaration of Pardon

LEADER: Hear the good news of the gospel: (reads Rom. 8:34; 6:8, 11). In Jesus Christ, our sins are pardoned and we are reconciled to God.

PEOPLE: **Thanks be to God!**

Passing of the Peace

LEADER: Since in Christ we are reconciled to God, so also we are reconciled to each other, the members of his body, the church. May God's peace extend throughout this congregation.

PEOPLE [to each other]:
God's peace be with you.

Prayers of the People

LEADER: As the united people of God, we offer our prayers to him.

(Prayers for the church. Prayers for the nation. Prayers for specific needs within the congregation. Prayers for the congregation's observance of Holy Week.)

Commentary: These prayers may be spoken by several members of the congregation or by one elder, deacon, or pastor. Special care should be given to relate the prayer to other elements in the service and in the congregation's observance of Holy Week. Other helpful forms for the prayers of the people may be found in the other services in this series.

Offertory

LEADER: (reads 2 Corinthians 8:9.) Let us bring our gifts to God.

PEOPLE: **We bring our gifts in joy.**

(The gifts are received.)

PEOPLE: (sing doxology.)

Commentary: An alternate doxology for use on Palm/Passion Sunday is the final verse of the hymn "O Love, How Deep, How Broad, How High." At this point, the elements for Communion and the gifts which have been received may be brought forward.

SERVICE OF HOLY COMMUNION

Approach to the Table

Invitation to the Table

LEADER: Friends in Christ, the table of the Lord is spread for us. "Come, taste and see that the Lord is good! Happy are those who find refuge in God." (Ps. 34:8)

Prayer of Thanksgiving

LEADER: Lift up your heart.

PEOPLE: **Lift them up to the Lord.**

LEADER: Let us give thanks to the Lord our God.

PEOPLE: **It is right of us to give thanks, it is our joy and our peace, at all times and in all places to give thanks to you, holy Father, almighty and everlasting God, through Christ, our Lord.**

LEADER: We praise you for creating this world and all who live in it. We praise you for redeeming this world and your people, when we followed false gods and ignored your will. Truly, your ways are higher than our ways and your thoughts are higher than our thoughts. Therefore, we join with your people of all ages and sing with joy:

PEOPLE: **Holy, holy, holy Lord, God of power and might,**
heaven and earth are full of your glory.
Hosanna in the highest.
Blessed is he who comes in the name of the Lord.
Hosanna in the highest.

Commentary: Most hymnals include a setting of this traditional canticle. For a list of service music found in a representative group of hymnals, consult the commentary to the Communion liturgy of the Advent service in this series.

LEADER 1: We acknowledge you, Christ Jesus, to be our Lord. We join our voices with the people of old in declaring, "Blessed is he who comes in the name of the Lord." We remember the triumphant spirit of your entry into Jerusalem and how, though the crowds had deserted you, you were lifted up high upon the cross and ultimately established your powerful kingdom by your resurrection on Easter and your ascension into heaven.

LEADER 2: We also praise you, Christ Jesus, for being our Savior. We thank you for enduring the depths of your passion, the torture of death by execution, the pathos of abandonment by God. We celebrate the gift of salvation which you offer to us and cling to the promise of your continued love. Amen.

Commentary: These two paragraphs, which form the Christocentric portion of the prayer of thanksgiving, each focus on of the two aspects held in tension during worship on Palm Sunday, the acclamation of Christ as Lord and the remembrance of his passion. If a choice is made to focus on one of these themes on Palm Sunday, worship leaders may wish to include only the paragraph appropriate to that choice.

Institution

LEADER: For the Lord Jesus, on the night when he was betrayed, took bread, and when he had given thanks, he broke it and said, "This is my body, which is for you; do this in remembrance of me." In the same way, he took the cup, after supper, saying, "This cup is the new covenant in my blood; do this, whenever you drink it, in remembrance of me." For whenever you eat this bread and drink this cup, you proclaim the Lord's death until he comes.

Memorial

PEOPLE: **We shall do as our Lord commands. We eat this bread and drink this cup, proclaiming his death. We do this now and until he comes again.**

COMMUNION
Prayer of Consecration

PASTOR: Gracious God, send your Holy Spirit upon us, we pray. Unite us, by this bread and wine, with our Lord Jesus Christ and with each other, the members of his body. Strengthen us for

service in his kingdom, that we may live in the power of his lordship until that day when we shall feast with him in heaven.

PEOPLE: **Amen.**

Breaking of the Bread and Pouring of the Cup

PASTOR: When we break the bread, is it not a sharing in the body of Christ?

PASTOR: When we give thanks over the cup, is it not a sharing in the blood of Christ?

Hymn

Lamb of God, you take away the sins of the world,
  have mercy upon us.
Lamb of God, you take away the sins of the world,
  have mercy upon us.
Lamb of God, you take away the sins of the world,
  grant us your peace.

Commentary: See the note to this hymn in the commentary to the Maundy Thursday service in this series.

Invitation

PASTOR: Friends in Christ, the Lord has prepared his table for his church. All who love him and trust in him alone for their salvation are now invited to come to the table of the Lord.

PEOPLE: **We come with gladness. Thanks be to God!**

PASTOR: The gifts of God for the people of God.

Sacrament

PASTOR: (as the people take the bread) Take eat, remember and believe that the body of the Lord Jesus Christ was given for the complete remission of all our sins.

PASTOR: (as the people take the cup) Take, drink, remember and believe that the precious blood of our Lord Jesus Christ was shed for the complete forgiveness of all our sins.

Commentary: During the sacrament, appropriate instrumental, choral, solo music may be played or sung, or the congregation may sing a series of Communion hymns. Preference should be given to texts that focus on either the lordship of Christ and our appropriate homage to him, or the passion of Christ and our appropriate response of penitence, depending on the focus of the service.

RESPONSE

Hymn: "What Wondrous Love is This?"

Commentary: An alternate response would consist of the reading of Psalm 103.

Prayer

LEADER: Ever-living God, we bring you thanks and praise for nourishing us at this table. Now may we live by the power of your Spirit as a continuing offering of thanksgiving to you.

PEOPLE: **Amen.**

Service of Dispersal

Charge to the People

LEADER: Go now into the world with the gospel of Jesus Christ. Never fail to wonder at the depth of his passion. Never fail to offer thanksgiving for the unsurpassable gift of reconciliation to God which he has give. Never fail to live as his servants, trusting in the power of his reign.

PEOPLE: **Amen.**

Commentary: The text may be revised in light of the specific call of the sermon.

Hymn of Dedication (Recessional)

Benediction

LEADER: (reads Philippians 4:7)

or

LEADER: Almighty God, look with favor on your family, we pray, the ones for whom Christ suffered and died. May the love of Christ be upon you all. Amen.

PEOPLE: **Amen.**

Dispersal of the Congregation
(with Organ, Piano, or Instrumental Postlude)

Commentary: Post-service music on Palm Sunday should anticipate the mood of the remainder of Holy Week, favoring meditative Passion hymns and the like.

John D. Witvliet

248 • A Creative Palm Sunday Service

This contemporary Palm Sunday service is appropriate for Protestant congregations who desire a more informal worship. Adapt the order below to local usage and style.

Order of Worship

Worship Space. You might want to hang Palm Sunday banners, and together with these, or if banners are not available, set an abundance of palm plants on the platform at obvious places along the aisles and at the entrance to the sanctuary. You might even want to supplement these special effects by hanging palm branches from the church walls. The altar or table should be prepared for Eucharist, with a prominently placed, lighted Christ candle.

Call to Worship

LEADER: In recollection of Jesus' entry into Jerusalem, every generation of believers, once yearly, welcomes Christ anew on this day which we call Palm Sunday. Today marks the beginning of Holy Week, the week prior to Christ's crucifixion, the most holy season of the Christian year.

As we prepare to walk this week with our Lord, let us begin by standing together, honoring, and receiving him in our opening worship hymns.

Opening Hymn: "All Glory, Laud and Honor"

Opening Prayer

ALL: **Our loving God, as we offer ourselves to you this morning, we humbly ask that our worship may join that of your angel hosts as they praise our Redeemer King on high.**

We want to know you more truly, and pray that your Holy Spirit would enlighten our minds and guide us into all truth. We seek to respond to your truth with an increased measure of love, and pray that your faithful and merciful hand would enlarge our hearts and teach us how to live our love. With confidence in the grace that you have abundantly

bestowed on your people through-out the ages, we ask these things in the name of your son, Jesus Christ. Amen.

LEADER: This morning, we want to accompany both the Israelites, as they antici-pated their Messiah, and Jesus' de-voted followers who welcomed him on that first Triumphal Entry. Let us walk with these people of God by re-ceiving them in the Scriptures.

1ST READER: Our first reading is from 2 Kings 9:1-7, 11-13. (Concludes with) This is the word of the Lord.

PEOPLE: **Thanks be to God.**

2ND READER: This reading is from the Old Testa-ment prophet Zechariah 9:9-17. (Con-cludes with) This is the word of the Lord.

PEOPLE: **Thanks be to God.**

3RD READER: Our response is from Psalm 118:1-9, 19-29. (Concludes with) This is the word of the Lord.

PEOPLE: "The Steadfast Love of the Lord Never Ceases" or "Gloria, Gloria" (Taizé) (sung response)

4TH READER: Let us stand for the reading of the gospel.

Commentary: Prior to the worship service, the leader can select a "crowd," composed of all age groups, including both infants and seniors. This crowd can be seated in the back seats of the church, and then gather in the foyer as the con-gregation stands for the reading from Matthew's gospel.

(reads Matthew 21:1-10) (Reader emphasizes v. 10: "Who is this?")

Commentary: After a few moments' pause, the crowd will begin to sing and will enter the wor-ship center in mid-song. Some in the crowd will be carrying palm branches, which they will pass among the congregation as they enter the church. Many in this crowd will be waving palm branches as they proceed, others will be preparing the way by laying down garments along the pathway of the procession. Still others will accompany with tambou-rines and other instruments, and with dancing.

The people join with the crowd in singing: "Make Way" (Kendrick). The members of the crowd joyously proceed to the front of the church, where they spread out and face the congregation, continuing to celebrate festively and freely, sing-ing: "Hosanna, Hosanna," "I Will Enter His Gates," "Hosanna to the Son of David," and "Awake O Is-rael."

The lights will slowly dim during the last song. The final song will be led to a slow, quiet finish, and at the close of the song the room will be dark. The Christ candle will be the sole light in the sanc-tuary. The crowd will quietly move to their seats at this time.

Out of the darkness, 4TH READER reiterates Matthew 21:6-10 and the dispersed "crowd" responds, ut-tering "Who is this?" in such a fashion that the question becomes a muttered echo throughout the sanctuary.

(silent pause)

VOICE 1: (shouts) He is a prophet! Never has one spoken as he has.

CROWD: "Who is this? . . .Who is this? . . .Who is this?"

VOICE 2: (shouts) He is a prophet! Never has one worked the wonders that he has.

CROWD: "Who is this? . . .Who is this? . . .Who is this?"

VOICE 3: He's a son of Satan! . . . He's leading the people astray.

CROWD: "Who is this? . . .Who is this? . . .Who is this?"

VOICE 4: (shouts) He is the Christ! The King! Bring on his kingdom! (silent pause)

(Lights slowly brighten.)

Homily

As the people were placing their garments before Jesus, perhaps they were remembering God's anointing of Jehu, and the spontaneous response of Jehu's guards, as they spread their cloaks be-fore him, shouting "Jehu is king!"

In like manner, the worshiping crowd spread their cloaks under Jesus of Nazareth, believing him to be their coming king. Little could they know, however, that their beloved teacher, healer, and prophet had come to Jerusalem not to be pro-claimed King, but to become their Passover lamb; not to be crowned, but to be crucified.

They wanted a king, they received a yielded lamb. They offered to this lord their garments, their only source of covering, of protection. Perhaps the palm branches, which we are more familiar with in connection with this day, were the gift of the poor, who did not have so much as a cloak to offer.

What do we, with palm branch in hand, offer to Christ? Are we in company with the poor, or with those who may have had several cloaks, several layers with which to cover themselves? Our palm branches are different from those that Jesus' followers carried. Our palm branch comes to us so that we might form it into a cross. The cross, then, becomes our ultimate link with Jesus, and with his challenge for us on this twentieth-century Palm Sunday.

We must ask ourselves, "What are our means of protection, our sources of security?" These people led a simple life; their greatest source of protection was obvious. In our more complex lives, are we aware of the people and situations from which our confidence comes? What comes between us and our experience of the cross?

Whom would we trust enough that we would totally yield up these things to him or her? We know that we should be as free to abandon ourselves to Christ as these enraptured followers were . . . and more so, since we know the outcome of the Palm Sunday story. But of course, in our humanness, we limit our trust. And we limit our trust because, in the depths of our being, the source of our motivation, we do not yet really know or love the God who moves among us and beckons us in the person of Jesus of Nazareth. Nor are we alone in the struggle.

"Who is this?", the people cried.

The enraptured followers, in their loving, neither knew nor understood: their hymns longings and basic needs prevented them from seeing. The Jewish leaders, with their learning, were too afraid to know or understand: the cost to their security and status was too great.

But what of us who are here today, with our own belief systems and tradition? How can we actively respond to the question, "Who is this Jesus, and what must I entrust to him?" What securities, what physical, spiritual, or psychological cloaks do we guard our personhood with? Let's consider these things, and silently place them before our Lord. (silent pause) Amen.

LEADER: We are encouraged to pray our personal prayers to God, but we also need to offer ourselves as a community. In the moments that follow we will allow time for those who would like to offer a prayer aloud. We will do so in the form of brief, bidding prayers. As you pray, try to express your prayer in a word or simple phrase, being as symbolic or as specific as you wish.

After a person confesses prayer aloud, let us confess our unity with that one by joining in a response of, "Lord, hear our prayer."

(Corporate prayer follows.)

LEADER: Will you please stand with me, and together let us receive God's word of absolution, taken from the epistle to the Colossians 1:13-14: "For God has rescued us from the power of darkness and transferred us into the kingdom of his beloved Son, in whom we have redemption, the forgiveness of sins."

We bless you, loving God, that you desire to strip us, layer by layer, in order that you may clothe us anew with Christ's faith, trust, and life. We submit ourselves to you with the prayer that you would indeed continue your work in us, and we offer our gratitude that as you undress us, you cover us with your forgiveness. Amen.

Eucharist/Communion

LEADER: The worshiping crowd of innocents and children was so filled with the immediacy of their joy that they little realized the holy poignancy of their celebration. However, even in their ignorance, they were right to yield themselves to God in the person of Jesus. This morning we want to symbolize that same receptivity, but we want to do so with a more conscious sense of who Christ is and of why he came.

As we come forward to receive Communion, Christ who has placed his Spirit within us comes forward as well. The religious leaders of Jesus' day were plotting Jesus' demise rather than welcoming him as the crowds did. In a conscious reversal of their denial of God's presence among them, we as the leadership of this church want to be the first to offer our cloaks to Christ on this Palm Sunday as he presents himself to us in all the diversity that you represent.

We place our [vestments/jackets/coats/sweaters] beside the Commnion table [or along the altar rail] and ask that you kneel upon these as you come to receive. You may wish to bring your sweater, jacket, or coat as well, to kneel upon it as you receive the bread and wine; and then to leave it here for the duration of the service as a symbol of your desire to place yourself before Jesus as he comes in the form of this Christian community.

Yes, they will all get creased and wrinkled, some will be soiled. Both of these inconveniences will become tangible reminders of that greater gift that was offered two thousand years ago, as people placed their garments before Jesus as he rode over them with his donkey. Let us allow ourselves to complement our earlier silent and verbal confessions with this simple, tangible gesture of humility.

Institution and Invitation to Eucharist:

LEADER:　(reads Matthew 26:26-29)

Prayer

ALL:　**We bless you, gracious Lord, that just as you intimately knew your disciples to whom you first offered yourself, in the bread and wine, that you know us. Thank you that you offer yourself to us on this day, receiving us as people you know to be as fickle or as ignorant as your first disciples and those early followers. We pray that you would consecrate this offering of bread and wine, that in our partaking, we would be able**

to follow you with a greater measure of faith, hope, and love. Amen.

Eucharist/Communion:

Commentary: Leaders come and place their garments around the table or along the altar and then the servers, prior to kneeling to receive the elements themselves, come forward and add their garment offering alongside. The congregation then joins.

LEADER:　Who is this Jesus? Our answers to that question would vary. We worship one Lord, but a Lord who comes to us in a variety of face. Let us now receive him in one another, by exchanging the kiss or hand of the peace of Christ.

Exchange of Peace

LEADER:　Today we have walked alongside those first followers of Christ. In closing, let us sing again, now with an enriched faith: "All Glory, Laud, and Honor."

Closing Hymn

Benediction

LEADER:　Now to him who is able to keep you from falling, and to make you stand without blemish in the presence of his glory with rejoicing, to the only God our Savior, through Jesus Christ our Lord, be glory, majesty, power, and authority, before all time and now and forever. Amen. (Jude 24-25)

Postlude: "Make Way" (Kendrick)

────────── **Commentary** ──────────

Preamble. Congregations that are used to celebrating Palm Sunday often associate the day with children waving palm branches or with hymns about children singing their "hosannas." Children waving palm branches are cute, and children singing hosannas for the Lord are sweet. Palm Sunday, which is rooted with Jesus' triumphal entry into Jerusalem is neither cute nor sweet.

Jesus came triumphantly—on a donkey; the crowds received him joyously, but with the mistaken notion that he would become their king and free them from Roman dominion. Meanwhile, the religious leaders were plotting to put him to death because he was upsetting their system. The challenge of the Palm Sunday service is to encourage us to celebrate while at the same time calling to mind the fickleness of the crowd and the backroom intrigue that would lead to Jesus' crucifixion.

Worship Space. Using palm plants and branches will immediately remind people that this is indeed Palm Sunday. This service will lead people beyond their familiar associations with the day, and so using traditional symbols will allow the service to begin on a comfortable note. The Christ candle, of course, enables us to draw our present understanding of Christ into this service which seeks to expand on what biblical history has to teach us.

Entrance. In this early portion of the service you will want to choose a hymn that both acknowledges the triumphal entry and includes the broader perspective of salvation history.

Word. The preliminary portion of many Palm Sunday services includes a procession of children waving palm branches. For a change, you might want to set the scene by moving quickly to the Service of the Word, which includes Old Testament and Gospel readings that make allusions to the triumphal entry. Such an order of service would help subordinate our traditions to the Service of the Word.

At some point in the service you will want the congregation to participate in the dynamic of the Triumphal Entry, and not simply hear of it via the reading of the Word. After *hearing* the Word, the congregation should be ready to have the Triumphal Entry portrayed loudly and clearly before them. The songs you choose should be songs of a festive, welcoming nature. The latter category should include pieces with a beckoning note.

This particular service lends itself very well to an incorporation of the arts in worship, particularly visual art, instrumental music, and dance. In place of the "crowd" motif, you could opt to have a liturgical dance to convey the mood and activity of Jesus' entry; such a dance could incorporate the procession and drama of the accompanying service by including both festivity and discord.

A homily could help to tie together the loose ends and complexities of the event. In particular, the homily could help the congregation to pre-

pare for a special Palm Sunday Eucharist, which, in turn, will prepare the congregation to receive Christ's strength for the spiritually challenging passage from Lent into Holy Week.

Along with a brief time for reflection following the homily, your congregation might also appreciate having some time to call to mind and write down those things that keep them from abandoning themselves fully in trust to Christ. These items can be anonymously noted on small slips of paper, collected in an offering basket, and brought forward as a confession and prayer offering to the Lord.

Eucharist/Communion. The depth of the sacrifice made by many in Jesus' crowd of followers needs to be acknowledged, as does the blindness and hypocrisy of the religious leaders. This Eucharist can be very powerful if it is planned in such a way as to offer the congregation a tangible means of identifying with that first community. The participants (and leadership in particular) need the opportunity to acknowledge our human pride and ignorance, and both of which are rooted in the certainty that Christ receives our praises and confessions, tainted though they are. The gesture of laying down "our garments" has the potential of providing a symbolic medium for expressing this acknowledgment. Depending on your church's specific social or ethnic culture, you may want to adapt this gesture accordingly.

Dismissal. Having walked through the triumphal entry in company with the earliest followers, repeating the opening hymn could serve as a meaningful voice of confession for the participants, "Thou didst accept their praises, accept the prayers we bring."

Diane S. George Ayer

249 ✦ A CONVERGENCE PALM SUNDAY SERVICE

This convergence Palm Sunday service will be compatible with congregations that are developing a worship style that draws on both traditional and contemporary worship forms.

Palm Sunday marks the beginning of the highest week of worship in the Christian church. While the main focus involves the services from Thursday through Easter Sunday, Palm Sunday provides the beginning point for seven days of intense prayer, Scripture reading, mediation, and spiritual preparation.

Banners and palms play a major part in setting the mood of worship. The highway to Jerusalem was filled with pilgrims who were welcoming their new king—Jesus. Little did they know how profound their welcome was. So it is today. The sanctuary must become a place of coronation as we proclaim the King and kingdom of God. Red, symbolizing the blood of Christ, is the principle color, used for paraments, frontals, stoles, and chasubles. Crosses and other symbols may be covered by a veil for Palm Sunday and the rest of Holy Week. Usually no flowers are present, only palm branches.

The front of the sanctuary may also have other symbols of his passion present: a crown of thorns, whip, sponge, spear, nails, hammer, a bag of coins, etc. These items should remain there all week.

The actual worship on Palm Sunday will be the same as the standard convergence service, with the following changes or modifications. Only the differences will be noted.

The Basic Pattern

ACTS OF ENTRANCE
Pre-processional Liturgy
Processional
Acts of Praise and Worship

MINISTRY OF THE WORD
Collect
Readings
Announcements

MINISTRY OF THE TABLE
Great Thanksgiving
Prayer after Communion

ACTS OF DISMISSAL
Blessing and Benediction
Distribution of Palms

Commentary

If weather and circumstances permit, the congregation may form a large processional outside the church sanctuary and proceed in together, carrying palm branches, shouting praises to God and singing to him.

Should the congregation not process, the processional should be larger than normal, with a crucifer, banners, singers, dancers, ministers, etc. The children may serve as a part of this processional, carrying palm branches and shouting "Hosanna!" The processional would come in with upbeat, victorious hymns or songs of praise.

When the processional has gathered, either outside the sanctuary or at the back entrance of the sanctuary if the congregation has already been seated, a pre-processional liturgy is offered by one of the ministers.

LEADER: The Lord be with you.
PEOPLE: **And also with you.**
LEADER: Let us give thanks to the Lord our God.
PEOPLE: **It is right to give him thanks and praise.**
LEADER: It is right and a good thing to give you praise, O Heavenly Father, for you sent your Son as a gift into the world. You sent him to a stable to be born, to people to be light, and to a cross to be killed that we might live eternally. On this day he entered the holy city of Jerusalem, and was proclaimed as King by those who spread their garments and branches before him. May these branches here today serve as a symbol of his kingly rule and his victory over the prince of darkness. Grant that we, who bear them in his name may always hail him as our King and follow him in the way everlasting; for he is Jesus Christ, who lives and reigns with you and the Holy Spirit, one God, world without end. Amen. Blessed is he who comes in the name of the Lord!
PEOPLE: **Hosanna in the highest.**
LEADER: Let us go forth in peace.
PEOPLE: **In the name of Jesus Christ. Amen.**

Commentary: In addition to the thematic treatment of hymns and worship songs, litanies and other forms of responsive readings may be used to focus our worship and attention upon Christ and his acts of love. In addition to the readings listed, dramatic presentations focusing on the Triumphal Entry or his passion may be used in this part of the service.

LEADER: Almighty God, who in your tender love for all mankind sent your Son our Savior Jesus Christ into the world and onto a cross: Help us stay true to the gospel, that we may never take his passion and death for granted, that we may, as Christ's own share in his sufferings and in his resurrection power; through Jesus Christ our Lord, who lives and reigns with you and the Holy Spirit, one God, for ever and ever. Amen.

First Reading: Isaiah 45:21-25 or 52:13–53:12; Psalm 22:1-21
Second Reading: Philippians 2:5-11
Gospel Reading: Matthew 26:36–27:54 or Mark 14:32–15:39 or Luke 22:39–23:49

Commentary: Please note that in announcing the Gospel, the following words are used: *The Passion of our Lord Jesus Christ according to* _____ .

At a designated time in the service, the minister should encourage the congregation to enter an intense time of prayer, fasting, reading, and meditation for the next seven days. He may even want to hand out special Scripture reading lists with a prayer and meditation theme for each day.

LEADER: Heavenly Father, we thank you for satisfying the hunger in our hearts through giving us the Bread of heaven. In sharing in this holy meal, may we remember his death which gives us salvation, his resurrection which gives us life, and his coming again which gives us hope. This we ask through Jesus Christ our Lord. Amen.

Commentary: Communion should be sober to reflect the mood of entrance into Holy Week. During Communion, keep silence. If songs are sung they should have to do with Jesus' journey to the cross. Observe stations for the anointing of oil.

LEADER: May God the Father, who loved you enough to send his Son to the world, bless you and keep you. May he give us peace. May Jesus Christ, the Bread of heaven, feed you by his grace and mercy. May he give us life. May the Holy Spirit, who dwells in you, order and direct all your days to the glory of God. Amen. Thanks be to God!

Commentary: As people leave the service, they are given palm leaves or palms in the shape of a cross to take with them as a reminder of this special day and the week that is to come.

Randolph W. Sly

250 ✦ A Palm Sunday Drama

The drama below is a production of the temple scene as it may have been during the Triumphal Entry. It may be used at the beginning of the Palm Sunday service. This service involves the children and gives them a greater sense of the meaning of Palm Sunday. The drama requires two money changers, the crowd (congregation), a lame person, a chief priest, a blind person, rabbi, Pharisee, children's nanny, narrator, Jesus, and temple children.

────── **Characters** ──────

MONEY CHANGER 1
MONEY CHANGER 2
RABBI
NARRATOR
CROWD
CHIEF PRIEST
PHARISEE
JESUS
LAME PERSON
BLIND PERSON
CHILDREN'S NANNY
TEMPLE CHILDREN

────── **Script and Stage Notes** ──────

MONEY CHANGER 1: Get your Gentile money exchanged here! Good prices for your pagan currency! *(Repeatedly)*

The two MONEY CHANGERS *are in position as the scene opens. The* RABBI *is also in position and is "davening" (reading the prayer).*

MONEY CHANGER 2: One shekel in exchange for 50 Roman denarii! Let me help with your temple gift! *(Repeatedly)*

The MONEY CHANGERS *begin hawking their wares, addressing the congregation.*

NARRATOR: The crowds went ahead of him, and

those that followed shouted, "Hosanna to the Son of David! Blessed is he who comes in the name of the Lord! Hosanna in the highest!" They took palm branches and went out to meet him, shouting,

CROWD: Hosanna! Blessed is he who comes in the name of the Lord! Blessed is the King of Israel!

(Note: The congregation will serve as the crowd.)

NARRATOR: When Jesus entered Jerusalem, the whole city was stirred and asked, "Who is this?"

The CHIEF PRIEST *and the* PHARISEE *enter and take position near the* RABBI. *The* RABBI *begins offering doves for sale.* JESUS *appears at the back of the sanctuary.*

CROWD: This is Jesus, the prophet from Nazareth in Galilee. Blessed is the king who comes in the name of the Lord! Peace in heaven and glory in the highest! Blessed is the coming kingdom of our father David! Hosanna in the highest!

RABBI: See, this is getting us nowhere.

PHARISEE: Look how the whole world has gone after him!

JESUS *comes down the aisle speaking*

JESUS: If you, even you, had only known on this day what would bring you peace—but now it is hidden from your eyes.

MONEY CHANGERS *go into action again.*

MONEY CHANGER 1: Get your Gentile money exchanged here! Good prices for your pagan currency! *(Repeatedly)*

MONEY CHANGER 2: One shekel in exchange for 50 Roman denarii! Let me help you with your temple gift! *(Repeatedly)*

NARRATOR: Then he entered the temple area and began driving out those who were selling and would not allow anyone to carry merchandise through the temple.

JESUS *overturns the money changers' table and confiscates the doves.*

JESUS: It is written, "My house will be a house of prayer"; but you have made it "a den of robbers."

Said toward the CHIEF PRIEST, PHARISEE, *and* RABBI. *They withdraw toward stage right.*

NARRATOR: Then the blind and the lame came to him at the temple, and he healed them.

BLIND PERSON *and* LAME PERSON *get up from their place in the crowd and start toward Jesus. They help each other. Jesus meets them.*

NARRATOR: The chief priests and the teachers of the law heard this and began looking for a way.

CHIEF PRIEST, PHARISEE, *and* RABBI *shun them and mutter together.*

JESUS: The hour has come for the Son of Man to be glorified.

NARRATOR: Yet they could not find any way to do it, because the whole crowd was amazed at his teaching.

BLIND PERSON: I can see! Wow, I can see!

JESUS *heals the* BLIND PERSON. *(Action involves touching and supporting as actor sees fit.)*

LAME PERSON: I can walk! I'm healed!

JESUS *heals the* LAME PERSON. *They fall on their knees before Jesus in gratitude.*

CHILDREN: Hosanna to the Son of David! Hosanna! Hosanna to the Son of David! Hosanna!

CHILDREN *enter from all aisles waving palm branches, gather around Jesus, (repeatedly) lay the palms around him, and sit around his feet.* JESUS *interacts with the* CHILDREN—*holds one in his arms, etc.*

NARRATOR: When the chief priests and the teachers of the law saw the wonderful things he did and heard the children shouting in the temple area, they were indignant.

The CHIEF PRIEST, PHARISEE, *and* RABBI *approach* JESUS.

RABBI: Do you hear what these children are saying?

The CHILDREN *cringe, back away, or cling to* JESUS.

PHARISEE: Listen to them! How awful!

CHIEF PRIEST: Do you hear what they call you? That is blasphemy!

JESUS: And have you never read, "From the lips of children and infants you have ordained praise?" Father, glorify your name!

The CHIEF PRIEST, PHARISEE, *and* RABBI *turn away in anger.*

NARRATOR: Then a voice came from heaven—"I have glorified it, and will glorify it again."

CHILDREN *look up.*

JESUS: This voice is for your benefit, not mine. I tell you the truth, if you have faith, and do not doubt, you can say to this mountain, "Go, throw yourself into the sea," and it will be done. I tell you the truth, unless a kernel of wheat falls to the ground and dies, it remains only a single seed. But if it dies, it produces many seeds. The man who loves his life will lose it, while the man who hates his life in this world will keep it for eternal life. Whoever serves me must follow men; and where, I am, my servant also will be. My Father will honor the one who serves me. Now is the time, for judgment on this world; now the prince of this world will be driven out. But I, when I am lifted up from the earth, will draw all men to myself.

Jesus points at the CHIEF PRIEST, PHARISEE, *and* RABBI. *They turn and sneer.* CHILDREN *gather upstage— toward choir pews (or area from which they can sing).* MONEY CHANGER #1 *starts to move toward Jesus.* #2 *watches him.* #1 *turns to* #2 *to pull him along.* MONEY CHANGER #2 *goes part way, then throws* #1's *hand off and stomps over to the* CHIEF PRIEST, PHARISEE *and* RABBI. #2 *points to Jesus. They shake their heads and mutter among themselves.* MONEY CHANGER #1 *sits at* JESUS' *right side.*

NARRATOR: The crowd spoke up,

CROWD: We have heard from the Law that the Christ will remain forever, so how can you say, "The Son of Man must be lifted up"? Who is this "Son of Man"?

JESUS: You are going to have the light a little while longer before darkness overtakes you. The man who walks in the dark does not know where he is going. Walk while you have the light, that you may become sons of light.

JESUS *reaches down and extends hand to* MONEY CHANGER #1, *who then stands as* JESUS *turns to the crowd. The* CHIEF PRIEST, PHARISEE, *and* RABBI *get more angry. As* JESUS *is speaking, he turns to the* CROWD *and begins to exit down the center aisle.* MONEY CHANGER #1 *follows him.*

NARRATOR: Even after Jesus had done all these miraculous signs in their presence, they still would not believe in him.

The CHIEF PRIEST, PHARISEE, *and* RABBI *come center stage.*

RABBI: See, this is getting us nowhere. Look how the whole world has gone after him!

PHARISEE: If we let him go on like this, everyone will believe in him.

PHARISEE *and* RABBI *begin to exit.*

CHIEF PRIEST: It is better that one die for the people than that the whole nation perish.

PHARISEE *and* RABBI *stop to listen, then continue to exit.* CHIEF PRIEST *exits.*

CHILDREN *sing "The King of Glory Comes." They move into final position to sing and proceed with their song.*

General Notes

• Plan to use costumes—especially robes, prayer shawls, head pieces and *yahmulkahs* or *kipots.* (Kipots can be obtained by contacting a local synagogue.)

• The presence of the children's nanny is both authentic (Gentile women were used to bring children to the outer courts of the temple) and practical for the presentation (the very small children need an older teenager or adult to guide them).

• For money, consider using gold foil-wrapped

chocolate candy, which can be distributed to the children after the worship service.

- The lines for the congregation (crowd) can be printed in the bulletin or projected on an overhead. Have the narrator give cues to the crowd.

- During church school in the preceding weeks, inform the children of the plan, the story, and their role in the drama. Practicing their processional with the nanny and the person who takes the part of Jesus will only heighten their anticipation and understanding. They should know the "Hosanna" lines and the Israeli song "The King of Glory Comes" (_Psalter Hymnal_ 370), preferably performed with rhythm instruments and descant. Perhaps the adults could sing some of the stanzas with the children.

- The action should not be rushed. Give time for the movement to occur and for people to absorb the symbolism.

- The scene takes about 10–12 minutes. It can serve as the opening of the worship service on Palm Sunday.

- Scripture references in the following order are found in the script: Matthew 21:9; John 12:13; Matthew 21:10-11; Luke 19:38; Mark 11:10; John 12:19; Luke 19:42; 19:45; Mark 11:16; Luke 19:46; Matthew 21:14; Mark 11:18; John 12:23; Luke 19:48; Mark 11:18; Matthew 21:15-16; John 12:28; 12:30; Matthew 21:21; John 12:24-26; 12:31-32; 12:34-37; 12:19; 11:48; 11:50.

Jonathan Levy Gerdan II
and Fred Walhof[33]

251 ◆ THE PASSION NARRATIVE

Traditionally the Passion narrative is read during the Service of the Word in the Palm Sunday service. The narrative represents the shift from the joy of the triumphant entry to be sober reality that this same crowd will deny Jesus and call for his crucifixion.

The Passion reading may also constitute the "Service of the Word" in an evening service on Passion (Palm) Sunday. The Scripture would also be most appropriate for a Good Friday service, for it is traditional to reserve John's Passion narrative for Good Friday. In either of these services the reading may be preceded or followed by a brief homily, if necessary.

The Passion reading may also serve as the central portion of a Tenebrae service, with its gradual extinguishing of lights, draping of chancel items in black, cessation of instrumental accompaniment, and silent recessing from the church.

The script requires an evangelist (narrator), Jesus, a servant girl, Peter, an official, a bystander, a servant, Pilate, a chorus of priests, several soldiers, and the crowd (the congregation).

Main readers, such as the evangelist and Jesus, may be positioned at the pulpit and a lectern; other roles may be spoken from the front pews and/or the side aisles.

The "crowd" parts (in John 18:40; 19:6; and 19:15) are spoken and shouted by the entire congregation; these lines must be rehearsed with the congregation just prior to the service. The congregation is expected to participate in the "crowd" parts by following the [NIV] text in their own Bibles.

——— John 18:1-14 ———

EVANGELIST: When Jesus had finished praying, he left with his disciples and crossed the Kidron Valley. On the other side there was an olive grove, and he and his disciples went into it. Now Judas, who betrayed him, knew the place because Jesus had often met there with his disciples.

So Judas came to the grove, guiding a detachment of soldiers and some officials from the chief priests and weapons. Jesus, knowing all that was going to happen to him, went out and asked them,

JESUS: Who is it that you want?

SOLDIERS: Jesus of Nazareth.

JESUS: I am he.

EVANGELIST: And Judas the traitor was standing there with them. When Jesus said, "I am he," they drew back and fell to the ground. Again Jesus asked them,

JESUS: I told you that I am he. If you are looking for me, then let these men go.

EVANGELIST: This happened so that the words Jesus had spoken would be fulfilled: "I have not lost one of those you gave me."

Then Simon Peter, who had a sword, drew it and struck the high priest's servant, cutting off his right ear. The servant's name was Malchus. But Jesus commanded Peter,

JESUS: Put your sword away! Shall I not drink the cup the Father has given me?

EVANGELIST: Then the detachment of soldiers with its commander and the Jewish officials arrested Jesus. They bound him and brought him first to Annas, who was the father-in-law of Caiaphas, the high priest that year. Caiaphas was the one who had advised the Jews that it would be good if one man died for [all] the people.

Following this reading, all shall pray in silence, and then sing: "What Wondrous Love."

―――――― **John 18:15-27** ――――――

EVANGELIST: Simon Peter and another disciple were following Jesus. Because this disciple was known to the high priest, he went with Jesus into the high priest's courtyard, but Peter had to wait outside at the door. The other disciple, who was known to the high priest, came back, spoke to the girl on duty there, and brought Peter in.

SERVANT GIRL: Surely you are not another of this man's disciples?

PETER: I am not.

EVANGELIST: It was cold, and the servants and officials stood around a fire they had made to keep warm. Peter was also standing with them, warming himself.

(Pause)

Meanwhile, the former high priest Annas questioned Jesus about his disciples and his teaching, to which Jesus replied,

JESUS: I have spoken openly to the world. I always taught in synagogues or at the temple, where all the Jews come together. I said nothing in secret. Why question me? Ask those who heard me. Surely they know what I said.

EVANGELIST: When Jesus said this, one of the officials nearby struck him in the face.

AN OFFICIAL: Is that any way to answer the high priest?

JESUS: If I said something wrong, testify as to what is wrong. But if I spoke the truth, why did you strike me?

EVANGELIST: Then Annas sent Jesus, still bound, to Caiaphas, the high priest.

(Pause)

As Simon Peter stood warming himself, he was asked,

A BYSTANDER: You are not one of his disciples, are you?

PETER: I am not.

EVANGELIST: One of the high priest's servants, a relative of Malchus, whose ear Peter had cut off, challenged him,

A SERVANT: Didn't I see you with him in the olive grove?

EVANGELIST: Again Peter denied it, and at that moment a rooster began to crow.

Following this reading, all shall pray in silence, and then sing: "Ah, Holy Jesus, How Have You Offended."

―――――― **John 18:28–19:3** ――――――

EVANGELIST: Then the Jews led Jesus from Caiphas to the palace of the Roman governor [Pilate]. By now it was early morning, and to avoid ceremonial uncleanness the Jews did not enter the palace; they wanted to be able to eat the Passover. So Pilate came out to them and asked.

PILATE: What charges are you bringing against this man?

PRIESTS: If he were not a criminal, we would not have handed him over to you.

PILATE: Take him yourselves and judge him by your own law.

PRIESTS: But we have no right to execute anyone.

EVANGELIST: This happened so that the words Jesus had spoken indicating the kind of death he was going to die would be fulfilled.

Then Pilate went back inside the palace, summoned Jesus and asked him,

PILATE: Are you the king of the Jews?

JESUS: Is that your own idea, or did others talk to you about me?

PILATE: Am I a Jew? It was your people and your chief priests who handed you over to me. What is it you have done?

JESUS: My kingdom is not of this world. If it were, my servants would fight to prevent my arrest by the Jews. But now my kingdom is from another place.

PILATE: You are a king, then!

JESUS: You are right in saying I am a king. In fact, for this reason I was born, and for this I came into the world, to testify to the truth. Everyone on the side of truth listens to me.

PILATE: What is truth?

EVANGELIST: With this Pilate went out again to the Jews and said to them,

PILATE: I find no basis for a charge against him. But it is your custom for me to release to you one prisoner at the time of the Passover. Do you want me to release "the king of the Jews"?

EVANGELIST: [But] the crowd shouted back,

CROWD: *(voices through each other)* No, not him! Give us Barrabas! (John 18:40)

EVANGELIST: Now Barabbas had taken part in a rebellion.

Then Pilate took Jesus and had him flogged. The soldiers twisted together a crown of thorns and put it on his head. They clothed him in a purple robe, and went up to him again and again, saying,

SOLDIERS: *(voice through each other)* Hail, king of the Jews!

EVANGELIST: And they struck Jesus in the face.

Following this reading, all shall pray in silence, and then sing: "O Sacred Head, Now Wounded."

——————— **John 19:4-18** ———————

EVANGELIST: Once more Pilate came out and said to the Jews,

PILATE: Look, I am bringing him out to you to let you know that I find no basis

for a charge against him.

EVANGELIST: Then Jesus came out wearing the crown of thorns and the purple robe.

PILATE: Here is the man!

EVANGELIST: As soon as the chief priests and their officials saw Jesus, they [all] shouted,

CROWD: *(voices through each other)* Crucify! Crucify! (John 19:6)

PILATE: You take him and crucify him. As for me, I find no basis for a charge against him.

PRIESTS: We have a law, and according to that law he must die, because he claimed to be the Son of God.

EVANGELIST: When Pilate heard this, he was even more afraid. He went back inside the palace and asked Jesus,

PILATE: Where do you come from?

EVANGELIST: But Jesus gave him no answer.

PILATE: Do you refuse to speak to me? Don't you realize I have the power either to free you or to crucify you?

JESUS: You would have no power over me if it were not given to you from above. Therefore the one who handed me over to you is guilty of a greater sin.

EVANGELIST: From then on, Pilate tried to set Jesus free, but the Jewish leaders kept shouting,

PRIESTS: If you let this man go, you are no friend of Caesar. Anyone who claims to be a king opposes Caesar.

EVANGELIST: When Pilate heard this, he brought Jesus out and sat down on the judge's seat at a place known as the Stone Pavement (which in Aramaic is *Gabbatha*). It was the Day of Preparation of Passover Week, about the sixth hour, [when] Pilate said,

PILATE: Here is your king.

EVANGELIST: But the crowd shouted.

CROWD: *(voices through each other)* Take him away! Take him away! Crucify him! (John 19:15)

PILATE: Shall I crucify your king?

PRIESTS: We have no king but Caesar.

EVANGELIST: Finally Pilate handed Jesus over to them to be crucified. So the soldiers took charge of Jesus. Carrying his own cross, he went out to the place of the skull (which in Aramaic is called *Golgotha*). Here they crucified him, and with him two others—one on each side and Jesus in the middle.

Following this reading, all shall pray in silence, and then sing: "Were You There."

--------- **John 19:19-30** ---------

EVANGELIST: Pilate had a notice prepared and fastened to the cross. It read: JESUS OF NAZARETH, THE KING OF THE JEWS. Many of the Jews read this sign, for the place where Jesus was crucified was near the city, and the sign was written in Aramaic, Latin, and Greek. The chief priests of the Jews protested to Pilate:

PRIESTS: Do not write "the King of the Jews" but that this man *claimed* to be king of the Jews.

PILATE: What I have written, I have written.

EVANGELIST: When the soldiers crucified Jesus, they took his clothing, dividing them into four shares, one for each of them, with the undergarment remaining. This garment was seamless, woven in one piece from top to bottom.

SOLDIERS: Let's not tear it, [but] decide by lot who will get it.

EVANGELIST: This happened that the Scripture might be fulfilled which said, "They divided my garments among them and cast lots for my clothing." So this is what the soldiers did.

(Pause)

Near the cross of Jesus stood his mother, his mother's sister, Mary, the wife of Clopas, and Mary Magdalene. When Jesus saw his mother there, and the disciple whom he loved standing nearby, he said to his mother,

JESUS: Dear woman, here is your son.

EVANGELIST: And to the disciple,

JESUS: Here is your mother.

EVANGELIST: From that time on, this disciple took Jesus' mother into his home.

(Pause)

Later, knowing that all was now completed, and so that the Scripture would be fulfilled, Jesus said,

JESUS: I am thirsty.

EVANGELIST: A jar of wine vinegar was there, so they soaked sponge in it, put the sponge on a stake of the hyssop plant, and lifted it to Jesus' lips. When he had received the drink, Jesus said,

JESUS: It is finished!

EVANGELIST: With that, he bowed his head and gave up his spirit.

Following this reading, all shall pray in silence, and then sing: "When I Survey the Wondrous Cross."

--------- **John 19:31-42** ---------

EVANGELIST: Now it was the day of Preparation, and the next day was to be a special Sabbath. Because the Jews did not want the bodies left on the crosses during the Sabbath, they asked Pilate to have the legs broken and the bodies taken down. The soldiers therefore came and broke the legs of the first man who had been crucified with Jesus, and then those of the other [man]. But when they came to Jesus and found that he was already dead, they did not break his legs. Instead, one of the soldiers pierced Jesus' side with a spear, bringing a sudden flow of blood and water.

The man who saw it has given testimony, and his testimony is true. He knows that he tells the truth, and he testifies so that you also may believe. These things happened so that the Scripture would be fulfilled: "Not one of his bones will be broken," and, as another Scripture says, "They will look on the one they have pierced."

(Pause)

Later, Joseph of Arimathea asked Pilate for the body of Jesus. Now Joseph was a disciple of Jesus, but secretly because he feared the [leaders of the] Jews. With Pilate's permission, he came and took the body away. He was accompanied by Nicodemus, the man who earlier had visited Jesus at night. Nicodemus brought a mixture of myrrh and aloes, about seventy-five pounds. Taking Jesus' body, the two of them wrapped it, with the spices, in strips of linen. This was in accordance with Jewish burial customs. At the place where Jesus was crucified, there was a garden, and in the garden a new tomb, in which no one had ever been laid. Because it was the Jewish day of Preparation and since the tomb was nearby, they laid Jesus there.

Following this reading, all shall mediate and pray in silence, and, after due time, sing: "I Will Sing of My Redeemer."

Bert Polman[34]

NINETEEN

Worship on Maundy Thursday

The Maundy Thursday service enacts the giving of the new commandment of love, the inauguration of the Lord's Table (Last Supper), and the journey of Jesus into the Garden of Gethsemane where he was captured and led captive toward his death. The resources of this chapter are presented to help a congregation recall these initial events of the Passion and to sense their significance for the Christian life.

252 ✦ AN INTRODUCTION TO THE MAUNDY THURSDAY SERVICE

Below is a description of the meaning and content of the ancient Maundy Thursday service. Adapt this material to current usage and style.

In the ancient church the service of Maundy Thursday began the great triduum, the three great days of the paschal celebration. These were days of fasting and prayer, days when the final acts of Christ's saving work were remembered by the church. The day gets its name from the Latin *mandatum novarum* ("a new commandment"—John 13:34), which was translated into the French *mande.* A primary meaning of this service is to celebrate the giving of the new commandment to love one another, a commandment given in the context of Jesus washing the disciples' feet. When we celebrate this service, the covenant between God and ourselves is renewed, and we are made ready for his death and resurrection. The agape meal that is celebrated with this service symbolizes, as meals in the Old Testament did, the relationship we have with God. After the agape meal, the people assemble to worship. Because of the solemnity of the moment, the service is opened in silence. A silent procession of the minister and choir is followed by the prayer. These two acts constitute the entrance to worship. The people are then seated for the Scripture readings and the sermon.

After the sermon, the ceremony of the washing of the feet is conducted. In some traditions all the people of the congregation are involved in the ceremony. In other congregations the washing of the feet is done by the minister to several people in the congregation. The minister may choose to wash the feet of several leaders of the church, representatives from among the leaders, or representatives from various groups or ages in the congregation. All that is needed is a pitcher of water, a basin, and a towel. The people, having removed their shoes, sit in a place visible to all. The minister then washes their feet as the choir and/or congregation sings suitable anthems or songs. After the washing of the feet, the service continues with the prayers of the people, followed by the Lord's Supper.

After the Last Supper, our Lord went to the Garden of Gethsemane to pray while his disciples watched and prayed with him. Consequently it has been customary to have a prayer vigil after the Maundy Thursday service, extending through the night in some churches. The church may either be open, allowing people to come and go as they please, or various persons may sign up to pray at designated half hours, or hours throughout the night. For those who are able to do the vigil, the tiredness of the body itself, which is often sustained through the three days, assists the spirit in experiencing to some small degree the pain and suffering of our Lord.

Robert E. Webber

253 ✦ A Traditional Maundy Thursday Service

The following service is a creative adaptation of the traditional pattern and texts for worship on Maundy Thursday. It will be of particular help to those who plan more formal Maundy Thursday worship. For others, the commentary included with this service will provide a guide to thoughtful planning.

GATHERING FOR WORSHIP

Commentary: Since the Maundy Thursday service centers around the events held in the Upper Room the night before Christ's death, the service should reflect the nature of these events. One important aspect in the Upper Room was Jesus' fellowship with his disciples. This may be emphasized in a congregation's celebration by holding a fellowship meal prior to the service.

The visual environment for the service can build on what is done for other services during Holy Week, including the use of purple and other dark colors, rough fabrics, somber lighting, and symbols of Christ's passion. Yet the unique emphases of this service—the institution of the Lord's Supper, the act of footwashing, and the preparation for Christ's death—may also be highlighted on banners, vestments, and the like. Since the visual environment should suggest a quiet and reflective intimacy, not a large-scale festival, this should also be reflected in the choice of music for the service.

Gathering of the Congregation

Call to Worship

This is the day that Christ, the Lamb of God, gave himself into the hands of those who would slay him.

This is that day that Christ gathered with his disciples in the Upper Room.

This is the day that Christ took a towel and washed his disciples' feet,
giving us an example that we should do to others as he has done to us.

This is the day that Christ our God gave us this holy feast,
that we who eat this bread and drink this cup may here proclaim
his holy sacrifice and be partakers of his resurrection

and at the last day may reign with him in heaven.[35]

LEADER: Taste and see that the Lord is good.

PEOPLE: **Happy are all who take refuge in him.**

LEADER: Let us bring our praise to God.

Commentary: Each line of this call to worship may be read by a different reader from within the congregation. The first several lines (up to "Taste and see. . .") need not be printed for the congregation.

Entrance Prayer

LEADER: Let us pray.

PEOPLE: **Lord Jesus, we worship you and offer you now the prayers of our hearts. Help us to enter the spirit of the Upper Room that we may be confronted by your presence and the depth of your love for us. Then prepare our hearts to be fed at your holy table that we may be bound to you in your suffering, that we may be raised with you into a new life. Amen.**

Greeting

PASTOR: Grace to you and peace from God our Father and the Lord Jesus Christ.

Hymn: "Go to Dark Gethsemane"

ACT OF PENITENCE

Call to Confession

LEADER: People of God, we gather to meet our Savior. We must come with humility and honesty to meet our Lord. Let us then confess our sins to God.

Prayer of Confession

LEADER: Almighty God, we have promised our love and renewed commitment to you, especially in this season of penitence [or season of Lent]. Instead, we have proven to be disobedient and ungrateful. We have promised our love and servanthood to each other. Instead, we have sown seeds of hate, envy, bitterness. We have promised to live in the power of our Lord, Jesus

Christ. Instead, we have listened to the powers of darkness. For the sake of your Son, Jesus Christ, the suffering and humble servant, forgive us, we pray, and renew us in his power. Amen.

Declaration of Pardon

LEADER: (reads Romans 5:8)
Therefore, people of God, we are assured that our sins are forgiven, that we are brought to new life in Christ.

PEOPLE: **Thanks be to God.**

The Passing of the Peace

LEADER: With the joy of knowing his love, let us greet each other in Jesus name.

PEOPLE: **(to each other) The peace of Jesus Christ be with you.**

LITURGY OF THE WORD

Prayer for Illumination

PEOPLE: **We are gathered now as the people of God, redeemed by Jesus' blood. Inspire us, Lord, by your example, that we may be the body of Christ, for each other and for our world. Amen.**

Scripture Readings

Old Testament: Exodus 12:1-14
Psalm: 89

Commentary: The Psalm may be sung by the choir or congregation. Musical resources for singing the Psalms are included in the commentary on the Pentecost service in this series.

New Testament: John 13:1-15; 1 Corinthians 11:23-26

Sermon

RESPONSES TO THE WORD

Act of Servanthood—The Footwashing

Commentary: For centuries, Christians remembered the powerful symbol of Jesus' servanthood by re-enacting the ritual of footwashing in communal worship. This serves as a powerful witness

The Chalice and Cross. The agony in Gethsemane is often represented by the use of a jeweled chalice from which a small cross with a pointed end emerges. The reference is to our Lord's prayer concerning the cup of suffering (see Luke 22:42).

of Jesus' humility as he approached his death. Congregations who do not traditionally re-enact this ritual may find this suggestion to interfere with the spirit of Maundy Thursday worship for many reasons. Worship planners in such congregations may wish instead to read the Gospel account of the footwashing, to ask for the members of the congregation to pledge their humility and servanthood toward each other, and to sing an appropriate hymn (see below.) In other congregations, the pastor may wish to share in this ritual with a few members. Either of these two means can introduce the congregation to the importance of this gesture given to us by Jesus, perhaps allowing for a more participatory use of the ritual in future years.

Introduction

LEADER: Fellow servants of our Lord Jesus Christ: On the night before his death, Jesus set an example for his disciples by washing their feet, an act of humble service. He taught that strength and growth in the kingdom of God come not by power, authority, or even miracle, but by such lowly service.

PASTOR: (If the pastor is to wash) We all need to remember his example, but none stand more in need to this reminder than those who the Lord has called to the ordained ministry. Therefore, I invite you who share in the royal priesthood of Christ to come forward that I may recall whose servant I am by following the example of my Master.

PASTOR: (If the representatives of the congregation are to wash) We need to remember the example of our Lord and model ourselves after his humility and servanthood. We come forward now, and in the act of this ceremony, we recall that we are servants of our Lord and of each other.

Come, remembering his admonition that what will be done for you is also to be done by you to others, for "a servant is not greater than his master, nor is one who is sent greater than the one who sent him. If you know these things, blessed are you if you do them."[36]

LEADER: The Lord Jesus, after he had eaten supper with his disciples and washed their feet, said to them, "Do you know what I, your Lord, and Master, have done to you? I have given you an example, that you should do as I have done.

PEOPLE: **Peace is my last gift to you, my own peace I now leave with you; peace which the world cannot give, I give to you.**

LEADER: I give you a new commandment: love one another as I have loved you.

PEOPLE: **Peace is my last gift to you, my own peace I now leave with you; peace which the world cannot give, I give to you.**

LEADER: By this shall the world know that you are my disciples: that you have love for one another.[37]

The Ritual (people come forward)

Commentary: The footwashing should be conducted in a place clearly visible to the congregation. Small children may be invited forward to witness and participate in the ceremony.

If the congregation is too large to have all participate in this ceremony, representatives of the people may be chosen to participate. Some worshipers may be designated to serve as footwashers for others. Otherwise, each worshiper may wash the feet of the person next to them.

Materials needed for footwashing include only a basin, towels, and several pitchers of warm water. Footwashers should kneel before the person whose feet they are washing, assist in the removal of footwear, pour water from the basin over the foot, which should be extended over the basin, and then towel dry the foot.

Hymn: "Where Charity and Love Prevail" (Ubi Caritas) or "They Will Know We Are Christians by Our Love"

Commentary: The hymn "Where Charity and Love Prevail" has been traditionally associated for centuries with the Gospel account of Christ's footwashing. Several fine choral and vocal solo settings of this text are available.

Act of Intercession

LEADER: Almighty and loving God, your Son, Jesus Christ, gave us a model of true humility and servanthood. Through your Spirit, work within us we pray:
that we may be servants to each other in this church,
that we may be servants to the community that surrounds this church,
that we, as members of the worldwide church, may be servants to our world.

Commentary: Each of these phrases may be followed by a period of silence or by spoken prayers offered by various members of the congregation which elaborate on these themes.

LEADER: As our Savior has taught us, we pray:
PEOPLE: **Our Father, who art in heaven . . .**

Act of Offering

LEADER: (reads 2 Corinthians 8:9)
PEOPLE: **Let us bring our gifts to our Lord.**

THE EUCHARIST

Commentary: The following Communion liturgy is organized around the phrases used by the

Gospel writers to describe Jesus' actions at the Last Supper. Though often unnoticed, almost all Communion liturgies follow this pattern of taking the elements, giving thanks, breaking the bread, and sharing the elements. Using these as headings in the Communion liturgy calls to the attention of the worshiper the intimate connection between the continuing celebration of the sacrament and Jesus' institution of it. While these divisions may be used anytime the Lord's Supper is celebrated, they are especially appropriate for use on Maundy Thursday.

The structure of the Communion liturgy may be highlighted by having a voice other than the worship leader read each of the headings included in the following liturgy.

JESUS TOOK BREAD AND WINE

Presentation of the Communion Elements

Commentary: Both the gifts collected during the offertory and the elements for Communion may be brought forward at this time.

Invitation to the Table

LEADER: Every time you eat of the bread and drink of the cup, you proclaim the Lord's death, until he comes. People of God, let us join now in proclaiming the death of God's humble and suffering servant, our Lord Jesus Christ.

JESUS GAVE THANKS

Great Prayer of Thanksgiving

LEADER: The Lord be with you.
PEOPLE: **And also with you.**
LEADER: Lift up your hearts.
PEOPLE: **We lift them up to the Lord.**
LEADER: Let us give thanks to the Lord, our God.
PEOPLE: **It is right to give our thanks and praise.**
LEADER: It is truly right for us to offer our praise to you, Lord God Almighty. You have created this world and rule over it through Jesus Christ, our Lord. You have made us in your image and freed us from slavery to the power of sin.

You claimed us as your people and made a covenant with us, first with Israel and then with all who called on the name of Jesus Christ. Therefore, we praise you and join the heavenly hosts in singing to the glory of your name:
PEOPLE: **Holy, holy, holy Lord, God of power and might,**
heaven and earth are full of your glory.
Hosanna in the highest.
Blessed is he who comes in the name of the Lord.
Hosanna in the highest.

Commentary: Most hymnals include a setting of this traditional canticle. For a list of service music found in a representative group of hymnals, consult the commentary on the Communion liturgy of the Advent service in this series.

LEADER: We offer our thanks and praise for Jesus Christ, our Lord, who came to live among us, to serve us in humility, and to deliver us from our slavery to sin. His passion and death gave payment for our sins that we may share in the glory of life everlasting. He sustains us in this life by humility, which he modeled in his life, by his gift to us of this feast, and by sending to us the Holy Spirit to comfort and strengthen us. By these gifts, we are able to long for the life to come when we will again feast with him at his table. For all these gifts, praise be to you, Lord Jesus Christ.

Commentary: References to Christ's life and passion that were mentioned in the sermon may be incorporated into this section of the Prayer of Thanksgiving.

Institution

LEADER: The Lord Jesus, on the night when he was betrayed, took bread, and when he had given thanks, he broke it and said, "This is my body, which is for you; do this in remembrance of me." In the same way, he took the cup after supper, saying, "This cup is the new covenant in my blood; do this, whenever you drink it, in remembrance of me." For whenever you eat this bread and drink this cup, you proclaim the Lord's death until he comes.

Response

PEOPLE: **We shall do as our Lord commands. As we share in this feast, we proclaim that Jesus Christ was sent by the Father into the world, that he was condemned to die that we might live, that he rose again in power, and that he will come again in glory.**

JESUS BROKE THE BREAD AND POURED THE CUP . . .

Prayer of Consecration

PASTOR: Eternal God, pour out your Spirit upon us, we pray. May these gifts of bread and wine be for us a communion with the body and blood of Jesus Christ. May they unite us with each other as fellow servants of Jesus Christ and allow us to know more fully the joy of knowing him. Amen.

Breaking of the Bread and Pouring of the Cup

Commentary: The following sentences are spoken as the minister breaks the common loaf and pours the wine or juice into the common cup.

PASTOR: The bread which we break is a sharing in the body of Christ.
PEOPLE: **We who are many are one body, for we all share the same loaf.**
PASTOR: The cup for which we give thanks is a sharing in the blood of Christ.
PEOPLE: **The cup which we drink is our participation in the blood of Christ.**

Hymn

Lamb of God, you take away the sins of the world, have mercy upon us.
Lamb of God, you take away the sins of the world, have mercy upon us.
Lamb of God, you take away the sins of the world, grant us your peace.

Commentary: This hymn at the breaking of the bread is set to numerous musical settings. It is often identified by its Latin name, Agnus Dei, and is appropriate for use in every service in the Christian year, either following the breaking of bread or during the sacrament.

Invitation

PASTOR: Friends in Christ, the Lord has prepared his table for his church. All who love him and trust in him alone for their salvation are now invited to come to the table of the Lord.
PEOPLE: **We come with gladness. Thanks be to God!**
PASTOR: The gifts of God for the people of God.

. . . AND GAVE IT TO HIS DISCIPLES

Sacrament

PASTOR: (as the people take the bread) Take eat, remember and believe that the body of the Lord Jesus Christ was given for the complete remission of all our sins.
PASTOR: (as the people take the cup) Take, drink, remember and believe that the precious blood of our Lord Jesus Christ was shed for the complete forgiveness of all our sins.

Commentary: Many congregations choose to alter their means of distribution of the Communion elements on Maundy Thursday, serving the elements to worshipers who are seated at tables. This method emphasizes the congregation's fellowship and mutual servanthood at the table and recalls the intimacy of the Last Supper itself.

During the sacrament, appropriate instrumental, choral, or solo music may be played or sung, or the congregation may sing a series of Communion hymns. Preference should be given to texts that focus on the events in the Upper Room and the appropriate attitudes of humility and servanthood that are central to Christ's sacrifice and to the church.

Response: "What Wondrous Love Is This"

Commentary: If the stripping of the church follows Communion, then only the first verse of this hymn should be sung.

Benediction

PASTOR: As Christ has loved you, love one another. And may God's peace attend you. Amen.

Stripping of the Church
Psalm 22

Commentary: Many congregations prepare for Good Friday by closing their Maundy Thursday service with the removal of all banners, paraments, and candles from the worship space. During this time, Psalm 22 may be read. It should be read slowly and quietly. Following this, worshipers should leave the worship space in silence.

Dispersal of the Congregation (in silence)

John D. Witvliet

254 ✦ A CREATIVE MAUNDY THURSDAY SERVICE

The creative Maundy Thursday service can be used in free-church and more informal traditions of worship. Adapt to local usage and style.

─────────── **Basic Pattern** ───────────

ENTRANCE
Scripture: Genesis 1:1-5a; John 1:1-5
Hymn of Invocation: "O Splendor of God's Glory Bright" (Ambrose of Milan)
Prayer
Hymn of Confession: "Jesus Thou Joy of Loving Hearts" (Bernard of Clairvaux)
Response: Romans 8:33-35a, 38-39
Congregation: "Alleluia" (Taizé)

SERVICE OF THE WORD
Scripture: Isaiah 42:1-9; Psalm 143; John 3:17-21; Matthew 26:6-13
Responsorial Prayer
Passing of the Peace

CELEBRATION OF THE TABLE
Scripture: John 13:1-17
Hymn: "The Song of the Supper" (Iona)
Scripture: Matthew 26:26-29
Prayer
Communion

DISMISSAL
Scripture: Matthew 26:36-56; John 9:4-5
(The congregation will depart in silence.)

─────────── **Full Text** ───────────

Worship Space. The altar or Communion table can be laid with a purple cloth, its only adornment being a dimly lit lantern and three unit candles. If the walls of the worship center can accommodate candles, unlit candles could also be placed along the walls. Banners for Lent/Holy Week can also be used.

Entrance. The Scriptures shown below will be read antiphonally by two readers from the front of the sanctuary. As they are being read, a server will slowly proceed to the altar, carrying a Christ candle, from which the other candles will be lit. Depending upon the number of candles available, the lights in the church can also be turned up as the candles are lit.

> Genesis 1:1-2
> John 1:1-3b
> (pause)
> Genesis 1:3-4a
> John 1:3c-4
> (pause)
> Genesis 1:4b-5a
> John 1:5
> (pause)

Hymn of Invocation: "O Splendor of God's Glory Bright" (Ambrose of Milan)

Opening Prayer

ALL: Blessed Father, gracious Son, and Holy Spirit, eternal Trinity, eternal light, we pray you would grace us with your presence during this hour. We pray that during our worship, your light would further penetrate our darkness, into spaces and thoughts that have heretofore remained shrouded. We pray for this for the sake of your kingdom, your glory, and our salvation. Amen.

LEADER: One of the liberating joys of worship is that worship brings us together with two millennia of believers who came, week after week, as we do, expressing their gratitude for God's salvation as well as their need of God's extension of mercy, love, and forgiveness. As a confession of both our contribution and our desire, let us join our spirits with the saints of ages past and sing the following hymn together.

Hymn of Confession: "Jesus, Thou Joy of Loving Hearts" (attr. Bernard of Clairvaux)

Leader's Response: Romans 8:33-35a, 38-39

Congregation's Response: "Alleluia" (Taizé)

SERVICE OF THE WORD
Scripture:

Old Testament: Isaiah 42:1-9

> CANTOR: The Lord calls us in righteousness.
> PEOPLE: **Lord, teach us the way.**

Responsorial Psalm: Psalm 143

> CANTOR: Lord, our spirit grows weak and faint.
> PEOPLE: **Revive us that we may serve you.**

Gospel Reading: John 3:17-21

> CANTOR: Lord, teach us the deeds of light,
> PEOPLE: **That we may do our deed in God.**

(silent prayer)

> CANTOR: Let us listen in order to receive the deeds of the light, that we might hear our call (reads Matthew 26:6-13).

(As the Gospel is being read, a woman will slowly proceed to the altar/Communion table. In the open palms of her outstretched hands, she will carry a bottle of [scented] anointing oil, which she will place on the altar/table.)

Responsorial Prayer

> LEADER: God's first act after creating the heavens and earth was to bring light.
> The prophets prophesied that God was going to send a light to the Gentiles, and Jesus came as a light to the world. When the woman of Bethany anointed Jesus' head, she offered a humble service to the light that was soon to be extinguished.
> We are called to perform the deeds of the light. During the worship, one

such service is to offer prayers for those whose light in life is precarious or will soon die. With the oil of God's Holy Spirit, let us jointly anoint these ones.

As we pray together, let us imagine ourselves, each with our own bottle of anointing oil, touching those for whom we are praying, or perhaps signing their foreheads with the sign of the cross. Many of these intercessions will apply to persons in this congregation.

Let us intercede together.

> LEADER: For all leaders of politically troubled countries,
> ALL: **We anoint each one with God's spirit of justice and light.**
> LEADER: For all families who suffer from political oppression,
> ALL: **We anoint each one with God's spirit of hope and light.**
> LEADER: For all those whose soul is being extinguished by the drives of power and greed,
> ALL: **We anoint each one with God's spirit of repentance and light.**
> LEADER: For all those who are dying of terminal illnesses,
> ALL: **We anoint each one with your spirit of comfort and light.**
> LEADER: For all those who are now saying good-bye to a beloved friend or family member,
> ALL: **We anoint each one with God's spirit of presence and light.**
> LEADER: For all those who see suicide as the only solution to their troubles,
> ALL: **We anoint each one with God's spirit of hope and pray God to fan a flame of light.**
> LEADER: For all those who are being consumed by poverty,
> ALL: **We anoint each one with God's spirit of comfort and the light of protection.**
> LEADER: For all those who are living lives of quiet desperation,
> ALL: **We anoint each one with God's healing spirit of peace and light.**

(silence)

LEADER: Let us seal our prayer with a hymn of faith.

Hymn: "God of Creation, All-Powerful" (Clarkson)

LEADER: The peace of Christ that we have extended through our prayers, let us now extend to one another.

Passing of the Peace

Celebration of the Table

Scripture: John 13:1-17

(As the Gospel is being read, a server will slowly proceed to the front of the sanctuary, carrying a laver and, draped over the arm, a white towel. The server will place these on the altar/Communion table.)

(pause)

LEADER: One of Jesus' last messages, taught by this powerful example, was that those of us who choose to follow him must become servants of one another. We are called to follow Jesus by serving those whom he came to save. But when the call comes, we realize that few of us can do this.

The daily calling of servanthood is one of the avenues God has provided to help draw us out of our darkness and into God's light. But in order to persevere along the tunnel of our darkness, we need God's constant nurture and forgiveness, and the hope of light.

On the night on which he was betrayed, Jesus provided the nurture, on the cross he provided the forgiveness, and through the Resurrection, he provided the light.

Hymn: "The Song of the Supper" (Iona)

Scripture: Matthew 26:26-29

(The servers will have memorized the Scriptures and will then proclaim their text as they slowly proceed to the altar/Communion table, carrying the bread and the wine. One will recite verses 26 and 29, the other, 27 and 28.)

Prayer (in unison):

Our loving God and Father,
We bless you
    that from the beginning of time,
    you have been calling your people
    out of the darkness of our human condition
    and into the light of your saving life.
We bless you
    that Jesus entered our darkness
    and wore it as his garment,
    that he exchanged the raiment of the starry heavens
    for the raiment of darkest death.
We bless you in this bread and this wine
    you are both calling us
    and enabling us
    to walk the path of your Son.
We pray that you would consecrate this bread and wine
    that in our partaking
We would be filled with the life of Christ
    that Christ's life would lighten our darkness,
    that Christ's blood would purify and invigorate us
    to follow his example of loving service in this our world.

Communion

(During the final half of Communion, the congregation may begin singing.)

Hymn: "Christ Is the World's Light" (Green)

(pause)

Scripture: Matthew 26:36-56

(As the final portion of the text is being read, the candles should be extinguished one at a time, each snuff corresponding to an action in the text, e.g., the arrival of Judas, the kiss, the arrest, etc. If lights were also used during the service, they should likewise be slowly and completely dimmed so that the only remaining light is that of the Christ candle on the altar/Communion table, which will be extinguished immediately after the reading of John 9:4-5.

While one attendant is seeing to the candles, another should be removing the banners as well as any other liturgical symbols, leaving the worship center as stark as possible.)

(All these actions will be done in silence.)

(pause)

(In the darkened room the following verses will be read, serving as a final cry and as a closing recapitulation of the theme of the service:)

Scripture: John 9:4-5

(The Christ candle is quickly blown out, leaving the room in near darkness. People will leave, without dismissal, with only the very dim lantern lighting the darkness.)

─────── **Commentary** ───────

Preamble. The Maundy Thursday service, traditionally and historically, can include any of several possible foci, so rich is the significance of the day. It marks the remembrance of the woman who risked shame and ridicule in order to anoint Jesus with her costly perfume; it marks the institution of the Lord's Supper, Jesus' final meal shared with his disciples; it marks Jesus' example that all who are called to follow him in discipleship are called to become servants; and it marks Jesus' betrayal by Judas and Peter's later denial of Jesus.

The accompanying service is a prayer service, drawing our attention to Jesus, who has come as the light of the world, a light that is soon to be extinguished. The service has a chiasmatic outline: light-service-Eucharist-service-light.

We begin by focusing our attention on the God of light—the light of creation and the light of Christ. In the light of Christ, we discover his message: servanthood. The Eucharist then comes to us as God's enabling gift, propelling us outward, in servanthood, to bring God's redeeming light. However, the close of this service has a surprise ending, bringing confusion to the call. As the light goes out, we are forced to wait; with no light, we have no message. Unless the light is somehow rekindled, we will have nothing to bring to the world but good and kindly teaching. In company with Jesus' disciples, we now enter and wait out three eternal days of darkness.

Worship Space. As the congregation enters the worship center, they will find it very dimly lit. The quiet peacefulness of the sanctuary will help the congregation to prepare themselves for the service. The light is dimmed. Why? they might ask. The question is partly answered by the opening Scriptures. The rest of the answer comes at the close of the service.

If the church has used banners for Lent and Holy Week, these can continue to enrich the worship of this service.

The Communion table will be largely unadorned. During the service, attendants will bring forward the oil (perfume), basin, and Communion elements. The act of bringing these elements into the service, rather than simply providing them, symbolically tells us that we are likewise called, with the disciples, to bring these signs and services into the world.

Entrance. The entrance of the service reminds the people that light has not always been present in our world. God brought light in creation, and Christ later came bringing light to our spirit, so we begin by celebrating that light. (By contrast, the close of the service—with Jesus' arrest and imminent death—will be more powerful and compelling and will appropriately lead the congregation into the starkness of Good Friday.) As we continue our approach to worship, the hymns and confessions lead us to seek further evidence of this light in our lives.

Service of the Word. During this portion of the service, you might also choose to substitute or add a brief homily. Depending upon the size of the congregation and the formality of its usual worship, following upon the reading of Matthew 26, the congregation could be invited to pray for one another. Those who wish to do so could come forward in company with fellow parishioners, dip their finger into the anointing oil, and then anoint and pray for one another. Others could be invited to prayerfully participate from their seats. While prayer is taking place, the congregation could be lead in some quiet songs of hope and intercession.

If you wish to retain the guided prayer service, you could easily include more personal petitions that would relate to needs connected to your congregation and its extended ministries.

Service of the Table. Prior to receiving Communion and following upon the reading from John 13 (again, depending upon the factors of size and formality mentioned above), the church could take part in a foot-washing service, with the leaders beginning by washing the feet of those who are subject to their leadership.

As an alternative to the literal foot-washing service, the Communion service could be carried out in a fashion whereby the participants come to the table, take a large piece of bread, and then go and share their bread with another member, can pray for them, or in serving them, express gratitude for them. Once the bread has been shared, the congregation can come forward to receive from the one cup. The members are scattered in service while extending the body of Christ, then are joined as they receive the cup.

Any of the above actions embodies Jesus' teaching on servanthood and would powerfully emphasize Christ's concern that we follow him in this manner.

Dismissal. We cannot be dismissed on this Maundy Thursday with the usual joy. Our Lord is about to be betrayed, denied, and crucified. But a picture is worth more than a directive.

The Matthean text matter-of-factly tells us the unfolding of events. We need no further explanation. The extinguishing of the candles draws into the possible emotions that would have been felt on that night so long ago as the unraveling of events began.

Then Jesus is taken. The disciples flee. What would we have done? Like the disciples then, we have little choice now but to wait and pray. In the darkness.

Diane S. George Ayer

255 ✦ A Convergence Maundy Thursday Service

This convergence Maundy Thursday service is presented for those congregations that seek to bring traditional and contemporary forms of worship together.

If a special or different style of worship service is going to take place, the front of the sanctuary could be redecorated to take on the appearance of the Upper Room. A long table with different Passover foods could be placed on the table, and all of the worship activities then would be focused on that particular arrangement.

Several options are available on ways to celebrate this most important event.

(1) **Passover Meal.** Many books and other resources with complete commentary are available for churches that desire to celebrate the meal.

Members of local synagogues or Messianic congregations can be very helpful in learning some of the fine points of this feast.

(2) **Living Lord's Supper.** Through narrative, drama, and dialogue, some churches have put on a Maundy Thursday drama of the Upper Room. As Jesus and the disciples dramatize the institution of Holy Communion, the whole congregation participates with the actors on the platform.

(3) **Walk through of the Stations of the Cross.** For those churches who do not have the stations of the cross already depicted, graphic representations are posted throughout the church, and the people are invited to move from station to station with a guide to Scripture readings, meditations, and prayer for each one. At the end, Communion may be received.

(4) **Dramatized Stations of the Cross.** (This is a tremendous youth project!) A group of people dramatically form each of the stations of the cross with accompanying commentary and direction for prayer and meditation. At the end, all share in Communion.

(5) **Come-and-Go Communion.** Very popular in recent years, the church sets up for Communion, and a minister waits in the sanctuary for those who desire to commune. As each person or family enters, they receive a guide who takes them through several Scripture readings, a spiritual inventory, prayer of confession, and Communion meditation. The minister then serves them as they come to receive.

(6) **Maundy Thursday Communion Celebration.** A full service with several special activities included.

Order of Service

ACTS OF ENTRANCE

Processional

Commentary: Any processional should be simple and low-key. The ministers and any others that are processing can come in silently or with a hymn.

Words of Invitation
Come, praise the Lord, for in his rich and
great mercy he has prepared a feast for us.
I will bless the Lord at all times. His
praise shall be continually on my lips.
Come and sit with him at the table of blessing.
I will open the door of my heart that I

may eat with him and he with me.
Come, let us praise the Lord together!
Yes, let us praise the Lord!

Acts of Praise and Worship

Commentary: If a footwashing service is to be held later in the service, this section may be shortened and more worship offered during the time of footwashing.

MINISTRY OF THE WORD

Prayer

ALL: **Almighty Father, whose own Son, Jesus Christ, met with his disciples on the night of his betrayal and instituted the holy sacrament of his body and blood: Grant that we who partake of these holy emblems may receive them with thankful hearts, knowing that through his death and passion, we have been given everlasting life; through Jesus Christ our Lord, who now lives and reigns with you and the Holy Spirit, one God, now and forever. Amen.**

Readings

First Reading: Exodus 12:1-14a
Psalm 78:14-20, 23-25
Second Reading: 1 Corinthians 11:23-26
Gospel Reading: John 13:1-15 or Luke 22:14-30

Footwashing Service

Commentary: Following the readings, the church may have a footwashing service for everyone or for selected representatives if the church is too large. After the washing of someone's feet, other expressions of love and support can be spontaneously offered. This part of the service needs no commentary and can either be done in silence or with singing.

MINISTRY AT THE TABLE

Commentary: The following prayers of thanksgiving pick up the themes of Maundy Thursday. Silence should be kept.

Great Thanksgiving

LEADER: The Lord be with you.
ALL: **And also with you.**
LEADER: Lift up your hearts.

ALL: **We lift them to the Lord.**
LEADER: Let us give thanks to the Lord our God.
ALL: **It is right to give our thanks and praise.**
LEADER: We give you thanks, O God, through your beloved Servant, Jesus Christ, who was heralded as king and welcomed into the city of his death and passion. It is he whom you have sent in these last times, becoming like us, that he might save us and redeem us, and be the messenger of your will. He is your Word, inseparable from you, through whom you made all things and in whom you take delight. And so, with your people on earth and all the company of heaven, we praise your name and join their unending hymn:
ALL: (singing)
Holy, holy, holy Lord, God of power and might, heaven and earth are full of your glory. Hosanna in the highest. Blessed is he who comes in the name of the Lord. Hosanna in the highest.
LEADER: You sent him from heaven into the Virgin's womb, where he was conceived and took flesh. Born of the Holy Spirit and the Virgin. He was revealed as your Son.

Having walked in sinless obedience, he gathered his disciples on the night before his crucifixion and prepared them for his suffering and death. In fulfillment of your will.

He stretched out his hands in suffering to release from suffering those who place their hope in you, and so he won for you a holy people. Of his own free choice, he was handed over to his passion in order to make an end of death and to shatter the chains of the evil one; to trample underfoot the powers of hell and to lead the righteous into light; to establish boundaries of death and to manifest the Resurrection.

And so on this night in which he was betrayed he instituted a holy sacrament, which he commanded we continue until his coming again. He took bread, and after giving thanks to you, he broke it and gave it to his disciples, saying, "Take and eat; this is my body which is broken for you." In the same way, after supper he took the cup; after he had given thanks, he gave it to them, saying, "This is my blood of the new covenant, which is shed for you. When you do this, you do it in memory of me."

ALL: **Remembering, therefore, his birth, his death and resurrection, and his coming again in glory, we offer you this bread and cup, thankful that you have counted us worthy to stand in your presence and to show you priestly service.**

LEADER: We entreat you to send your Holy Spirit upon the offering of the holy church. Gather into one all who share in these sacred mysteries, filling them with the Holy Spirit and confirming their faith in the truth, that together we may praise you and give you glory through your Servant, Jesus Christ. And now with the confidence of the children of God, let us pray: (here the Lord's Prayer is said)

ALL: **All glory and honor is yours, Father and Son, with the Holy Spirit, in the holy church, now and forever. Amen.**

Prayer after Communion

ALL: **Heavenly Father, on this holy eve we thank you for the remembrance of your Son, Jesus Christ, which we have received in partaking of this bread and wine. Make this night, for us, a memorial of his death and passion, which was sealed by his resurrection. This we ask through Jesus Christ our Lord. Amen.**

Tenebrae, or Stripping of the Church

Commentary: A Tenebrae (which means "shadows") service, or the stripping of the church, may follow Communion. Here, people are instructed in the removal of all hangings, all furnishings on the altar, and all candles. The sanctuary is left barren until the Easter Vigil on Saturday evening.

Randolph W. Sly

256 ◆ A DANCE FOR MAUNDY THURSDAY

The dance below is meant to express a note of joy in an otherwise sober service. The expression of joy in a service of sobriety reminds us of the gospel that is always present, even in the darkest moment.

Every day we should move as the resurrected body of Christ. Every Holy Thursday celebration should incorporate the joy of the Resurrection, even as we remember the crosses ahead; for the cross itself has meaning only in the context of Resurrection. The celebrational joy of the Lord's Supper moves us beyond ourselves and out into the world. The following simple historic Jewish and Christian dance patterns may be used with many of the hymns planned for the Maundy Thursday celebration. The Christian tripudium dance pattern is especially helpful to incarnate the recessional hymn of the celebration. The following descriptive material on the biblical and historical uses of dance in worship could be incorporated in the homily or presented as instructions just before the congregation is invited to do (or watch) the dances that embody our faithful response to setbacks or hardships.

Dancing is particularly appropriate during Maundy Thursday celebrations because such celebrations are popularly associated with the Jewish Passover. The very word _Passover_ (_pesach_ in Hebrew) means "leaping" or "limping." Scholars conclude that such limping dances were a part of the original Israelite celebrations. They recall the Passover conditions prior to the Exodus experience. Such limping, or mourning, dances were common in Near Eastern religions and recalled the slavery condition of the people before their exodus to freedom. (C. H. Toy, "The Meaning of Pesach," _The Journal of Biblical Literature_ 16 [1897]: 178–79; and Theodor H. Gaster, _Passover, Its History and Traditions_ [Boston: Beacon, 1968], 23–25.)

This pesach dance is appropriate for those who are without hope and those who are utterly dependent—people for whom God has not yet acted decisively. A likely recreation of this dance step is outlined by Jewish dance expert Florence Freehold:

1. Step forward with the right foot.
2. Flex the right knee.
3. Draw the left toes up to the right heel as the right knee is straightened.
4. Step forward with the right foot and continue repeating this limping sequence. (Florence Freehol, *Jews Are a Dancing People* [San Francisco: Stark-Rath Publishing, 1954], 56.)

Dancers moving in a circle may demonstrate this limping dance as the speaker continues to provide background information such as the following discussion.

In an effort to disassociate themselves from surrounding Near Eastern religions, Israelites eventually rejected all mourning dances and used only joyful dances in worship. The only other instance of mourning dance (pesach) in the Old Testament is the dance done by the priests of Baal mocked by the prophet Elijah (1 Kings 18:28). That Baal dance was mournful for it was based on a belief that the world's problems were traceable to God being asleep or away. Until the return of God, there was little the people could do except the mourning dance. The Israelites eventually rejected the mourning dance and embraced only joyful dances. This expressed a belief that the world's problems were traceable to the fact that people were asleep to God, who was very much alive and active for them. The joyful dance was to wake the people up to all that they could do. (For a detailed study of these shifting emphases in Jewish dance, see Doug Adams, *Congregational Dancing in Christian Worship* [Austin, Tex.: The Sharing Company, 1977], especially pp. 83–94 on "Jewish Rejoiceful Dance and Recognition of Possibility.") Christianity followed in the Jewish tradition and stressed a joyful dance pattern used whenever hymns were sung in worship.

The homily or instruction would climax with the introduction of the joyful tripudium dance, which contrasts strongly with the mourning Pesach step. It is this simple tripudium dance step that all would be invited to join in doing as they move out of the church singing the recessional hymn at the end of the celebration. The tripudium dance step was the most common dance step in Christian church processions and recessions for a thousand years. It fits with any hymn of 2/4, 3/4, or 4/4 time. *Tripudium* means literally "three-step" and comes to be translated "jubilation" because of the joy it produces in those who do it. To do this dance, simply take three steps forward and one back, three steps forward and one back, time after time. People did not do this step in a single file or in a circle. Rather they did it in processions with many abreast, with arms linked in row after row. They would move through the streets and into the church, around inside the church during the hymns of the service, and then they would go back through the streets as a recessional. Moving three, four, or more abreast with arms linked makes this step much easier to do. One can hardly fall behind. This manner of dance, which has the character of a march that does not simply go in circles, is more reflective of a faith that believes in a God of history rather than of a view that sees the world caught forever in its own cyclical return. Taking three steps forward and one back, three steps forward and one back, time after time, leads to a spirit that sees setbacks in the context of forward progress. (For a more complete history of the tripudium step in Christian worship, see Adams, *Congregational Dancing*, 19–20, 96–97.)

A most effective closing to a Maundy Thursday worship combines a meaningful gesture of benediction within the context of a joyful recessional use of the tripudium step. Through this dance, people sense a heightening of community, repentance, rejoicing, and rededication. The music leaders begin singing the recessional hymn (e.g., the simple "Alleluia" by Richard Horn as contained in *Gather 'Round*, edited by Paul F. Page and available through the Modern Liturgy Bookstore). After the congregation has joined in the singing and can continue without needing to look at any song sheets, the dancers and music leaders begin moving (with the tripudium step) around and around the altar Communion table as they continue singing. They do this not in single file, nor in rows of two or three abreast with arms linked, although the latter method is an alternative way of recessing. Instead, they move as a massed group. Each person places a hand on the shoulder of one person ahead of them (as a gesture of benediction). After they have moved around the altar this way for a time, one or more of them invite others in the congregation to join them as they continue to move around the altar. After a few more times around the altar, they move through the aisles of the church signaling others to join them in the singing and in the recessional, as all move out of the church.

Doug Adams[38]

257 ❖ A DRAMA FOR MAUNDY THURSDAY

The following drama could be used in a gathering on Maundy Thursday, perhaps during a preservice congregational meal or in conjunction with reading the Scripture lessons during worship.

The story line, a device to employ the dramatic and living aspect of this liturgy of the Word, is formed by a line of children divided into two groups—Chorus One and Chorus Two. The story line forms a circle around the story center. Within the circle will be the story figures. They may be children of the same age, older children, even adults. Simplicity is important. The bodily positions and movements take precedence over production. All participants in the liturgy, if the group is small enough, can be involved in the story line with their responses printed on a song sheet. The content for this dramatic liturgy is based on the three readings for Holy Thursday and incorporates the actual scriptural texts.

PART ONE

(Within the circle are MOSES, AARON, and VOICE OF GOD—a person on a box or standing to one side. The action and props may all be pantomimed. MOSES and AARON are on their knees, hands folded and heads bowed in prayer.)

CHORUS ONE: "It is a Passover in honor of Yahweh" (Exod. 12:11).

CHORUS TWO: "This day is to be a day of remembrance for you" (Exod. 12:14).

CHORUS ONE: "It is a Passover in honor of Yahweh." But who is Yahweh? And what is Passover?

CHORUS TWO: "This is to be a day of remembrance for you." Let's listen to the story to learn what God wants us to do.

VOICE OF GOD: "Speak to the whole community of Israel" (Exod. 12:3). "I will go through the land of Egypt and strike down all the first-born in the land of Egypt, man and beast alike, and I shall deal out punishment to all the gods of Egypt, I am Yahweh!" (Exod. 12:12).

MOSES: (rising, looking heavenward, arms raising to outstretched position) Moses, your servant listens. (bows his head and then instructs) "This is Yahweh's message. 'Towards midnight I shall pass through Egypt. All the first-born in the land of Egypt shall die, from the first-born of Pharaoh, heir to his throne, to the first-born of the maidservant at the mill and all the first-born of the cattle '" (Exod. 11:4-5).

CHORUS ONE: Oh no! Oh, no!

CHORUS TWO: Yahweh is God. Why did God do that?

MOSES: "And throughout the land of Egypt there shall be such a wailing as never was heard before, nor will be again. But against the sons of Israel, against man or beast, never a dog shall bark" (Exod. 11:6-7).

AARON: (rising now, like MOSES) Aaron, your servant, listens. This is Yahweh's message. "On the tenth day of this month each man must take an animal from the flock, one for each family." (steps forward holding a sheep in his arms, instructs) "You must keep it 'till the fourteenth day of the month when the whole assembly of the community of Israel shall slaughter it between the two evenings." (He places the animal upon a table. Now speaking slowly, in deliberate, hushed tones) "Some of the blood must then be taken and put on the two doorposts and the lintel of the house where it is eaten." (He places a mark on the door. Then he joins Moses at a table; both begin eating.) "That night the flesh is to eaten with unleavened bread and bitter herbs" (Exod. 12:3-8).

MOSES: (speaking to AARON) "You shall eat it hastily! It is a Passover in honor of Yahweh" (Exod. 12:11).

VOICE OF GOD: (low, reassuring voice) "The blood shall serve to mark the houses that you live in. When I see the blood I will pass over you and you shall escape the destroying plague when I strike the land of Egypt" (Exod. 12:13).

(Allow a few moments to pass unspoken. AARON and MOSES rise, extend hands outward, speaking to everyone.)

AARON: "This day is to be a day of remembrance for you" (Exod. 12:14).

MOSES: "It is a Passover in honor of Yahweh" (Exod. 12:11). "For all generations you are to declare it a day of festival forever" (Exod. 12:14).

CHORUS ONE AND TWO: (All join hands and raise their arms high over their heads) "It is a Passover in honor of Yahweh. This day is to be a day of remembrance for you."

PART TWO

(The story line opens and story figures leave. A song such as "This Is the Day" may be sung while the circle rotates slowly. The figures of JESUS and THE TWELVE enter the circle and sit at a table, apparently eating a meal.)

CHORUS ONE: Jesus was a Jew. Was it a Passover festival he knew?

CHORUS TWO: If he knew the law, what offering would he give?

CHORUS ONE: The Passover was a meal. A gift of himself as the sacrifice would make it real.

JESUS: (He takes some bread, thanks God for it, and breaks it. As he says the words, he looks at each and every one of the Twelve.) "This is my body which is for you. Do this as memorial of me" (1 Cor. 11:24). (He passes the bread to each of the Twelve. They respond, saying "thank you," looking at one another questioningly, or with heads bowed prayerfully—some of each.)

CHORUS ONE: He celebrates the Passover. He gives bread to each and every one.

CHORUS TWO: That is the mark. What will be the plague that is to come?

JESUS: (He pushes the plate away, indicating the end of the meal. He takes the cup

and raises it, again looking at each of his friends.) "This cup is the new covenant in my blood. Whenever you drink it, do this as memorial of me" (1 Cor. 11:25).

THE TWELVE: (in unison, speaking to everyone) "Until the Lord comes, therefore, every time you eat the bread and drink this cup, you are proclaiming his death" (1 Cor. 11:26).

PART THREE

(The story line joins hands and rotates once silently saying:)

CHORUS ONE: "They were at supper" (John 13:2).

CHORUS TWO: "It was before the festival of the Passover" (John 13:1).

JESUS: (He gets us from the table, removes his outer garment, and takes a towel and wraps it around his waist. He then pours water into a basin and begins to wash the disciples' feet and to wipe them with the towel he is wearing.) (John 13:4-5)

(THE TWELVE react with loving gestures, bend forward, hands on Jesus' shoulders.)

SIMON PETER: (one of the Twelve) "Lord, are you going to wash my feet?" (John 13:6).

JESUS: "At the moment you do not know what I am doing, but later you will understand" (John 13:7).

PETER: "Never! You shall never wash my feet" (John 13:8).

JESUS: "If I do not wash you, you can have nothing in common with me" (John 13:8).

PETER: "Then Lord, not only my feet, but my hands and my head as well!" (John 13:9).

JESUS: "No one who has taken a bath needs washing, he is clean all over. You, too, (he looks at some of the others) are clean, though not all of you are." (One of the Twelve looks to the ground) (John 13:10.) (Jesus returns to the table and puts on his clothes again.)

JESUS: "Do you understand what I have done to you?" (John 13:12).

THE TWELVE: (Some nod yes; some nod at each other; some raise their shoulders questioningly.)

JESUS: "You shall call me Master and Lord, and rightly; so I am" (John 13:13).

CHORUS ONE: Master and Lord!

CHORUS TWO: The sacrifice of this Passover meal. The sacrifice is real—Master and Lord, the sacrifice is real.

Author Unknown[39]

✥ TWENTY ✥

Worship on Good Friday

Good Friday has always been a solemn day for prayer, repentance, and the remembrance of Jesus' death on the cross. The resources of this chapter will help congregations understand the meaning of this day of bright sadness and will provide services to order and organize the spiritual journey of the congregation through corporate worship. Adapt these services to local usage and style.

258 ✦ An Introduction to Good Friday Worship

This article traces the most ancient traditions of Good Friday worship. With these in mind, the reader and worship planner will be able to put into context the articles and resources that follow.

In the ancient church, the paschal celebration from Thursday of Holy Week through the great vigil of Saturday night (which ended on Sunday morning) was one ongoing service with occasional breaks.

On the morning of Good Friday, the people paid tribute to the wood of the cross, the instrument upon which our salvation was attained. A casket containing a cross was often placed on a table covered with a linen cloth. The bishop stood behind the table as the people filed by touching and kissing the cross and sometimes bowing before it or lying prostrate in front of it. This was not a worship of the cross but a worship of God, who sent his Son to die on the cross for the salvation of the world.

At noon the people gathered until three o'clock to hear Scripture readings about the passion of our Lord. Scripture readings were taken from the Psalms, the prophets, the Epistles, Acts, and the Gospels. In between these readings, there were prayers and sermons to help guide the devotion of people as they observed the hours when Jesus hung on the cross. At three o'clock the passage from John's Gospel regarding the death of Christ was read.

In the evening, the Christians gathered again to hear the story of the burial of Christ read. Usually a great crowd remained there in vigil all night long.

While these practices are not observed today in the same way they were in the ancient traditions, a new emphasis has emerged stressing the importance of Good Friday as a day of worship. Three services in particular are observed today in various traditions: the Veneration of the Cross; the Way of the Cross; and the Three Hours' Devotion.

Robert E. Webber

259 ✦ The Origin and Meaning of the Veneration of the Cross Service

The aim of this essay is to set forth the origin and the significance of the Veneration of the Cross service with the hope that it will provide the basis for a more faithful interpretation and practice of the Veneration of the Cross service.

─────── **Origin and Development** ───────

At the outset it must be emphasized that veneration of the cross was not part of the ancient Roman liturgy. Until the seventh century, the Good Friday service at Rome consisted only of the scriptural readings and solemn orations. The custom of venerating the cross, therefore, arose not at Rome, but at Jerusalem where the true cross was discovered during the second quarter of the fourth century. Tradition credits St. Helena, the mother of Constantine, with this discovery.

Once unearthed, the sacred wood immediately became the object of great popular devotion. In 403, Paulinus of Nola reported that "every year during the Lord's Pasch the bishop of that city [Jerusalem] brings it [the cross] out to be venerated by the people; he leads them in this show of respect" *(Letters of St. Paulinus of Nola II,* "Letter 31," trans. P. G. Walsch, in *Ancient Christian Writers* [ACW] [Westminster, Md.: Newman Press, 1967], 36:132).

At the end of the fourth century, the pilgrim Egeria visited the Holy City and left us an eyewitness account of the Good Friday liturgy. It began at about eight o'clock in the morning when a throne was set up for the bishop at the site of our Lord's crucifixion. Then the cross was publicly exposed. "The gilded silver casket containing the sacred wood of the cross is brought in and opened. Both the wood of the cross and the inscription are taken out and placed on the table. As soon as they have been placed on the table, the bishop, remaining seated, grips the ends of the sacred wood with his hands, while the deacons, who are standing about, keep watch over it" *(Egeria: Diary of a Pilgrimage,* trans. George E. Ginrasin, in *ACW* [1970], 38:111).

Having described the exposition of the cross, Egeria states that "all the people pass through one by one, all of them bow down, touching the cross and the inscription, first with their foreheads, then with their eyes; and, after kissing the cross, they move on." Veneration came to an end at noon. For the next three hours, the throng of devout pilgrims listened to Scripture reading, sang psalms, and prayed. "After this," Egeria recounts "when the ninth hour is at hand, the passage is read from the Gospel according to Saint John where Christ gave up His spirit" *(ACW,* 38:112–13).

Paulinus tells that the bishop of Jerusalem frequently made "tiny fragments of the sacred wood" available to others so that they might "win great graces and faith and blessings" *(Letters of St. Paulinus of Nola II,* "Letter 31," *ACW,* 36:132). This statement is confirmed by Cyril of Jerusalem who confesses that the wood of the cross is "now distributed piecemeal from Jerusalem over all the world." Because of this, adoration of the cross developed in other churches in the East.

At Antioch, a segment of the true cross was pub-licly venerated on Good Friday; at Constantinople, it was honored throughout the last three days of Holy Week. Hymns from the Byzantine liturgy disclose some of the significance of this practice. One of them addresses Adam and Eve, saying, "O you first-created Couple, fallen from heavenly status . . . through the bitter pleasure from the olden tree: come!! See here the true and most revered Tree; hasten to kiss it and to cry out with faith: 'You are our help, most revered Cross.' " Another hymn summons the faithful: "Come, O Faithful, let us adore the life-giving Cross of Christ, the King of Glory, for when he extended his arms on it of his own free will, He restored us to the original bliss." *(Byzantine Daily Worship,* ed. Joseph Raya and Jose de Vinck [Allendale, N.J.: Alleluia Press, 1969], 802, 805.) Here the wood of the cross is seen as the tree of life from which Adam and Eve were banished, but to which the faithful have access through Christ.

By the end of the seventh century, apparently under the influence of Constantinople, veneration of the cross had been adopted at Rome. The papal liturgy, as is known from the Ordo of Einsideln, began at two in the afternoon and was characterized by an elaborate procession from Saint John Latern to the Church of the Holy Cross. In the procession the ministers walked barefoot. A deacon bore the wood of the cross in a gold reliquary adorned with precious gems. The pope himself carried a censer before the cross. During the procession, Psalm 118 was chanted, probably with the antiphon "Behold the wood of the cross on which hung the salvation of the world" *(Les Ordines Romani du haut moyen age III* [Louvain: Spicilegium Sacrum Lovaniense, 1961], 270).

Having arrived "at Jerusalem," as the ordo phrases it, the pope, clergy, and faithful prayed together, then kissed the holy relic. After this the traditional Service of the Word took place at which John's Passion was read. Except for the procession, the order of the papal service reflects that of the Jerusalem church as reported by Egeria. The procession itself constitutes a kind of pilgrimage to the Holy City.

In the titular and suburban churches of Rome served not by the pope but by other bishops and presbyters, a relic of the cross was also exposed and venerated. These services began at three in the afternoon while the papal liturgy was still in progress, but they did not include a procession.

Moreover, the sequence of parts is different. According to the Ancient Gelasian Sacramentary, the holy cross was placed on the altar without any ceremony before the liturgy began. After the ministers had entered, the Scripture readings and solemn orations took place, at the end of which "all adore the holy cross and communicate" (Cunibert Mohlberg, ed., *Liber sacramentorum Romanae aeclesiae ordines anni circuli* [Rome: Herder, 1960], 418). Whereas in the papal rite, veneration of the cross preceded the Service of the Word, in other churches it followed the intercessory prayers. Churches north of the Alps also incorporated the veneration of the cross into the Good Friday service. Their obvious source of inspiration is Roman suburban practice, since they provide for no procession and locate the veneration after the solemn orations. Some Frankish ordines simply repeat the Gelasian rubrics more or less verbatim. On the other hand, Ordo XXIV, from the second half of the eighth century, offers a more detailed description of the action and mentions that Psalm 118, with the antiphon "Ecce lignum crucis," is chanted while the cross is being honored. Thus the Psalm and antiphon which were sung during the procession at the Roman papal rite are now executed during the veneration. This may have been the case already in the suburban churches of Rome from which this ordo derives.

At this point it might be well to point out that the antiphon "Ecce lignum crucis" is composed of phrases strongly reminiscent of various accounts of the finding of the true cross. St. Paulinus, for example, states, "Once you think that you behold the wood on which our salvation, the Lord of Majesty, was hanged with nails whilst the world trembled, you, too, must tremble, but you must also rejoice" (*Letters of St. Paulinus of Nola II*, "Letter 31," 36:126). Another pertinent text is furnished by Rufinus, who reports that as Helena searched for the cross she prayed that God would reveal to them "the blessed wood on which hung our salvation" (Rufinus, *Historia Ecclesiastica I*, in *Patrologia Latina*, 21:476). Both these passages find a clear echo in the words of the acclamation: "Behold the wood of the cross on which hung the salvation of the world." Whether this acclamation is sung in procession during the veneration or during the exposition (as will be the case later), it calls attention to the wood of the cross in a quite

literal sense: the wood of the very cross by which Christ saved the world. The hearer is thereby made to participate in the original discovery. If these words are to bear their intended meaning, a relic of the true cross is required.

Ordo XXXI, stemming from the second half of the ninth century, is of particular interest, for it shows that the exposition of the sacred wood has been considerably embellished with a view to making of it a veritable theophany—which, of course, is fully consistent with St. John's presentation of the Crucifixion as the revelation of divine glory. The cross, covered with a veil, is carried to the front of the altar by two acolytes. They stop three times along the way. Each time they do so the chanters bow and sing in Greek: "Holy God, holy Mighty One, holy Immortal One, have mercy on us." The choir answers with the same words in Latin. After the third time, the bishop unveils the cross all at once and sings in a loud voice: "Behold the wood of the Cross."

The cross is here treated as the revelation of God, as the visible manifestation of his presence and saving power. Hence, the appearance of the cross calls forth the awesome Trisagion. The custom mentioned in the Roman-Germanic pontifical of genuflecting or even prostrating before the sacred wood is likewise consistent with this understanding. Commenting on this practice, Pseudo-Alcuin declares, "When we adore this cross, our whole body clings to the earth; and him whom we adore, we mentally discern as if hanging upon it. The power which it received from the Son of God, that we adore" (*De Divinus Officiis Liber XVIII*, in *Patrologia Latina*, 101:1210). The same text also proves, incidentally, the figure of the crucified Christ was not affixed to the cross. It was discerned only mentally.

Medieval rituals also prescribe that the hymn "Pange lingua" with its recurring refrain *"crux fidelis"* should be sung either during the adoration or at Communion. This splendid composition was written by Venatius Fortunatus in 569 for the reception of a relic of the true cross sent to Queen Radegunde at Poitiers by the Byzantine emperor Julian II. It is intended for processional use. As the wood of the cross appears to sight, it prompts the narration of how Christ in the fullness of time assumed our flesh and redeemed mankind by his death on the tree, thereby restoring creation by means of the very material that caused its fall. The wood of the cross, therefore, is a trophy, a sign of victory. The eighth verse, used as a refrain on Good Friday, addresses the sacred wood directly, proclaiming it to be "alone in its glory among all other trees; no forest ever yielded its equal in leaf, flower and fruit" for the fruit of the cross is the salvation of the world (Joseph Connelly, *Hymns of the Roman Liturgy* [Westminster, Md.: Newman Press, 1957], 84). This hymn, like the "Vexilla regis," also composed by Fortunatus and for the same occasion, is an outstanding example of how the mystery of the cross was understood in the West and what kind of response it stirred. It is an excellent commentary not only on the veneration of the cross but on the entire Good Friday liturgy.

During the eleventh and twelfth centuries especially, under the influence of Cluny and other centers of ecclesiastical reform, Frankish and Germanic practices were brought down to Rome and given fresh expression in the Roman pontifical of the twelfth century. According to this document, the pontiff removes his shoes and prostrates three times before kissing the cross, which, as was mentioned in Ordo XXXI, is covered with a veil. Then, unlike the procedure described in Ordo XXXI, he intones "Ecce lignum crucis" three times, each time unveiling a portion of the cross. The Trisagion, "Pange lingua," and other anthems are sung during the period of veneration. The first printed edition of the Roman Missal in 1474 attests the same format, except that the priest exposes the cross first and only then removes his shoes, prostrates, and kisses it. Thus was the rite transmitted to our own day.

The texts and fundamental gestures employed in this rite have remained the same from the early Middle Ages to the present. Missals of more recent centuries as well as the Sacramentary of Paul VI continue to speak of the veneration of the cross. Nevertheless, there is literary evidence from at least the fourteenth century to indicate that the crucifix was replacing the cross as the object of adoration. This shift in devotion from the wood of the cross itself to a naturalistic representation of the crucified Christ corresponds to the collapse of the symbolic universe of the Middle Ages and the advent of secular, humanistic thought, which would eventually issue in the Renaissance. It also marks a low point in sacramental life and the emergence of a piety and spirituality that have no foundation in doctrine—a state of affairs that the modern liturgical renewal has not altogether succeeded in remedying. Moreover the pontifical revised by Innocent III in the early years of the thirteenth century explicitly restricted Communion on Good Friday to the celebrant alone. From then until 1956, Communion of the faithful was forbidden. Dom Bernard Capelle surmises that this measure did not bring a sudden halt to existing practice, but merely accorded official recognition to what had already become a fact. In any case, it is interesting to speculate whether the appearance of the corpus upon the cross used for veneration on Good Friday advanced in proportion to decline in the reception of the *corpus Domini* sacramentally. Capelle has shown that the absence of general Communion in the thirteenth century was compensated for by considerably augmenting the rites surrounding the presanctified bread. The tendency to represent the body of Christ in the form of a figure on the cross may be yet another compensation for its disappearance in sacramental form. But this is merely a hypothesis and requires further testing.

Significance

Before drawing any practical conclusions, it is necessary to comment briefly on the significance of the holy cross. The cross is first of all and most obviously the instrument of redemption. Because of Adam's transgression, the wood of a tree brought sin and death; because of Christ's obedience, the wood of the cross brings forgiveness and life. Salvation, therefore, does not substitute for creation, but rather heals it at its root and brings it to completion. God's fidelity to the work of his hands remains unshaken. In his infinite wisdom, he makes the very element that provoked the world's downfall to be the source of its restoration and ultimate perfection. In retrospect, the early church fathers perceived the entire movement of salvation history as being oriented to the cross and partaking of its power. "Life ever comes from wood," declared Cyril of Jerusalem. "In the time of Noah the preservation of life came from a wooden ark. In Moses' time the sea, on beholding the figurative rod, gave way before him who struck it." When the plan of salvation had reached fulfillment, Pseudo-Chrysostom could acclaim the cross as the foundation, goal, and content of all creation: "This Tree, vast as heaven itself, rises from earth to the skies, a plant immortal, set firm in the midst of heaven and earth, base of all that is, binding force of all creation, holding within itself all the mysterious essence of man." To kiss the cross, then, is to thankfully and humbly embrace the gift of creation now made whole by the sacrifice of him whose body was raised upon the wood.

Secondly, the cross is understood as a royal throne from which the divine presence reigns. In the desert, Yahweh directed Moses to construct a wooden ark surmounted by a covering, called the propitiatory, or throne of mercy, at each side of which were winged figures, or cherubim. "There I shall come to meet you," he said, "there, from above the throne of mercy" (Exod. 25:22). Because God had chosen the lid of the ark as the place where he made himself present to rule his people, he is said to be "enthroned on the cherubim" (1 Sam. 4:4; 2 Sam. 6:2) and is invoked as such in prayer (2 Kings 19:15; Ps. 80:1).

Each year on the Day of Atonement, the priest was required to sprinkle the blood of sacrificed animals on the propitiatory and to burn incense before it (Lev. 16:11-16), thereby obtaining forgiveness, mercy, and life from God. The letter to the Hebrews, now read on Good Friday, recalls this ritual to present the sacrifice of Christ and the sprinkling of his blood as the "source of eternal salvation" (Heb. 5:9). In the body of the crucified One, God has once for all abolished sin and manifested his gracious presence to mankind. The cross, then, is the throne upon which his grace reigns victorious. It is the place where his glory is revealed. As St. John's Passion narrative emphasizes, Christ is king; but his kingdom "rests on the wood." Hence the ancient Christian gloss on Psalm 96:10, known as early as St. Justin: "The Lord hath reigned from the tree." This famous gloss recurs in the "Vexilla regis" of Fortunatus: "The words of David's true prophetic song were fulfilled in which he announced to the nations: 'God has reigned from a tree'" (Connelly, _Hymns_, 80).

These reflections demonstrate once again why the unveiling of the sacred wood prompted the chanting of the Trisagion, accompanied by profound bows. Like the lid of the ark, the cross is the throne where the glory of God is revealed unto judgment and salvation. Catching sight of it, the people of the new covenant shield their eyes and cry for mercy. They also remove their shoes as did Moses (Exod. 3:5) and Joshua (Josh. 5:15) in the

presence of the Holy One. The bearing of incense before the relic of the cross, as in the ancient papal rite, may likewise be intended to evoke, among other things, the liturgy of the Day of Atonement.

Finally, and perhaps most important of all, the cross is the sign of the Lord's eschatological presence. Christ, once taken up to heaven, was expected to return from the east. Matthew had announced the "coming of the Son of Man will be like lightning striking in the east and flashing far into the west!" (Matt. 24:27). As the immediate prelude to this occurrence, he adds that "the sign of the Son of Man will appear in heaven" (Matt. 24:30). Patristic literature is practically unanimous in interpreting this sign as the cross. Commenting on the text of the Gospel, Cyril of Jerusalem declares, "The true sign, Christ's own, is the Cross. A sign of a luminous cross precedes the King, showing Him who was formerly crucified." In another lecture, he explains that "the Cross will appear again with Jesus from heaven; for His emblem will precede the King; . . . and we shall glory, taking pride in the Cross, worshipping the Lord who was sent, and was crucified for us."

Because Christ was expected to come from the east, Christians at a very early date prayed facing that direction in order to show themselves ready for his appearing and actually looking forward to the great event that would consummate the union with him already experienced in prayer. For that same reason, the sign of the cross was frequently traced on the eastern wall of places of prayer, thereby indicating the direction of prayer but also rendering the Lord's coming a present reality in the sign that heralds it. In other words, through the cross the anticipated eschatological appearance becomes Parousia: presence.

This joining of prayer with the eschatological presence of Christ, unseen to the eye but revealed in the cross, obviously underlies the widely attested practice of prostrating before the sacred wood while praying to him who hung upon it. The public exposition of the cross signals the dawning of the Day of the Lord. On beholding it, the believer reverently kneels before the mysterious sign that reveals yet conceals the Lord whom he awaits. Looking with faith at the one who was pierced (Zech. 12:10; John 19:37), he mourns his sins—confident of being cleansed by the fountain of salvation flowing from the pierced one's side (Zech. 13:1; John 19:34).

Practical Application

Given the origin, development, and significance of this portion of the Good Friday liturgy, it is clear that a relic of the true cross should be the preferred object of veneration. Without it, the words and gestures of the ritual lose their immediacy and cease to convey their intended meaning, for they were fashioned as a response to the true cross and still depend upon its presence for their sense. The size of the relic is of no account, for as Paulinus of Nola urged long ago, "Let not your faith shrink because the eyes of the body behold evidence so small; let it look with the inner eye on the whole power of the cross in this tiny segment" (*Paulinus of Nola*, "Letter 31," *ACW*, 36:126).

But because the sacred wood will usually be merely a fragment, it should be mounted within a much larger wooden cross, preferably Greek or Celtic in form, and suitably adorned by competent hands. The design and ornamentation of the larger cross should radiate the mystery it carries, that is "the mystery wherein the creator of man's flesh in His own flesh hung on the gibbet" "Vexilla regis," first stanza, trans. Connelly, in *Hymns of the Roman Liturgy*, 80). Hence infantile or amateurish dabblings in this important matter must be avoided.

Lacking a relic of the true cross, a large wooden cross will suffice. Pseudo-Alcuin had already observed that "those who do not have the wood of the Lord, in good faith adore that which they have" (Pseudo-Alcuin, *De Divinus Officialis Liber XVIII*, in *Patrologia Latina*, 101:1210C). In the ninth century, Amalarius of Metz, while wishing that every church possessed a portion of the sacred wood, was nevertheless convinced that "the power of the holy cross is not lacking in those crosses which are made in the likeness of the Lord's cross" (*Liber Officialis I*, 14:10, ed. J. M. Hanssens, in *Amalarii Episcopi Opera Liturgica Omnia* [Vatican City: Biblioteca Apostolica Vaticana, 1948], 2:102).

Besides enabling the texts and gestures of the liturgy to regain their authenticity, veneration of the cross rather than a crucifix on Good Friday would restore a truly universal Catholic tradition. It would bring Christians of today into living contact with the one, undivided church of past centuries, with the ancient Jerusalem church, and ultimately with Calvary itself. And having devoutly kissed the instrument of salvation, they could then commune sacramentally with him who once hung upon it, but who now reigns in glory and will one day come again in order to manifest his universal kingship over all creation.

Patrick Regan[40]

260 ✦ An Explanation of the Veneration of the Cross Service

The comments below explain the modern practice of the Veneration of the Cross service. This ancient service was recovered and mandated for use in Roman Catholic parishes in 1956 and has provided the basis for many reforms in Protestant worship on Good Friday since that time. Adapt to local usage and custom.

The modern service venerating the cross is made up of three parts: the Liturgy of the Word, the Veneration of the Cross, and the Communion.

The Service of the Word, like other solemn services, begins in silence. The opening prayer catches the full meaning of the event: "Almighty God, we pray you graciously to behold this your family, for whom our Lord Jesus Christ was willing to be betrayed, and given into the hands of sinners, and to suffer death for sinners." Readings from the Old Testament, the Psalms, and epistle then follow. After these readings, the congregation is involved in the hearing of the Passion from St. John. The Passion reading may be read again as it was on Palm Sunday, or it may be sung. After a sermon and hymn, the solemn prayers are prayed.

The specific origin of the solemn prayers is not known; nevertheless, it is known that they go back to prayers said in the church, prayers developed perhaps in Rome to be used as intercession at the Eucharist. These prayers cover a wide range of subjects, such as prayers for leaders of government, the poor and oppressed, and those who have never heard of Christ.

Next comes the Veneration of the Cross. This service originated in Jerusalem, but was not incorporated into the Western liturgy until the end of the seventh century. Throughout the medieval era, it gained considerable popularity and became known as "Creeping to the Cross."

Although the occasion of this service is very

solemn, the solemnity is enhanced through the use of a dramatic visual. A large cross may be carried through the congregation by the celebrant, flanked by acolytes with candles. The cross may be draped with a purple cloth. The celebrant with attendants carries the cross one third of the way up the aisle of the church, stops, removes the cloth from a part of the cross, raises the cross high into the air, and sings: "This is the wood of the cross on which hung the Savior of the world," to which the people respond, "Come, let us worship." Then all kneel for a moment, observing the cross. The same order is followed two more times, bringing the cross to the front of the sanctuary, where it is placed in sight of all the people.

The service now continues with the saying or singing of the reproaches. The reproaches, which are Scriptures freely collected and translated, are put into the mouth of Jesus (written in the ninth century). Jesus, while hanging on the cross as it were, utters his lament that the world has turned its back on his love. In moving words of intense feeling, Christ calls on the world to repent and be converted to him. He recounts how he led his people out of Egypt, through the desert, and yet "thou has hanged me on the gibbet of the cross." These reproaches are followed by anthems of praise and a concluding prayer for grace.

If the reproaches are sung by a choir, the Veneration of the Cross can take place during the singing. The Veneration itself is a very simple gesture. The cross is in display at the front of the sanctuary, and the people, moving in rows, come to the cross, where they may touch it, kiss it, bow before it, or lie prostrate on the floor before it. Or people may simply walk by it, acknowledging that it is the instrument of death through which Christ overcame the power of the evil one and gained the salvation of the world.

The third part, and ending of the service, is the reception of the bread and wine retained from the service of Maundy Thursday. In this service, typical prayers of thanksgiving are not said, since the bread and wine was blessed the evening before. In the early church, it was a tradition not to celebrate Communion on the Friday of his death, a tradition that is being observed once again in contemporary worship. When this ancient custom is followed, the Good Friday service ends with the Veneration of the Cross. In either event, all the people leave in silence.

This service may be celebrated at noon, but it is best celebrated on Good Friday evening.

261 ✦ AN ORDER FOR THE VENERATION OF THE CROSS SERVICE

The following liturgy is based on the historical insights described in the last two articles. Adapt the service below to local usage and custom.

THE ENTRANCE

The ministers, wearing black, enter into the sanctuary in silence and take their seats. All kneel or stand for silent prayer.

> MINISTER: Blessed be our God.
> PEOPLE: **Forever and ever. Amen.**
> MINISTER: Let us pray.
>
> Almighty God, we pray you graciously to behold this your family, for whom our Lord Jesus Christ was willing to be betrayed, and given into the hands of sinners, and to suffer death upon the cross; who now lives and reigns with you and the Holy Spirit, one God, forever and ever. Amen.

THE SERVICE OF THE WORD

The Readings
The Old Testament Lesson: Isaiah 52:13–53:12 or Genesis 22:1-18
The Responsorial Psalm: 22:1-11 (12-21) or 40:1-14 or 69:1-23
The Epistle: Hebrews 10:1-25

The Reading of the Passion Story

Commentary: The Passion story may be read as it was on Palm Sunday or it may be sung.

The Sermon

Hymn: "When I Survey the Wondrous Cross"

The Solemn Prayers of the People

Commentary: The people stand. They are led in prayer with the following solemn collects. (Adapt these prayers to local use and custom.)

> MINISTER: Dear People of God: Our heavenly Father sent his Son into the world,

not to condemn the world, but that the world through him might be saved; that all who believe in him might be delivered from the power of sin and death, and become heirs with him of everlasting life.

We pray, therefore, for people everywhere according to their needs.
Let us pray for the holy catholic church of Christ throughout the world;
For its unity in witness and service,
For all bishops and other ministers and the people whom they serve
For _____ , our bishop, and all the people of the diocese,
For all Christians in this community,
For those about to be baptized (particularly _____)

That God will confirm his church in faith, increase it in love, and preserve it in peace.

(Silence)

Almighty and everlasting God, by whose Spirit the whole body of your faithful people is governed and sanctified: Receive our supplications and prayers which we offer before you for all members of your holy church, that in their vocation and ministry they may truly and devoutly serve you; through our Lord and Savior Jesus Christ.
Amen.

Let us pray for all nations and peoples of the earth, and for those in authority among them;
For_____ , the president of the United States,
For the Congress and the Supreme Court,
For the members and representatives of the United Nations,
For all who serve the common good,

That by God's help they may seek justice and truth, and live in peace and concord.

(Silence)

Almighty God, kindle, we pray, in every heart, the true love of peace, and guide with your wisdom those who take counsel for the nations of the earth; that in tranquillity your dominion may increase, until the earth is filled with the knowledge of your love; through Jesus Christ our Lord.
Amen.

Let us pray for all who suffer and are afflicted in body or in mind;
For the hungry and the homeless, the destitute and the oppressed,
For the sick, the wounded, and the crippled,
For those in loneliness, fear, and anguish,
For those who face temptation, doubt, and despair,
For the sorrowful and bereaved,
For prisoners and captives, and those in mortal danger

That God in his mercy will comfort and relieve them, and grant them the knowledge of his love, and stir up in us the will and patience to minister to their needs.

(Silence)

Gracious God, the comfort of all who sorrow, the strength of all who suffer: Let the cry of those in misery and need come to you, that they may find your mercy present with them in all their afflictions; and give us, we pray, the strength to serve them for the sake of him who suffered for us, your Son, Jesus Christ our Lord.
Amen.

Let us pray for all who have not received the gospel of Christ;
For those who have never heard the word of salvation,
For those who have lost their faith,
For those hardened by sin or indifference,
For the contemptuous and the scornful,
For those who are enemies of the cross of Christ and persecutors of his disciples,

For those who in the name of Christ have persecuted others,

That God will open their hearts to the truth, and lead them to faith and obedience.

(Silence)

Merciful God, creator of all the peoples of the earth and lover of souls: Have compassion on all who do not know you as you are revealed in your Son, Jesus Christ; let your gospel be preached with grace and power to those who have not heard it; turn the hearts of those who resist it; and bring home to your fold those who have gone astray; that there may be one flock under on shepherd, Jesus Christ our Lord. *Amen.*

Let us commit ourselves to our God, and pray for the grace of a holy life, that, with all who have departed this world and have died in the peace of Christ, and those whose faith is known to God alone, we may be accounted worthy to enter into the fullness of the joy of our Lord, and receive the crown of life in the day of resurrection.

(Silence)

O God of unchangeable power and eternal light: Look favorably on your whole church, that wonderful and sacred mystery; by the effectual working of your providence, carry out in tranquillity the plan of salvation; let the whole world see and know that things which were cast down are being raised up, and things which had grown old are being made new, and that all things are being brought to their perfection by him through whom all things were made, your Son, Jesus Christ our Lord; who lives and reigns with you, in the unity of the Holy Spirit, one God, forever and ever. *Amen.*

Commentary: This service may be concluded here with the singing of a hymn or anthem, and prayer. If the service continues with the Veneration of the Cross the following takes place: A person carrying a wood cross proceeds up the center aisle of the church, stopping three times during which the congregation says or sings Anthem 1, 2, and 3.

Anthem 1
(The cross is carried one third of the aisle. The carrier stops and the following is said or sung)

We glory in your cross, O Lord,
and praise and glorify your holy resurrection;
for by virtue of your cross,
joy has come to the whole world.

May God be merciful to us and bless us, show us the light of his countenance, and come to us.
Let your ways be known upon earth,
your saving health among all nations.

Let the peoples praise you, O God;
let all the peoples praise you.

We glory in your cross, O Lord,
and praise and glorify your holy resurrection;
for by virtue of your cross,
joy has come to the whole world.

Anthem 2
(The carrier of the cross proceeds to walk the second third of the aisle. The carrier stops and the following is said or sung)

We adore you, O Christ, and we bless you,
because by your holy cross you have redeemed the world.

If we have died with him, we shall also live with him;
if we endure, we shall also reign with him.

We adore you, O Christ, and we bless you,
because by your holy cross you have redeemed the world.

Anthem 3
(The carrier walks to the front of the sanctuary and places the large wooden cross in a place where all may see. Then the following is said or sung)

O Savior of the world,
who by thy cross and precious blood hast redeemed us:

Save us and help us, we humbly beseech thee, O Lord.

Commentary: The people may now walk to the cross, touch it, embrace it, or kiss it. This action may be done in silence or to a hymn, such as "Sing, My Tongue, the Glorious Battle" or some other hymn extolling the glory of the cross. The service may be concluded here with the Lord's Prayer and the final prayer below.

Lord's Supper

Commentary: If Holy Communion is to be administered from the reserved sacrament, the following order is observed:

A Confession of Sin

The Lord's Prayer

The Communion

Commentary: The service concludes with the following prayer. No blessing or dismissal is added.

LEADER: Lord Jesus Christ, Son of the living God, we pray you to set your passion, cross, and death between your judgment and our souls, now and in the hour of our death. Give mercy and grace to the living; pardon and rest to the dead; to your holy church, peace and concord; and to us sinners, everlasting life and glory; for with the Father and Holy Spirit you live and reign, one God, now and forever. *Amen.*

262 • A CREATIVE GOOD FRIDAY SERVICE

The following outline for Good Friday worship does not follow the traditional pattern described in the preceding articles. This plan will be especially helpful for congregations that worship in a more informal manner.

Basic Pattern of Worship

Preparation and Reflection
Opening Prayer
Introduction to Good Friday
Scripture Readings: Luke 1:26-33, 46-55; 2:8-11, 16-19, 27-35
Dramatic Presentation
Silent Prayer

Hymn: "Come and See" (Kendrick)
Scripture Reading: 2 Corinthians 4:6-11, 16-18
Guided Reflection Time
Benediction

Commentary

Preamble. Good Friday is a difficult day for Christians to appreciate fully. First, they are nearly two millennia removed from the Crucifixion and have known Jesus of Nazareth only through the eyes of faith. Second, Christians cannot really identify with the suffering of "a god who loves his son." However, as believers read the Passion narrative, they can often find themselves identifying with the feelings and response of, say, a self-righteous Pharisee, a frightened disciple, or a confused person in the crowd.

If this worship service is offered from the perspective of one of these secondary players rather than from the more usual perspective of Jesus or the Father, those who attend the service might be enabled to receive the challenge of the cross in a more personal way.

Worship Space. The service is a solemn one. A black cloth, draped over the cross, and dimmed lights can quietly convey the soberness of the occasion. Light is present, but shrouded. We know God is always present, but at times such as these, his presence is veiled. Using lanterns rather than candles as the source of light convey this truth well. Either silence, which would draw attention to the symbols, or quiet music, which might allow for a more interior focus, can be helpful.

Entrance. If at the outset of the service you can honestly acknowledge the difficulty of the day, you can dispel the unwarranted personal expectations people might bring to the Good Friday service, and open the way for participants to freely receive the graces God has for them.

You can most easily maintain this sense of quiet sobriety if you can lead the people to the Scriptures for the service following the opening prayer and avoid breaking for a hymn or worship songs, leaving these until a more appropriate time for response.

Word. The service described below leads the congregation toward Good Friday by presenting the Passion from the perspective of Mary, the mother of Christ. The Scriptures were chosen to this end. Likewise, if you want the congregation to see

Good Friday through, Peter's eyes or those of Mary Magdalene, you would then draw from to use parts of the Gospel narratives that present the events from the perspective of Peter or Mary. (In order to allow the participants to identify as fully as possible with the character or group that you highlight, be sure to choose Scriptures that will give as inclusive and broad a perspective as possible. For example, Mary of Nazareth's role in the Passion story began with the Annunciation, hence the inclusion of those Scriptures in the liturgy.)

If the church is not too large, the Scriptures can most effectively be read from within the congregation rather than from the podium. This style of presentation symbolically conveys that everyone present is wrestling with the meaning of the word and its application to us. In the pathos of the Good Friday service, the word comes from the God who is among and alongside us, not from a disinterested bystander.

You could perform a drama based on a character in the narrative, or you could instead present a dramatic reading in the form of a collage that juxtaposes a variety of Scriptures from the Passion narratives.

If you present a drama or a Scripture collage instead of a sermon or a homily, you might want to allow the participants time to pray quietly and then, if the number of people present is not too large, allow them time to stand and offer their response to the service. Was their understanding broadened? How did they feel as they looked at the Crucifixion through someone else's eyes?

Table. Some churches will want to receive Eucharist on Good Friday, but others believe that we are called simply to wait out the coming three days. Both approaches affirm that we come to Good Friday as people of the Resurrection, but each expresses this truth differently.

If you choose not to celebrate the Lord's Supper, you can focus the celebrative portion of the worship service on the hope God promises to us for our times of despair or darkness. By including this personal reflection time, the participants learn that the purpose of Good Friday is not to relive history but to receive power from Good Friday as they link their present suffering with the life and sufferings of Christ.

You will want to lead the people toward a hope that is tempered by sobriety. Therefore, if you choose to respond in song at this time, the most appropriate hymns will be those that acknowledge our human fickleness and sin while proclaiming God's faithfulness and promises to be with us always. Hymns and worship songs should honor Christ without being inappropriately cheerful.

The Scripture that, earlier in the service, brought evidence of cruelty and seeming despair, can at this time infuse human suffering with hope, a hope that respects the mysteries of life and faith.

Dismissal. Since the service could tend to evoke profound emotional responses in the participants, the prayer of benediction should be a simple, personal restatement of the central truths of the Christian life, namely that death is necessary to life and that we worship a God who is committed to bringing life from death.

Diane S. George Ayer

263 ✦ AN ORDER FOR "THE SEVEN LAST WORDS" SERVICE

Many congregations order their worship on Good Friday around the seven statements that Christ spoke on the cross. The following liturgy provides an example of this type of service.

──────── **Introduction** ────────

In the early church, devotions were held during the three hours Christ hung on the cross, from twelve noon to three o'clock. Although records of this devotion are available from the writings of Egeria, the devotion itself did not survive and develop into a traditional devotion of the church as did other devotions of Holy Week.

In the late seventeenth century, the idea of the ancient church observing three hours of devotion during the time Jesus hung on the cross was revived in Peru. This service has since been adopted by many Catholic and Protestant churches.

The content of the service consists of a reflection on the last seven words of Jesus. Usually, a brief service of Scripture reading, sermon, and prayer are offered around each of Jesus' last words. A period of silence is maintained between each of the services so that people may reflect on the meaning of the words. In most churches, people are free to come and go between services rather than stay for all seven of them. Adapt to local usage and custom.

---------- **Order of Service** ----------

Commentary: The people are seated in silence. The ministers process to their places. Silence is kept for a period of time. The minister begins.

The Opening Prayers

LEADER: The Lord be with you.
PEOPLE: **And also with you.**
LEADER: Let us pray.
PEOPLE: **Lord Jesus Christ, you who were led forth into the pain of the cross for the salvation of the world: Help us to enter into your passion and death, forgive us all our sin, and bring us to eternal salvation through Jesus Christ our Lord, who lives and reigns with you and the Holy Spirit forever. Amen.**
LEADER: O Savior of the world, who by your cross and precious blood has redeemed us,
PEOPLE: **Save us and help us, we pray. Amen.**

(Silence)

Hymn: "Glory Be to Jesus"

THE FIRST WORD: "Father forgive them for they know not what they do" (Luke 23:34).

The Homily

(Silence)

The Prayer

LEADER: Most blessed Jesus, through your suffering, you paid for our sins. Give us a deep hatred of sin. Grant us a tender spirit toward sinners, and help us to forgive those who have sinned against us. Teach us to confess our own sin and to seek reconciliation with those whom we have sinned against, through Jesus Christ our Lord who lives and reigns with you and the Holy Spirit.
PEOPLE: **Amen.**

(Silence)

LEADER: Savior of the world, who by your

cross and precious blood has redeemed us,
PEOPLE: **Save us and help us, we pray. Amen.**

(Silence)

Hymn (one of the following):
"Search Me, O God"
"Jesus, Thy Blood and Righteousness"
"We Sing the Praise of Him Who Died"

THE SECOND WORD: "Truly I say to you, today you will be with me in Paradise" (Luke 23:43).

The Homily

(Silence)

The Prayer

LEADER: Most blessed Lord Jesus, you forgave the thief on the cross. Look on us with mercy and compassion. Give us a strong faith in you, a humble remembrance of our sins, and the strength to confess you before others, and so wash us in your blood that we may share in your glory forever, through Jesus Christ, your only beloved Son, and our Lord.
PEOPLE: **Amen.**

(Silence)

LEADER: O Savior of the world, who by your cross and precious blood has redeemed us,
PEOPLE: **Save us and help us, we pray. Amen.**

(Silence)

Hymn (one of the following):
"Teach Me Thy Way"
"Amazing Grace"
"Jesus Said It All"
"In the Cross of Christ I Glory"

THE THIRD WORD: "Woman behold your Son!" Then he said to the disciple, "Behold your mother!" (John 19:26–27).

The Homily

(Silence)

The Prayer

LEADER: O most Holy Lord Jesus, you left us

an example of holy love by leaving your mother in the care of the disciple. Purify our own feelings and pour out your blessings on our homes and relationships. Comfort the homeless, and cause us to act tenderly toward them, and bring us to your home above, where we with your mother and all the saints may worship and adore you with your Father and the Holy Spirit forever.

PEOPLE: **Amen.**

(Silence)

LEADER: O Savior of the world, who by your cross and precious blood has redeemed us,

PEOPLE: **Save us and help us, we pray. Amen.**

Hymn (one of the following):
"Go to Dark Gethsemane"
"The Old Rugged Cross"
"Alone Thou Goest Forth, O Lord"

THE FOURTH WORD: "My God, my God, why hast thou forsaken me?" (Matt. 27:46).

The Homily

(Silence)

The Prayer

LEADER: O blessed Lord Jesus, you bitterly suffered alone on the cross and experienced the anguish of separation. Come, and be with us in times of despair and loneliness, and transform our sadness into fellowship with you. We pray also for our sisters and brothers throughout the world who experience alienation, oppression, and aloneness. Comfort and support them with your presence, and bring them to a place of rest in you, through Jesus Christ, our Savior and Lord.

PEOPLE: **Amen.**

(Silence)

LEADER: O Savior of the world, who by your cross and precious blood has redeemed us,

PEOPLE: **Save us and help us, we pray. Amen.**

Hymn (one of the following):
"Alas, and Did My Savior Bleed"
"Jesus Paid It All"
"Ah, Holy Jesus, How Hast Thou Offended"

THE FIFTH WORD: "I thirst" (John 19:28).

The Homily

(Silence)

The Prayer

LEADER: O most blessed Jesus, you who thirsted and experienced pain for us. Kindle in our hearts a thirst for you that we may love and serve you and lead others to find their rest in you. Remember, O Lord, all the sick and dying and deliver them from pain, granting them a happy ending through Jesus Christ our Lord, who lives and reigns with you and the Holy Spirit forever.

PEOPLE: **Amen.**

(Silence)

LEADER: O Savior of the world, who by your cross and precious blood has redeemed us,

PEOPLE: **Save us and help us we pray. Amen.**

(Silence)

Hymn (one of the following):
"O Sacred Head Now Wounded"
"Alas, and Did My Savior Bleed"
"Wounded for Me"

THE SIXTH WORD: "It is finished" (John 19:30).

Homily

(Silence)

The Prayer

LEADER: O most blessed Savior, you proclaimed the perfect fulfillment of your work and bowed your wounded head in completion. Work in us the grace of your salvation that we might live in union with you. And whatever good work you have begun in us, continue it throughout our days that we might be full of your calling and be patient in doing well to others through Christ our Lord, who lives and reigns with the Father and the Holy Spirit forever.

PEOPLE: **Amen.**

(Silence)

LEADER: O Savior of the world, who by your cross and precious blood has redeemed us,

PEOPLE: **Save us and help us, we pray. Amen.**

Hymn (one of the following):
"Jesus, Thy Blood and Righteousness"
"Calvary Covers It All"
"In the Cross of Christ I Glory"

THE SEVENTH WORD: "Father into thy hands I commit my spirit!" (Luke 23:46).

The Homily

(Silence)

The Prayer

LEADER: O most blessed Savior, you gave up your precious life to atone for sin and conquer the powers of evil. Grant us the power to live in your name. Do not forsake us in our hour of need. Confirm our faith, deepen our repentance, and strengthen us with your body and blood, and may we come to that heavenly rest where you dwell forever with your Father in the fellowship of the Spirit.

PEOPLE: **Amen.**

LEADER: O Savior of the world, who by your cross and precious blood has redeemed us,

PEOPLE: **Save us and help us, we pray. Amen.**

(Silence)

Hymn (one of the following):
"Just As I Am"
"When I Survey the Wondrous Cross"
"We Sing the Praise of Him Who Died"

THE CLOSING PRAYER

O most blessed Jesus, Son of the living God: See us poor sinners through your passion and death, forgive us our sins which we have committed against you and our neighbor. Give us eternal life and everlasting joy through the blood of your cross. We give ourselves to you in faith and submission. Keep us always as your own and grant us eternal life through Jesus Christ our Lord. Amen.

(The people leave in silence.)

Adapted by Robert E. Webber[41]

TWENTY-ONE

Other Services for Holy Week

Below are services that may be used in a number of different worship settings of Holy Week. Of particular interest are the various services of Tenebrae and the Way of the Cross. These services order the spiritual pilgrimage of the congregation and communicate the significance of the death of Jesus in a dramatic way.

264 ✦ AN INTRODUCTION TO TENEBRAE WORSHIP

The word tenebrae *means "darkness" and refers specifically to a service of worship in which the progressive extinguishing of candles represent the snuffing out of the life of Christ. It is becoming an increasingly popular devotion for Holy Week and is celebrated on Wednesday, Thursday, or Friday of Holy Week.*

The word *tenebrae* appears after the twelfth century and is used to refer to Matins and Lauds (prayers at dawn and sunset) on the last three days of Holy Week. These services were sung on the night before the day to which they refer, beginning on Wednesday night before Maundy Thursday. Originally the Matins and Lauds for the three great days were simply the ordinary office sung in monastic communities of the medieval era.

The Matins and Lauds for the last three days of Holy Week consisted of a series on the events of salvation that took place from the Last Supper to the entombment. On Thursday the betrayal is emphasized; on Friday the judgment, crucifixion, and death of Christ; and on Saturday the burial and expected resurrection.

The services featured a triangular candlestick holding fifteen candles. Nine for the Matins reading and five for the Lauds, with one remaining. Although the one remaining may have originally been for the purpose of light for the departing worshipers, it gradually came to represent the Resurrection and the enduring light of Jesus.

The service begins with all fifteen candles lighted. Then the minister, readers, and choir or singer process into the sanctuary in silence. The first antiphon is read or sung, followed by the reading or singing of the Psalm. Then a candle is snuffed out. This order of service progresses throughout until all the candles except the middle (or top) one has been snuffed out (in addition to the Psalms, a candle is snuffed out after the reading of the Song of Hezekiah).

By the time Canticle 16: *Benedictum Dominus Deus Israel* is sung, only one candle is burning. During the Benedictus the only lighted candle may be taken and hidden in the sanctuary to represent the death and burial of Jesus. After Psalm 51 has been said, a noise may be made representing the opening of the grave. The remaining candle representing the Resurrection may be returned to the candlestick to provide light for the people as they leave the sanctuary in silence.

265 ✦ A SERVICE OF TENEBRAE

The Tenebrae service is one of prolonged meditation on the suffering of Christ. Various readings trace the story of Christ's passion, the music expresses his pathos, and the darkness with the accompanying silence suggests the drama of this momentous day.

ENTRANCE TO WORSHIP
(Enter in Silence)

Scripture Reading: Psalm 22:1-18

(Silence)

Opening

LEADER: The Lord be with you.

PEOPLE: **And also with you.**
LEADER: The Light has come into the world.
PEOPLE: **But the world loved darkness rather than light.**
LEADER: Come, let us worship the Lord, who was obedient to death, even death on a cross.

Entrance Prayer

CHOIR: Let thy merciful ears, O Lord, be open unto the prayers of thy humble servants; and that they may obtain their petitions make them to ask such things as shall please thee;through Jesus Christ, our Lord, Amen. (by Richard Mudd)
Leader: We know that Jesus Christ was willing to be betrayed,
People: **And to suffer death on a cross for our sake.**
Leader: Hear our prayers, O God,
People: **Through Jesus Christ, our Lord. Amen.**

Commentary: As worshipers enter, the Tenebrae candles should be lit. The traditional arrangement would include fifteen taper candles in a triangular candle stand. Alternatively, fifteen thick candles may be arranged asymmetrically on stands or in the front of the worship space. In either case, the fourteen candles that will be extinguished may be purple and the fifteenth may be white, symbolizing the light of Christ. The sanctuary may be darkened. Purple and black fabrics that recall the overarching themes of Lent and Holy Week may be displayed in the sanctuary.

The Psalm may be read from the back of the worship space, breaking the silence with a soft yet passionate reading. The Psalm may also be sung.

Periods of silence may be added throughout the service. This early reprise of the opening silence establishes the meditative character of the service and allows time for meditation on the words of the opening reading.

The reference to darkness and light—essential to the Tenebrae service—is prominent in each part of the service.

The prayer may be spoken and/or sung. This example demonstrates how music may be used with a clearly identified liturgical function.

PROCLAMATION OF THE WORD

Sermon Hymn: "O Love, How Deep, How Broad, How High"

stanza 1: ALL	stanza 2: MEN
stanza 3: WOMEN	stanza 4: CHOIR
omit stanza 5	stanza 6: ALL

Old Testament Lesson: Isaiah 52:13–53:12

New Testament Lesson: Hebrews 4:14-15; 5:7-9

Sermon Prayer

Organ Chorale Prelude: "O Sacred Head, Now Wounded," (arr: Johann Gottfried Walther)
What language shall I borrow
to thank you dearest Friend,
for this, your dying sorrow,
your mercy without end?
Lord, make me yours forever,
a loyal servant true,
and let me never, never
outlive my love for you.

Commentary: The sermon hymns should be chosen to complement the theme of the sermon. It is advisable to choose a strong hymn at this point in the service and to accompany the hymn with strength. Ensuing hymns in the "Service of Shadows" will naturally be more reflective, creating a musical decrescendo that extends throughout the service. Other possible sermon hymns include "Lift High the Cross," "What Wondrous Love Is This," and "Hallelujah, What a Savior." In the hymn "O Love, How Deep" the stanza that refers to Easter should be omitted.

The Psalm has already been read and the Gospel reading is included in the following portion of the service, leaving as necessary only the reading of the Old and New Testament lessons.

Like silence, instrumental music enhances the meditative spirit of the service. Hymn-based instrumental music focuses the attention of the worshiper on texts appropriate for the service. Such may be interspersed throughout the service and should be accompanied by the printed text of the hymns.

THE SHADOWS

Jesus Prays on the Mount of Olives

Scripture Reading: Luke 22:39-46

(Silence)

Refrain: "Stay With Me," Jacques Berthier (Taizé)
The people repeat the refrain, "Stay with me, re-main here with me" several times; the cantor and choir will sing the verses.

Commentary: The readings are chosen to follow the complete Passion account. See the appendix for readings from the other gospels. Readings may be read by several readers, with at least one voice reading narrative passages and other voices taking the roles of the various characters in the Passion account, reading all direct quotations (such as the words of Christ found in Luke 22:40, 42, and 46).

Each reading may conclude with the words "The Word of the Lord" or "The Gospel of our Lord Jesus Christ," to which the congregation may respond, "Thanks be to God" or "Praise be to you, O Christ." Alternatively, each reading may conclude with the words of Paul: "God proves his love for us in this: While we were yet sinners Christ died for us," to which the congregation may respond, "Thanks be to God." The repetition of the this text quickly becomes a dramatic refrain that suggests the significance of Christ's passion.

During each period of silence, a member of the congregation, perhaps a dancer, moves to the candles at the front of the sanctuary, and extinguishes one or two candles. The number of candles will depend on the number of readings used.

Each lesson may be followed by an appropriate hymn or anthem. Words not sung by all the people should be printed to guide each worshiper's meditation.

Alternate hymns for the refrain include "Tis Midnight, and on Olive's Brow," and "Go to Dark Gethsemane."

Jesus Is Arrested

Scripture Reading: Luke 22:47-53

(Silence)

Hymn: "Christ, the Life of All the Living"
   stanza 1: ALL
   stanza 2: WOMEN
   stanza 3: ALL

Commentary. It may not be possible to find familiar congregational hymns that correspond with each event in the Passion narrative. In such a case, an appropriate vocal solo or choral anthem maybe easier to find. Alternatively, an instrumental mu-sical selection or more general Passion hymn may be used.

Peter Disowns Jesus

Scripture Reading: Luke 22:54-62

(Silence)

Musical Reflection: "Ah, Holy Jesus, How Have You Offended," (organ chorale prelude by Helmut Walcha)

Hymn: "Ah, Holy Jesus, How Have You Offended"
   stanza 1: ALL
   stanza 2: MEN
   stanza 3: ALL
   stanza 4: ALL, without accompaniment

Jesus Before Pilate and Herod

Scripture Reading: Luke 22:63–23:12

(Silence)

Hymn: "Go to Dark Gethsemane" (all sing stanzas 1 and 3)

Jesus Is Sentenced

Scripture Reading: Luke 23:13-25

(Silence)

Spiritual: "He Never Said a Mumbalin' Word"

Commentary: An alternate hymn is "A Purple Robe, a Crown of Thorns"

Jesus Is Crucified

Scripture Reading: Luke 23:26-43

(Silence)

Hymn: "O Perfect Life of Love"

Commentary: Alternate hymns include "There Is a Green Hill Far Away," "At the Cross, Her Station Keeping" (the Stabat Mater), "Lamb of God" (O Lamm Gottes, Unschuldig), and "Beneath the Cross of Jesus."

Jesus Dies

Scripture Reading: Luke 23:44-46

(Silence)

Hymn: "O Sacred Head Now Wounded"
   stanza 1: ALL
   stanza 2: organ and dance interpretation
   stanza 3: ALL, without accompaniment

Commentary: Following this lesson, all candles should be extinguished except for one, which represents the light of Christ.

Alternate hymns include "O Perfect Life of Love," "Glory Be to Jesus," and "He Never Said a Mumbalin' Word." By this point in the service, all musical accompaniment should be minimized or removed to allow for quiet, meditative singing.

Jesus Is Buried

Scripture Reading: Luke 23:47-56a

Spiritual: "Were You There" (arr. Robert Scholz)

(Silence)

Strepitus

Hymn: "When I Survey the Wondrous Cross"

Commentary: "Were You There" may be effectively sung by an unaccompanied solo voice from outside the worship space or from the back of the worship space. The final verse—"Were you there when God raised Him from the tomb"—may be omitted.

Alternate hymns include "Worthy is the Lamb" and "Calvary" (alternate title, "Every Time I Think About Jesus").

Benediction

LEADER: May Jesus Christ, who for our sakes became obedient unto death, even death on a cross, keep you and strengthen you.

PEOPLE: **Amen.**

(People leave in silence)

Commentary: After the hymn, the remaining candle should be removed from the sanctuary. It may be carried by any member of the congregation, including a liturgical dancer who may lift the candle high above his or her head and encircle the people before exiting the worship space. Silence should be observed throughout.

The silence is broken with a loud, resounding noise (hence the Latin name *strepitus,* which means "crashing" or "rumbling"). The noise may be one striking sound, such as that made by clapping two boards together or—perhaps more effectively—an extended peal of sound that begins quietly and continues to increase in volume until it overwhelms the worshiper, such as that made

by an firm roll on a suspended cymbal. This sound signifies the earthquake on Good Friday or may remind the worshipers more generally of the cataclysmic nature of Christ's sacrifice, without reference to the specific earthquake.

Afterward the single candle may be brought back in to the sanctuary. Alternatively, the candle may be brought back in to the sanctuary on the Easter service, most appropriately at Easter Vigil.

———— Alternate Scripture Readings ————

The following texts may be divided into any number of readings. Eight readings allows for two candles to be extinguished after each of the first seven lessons, and the final candle to be removed following the eighth lesson.

I. Readings from Matthew

Matthew 26:31-46	Jesus Predicts Peter's Denial and Prays in Gethsemane
Matthew 26:47-56	Jesus Is Arrested
Matthew 26:57-68	Jesus Is Tried Before the Sanhedrin
Matthew 26:69-75	Jesus Is Disowned by Peter
Matthew 27:1-23	Judas Hangs Himself and Jesus Is Tried by Pilate
Matthew 27:45-50	Jesus Dies
Matthew 27:51-56	The Response to Jesus' Death

II. Readings from Mark

Mark 14:27-42	Jesus Predicts Peter's Denial and Prays in Gethsemane
Mark 14:43-52	Jesus Is Arrested
Mark 14:53-65	Jesus Is Tried Before the Sanhedrin
Mark 14:66-72	Jesus Is Disowned by Peter
Mark 15:1-15	Jesus Is Tried by Pilate
Mark 15:16-32	Jesus Is Crucified
Mark 15:33-37	Jesus Dies
Mark 15:38-39	The Response to Jesus' Death

John D. Witvliet

266 • A PSALM/TENEBRAE SERVICE

The Tenebrae service that features the extinguishing of lights to represent the fading life of Jesus may take many forms. *The Tenebrae service that follows is reading or singing of the Psalms.*

———————— **Order of Worship** ————————

(People enter in silence)

Procession

Psalm 69

> CANTOR: Zeal for your house has consumed me; the insults of those who insult you have fallen upon me.
>
> PEOPLE: **(read in unison Psalm 69)**
>
> CANTOR: Zeal for your house has consumed me; the insults of those who insult you have fallen upon me.

Silence and Extinguishing of Candles

Psalm 70

> CANTOR: Let those be put to shame and confusion who delight in my misfortune.
>
> PEOPLE: **(chant in unison Psalm 70)**
>
> CANTOR: Let those be put to shame and confusion who delight in my misfortune.

Silence and Extinguishing of Candles

Psalm 74

> CANTOR: Deliver me, my God, from the hand of the wicked, from the clutches of the unjust and cruel.
>
> PEOPLE: **"O God, Why Have You Cast Us All Away" (a metrical setting of Psalm 74 as found in the *Psalter Hymnal* [Grand Rapids: CRC Publications, 1987])**
>
> CANTOR: Deliver me, my God, from the hand of the wicked, from the clutches of the unjust and cruel.

Silence and Extinguishing of Candles

Lamentations 1:1-5

Response

> CANTOR: Jerusalem, Jerusalem, return to the Lord your God!
>
> READER: On the Mount of Olives Jesus prayed:
>
> PEOPLE: **My Father, if it be possible, let this cup pass from me.**
> **The spirit is willing, but the flesh is weak.**

> READER: Watch and pray, that you may not enter temptation.
>
> PEOPLE: **The spirit is willing, but the flesh is weak.**

Lamentations 1:6-9

Response

> CANTOR: Jerusalem, Jerusalem, return to the Lord your God!
>
> READER: My soul is very sorrowful, even to death;
>
> PEOPLE: **Remain here, and watch with me.**
> **Now you shall see the crowd who will surround me;**
> **you will flee, and I will go to be offered up for you.**

> READER: Behold, the hour is at hand, and the Son of Man is betrayed into the hands of sinners.
>
> PEOPLE: **You will flee, and I will go to be offered up for you.**

Lamentations 1:10-14

Response

> CANTOR: Jerusalem, Jerusalem, return to the Lord your God!
>
> READER: Lo, we have seen him without beauty or majesty.
>
> PEOPLE: **Nothing in his appearance that we should desire him.**
> **He bore our sins and grieved for us, he was wounded for our transgressions,**
> **and by his scourging we are healed.**

> READER: Surely he has borne our griefs and carried our sorrows:
>
> PEOPLE: **And by his scourging we are healed.**

Psalm 63

> CANTOR: God did not spare his own Son, but delivered him up for us all.
>
> PEOPLE: **(Psalm 63, sung to chant setting in *The Celebration Psalter* [St. Louis: Cathedral Music Press)])**
>
> CANTOR: God did not spare his own Son, but delivered him up for us all.

Silence and Extinguishing of Candles

Psalm 90

> CANTOR: Like a lamb led to slaughter, he opened not his mouth.

PEOPLE: **"Lord, You Have Been Our Dwelling Place" (a metrical setting of Psalm 90, from the *Presbyterian Hymnal* [Louisville: Westminster/John Knox, 1990])**

CANTOR: Like a lamb led to slaughter, he opened not his mouth.

Silence and Extinguishing of Candles

Psalm 143

CANTOR: They shall mourn for him as one mourns for an only child; for the Lord, who is without sin, is slain.

PEOPLE: **(chanted in unison Psalm 143)**

CANTOR: They shall mourn for him as one mourns for an only child; for the Lord, who is without sin, is slain.

Silence and Extinguishing of Candles

Canticle of Hezekiah (Isaiah 38:10-20)

CANTOR: From the gates of hell, O Lord, deliver my soul.

PEOPLE: **(read Isaiah 38:10-20)**

CANTOR: From the gates of hell, O Lord, deliver my soul.

Silence and Extinguishing of Candles

Psalm 150

CANTOR: O Death, I will be your death; O Grave, I will be your destruction.

READER: (Psalm 150)

CANTOR: O Death, I will be your death; O Grave, I will be your destruction

Silence and Extinguishing of Candles

Canticle of Zechariah (Luke 1:68-79)

CANTOR: Now the women sitting at the tomb made lamentation, weeping for the Lord.

PEOPLE: **(Canticles S190–95 chanted in unison (from *Hymnal 1982*, New York: Church Hymnal Corporation, 1982)**

CANTOR: Now the women sitting at the tomb made lamentation, weeping for the Lord.

Psalm 51

Prayer

LEADER: Almighty God, behold this your family,

for whom our Lord Jesus Christ was willing to be betrayed and given into the hands of sinners, and to suffer death upon the cross.

(Silence)

The Strepitus

(People leave in silence)

Additional Psalm Readings for Refrains

Ps. 2: The kings of the earth rise up in revolt, and the princes plot together, against the Lord and against his Anointed.

Ps. 22: They divide my garments among them; they cast lots for my clothing.

Ps. 27: False witnesses have risen up against me, and also those who speak malice.

Ps. 54: God is my helper; it is the Lord who sustains my life.

Ps. 76: At Salem in his tabernacle, and his dwelling is in Zion.

Ps. 88: I have become like one who has no strength, lost among the dead.

Commentary

The Psalter. As worshipers enter, the Tenebrae candles should be lit. The traditional arrangement would include fifteen taper candles in a triangular candle stand. Alternatively, fifteen thick candles may be arranged asymmetrically on stands in the front of the worship space. In either case, the fourteen candles that will be extinguished may be purple and the fifteenth may be white, symbolizing the light of Christ. The sanctuary may be darkened. Purple and black fabrics that recall the overarching themes of Lent and Holy Week may be displayed in the sanctuary.

The several Psalms and canticles in this service may be read or sung. Whether read or sung, the antiphon (or refrain) should be prominent, because it indicates the significance of a given Psalm or canticle for Holy Week meditation. When the Psalms or canticles are read, they may be read in unison, responsively, or by a solo reader or group of readers. When the Psalms and canticles are sung, they may be chanted or sung to a metrical setting by a choir, soloist, or the congregation. This sample service uses several of these styles.

This sample service features the prominent use

of a cantor whose only role it is to sing or read the antiphon for each Psalm or canticle and the recurring injunction following each lesson from Lamentations. Whether the Psalms or canticles are sung or read, whether they are offered by the choir, single reader, or the whole congregation, only the lone voice of the cantor offers the various refrains, calling attention to these important words. In this sample service, the cantor sings each antiphon both before and after each Psalm or canticle, using the same tone for each antiphon, but varying the pitch according to the key of the music in which the Psalm is sung. A moment of silence should precede and follow each singing of the antiphon to allow each to be heard as a separate musical entity and to heighten the drama of these poignant texts. The cantor may be stationed near the rear of the sanctuary or in a balcony. Alternatively, the congregation may read each antiphon, leaving the reading and singing of the Psalms to the choir or solo voices. In any case, the alternation between the people and a leader calls attention to the antiphon. Priority should always be given to the participation of the congregation and the interpretive significance of the indicated refrain. Psalm tones for the singing of any of the Psalms and antiphons can be found in Hal H. Hopson's _Psalm Refrains and Tones_ (Carol Stream, Ill.: Hope Publishing, 1987).

The worship leaders process to their places in silence. A cross may go before them in procession.

The refrains that accompany each Psalm are based on a verse within the Psalm itself that is essential to the interpretation of the Psalm itself and its appropriation for its use during Holy Week. The refrains used in this service should be adapted to correspond with the nuances found in the given version of the Bible that a congregation is using.

Appropriate musical settings of Psalm 69 include "Save Me, O God; I Sink in Floods" (_Psalter Hymnal,_ 1987) and "When Waters Cover Me" (_Psalms for Today_ [London: Hodder and Stoughton, 1989]).

Periods of silence may be added throughout the service. This early reprise of the opening silence establishes the meditative character of the service and allows time for meditation on the words of the opening reading.

During each period of silence, a member of the congregation, perhaps a dancer moves to the candles at the front of the sanctuary, and extinguishes one or two candles. The number of candles extinguished each time will depend on the number of readings used.

Psalm tone for chanting from Hal H. Hopson, _Psalm Tones and Refrains,_ p. 42, no. 1. Other appropriate musical settings of Psalm 70 include "Come Quickly, Lord, to Rescue Me" (_Psalter Hymnal,_ 1987) and "Come Quickly, Lord" (_Psalms for Today_).

Alternatively, the Psalm may be read antiphonally or chanted in unison.

Lessons. These lessons may be read by one voice from the lectern or may be read by several voices from within the congregation.

The complete, traditional Tenebrae service continues here with Psalms 2, 22, and 27, followed by lessons from Isaiah 52–53 and Psalms 54, 76, and 88, followed by lessons from Hebrews 4, 5, and 9. The complete service, then, includes three sets of Psalms and lessons, followed by the final set of Psalms and canticles. This derives from the origins of this service as a three-day observance. This sample service only includes the first of these three sets, followed by the concluding Psalms and canticles. The refrains for the Psalms not included in this sample service are found in the appendix to this service. These additional Psalms may be used as alternatives to the first three Psalms of this service.

Psalms/Canticles. Appropriate musical settings of Psalm 63 include "My Soul Is Longing" (_Psalms for the Church Year,_ vol. 4, GIA Publications), "Your Love Is Finer Than Life" (_Psalms for the Church Year,_ vol. 1; GIA Publications), "O God Eternal, You Are My God" (_Trinity Hymnal_ [Atlanta: Great Commission Publications, 1990]), and "O God, You Are My God" (two settings in _Presbyterian Hymnal_ [Louisville: Westminster-John Knox, 1990]).

Appropriate musical settings of Psalm 90 include a responsorial setting found in _The Celebration Psalter,_ the familiar hymn "O God Our Help in Ages Past," and "Lord You Have Been Our Dwelling Place" (_Psalter Hymnal,_ 1987).

Other appropriate musical settings of Psalm 143 include "When Morning Lights the Eastern Skies" (_Presbyterian Hymnal,_ 1990), and "Lord Hear My

Prayer, My Supplication" (*Psalter Hymnal*, 1987).

As the refrain indicates, Psalm 143 brings a note of hope to the service. Any musical setting used must do justice to both the injunction of praise found in the Psalm and the evident solemnity of the service. It may be most appropriate to save a common musical setting of the Psalm for Eastertide, allowing only a single voice to read the Psalm in Tenebrae.

Other appropriate musical settings of Zechariah are found in the *Lutheran Book of Worship, Songs of Rejoicing*, (Accord, N.Y.: Selah Publications, 1989), *Presbyterian Hymnal*, (1990), *United Methodist Hymnal* (Nashville: Abingdon, 1989), *Psalter Hymnal*, (1991), and most other hymnals.

During the final antiphon the final candle, symbolizing the light of Christ, is removed from the sanctuary. All other sources of light should be extinguished. It may be carried by any member of the congregation, including a liturgical dancer, who may lift the candle high above his or her head and encircle the people before exiting the worship space.

Psalm 51 should be read quietly, but urgently, perhaps by a group of voices.

The silence is broken with a loud, resounding noise (strepitus). The noise may be one striking sound, such as that made by clapping two boards together or—perhaps more effectively—an extended peal of sound that begins quietly and continues to increase in volume until it overwhelms the worshiper, such as that made by a firm roll on a suspended cymbal. This sound signifies the earthquake on Good Friday or may remind the worshipers more generally of the cataclysmic nature of Christ's sacrifice, without reference to the specific earthquake.

Finally, the single candle may be brought back into the sanctuary. Alternatively, the candle may be brought back into the sanctuary on an Easter service, most appropriately at the Easter vigil.

John D. Witvliet

267 • A Combined Tenebrae and Seven Last Words Service

Tenebrae has been observed in the church since the fourth century. In this service, the church remembers the death of Jesus and recalls his seven last words on the cross. The gradual extinguishing of the candles is accompanied by prayers, hymns, choral anthems, and readings from Scripture.

Call to Worship (Isaiah 53:4-6)

LEADER: Surely he took up our infirmities and carried our sorrows,

PEOPLE: **yet we considered him stricken by God, smitten by him, and afflicted.**

LEADER: But he was pierced for our transgressions, he was crushed for our iniquities;

PEOPLE: **the punishment that brought us peace was upon him, and by his wounds we are healed.**

LEADER: We all, like sheep, have gone astray, each of us has turned to his own way;

PEOPLE: **and the Lord has laid on him the iniquity of us all.**

Hymn: "I Greet thee, Who My Sure Redeemer Art"

Litany of Remembrance

LEADER: Let us remember Jesus:
who, though rich, became poor and dwelt among us,
who was mighty indeed, healing the sick and the troubled,
who, as a teacher to his disciples, was their companion and servant.

PEOPLE: **May we ever be grateful for Jesus the Christ and what he has done for us.**

LEADER: Let us remember Jesus:
who prayed for the forgiveness of those who rejected him
and for the perfecting of those who received him,
who loved all people, and prayed for them,
even if they denied and rejected him
who hated sin because he knew the cost of pride and selfishness,
of cruelty and hatred, both to people and to God.

PEOPLE: **May we ever be grateful for Jesus the Christ and what he has done for us.**

LEADER: Let us remember Jesus:
who humbled himself, obedient unto the cross.
God has exalted him who has redeemed

us from the bondage of sin and given us new freedom.

PEOPLE: **May we ever be grateful for Jesus the Christ and what he has done and continues to do for us.**

Anthem: "Thy Will Be Done" (Courtney)

THE FIRST WORD: "Father, forgive them, for they do not know what they are doing" (Luke 23:34).

Reading: Psalm 51:1-14

Prayer on the First Word from the Cross

LEADER: Almighty God, to whom your crucified Son prayed for the forgiveness of those who did not know what they were doing, grant that we, too, may be included in that prayer. Whether we sin out of ignorance or intention, be merciful to us and grant us your acceptance and peace: in the name of Jesus Christ, our suffering Savior.

PEOPLE: **Amen.**

Hymn: "Ah, Holy Jesus, How Have You Offended? (RL 285)

Extinguish the first candle.

THE SECOND WORD: "Today you will be with me in paradise" (Luke 23:43).

The Two Scourges. The scourges received by our Savior are represented by two rods to which are attached to a number of straps with lead and bone woven into them.

Reading: John 14:1-6

Prayer on the Second Word from the Cross

LEADER: O Lord Jesus Christ, in your agony you showed compassion to a man who recognized his sinfulness and your holiness. You gave him the gift of life eternal. We thank you for that same indescribable gift you give to us. Help us to show such compassion to the lost so that they may too dwell in paradise with you. In your holy name we pray,

PEOPLE: **Amen.**

Hymn: "Lord Jesus Think on Me"

Extinguish the second candle.

THE THIRD WORD: "Dear woman, here is your son," . . . "Here is your mother" (John 19:26-27).

Reading: Mark 3:31-35

Prayer on the Third Word from the Cross

LEADER: O Blessed Savior, who in your hours of greatest suffering expressed compassion for your mother and made arrangements for her care, grant that we who seek to follow your example may show our concern for the needs of others, reaching out to provide for those who suffer in our human family. Hear this our prayer for your mercy's sake.

PEOPLE: **Amen.**

Hymn: "Beneath the Cross of Jesus"

Extinguish the third candle.

THE FOURTH WORD: "My God, my God, why have you forsaken me?" (Matt. 27:46).

Reading: Psalm 22:1-11

Prayer on the Fourth Word from the Cross

LEADER: Almighty God, who forsook your Son upon the cross showing the world your judgment upon human sin and guilt, grant us, upon hearing his cry, the grace to know and believe that we will never be forsaken, that he is present with us even to the end of the age. For the sake of Jesus Christ who bore our sins on the cross.

PEOPLE: **Amen.**

Anthem: "He Was Wounded" (Courtney)

Extinguish the fourth candle.

THE FIFTH WORD: "I am thirsty" (John 19:28).

Reading: Isaiah 55:1-5

Prayer on the Fifth Word from the Cross

LEADER: O blessed Savior, whose lips were dry and whose throat was parched, grant us the water of life that we who thirst after righteousness may find it quenched by your love and mercy, leading us to bring this same relief to others.

PEOPLE: **Amen.**

Hymn: "When I Survey the Wondrous Cross"

Extinguish the fifth candle.

THE SIXTH WORD: "It is finished" (John 19:30).

Reading: Luke 13:31-35

Prayer on the Sixth Word from the Cross

LEADER: O Lord Jesus Christ, who finished the work that you were sent to do, enable us by your Holy Spirit to be faithful to our call. Grant us strength to bear our crosses and endure our sufferings, even unto death. Enable us to live and love so faithfully that we also become good news to the world, joining your witness. O Christ, in whose name we pray.

PEOPLE: **Amen.**

Hymn: "It Is Finished"

Extinguish the sixth candle.

THE SEVENTH WORD: "Father, into your hands I commit my spirit" (Luke 23:46).

Reading: Luke 2:29-35

Prayer on the Seventh Word from the Cross

LEADER: Father, into whose hands your Son Jesus Christ commended his spirit, grant that we too, following his ex-

ample, may in all of life and at the moment of our death entrust our lives into your faithful hands of love. In the name of Jesus who gave his life for us all.

PEOPLE: **Amen.**

Hymn: "O Sacred Head, Now Wounded"

Extinguish the seventh candle.

Darkness

Tolling of the Bell

Return with the seventh candle, lit.

Benediction

After a moment of meditation, the congregation is asked to leave in silence.

Norman D. Palsma

268 ✦ THE WAY OF THE CROSS SERVICE

The Way of the Cross service below is especially designed for use in the free church tradition. Adapt to local usage and style.

In the ancient church pilgrims came to Jerusalem during Holy Week to reenact the final events of the life of Jesus. In the course of time a tradition grew up which followed the course of events from Pilate's house to Calvary. Scripture readings and prayers were said at each of these stations.

At first the number of stations or devotional stops varied widely. By the sixteenth century fourteen stations became the fixed number of devotional stops. Of these fourteen, eight are based directly on events recorded in the Gospels while six (numbers 3, 4, 6, 7, 9 and 13) are rooted in inferences from the Gospels or from legend.

In modern times this devotional, which carries the worshiper from the condemnation of Jesus at the cross to the entombment, became established in almost all Catholic churches throughout the world. Artistic renditions of these stations were placed in the walls of the church either permanently or in a removable fashion to be brought out for use during Lent and especially during Holy Week.

Among Catholics, the service begins with a set of prayers, followed by the movements of the congregation from station to station. A Scripture is read before the station, prayers are said, and a hymn is sung. Then the congregation moves on to the next station.

In Protestant churches that do not have visuals of the stations of the cross, a visual image of movement may be made by three persons dressed in black who walk through the congregation. The person in the middle carries a cross and represents Jesus. The other two represent the crowd that accompanied Jesus to Golgotha.

In this arrangement the congregation remains seated while these three persons move as the congregation sings to symbolize the journey from one station to the other. Pace out the journey down the aisle of the church into fourteen sections. On Station 12 the cross bearer and attendants kneel; on Station 13 they kneel again with hands outstretched, on Station 14 they lie face down on the floor. They remain in this position until after the closing prayer. The congregation may kneel on Station 12 and remain in that position until the close of the service.

This service may be adapted to the noon to 3:00 P.M. time or it may be used throughout Lent. The service printed here was developed for an evangelical Protestant tradition. Many different services are available. Adapt to local usage and style.

The Way of the Cross Service

The service begins in silence and semi-darkness as the people gather. People who represent Jesus and the crowds may stand in an obvious place as people enter. The service may begin with a prayer followed by the announcement of each station, the reading , the prayer, the hymn, and movement of the symbolic figures. The service should commence slowly with periods of silence between the acts of worship.

1. Jesus Is Condemned to Death

Scripture Reading: John 19:1-3, 5
Then Pilate took Jesus and had him flogged. The soldiers twisted together a crown of thorns and put it on his head. They clothed him in a purple robe. . . . When Jesus came out wearing the crown of thorns and the purple robe, Pilate said to them, "Here is the man!"

Prayer

LEADER: Let us pray. (silence)
Holy Father, you gave your only begotten Son to become one of us, to stand in our place and be condemned for us: grant that we who are in him may now journey by faith into his glorious death; through Jesus Christ your Son, our Lord. Amen.

Hymn: "Go to Dark Gethsemane" (the symbolic figures move to the next station)

2. Jesus Takes up His Cross

Scripture Reading: John 19:15-17
But they shouted, "Take him away! Take him away! Crucify him!" "Shall I crucify your king?" Pilate asked. "We have no king but Caesar," the chief priests answered. Finally Pilate handed him over to them to be crucified. So the soldiers took charge of Jesus. Carrying his own cross, he went out to the place of the Skull (which in Aramaic is called Golgotha).

Prayer

LEADER: Let us pray. (silence)
Most merciful God, whose Son came to be the light to shine in the darkness: Shine forth in our hearts and dispel the darkness within us so that we might not join those who turn their hearts from the light of truth; through Jesus Christ our Lord. Amen.

Hymn: "Alas and Did My Savior Bleed" (the symbolic figures move to the next station)

3. Jesus Falls the First Time

Scripture Reading: Philippians 2:5-11
Your attitude should be the same as that of Christ Jesus:
Who, being in very nature God,
    did not consider equality with God something
        to be grasped,
but made himself nothing,
    taking the very nature of a servant,
    being made in human likeness.
And being found in appearance as a man,
    he humbled himself
    and became obedient to death—
        even death on a cross!

Therefore God exalted him to the highest place
and gave him the name that is above every
name,
that at the name of Jesus every knee should bow,
in heaven and on earth and under the earth,
and every tongue confess that Jesus Christ is
Lord,
to the glory of God the Father.

Prayer

LEADER: Let us pray. (silence)
Almighty God, you have exalted the
name of your Son above every name
in heaven and on earth: grant that we
in the hour of his death might bow
our knee and humbly confess with
our mouths that Jesus is Lord;
through Jesus Christ our Lord. Amen.

Hymn: "The Old Rugged Cross" (the symbolic figures move to the next section)

4. Jesus Meets His Afflicted Mother

Scripture Reading: Luke 1:46-55
And Mary said:
"My soul glorifies the Lord
and my spirit rejoices in God my Savior,
for he has been mindful of the humble state of
his servant.
From now on all generations will call me
blessed,
for the Mighty One has done great things for
me—
holy is his name.
His mercy extends to those who fear him,
from generation to generation.
He has performed mighty deeds with his arm;
he has scattered those who are proud in their
inmost thoughts.
He has brought down rulers from their thrones
but has lifted up the humble.
He has filled the hungry with good things
but has sent the rich away empty.
He has helped his servant Israel,
remembering to be merciful
to Abraham and his descendants forever,
even as he said to our fathers."

Prayer

LEADER: Let us pray. (silence)

Heavenly Father, you who chose Mary
to be your bondslave and bring forth
the Savior of the world: Grant that we
like Mary might share in his passion
so that we might rejoice with her in
his glorious resurrection; through
Jesus Christ our Lord. Amen.

Song: "Jesus, I My Cross" (the symbolic figures move to the next station)

5. The Cross Is Laid on Simon of Cyrene

Scripture Reading: Luke 23:26; Matthew 11:28-30
As they led him away, they seized Simon from
Cyrene, who was on his way in from the country,
and put the cross on him and made him carry it
behind Jesus.

"Come to me, all you who are weary and burdened, and I will give you rest. Take my yoke upon
you and learn from me, for I am gentle and humble
in heart, and you will find rest for your souls. For
my yoke is easy and my burden is light."

Prayer

LEADER: Let us pray. (silence)
Lord Jesus Christ, you who came not
to be served but to serve, you gladly
gave your life over to suffering and
death for us: Give us the grace to follow in your way, to live lives of self-sacrifice for those who suffer and are
in need; grant this through the power
of the Holy Spirit we pray. Amen.

Hymn: "Must Jesus Bear the Cross" (the symbolic figures move to the next station)

6. A Woman Wipes the Face of Jesus

Scripture Reading: Isaiah 53:1-3
Who has believed our message
and to whom has the arm of the LORD been revealed?
He grew up before him like a tender shoot,
and like a root out of dry ground.
He had no beauty or majesty to attract us to him,
nothing in his appearance that we should desire him.
He was despised and rejected by men,
a man of sorrows, and familiar with suffering.

Like one from whom men hide their faces
  he was despised, and we esteemed him not.

Prayer

LEADER: Let us pray. (silence)
Loving God, you who gave us the most costly gift of your Son to endure the penalty of our sin in his own body: turn our eyes upon your Son that we, beholding your mercy in him, may by faith take up his cross and enter into his suffering; we offer this prayer in the name of your Son Jesus. Amen.

Hymn: "Christ Has for Sin Atoned" (the symbolic figures move to the next station)

7. Jesus Falls a Second Time

Scripture Reading: Isaiah 53:4-6
  Surely he took up our infirmities
    and carried our sorrows,
  yet we considered him stricken by God,
    smitten by him, and afflicted.
  But he was pierced for our transgressions
    he was crushed for our iniquities;
  the punishment that brought us peace was
    upon him,
    and by his wounds we are healed.
  We all, like sheep, have gone astray,
    each of us has turned to his own way;
  and the LORD has laid on him
    the iniquity of us all.

Prayer

LEADER: Let us pray. (silence)
O blessed Jesus, you who are the lover of souls, the innocent one, upon whom the iniquity of all peoples of every generation has been laid: grant that we, having been healed by your wounds, may be set free to love and serve you with singleness of mind; who lives and reigns forever and ever. Amen.

Hymn: "Lead Me to Calvary" (the symbolic figures move to the next station)

8. Jesus Meets the Women of Jerusalem

Scripture Reading: Luke 23:27-28

A large number of people followed him, including women who mourned and wailed for him. Jesus turned and said to them, "Daughters of Jerusalem, do not weep for me; weep for yourselves and for your children."

Prayer

LEADER: Let us pray. (silence)
Holy Spirit of life everlasting, you who bring us the benefits and salvation purchased by Jesus the Christ; turn our mourning into rejoicing that we, having suffered with Christ, may be raised in newness of life with him; through Jesus our Lord. Amen.

Hymn: "When I Survey the Wondrous Cross" (the symbolic figures move to the next station)

9. Jesus Falls a Third Time

Scripture Reading: Isaiah 53:7-9
  He was oppressed and afflicted,
    yet he did not open his mouth;
  he was led like a lamb to the slaughter,
    and as a sheep before her shearers is silent,
    so he did not open his mouth.
  By oppression and judgment, he was taken away.
    And who can speak of his descendants?
  For he was cut off from the land of the living;
    for the transgression of my people he was
    stricken.
  He was assigned a grave with the wicked,
    and with the rich in his death,
  though he had done no violence,
    nor was any deceit in his mouth.

Prayer

LEADER: Let us pray. (silence)
Lord Jesus Christ, you who humbled yourself on earth for our sake and are now seated at the right hand of the Father: grant that we be so moved by your compassion for us that we might not only believe in you, but that we might emulate your humility and participate in your suffering; who lives and reigns with the Father and the Holy Spirit forever and ever. Amen.

Hymn: "Alas and Did My Savior Bleed" (the symbolic figures move to the next station)

10. Jesus Is Stripped of His Garment

Scripture Reading: Luke 23:32-38

Two other men, both criminals, were also led out with him to be executed. When they came to the place called the Skull, there they crucified him, along with the criminals—one on his right, the other on his left. Jesus said, "Father, forgive them, for they do not know what they are doing." And they divided up his clothes by casting lots. The people stood watching, and the rulers even sneered at him. They said, "He saved others; let him save himself if he is the Christ of God, the Chosen One." The soldiers also came up and mocked him. They offered him wine vinegar and said, "If you are the king of Jews, save yourself." There was a written notice above him, which read: THIS IS THE KING OF THE JEWS.

Prayer

LEADER: Let us pray. (silence)
Most blessed Jesus, you who knew no sin was made sin for us, that we might be made righteous: give us the grace of your salvation that being made one in you we might rejoice in your suffering and await with hope your glorious resurrection; who lives and reigns forever and ever. Amen.

Hymn: "Let All Mortal Flesh Keep Silence" (the symbolic figures move to the next station)

11. Jesus Is Nailed to the Cross

Scripture Reading: Isaiah 53:10-12

Yet it was the LORD's will to crush him and cause him to suffer,
and though the LORD makes his life a guilt offering,
he will see his offspring and prolong his days,
and the will of the LORD will prosper in his hand.
After the suffering of his soul,
he will see the light of life and be satisfied;
by his knowledge my righteous servant will justify many,
and he will bear their iniquities.
Therefore I will give him a portion among the great,
and he will divide the spoils with the strong,

because he poured out his life unto death,
and was numbered with the transgressors.
For he bore the sin of many,
and made intercession for the transgressors.

Prayer

LEADER: Let us pray. (silence)
Almighty and everlasting God, because of your love and mercy you choose to lay upon your only Son the iniquity of us all: turn us, dear one, from the iniquity of our ways, from our oppression of others, and from the love of evil; that we may die to sin through Jesus your Son. Amen.

Hymn: "Were You There?" (the symbolic figures move to the next station)

12. Jesus Dies on the Cross

Scripture Reading: Luke 23:44-46

It was now about the sixth hour, and the darkness came over the whole land until the ninth hour, for the sun stopped shining. And the curtain of the temple was torn in two. Jesus called out with a loud voice, "Father, into your hands I commit my spirit." When he said this, he breathed his last.

Prayer

LEADER: Let us pray. (silence)
O Jesus , you who are one of us, you who participated in the joys and sorrows of human existence, you who went to death for us: take our hate and greed, our self-centeredness and rebellion to the cross with you, and by the power of the Holy Spirit release us from the death that grips our lives; we prayer this for the sake of your glorious name. Amen.

Hymn: "O Sacred Head" (the symbolic figures move to the next station)

13. The Body of Jesus Is Placed in the Arms of His Mother

Scripture Reading: Isaiah 54:4-6

"Do not be afraid; you will not suffer shame.
Do not fear disgrace; you will not be humiliated.

You will forget the shame of your youth
  and remember no more the reproach
  of your widowhood.
For your Maker is your husband—
  the Lᴏʀᴅ Almighty is his name—
the Holy One of Israel is your Redeemer;
  he is called the God of all the earth.
The Lᴏʀᴅ will call you back
  as if you were a wife deserted and distressed
  in spirit—
a wife who married young,
  only to be rejected," says your God.

Prayer

LEADER: Let us pray. (silence)
O peaceful Jesus, you who were enveloped in the loving arms of your mother, you who rested your head against the heart broken with grief: touch us in the hour of your death and bring us to everlasting peace; through the power of your Holy Spirit. Amen.

Hymn: "Glory Be to Jesus" (the symbolic figures move to the next station)

——— 14. Jesus Is Laid in the Tomb ———

Scripture Reading: Luke 23:50-56
Now there was a man named Joseph, a member of the Council, a good and upright man, who had not consented to their decision and action. He came from the Judean town of Arimathea and he was waiting for the kingdom of God. Going to Pilate, he asked for Jesus' body. Then he took it down, wrapped it in linen cloth and placed it in a tomb cut in the rock, one in which no one had yet been laid. It was Preparation Day, and the Sabbath was about to begin. The women who had come with Jesus from Galilee followed Joseph and saw the tomb and how his body was laid in it. Then they went home and prepared spices and perfumes. But they rested on the Sabbath in obedience to the commandment.

Prayer

LEADER: Let us pray. (silence)
O loving Jesus, you who were stretched forth on the bed of death and entered the gates of hell to proclaim your victory over the power of the evil one: enter the gates of my heart and trample to death the evil that lurks within, that I might rejoice in your resurrection; for your sake. Amen.

Hymn: "Just As I Am"

The people leave in silence.

269 ✦ A Combined Way of the Cross and Tenebrae Service

The service below requires two narrators, a song leader, three characters dressed in black (one of whom carries a cross and represents Jesus), one or two people to extinguish candles, two readers, and a person to offer prayer. The room should be semidark. Ten candles should be lit; one will represent Christ and should be larger or made of a different color. The three symbolic figures may take their place in the back of the church and stand in silence as the people enter.

Invocation: (Pastor or song leader)

I.

NARRATOR 1: Station 1 (Matt. 27:11-26)—Jesus is condemned to death.

NARRATOR 2: Jesus stood before the governor, and the governor asked him, "Are you the king of the Jews?"

NARRATOR 1: "Yes, it is as you say."

NARRATOR 2: When he was accused by the high priests and elders, he gave no answer. Then Pilate asked Him, "Don't you hear how many things they are accusing you of?" But Jesus made no reply, not even to a single charge—to the great amazement of the governor.

NARRATOR 1: Now it was the governor's custom at the Feast to release a prisoner chosen by the crowd. at that time they had a notorious prisoner, called Barabbas. So when the crowd had gathered, Pilate asked them, "Which one do you want me to release to you: Barrabas, or Jesus who is called Christ?" For he knew it was out of envy that they had handed Jesus over to him.

NARRATOR 2: While Pilate was sitting on the

judge's seat, his wife sent him this message: "Don't have anything to do with that innocent man, for I have suffered a great deal today in a dream because of him."

NARRATOR 1: But the chief priests and the elders persuaded the crowd to ask for Barabbas and to have Jesus executed. "Which of the two do you want me to release to you?" asked the governor.

NARRATOR 2: "Barabbas," they answered.

NARRATOR 1: "What shall I do, then, with Jesus who is called Christ?"

NARRATOR 2: "Crucify him!"

NARRATOR 1: "Why? What crime has he committed?"

NARRATOR 2: But they shouted all the louder, "Crucify him!"

NARRATOR 1: When Pilate saw that he was getting nowhere, but that instead an uproar was starting, he took water and washed his hands in front of the crowd. "I am innocent of this man's blood, it is your responsibility!"

NARRATOR 2: All the people answered, "Let his blood be on us and on our children!"

(Pause)

NARRATOR 1: Then he released Barabbas to them. But he had Jesus flogged, and he handed him over to be crucified.

Hymn: "What Wondrous Love Is This" (the figures move to the next station)

Prayer

Candle 1 is extinguished.

II.

NARRATOR 1: Station 2 (Matt. 27:27-31)—The soldiers mock Jesus

NARRATOR 2: Then the governor's soldiers took Jesus into the Praetorium and gathered the whole company of soldiers around him. They stripped him and put a scarlet robe on him, and then wove a crown of thorns and set it on his head.

NARRATOR 1: They put a staff in his right hand and knelt in front of him and mocked him. "Hail, king of the Jews!" they said. They spit on him, and took the staff and struck him on the head again and again. (Pause) After they had mocked him, they took off the robe and put his own clothes on him. Then they led him away to crucify him.

CHORUS: "Sing Hallelujah to the Lord" (the figures moves to the next station)

Prayer

Candle 2 is extinguished.

III.

NARRATOR 1: Station 3 (Luke 23:26)—The cross is laid on Simon of Cyrene

NARRATOR 2: As they led him away, they seized Simon from Cyrene, who was on his way in from the country, and put the cross on him and made him carry it behind Jesus.

Hymn: "Near the Cross" (the figures lift the cross)

Prayer

Candle 3 is extinguished.

IV.

NARRATOR 1: Station 4: (Luke 23:27-31) Jesus meets the women of Jerusalem

NARRATOR 2: A large number of people followed him, including women who mourned and wailed for him. Jesus turned and said to them,

NARRATOR 1: "Daughters of Jerusalem, do not weep for me; weep for yourselves and for your children. For the time will come when you will say, 'Blessed are the barren women, the wombs that never bore and the breasts that never nursed!' Then they will say to the mountains, 'Fall on us!' and to the hills, 'Cover us!' For if men do these things when the tree is green, what will happen when it is dry?"

Hymn: "Beneath the Cross of Jesus"

Prayer (the figures remain in place as the cross is lowered)

Candle 4 is extinguished.

V.

NARRATOR 1: Station 5 (Isa. 53:4, 5)—Jesus is nailed to the cross

NARRATOR 2: Surely he took up our infirmities and carried our sorrows, yet we considered him stricken by God, smitten by him, and afflicted. But he was pierced for our transgressions, he was crushed for our iniquities; the punishment that brought us peace was upon him, and by his wounds are healed.

The cross is laid down, and one nail is driven into it by assistants.

Hymn: "The Old Rugged Cross" (a cappella)

Another nail is driven into the cross.

"The Old Rugged Cross" (a cappella)

The third nail is driven into the cross.

"The Old Rugged Cross" (a cappella)

Prayer

Candle 5 is extinguished.

VI.

NARRATOR 1: Station 6 (John 19:23, 24)—Jesus is stripped of his garments

NARRATOR 2: When the soldiers had crucified Jesus, they took his clothes, dividing them into four shares, one of each of them, with the undergarment remaining. This garment was seamless, woven in one piece from top to bottom.

NARRATOR 1: "Let's not tear it," they said to one another. "Let's decide by lot who will get it." This happened that the scripture might be fulfilled which said, "They divided my garments among them and cast lots for my clothing."

Hymn: "When I Survey the Wondrous Cross" (the cross with nails is lifted for all to see)

Prayer

Candle 6 is extinguished.

VII.

NARRATOR 1: Station 7 (Luke 23:39-43)—Jesus welcomes the repentant thief

NARRATOR 2: One of the criminals who hung there hurled insults at him:

NARRATOR 1: "Aren't you the Christ? Save yourself and us." But the other criminal rebuked him.

NARRATOR 2: "Don't you fear God, since you are under the same sentence? We are punished justly, for we are getting what our deeds deserve. But this man has done nothing wrong." Then he said, "Jesus, remember me when you come into your kingdom."

NARRATOR 1: "I tell you the truth, today you will be with me in paradise."

Hymn: "Amazing Grace" (v. 1, 3, 5 sung; v. 2, 4 read by song leader)

(The cross remains lifted for all to see.)

Prayer

Candle 7 is extinguished.

VIII.

NARRATOR 1: Station 8: (Matt. 27:45-49) Jesus cries out

NARRATOR 2: From the sixth hour until the ninth hour (that is, noon to 3 P.M.) darkness came over all the land. About the ninth hour, Jesus cried in a loud voice,

NARRATOR 1: *"Eloi, Eloi, lama sabachthani?"* — which means, "My God, my God, why have you forsaken me?"

NARRATOR 2: When some of those standing there heard this, they said, "He's calling Elijah."

NARRATOR 1: Immediately one of them ran and got a sponge. He filled it with wine vinegar, put it on a stick, and offered it to Jesus to drink. The rest said,

NARRATOR 2: "Now leave him alone. Let's see if Elijah comes to save him."

Hymn: "Jesus Paid It All" (the cross is lifted but turned upside down)

Prayer

Candle 8 is extinguished.

IX.

NARRATOR 1: Station 9 (Luke 23:44-49)—Jesus dies on the cross

NARRATOR 2: It was now about the sixth hour, and darkness came over the whole land until the ninth hour, for the sun stopped shining. And the curtain of the temple was torn in two.

NARRATOR 1: Jesus called out with a loud voice, "Father, into your hands I commit my spirit." When he had said this, he breathed his last.

NARRATOR 2: The centurion, seeing what had happened, praised God and said, "Surely this was a righteous man." When all the people who had gathered to witness this sight saw what took place, they beat their breasts and went away.

NARRATOR 1: But all those who knew him, including the women who had followed him from Galilee, stood at a distance, watching these things.

Hymn: "O Sacred Head Now Wounded" (the cross is laid down and the symbolic figures kneel)

Prayer

Candle 9 is extinguished.

X.

NARRATOR 1: Station 10 (Luke 23:50-56)—Jesus is laid in the tomb

NARRATOR 2: Now there was a man named Joseph, a member of the Council, a good and upright man, who had not consented to their decision and action. He came from the Judean town of Arimathea and he was waiting for the kingdom of God.

NARRATOR 1: Going to Pilate, he asked for Jesus' body. Then he took it down, wrapped it in linen cloth and placed it in a tomb cut in the rock, one in which no one had yet been laid. It was Preparation Day, and the Sabbath was about to begin.

NARRATOR 2: The women who had come with Jesus from Galilee followed Joseph and saw the tomb and how his body was laid in it. Then they went home and prepared spices and perfumes. But they rested on the Sabbath in obedience to the commandment.

Hymn: "Were You There?" (the symbolic figures lie prostrate near the cross)

Candle 10 is extinguished.

Closing prayer

The lights slowly rise to half, and the congregation leaves in silence.

William Wells

270 ◆ A MIME FOR THE STATIONS OF THE CROSS SERVICE

The following mime outlines the stations of the cross. It may be used in conjunction with either of the two previous services, or in conjunction with another service presented earlier in this section.

The only spoken word is done by a girl who merely stands at the microphone and announces each station. The children then proceed to act out each station in turn. At the end of the fifteenth station, after everyone has left the setting, the narrator slips out, too.

Pontius Pilate walks out with **two guards** smaller than he. They start at the right side and walk in front of the altar. Pilate condemns Jesus to death by crossing his hands and then turns to the right where the first guard washes this hands. Then the three of them walk up behind the altar and Pilate sits in a chair with a guard standing on either side of him. They remain in that position until the tenth station. The guards return in the eleventh station.

Jesus slowly walks towards Pilate—the expression on his face is sad when the cross is presented. With a guard on either side he walks to and fro. He is like one chained. His first fall appears painful. The meeting with his mother, **Mary**, is tender, and he slowly blesses her.

Then **Simon** is pulled into the team to help carry the cross. **Veronica** walks to Jesus: she kneels and wipes his face. She then goes to the center, faces the congregation, and stands poised, holding up her arms to display the imaginary towel.

Women of Jerusalem come in. Those nearest Jesus kneel and he warily motions to them. They slowly turn and retreat.

The guards with Jesus and Simon take care to lift the cross to the other shoulder as Christ walks back and forth. One of the guards lifts his hand as if to strike Christ occasionally. With each fall Jesus falls into more of a slump, trying to display more and more pain and exhaustion.

At the tenth station Jesus is in the center and the guards painfully strip him of his garments. Two guards hold the cross behind Jesus and another guard slowly pretends to hammer nails into his hands.

At the twelfth station, **Mary, Mary Magdalene**, and **John** come and stand at the foot of the cross. Jesus slowly dies; he raises his head and eyes upward, and then closing his eyes, he bows his head and dies. Mary and her companions walk away. She sits on a bench and the other two stand behind her.

Then all the guards gather round the cross and pretend to carry Jesus off and place him on the bench in his mother's arms.

For the fourteenth station the guards again gather around Jesus. With hands raised in position for carrying someone, they make way to the tomb which is behind the altar. Then the guards take their places on and around the altar as if they were guarding a tomb.

At the fifteenth station Christ, robed in white, slowly walks out and around the altar. As this is done the guards motion as if they see a dazzling light and fall gently to the floor. As Christ passes, each guard is motionless until he has returned to the tomb.

One by one the mimists leave the sanctuary.

Virginia Kimball[42]

271 ✦ GUIDELINES FOR THE CHRISTIAN USE OF THE SEDER

In recent years it has become popular for congregations to conduct the Passover meal, or some combination of the Seder and Communion during Holy Week, particularly on Maundy Thursday. This article challenges such practices, urging Christians to observe the Seder authentically. Full Seder services are usually available through local bookstores.

The Christian use of the Jewish Passover Seder is as much an _interreligious_ (affecting relationships between Christianity and other world religions) as a liturgical concern. Improving Jewish-Christian relations in the post-Holocaust era requires that Christians be especially sensitive to Jewish difficulties with the uncritical Christian use of the Seder, and with the Christianizing of any of its elements in particular.

The Seder (order) or Pesach (Passover), celebrated according to the traditional Haggadah (telling), is the key rite of Judaism's central festival. Although the biblical account of Passover (Exod. 12:1-28) is part of the heritage common to Jews and Christians, the Seder Haggadah, while based on the biblical account, evolved into its basic form between the destruction of the temple in 70 of the Common Era (A.D.) and the thirteenth century C.E. Thus, the traditional Haggadah belongs to the Jews; it is not the common property of Jews and Christians. Christians are not free to use or adapt the Haggadah without regard for its Jewish origins. "Good ecumenical (interreligious) relations require respect for the religious heritage of others and the integrity of their rituals" (Alfred Tegels, "Seder Meals and Passion Plays," _Worship_ 60 [1986], 74).

The Seder Haggadah used by the Jewish community today cannot accurately be represented to Christians as "what Jesus did" or as the "roots" of the Lord's Supper (Communion). The basic text of the Haggadah did not reach its present form until the thirteenth century C.E. While its primary elements (the Passover story, unleavened bread, bitter herbs, cups of wine) are undeniably from the time of Jesus or before, the Haggadah contains much material that was added _after_ the time of Jesus (including the placing of the questions _before_ instead of _after_ the meal; the sequence and content of the questions; the use of the ceremonial Seder tray and its arrangement; the addition of the _haroset_ to the menu of symbolic foods; the ritual recitation of the plagues as drops of wine are spilled from the second cup of wine; the cup, chair and opening of the door for Elijah; "next year in Jerusalem," and the final songs, including "Dayenu"). None of these elements would have been familiar to Jesus (nor would the terms "Seder" or "Haggadah" been known to Jesus in connection with the Passover meal).

Because so many elements were added to the Seder Haggadah after the time of Jesus, it is obviously inappropriate to _substitute_ the Seder for the Lord's Supper on Holy (Maundy) Thursday.

It is also misleading (as well as insensitive to Jewish-Christian relations) to conclude a Seder with an abbreviated form of the Lord's Supper on Holy Thursday, as though the thirteenth century C.E. Haggadah somehow represents "what Jesus did" at the Last Supper. The order of the Passover meal followed by Jesus was much less elaborate. After a brief introduction, the meal was eaten with its symbolic foods (Exod. 12:8: lamb, unleavened bread, bitter herbs) and a cup or cups of wine were blessed and shared. The meal was followed by suggestive rather than prescriptive questions and answers concerning the meaning of the foods, and may have concluded with a form of Grace after Meals (the common Jewish table prayer) and the singing of a Psalm or Psalms. The narratives of the Lord's Supper (1 Cor. 11:23-26; Matt. 26:26-29; Mark 14:22-25; Luke 22:15-20) mention only bread and wine; the customary word for unleavened bread is not used, nor are lamb and bitter herbs mentioned. The use of lamb at the Seder was discontinued by most Jews after the sacrificial system came to an end with the destruction of the Jerusalem temple by the Romans in 70 C.E.; it has not been reintroduced.

Because the Christian Passover (Pascha) is a comprehensive three-day (Holy Thursday, Good Friday, Easter Day) liturgy of Christ's "passing over" from death to life, the Christian equivalent of the Seder is not the Lord's Supper of Holy Thursday, but the Eucharist of Easter day, preferably at the climax of the Paschal Vigil. The Christian equivalent of the Seder Haggadah is not the medieval Jewish Haggadah celebrated on Holy Thursday, but the Great Paschal Vigil of the Resurrection celebrated late on Easter eve or early on Easter day (see *Handbook of the Christian Year* [Nashville: Abingdon, 1986], 191–209). As the historic and distinctive "telling" of the Christian Passover, the Paschal Vigil begins with the Paschal Proclamation of Christ's Passover Victory (Exulted) during the introductory Service of Light. The Service of the Word consists of Old Testament prophetic readings that rehearse God's saving deeds in history (always including the Exodus) in anticipation of their fulfillment in Christian baptism. New Christians are initiated during the Service of the Water, and the Vigil concludes with the Service of the Bread and Cup which is the Christian Passover meal *par excellence*. As the Seder Haggadah directs its participants to regard themselves as if they too had come forth out of Egypt, so the Paschal Proclamation at the beginning of

the Paschal Vigil involves Christians in the events of their liberation with its repeated reminder, "This is the night . . . "

The Jewish Seder is best experienced by Christians, not as background to the institution of the Lord's Supper in Holy Week, but as an exercise in interreligious understanding. The Seder Haggadah is not primarily a lesson in Christian origins, so much as it is the Jewish understanding of Passover as it evolved in reaction to Christianity and to persecution during the Common (Christian) Era. The questions and answers, for example, originally came in natural sequence after the meal, but between 70 and 200 C.E., they were moved to their present position *before* the meal, probably to avoid any possible confusion with the new significance being attached to bread and wine during the Passover meal observed by Jewish Christians. The opening of the door for Elijah—unknown to Jesus, but introduced between the tenth and the thirteenth centuries C.E.—may have originally served a purely utilitarian function: it was opened during the Seder to demonstrate to a suspicious and hostile Christian community that the Jews had nothing to hide.

As an exercise in Jewish-Christian understanding, the Seder experienced by Christians should be as authentic as possible. Because the Seder is a ritual of home and family around the dinner table, often of several hours' duration, it is most authentically experienced by Christians as the invited guests of a Jewish household where such arrangements can be made.

Where it is not possible for Christians to be the guests of a Jewish family for the Seder, a rabbi or other informed Jew should be invited to lead a Seder for the congregation (or to participate actively in the planning of a Seder if such leadership is not possible). The Haggadah should be followed without abbreviation, including the service of the full meal (without lamb).

Care should be taken to preserve as much of the Seder's essential family intimacy and informality and length as possible.

The Seder is experienced most authentically by Christians with a Jewish family on the first or second night of the Jewish festival of Pesach (Passover), regardless of the dates of the Christian Holy Week. When Passover coincides with Holy Week, the Seder should not be scheduled for Holy Thursday.

Where the custom of the Christian use of the Seder in Holy Week persists, despite the interreligious, historical, theological, and liturgical problems it raises, it would be less susceptible to misinterpretation and offense if it were held on Wednesday of Holy Week or earlier, rather than on Holy (Maundy) Thursday.

John D. Grabner

272 ✦ A SERVICE FOR HOLY SATURDAY

The third day of the triduum _is a day for silence. During this day, Christians may gather for prayer, to feel the silence and to sense the weight of Jesus' death. This service prepares worshipers for the Great Paschal Vigil on Saturday evening (see chapter 23)._

In the early church the commemoration of the paschal event allowed for a connection between Good Friday and the great Paschal Vigil of Saturday night (which was the Easter day celebration). During the day of Saturday, Christians gathered for prayer and meditation of the sixth and ninth hours.

Today the unitive nature of the three days has been largely lost. However, churches seeking to restore the entire three days as a time of solemn worship conduct a service on Saturday of Holy Week and also keep the church open during the day for prayers.

The Saturday service is a very simple service of prayer, Scripture reading, a sermon, and the anthem "In the Midst of Life," which is normally used in the burial office. This service begins and ends in silence in keeping with the solemnity of the day.

It is good to have a devotional guide for prayer, reading, and meditation available for those who wish to come to the church during the day. This may be an especially profitable time to focus on the meaning of Christ's death and the application of Christ's death to one's life.

An Order for the Holy Saturday Service

(The people take their places in silence.)

The minister steps forward and says, "Let us pray: O God, Creator of heaven and earth: Grant that, as the crucified body of your dear Son was laid in the tomb and rested on this holy Sabbath, so we may await with him the coming of the third day, and rise with him to newness of life; who now lives and reigns with you and the Holy Spirit, one God, for ever and ever. Amen.

The Scripture Readings
Old Testament: Job 14:1-14
Psalm 130 or 31:1-5
Epistle: 1 Peter 4:1-8
Gospel: Matthew 27:57-66, or John 19:38-42

The Sermon

The Prayers

(After the gospel and homily, in place of the Prayers of the People, the anthem "In the Midst of Life" is sung or said. The service then concludes with the Lord's Prayer and the Grace.)

Robert E. Webber

PART SEVEN

The Season of Easter and Pentecost

The season of Easter is the season of celebration. Christ is risen! Death is conquered! Let all the people worship the Lord! The solemn preparation of Lent and somber meditation of Holy Week gives way to victorious festivity during the fifty days of Easter.

It is important to see the fifty days of Easter as a season, anchored by Easter Sunday on one end and Pentecost on the other. Neither would be complete without the other. The church's worship centers on the paschal mystery of Christ's dying and rising. It is inspired and guided by the Holy Spirit. The following chapters both introduce this season of celebration and provide resources for planning worship.

ꙮ TWENTY-TWO ꙮ

Introduction to the Season of Easter

Many Christians may assume that Easter is just one day. In fact, the church celebrates Easter for fifty days. During this season, it remembers the post-resurrection appearances of Christ, it celebrates Christ's ascension into heaven, the coming of the Spirit on Pentecost, and begins to explore the implications of the Resurrection for the future of God's kingdom. This chapter introduces these themes of Easter worship and describes their significance in the history of the worship of the church.

273 ◆ AN INTRODUCTION TO WORSHIP FROM EASTER TO PENTECOST

The tenor of the Easter season is the opposite of the that of Lenten worship. While Lent is characterized by austerity, during Easter the church celebrates. Fasting and kneeling are replaced by alleluias of celebration.

Easter is the annual festival that forms the center around which our liturgical life, indeed our faith, moves in orbit. We are *Easter people* precisely because it is in the unitive, historical event of cross and resurrection that we find the source of our salvation.

While the details are far from clear, there seems to be wide agreement among scholars that, in addition to the weekly celebration of the Resurrection, an annual observance of Easter became standard fare very early in the life of the ancient church. Indeed, there is every reason to suspect that the primitive Christian community of Jewish origin would have observed the "Passover of God in Christ" the very next year after the Crucifixion. There seems to be little doubt that the original annual observance was celebrated on the night from the fourteenth to the fifteenth of Nisan, the night of Passover. The impact of this conjunction of festivals is no doubt responsible for the rich paschal theology and liturgical shape of the Christian celebration of the Resurrection. The influence of Passover can be seen in the very name of the event—*Pascha*. The writings of the early church

fathers regularly used *Pascha* to refer to the cross/Resurrection event and the annual liturgical observance of it. Until the fourth century, the word was understood to derive from the Greek word *paschein*, meaning "to suffer." Augustine, however, rightly pointed out that the term was derived from the Hebrew word *pesach*, that is, Passover. The cross and resurrection of Christ is his passover, his passage out of death into life. The liturgical observance of the passover of Christ, concerned not with the Passion or Resurrection, but with both together as one salvific event, is the Paschal Vigil.

The liturgy for the Vigil of Easter, the Christian Passover, as set forth in the worship books or supplemental resources of many churches, is comprised of four major components, all of which have enjoyed centuries of Christian liturgical usage. It is important to examine each part separately.

The Vigil begins with the kindling of the new fire—the Service of Light. In the pre-electric world, the dawning and setting of the sun were daily events of nature that both regulated life and worship. The lighting of the evening lamps was a moment of ritual significance in the Jewish meal traditions for sabbaths and major feasts. The early Christians also included a lamp lighting, the *lucernarium*, in their daily offering of evening prayers. The particular lamp lighting of the vigil may have more definite origins in the eighth-century Gallican liturgies. There it appears that the lights in the church were progressively extinguished in the last days of Holy Week and a new light had to be kindled for the evening.

It is often suggested that the service begin apart from the church building, preferably outdoors. The new paschal candle is lit and the procession moves into the dark church led by the light of Christ. The rekindling of the light of Christ that was earlier extinguished during Holy Week, and the solemn procession into the church—the passage out of darkness into light—is a moving liturgical experience which forms a candid backdrop against which the vigil continues.

This Service of Light continues as the deacon (or liturgical assistant) sings the *Exultet:* "Rejoice, now, all heavenly choirs of angels . . ."The *Exultet,* in one of its several forms, was in widespread use by the eighth century, but it seems clear that the inspiration for it was well in place several centuries earlier. An examination of the text will reveal its deep paschal imagery and theology. *This is the night* of the new Passover. *This is the night* when darkness becomes light, sadness becomes joy, despair becomes hope, death becomes life.

At the conclusion of the *Exultet,* the congregation extinguishes its candles and a Service of Readings begins. Most traditions appoint from nine to twelve readings from the Old Testament or Apocrypha. Whatever the number, the story of creation (Genesis 1:1–2:2), the account of the flood (Genesis 7:1-15, 11-18; 8:6-18; 9:8-13), the narrative of Israel's deliverance at the Red Sea (Exodus 14:10–15:1), and the story of the valley of dry bones (Ezekiel 37:1-14) are normally included. Most traditions provide psalms, canticles, and prayers to accompany the readings. This lengthy service of readings guides the congregation's "watching and waiting" through the hours of the night—awaiting the cockcrow announcing the dawning of the new day, the day of resurrection. The readings, canticles, and prayers are separated by extended periods of quietness for meditation; this entire portion of the vigil can take hours to complete.

Following the readings, the sacrament of Holy Baptism may be celebrated, or a rite for the renewal of baptismal life. The liturgy that celebrates the passage of Christ out of death into life is the time for the celebration of the sacrament which buries us with him in death and raises us with him

to new life. Pastors and laity responsible for worship planning should encourage the formation of groups of baptismal candidates, both children and adults, so that the powerful implications, pastoral and theological, of paschal baptism are not missed either by those being initiated into God's family or to the congregation that witnesses and participates in the sacramental action of God.

At the conclusion of the initiation rites, the Holy Eucharist is celebrated in all of its splendor. Some have argued that the vigil Eucharist should not be too resplendent so as not to detract from the power of the Sunday celebration. This is hardly a worry. The celebration of the total mystery of redemption at the Paschal Vigil need not in any way lessen the joy of Easter day. In fact, the opposite is likely to be the case. The vigil observes the historic and continuing redemption of the people of God into which salvatory mainstream we are inserted by water and the Spirit. The Paschal Vigil brings before the people all that they are, know, and experience as God's people.

We noted earlier that the original annual observance of *Pascha* coincided with the Passover regardless of the day of the week upon which it fell. That is to say that while the *weekly* celebration of resurrection took place on Sunday, the annual celebration, in its primitive form, was celebrated in conjunction with the date of Passover. Some scholars argue for an early institution of Sunday observance but it is not until the second century, and in some places late in the century, that we can speak with certainty about the annual observance of Easter being regularly celebrated on Sunday. It is indeed unfortunate that the Sunday celebration of Easter, particularly the so-called "sunrise service," has in much of Protestantism replaced the noctural Paschal Vigil. The Vigil that the liturgical and sacramental rite celebrates encompasses *all* upon which our salvation depends. Certainly we can be zealous enough to "pull out all the stops" at the vigil only to find ourselves anxious to return in the morning to celebrate the "yet more glorious day!"

It hardly needs to be said that our Eastertide festivities do not end with Easter day. In addition to the celebration of our redemption every Lord's Day, we have set aside fifty days of paschal rejoicing. Easter day is not the climax, but the beginning of our season of holy rejoicing. Our worship comes to its resounding climax on the day of Pentecost—the fiftieth day of Easter. It is unfortunate that many of our parishes treat the Sundays after Easter day as "business as usual" with no special music, decorations, or festivity. What would happen if we asked people to spread their offering of Easter lilies over the eight Sundays rather than packing them all into the church on Easter day so that we have to walk around them and choke on their overwhelming odor? Or, what about a major musical service on the sixth Sunday of Easter, a day which in many traditions honor the importance of music to Christian life and worship?

Many congregations that are still struggling to restore the full Sunday liturgy of Word and sacrament have found that the Sundays of Easter are an ideal time to experiment with weekly Eucharists. It is difficult to argue against weekly Eucharists, the weekly banquet of the Resurrection, during the weeks of Easter, and it is a long enough period for the congregation to become acquainted with the rhythm of the weekly celebration.

Contained within the Easter season is the festival of the Ascension of Our Lord. Ascension is one of the annual festivals of the church's life that _always_ falls on a weekday, the fortieth day of Easter. Like Epiphany, Ascension often fails to get the treatment it deserves in the life of many congregations. The ascension of Christ into heaven and his exaltation in the kingdom over which he reigns is a critical piece of the Easter proclamation and essential part of the history of our redemption. In the words of the Moravian liturgy, "Christ our crucified, risen, and ascended Redeemer, shall remain our confession of faith."

Our celebration of the fiftieth day of Easter, the day of Pentecost, brings our annual observance of our Lord's resurrection to a joyful close. The day should parallel the Easter day festivities closely, perhaps with the inclusion of a vigil for Pentecost. The music should be every bit as exultant. The decoration of the church should visually impress upon one's eyes the celebrative nature of the day. The preaching should be carefully planned and executed. On the fiftieth day, the church should be filled to overflowing, just like it was on the first day of Easter. If our keeping of the fiftieth day fails to parallel the beginning of the season and move us to a powerful conclusion of our Resurrection proclamation, we have work to do. It is unfortunate that we have designated the day of Pentecost as its own festival commemorating the sending of the Holy Spirit to the church. It is far better to embrace the sending of the Spirit as the completion, the fulfillment, of the resurrection promises of the risen Christ, the climax of the Easter message, and not as a separate event. The day of Pentecost must stand alongside of Easter in importance, and our liturgical expressions must show that vividly. This understanding of Pentecost would suggest that, while baptism and confirmation certainly have their historic and pastoral place on this day, other possibilities should be explored for their celebration so as not to take anything away from the major proclamation of the day. Another Sunday of Easter, the Sunday of Holy Trinity, or best of all, the Vigil of Pentecost on the evening before, are appropriate alternatives.

It would be possible to fill pages with little details that would underscore the thrust of our liturgical celebrations of Easter. But the point is a very simple one: From the first notes of the _Gloria in Excelsis_ at the Paschal Vigil to the dismissal at the close of the Eucharist for Pentecost there should be no letup in our resounding, if at times rowdy, celebration of the resurrection of our Lord. The cross and resurrection of Christ was a reckless act of pure love, for us. Our response must be no less so. "Christ, our crucified, risen, and ascended Redeemer, shall remain our confession of faith!"

Neil Alexander

274 • RECOVERING THE WORD _PASCHA_

More than a language lesson, this article challenges us to understand Easter in light of the rich Old Testament imagery of the Passover.

English is the unfortunate inheritor of the word _Easter,_ a word that lacks the power and significance of the more accurate _Pascha._ Greek and Latin transmitted the Hebrew word _pascha_ (passover), and so have other European languages (French: _paques_; Spanish: _pascua_; Dutch: _pasen_; Scottish: _pask_). In every case we can still hear the Old Testament meaning of liberation, wedded to the passion of Christ and the New Testament celebration of the Resurrection.

In many European traditions the Communion bread was also called _pascha,_ as was the lamb of paschal sacrifice. Those language treasures of deliverance and sacrifice enable us to sense the richness of Paul's phrase in 1 Corinthians 5:7: "Christ our pascha [Passover lamb] is sacrificed for us." Christ, the lamb, the bread, the Passover.

In contrast we can see how utterly impoverished is the translation of *pascha* as "Easter." "Christ our Easter is sacrificed for us" in a nonsensical statement. So is using the word *Easter* as a designation for the central celebration of the Paschal reality of the Christian tradition. If we primarily commemorate the Paschal mystery, we must recover the biblical usage with long and rich tradition and speak again of "Pascha."

Arlo Duba[43]

275 ✤ How to Celebrate the Fifty Days

The current renewal of Easter (Pascha) has not only recovered the festal character of Sunday and of the special events of the Christian year, but the celebratory character of the entire season. This article challenges the church to make pascha a full fifty-day experience of Resurrection joy.

A Week of Sundays: Celebrating the Great Fifty Days

Celebrating Easter for fifty days is a Christian practice almost as ancient as the annual observance of Easter. Almost as soon as Christians began observing an annual feast in honor of Christ's resurrection, they extended the celebration for fifty days, or seven weeks. Moreover, this "Great Fifty Days," as it is sometimes called, predated the observance of a day of Pentecost by nearly two hundred years. In fact, the term *Pentecost* was first used by Christians to refer to this seven-week period as a unit: "the Pentecost," or the fifty days. It was only later that the term was applied to the fiftieth day, at which time then the fifty days was called the Easter season.

The importance of this period for the ancient church is reflected in the language used by early writers when speaking of it, and the practices which their comments reveal. Tertullian refers to the period, which he called the Pentecost, as a *laetissimum spatium*, a "most joyous space", in which it is especially fitting that baptisms take place. Athanasius, bishop of Alexandria, wrote an annual "Festal Letter" to the churches in which he announced the date of Easter, which "extends its beams, with unobscured grace, to all the seven weeks of holy Pentecost." In every letter Athanasius emphasizes the centrality of the Easter observance for Christians, speaking of the fifty days especially as a time of joy and fulfillment: "But let us now keep the feast, my beloved, not as introducing a day of suffering but of joy in Christ, in whom we are fed every day." It was, quite simply, a "Great Sunday" which lasted for seven weeks, *a week of Sundays,* wherein the church celebrated on a large scale the resurrection of Christ. "All of Pentecost," writes Basil of Caesarea, "reminds us of the resurrection which we await in the other world."

This festal Sunday character of the period was expressed in the extension of Sunday practices to all fifty days, such as replacing the Lenten fast with the paschal feast, replacing penitential kneeling with prayers while standing and the singing of alleluias.

All of this would be of only historic interest to us today were it not for the fact that all of the contemporary reformed calendars from the 1969 Roman calendar to that assumed by the compilers of the Common Lectionary restore this fifty-day period in the church year. These calendars and lectionaries designate the Sundays "of Easter" rather than "after Easter" and they employ Scripture texts that bear witness to the essential unity of this period of the church year.

However, having reformed calendars and lectionaries—while it is a beginning toward a restoration of the ancient paschal observance—is not enough in itself. Books and resources must come to expression in our Sunday worship, resulting in assemblies that bear fruit in transformed communities and lives. Otherwise, we have done nothing but satisfy the nostalgia of a few liturgical scholars.

The difficult question then is how would the observance of the Great Fifty Days look in a congregation not of the ancient past but of the present day? What are the challenges of observing such a celebration, and what are the values?

The Challenge of the Fifty Days

We must acknowledge that the celebration of this season presupposes certain practices that are by no means common to average churches. *First,* the season of feast presumes a preceding season of fast. An intentional congregational observance of Lent as a time of self-examination, disciplines, and renewal sets the stage for the festivity of Easter. _Further,_ the presence of catechumens during Lent, who bear evangelical witness to the congregation, provides the baptismal framework that keeps the observance of the annual celebration of the resurrection of Christ from becoming a mere historical reminiscence. _Third_, as is evident from the quotations from early Christian writers, the strength of the season of celebration depends upon the presence of a community that is able to celebrate the Resurrection on a weekly basis, for whom the event of the Resurrection is not the past remembered but a present reality recognized and celebrated.

There is some reason to ask whether any of these presuppositions can be granted in most congregations, in which baptisms are casual and occasional, Lenten discipline at best is an optional, individual exercise, and Sunday is the end of the weekend, not the first day of the new creation.

However, it might be that a better grasp of the inter-connection of baptismal practice and its preparation, the resurrection message of the Lord's Day, and the celebration of the annual paschal fast and feast would strengthen the observance of each one, and that beginning with a celebration of the fifty days is as good a place to start as any. Accordingly, we will look at the characteristic theological themes of this period as observed in the early church, the way in which those themes are expressed in the Scripture texts chosen for this season in the Common Lectionary, and finally some specific practices that are suggested by the themes and texts themselves.

The Character of the Season

The entire season, as we have seen, was but an extension of the Lord's Day celebration. Sunday is not, as is so commonly said, a "little Easter"; Easter (as spread out over seven weeks) is a "big Sunday." Its theme, therefore, is the theme of every Lord's Day: the death and resurrection of Jesus Christ, and his life-giving presence in the community through the power of the Spirit. By the time of the development of the Easter season, this central theme was expressed by emphasis on the new creation in Christ. On the Lord's Day, and therefore during the period of the "Great Sunday," the

eschatological hope of Christians was partially realized. The One whose return was longed for was present in the midst of the community; the liturgy itself provided for the community a foretaste of the anticipated reign of Christ. The prevailing atmosphere was one of joy in the presence of Christ and freedom within his reign. (See Patrick Regan, "The Fifty Days and the Fiftieth Day," in _Worship_ 55 [1981]: 194–218.)

This realized eschatology expressed itself in several powerful actions in the liturgy. _First_, there was great emphasis on the feast. The Paschal feast was the prototypical Christian feast, prepared for by the preceding Lenten fast. Mindful of Jesus' saying that the wedding guest do not fast when the bridegroom is with them (Mark 2:19), the early church forbade fasting during the fifty days, a period full of the presence of Christ. Positively, the church recalled the post-resurrection meals of Christ with his disciples and behaved accordingly.

Second, the church prayed standing during this period, as a physical sign of the Resurrection and of the dignity that comes from participation in the reign of Christ. Standing, as opposed to kneeling, also gave physical expression to the joy characteristic of this season.

Third, the singing of "alleluia," which had been curtailed during Lent, marked the community's participation in the heavenly liturgy during the Easter season and was a further sign of the joy of the church in the presence of the risen Christ.

Finally, in some places, post-baptismal training in the form of mystagogical catechesis, or instruction in the mysteries of the faith, took place during part of this season, usually the first week. Thus there is also a practice that bears witness to the revelation of the mysteries of God to God's people, as well as a continuation of the baptismal character of the Lenten season.

The Biblical Texts

The lectionary texts for this season, for all three years of the three-year cycle, are drawn primarily from the Acts of the apostles and the Gospel of John. By replacing the Old Testament reading with readings from Acts, the lectionary attests that this period is the time of the church. In particular, these readings emphasize the evangelical nature of the church's faith. The Gospel readings from John are revelatory concerning the nature of the risen Christ. The second reading for each of the three years is taken from 1 Peter (Year A), 1 John (Year B), or Revelation (Year C).

A review of the readings for the seven weeks for all three years reveals several prominent themes which in turn suggest possible liturgical and other congregational expressions.

The presence of the risen Christ is a prominent theme through the season. Particular Sundays bring up different aspects of this reality. For example, the third Sunday of Easter includes an account of one of Jesus' post-resurrection meals with his disciples (in Year A, Luke 24:13-35; in Year C, John 21:1-19). The fifth Sunday, in Years A and B, includes Jesus' "I am" sayings, which bear witness to the revelation of the risen Christ. The fourth Sunday is always "Good Shepherd" Sunday, with the use of Psalm 23 and a portion of the "Good Shepherd" discourse from John 10. Here the tension between the suffering Christ and the reigning, risen Christ is particularly sharp, especially in the Revelation text for Year C, where the Lamb who was slain is also the Shepherd. The seventh Sunday reveals Jesus as High Priest with the use of his high-priest prayer in John 17.

A second prominent theme of the season is the *presence and work of the Holy Spirit*. These texts make it clear that the Holy Spirit is present in the church before the fiftieth day through the use of texts from the Acts of the apostles. Peter's sermons, Saul's conversion, healings by the apostles in Jesus' name, and the unity of the church all are presented by the writer of Acts as signs of the active presence of the Spirit in the church. Moreover, the gospel texts for the second Sunday and the sixth Sunday emphasize the presence of the Spirit with the use of the Johannine interpretation of the giving of the Spirit by Jesus to his disciples in John 14–15 and 20. The second Sunday in particular always includes the John 20 text, with its account of the appearance of the risen Christ to the disciples and to "doubting" Thomas and Christ's bestowing of the Spirit by breathing on them.

A third prominent theme of this period is *the nature of the baptismal life*. The texts from Acts, of course, bear witness to the mission of the community of the baptized to preach and to heal and to form believers into evangelical communities. Texts from Revelation emphasize the ethos of praise that characterizes the community of the faithful both on earth and before the throne of the Lamb. Readings from 1 John especially draw attention to the Christian ethic of love as an essential characteristic of the baptized believer, while 1 Peter provides running commentary on the demands and the blessings of the new life of those who have been made "God's people."

The presence of the risen Christ, the work of the Holy Spirit, and the significance of the baptismal life are the fundamental themes that permeate the texts for the Easter season. They are, of course fundamental themes of all of Christian worship, since they are at the foundation of the Christian faith.

Practical Considerations

These fundamental biblical themes in turn direct our attention to fundamental Christian liturgical practices: baptism and confirmation, the eucharistic meal, proclamation of the Resurrection, and joyful singing.

The baptismal character of the entire paschal season suggests a myriad of possible practices. Following a Lenten preparation for baptism or its renewal, the Easter season provides the opportunity to assimilate new members into the congregation's life and to celebrate the renewal of the baptism of all.

Environmentally, this means keeping the lighted paschal candle and baptismal font prominently displayed during the fifty days, and seeing to it that the church is dressed in its finest. Although the use of white, perhaps trimmed with gold and red, is common during this period, the color used is less important than that the environment as a whole bear witness to the joy of the season. The use of textiles and art which reflect the best of the local culture might be more fitting than satins and brocades.

Ritually, the newly baptized should be prayed for by name in the intercessions during this period as a sign of the community's support of their new life in Christ. Teaching and preaching might appropriately include attention to the meaning of baptismal life, which would be addressed to the entire community of the faithful. Many of the texts assigned to this season provide ample basis for such preaching.

If the congregation is very large, the inclusion of new members in small groups for study, prayer, and mission would be important and might begin during this period. If the congregation is small, an all-church dinner in honor of all those who have joined the congregation since last Easter is appropriate during this period (perhaps on Pentecost Sunday) and also has the advantage of enacting another theme of the season: the risen Christ's meals with his disciples.

Of course, if baptisms have not been part of the Easter Vigil, or if there are too many candidates to be conveniently included in the vigil, any Sunday during the Great Fifty Days is, as Tertullian noted, a "most joyous space" for baptisms. Many of the texts contain specific references to baptism and the Spirit, as already noted, and would provide a most appropriate occasion. Likewise confirmation (if separated from baptism) as well as congregational baptismal renewal would be most fitting during this period.

The eucharistic character of the Easter season can hardly be ignored. The emphasis both on the presence of the risen Christ and the extension of the paschal feast as a kind of post-Resurrection meal with him seems to demand the celebration of the Lord's Supper weekly during this great Lord's Day. Such practice, of course presumes a shift in eucharistic piety, away from the penitential medieval focus of the Crucifixion to a more ancient emphasis on joyful Resurrection meal. If this shift seems drastic for a congregation (as well it might), preparation might take place during Lent, in the form of a study of some of the diverse emphases which have been associated with the holy meal over the centuries.

Beyond the weekly celebration of the Eucharist, the festal character of the season is well expressed in the form of noneucharistic meals as well, such as church dinners or agape meals. The missional character of the season might be expressed in the congregation preparing meals for the homeless of that congregation's neighborhood or city.

The resources of the lectionary for preaching on the themes of the period have already been mentioned, and in particular the value of preaching on baptismal life. This is a concern primarily, if not exclusively, however, of the preacher. The responsibility of the community to witness to the Resurrection might take the form of social action or social service. The transformation engendered by the Resurrection is not limited to personal or even congregational transformation, but is social and cultural as well. The congregation has a particular obligation to identify the needs of the community in which it resides, and to address those needs as a form of proclamation of the gospel.

The season of joy is best expressed in the use of joyous music. To sing for joy is a most natural human reaction, and in this season above all others this reaction should be fostered and encouraged. Trained musicians will want to perform the most joyous music that they are able, but such performance must never stifle the congregation's confidence in its own ability to sing for joy to God. Nor do singing and other forms of music needs to be limited to the liturgy (although the liturgy during this season especially should be richly musical). Concerts, hymn-sings, and musical events of all kinds can give further expression to the "alleluia" character of the Easter season.

Marjorie Proctor-Smith[44]

TWENTY-THREE

The Easter or Paschal Vigil

This chapter contains the great vigil of Easter (Pascha), which is the primordial service of the Christian faith. For in this service the church recalls the great acts of salvation that culminate in the resurrection of Christ. It marks this sign of a new beginning for human history. The following articles should be studied with care so that the reader will begin to see how the themes and images of this service are the foundation for the entire Christian year.

276 ◆ An Introduction to the Paschal Vigil Service

The Paschal Vigil is the foundational service of all Christian worship. In this service the great theme of Christian salvation is enacted in recollection of the days of salvation.

Inasmuch as the purpose of worship is to celebrate the death and resurrection of Christ for the salvation of the world, the Paschal Vigil is the source of all Christian worship. It is the single most important service of the year, the fount from which all the praises of the church flow.

In a most primitive and basic sense, it can also be regarded as the oldest service of the church. Its roots go clear back to the original day of the Resurrection and the great rejoicing of the people of God on that day. The contemporary forum of the Paschal Vigil consists of four parts (the Service of Light; the Service of the Word; the Service of Baptism; the Service of the Eucharist) that originated in the early church.

In the first century the Paschal Vigil centered on the Eucharist: "For indeed, Christ our Passover was sacrificed for us. Therefore, let us keep the feast" (1 Cor. 5:7-8). During the second century the baptism of new members into the church was added to the feast. The third element, the emphasis on light, probably came from the Jewish observance of lighting the lamps on the eve of the Sabbath. And the Scriptures, the fourth element of the service, was always there, but underwent a significant development in the late second and third century as it was honed into the final instruction to the catchumenates who were to be baptized at dawn. By the end of the fourth century, all the elements of this service were in place. Although the service underwent a number of changes through the centuries, the recent revisions in the service due to the liturgical renewal of the twentieth century have brought it back to the original simplicity and beauty. Although the service begins with the Service of Light, the real focal point and ultimate purpose of the service is to bring the worshiper to the Eucharist, which is the ultimate celebration of the Resurrection.

The Paschal Vigil begins with the Service of Light. The people gather in the vestibule in darkness and remain silent. The minister, attendants, and choir gather around the place where a fire will be lit. (Use whatever is appropriate—from a small fire in a grill to a large match.) The first action is the lighting of the fire from which a large candle (the paschal candle) will be lighted. This light symbolizes the coming of the light of Christ to dispel all darkness. An opening address and prayer follows. Then the paschal candle is lit. The candle bearer leads a procession of the people into the church, stopping three times to raise the paschal candle high and sing, "The Light of Christ," to which the people respond, "Thanks be to God." Simultaneously, the candles of each worshiper are lit so that when the candlebearer reaches the front of the sanctuary, and when final candle is lifted, the entire sanctuary, previously dark, is now lit up with the light of the flaming candles. The service continues with the singing of the Exultet. This is the Easter proclamation in which the saving events of both the Hebrew and New Testament covenants are proclaimed. This great song of faith moves from the night of the Passover in Egypt to the proclamation of Christ's victory over the powers of evil won through his death.

It should be noted that the Service of Light contains three parts: (1) the lighting of the fire; (2) the greeting of the light; and (3) the praise of the light. While this moving service may give one the feeling of the Resurrection, it is not yet the moment to celebrate the Resurrection; it is only a powerful precursor of the event.

The second part of the Paschal Vigil is the Service of the Word. Although the reading of the Word is instructive, the mood is more like a prayer. What is important about these readings is their content. For they review the salient features of salvation history from Creation to the Fall, to the covenants made with Abraham and Israel, to the covenants God made with their descendants, to the coming of Christ and beyond to the new heavens and the new earth. While the readings provide a solid history of the salvific events of the Scripture, it is not necessary to read them all. However, take care to choose readings that adequately communicate the breadth of salvation history. After the readings, a sermon based on the theme of these Scripture passages may also be delivered.

A high point in the Service of the Word comes just before the reading of the epistle. For it is here that the announcement is made that Christ is risen. Contemporary churches are making much of this moment through an environmental action. Actions such as the ringing of bells, the bursting forth of the organ, the bringing of flowers to the pulpit and table area, and dancing and the like are all ways to make a joyful noise to the Lord. After the reading of the epistle the gospel is read, followed by the sermon (usually very short and to the point of the Resurrection).

Now the congregation is ready for the third part of the vigil: the baptism. In the early church, converts to Christ who had undergone a period of instruction were admitted to the waters of baptism on Easter Sunday morning. Soon the sacrament of baptism was celebrated, not only for these catechumenates, but also for the faithful who used this occasion to renew their baptismal vows. Consequently, the baptismal service is always a part of the vigil, whether or not there are new converts to baptize.

The climax of the service is in the celebration of the Table. Here the risen Lord comes to meet the church in fulfillment of his promise that he will be "in the midst." It is not that Christ has not already been in the midst, for he has. But the Eucharist has always been and is now the most intense experience of the presence of Christ.

Each of the readings, psalms, and hymns are united by their reference to three images: light, water, and the heavenly banquet. These symbols, common to nearly all human religious expression, but given unique significance by the Christian Scriptures, are perhaps the richest symbols of Christian experience. These symbols point to the key themes of the service: deliverance from bondage and union with Christ.

Robert Webber

The Paschal Candle. The paschal candle symbolizes Christ the light, who has overcome the darkness of this world. In liturgical churches it stands at the side of the Communion table for the entire Easter season (Easter morning through the day of Pentecost).

277 ✦ LECTIONARY READINGS FOR THE EASTER VIGIL

These are suggested readings for Years A, B, C from the Revised Common Lectionary.

THE VIGIL READINGS

Old Testament Readings	Psalm or Canticle
Genesis 1:1–2:2, the account of creation	Psalm 33
Genesis 7:1-5, 11-18; 8:6-18, 9:8-13, the covenant between God and the earth	Psalm 46
Genesis 22:1-18, Abraham's obedience on Mt. Moriah	Psalm 16
Exodus 14:10–15:1, Israel's deliverance from Pharaoh	Exodus 15:1-6, 11-13, 17-18
Isaiah 54:5-14, the covenant of peace	Psalm 30
Isaiah 55:1-11, salvation is offered to all	Isaiah 12:2-6
Baruch 3:9-15, 3:32–4:4, God's wisdom	Psalm 19
Ezekiel 36:24-28, a new heart and a new Spirit	Psalm 42
Ezekiel 37:1-14, dry bones come to life	Psalm 143
Zephaniah 3:14-20, the salvation of the Lord	Psalm 98

READINGS FOR PROCLAMATION

Romans 6:3-11, dying and rising with Christ	Psalm 114
Matthew 28:1-10 (A), Mark 16: 1-8 (B), Luke 24:1-12 (C), the resurrection of Jesus	

Revised Common Lectionary

278 ✦ A TRADITIONAL SERVICE OF THE PASCHAL VIGIL

The following service is a creative adaptation of the traditional pattern and texts for the Easter Vigil. It will be of particular help for those who plan a more formal Easer Vigil service. For others, the commentary included with this service will provide a guide to thoughtful planning for the Advent season.

I. Service of Light

Commentary: Since participation in this service becomes meaningful especially when worshipers are familiar with the complex nature and history of the service, congregations who are holding an Easter Vigil service for the first time should find a forum for informing worshipers about the service, perhaps through a church education session or newsletter.

Easter Vigil is traditionally observed on either the Saturday evening before Easter or early on Easter morning. The visual environment for Easter Vigil should attempt to portray the poignant juncture between the remembrance of Christ's passion and the celebration of Easter. The symbols and colors of Holy Week may be present—the black and purple, the cross, thorns, and nails. But against this backdrop, the symbols and colors of Easter should predominate: the white and gold, the trumpets, empty tomb, and lilies. This juncture between Lent and Easter can be dramatized by beginning the service with the Lenten banners, paraments, and vestments and replacing or covering them by the Easter symbols as the service progresses toward its grand climax. This transformation can take place during the lighting of the paschal candle, the moments following baptismal renewal, the offertory, and the final reading of the Easter Gospel.

The images that are uniquely important to the Easter Vigil service are light, water, and the heavenly banquet, with each mentioned frequently in the prescribed readings for the service. These symbols point to the key themes of the service—deliverance from bondage and union with Christ—and could appropriately be displayed on banners, paraments, or vestments.

Gathering of the Congregation

Commentary: The service may begin with the gathering of the congregation outside the worship space. The first portion of the service, through the lighting of the paschal candle, would then be held outside and be followed by a congregational processional into the worship space.

If the congregation does gather in the worship space, the service may begin in silence. If instrumental, organ, or piano prelude music is played, it should retain the very quiet, reflective mood Holy Week. Post-service music, in contrast, should be celebrative and exuberant.

Hymn Antiphon: "Christ Jesus Lay in Death's Strong Bands," stanza 1

CANTOR OR CHOIR:
> Christ Jesus lay in death's strong bands for our offenses given.
> But now at God's right hand he stands, and brings us life from heaven.
> Therefore let us joyful be, and sing to God right thankfully loud songs of Alleluia! Alleluia!

Commentary: This sample service suggests the use of one verse from the hymn, "Christ Jesus Lay in Death's Strong Bands" at the beginning of each section of the service. Use of this hymn in this way serves as both a unifying device in the service and as an appropriate textual introduction to each section of the service. This hymn is particularly appropriate because the text of the hymn mirrors the structure of the service. In addition, the chant-like quality of this hymn tune is appropriate for the meditative nature of the service. This hymn-antiphon may be sung by the congregation, but can also be effectively sung by a small group of singers located some distance from the congregation, perhaps in the back corner of the balcony or transept of the worship space.

Statement of Purpose

LEADER: Sisters and brothers in Christ: On this holy night, when our Lord Jesus passed over from death to life, members of the Christian community, dispersed throughout the world, gather in vigil and prayer. We join with the whole company of God's people in recalling and celebrating his victory over death, and our deliverance from the bondage of sin and darkness to everlasting light.

New Testament Reading: John 1:1, 4-5

Prayer

PEOPLE: **Eternal Lord of life, through your Son you have given your people the brightness of your light. Sanctify this new fire, and kindle in our hearts and minds a holy desire to shine forth with the brightness of Christ's rising until we feast at the banquet of eternal light; through Jesus Christ, the Sun of righteousness. Amen.**

Lighting of the Paschal Candle

LEADER: The light of Christ rises in glory, overcoming the darkness of sin and death.

PEOPLE: **Thanks be to God!**

Commentary: The paschal candle (a large white candle, on which may be engraved the chi-rho) symbolizes the eternal victory of Jesus Christ over death, which brings light to our dark world of sin. This symbol is different from other candles, such as those used in an Advent wreath, because it is designed to focus on themes explicitly tied to Easter. Hence, the paschal candle is traditionally lit each Sunday of Eastertide through Pentecost. It may also be lit at every baptism, where the Christian community celebrates that Christians are "raised with Christ," and at every memorial or funeral service, where we celebrate Christ's victory over death.

If the first part of the service is held outside the worship space, the congregational processional would begin at this point. During the processional, the entire congregation or a group of appointed singers may sing the acclamation, "The light of Christ; Thanks be to God."

Canticle: "The Exultet"

Commentary: After the Paschal candle is lit and all worship leaders and worshipers are in place, traditional Easter Vigil services include the singing of the fourth-century canticle, "The Exultet." The first option printed here is one translation of the ancient canticle that may be sung or read. Musical settings of the canticle are available in *The Liturgical Year: The Worship of God*, Supplemental Liturgical Resource 7 (Louisville: Westminster/John Knox, 1992). The second is a rough metrical translation suitable for singing to the tune TALLIS CANON. Third, the text printed here may be used in a choral reading by a group of voices. Fourth and finally, the hymn "Christ Whose Glory Fills the Skies" may be substituted for the canticle, as it uses many of the same images.

> Rejoice now, heavenly hosts and choirs of angels, and let your trumpets shout salvation for the victory of our mighty King.
>
> Rejoice and sing now, all the round earth, bright with a glorious splendor for the darkness has been vanquished by our eternal King.
>
> Rejoice and be glad now, holy church, and let your holy courts, in radiant light, resound with the praises of your people.
>
> It is truly right and good, always and everywhere, with our whole heart and mind and voice, to praise you, the invisible, almighty, and eternal God, and your only begotten Son, Jesus Christ, our Lord; for he is the true Paschal Lamb, who at the feast of the Passover paid for us the debt of Adam's sin, and by his blood delivered your faithful people.
>
> This is the night, when you brought our forebears, the children of Israel, out of bondage in Egypt, and lead them through the Red Sea on dry land. This is the night, when all who believe in Christ are delivered from the gloom of sin, and are restored to grace and holiness of life. This is the night, when Christ broke the bonds of death and hell, and rose victorious from the grave.

> Holy Father, accept our evening sacrifice, the offering of this candle in your honor. May it shine continually to drive away all darkness. May Christ, the Morning Star who knows no setting, find it ever burning—he who gives his light to all creation, and who lives and reigns forever and ever. Amen.[45]

[or]

> O Christ, you are the Light and Day,
> You drive our death and night away!
> We know you as the Light of light,
> Illuminating mortal sight.[46]
>
> O sing you angels, now rejoice,
> To Christ, our Light, lift up your voice,
> Exult the Lord, our reigning king,
> With joyful hearts your worship bring.
>
> Praise God, from whom all blessings flow;
> Praise him, all creatures here below;
> Praise him above, you heavenly hosts,
> Praise Father, Son, and Holy Ghost. Amen.

II. Service of the Word

Hymn Antiphon: "Christ Jesus Lay in Death's Strong Bands," stanza 2

CANTOR: It was a strange and dreadful strife
when life and death contended.
The victory remained with life; the
reign of death was ended.
Holy Scripture plainly says his death
has swallowed up our death;
Its sting is lost forever. Alleluia!

Statement of Purpose

LEADER: Sisters and brothers in Christ, we now begin our solemn vigil. We hear the Word of God, recalling God's saving deeds in history and how God's own Son was sent to be our Redeemer. May the Holy Spirit illumine our hearts and minds in the hearing of his Word.

Commentary: The following lessons trace the broad sweep of salvation history. Each of the events described in these Old Testament lessons is in some significant way an anticipation of or are fulfilled by Christ's victory on Easter. Information given to the congregation prior to the service should include a list of which readings are chosen and how they relate to Christ's resurrection.

Because of time constraints, many congregations will choose not to incorporate the entire portion of the vigil service. Yet worship planners should remember that a vigil service is designed to capture that emotion or feeling that seems so elusive in modern culture—that of patient but earnest yearning for a given event. And the readings that precede the sacraments are essential to create this sense of longing or waiting. The following portion of the service may be shortened by excluding many of the musical responses to the readings. The readings from Genesis 1 and Exodus 14–15 are especially essential and should not be omitted.

THE CREATION[47]

Old Testament Reading: Genesis 1–2:3

Response

LEADER: Give thanks to the Lord for he is good.

PEOPLE: **His love endures forever!**

Commentary: This response is based on the familiar Old Testament refrain found in many psalms and canticles (including Psalms 118 and 136). This verse is especially appropriate for Easter Vigil because of its frequent use within the Old Testament as a response to God's acts of creation and salvation. Worship planners may, however, wish to substitute a more familiar response (e.g., LEADER: The Word of the Lord, PEOPLE: **Thanks be to God.**)

Psalm 33

Commentary: This Psalm may be sung by the congregation or choir. Metrical settings of this and other psalms can be found in *A New Metrical Psalter* (New York: Church Hymnal Corporation, 1984); *The Psalter Hymnal* (Grand Rapids: CRC Publications, 1987); *Rejoice in the Lord* (Grand Rapids: Eerdmans, 1985); *Trinity Hymnal* (Atlanta: Great Commission Publications, 1990); *The Presbyterian Hymnal* (Louisville: Westminster/John Knox, 1990). Responsorial settings can be found in *The Celebration Psalter* (St. Louis: Cathedral Music Press, 1991); *Psalm Refrains and Tones* (Carol Stream, Ill.: Hope Publishing, 1988); *Lead Me, Guide Me* (Chicago: GIA Publications, 1987); *Psalms for the Church Year*, vols. 1–4 (Chicago: GIA Publications), *United Methodist Hymnal* (Nashville: Abingdon, 1989). Additional settings of the Psalms can be found in *Psalms for Today* and *Songs from the Psalms* (London: Hodder and Stoughton, 1990).

[or]

Hymn: "All Creatures of Our God and King" "Morning Has Broken"

Commentary: Each reading may be followed by a psalm or a hymn. The use of hymns tends to reinforce the New Testament appropriation of the Old Testament lessons, some with explicit reference to Christ's resurrection.

Prayer

PEOPLE: **Almighty and eternal God, you created all things in beauty and order. Help us now to perceive how still more wonderful is your new creation, in which you redeemed your people through the sacrifice of our Passover, Jesus Christ, who lives and reigns for ever and ever. Amen.**

THE COVENANT BETWEEN GOD AND THE EARTH

Old Testament Reading: Genesis 7:1-5, 11-18; 8:6-18; 9:8-15

Response

LEADER: Give thanks to the Lord for he is good.

PEOPLE: **His love endures forever!**

Psalm 46

[or]

Hymn: "A Mighty Fortress" "Your Are Our God; We Are Your People"

Commentary: This second hymn, found in the *Psalter Hymnal,* is less familiar but perfectly suited to this lesson.

Prayer

PEOPLE: **Faithful God, you placed the rainbow in the skies as the sign of your covenant with all living things. May we who are saved through water and the Spirit, offer to you our sacrifice of thanksgiving with right hearts. We**

ask this in the name of Jesus Christ
our Lord. Amen.

ABRAHAM'S OBEDIENCE

Old Testament Reading: Genesis 22:1-18

Response
LEADER: Give thanks to the Lord for he is
           good.
PEOPLE: His love endures forever!

Psalm 16

[or]

Hymn: "You Are Our God; We Are Your People"

Commentary: See the note to the last lesson.

Prayer
PEOPLE: Gracious God of all believers,
           through Abraham's obedience you
           made known your faithful love to
           countless numbers, by the grace of
           Christ's sacrifice fulfill in your church
           and in all creation the joy of your
           promise and new covenant. Amen.

ISRAEL'S DELIVERANCE AT THE RED SEA

Old Testament Reading: Exodus 14:10-31; 15:20-21

Response
LEADER: Give thanks to the Lord for he is
           good.
PEOPLE: His love endures forever!

Canticle: Exodus 15:1b-6, 11-13, 17-18

[or]

Hymn: "Come, You Faithful, Raise the Strain"
"How Firm a Foundation"

Prayer
PEOPLE: O God, our Savior, you once deliv-
           ered by the power of your mighty
           arm your chosen people Israel
           through the water of the sea; so now
           deliver your church and all the
           peoples of the earth from bondage
           and oppression to rejoice and serve
           you in freedom, through Jesus
           Christ our Lord, Amen.

THE PROMISE OF A RENEWED ISRAEL

Old Testament Reading: Isaiah 4:2-6

Response
LEADER: Give thanks to the Lord for he is
           good.
PEOPLE: His love endures forever!

Psalm 122

[or]

Hymn: "Glorious Things of You Are Spoken"
"Guide Me, O My Great Redeemer"

Prayer
PEOPLE: O God, our Guide, you led your an-
           cient people by a pillar of cloud by
           day and a pillar of fire by night. May
           we, who serve you now on earth,
           come to the joy of that heavenly
           Jerusalem, where all tears are wiped
           away and where your saints forever
           sing your praise, through Jesus
           Christ our Lord. Amen.

ETERNAL COVENANT OF PEACE

Old Testament Reading: Isaiah 54:1-10

Response
LEADER: Give thanks to the Lord for he is
           good.
People: His love endures forever!

Psalm 30

[or]

Hymn: "Great Is Your Faithfulness"

Prayer
PEOPLE: Holy One of Israel, Our Redeemer,
           your love is unending and your cov-
           enant is not shaken, even when our
           sin carries us away from you; take
           pity again, establish us in righteous-
           ness, and through our baptism lead
           us to salvation in Jesus Christ our
           Lord. Amen.

SALVATION FREELY OFFERED

Old Testament Reading: Isaiah 55:1-11

Response
LEADER: Give thanks to the Lord for he is
           good.
PEOPLE: His love endures forever!

Canticle: Isaiah 12:2-6

[or]

Hymn
"God Is My Strong Salvation"
"Amazing Grace"

Prayer

PEOPLE: O God, you have created all things by the power of your Word, and you renew all things by your Spirit; Give now the water of life to those who thirst for you, that they may bring forth abundant fruit in your glorious kingdom; through Jesus Christ our Lord, Amen.

A NEW HEART AND A NEW SPIRIT

Old Testament Reading: Ezekiel 36:24-28

Response
LEADER: Give thanks to the Lord for he is good.
PEOPLE: **His love endures forever!**

Psalm: Psalms 42 and 43

[or]

Hymn: "Spirit of God, Descend upon My Heart"
(see also hymns for the next lesson)

Prayer
PEOPLE: God of holiness and light, in the mystery of dying and rising with Christ you have established a new covenant of reconciliation; cleanse our hearts and give a new spirit to all your people, that your saving grace may be proclaimed to the whole world; through Jesus Christ our Lord. Amen.

NEW LIFE FOR GOD'S PEOPLE

Old Testament Reading: Ezekiel 37:1-14

Response
LEADER: Give thanks to the Lord for he is good.
PEOPLE: **His love endures forever!**

Psalm 143

[or]

Hymn: "Come Holy Ghost, Our Souls Inspire"
"Come Down, O Love Divine"
"For Your Gift of God the Spirit"

Prayer
PEOPLE: Eternal God, you raised from the dead our Lord Jesus Christ, and by your Holy Spirit brought to life your church; breathe upon us again with your Spirit and give new life to your people, through the same Jesus Christ our Lord. Amen.

GATHERING OF GOD'S PEOPLE

Old Testament Reading: Zephaniah 3:14-20

Response
LEADER: Give thanks to the Lord for he is good.
PEOPLE: **His love endures forever!**

Psalm 98

[or]

Hymn: "Joy to the World"
"The Church's One Foundation"
"Glorious Things of You Spoken"

Prayer
People: **Ever-living God of power and light, look with mercy on your whole church, we pray; bring to completion your lasting salvation, that the whole world may see the fallen lifted up, the old made new, and all things brought to perfection in him through whom all things were made, our Lord Jesus Christ. Amen.**

Hymn Antiphon: "Christ Jesus Lay in Death's Strong Bands"

CANTOR OR CHOIR:
Here the true Paschal Lamb we see, whom God so freely gave us.
He died on the accursed tree—so strong his love to save us.
See his blood now marks our door; faith points to it, death passes o'er;
and Satan cannot harm us. Alleluia!

New Testament Reading: Romans 13:11b-12 or 6:3-11

Commentary: The reading should be chosen as the text for the sermon which will follow.

Response
LEADER: The Word of the Lord.
PEOPLE: **Thanks be to God!**

Sermon

Commentary: The sermon for Easter Vigil may serve to briefly summarize the relationship between the Old Testament lessons and the resurrection of Christ.

III. Service of Easter Baptism

Commentary: Baptism has long been associated with the Easter Vigil. In the early church, candidates for baptism prepared for their baptism during a season of study, prayer, and renewal that later became known as Lent. They were baptized as a part of the Easter Vigil service. Today Easter Vigil is still a most appropriate occasion for baptism, as well as a fine opportunity for all baptized members of the church to either renew their baptismal vows or to recall their own baptism, depending on the theological understanding of baptism in the given congregation.

Hymn Antiphon: "Christ Jesus Lay in Death's Strong Bands"

CANTOR OR CHOIR:
> So let us keep the festival to which the Lord invites us.
> Christ is himself the joy of all, the sun that warms and lights us.
> Now his grace to us imparts eternal sunshine to our hearts;
> the night of sin is ended. Alleluia!

Invitation

LEADER: Sisters and brothers in Christ, our baptism is the sign and seal of our cleansing from sin and of our being grafted into Christ. Through the birth, life, death, and rising of Christ, the power of sin was broken and God's kingdom entered our world. Through our baptism we were made citizens of God's kingdom, and freed from the bondage of sin. Join me now in celebrating our freedom and redemption in Christ and renewing our commitment to the one in whom we are baptized.

Renunciation of Sin

LEADER: Do you renounce the spiritual forces of wickedness, reject the evil powers of this world, and repent of your sin?

PEOPLE: **We do.**

LEADER: Do you accept the freedom and power God gives you to resist evil, injustice, and oppression in whatever forms they present themselves?

PEOPLE: **We do.**

LEADER: Do you confess Jesus Christ as your Savior, put your whole trust in his grace, and promise to serve him as your Lord, in union with the church which Christ has opened to people of all ages, nations, and races?

PEOPLE: **We do.**

LEADER: According to the grace given you, will you remain faithful members of Christ's holy church and serve as Christ's representatives in the world?

PEOPLE: **We do.**

LEADER: Let us join together in professing the Christian faith as contained in the Scriptures of the Old and New Testaments.[48]

Profession of Faith: The Apostles' Creed

LEADER: Do you believe in God the Father?

PEOPLE: **I believe in God, the Father almighty,**
creator of heaven and earth.

LEADER: Do you believe in Jesus Christ, the Son of God?

PEOPLE: **I believe in Jesus Christ, his only Son, our Lord,**
who was conceived by the Holy Spirit
and born of the virgin Mary.
He suffered under Pontius Pilate,
was crucified, died, and was buried;
he descended to hell.
The third day he rose again from the dead.
He ascended to heaven
and is seated at the right hand of God the Father almighty.
From there he will come to judge the living and the dead.

LEADER: Do you believe in God the Holy Spirit?

PEOPLE: **I believe in the Holy Spirit,**
the holy catholic church,
the communion of saints,
the forgiveness of sins,

the resurrection of the body,
and the life everlasting. Amen.

Hymn: "We Know that Christ Is Raised"

Commentary: The text of the hymn should ideally make the connection between baptism and Christ's resurrection quite explicit.

Prayer

PEOPLE: **Almighty God, the Father of our Lord Jesus Christ, you have given us a new birth by water and the Holy Spirit and have forgiven our sins. Continue to give us your grace that we may live in obedience to you, in the power of the Resurrection which we now celebrate, through Jesus Christ our Lord. Amen.**

Charge to the People

LEADER: Remember your baptism and be thankful. In the name of the Father and of the Son and of the Holy Spirit.

PEOPLE: **Amen.**

IV. Service of the Table

Hymn Antiphon: "Christ Jesus Lay in Death's Strong Bands"

ALL SINGING: **Then let us keep this holy day on Christ, the bread of heaven. The Word of grace has purged away the old and evil leaven. Christ alone our souls will feed; he is our meat and drink indeed; faith lives upon no other! Alleluia!**

Offertory

LEADER: People of God, as an offering of thanksgiving to God for his inestimable gift to us, let us bring our gifts to him.

PEOPLE: **Amen.**

(The gifts are received.)

Commentary: At this point, the elements for Communion and the gifts which have been received may be brought forward.

Invitation

LEADER: Friends in Christ Jesus: According to Luke, when our risen Lord was at table with his disciples, he took the bread, and blessed and broke it, and gave it to them. Then their eyes were opened and they recognized him. Come now to the joyful feast of our Lord.

Prayer of Thanksgiving

LEADER: O holy God, Father almighty, Creator of heaven and earth, with joy we give you thanks and praise. By your power you raised Christ Jesus from death to life. Through his victory over the grave we are set free from the bonds of sin and fear of death to share the glorious freedom of the children of God. How wonderful are your ways, almighty God.

How marvelous are your ways, O holy God. With the church of all ages we bless you and proclaim:

PEOPLE: **"Holy, holy, holy Lord, God of power and might.
Heaven and earth are full of your glory.
Hosanna in the highest."**

Commentary: This canticle may be read or sung. Most hymnals include several settings of it. For a list of service music found in a representative group of hymnals, consult the commentary to the Communion liturgy of the Advent service in this series.

In remembrance of your mighty acts in Jesus Christ,
we bless you and give you thanks.

Pour out your Holy Spirit upon us,
that we may be one with Christ and he with us.
Fill us with eternal life,
that with joy we may be his faithful people until we feast with him in glory.
Through Jesus Christ, our Lord. Amen.

Institution

LEADER: The Lord Jesus, on the night when he was betrayed, took bread, and when he had given thanks, he broke it and said, "This is my body, which is for you; do this in remembrance of me." In the same way, he took the cup, after supper, saying, "This cup is the new covenant in my blood; do this, whenever you drink it, in remembrance of me." For whenever you eat this bread and drink this cup, you proclaim the Lord's death until he comes."

Memorial

PEOPLE: **Christ has died. Christ has risen. We remember his death. We celebrate his life!**

Prayer of Consecration

Leader: Gracious God, pour out your Holy Spirit upon us, gathered here, and upon these gifts, we pray. By them, may we be united with Christ, our Lord, and raised with him to a new life. By your power, may this sacrament be a bold witness to joy of our baptism and the power of Christ's coming to life. Amen.

Invitation

PASTOR: Friends in Christ, the Lord has prepared his table for his church. All who love him and trust in him alone for their salvation are now invited to come to the table of the Lord.

PEOPLE: **We come with gladness. Thanks be to God!**

Pastor: The gifts of God for the people of God.

Sacrament

PASTOR: (as the people take the bread) The body of Christ for you.

PASTOR: (as the people take the cup) The blood of Christ for you.

Commentary: Appropriate hymns and anthems may accompany the sacrament.

The Easter Gospel

Lesson: Matthew 28:1-10

Commentary: Traditional Easter Vigil services do not call for the reading of the Easter Gospel at this point in the service, leaving that for the Easter morning service. While this option is certainly appropriate, including the Easter Gospel in the Vigil service provides a fittingly dramatic and victorious way to complete the service, especially if Easter Vigil is held early on Easter morning.

Hymn: "Were You There?" (final verse only)

Commentary: The final verse of this spiritual— "Were you there when God raised him from the tomb?"—is most appropriate for use at this point. It may be sung by an unaccompanied solo voice, especially if the first verses of this spiritual were sung in this manner on Good Friday. (See the service on Good Friday Tenebrae in this series.)

Acclamation: Alleluias

Commentary: The reading of the Gospel lesson or the singing of the final verse of "Were You There" may be followed by an acclamation sung by a choir or played on a variety of instruments. For example, this acclamation could begin with the peal of handbells from around the worship space, followed by the singing of Alleluias by members of the choir or congregation. Other instruments, even loud orchestra bells, can join the acclamation, which can conclude as the organ triumphantly introduces the final hymn. Church musicians can easily compose or prescribe such a sequence, giving each musician a melody for their sung Alleluia or bell or instrumental peal that falls within a common major key (e.g., G Major). The aleatoric effect of this acclamation can provide drama to the proclamation of the Easter gospel.

Hymn: "Christ the Lord Is Risen Today"

Dismissal

LEADER: Go in peace to love and serve the Lord.

PEOPLE: **We are sent in the power of Christ's resurrection. Alleluia!**

Blessing

LEADER: The blessing of Almighty God, Father, Son and Holy Spirit, be with you always. Amen.

PEOPLE: **Amen. Alleluia, alleluia!**

Dispersal of the Congregation

Commentary: Post-service music should be celebrative, reflecting the full joy of Easter.

John D. Witvliet

279 • A Convergence Service of the Paschal Vigil

The service below is meant for use by those congregations who desire to combine historical traditions of wor-

ship with a contemporary style. It can be amended to suit the particular needs or traditions of the congregation.

People are given a small candle and handout upon entering the sanctuary. Music is soft and subdued. Banners and the large wooden cross are in place around the platform.

The basic body for the Great Easter Vigil is taken from the *Book of Common Prayer*, beginning on page 285.

Decoration. If the service of Tenebrae was held, the sanctuary will be barren. The articles and furnishings can be brought in as a part of the processional and placed in their appropriate locations.

ACTS OF ENTRANCE

Solemn Processional. The lights are darkened in the sanctuary, except for a small reading candle on the altar. The only other items on the altar are the bowl for the kindled fire and the paschal candle. Pre-service music is stopped and a period of silence is observed. The celebrants then gather at the altar to begin the service. Words of instruction are shared giving the history and purpose of the Easter.

Lighting the Paschal Fire. One of the celebrants lights the kindled fire in the bowl, then another reads the words of invitation and prayer, *Book of Common Prayer*, p. 285. A small candle is used to light the Paschal candle from the kindled fire, which is slowly burning down. Celebrants continue in the *Book of Common Prayer*, pp. 285–287.

LITURGY OF THE WORD

Scripture Reading. Readers should come forward at the appropriate times for their readings. Following each lesson, a celebrant will lead in the collect (*Book of Common Prayer*, pp. 288–291) and then a time of extemporaneous praying for each topic. After prayer, the congregation joins in a song or hymn as directed. The tone must remain somber and reverent at all times.

The Abrahamic Covenant: Genesis 15
    Collect and Extemporaneous Prayers
    Music: Hymn or chorus
Abraham's Sacrifice of Isaac: Genesis 22:1-18
    Collect and Extemporaneous Prayers

    Music: Hymn or chorus
Israel's Deliverance at the Red Sea: Exodus 14:10-15
    Collect and Extemporaneous Prayers
    Music: Hymn or chorus
Salvation Offered Freely to All: Isaiah 55:1-11
    Collect and Extemporaneous Prayers
    Music: Hymn or chorus
A New Heart and a New Spirit: Ezekiel 36:20-28
    Collect and Extemporaneous Prayers
    Music: Hymn or chorus

MINISTRY OF RENEWAL

Renewal of Baptismal Vows. Instructions are given about the lighting of candles after the last song. Those designated as candle lighters will then come forward, taking their light from the paschal candle and then lighting the candles of those on the end of each row. The light is then passed down the row until all candles are lit. When everyone has received the light of the paschal candle, the celebrants will begin leading the people through the renewal of baptismal vows as printed. The people are then instructed to extinguish their lights, while being reminded that although the candles have gone out, the light of Christ continues to burn brightly in their hearts.

The Passion and Resurrection of Christ. Readers will take their place and begin the readings with appropriate music and sound effects as directed. At the end of the reading the congregation will join in singing the hymn.

Text: John 19
Hymn: "When I Survey the Wondrous Cross" or "Christ the Lord is Risen Today"

Eucharist. A great and celebrative Eucharist expresses the joy of the Resurrection; sing numerous Alleluias and sing hymns, songs, and choruses of the Resurrection during Communion. Offer the laying on of hands.

Acts of Praise and Worship. The celebrants will then give time for ministry and worship. Praise choruses can be used along with any prophetic, exhortative, or Scripture offerings from the congregation.

ACTS OF DISMISSAL

Solemn Recessional. When ministry seems to be finished, the banner carriers and crossbearer will come forward. Banners will be furled and tied and a draped cloth will be placed over the cross. The cross bearer will take up the cross and lead the recessional, followed by the furled banners and celebrants. The lights will be turned on after all have recessed.

280 ♦ CREATIVE WAYS TO PROCLAIM THE EASTER VIGIL SCRIPTURE READINGS

The Easter Vigil readings span the history of salvation and recall for the worshiper the great acts of God's mercy. Sometimes the readings are not heard. The article below suggests how the readings may take on new life through dramatic forms of communication.

Our Episcopal parish values freedom for creative expression in its worship life, believing that, at its best, this expression can reflect the surprising and refreshing ways the living God encounters us.

With the introduction of the 1979 _Book of Common Prayer_, we were delighted to find the Great Vigil of Easter, one of the oldest of all liturgies, included for the first time. The service consists of four parts: the Service of Light; the Service of Lessons; Christian Initiation or the Renewal of Vows; and the Holy Eucharist with the administration of Easter Communion. The Service of Lessons is the record of God's saving acts in history and the witness of God's continued presence with God's people. The rubrics read, "It is customary for all the ordained ministers present, together with lay readers, singers, and other persons, to take active parts in the service" (p. 284). Our worship committee has taken these directions to heart. We work with the familiar stories in different ways to awaken the congregation into new awareness of God's life, as they are waking to another Easter through the pre-dawn darkness in which the Great Vigil begins.

The service begins an hour before sunrise in the church yard around a bonfire from which the paschal candle is lit. The candle speaks to the heart as well as the mind as we follow the subdeacon, priest, and cantor in a procession to the darkened church, responding to the cantor's "The Light of Christ" with our response, "Thanks be to God." At the door of the church we are given small, lighted candles. In the darkened church the smell of the lilies alerts our senses to our surroundings. As we become more accustomed to the candlelight, we can appreciate the Easter beauty of the sanctuary after the Lenten barrenness. One strength of the vigil is its appeal to all senses, and the readings for this service are always multimedia events. The singing of the Exultet sets the stage for the Service of Lessons.

The Story of Creation (Gen. 1:1–2:2)
We have used two approaches to the story from Genesis. We have accumulated a connoisseur's collection of slides, garnered from all over the world by members of our worship committee. We use them to visualize the creation as the story is read. We even have one slide of Halley's Comet on its last appearance, caught by the camera of a local astronomer-photographer. For many of us, this slide gives new meaning to the words, "Let there be lights in the firmament."

This past Easter we discovered James Weldon Johnson's _God's Trombones_, which contains "Creation Story." One member of our group, a dancer, created graceful mime movements that she performs as the story is read. Her portrayal of God as sculptor is vividly set forth as the reader recites this portion:

> This Great God,
> Like a mammy bending over her baby,
> Kneeled down in the dust
> Toiling over a lump of clay
> Til he shaped it in his own image.

We used a background tape to enhance the dancer's actions. The sanctuary lights were gradually turned on as the reading suggested. At the line, "And flung it against the darkness, spangling the night with the moon and stars," the lights became full.

The Flood (Gen. 7:1-5, 11-18; 8:6-18; 9:8-13)
Our telling of the Flood has gone from the children in animals' masks parading during the reading to the reading of a riveting interpretation which we adapted from _History, Herstory, Ourstory_ by Rev. David Steele. We have an eighty-two-year-old storyteller who gives a great deal of time and care to preparation. Everyone is with her as she brings this story to its final paragraph: "Now the story is of a lethal rain that wipes out all humanity. It is not within the mind of God but has

emerged from human laboratories. . . ." Fayetteville is a military town, and these words are not lost on the listeners.

Abraham's Sacrifice of Isaac (Gen. 22:1-18)

We took it upon ourselves to look at this reading and imagine what was going on with another principal in the drama, Sarah. After writing Sarah's part, we felt that her agonizing prayers to God gave life to the angel who intervened and stopped Abraham's knife. For that reason we also had Sarah speak the angel's part. The music which followed this reading was composed by our guitarist and was a song telling of his love for his own young son.

Israel's Deliverance at the Red Sea (Exod. 14:10–15:1)

We first did this reading with musical sound effects. We read it straight with background music in which you could hear chariots and horses. We have also rewritten the story in the style of rap music.

A New Heart and a New Spirit (Ezek. 36:24-28)

This reading uses two readers. One reader reads the lesson and the other responds to it. There are also two mimes. Both mimes wear black robes under which they wear identical, colorful outfits. Mime one wears a black mask. We used a large grocery bag painted with tempera black, with slits cut so the mime could see. This large bag worked well and did not smear the makeup which mime one had on underneath. Mime two wears white makeup only.

The readers take places on each side of the altar. Mime two, with white face, comes in, walks to front of altar, faces the congregation, and stands at attention, frozen until reader two responds to reader one.

READER 1: Thus says the Lord God, "I will take you from the nations, and gather you from all the countries, and bring you into your own land."

READER 2: Me, God? You want me? Are you sure you want me? I have sure strayed a long way from home!

(Mime two points to self while saying, "You want me?" then points skyward and back to self. At mention of *straying,* he (or she) puts both pointing fingers together under chin and, while moving

them out from his (or her) body, separates them from each other. Mime one comes in and takes his place beside the baptismal font, which is in front of mime two.)

READER 1: I will sprinkle water upon you, and you shall be clean from all your uncleannesses, and from all your idols I will cleanse you.

(Mime one sprinkles water on mime two, who is frozen.)

READER 2: Gee, God, now I can give up all those things I have worshiped . . . my good looks, all my money . . . all those things I have given so much power to.

(Both mimes look into imaginary mirrors, study themselves with admiration, and then throw the mirrors away over their shoulders; they pull out the pockets of their robes to show they are empty of money. Then they shrug shoulders at each other.)

READER 1: A new heart I will give you.

(Mime one creates a pulsing heart in his hand and puts it to breast of mime two. He keeps it pulsing until mime two gets his hand there to take over the pulse movement.)

READER 2: With my new heart I learn to feel compassion for all the hurting people in the world. And I learn about tears. Tears are so important, aren't they, God?

(Mime one uses a makeup pencil and puts tears on the face of mime two.)

READER 1: A new spirit I will put within you.

READER 2: You will change that innermost part of me. Red must be your most favorite color, God, for you use it for such important things: Sunsets. Santa's suits. Cherries. Rhubarb. Fire trucks. Blood. Blushes! It's a wonderful color for spirit. It's hot. It's cool. It's lively. It's shy. It's a delicious, sacred, sad, happy, brave kind of color!

(Mime one uses a pallet with red makeup on it to put a red nose, red happy mouth, and round red dot on the cheek of mime two.)

READER 1: I will take out of your flesh the heart of stone and give you a heart of flesh.

READER 2: You will change me by loving me and I will become loving too . . . for how can I ever love another if I have never experienced love myself?

(Mime one hugs mime two, who shows great delight in it. Mime two then hugs himself with great gusto. Then he goes back to hugging mime one, then hugging self, back and forth, as time allows.)

READER 1: And I will put my spirit within you, and cause you to walk in my statutes, and be careful to observe my ordinances. You shall dwell in the land which I gave your fathers.

READER 2: Does this mean we have a contract, God? You're going to love all of us into being new and changed people? I get it . . . and when I have tears or see that wonderful color red, I will be reminded of my new life and my new spirit!

(Mimes slap hands as in "high five" and "low five," showing contract. Mime two removes robe with quite a flair to reveal colorful clown clothes. He then shows interest in mime one's mask and begins to study it. He removes the mask from mime one, revealing a face exactly like his own. He is delighted and begins to walk around mime one looking at the robe, up and down, studying it, peeking into the collar. He prayerfully asks mime one to take off robe, which mime one does. They face the congregation together, holding hands, identical in makeup and costume. They hold hands aloft and freeze.)

READER 1: You shall be my people and I will be your God.

(Mimes turn and bow to each other and exit joyfully.)

READER 2: The Word of the Lord.

The Valley of Dry Bones (Ezek. 37:1-14)

During an arts conference at the Church Divinity School of the Pacific in 1984, several of our members joined Doug Adams to visit George Segal's Holocaust memorial in Lincoln Park, San Francisco. The subject matter of the memorial is eleven corpses heaped upon one another in chaos and disorder. One lone, living figure stands in front of the bodies. He is a figure with eyes downcast, one hand holding a strand of the high-barbed wire fence that imprisons him. The stoop of his body portrays his weariness and the toll of horrors in his life. The figures are life-sized, cast in whitened bronze. Friends of the sculptor served as models.

With the models' experience in mind, Doug asked us to duplicate the statuary with our bodies. The effect was very dramatic for each of us. From that experience arose the idea that the dry bones of Ezekiel must have shared something in common with these statues. We chose four people, dressed in black with simple mime faces. They entered the sanctuary in darkness and stretched out on the floor in front of the altar with their bodies related in some way, reminiscent of Segal's work. We used music as background, part from the soundtrack of the movie, _Doctor Zhivago,_ and part from Prokofiev's "Alexander Nevsky." The music followed the reader, and as the bones were enlivened, so was the music. The mimes began to come alive very slowly, one at a time. They responded to the words of the reading, showing the breath coming into them and pushing open their graces until they exited in single file with their heads up and arms held aloft in praise.

The Gathering of God's People (Zeph. 3:12-20)

We are brooding over this reading now, along with our increasing experience of being lame and outcast as we live with AIDS, for offering on next Easter.

Betsy L. Willis[49]

✎ TWENTY-FOUR ✎

Worship on Easter Sunday

Easter Sunday is a Sunday for witness. This is a Sunday when the whole church gathers for worship and when nominal Christians or non-Christians may attend worship services. Thus, worship on Easter Sunday must clearly announce the power of Christ's victory over sin and death. The following articles include several suggestions for proclaiming that Good News to the world.

281 ♦ LECTIONARY READINGS FOR EASTER SUNDAY

The following are the recommended readings for Easter Sunday in the Revised Common Lectionary.

SUNDAY	ACTS	PSALM	EPISTLE	GOSPEL
Year A	Acts 10:34-43, Peter: they killed Jesus, but God raised him; or Jeremiah 31:1-6, the return of the exile.	Psalm 118:1-2, 14-24	Colossians 3:1-4, you are raised to life with Christ.	John 20:1-18 or Matthew 28:1-10, Mary and the empty tomb.
Year B	Acts 10:34-43 (above) or Isaiah 25:6-9, the mountain of the Lord.		1 Corinthians 15:1-11, the resurrection of Christ and his appearances.	John 20:1-18 or Mark 16:1-8
Year C	Acts 10:34-43, (above) or Isaiah 65:17-25, the new creation.		1 Corinthians 15:19-26, Christ's resurrection and ours.	John 20:1-18 or Luke 24:1-12
If the Old Testament lesson is chosen, the reading from Acts 10 may be substituted for the Epistle reading.				

282 ♦ A TRADITIONAL EASTER (PASCHA) SERVICE

The following service is a creative adaptation of the traditional pattern and texts for worship on Easter. It will be of particular help for those who plan more formal Easter worship. For Christians in nonliturgical churches, the commentary included with this service will provide a guide to thoughtful planning.

WE ENTER TO WORSHIP

Commentary: Every aspect of the congregation's gathering on Easter should be marked by celebrative joy. The colors of white (purity) and gold (regality) should dominate the worship space. Images of the Easter event—the opening tomb, the lily, the butterfly, the herald's trumpet, the empty cross, the chi rho—can be featured on banners, paraments, and printed liturgy covers. Lilies can adorn the worship space, adding their white brilliance and springtime odor to the worship space. Members of the congregation can be appointed to greet worshipers as they arrive with the joyous news of the Lord's victory.

Gathering of the Congregation (with organ, piano, or instrumental prelude)

Commentary: If the service begins early on Easter morning, perhaps even before sunrise, the service can begin in quietness and darkness—the last shadow of Lent. Then the opening acclamation of Christ's victory can shatter the silence as the rising sun and other lights break the darkness. Following this opening announcement, the Easter banners, paraments, and flowers can be brought in, perhaps by the children of the congregation or by various members of the congregation, while the congregation sings the first hymn. The Paschal candle can also be lit at this point. (See below).

If the service begins at a later time, or after an Easter Vigil service, then the festive mood should be present from the beginning. As the congregation gathers, instrumental, organ, or piano music, perhaps based on Easter hymns, can serve to call the people to worship. As another option, the gathering congregation may sing these same hymns as if they cannot hold back their exuberant praise. As more people arrive the song will naturally crescendo.

Acclamation

LEADER(S): The Lord is risen!
PEOPLE: **The Lord is risen indeed!**

Commentary: This joyous announcement should be done with vigor. Perhaps several people, stationed at various places within the worship space or at each entrance, can begin by exclaiming, "The Lord is risen," followed the congregation, led the by choir or a speech choir responding with, "The Lord is risen indeed." This final response can be repeated several times, each growing in vitality.

Hymn of Praise: "Christ the Lord Is Risen Today"

Commentary: The introduction to the hymn should follow the opening acclamation without pause. Other appropriate hymns include "The Day of Resurrection," "Come, You Faithful, Raise the Strain," and "Good Christians All, Rejoice and Sing."

Greeting

PASTOR: Grace to you and peace, from him who is and who was and who is to come, and from Jesus Christ, the faithful witness, the firstborn of the dead, and the Ruler of kings on earth.
PEOPLE: **Alleluia, Amen!**

Commentary: The reference in this text to Christ as the "firstborn of the dead" makes its use especially appropriate for Easter.

Mutual Greeting

LEADER: Even now as we have received God's greeting, let us greet each other, in Jesus' name.
PEOPLE: (to each other) **The Lord is risen!**

Commentary: Placing the mutual greeting (or passing of the peace) at this point in the service may be especially important on Easter Sunday because of the number of visitors often present on this day. Members of the congregation should be especially alert to greet visitors, to assist them with questions they may have, and to ensure that they have all necessary worship materials (hymnals, printed liturgies, prayer books, the Bible).

Lighting of the Paschal Candle

LEADER: Sisters and brothers in Christ: On this joyous morning, we celebrate that our Lord Jesus passed over from death to life. We join with the whole company of God's people in recalling and celebrating his victory over death, and our deliverance from the bondage of sin and darkness to everlasting light.
LEADER: (reads John 1:1, 4-5)
PEOPLE: **Eternal Lord of Life, through your Son you have given your people the brightness of your light. Sanctify this new fire, and kindle in our hearts and minds a holy desire to shine forth with the brightness of Christ's rising until we feast at the banquet of Eternal light; through Jesus Christ, the Sun of righteousness. Amen.**
LEADER: The light of Christ rises in glory, overcoming the darkness of sin and death.
PEOPLE: **Thanks be to God!**

Commentary: The paschal candle (a large white candle, on which may be engraved the chi rho) symbolizes the eternal victory of Jesus Christ over death, which brings light to our dark world of sin. Unlike other candles in Christian symbolism, the paschal candle is explicitly tied to the Easter message. Hence, the paschal candle is traditionally lit each of Sunday of Eastertide through Pentecost.

It may also be lit at every baptism, where Christians celebrate that they "are raised with Christ," and at every memorial or funeral service, where we celebrate Christ's victory over death. This candle is traditionally lit at Easter Vigil, but congregations who do not hold such services may incorporate this into the opening of Easter morning worship.

Acclamations of Praise

Psalm 118:1-2, 14-16
Hymn: "Come, You Faithful, Raise the Strain"
Psalm 118: 16-21
Hymn: "The Strife Is O'er, the Battle Done"
Psalm 118:22-24
Hymn: "O Sons and Daughters of the King"

Commentary: This service features the use of Psalm 118, which has long been associated with Easter celebrations, in the opening section of the service. This serves to extend the opening time of celebration and adoration, certainly appropriate for Easter. The Psalm may otherwise be read or sung in its usual place between the Old and New Testament readings.

Psalm 118 may be sung by the congregation, choir, or by cantor and congregation in a responsorial form. This service, however, features readings of portions of the Psalm, alternating with Easter hymns. Other scriptural songs and choral or solo anthems may also used. This alternation reinforces the appropriation of these Old Testament words to express the faith and joy of New Testament experience.

WE HEAR GOD'S WORD

Prayer for Illumination

PEOPLE: **Almighty God, we celebrate today the victory of Jesus Christ over death. As we now hear your Word of grace, inspire us by the power of your Spirit, that we may respond with joy and boldness in declaring our union with Christ, share in the feast of his victory, live in the power of his resurrection; through Jesus Christ our Lord, who now lives and reigns with you and the Holy Spirit, one God forever. Alleluia! Amen!**

The Old Testament and New Testament Readings

Jeremiah 31:1-6, Acts 10:34-43, Colossians 3:1-4

Commentary: If Psalm 118 is not read or sung earlier in the service, it may be used at this point.

The Easter Gospel: Matthew 28:1-10

Commentary: The Easter Gospel may be read dramatically by several readers, each reading the words of one of the persons in this scriptural account, with one reader reciting the narration. If this is done, the reading may be extended to include some of the post-resurrection appearances of Jesus, such as the appearance on the road to Emmaus. This type of reading is uniquely well-suited to capturing the spirit of joy inherent the account of Christ's resurrection and post-resurrection appearances.

Response

LEADER: The Gospel of Jesus Christ.
PEOPLE: **Praise to you, Lord Christ!**

Commentary: This response to the reading of the Gospel lesson is appropriate for every service in the Christian year.

Sermon

WE CELEBRATE OUR NEW LIFE

Service of Christian Baptism or Reaffirmation of the Baptismal Covenant

Introduction
Renunciation of Sin
Statement of Faith: (Nicene or Apostles' Creed)
Prayer

Commentary: Easter morning is perhaps the most appropriate occasion in the Christian year for prospective members and newborn children of the church to be baptized, according to the practice of a local congregation. If there are no candidates for baptism, it is appropriate for each member of the congregation to remember their own baptism and to declare their union with Christ, by reaffirming their place in the baptismal covenant. See the Easter Vigil service for a complete text of the renewal of the baptismal covenant. If this is not included, it should be replaced by the statement of the Nicene or Apostles' Creed, unless the creed is used to structure the Communion liturgy, as is the case in this sample service.

Prayers of the People

Adoration
Lord God, of power and might,

We praise you because of your power over sin and death.

We praise you for raising Jesus Christ from the dead.

We praise you for binding us together as the body of Christ.

We praise you for ruling over your kingdom in power and might.

Petition

We petition you to extend your power in our world, to crush the effects of evil that we see in our neighborhood, community, state, nation, and world.

We petition you to extend and strengthen the body of Christ, the church.

We petition you to assure us and strengthen us in our faith.

Confession

We confess that our faith has not always remained firm.

We confess that we have not always lived in the power of Christ's resurrection.

We confess that we not have brought the news of Christ's victory to our world.

Commentary: Worship in many Protestant churches has long featured a balance between printed and extemporaneous prayers. The latter can be best developed by following a pre-written pattern, as is printed here. Under each category of prayer are listed theme sentences upon which can be elaborated by the pastor or other worship leaders. Care should be given to make each section of the prayer specifically relevant to the needs and concerns of the local congregation.

Declaration of Pardon

LEADER: Friends in Christ: hear the good news: (reads Romans 12:1-2). In Jesus Christ, we are forgiven.

PEOPLE: **Thanks be to God.**

Offertory

LEADER: In thanksgiving for Christ's victory, we bring our offerings to God.

PEOPLE: **Amen.**

[The gifts are received.]

PEOPLE (SING):
Praise God, from whom all blessings flow . . .

Commentary: At this point, the elements for communion and the gifts which have been received may be brought forward.

WE CELEBRATE THE SACRAMENT

Preface

LEADER: According to Luke, when our risen Lord was at table with his disciples he took bread, and blessed and broke it, and gave it to them. Then their eyes were opened and they recognized him. Friends, this is the joyful feast of the people of God. Come, taste, and see the that the Lord is good.

Declaration of Faith and Prayer of Thanksgiving

Commentary: The prayer of thanksgiving that is a part of the Communion liturgy traditionally features a Trinitarian structure. (See Pentecost Service.) The following Communion liturgy integrates the statement of the three parts of the Apostles' Creed, itself reflecting Trinitarian structure, with the traditional structure of the Lord's Supper liturgy. This is especially appropriate for Easter Sunday, when Christians emphasize the proclamation of their faith in the risen Lord and recall the fundamental tenets of the Christian faith which are important to the act of baptism or entry into the body of Christ.

LEADER: What do you believe concerning God the Father?

PEOPLE: **I believe in God, the Father almighty, creator of heaven and earth.**

LEADER: O Lord, our God, Father almighty, creator of heaven and earth, with joy we give you thanks and praise. By your power you raised Christ Jesus from death to life. Through his victory over the grave we are set free from the bonds of sin and the fear of death. In his rising to life you promise eternal life to all who believe in him. We praise you that as we break bread in faith, we shall know the risen Christ among us. Therefore, with all Christians we praise your name and sing with joy:

PEOPLE: **Holy, holy, holy Lord, God of power and might,**
heaven and earth are full of your glory.

Hosanna in the highest.
Blessed is he who comes in the
name of the Lord.
Hosanna in the highest.

Commentary: Most hymnals include a setting of this traditional canticle. For a list of service music found in a representative group of hymnals, consult the commentary to the Communion liturgy of the Advent service in this series. For Easter, the most celebrative version of the canticle should be chosen.

LEADER: What do you believe concerning Jesus Christ, the Son of God?

PEOPLE: **I believe in Jesus Christ, his only Son, our Lord,**
who was conceived by the Holy Spirit and born of the virgin Mary.
He suffered under Pontius Pilate, was crucified, died and was buried; he descended to hell.
The third day he rose again from the dead.
He ascended to heaven and is seated at the right hand of God the Father almighty.
From there he will come to judge the living and the dead.

LEADER: We praise you, O risen Christ, as the Lord of all creation. We bless you for your sacrifice in dwelling with us on this earth and sustaining even death on a cross. We worship you for your powerful victory over death and for your glorious ascension into heaven. And we thank you for leaving us with a constant reminder of your death and resurrection and means to declare our love for you: the sacrament of our Lord. Amen.

Institution

LEADER: For the Lord Jesus, on the night when he was betrayed, took bread, and when he had given thanks, he broke it and said, "This is my body, which is for you; do this in remembrance of me." In the same way, he took the cup, after supper, saying, "This cup is the new covenant in my blood; do this, whenever you drink it, in re-

membrance of me." For whenever you eat this bread and drink this cup, you proclaim the Lord's death until he comes.

Memorial

LEADER: People of God, what do you proclaim in this feast?

PEOPLE: **We proclaim that Christ has died, Christ is risen, and Christ is coming again.**

LEADER: What do you believe concerning God the Holy Spirit?

PEOPLE: **I believe in the Holy Spirit,**
the holy catholic church,
the communion of saints,
the forgiveness of sins,
the resurrection of the body,
and the life everlasting. Amen.

Prayer of Consecration

LEADER: Holy Spirit of God, descend upon us now, we pray. By these gifts, inspire in us a knowledge of our union with Christ and his church, an assurance of the forgiveness of our sins, a vision of our coming resurrection with Christ, and the comfort of knowing we will live and reign forever with our Lord. Amen.

Invitation

PASTOR: Friends in Christ, the Lord has prepared his table for his church. All who love him and trust in him alone for their salvation are now invited to come to the table of the Lord.

PEOPLE: **We come with gladness. Thanks be to God!**

PASTOR: The gifts of God for the people of God.

Sacrament

PASTOR: (as the people take the bread) Take, eat, remember, and believe that the body of the Lord Jesus Christ was given for the complete remission of all our sins.

PASTOR: (as the people take the cup) Take, drink, remember, and believe that the precious blood of our Lord Jesus Christ was shed for the complete forgiveness of all our sins.

Commentary: Music that accompanies the Lord's Supper on Easter should be distinctly celebrative in tone. While it has been common practice in some parishes to accompany the sacrament with somber tones that focus on Christ's sacrifice, this is certainly one occasion where the emphasis should fall on the celebration of his victory.

This mood of celebration may also influence the method of distribution for the sacrament. Congregations who normally serve the elements of Communion to the people in their seats may wish to invite the people to come forward to receive them.

Thanksgiving

PASTOR: You have given yourself to us, Lord.

PEOPLE: **Now we pledge to give ourselves to each other.**

PASTOR: You have raised us with Christ, and made us a new people.

PEOPLE: **As people of the resurrection, we will serve you with joy.**

PASTOR: You glory has filled our hearts.

PEOPLE: **Help us to glorify you in all things. Amen.**

WE DEPART TO SERVE

Charge to the Congregation

PASTOR: Go in the power of our risen Lord, to love and serve him in all you do.

[or]

(reads Colossians 3:1-4)

PEOPLE: **We go in his name and for his glory.**

Hymn of Dedication (Recession): "This Joyful Eastertide"

Benediction

PASTOR: May the God of peace, who raised to life the great Shepherd of the sheep, make us ready to do his will in every good thing, through Jesus Christ, to whom be glory forever and ever.

[or]

PASTOR: May God, who through the water of baptism has raised us from sin into newness of life, bring you into all the riches of union with Christ Jesus, his Son, through the power of the Holy Spirit.

PEOPLE: **Amen. Alleluia! Amen!**

Dispersal of the Congregation
(with organ, piano, or instrumental postlude)

Commentary: Post-service music on Easter should be triumphant. The use of brass instruments is especially effective.

John D. Witvliet

283 ✦ A CONVERGENCE EASTER SERVICE

The service below is intended to be used as a guideline for the congregation that desires to bring together traditional and contemporary styles of worship. Adapt to local usage and style during the Easter (Pascha) season.

Environment. After the solemnity of the week and the red paraments and frontals of earlier services, the white colors seem to brighten the whole sanctuary. Before the service, lilies and other floral arrangements can be placed in the front to give the room a sense of life.

ACTS OF ENTRANCE

Solemn Processional/Declaration of Resurrection. The crucifer and banner carriers, dancers, and other participants from the previous night silently process in with the same veiled cross and furled banners to a single, low tone on the keyboards. After they are in place, a reader shares the Resurrection account.

Reading/Response. Luke 23:50–24:12 is read. After the reading of the Scripture the minister leads the congregation in a threefold declaration: He is risen—**He is risen indeed!** As the declaration continues, the cross is undraped and the banners are unfurled, with shouts of praise coming from everyone throughout the sanctuary.

Hymn. The worship team leads the congregation in "Christ the Lord is Risen Today."

Acts of Praise and Worship. Worship continues under the theme of resurrection and new life. Encouragement is given for gifts to operate as people celebrate the power of the Christ, risen from the dead. An Easter litany and other expressions of worship may also be added to this section.

Resurrection Praise Reports. Out of the time of praise and worship, opportunity is given for members of the congregation to express ways in which they have experienced Resurrection power in recent months. This can be spontaneous or preplanned concerning those who give testimony.

MINISTRY OF THE WORD

Collect for Easter Sunday. "Almighty God, who through your only begotten Son Jesus Christ destroyed the sting of death and opened to those who repent the way of everlasting life: grant that we, who celebrate with joy the day of the Lord's resurrection, may continually be raised from the death of sin by the same power that raised from the dead our Lord Jesus Christ, who lives and reigns with you and the Holy Spirit, one God, now and forever. Amen."

Readings. Good first reading selections are Isaiah 51:9-11, or Acts 10:34-43, or Exodus 14:10-14, 21-25; 15:20-21. An appropriate Psalm would be Psalm 118:14-29. The second reading could be either Acts 10:34-43 or Colossians 3:1-4. Fitting Gospel readings include Matthew 28:1-10, Mark 16:1-8, Luke 24:1-10, and John 20:1-10.

MINISTRY OF THE TABLE

Offertory. Easter is a perfect time to take a special offering for missions, emphasizing the work of the gospel, proclaiming the richness of the risen Christ to every nation. This could be done with the regular offering or as a special event afterward. People could even be invited to come forward and place their gift on the altar either before or during Communion.

Great Thanksgiving. Communion during the Easter season should be celebrated with added joy. Express this joy with Communion songs of resurrection, victory and exaltation, and observe the laying on of hands with anointing.

Prayer after Communion. "Heavenly Father, we thank you for satisfying the hunger in our hearts through giving us the Bread of heaven. In sharing in this holy meal, may we remember his death which gives us life, and his coming again which gives us hope. This we ask through Jesus Christ our Lord. Amen."

ACTS OF DISMISSAL

Blessing/Benediction. "May the God of peace, who through the blood of eternal covenant, brought back from the dead our Lord Jesus, that great Shepherd of the sheep, equip you with everything good for doing his will, and may he work in us what is pleasing to him through Jesus Christ, to whom be glory for ever and ever. Amen."

LEADER: Go forth in the resurrection power of Jesus Christ!

PEOPLE: **Thanks be to God!**

Randolph W. Sly

284 ◆ A LITANY OF THE RESURRECTION

This litany may be used on Easter day or on any of the Sundays of Easter.

LEADER: "Who is it you are looking for?" (Matt. 20:15).

PEOPLE: **"Sir, . . .we would like to see Jesus"** (John 12:21).

LEADER: "Do not be afraid, for I know that you are looking for Jesus, who was crucified. He is not here; he has risen just as he said. Come and see the place where he lay" (Matt. 28:5-6).

PEOPLE: **"Praise be to the Lord God, the God of Israel, who alone does marvelous deeds"** (Ps. 72:18).

LEADER: "Christ has indeed been raised from the dead, the firstfruits of those who have fallen asleep" (1 Cor. 15:20).

PEOPLE: **"Praise be to the Lord, for he showed his wonderful love to me"** (Ps. 31:21).

LEADER: "Praise be to the God and Father of our Lord Jesus Christ! In his great mercy he has given us new birth into a living hope through the resurrection of Jesus Christ from the dead" (1 Pet. 1:3).

PEOPLE: **"Praise be to the name of God for-ever and ever; wisdom and power are his"** (Dan. 2:20).

LEADER: "Where, O death, is your victory? Where, O death, is your sting? The sting of death is sin, and the power

PEOPLE: "Thanks be to God! He gives us the victory through our Lord Jesus Christ" (1 Cor. 15:57).

LEADER: "Therefore God exalted him to the highest place and gave him the name that is above every name" (Phil. 2:9).

PEOPLE: "Praise be to his glorious name forever; may the whole earth be filled with his glory. Amen and Amen" (Ps. 72:19).

LEADER: "Since, then, you have been raised with Christ, set your hearts on things above, where Christ is seated at the right hand of God" (Col. 3:1).

PEOPLE: "Praise be to the Lord, the God of Israel, from ever-lasting to everlasting. Let all the people say, 'Amen'" (Ps. 106:48).

TOGETHER: "Hallelujah! For our Lord God Almighty reigns. Let us rejoice and be glad and give him glory!" (Rev. 19:6-7).

Robert D. Gray

285 ◆ AN EASTER PROCLAMATION OF FAITH

This proclamation of faith may be used in response to the sermon on Easter Day or on any of the Easter Sundays.

LEADER: The manifold wisdom of God has been revealed.

PEOPLE: Rulers and authorities in heavenly realms now know of his marvelous plan.

LEADER: For the Son of God, Jesus Christ died on a cross for our sin.

PEOPLE: His body was pierced, His blood was shed as the perfect sacrifice lamb.

LEADER: After he died the death of man, his lifeless body was placed in a tomb.

PEOPLE: He was wrapped in linens and spices and a large stone sealed him in darkness.

LEADER: But God broke the darkness with the light of life; on the third day Jesus rose from the dead.

PEOPLE: Resurrection power surged through every part of his being.

LEADER: He became the Risen Christ—conqueror of sin and death.

PEOPLE: The firstborn from the dead, that we, too, might taste the power of light and life.

LEADER: He who rose now sits at the right hand of the Father.

PEOPLE: The Risen One is the Ascended Christ—the high priest of heaven and head of the church, his body.

LEADER: We declare today that we, as his church, are his blood-bought bride.

PEOPLE: That we are his people, a royal priesthood, a new and holy nation in his sight.

LEADER: He will come again for us . . . Maranatha!

PEOPLE: That we might be where he is . . . Maranatha, Lord Jesus!

LEADER: Glory be to the Father and to the Son and to the Holy Spirit.

PEOPLE: Who was in the beginning, is now, and ever shall be. World without end. Amen.

Randolph W. Sly

286 ◆ AN EASTER DRAMA

Below is an ancient play, Quem quaeritis? *(Whom do you seek?), that was traditionally performed on Easter Sunday. It can be used in this form or altered to suit the talents or needs of your congregation.*

The three women, with bowed heads and gestures of mourning, weave their way down the aisle to the altar, saying to one another, "Who will roll the stone for us?" "Who will roll away the stone?"

At the altar, the angel suddenly appears. The women cry out and fall back, covering their faces. The angel says, "Don't be afraid. Whom are you looking for?"

The women rise and call, "Where is Jesus, the man who was crucified?'

The angel indicates the empty tomb: "He isn't here!" Raising arms slowly and majestically, the angel continues: "As he said, he has risen!" The angel gestures toward the assembly: "Now go and tell everybody!"

The women turn and call, "Peter! Andrew! James! John! Everyone! Hurry up! Come to the tomb!" They repeat this, running down the steps to the aisle. Then, dancing and spinning in joy, they cry out such phrases as "Jesus is risen!" "The tomb! It's empty!" "Jesus is alive!" Hurry, come and see!" "Run and tell everyone!" to people in each row.

When they reach the back of the assembly, the disciples (and anyone else who wants to join in) run and skip and cartwheel forward, with ringing and jingling bells. Some call out: "Oh, Hallelujah! Jesus is risen!" Simultaneously, others cry: "Jesus is risen? I can't believe it!" Others, "Christ is alive! How can it be?" All converge at the altar, point out "the empty tomb" to each other, then are joined by the choir in leading the assembly in a favorite hymn of the Resurrection.

Rick Hodson[50]

Worship During the Season of Easter

The services of the Easter season also continue to celebrate the broad sweep of salvation history and invite the church to engage in the most festive days of its history. In contemporary worship renewal, ancient services are being restored to the life of the church. They continue to make the church stand out in a unique way in the midst of a secular culture. Note that this collection of services also includes the Pentecost service. The Easter season concludes on Pentecost Sunday.

287 ◆ LECTIONARY TEXTS FOR THE SUNDAYS OF EASTER

The following are the texts suggested for the Sundays of Easter in the Revised Common Lectionary. Brief descriptions of each lesson are provided to aid in recalling the basic theme of each passage.

——— **Year A** ———

SUNDAY	ACTS	PSALM	EPISTLE	GOSPEL
Second Sunday of Easter	Acts 2:14a, 22-32, Peter proclaims the good news about Jesus.	16	1 Peter 1:3-9, God's raising Christ; our living hope.	John 20:19-31, Jesus appears to disciples and to Thomas.
Third Sunday of Easter	Acts 2:14a, 36-41, response of people, who believed and were baptized.	116:1-4	1 Peter 1:17-23, have confidence in God who raised Christ.	Luke 24:13-35, appearance on the road to Emmaus.
Fourth Sunday of Easter	Acts 2:42-47, the life of the Christian community.	23	1 Peter 2:19-25, the example of Christ's suffering.	John 10:1-10, parables: shepherds and thieves.
Fifth Sunday of Easter	Acts 7:55-60, Stephen stoned.	31:1-5, 15-16	1 Peter 2:2-10, Lord is living stone, you are kingdom of priests.	John 14:1-14, don't worry; I am the way, the truth, life.
Sixth Sunday of Easter	Acts 17:22-31, Paul's sermons to the Athenians.	66:8-20	1 Peter 3:13-22, Christ died for our sins, suffer for doing right.	John 14:15-21, promise of the Holy Spirit.

continued...

———— Year A cont. ————

SUNDAY	ACTS	PSALM	EPISTLE	GOSPEL
Ascension Day	Acts 1:1-11, Jesus taken up to heaven.	47 68:1-10	Ephesians 1:15-23, I give thanks for you in my prayers .	Luke 24:44-53, final appearance; Jesus is taken up
Seventh Sunday of Easter	Acts 1:6-14, account of the ascension; disciples pray.		1 Peter 4:12-14, 5:6-11, suffer gladly as a Christian, be on the alert	John 17:1-11, Jesus' prayer for his disciples

———— Year B ————

SUNDAY	ACTS	PSALM	EPISTLE	GOSPEL
Second Sunday of Easter	Acts 4:32-35, believers share their possessions.	133	1 John 1:1–2:2, the Word; God is light; if we sin, we have advocate.	John 20:19-31, Easter appearances to disciples.
Third Sunday of Easter	Acts 3:12-19, Peter in temple: "you rejected Christ."	4	1 John 3:1-7, we are God's children; be like Jesus.	Luke 24:36b-48, Resurrection appearance, wait for Spirit.
Fourth Sunday of Easter	Acts 4:5-12, Peter and John before the Council.	23	1 John 3:16-24, God's commands: believe in Son, love others.	John 10:11-18, "I am the Good Shepherd."
Fifth Sunday of Easter	Acts 8:26-40, Philip and the Ethiopian official.	22:25-31	1 John 4:7-21, God is love; we love because he first loved us.	John 15:1-18, "I am the True Vine."
Sixth Sunday of Easter	Acts 10:44-48, Gentiles receive the Holy Spirit.	98	1 John 5:1-6, victory over the world by those who believe.	John 15:9-17, love one another as I have loved you.
Ascension Day	Acts 1:1-11, Jesus taken up to heaven.	47	Ephesians 1:15-23, I give thanks for you in my prayers .	Luke 24:44-53, final appearance; Jesus is taken up.
Seventh Sunday of Easter	Acts 1:15-17, 21, 26, apostle chosen to replace Judas.	1	1 John 5:9-13, the witness about Jesus; life through Son.	John 17:6-19, Jesus' prayer: may they be one.

———— Year C ————

SUNDAY	ACTS	PSALM	EPISTLE/REVELATION	GOSPEL
Second Sunday of Easter	Acts 4:32-35, believers Acts 5:27-32, Peter to Council: "We obey God, not humans."	150	Revelation 1:4-8, greeting to seven churches: "He is coming."	John 20:19-31, Jesus appears to disciples and Thomas.

——— **Year C cont.** ———

SUNDAY	ACTS	PSALM	EPISTLE/REVELATION	GOSPEL
Third Sunday of Easter	Acts 9:1-20, Paul is converted on road to Damascus.	30	Revelation 5:11-14, multitude around the throne, "worthy is the lamb."	John 21:1-19, Jesus appears in Galilee and to Peter.
Fourth Sunday of Easter	Acts 13:15-16, 26-33, Paul preaches good news in Antioch of Pisidia.	23	Revelation 7:9-17, crowd from every nation, robes washed with blood.	John 10:22-30, "Are you Messiah?" "Father and I are one."
Fifth Sunday of Easter	Acts 14:8-18, Paul in Lystra and Derbe, thought to be a god.	148	Revelation 21:1-16, I saw a new heaven and new earth.	John 13:31-35, the new commandment.
Sixth Sunday of Easter	Acts 15:1-2, 22-29, debate with apostles in Jerusalem over the law.	67	Revelation 21:10, 22-27, the Holy City and the Lamb.	John 14:23-29, "I will give you a helper, the Spirit."
Ascension Day	Acts 1:1-11, Jesus taken up to heaven.	47	Ephesians 1:15-23, I give thanks for you in my prayers .	Luke 24:44-53, final appearance; Jesus is taken up.
Seventh Sunday of Easter	Acts 16:16-34, Paul and Silas bound in jail; doors open.	97	Revelation 22:12-14, 16-17, 20, "I am coming soon. I am the First and Last."	John 17:20-26, "Pray that they may be one as you and I are one."

Revised Common Lectionary, descriptions by H. A. Tillinghast

288 ✦ CALLS TO WORSHIP FOR THE SUNDAYS OF EASTER

The following litanies of praise from the ancient Eastern churches can be used in the Entrance Rites for the Sundays of Easter. They can be said or sung before the Entrance hymn or afterward in place of the hymn of praise.

——— **Easter Day** ———

MINISTER: Accept our praise, O holy Lord.

PEOPLE: **For you have manifested the Resurrection to the world.**

MINISTER: Come, O people. Fall down before Christ and glorify his resurrection from the dead.

PEOPLE: **He is our God who has delivered the world from the enemy.**

MINISTER: Let the heavens shout. Let the trumpets shake the foundations of the earth.

PEOPLE: **Behold Christ who has nailed our sins to the cross and has destroyed death.**

MINISTER: Let us praise him who was crucified in the flesh for our sake.

PEOPLE: **He suffered, was buried, and rose from the dead.**

MINISTER: We stand before your life-giving tomb and glorify your unspeakable tenderness of heart.

PEOPLE: **O sinless one, you accepted the cross to give resurrection to us and to the world.**

MINISTER: Let us praise the Lord.

PEOPLE: **Glory to thee, O life-giving Lord, the Savior of the world.**

MINISTER: We have been freed from suffering by your suffering, O Christ. We have been delivered from corruption by your resurrection, O Lord.

PEOPLE: **The Lord is King. He is robed in majesty.**

MINISTER: Let creation rejoice, let the heavens be glad. Let the nations clap their hands. Alleluia!

PEOPLE: **Alleluia! Alleluia! Amen.**

——— Second Sunday of Easter ———

MINISTER: Come, Let us worship the Word of God.

PEOPLE: **He is risen from the dead.**

MINISTER: Christ our Savior destroyed the dominion death.

PEOPLE: **We fall down before his resurrection.**

MINISTER: Let us join the archangels who praise the Resurrection.

PEOPLE: **He is our Savior, our Redeemer.**

MINISTER: The angel proclaimed "Come see the place where he lay. He is risen, as he said, for he is almighty."

PEOPLE: **We worship you, O Christ, O giver of life.**

MINISTER: By his cross he destroyed the curse of the tree.

PEOPLE: **By his burial he overcame death.**

MINISTER: By his rising he began the new creation.

PEOPLE: **Glory to you, O Christ.**

MINISTER: When the guards of hell saw him they were afraid. For he demolished the gates and smashed the iron chains.

PEOPLE: **He has led as from darkness and opened heaven to us.**

MINISTER: Come, let us worship in the house of the Lord. Let us sing the hymn of salvation. For the one who was crucified is risen from the dead. Alleluia!

PEOPLE: **Alleluia! Alleluia! Amen.**

——— Third Sunday of Easter ———

MINISTER: Come, let us worship Christ our Savior. By his resurrection, death has been shattered and the devil destroyed.

PEOPLE: **We sing to you, we praise your holy name, O Christ.**

MINISTER: Come, let us worship Christ our Savior. By his resurrection we have been enlightened, and paradise has been opened again.

PEOPLE: **All creation sings to you, all Creation praises your holy name, O Christ.**

MINISTER: Bow down before his precious cross. Glorify and praise his resurrection for by his wounds we have been healed.

PEOPLE: **We praise the incarnate one, the one who was crucified for us, the one who rose on the third day.**

MINISTER: Praise Christ who descended into hell and cried, "I have shattered the gates of hell."

PEOPLE: **We stand in your house, O Christ, and we cry from our depths offering you the song of our praise.**

MINISTER: Let the heavens rejoice! Let the earth be glad! For the Lord has trampled down death by death and has delivered us from the mouth of hell. Alleluia!

PEOPLE: **Alleluia! Alleluia! Amen.**

——— Fourth Sunday of Easter ———

MINISTER: We glorify your resurrection, O Christ, for by it you have renewed our corrupt nature and opened the way to heaven.

PEOPLE: **Praise be to you, O Christ.**

MINISTER: Praise be to you. You were nailed to the tree. You descended to hell. You broke the bonds of death.

PEOPLE: **We adore you, O resurrected one.**

MINISTER: You smashed the gates of hell. You demolished the kingdom of death. You delivered us from the jaws of death.

PEOPLE: **Glory to you, all powerful one.**

MINISTER: Come, let us sing of the resurrection for by it we have been freed from the bonds of hell. By it, we have received new life!

PEOPLE: **We hail you and praise your holy name.**

MINISTER: Angels sing of your resurrection, O Lord. By it, the ends of the earth have been illuminated. By it, we have been delivered from the hand of the enemy.

PEOPLE: **O Lord, risen from the dead, glory to you!**

MINISTER: By your cross, O Lord, you have annulled the curse. By descending to hell you have freed the prisoners. By rising from the dead you have brought new life! Alleluia!

PEOPLE: **Alleluia! Alleluia! Amen.**

Fifth Sunday of Easter

MINISTER: We praise your cross, O Christ, for by taking it you put the devil to shame. We bless your resurrection from the dead, for by it you have blunted the sting of sin and saved us from death.

PEOPLE: **Glory to you, only begotten one.**

MINISTER: O Christ, you were led as a sheep to the slaughter, the princes of hell were frightened and the gates of sorrow were lifted.

PEOPLE: **O great wonder!**

MINISTER: O great wonder! The creator rose again. Come, let us worship him. Let us sing his praises.

PEOPLE: **Glory be to you, Father, Son and Holy Spirit.**

MINISTER: We glorify you, O leader of our salvation, for by your resurrection the world was saved from deceit, the devil fell and fallen Adam arose.

PEOPLE: **Angels and archangels sing glory to you, O Christ.**

Easter Lily. The lily is a powerful symbol of the Resurrection because of the new flower that sprouts from the seemingly dead bulb.

MINISTER: O Lord, you have captured hell and trampled down death, you have overcome evil and saved as from the enemy! Alleluia!

PEOPLE: **Alleluia! Alleluia! Amen.**

Sixth Sunday of Easter

MINISTER: Come, let us worship the one who is victor over hell. He ascended on the cross so that we who sit in the shade of death might be raised with him!

PEOPLE: **We worship and adore you, O Savior of the world.**

MINISTER: Today Christ tramples on death, he is risen, and he has granted joy to the world, so let us sing his praises.

PEOPLE: **We will sing to the Lord.**

MINISTER: Through your cross we sing and praise you, O Christ. We sing and glorify your resurrection for you are God and you only do we praise.

PEOPLE: **Sing praises, sing praises to the Lord.**

MINISTER: You endured the cross. You trampled down death by death. We bless you and sing of your resurrection!

PEOPLE: **We bless you and sing of your resurrection.**

MINISTER: Glory to you, O Lord for you overthrew the prince of death and you gave us new and life.

PEOPLE: **O Lord, glory to you.**

MINISTER: O Christ, because of your resurrection the angels sing and the archangels dance. Alleluia!

PEOPLE: **Alleluia! Alleluia! Amen.**

Seventh Sunday of Easter

MINISTER: Come, let us rejoice in the Lord, who destroyed the dominion of death! Let us sing to him, the Maker and Savior of all.

PEOPLE: **He is the King, the Lord of all.**

MINISTER: Come, let us rejoice in the Lord. He endured the cross and burial and by his resurrection he began all things anew.

PEOPLE: **Glory to you, O Christ.**

MINISTER: When the apostles saw the resurrection, they were amazed and sang his praise.

PEOPLE: **He is the glory of the church.**

MINISTER: O Lord, you were smitten on the cheek. You were nailed to the cross. You were buried in the tomb and you rose again on the third day.

PEOPLE: **Glory, to you Lord Jesus Christ.**

MINISTER: O Lord, when you were placed in the tomb the sight was terrifying, but when you rose from the dead, the sight was awesome!

PEOPLE: **Glory to the Father, to the Son and to the Holy Spirit, now and unto ages of ages.**

MINISTER: Glory to you triune God, let the heavens rejoice, let the earth be glad, let the mountains skip with joy. Alleluia!

PEOPLE: **Alleluia! Alleluia! Amen.**

Adapted from traditional Easter sources

289 ✦ TRADITIONAL OPENING PRAYERS FOR THE SEASON OF EASTER

The prayers below, some of which are based on centuries-old texts, express the themes of Easter (Pascha) worship. Adapt these prayers to local usage and style.

Easter Day
(Easter Eve or Dawn)
O God, who for our redemption gave your only begotten Son to the death of the cross, and by his glorious resurrection delivered us from the power of our enemy; grant us so to die daily to sin, that we may evermore live with him in the joy of his resurrection; through Jesus Christ your Son to our Lord, who lives and reigns with you and the Holy Spirit, one God, now and forever. **Amen.**

or

O God, who made this most holy night to shine with the glory of the Lord's resurrection: Stir up in your church that Spirit of adoption which is given to us in baptism, that we, being renewed both in body and mind, may worship you in sincerity and truth; through Jesus Christ our Lord who lives and reigns with you, in the unity of the Holy Spirit, one God, now and forever. **Amen.**

or

Almighty God, who through your only begotten Son Jesus Christ overcame death and opened to us the gate of everlasting life: Grant that we, who celebrate with joy the day of the Lord's resurrection, may be raised from the death of sin by your life-giving Spirit; through Jesus Christ our Lord who loves and reigns with you and the Holy Spirit, one God, now and forever. **Amen.**

Second Sunday of Easter
Almighty and everlasting God, who in the Paschal mystery established the new covenant of reconciliation: Grant that all who have been reborn into the fellowship of Christ's body may show forth in their lives what they profess by their faith; through Jesus Christ our Lord, who lives and reigns with you and the Holy Spirit, one God, forever and ever. **Amen.**

Third Sunday of Easter
O God, whose blessed Son made himself known to his disciples in the breaking of bread: Open the eyes of our faith, that we may behold him in all his redeeming work; who lives and reigns with you, in the unity of the Holy Spirit, one God, now and forever. **Amen.**

Fourth Sunday of Easter
O God, whose Son Jesus is the Good Shepherd of your people: Grant that when we hear his voice we may know him who calls us each by name, and follow where he leads; who, with you and the Holy Spirit, lives and reigns, one God, forever and ever. **Amen.**

Fifth Sunday of Easter
Almighty God, whom truly to know is everlasting life: Grant us so perfectly to know your Son Jesus Christ to be the way, the truth, and the life, that we may steadfastly follow his steps in the way that leads to eternal life; through Jesus Christ your Son our Lord, who lives and reigns with you, in the unity of the Holy Spirit, one God, forever and ever. **Amen.**

Sixth Sunday of Easter
O God, you have prepared for those who love you such good things as surpass our understanding: Pour into our hearts such love towards you, that we, loving you in all things and above all things, may obtain your promises, which exceed all that we can desire; through Jesus Christ our Lord, who lives and reigns with you and the Holy Spirit, one God, forever and ever. **Amen.**

Ascension Day (Thursday between Sixth and Seventh Sundays of Easter)

Almighty God, whose blessed Son our Savior Jesus Christ ascended far above all heavens that he might fill all things: Mercifully give us faith to perceive that, according to his promise, he abides with his church on earth, even to the end of the ages; through Jesus Christ our Lord, who lives and reigns with you and the Holy Spirit, one God, in glory everlasting. **Amen.**

or

Grant, we pray, Almighty God, that as we believe your only begotten Son our Lord Jesus Christ to have ascended into heaven, so we may also in heart and mind there ascend, and with him continually dwell; who lives and reigns with you and the Holy Spirit, one God, forever and ever. **Amen.**

Seventh Sunday of Easter (The Sunday after Ascension Day)

O God, the King of glory, you have exalted your only Son Jesus Christ with great triumph to your kingdom in heaven: Do not leave us comfortless, but send us your Holy Spirit to strengthen us, and exalt us to that place where our Savior Christ has gone before; who lives and reigns with you and the Holy Spirit, one God, in glory everlasting. **Amen.**

The Day of Pentecost (The Last Day of the Easter Cycle/Season)

Almighty God, on this day you opened the way of eternal life to every race and nation by the promised gift of your Holy Spirit: Shed abroad this gift throughout the world by the preaching of the gospel, that it may reach to the ends of the earth; through Jesus Christ our Lord, who lives and reigns with you, in the unity of the Holy Spirit, one God, forever and ever. **Amen.**

or

O God, who on this day taught the hearts of your faithful people by sending to them the light of your Holy Spirit: Grant us by the same Spirit to have a right judgment in all things, and evermore to rejoice in his holy comfort; through Jesus Christ your Son our Lord, who lives and reigns with you, in the unity of the Holy Spirit, one God, forever and ever. **Amen.**

Book of Common Prayer

290 ❖ RESOURCES FOR ASCENSION DAY

Ascension Day is the fortieth day after Easter. On this day, the church recalls the ascension of Christ into heaven and celebrates his rule over all Creation. The following information provides a helpful start for local congregations that want to revive the observance of this day.

Originally the Ascension was celebrated with Pentecost as a unitive festival. Their evolution into two different festivals took place during the end of the fourth century.

The date for the Ascension is always forty days after Easter, following the tradition of Acts 1:3: "appearing to them during forty days and speaking of the kingdom of God."

It has never been a day of great ceremony, even though it is a day of celebration. The impact the celebration of Ascension is to make on us is announced in the words of the preface prayer. "O Almighty God, whose blessed Son our Savior Jesus Christ ascended far above all heavens that we might fill all things: mercifully give us faith to perceive that, according to his promise, he abideth with his church on earth, even unto the end of the ages." The same theme is captured in the texts for the day from Acts 1:1-11, Ephesians 1:15-23, and either Luke 24:49-53 or Mark 16:9-15, 19-20.

If a congregation desires to celebrate the Eucharist, use the Eucharist suggested for the Sundays of Easter and add music and hymns of the Ascension theme. Other ascension hymns include "Hail the Day That Sees Him Rise," "See the Conquering Mounts in Triumph," "Hail the Festival Day," and "Rejoice, the Lord of Life Ascends."

SENTENCES OF SCRIPTURE

1
Since we have a great high priest
who has passed through the heavens,
Jesus, the Son of God,
let us approach the throne of grace with boldness,
so that we may receive mercy
and find grace to help in time of need.
(Heb. 4:14, 16)

2
Go and make disciples of all nations, says the Lord;
I am with you always,
to the end of time. _(Matt. 28:19a, 20b)_
Alleluia!

3
Why do you stand looking up toward heaven?
This Jesus will come in the same way as you saw
    him go into heaven. *(Acts 1:11)*
Alleluia!

PRAYER OF THE DAY

1
God of majesty,
you led the Messiah through suffering into risen
    life,
and took him up to the glory of heaven.
Clothe us with the power
    promised from on high,
and send us forth to the ends of the earth
    as heralds of repentance
and witnesses of Jesus Christ, firstborn from the
    dead,
who lives with you now and always in the unity of
    the Holy Spirit,
God forever and ever. **Amen.**

2
Almighty God,
your Son Jesus Christ ascended to the throne of
    heaven
that he might rule over all things as Lord.
Keep the church in the unity of the Spirit
    and in the bond of peace;
bring all creation to worship at his feet,
who is alive and reigns with you and the Holy
    Spirit,
one God, now and forever. **Amen.**

3
Eternal God,
by raising Jesus from the dead
    you proclaimed his victory,
and by his ascension,
you declared him Lord of all.
Lift up our hearts to heaven
    where he lives and reigns with you and the Holy
    Spirit,
one God, now and forever. **Amen.**

LITANY FOR ASCENSION

Arise, O Lord, in your strength.

We will praise you for your glory!

Let us pray with joy to Christ at the right hand of
    God, saying:

You are the king of glory!

You have raised the weakness of our flesh.
Heal us from our sins,
and restore to us the full dignity of life.

You are the king of glory!

May our faith lead us to the Father
as we follow the road you trod.

You are the king of glory!

You have promised to draw all people to yourself;
let no one of us be separate from your body.

You are the king of glory!

Grant that by our longing we may join you in your
    kingdom
where your humanity and ours is glorified.

You are the king of glory!

You are true God, and you will be our judge,
so lead us to contemplate your tender mercy.

You are the king of glory!

(After a brief silence, the leader concludes the
litany:)

O King of glory and Lord of hosts,
who ascended triumphantly above the heavens,
do not abandon us,
but send us the promised one,
the Spirit of truth.
Blessed be the holy and undivided Trinity,
now and forever.

PRAYER OF CONFESSION

Almighty God,
you have raised Jesus from death to life,
and crowned him Lord of all.
We confess that we have not bowed before him,
or acknowledged his rule in our lives.
We have gone along with the ways of the world,
and failed to give him glory.

Forgive us,
and raise us from sin,
that we may be your faithful people,
obeying the commands of our Lord Jesus Christ,
who rules the world
and is head of the church, his body.

Book of Common Worship[51]

291 ✦ PRAYER OF THANKSGIVING FOR EASTER LORD'S SUPPER

The following prayer of thanksgiving may be used at the service of the Lord's Supper for any or all of the Sundays of the Easter season. Notice how this text transforms the Lord's Supper into a meal of celebration, an act of thanksgiving (Eucharist) to the Lord.

MINISTER: The Lord be with you.
PEOPLE: **And also with you.**
MINISTER: Lift up your hearts.
PEOPLE: **We lift them to the Lord.**
MINISTER: Let us give thanks to the Lord our God.
PEOPLE: **It is right to give our thanks and praise.**
MINISTER: It is truly right and our greatest joy
to give you thanks and praise, eternal God,
Creator and rule of the universe.
At your word the earth was made
and spun on its course among the planets.
Your hand formed us from the dust of the earth
and set us among all your creatures
to love and serve you.

When we were unfaithful to you,
you kept faith with us,
your love remained steadfast.
When we were slaves in Egypt,
you broke the bonds of our oppression,
brought us through the sea to freedom,
and made covenant to be our God.
By a pillar of fire you led us through the desert
to a land flowing with milk and honey,
and set before us the way of life.

You spoke of love and justice in the prophets,
and in the Word made flesh you lived among us,
manifesting your glory.
He died that we might live,
and is risen to raise us to new life.
Therefore we praise you,
joining our voices with angels and archangels

and with all the faithful of every time and place,
who forever sing to the glory of your name:

(The people may sing or say:)

Holy, holy, holy Lord, God of power and might,
heaven and earth are full of your glory.
Hosanna in the highest.
Blessed is he who comes in the name of the Lord.
Hosanna in the highest.

(The minister continues:)

You are holy, O God of majesty,
and blessed is Jesus Christ, your Son, our Lord,
whom you sent to save us.
He came with healing in his touch,
and was wounded for our sins.
He came with mercy in his voice,
and was mocked as one despised.
He came with peace in his heart,
and met with violence and death.

By your power he broke free from the prison of the tomb,
and at his command the gates of hell were opened.
The one who was dead now lives.
The one who humbled himself is raised to rule over all creation,
the Lamb upon the throne.
The one ascended on high is with us always, as he promised.

(If they have not already been said, the words of institution may be said here, or in relation to the breaking of the bread.)

MINISTER: We give you thanks that the Lord Jesus,
on the night before he died,
took bread,
and after giving thanks to you,
he broke it, and gave it to his disciples, saying:
Take, eat.
This is my body, given for you.
Do this in remembrance of me.

In the same way he took the cup, saying:
This cup is the new covenant sealed
    in my blood,
shed for you for the forgiveness of
    sins.
Whenever you drink it,
do this in remembrance of me.
Remembering all your mighty and
    merciful acts,
we take this bread and this wine
from the gifts you have given us,
and celebrate with joy
the redemption won for us in Jesus
    Christ.
Accept this our sacrifice of praise and
    thanksgiving
as a living and holy offering of our-
    selves,
that our lives may proclaim the One
    crucified and risen.

(The people may sing or say one of the following:)

1
Minister: Great is the mystery of faith:
PEOPLE: **Christ has died,**
           Christ is risen,
           Christ will come again.

2
MINISTER: Praise to you, Lord Jesus:
PEOPLE: **Dying you destroyed our death,**
          rising you restored our life.
          Lord Jesus, come in glory.

3
MINISTER: According to his commandment:
PEOPLE: **We remember his death,**
          we proclaim his resurrection
          we await his coming in glory.

4
MINISTER: Christ is the bread of life:
PEOPLE: **When we eat this bread and drink**
          this cup,
          we proclaim your death, Lord Jesus,
          until you come in glory.

(The minister continues:)

Gracious God,
pour out your Holy Spirit upon us

and upon these your gifts of bread
    and wine,
that the bread we break
and the cup we bless
may be the communion of the body
    and blood of Christ.
By your Spirit make us one with
    Christ,
that we may be one with all who share
    this feast,
united in ministry in every place.
As this bread is Christ's body for us,
send us out to be the body of Christ
    in the world.

(Intercessions for the church and the world may
be included here.)

Nourished at this table, O God,
may we know Christ's redemptive
    love
and live a new life in him.
Help us who recognize our Lord in
    the breaking of bread
to see and serve him in all whose lives
    are broken.
Give us who are fed at his hand,
grace to share our bread with the
    hungry
and with the hungry of heart.
Keep us faithful in your service
until Christ comes in final victory,
and we shall feast with all your saints
in the joy of your eternal realm.
Through Christ,
all glory and honor are yours, al-
    mighty Father,
with the Holy Spirit in the holy church,
now and forever.

PEOPLE: **Amen.**

Book of Common Worship[52]

292 ✦ BLESSINGS FOR THE EASTER SEASON

*The following blessings are appropriate for use during
the season of Easter.*

May Almighty God, who has redeemed us and
made us his children through the resurrection of
his Son our Lord, bestow upon you the riches of
his blessing. Amen.

May God, who through the water of baptism has raised us from sin into newness of life, make you holy and worthy to be united with Christ forever. Amen.

May God, who has brought us out of bondage to sin into true and lasting freedom in the Redeemer, bring you to your eternal inheritance. Amen.

The God of peace, who brought again from the dead our Lord Jesus Christ, the great Shepherd of sheep, through the blood of the everlasting covenant, make you perfect in every good work to do his will, working in you that which is well-pleasing in his sight; and the blessing of God Almighty, the Father, the Son, and the Holy Spirit, be among you, and remain with you always. Amen.

Book of Occasional Services[53]

TWENTY-SIX

The Arts in Easter Worship

═══

Because Easter is the primary season of the Christian year, the season that celebrates the saving events of our Lord, it is important to festoon the entire season and not just one day. These resources will help a local congregation add color and festivity to the services of Easter and to fill these services with joyful sounds and actions. Adapt to local customs and style.

═══

293 • THE ENVIRONMENT FOR EASTER WORSHIP

During the Christian Passover—the three days from Holy Thursday sundown to Easter Sunday sundown—we carry into our worship halls certain elemental things. They remain among us through the year as the property of all the baptized. And they deserve prominence throughout Eastertime—the fifty days from Easter Sunday to Pentecost.

Oil and chrism. On Holy Thursday night we bring the oil of the sick, the oil of catechumens, and the sacred chrism to the assembly. These oils are the Easter gifts of the bishop to the people. The parish's containers should each be different, with the chrism in the finest vessel. The ministers to the sick and to the catechumens, and the deacons and priests carry the oils from the bishop to the parish.

The oils can be placed in the ambry, which may be decorated throughout Eastertime with a victory wreath of olive branches or with vigil lights—or with perhaps an oil lamp to consume the previous year's stock. If the ambry is homely, use a side altar or shrine to display the oils.

Wood. On Good Friday afternoon we carry into our midst the wood of the cross. The argument of whether to use a cross or a crucifix is settled by the words of the liturgy: "This is the wood of the cross. . . ." We are invited to regard this wood as the very cross of Christ " . . . on which hung the Savior of the world." In mystery this wood is Isaac's pyre and the ark of the covenant. It is the burning bush and the staff Moses held over the Red Sea. It is the great boat chock-full of creation's second chance, and it is the tree of paradise.

This holy wood deserves a place of honor in the assembly throughout Eastertime. Other symbols on the cross, such as a shroud or crown, can detract from the wood. Ideally, the Good Friday cross is used as the processional cross, the only cross in the worship hall. If the parish has a permanent cross/crucifix in the worship space, it doesn't make sense to add another cross; perhaps the Good Friday cross can be kept throughout Eastertime in the gathering place or in a shrine.

Fire and wax. During the night between Holy Saturday and Easter Sunday, a bonfire is kindled and flame from this fire is used to light the paschal candle. A fire can be built right on a lawn with a foot of sand laid over a large tarp. Keep the fire burning all night and into the morning. It should give evidence of Easter.

Throughout Eastertime, lighting and extinguishing the paschal candle should be done privately, giving the appearance that it is ever-burning. Lighting the other candles from the paschal candle is a gracious gesture that speaks of the candle's significance. It should be lit for all gatherings during the season, even weddings, and looks good rising from spring flowers, especially cut branches arranged in enormous pots of moist sand. Thanks to demand, there are fine, affordable, commercial candles over five feet tall. Such tremendous candles do not ship easily; buy yours in advance so you can exchange it if it comes cracked.

A paschal candle is ordinarily placed near the ambo. Easter casts a new light upon the Scripture. Especially where the font is in the midst of the assembly, so too the candle may be there. While an unadorned wax pillar is impressive, the candle deserves its customary decoration—a cross formed of five grains of incense, the Alpha and Omega, and the numerals of the current year—to make what Abbot Patrick Regan calls the "center pole of the new creation."

Water. Parishes with handsome fonts will keep them babbling through the season. During Eastertime, parishes with fonts that are hidden away may be tempted to display water near the altar, ambo, and chair. Wouldn't it be better to focus attention on the font no matter where it is located, rather than clutter up an area with something that often resembles a punch bowl or a rock garden? An Eastertime sprinkling rite can begin by walking to the font and drawing a bucketful of water, then carrying this bucket to the assembly for the prayer of thanksgiving.

To permit baptism by immersion in parishes without such fonts, temporary pools are sometimes constructed. (A serviceable font can be made from a horse water trough.) The redundancy of two fonts can be lessened by placing the temporary font next to or around the old one.

Eastertime enthusiasm. If the parish has paid attention to the Eastertime worship environment—the cross, candle, and font—the overwhelming joy of this season can be expressed in many ways. Garlands and flowers and wreaths and lights are all lively signs of rejoicing at any season. Yew and boxwood, peacock feathers and pussywillows, birch twigs, and hazel catkins are customary. Banks of flowers are commonly seen, but if you can't sustain such a display during all of Eastertime, spend your money some other way.

One of the most splendid Easter ornaments I've seen was a five-foot-wide ribboned grapevine wreath with a cluster of fresh flowers added weekly (in water-pics). This was hung over the assembly space. The rest of the worship hall was made bright with sheer pastel fabrics that flew from ceiling to wall. Another parish wired handmade silk blossoms to thirty-foot horizontal branches and hung them with eggs. A ribboned maypole with bells was used as a processional banner. The success of all this merriment was dependent on placement; at worship you couldn't see any of it unless your eyes wandered straight up. Even such commonplace details as washing the windows to let in the springtime sun had been attended to. And in the end, what the parish communicated was great enthusiasm through all fifty days of Easter. Their worship environment said that they were a people keeping their Great Sunday, a foretaste of heaven on earth.

Peter Mazar[54]

294 • AN ANTHOLOGY OF HYMNS, SONGS, AND CHORUSES FOR THE EASTER SEASON

Hymns, songs, and choruses in this section emphasize the finished climax to Christ's once-for-all redemptive sacrifice at Calvary: his resurrection from the dead, his conquest of death, his exaltation as eternal Lord and Savior, and his completed and absolute purchase of the believer from the wages of sin. Consult this list for representative songs for the Easter season.

In the history of Easter liturgical music, some of the earliest settings were tropes or additions to the liturgy of dramatic elements, such as the dramatic dialogue: "Whom do you seek?" "Do not be afraid; for I know that you seek Jesus who was crucified. He is not here; for he is risen, as he said." Known by the Latin text as "Quem Quaeritis" plays, these medieval church enactments were the beginning of a larger spectrum of liturgical dramas. The sense of dramatic joy suggested in these early dialogues has been maintained in the vast hymnodic repertory for Easter.

The following is a sampling of both traditional hymns and contemporary chorus for worship during the season of Easter, including Ascension Day.

TITLE	AUTHOR/COMPOSER	TUNE	STYLE	SCRIPTURE REFERENCE
Alive Forevermore	Anon. (1989)		Scripture Chorus	Luke 24:5–7
All Hail the Power of Jesus Name	E. Perronet/J. Ellor	DIADEM	Traditional	Revelation 4:11
At The Lamb's High Feast We Sing	17th cent. Bohemian/ 16th cent. tune	SONNE DER GERECHTIGKEIT	Traditional	John 19:34; Luke 22:17-20
Because He Lives	G. and W. Gaither	RESURRECTION	Southern Gospel	John 14:19
Christ Above All Glory Seated	Latin/W. Boyce	SHARON	Traditional	Matthew 28:18
Christ Is Risen! Shout Hosanna!	B. Wren/W. Rowan (1986)	JACKSON NEW	Hymn Renaissance	John 15:15
Christ the Lord Is Risen Today.	Latin/R.H. Williams	LLANFAIR	Traditional	1 Corinthians 15:54
Come, Ye Faithful, Raise the Strain	John of Damascus/ A. Sullivan	ST. KEVIN	Traditional	Psalm 68:18
Cristo Vive	N. Martinez/P. Sosa (1962)		Argentinian	Luke 24:5b
Crown Him with Many Crowns	M. Bridges, G. Thring/ G. Elvey	DIADEMATA	Traditional	Revelation 19:12
The Day of Resurrection	John of Damascus/ H. Smart	LANCASHIRE	Traditional	Matthew 28:19
God Sent His Son, They Called Him Jesus	G. and W. Gaither	RESURRECTION	Southern Gospel	John 14:19
Good Christian Friends, Rejoice and Sing	C. Alington/M. Vulpius	GELOBT SEI GOTT	Traditional	John 16:33
Hail Thee, Festival Day	V. Fortunatus/ R. Vaughan Williams	SALVE FESTA DIES	Traditional	Hebrews 1:2-4
Hail, Thou Once Despised Jesus	J. Bakewell/*Christian Lyre*, 1830	PLEADING SAVIOR	Early America	Matthew 27:29; Heb. 10:12
He is Lord	Anon. (1987)		Scripture Chorus	Philippians 2:11
He Lives	A. H. Ackley	ACKLEY	Gospel Song	Matthew 28:7
He's Back in the Land of the Living	F. Kaan/M. Metcalf (1972)	EASTER	Hymn Renaissance	Acts 2:23-24, Acts 8:52b
He's Risen, He's Risen	F. Walther	WALTHER	Traditional	Hosea 13:14; 1 Corinthians 15:55

Continued...

TITLE	AUTHOR/COMPOSER	TUNE	STYLE	SCRIPTURE REFERENCE
The Head that Once Was Crowned with Thorns	Kelly/attr. J. Clark	ST. MAGNUS	Traditional	Philippians 2:9
Hear the Bells Ringing	A. Herring (1974)	EASTER SONG	Contemporary	Matthew 28:6
I Know that My Redeemer Lives	American folk	SHOUT ON	Traditional	Job 19:25
Jesus Christ Is Risen Today	14th cent. Latin/ London, 1708	EASTER HYMN	Traditional	Matthew 28:6
Lo, Judah's Lion Wins the Strife	16th cent. Bohemian/ R. Schultz	BRONXVILLE	Traditional	Revelation 5:5
Low in the Grave He Lay	R. Lowry	CHRIST AROSE	Gospel Song	Matthew 28:2
Majesty	J. Hayford (1981)		Scripture Chorus	
Make Songs of Joy	J. Tranovsky/*Chorvát* 1936	ZPIVEJMEZ VSCKNI VESELE	Traditional	
Night is Over	C. Landry (1979)		Contemporary Easter Carol	Song of Songs 2:11-12; Acts 2:24
O Christ the Lord	R. Brooks/A. Warrell (1984)	FARMBOROUGH		Matthew 28:2; Philippians 2:9-11
O Sons and Daughters of the King	J. Tisserand/J. M. Neale	A FILII ET FILAE	Traditional	John 20:27-29
Risen Lord	F. Fabing, S. J.			Psalm 150
The Strife Is O'er, the Battle Done	tr. F. Pott/Palestrina, arr. Monk	VICTORY		1 Corinthians 15:54
See the Splendor of the Morning	F. Feliciano (1977)	TINMINAGO	Easter Carol	1 Corinthians 15:54
Surrexit Dominus Vere	Br. Robert/J. Berthier (1981)		Taizé canon	Mark 16:6
Thine Is the Glory	E. Budrey/G. Handel	JUDAS MACCABEUS	Traditional	Matthew 6:13
This Joyful Eastertide	G. Woodward/ 17th cent. Dutch	VREUCHTEN	Traditional	1 Corinthians 15:17, 20
Welcome, Happy Morning	V. Fortunatus/English tune, arr. G. Holst	PRINCE RUPERT	Traditional	Ephesians 4: 8-10
Wounded for Me	W. Ovens, G. Roberts, W. Ovens	FOR ME	Gospel Song	Isaiah 53:8

Steve Cushman

295 ✦ CAROLS FOR EASTER (PASCHA)

Most people associate carols with Christmas only. In recent years the Easter carol is being recovered and introduced into the services of the Easter season. The article below introduces these carols and urges their recovery.

If you're like most choir directors, you occasionally have problems filling your choir's repertoire for Easter. Perhaps you've noticed the sameness and even shallowness of some Easter hymns and anthems and have longed for music similar to Christmas carols—music which is simple and appealing and which can readily involve large numbers of people. If so, this may be the year you should try Easter carols—songs like "My Dancing Day" or "Easter Eggs." Singing Easter carols can expand your choir's repertoire and horizons into a fresh and significant area.

What is a Carol?

When most people use the word _carol_ today, they are referring to a strophic song associated with Christmas. However, this definition is both too broad (encompassing everything from "The Coventry Carol" to "Silent Night" to "Rudolph the Red-Nosed Reindeer") and too narrow (in subject).

Carols, it seems, are as hard to define as they are fun to sing. We usually think of them as "religious" songs, but some medieval carols are amorous, humorous, satirical, political, or convivial. We also think of them as "popular" songs, but not in the same sense that folk songs are popular. While folk songs are "popular by origin," carols are "popular by destination" (see Richard L. Greene, _The Early English Carols_ [Oxford, 1935], xciii). That is, carols were often written by educated men and women whose goal was to provide songs that were attractive as well as instructive. These were neither true folk songs nor hymns intended for the liturgy; rather, they were songs that corresponded roughly to some of today's "contemporary Christian" hits. In contrast to medieval hymns, which were doctrinal and contemplative, these popular carols showed a tender compassion for the poverty, pain, and emotions of real people.

In the Middle Ages, the one indispensable element of a carol was its literary structure: the carols had uniform stanzas and a "burden," that is, a refrain sung at the beginning of each song as well as after each stanza. A familiar example of a song with a burden is "All Things Bright and Beautiful."

In the oldest carols the stanza was sung by soloists, the refrain probably by a larger group. In the polyphonic carols of the fifteenth century we often find two refrains: one for soloists, the other for a chorus. Today this stanza-refrain structure makes it possible for the audience or congregation to join the choir in music making; the choir sings the stanzas, the larger group the refrain.

However, this stanza-refrain structure, although still present in many carols in later centuries, was no longer considered essential to the genre. Gradually the term _carol_ took on a broader meaning.

The Uses of Carols

Understanding ways in which carols were used in previous centuries can help us discover their appropriate use today.

The carol came to England from France, where it was a song to accompany a round dance (which accounts for the lively, generally triple-meter character of medieval carols). By the later fourteenth century, carols were sometimes associated simply with festive occasions, such as banquets.

During this same period Franciscan friars fostered the development of popular songs which taught spiritual truths and encouraged virtue. Often these religious leaders simply wrote new sets of words for the popular songs (frequently carols) of the day. Thus, the early "religious" carols had an educational purpose and generally were not associated with public worship. Many carols were apparently sung as "household music" in palaces and wealthy homes—either for devotional use or for nonreligious ceremonies such as New Year's feasts. Scholars have found some evidence that by the fifteenth century some of these carols may have been used in the liturgy, usually as processionals that replaced the Latin processional hymns. (Some still would serve well as processionals today.)

During the Christmas season today, of course, carols are usually used informally—either in homes or in caroling parties to neighbors and shut-ins. (We'll ignore the streams of carol-like noise that issue from the ceilings and walls of shopping malls!) But in a growing number of churches and schools a ceremony of lessons and carols, a service that intersperses carols and anthems with appropriate Bible readings, has become a popular special event.

Carols, then, are suitable for virtually any time that an edifying "contemporary Christian" song is appropriate. In the appendix to *The English Carol*, Erik Routley includes an order for a service of lessons and carols for Lent (which could be adapted or expanded) as well as suggestions for as Easter service.

Lessons and Carols for Easter

The following service ideas are adapted from *The English Carol* by Erik Routley (pp. 252–53). These ideas may be expanded to form a complete service.

Prelude

Processional Hymn: "Praise, My Soul, the King of Heaven"

Call to Worship: "The Crucified is risen from the dead. Alleluia! Tell it out among the nations that the Lord reigns. 'For we know that since Christ was raised from the dead, he cannot die again; death no longer has mastery over him. The death he died, he died to sin once for all; but the life he lives, he lives to God'" (Rom. 6:9-10).

Hymn: "O Love, How Deep, How Broad, How High"

Prayers: (leading to the Lord's Prayer said in unison)

First Lesson: Exodus 14:13-21

Carol or Hymn

Second Lesson: John 20-11-19

Carol

Third Lesson: Daniel 7:13-15

Carol

Fourth Lesson: Hebrews 1:1-13 or 4:14-16; 5:1-10

Carol

Prayer

Blessing

Recessional hymn

Postlude

Usable Carols

Hymnals are one source for Easter carols. Two examples included in many recent hymnals are "This Joyful Eastertide" and "O Sons and Daughters of the King ." In addition to hymnals, the choir director in search of carols will find two books invaluable. The first, *The Oxford Book of Carols* (hereafter abbreviated as *OxBC*), contains nearly 200 carols for all occasions. The second, R. L. Greene's *The Early English Carols,* contains the texts (without tunes) of 474 carols.

It may seem curious that very few old carols are specifically and only for Easter. However, many are appropriate for Lent and Passiontide as well as for Easter. Even many Christmas carols include stanzas that deal with the Crucifixion and even with the entire history of redemption. Perhaps the medieval friars who wrote those texts had a valuable insight that later generations have forgotten: the importance of a holistic view of the life and ministry of Jesus. Perhaps singing all eleven stanzas of "My Dancing Day" (*OxBC* #71), for example, or the nine stanzas of "All in the Morning" (*OxBC* #17) will help us remember that Christmas and Easter would be meaningless without each other.

Several of the *OxBC* carols most appropriate for Easter have been arranged for choir by Alice Parker and Robert Shaw and published as octavos by G. Schirmer. These accessible and well-arranged carols include the following: "Hilariter" (German; *OxBC* #96), order no. 9952; "Easter Eggs" (Russian; *OxBC* #94), order no. 9956; "Love Is Come Again" (French; *OxBC* #149), order no. 9959; and "The World Itself Keeps Easter Day" (*OxBC* #150), order no. 9942. Another recommended octavo is "Polish Easter Carol," arranged by Mary E. Caldwell (H. W. Gray [Belwin-Mills], GCMR 2778). Also, if you have a very capable choir, you may want to look at Gustav Holst's magnificent setting of "This Have I Done for My True Love" (the same text as "My Dancing Day," available in the U.S. from Galaxy Music, 1.5080). A much shorter but also challenging carol is Max Bruch's setting of "Christus ist auferstanden" ("Jesus Our Lord Has Risen") (Arista Music, AE 529) which would serve as an exciting fanfare or opening number.

The best recent collection devoted entirely to carols for this season is _The Easter Carol Book,_ edited by Mervyn Harder (London: Stinz & Schott, 1982; edition Schott 12072). The twenty-eight carols (in the modern sense) in this collection are all well-suited for group and informal singing and are adaptable for choral performance.

Songs of Jesus, by Salli Terri, is a set of nine lovely Flemish carols for an unaccompanied chorus of women's voices; handbells are optional (Lawson-Gould, LG 51799). All of the carols in this collection are appropriate for Easter; "Our Father" and "The Bells," both three-part canons, are also suitable for other occasions. The Easter carols include "The Last Supper," "The Death of Jesus," "The Song of Maria Magdalena," and "The Seven Days of the Week."

Once you and your singers have sampled Easter carols, you'll probably want to branch out and use some of the wealth of carols for other occasions too. _OxBC_ includes a valuable list of "Carols Arranged for Use Throughout the Year." You may well find yourself consulting it often.

Robert Copeland[55]

296 • AN EASTER HYMN FESTIVAL

The hymn festival below recalls the entire scope of the Easter season from the triumphant entry to Pentecost. Congregations may want to sing this festival early in the Easter season as a way of recalling the saving events just past and those yet to come. Adapt to local usage and style.

Reading: Philippians 2:5-11
Hymn: "O Love, How Deep, How Broad, How High"

CHRIST'S TRIUMPHAL ENTRY INTO JERUSALEM
Reading: Luke 19:29-38
Hymn: "All Glory, Laud, and Honor"
Hymn: "Hosanna, Loud Hosanna"

THE LAST SUPPER
Reading: Luke 22:14-20
Hymn: "Let Us Break Bread Together"

THE AGONY IN THE GARDEN
Reading: Mark 14:32-36

Hymn: "Go to Dark Gesthemane"

THE TRIAL AND SCOURGING
Reading: Matthew 27:11-14, 20-24, 27-31
Hymn: "O Sacred Head Now Wounded"

THE CRUCIFIXION
Reading: "O dearest Lord, thy sacred head with thorns was pierced for me; O pour thy blessing on my head that I may think for thee.

"O dearest Lord, thy sacred hands with nails were pierced for me; O shed thy blessing on my hands that they may work for thee.

"O dearest Lord, thy sacred feet with nails were pierced for me; O pour thy blessing on my feet, that they may follow thee.

"O dearest Lord, thy sacred heart with spear was pierced for me; O pour thy spirit in my heart, that I may live for thee." (H. E. Hardy, 1869–1946)
Hymn: "When I Survey the Wondrous Cross"

THE RESURRECTION
Reading: Matthew 28:1-8
Hymn: "Christ Is Alive" or "The Strife Is O'er"

EASTERTIDE
Reading: John 19:24-29
Hymn: "These Things Did Thomas Count as Real"

ASCENSION
Reading: Luke 24:49-53
Hymn: "See, The Conqueror Mounts in Triumph"

PENTECOST
Reading: 1 Corinthians 12:4-13
Hymn: "For Your Gift of God the Spirit"

TRINITY
Closing Collect: Almighty and everlasting God, you have given grace to us, your servants, to acknowledge the glory of the eternal Trinity, and in the power of your divine Majesty to worship the Unity: Keep us steadfast in this faith and worship, and bring us at last to see you in your one and eternal glory, O Father; who with the Son and the Holy Spirit live and reign, one God, for ever and ever. _Amen._
Hymn: "Rejoice, the Lord is King"

Sue Mitchell Wallace[56]

TWENTY-SEVEN

Worship on Pentecost Sunday

Pentecost Sunday is an end and a beginning. It is the culmination of the season of Easter. It is the day when the church senses the all-pervasive power of Easter as the Spirit is unleashed on Creation. It is also the dawn of a new day in the life of the church. For as the church is empowered by the Spirit, the message of the risen Lord is trumpeted around the world. The following chapters provide a variety of helpful suggestions for worship planners and challenge the reader to appreciate the signficance of the gift of the Spirit to the church.

297 ◆ LECTIONARY READINGS FOR PENTECOST SUNDAY

The following are the recommended readings for Pentecost Sunday in the Revised Common Lectionary.

SUNDAY	ACTS	PSALM	EPISTLE	GOSPEL
Year A	Acts 2:1-21, account of Pentecost and descent of the Spirit, or Numbers 11:24-30, gathering of the elders, with the Spirit of the Lord.	104:24-34	Acts 2:1-21 or 1 Corinthians 12:3b-13, different gifts from the Spirit, one body.	John 7:37-39, thirsty? come, drink; Holy Spirit promised, or John 20:19-23.
Year B	Acts 2:1-11 or Ezekiel 37:1-14, new life by the Spirit.	104:24-34	Acts 2:1-21 or Romans 8:22-27, all creation groans; Spirit pleads for us.	John 15:26-27; 16:4b-15, the work of the Holy Spirit.
Year C	Acts 2:1-11 or Genesis 11:1-9, the tower of Babel and the confusion of languages.	104:24-34	Acts 2:1-21 or Romans 8:14-17; Spirit makes us God's children; we inherit God's riches.	John 14:8-17, "I will send a Comforter; peace be with you."

Revised Common Lectionary, descriptions by H. A. Tillinghast

298 ◆ A TRADITIONAL SERVICE FOR PENTECOST

The following service is a creative adaptation of the traditional pattern and texts for worship for Pentecost Sunday. It will be of particular help for those who plan a more formal Pentecost service. For others interested in worship renewal, the commentary included with this service will provide a guide to thoughtful planning.

Commentary: The order of the following service varies from most traditional Protestant services, especially in the sections that open the service and immediately precede the Lord's Supper. Each of the traditional acts of worship are present, but are reordered as indicated below. The commentary which accompanies the following service will explain the reasons for each change in order. If a more traditional order is desired, the readings, hymns, and prayers suggested here may easily be placed in a more traditional form of service, following the outlines of other services in this series (e.g., Advent service).

CELEBRATING THE COMING OF THE HOLY SPIRIT

Commentary: The visual artists of the church can make several meaningful contributions to the setting for Pentecost worship. They can design banners, paraments, vestments, clothe streamers, and covers for printed liturgies, bulletins, or newsletters that reflect the colors and symbols of the celebration. The traditional Pentecost colors are all associated with the primary symbol of the day: the flame. Bright red and gold hues should be used most pervasively. In addition to the flame, other appropriate symbols include the descending dove or the rushing wind, symbolizing the Holy Spirit, or various symbols for the church, such as a ship.

Gathering of the Congregation
(with organ, piano, or instrumental prelude)

Commentary: The order of this opening section is designed to mirror the believer's response to the Pentecost gospel. The service begins with a reading of the promise of the Spirit's coming. The response of the believer is to pray for the fulfillment of that promise in the present gathering. Then, the account of the fulfillment of that promise is read, using passages that refer both to the first advent of the Spirit on Pentecost and to the continued presence of the Spirit with us. The appropriate response of the believer is then to celebrate and offer praise for this gift.

The sermon text, the text on which the prelude music is based, or another thematically important verse in the service may be printed at this point in the order of service to guide the meditation of the people as they gather for worship.

Gospel Promise
Lay Reader or Pastor: People of God, gathered now in the name of Jesus Christ, before our Lord ascended into heaven, he left us with this promise:

You will receive power when the Holy Spirit comes upon you; and you will be my witnesses in Jerusalem, and in all Judea and Samaria, and to the ends of the earth (Acts 1:8). We join now in prayer that this promise may be fulfilled even in this place and hour.

Prayer for God's Spirit: (Hymn)
   "Breathe on Me, Breath of God"
   "Spirit Divine, Inspire Our Prayer"
   "Eternal Spirit, God of Truth"
   "Holy Spirit Truth Divine"
   "Spirit of the Living God"
   "Creator Spirit, By Whose Aid"
   "Come Down, O Love Divine"

Commentary: Each of these hymns are prayers of petition for the presence of the Holy Spirit. It is important that the congregation be aware that these are not primarily hymns of praise (as are most opening hymns), but of petition. The hymn of praise follows the greeting in this service.

Gospel Fulfillment
PASTOR:	(reads Acts 2:1-4)
PEOPLE	**Praise God for the gift of the Spirit!**
PASTOR:	(reads Romans 5:5)
PEOPLE	**Praise God for the gift of the Spirit!**

Greeting
Pastor:	The Spirit of the Lord be with you.
PEOPLE	**And also with you.**
ALL:	**Thanks be to God!**

Hymn of Praise: "For Your Gift of God the Spirit"

Commentary: This hymn of praise may be used as a processional for the choir and other worship leaders. The festive nature of the occasion may be heightened by including liturgical banners in the procession or beginning the procession with liturgical dancers, who may carry red streamers or fabrics that can be added to the paraments or banners.

Another appropriate acclamation of praise used in many traditions is the hymn, "Hail, Thee Festival Day," which features several stanzas appropriate for use on Pentecost.

HEARING THE PROCLAMATION OF GOD'S WORD

Prayer for Illumination
   LEADER: Let us pray for the presence of the

PEOPLE: Spirit as we listen to the Word of God. **Come, Holy Spirit, lead us into all truth. Amen.**

Old Testament Reading: Ezekiel 37: 1-14, Joel 2

Psalm: Psalm 104: 24-34

Commentary: This psalm may be sung by the congregation or choir. Metrical settings of this and other psalms can be found in *A New Metrical Psalter* (New York: Church Hymnal Corporation, 1984; *The Psalter Hymnal* (Grand Rapids: CRC Publications, 1987); *Rejoice in the Lord* (Grand Rapids: Eerdmans, 1985); *Trinity Hymnal* (Atlanta: Great Commission Publications, 1990); and *The Presbyterian Hymnal* (Louisville: Westminster/John Knox, 1990). Responsorial settings can be found in *The Celebration Psalter* (St. Louis: Cathedral Music Press, 1991); *Psalm Refrains and Tones* (Carol Stream, Ill.: Hope Publishing, 1988); *Lead Me, Guide Me* (Chicago: GIA Publications, 1987); *Psalms for the Church Year,* vols. 1–4 (Chicago: GIA Publications); and *United Methodist Hymnal* (Nashville: Abingdon, 1989). Additional settings of the Psalms can be found in *Psalms for Today* and *Songs from the Psalms* (London: Hodder and Stoughton, 1990).

New Testament Readings: John 15:26-27, 16:4-15; Acts 2:1-21

Commentary: Another possibility for the Pentecost readings consists of surveying the themes of either the entire Christian year or the entire account of Christ's passion, resurrection, and ascension. This would be appropriate when the sermon is designed to relate the coming of the Spirit with these events of Christ's life, pointing to how the Spirit's presence with us is an extension of Christ's presence (see John 14).

Response

LEADER: The Word of the Lord, by the power of the Spirit.

PEOPLE: **Thanks be to God.**

Sermon

RESPONDING IN TESTIMONY AND PRAYER

Statement of Faith: The Apostles' Creed

LEADER: Do you believe in God the Father?

PEOPLE: **I believe in God, the Father almighty, creator of heaven and earth.**

LEADER: Do you believe in Jesus Christ, the Son of God?

PEOPLE: **I believe in Jesus Christ, his only Son, our Lord, who was conceived by the Holy Spirit and born of the virgin Mary. He suffered under Pontius Pilate, was crucified, died and was buried; he descended to hell. The third day he rose again from the dead. He ascended to heaven and is seated at the right hand of God the Father almighty. From there he will come to judge the living and the dead.**

LEADER: Do you believe in God the Holy Spirit?

PEOPLE: **I believe in the Holy Spirit, the holy catholic church, the communion of saints, the forgiveness of sins, the resurrection of the body, and the life everlasting. Amen.**

Commentary: This division of the Apostles' Creed highlights its Trinitarian structure. It also suggests the important link between the Holy Spirit and the Spirit's work in the holy catholic church, which may be appropriately emphasized on Pentecost Sunday.

Hymn

Commentary: The creed may be followed by a doxology or by a hymn which addresses the specific theme of the sermon. Especially appropriate are hymns which focus on the mission of the church, offering both petitions for the Spirit's presence with the church and promises of commitment to that service by the people. This hymn may also follow the testimonies of faith.

Testimonies of Faith or of Church Mission

Commentary: This would be a most appropriate time for representatives of various church ministries to give testimony to the presence of the Spirit in their life and work throughout the past year. A congregation wishing to emphasize its unity with the worldwide church may wish to invite representatives of neighboring churches, missionaries, or members of overseas churches to join them for the service or give words of welcome at this time. Other concerns and occasions for prayer may also be mentioned at this time.

Prayers of Petition
- for renewal of the church

LEADER: We pray for the church, . . .

- for the mission of the church, . . .

Commentary: At this point or other appropriate points in the prayer, specific references to the testimonies and reports of church ministries that were just heard should be made.

- for the unity of the church,
- for the holiness of the church,
- for the faithfulness of the church.

Commentary: Each phrase may be followed by a period of silence or by sentences spoken by various members of the congregation which elaborate on the specific nature of each petition.

PEOPLE: **Come Holy Spirit, renew the church, we pray.**

- for renewal of the earth

LEADER: We pray for our earth,
for the sustaining resources of water, soil, and air,
for the enriching resources of minerals,
for the gifts of living creatures,
for the gifts of natural beauty,

PEOPLE: **Come Holy Spirit, renew the earth, we pray.**

- for renewal of human culture

LEADER: We pray for our culture,
that governments may provide justice and protection,
that businesses may provide helpful goods and services,
that fine arts may stimulate us to creativity in expressing the truth,
that entertainment may delight us.

PEOPLE: **Come Holy Spirit, renew our culture, we pray.**

Prayer of Confession
PEOPLE: Almighty God,
we have fractured your church,
we have wasted the resources of this earth,

we have corrupted our culture,
Forgive us, we pray, renew us by the power of your Spirit,
and draw us to you as we now approach your table.
Amen.

Commentary: This prayer of confession is modeled after the structure of the prayers of the people that precede it.

Declaration of Pardon
PASTOR: (reads Titus 3:3-7)

Call to Discipleship
PASTOR: Walk now in the power of the Holy Spirit: (reads Galatians 6:22-25)

PEOPLE: **We will walk in the power of the Spirit.**

Passing of the Peace
PASTOR: As you walk in the Spirit's power, may the peace of Christ be with you.

PEOPLE: **And also with you.**

PEOPLE: (to each other)
God's peace be with you.

Commentary: The confession, declaration of pardon, and call to discipleship are placed at this point in the service as a way of focusing the attention of the worshiper on the personal challenge of living with the Spirit, even as the prayers move from worldwide to very personal concerns. This act of penitence is also very appropriate just before the celebration of the sacrament.

CELEBRATING THE SACRAMENT OF THE LORD

Offertory
LEADER: People of God, as a pledge to our commitment
to walk in the power of God's Spirit in service to him,
we bring our gifts to God.

PEOPLE: **Amen.**

(the gifts are received)

(People sing doxology)

Commentary: The doxology sung at Pentecost can appropriately be a Trinitarian expression of praise, such as the final doxological stanza of the Pentecost hymn, "O Holy Spirit, by Whose Breath," or any other translation of the ancient Pentecost hymn "Veni Creator Spiritus." During the singing of the doxology, the elements for Communion and the gifts which have been received may be brought forward.

The following Communion liturgy is replete with references to the work of the Spirit and is therefore appropriate for use on Pentecost and other Sundays on which the sermon text of the day may focus on the Spirit's work among the church.

Invitation to the Table

LEADER: Jesus said, "I will ask the Father, and he will give you another Counselor to be with you forever—the Spirit of truth." Friends in Christ, today we celebrate the fulfillment of this promise. We know that Christ is with us through his Spirit and now we realize this presence at his holy meal. As we approach his table, let us bring our praise to God.

Prayer of Thanksgiving

Commentary: The divisions of the following prayer of thanksgiving highlight the Trinitarian pattern that the prayer follows. Though often unnoticed, many Communion liturgies and prayers of thanksgiving follow this Trinitarian pattern. Use of these division calls this feature of the structure to the immediate attention of the worshiper and is especially appropriate for Pentecost and Trinity Sundays.

In Praise of God, the Father, Our Creator

LEADER: Blessed are you, God most high, creator of heaven and earth. You fashioned us in your image that we might live in joyous fellowship with you. Even after we broke the bonds of that fellowship, you loved and sought us. Therefore, we offer our praise to you and sing with joy:

PEOPLE: **Holy, holy, holy Lord, God of power and might,**

heaven and earth are full of your glory.

Hosanna in the highest.

Commentary: Most hymnals include a setting of this traditional canticle. For a list of service music found in a representative group of hymnals,

consult the commentary to the Communion liturgy of the Advent service in this series.

In Praise of God, the Son, Our Redeemer

LEADER: Blessed are you, Jesus Christ, Son of God, our Lord. You came to be our Immanuel, God with us. You brought us again into fellowship with God by your victory over sin and death. You promised that you would not leave us, and indeed you sent the Spirit to be our comforter and sustainer. You gave us this joyful feast, by which we realize again our union with you and proclaim to the world your death and resurrection. Therefore, we offer our praise to you and sing with joy:

PEOPLE: **Blessed is he who comes in the name of the Lord.**

Hosanna in the highest.

Commentary: In this Communion liturgy, the "Blessed is he who comes in the name of the Lord" is separated from the "Holy, Holy, Holy," contrary to most traditional forms. Given the strict Trinitarian structure of this liturgy, this separation allows the "Holy, Holy, Holy" to be sung as an acclamation of praise to God the Father and "Blessed is he who comes in the name of the Lord" to be sung to God the Son. These and other portions of the Communion liturgy may be sung. A representative list of musical resources is included in the commentary with Advent service in this series.

[Institution]

LEADER: People of God, remember that the Lord Jesus, on the night when he was betrayed, took bread, and when he had given thanks, he broke it and said, "This is my body, which is for you; do this in remembrance of me." In the same way, he took the cup, after supper, saying, "This cup is the new covenant in my blood; do this, whenever you drink it, in remembrance of me." For whenever you eat this bread and drink this cup, you proclaim the Lord's death until he comes."

[Memorial]

PEOPLE: **We shall do as our Lord commands. We celebrate this feast, proclaiming to the world that our Lord died, is risen, and is coming again, and until that day is with us, through the power of his Spirit!**

In Praise of God, the Spirit, Our Comforter

LEADER: Blessed are you, Holy Spirit, our comforter. At Creation you brought order out of chaos and breathed into humankind the breath of life. You led Abraham and Sarah to the chosen land and through them called a people to be your very own. You overshadowed Mary, and she conceived a Son who would save his people from their sins. At Pentecost you came like the rush of mighty wind, filling the apostles with power from on high, making of their many tongues the one new tongue of witness to you. You have been present with the church through many ages and in many lands, inspiring her witness to the gospel of Jesus Christ. Therefore, we offer our praise to you and sing with joy:

Commentary: This section of the prayer recites many of the aspects of the Spirit's work. Other aspects that may have been referred to in the sermon or in church education classes could be added to this list.

PEOPLE: **We give you thanks, God of power and might,**
that you send your Spirit to us now, breathing life
into your people and strengthening us with these gifts,
that we may receive again Christ's own life.

Prayer of Consecration

LEADER: Spirit of God, descend upon us now, we pray. Breath into your people and strengthen us with these gifts. By your power, unite us with our Lord, that we may remember his death and celebrate his resurrection. Then may we live in your power, as a bold wit-

ness to the world of the gospel of our Lord. Amen.

Breaking of the Bread

PASTOR: When we break the bread, is it not a sharing in the body of Christ?
PASTOR: When we give thanks over the cup, is it not a sharing in the blood of Christ?

Commentary: These sentences should be spoken as the pastor prepares the elements for Communion, breaking the common loaf and pouring the common cup.

Invitation

PASTOR: Friends in Christ, the Lord has prepared his table for his church and has given us his Spirit to guide us into all truth. All who love him and trust in him alone for their salvation are now invited to come to the table of the Lord.
PEOPLE: **We come with gladness. Thanks be to God!**
PASTOR: The gifts of God for the people of God.

The Sacrament

PASTOR: (as the people take the bread) The body of Christ, the bread of heaven, for you by the power of the Spirit.
PASTOR: (as the people take the cup) The blood of Christ, the cup of salvation, for you by the power of the Spirit.

Commentary: During the sacrament, appropriate hymns or anthems may be sung. Many Pentecost hymns are prayers for the presence of the Holy Spirit and are most appropriate for use during the sacrament.

The Thanksgiving

LEADER: Bless the Lord, O my soul; and all that is within me, bless his holy name!
PEOPLE: **Bless the Lord, O my soul, and forget not all his benefits. (Ps. 103:1-2)**

DEPARTING TO SERVE

Charge to the People

PASTOR: Go now in the power of the Spirit to love and serve the Lord.

Prayer of Dedication

PEOPLE: **Gracious God, we praise you for this feast of victory. By your Spirit, we** are strengthened for life in your service. With thanksgiving and joy, we dedicate ourselves to you. We promise to walk in your ways, clinging to your promise that your Spirit will never depart from us. We offer ourselves to you, Lord God. Amen.

Hymn of Dedication (Recessional)

Commentary: The closing hymn may be chosen from the list of petitioner hymns listed at the beginning the service. Especially appropriate are hymns that either ask for the Spirit's presence in the daily lives of the worshipers or that allow worshipers to make a declaration of their commitment to God's service by the power of the Spirit.

Benediction

PASTOR: Now may the God of hope fill you with all joy and peace in believing, so that by the power of the Holy Spirit you overflow with love and joy.

or

PASTOR: May the Spirit of truth lead you into all truth, that you may confess that Jesus is Lord, and may proclaim the wonderful works of God. May the blessing of God, the Father, the Son, and the Holy Spirit, remain with you always.

PEOPLE: **Amen.**

Commentary: The benediction may be given in several languages, pointing to the many languages that were unified on the day of Pentecost and the diversity that is brought together under Christ's lordship through the power of the Spirit. The use of other languages may also accompany the Scripture readings or a portion of the prayers of the people. Worship planners should take care that everyone present fully understands, through printed text or by respeaking the text in English, what is being said. The portions of the service spoken in more than one language should be kept very brief so as not to interfere with the worship of the people.

Dispersal of the Congregation (with instrumental, piano, or organ postlude or congregational singing)

Commentary: The service could appropriately conclude with triumphant instrumental or organ music that points to the power of the Spirit that accompanies the worshiper into the world. Another option consists of following the service with a time of congregational singing, which would encourage worshipers to linger, to sing psalms and hymns about the mission of the church, and even to participate in informal discussions about the mission of the local congregation.

John D. Witvliet

299 ◆ A CREATIVE/TRADITIONAL PENTECOSTAL SERVICE

The following service adapts traditional texts and patterns for Pentecost worship. Adapt to the needs of the local congregation.

In the early church Pentecost was not the beginning of a new season, but the end of the Easter season (as in the Jewish calendar from Passover to the Feast of Weeks). In the twentieth century, Pentecost has received greater attention because of the renewed emphasis on the Holy Spirit, especially from the charismatic movement. More churches are coming into a greater experience of the Holy Spirit, making Pentecost Sunday a time to celebrate not only the primitive church's experience, but also the experience of the twentieth-century church with the new outpouring of the Spirit.

The service below is an adaptation of the ancient St. John Chrysostom liturgy. Unlike Western worship, which moves in linear fashion from one point of worship to another, this Pentecost worship ties all the themes of worship into a single tapestry.

——————— **A Pentecost Liturgy** ———————

Entrance Hymn [all standing]

MINISTER: Blessed is the kingdom of the Father, and of the Son, and of the Holy Spirit: now, and forever: world without end.

PEOPLE: **Amen.**

MINISTER: In peace let us pray to the Lord.

PEOPLE: **Lord, have mercy.**

MINISTER: For the peace from on high and for the protection of the holy churches of God, let us pray to the Lord.

ALL: **Lord, have mercy.**

MINISTER: Lord our God, you are very great.

PEOPLE: **Praise the Lord, O my soul.**

MINISTER: You are clothed with splendor and majesty, and wrapped in light as with a garment.

PEOPLE: **Praise the Lord, O my soul.**

MINISTER: You have made the winds your messengers and flames of fire your servants.

PEOPLE: **Praise the Lord, O my soul.**

MINISTER: You have made the waters flow and the grasses grow and bread and wine to fill our hearts.

PEOPLE: **Praise the Lord, O my soul.**

MINISTER: How many are your works, O Lord. In wisdom you made them all: the earth is full of your creatures.

PEOPLE: **You open your hand and give us all good things. Send us your Spirit. Create in us a new heart and renew the face of the earth.**

MINISTER: Lord, may your glory endure forever. We will sing praise to you as long as we live.

ALL: **Praise the Lord, O my soul.**

(Alleluia sung)

MINISTER: Sovereign Lord, You promised to create new heavens and a new earth.

PEOPLE: **Hear us, O Lord.**

MINISTER: You promised to forget our former offenses and to remove the sound of weeping from our ears.

PEOPLE : **Hear us, O Lord.**

MINISTER: You are the Lord who is merciful and gracious, slow to anger, and abounding in love.

PEOPLE : **Hear us, O Lord.**

MINISTER: Remember to rejoice over your city, and take delight in your people.

PEOPLE: **Compassionate God, when you called, we did not answer. When you spoke, we did not listen.**

MINISTER: Lord, have mercy.

PEOPLE: **We confess we have done evil in your sight.**

MINISTER: Lord, have mercy.

PEOPLE: **We have not heard the cries of the poor. We have not answered the needs of our neighbors. We have not loved you as you love us.**

MINISTER: Lord, have mercy.

PEOPLE: **We are truly sorry and want to repent.**

MINISTER: Lord, have mercy.

PEOPLE: **Take away all our sins, heal our wounded souls, and fill us with your holiness.**

ALL: **Lord, have mercy.**

MINISTER: God has promised, "I will help you. I will give you peace like a flowing river. As a mother comforts her child, so I will comfort you. I will gather you from all nations and you will be my people. Let your hearts rejoice and be glad."

PEOPLE: **Let our hearts rejoice and be glad.**

(Alleluia sung)

MINISTER: Knowing that we are healed, that we are truly forgiven and gathered into the very peace of Christ, we offer this space to each other.

Hymn: "Glory to God" [Taizé]
(all seated)

MINISTER: By sending down a confusion of languages, the Most High scattered the nations. By distributing the tongues of fire, God calls all peoples into unity.

PEOPLE: **In harmony we glorify the all-holy Spirit.**

MINISTER: In a might wind rushing down from the heavens, the Most High trumpets good news over the earth. And those who cast nets to fish in the sea now cast your words to fish among people.

PEOPLE: **We worship and glorify the all-holy Spirit.**

ALL: **May the Savior who opens the gates of Paradise open our hearts to wisdom and truth.**

READER: (First Reading, ending with "This is the Word of the Lord")

PEOPLE: **Thanks be to you, O Lord.**

Responsorial Psalm: [psalm and antiphon]

READER: (Second Reading, ending with "This is the gospel of our Lord Jesus Christ")

PEOPLE: **Thanks be to you, O Christ.**

Children's Procession

Hymn (standing)

Sermon

Holy Silence

Response (sung—seated)

Prayers of Intercession

Apostles' Creed (all standing)

MINISTER: And now with the church at all times and in all places let us together say the Apostles' Creed.

ALL: (repeat the Apostles' Creed)

The Lord's Supper

Offertory (all standing)

MINISTER: Come Jesus, come, stand in our midst as you stood in the midst of your disciples. As you received the tears of Mary Magdalene, the hospitality of Zachaeus, and small coins from the widow. Accept our earthly gifts and make them holy. Give us your heavenly food and make us worthy to be your servants.

(At this point, a representative of each family comes forward and places alms in the collection basket. After the collection has been taken, a family brings forward the bread and wine for Communion. When all have returned to their seats, the people sing.)

Response of the People

The Thanksgiving

MINISTER: The Lord be with you.
PEOPLE: **And with you also.**
MINISTER: Lift up your hearts.
PEOPLE : **We lift them up to the Lord.**
MINISTER: Let us give thanks to the Lord our God.
PEOPLE: **It is fitting for us to give thanks.**
It is right and fitting,
our joy and our salvation,
that we should at all times and in all places
give thanks to you, O Lord, Holy Father,
almighty, everlasting God, through Christ our Lord.

MINISTER: We thank you for the Spirit, the Lord among us.
Always with your people,
Inviting us to hover over your creation with you,
a mother above the crib.
Where could we go to say, "And, the Lord is missing?"
How could we ever accuse you of infidelity?
Unconjurable but always nearby,
your visits are gifts.

You come to those who cry to you.
You come to those who need but do not expect.
You surprise us with children in age and in virginity.
You help the poor,
and show up at the door of the shut-in, bearing food.

You promise the earth to the meek.
You invite forgotten prisoners to sit at the head table of heaven.
So with all the poor, the lame, the foolish,
the orphaned and the forgotten,
we sing of your friendliness,
with laughter and joy.

ALL: **Holy, holy, holy Lord,
God of power and might;
heaven and earth are full of your glory.
Hosanna in the highest.**

The institution (all seated)

MINISTER: We give thanks to God
that our Savior Jesus Christ, before he suffered,
gave us this memorial of this sacrifice, until his coming again.
For on the night of his arrest he took bread,
and after giving thanks to God, broke it saying,
"This is my body, given for you;
do this to commemorate me."
Then he took the cup, gave thanks,
offered it to them, saying,
"This is the blood of the new covenant,

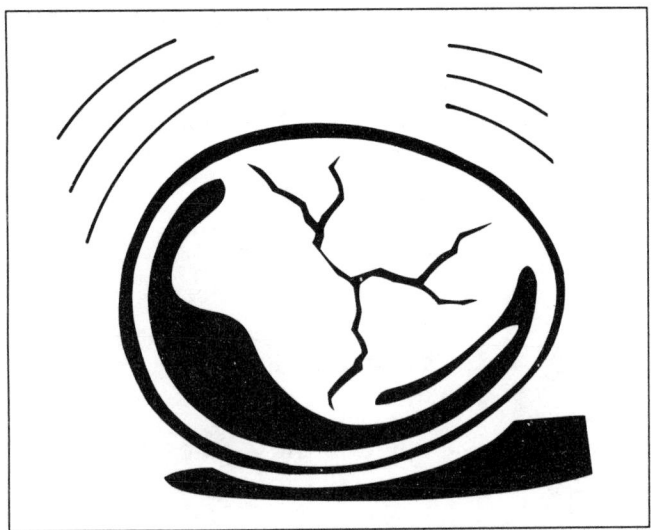

Egg. The egg is a symbol of the Resurrection, because the chick enclosed in the shell emerges with new life. In the same way, Jesus emerged from the tomb with new life.

which is poured out for many.
Whenever you drink it,
do this to commemorate me."

ALL: **We remember Christ's death,**
we proclaim his resurrection,
we await his coming in glory.

MINISTER: Send your Spirit, Lord,
to make a place for you, among and within us.
May our receiving of the bread and wine,
be our receiving of you.

PEOPLE: **Send us, O God, your Spirit.**

MINISTER: The bread which we break,
is it not a sharing in the body of our Lord Jesus Christ?

PEOPLE: **We who are many**
become one with our suffering Lord
for we all partake of one loaf.

MINISTER: The wine for which we give thanks,
is it not a sharing in the blood of Christ?

PEOPLE: **The wine which we all drink**
is our unity with Christ
who bled and died and arose.

MINISTER: Lord God,
rend the heavens and come down.
Send the Spirit of Jesus upon us,
that we may be moved to oneness
with each other
and with all those who suffer.

As Moses raised the serpent, raise us up,
that seeing our love,
all may find peace and joy.

PEOPLE: **Send us, O God, your Spirit.**

MINISTER: For the peace of the earth:
for the reconciling of nation with nation,
race with race, male with female;
we pray to you, Lord.
May this bread and wine be the sign of life
which flows from you through us to all creation.

PEOPLE: **Send us, O God, your Spirit.**

The Invitation (all standing)

MINISTER: Congregation of Jesus Christ,
our Lord has prepared this table
for all how love and trust in him for their salvation.
All who are truly sorry for their sins,
who sincerely believe in Jesus as their Savior,
and who desire to live in obedience,
are now invited to come with gladness to this holy meal.

The Dedication

PEOPLE: **We long for your salvation.**
We trust in you.
We offer ourselves,
alive to your will, dead to our own.
We shall eat the bread of affliction,
We shall drink the cup of sorrow,
O Risen Lord.

MINISTER: Come then, the table is ready.
The gifts of God for the people of God.

Communion

(The people come forward and are served in groups. As they pass the bread and wine, they say to each other, "The body of Christ for you" and "The blood of Christ for you" or other appropriate words.)

Thanksgiving after Communion

MINISTER: Bless the Lord, O my soul.

PEOPLE: **And all that is within me, bless**

God's holy name.

MINISTER: Bless the Lord, O my soul.

PEOPLE: **May the glory of the Lord endure forever.**

May the Lord rejoice over all creation.

MINISTER: Bless the Lord, O my soul.

PEOPLE: **I will sing to the Lord all my life;**

I will sing praise to my God as long as I live.

ALL: **Bless the Lord, O my soul.**

Praise the Lord!

MINISTER: Now may the God of hope

fill you with all joy and peace in believing,

so that by the power of the Holy spirit,

you overflow with love and hope.

PEOPLE: **Thanks be to God.**

MINISTER: And remember,

the harvest of the Spirit is love,

joy, peace, patience, kindness, goodness,

faithfulness, gentleness, and self-control.

The Spirit is our source of life.

Let us therefore walk by the Spirit.

PEOPLE: **Amen.** [Alleluia, possibly repeated]

300 ❖ A CREATIVE PENTECOST SERVICE

The service below is intended primarily for churches that emphasize informal worship. Although it lacks the structure of more familiar liturgies, it presents clearly th traditional themes of Pentecost worship.

—————— **Order of Worship** ——————

Processional: "For Your Gift of God the Spirit" (Clarkson)

LEADER: As we gather for worship this Pentecost Sunday, we want to place ourselves before God, to be birthed anew with the breath of God's benevolent life through his Holy Spirit. We want to be led to Pentecost, but wish to do so without preempting the history of the Spirit's work in Israel. Today we worship God the Holy Spirit by beginning at the beginning, with the hovering, birthing Spirit of creation.

FIRST READER: (dramatic reading of Genesis 1:1-31a, followed by silent pause, then:) Our loving God, we are awed by creation, by your ordered explosion of artistry.

PEOPLE: **We bless you, Creator God, for your gift of love and delight.**

ALL: "Gloria, Gloria" (Taizé)

SECOND READER: And God saw that it was very good. For a time, perfect. But following upon the disobedience of Adam, during the generations of Noah: "The Lord saw that the wickedness of humankind was great in the earth, and that every inclination of the thoughts of their hearts was only evil continually. And the Lord was sorry that he had made humankind on the earth, and it grieved him to his heart" (reads Gen. 6:5-6, followed by a silent pause).

LEADER: Lord, have mercy upon us.

PEOPLE: **O Lord, hear our prayer, and rescue us.**

(silent pause)

HOMILETIC REFLECTION: God grieved, and God judged sin. But even so, over the course of Israel's history, God poured out his Holy Spirit upon chosen leaders and messengers, in order to continue God's salvation mission toward his creation. Listen to a sampling of the Spirit's ministry in Israel. Pharaoh, the leader of the Egyptians, asked regarding Joseph, "Can we find anyone else like this—in whom is the Spirit of God?" An outsider, a man of power and position, recognized God's discernment in Joseph, who was at the time a prisoner of Pharaoh's in Egypt. Yahweh filled Bezalel, an artist, "with divine spirit, with ability, intelligence, and knowledge in every kind of craft, to devise artistic designs." Moses then confirmed, very specifically, the particular kind of anointing on Bezalel, whose mission was to function as a Spirit-anointed artist in the temple. The Spirit's presence in Joseph led him to work for good, both for Pharaoh and for his fellow Israelites; and the Spirit in Bezalel directed Bezalel to produce works of beauty and glory to God.

In contrast to this is the mysterious work of the Spirit recorded in the book of the Judges. The Spirit of the Lord came upon Gideon, Jephthah, and Samson, each of whom, though a judge in Israel, is of questionable character. Jephthah sacrificed his only child, a young woman, as a burnt offering to Yahweh, and Samson died in disgrace. Mystery and grace continue in the period of the kings and the restoration. The "spirit of the Lord" came mightily upon David, the shepherd, poet and king, whose story is rich with the rise and fall of character, as seen both in himself and in others. The rise of the Spirit in David contrasts the decline and departure of the Spirit in Saul. In God's grace-filled irony, God's Spirit in David then comforts the tormented and tragic Saul. Years later, the prophet Nehemiah reminds Israel that God warned Israel by his good Spirit through the prophets, but Israel would not listen. The Spirit instructs, but humans are called to respond. Today we are called to listen, and today we are called to respond to our particular heritage of God's Spirit in this new covenant.

THIRD READER: (reads Acts 2:1-13) Our loving God, we offer our gratitude for your benevolence.

PEOPLE :   **Renew our hearts, that we may respond with due amazement.**

Hymn: "Wind Who Makes All Winds that Blow" (Troeger)

LEADER: What does Pentecost mean for us, but that we allow God to lead us beyond the perimeter of our limited assumptions and presumptions and into God's vision for our life in faith. How does this happen?

FOURTH READER: (reads John 3:1-10)

LEADER: Many of us here this morning have already entered the kingdom of God, and have received the gift of the Holy Spirit. But perhaps we are not too old in faith to extend Nicodemus' question to ask, "Even at this stage can I participate in new birth: can I choose to submit myself to the unpredictable movement of the Spirit within and experience new life and growth?" Let us offer ourselves in prayer to the Lord.

LEADER: Our gracious God, we thank you for your Holy Spirit, messenger of hope, judgment and grace.

PEOPLE: **We bless you, Lord, for endowing us with your Holy Spirit.**

LEADER: Our merciful God, we thank you for your Spirit's messages to the prophets, to John the Baptist, and to Jesus, to reveal to us our sin and our need for forgiveness. Have mercy on us, we pray, and pierce our limited self-contained worlds.

ALL: "Confitemeni Domino" (Taizé); Psalm 51, followed by silent response, then "Spirit of the Living God, Fall Fresh on Me."

INSTITUTION AND CELEBRATION OF EUCHARIST

READER: (Romans 8:12-17)

LEADER: The Holy Spirit has come upon us, and the Holy Spirit continues to come, enlightening and enlivening us in our journey after Christ.

READER: (John 14:15-19)

LEADER: The Holy Spirit came to us, because Jesus left us in order to return to the Father. Reflection of the gift of the Spirit is inseparable from reflection upon Jesus' gift of himself to us.

READER: (John 14:25-27; 16:7, 12-15)

LEADER: We desire to follow Jesus, and we desire to allow the Spirit to lead us after him, but, on our own, we stumble on the cross that comes between the two. Jesus does not ask of us greater courage than he asked of his disciples, to whom he gave this meal in remembrance of himself. Let us quietly and courageously confess our desires and our fears to the Father, asking that we might be freed to gratefully allow the Spirit to bear new life within us. For Christ's sake. (silent pause)

PRAYER: Our loving Father, God of creation, God of the ages, God of our Lord Jesus Christ. We confess to you that we are companions with your disciples in their confusion and fear. That we are oft-times caught between our desire to follow you and our desire to remain with that which is known and recognizable. We pray you would pour your Holy Spirit upon this bread and wine; consecrate it, that we might be nourished with truth, courage, and hope in our journey with Jesus to the Father.

COMMUNION

Hymns: "Spirit, Working in Creation" (Iona); "No One Will Ever be the Same" (Iona) (can be sung during Communion)

Declaration of Faith and Hope: "God's Grandeur" (poem by Gerald Manley Hopkins)

Benediction: May God nurture his gift within you as God likewise liberates you from your fears. Go in the peace and protection of God's Spirit.

Recessional Hymn: "Come, Holy Spirit" (Petersen)

———— Commentary ————

Preamble. This is a celebrative occasion, in which we offer our gratitude for the participation by God's Spirit in creation life, the presence of God's Spirit throughout the course of our salvation history, and for the gift of the Holy Spirit at Pentecost. Pentecost is the final aspect of the Easter event, following ten days after the Ascension of Jesus into heaven. Like each of the great events of the church year, the focus in celebrating Pentecost is not to relive a historical event, but to yield ourselves to God and to be drawn deeper into the graces that God has already bestowed on us. The Holy Spirit has already been poured out on the church, but the prayer of our human spirit is always "purify me and fill me yet more."

Worship Space. Whatever is present in the worship center should convey the fullness, or permeating presence, of God's Spirit; the longevity of the Spirit's presence in creation life and salvation history; as well as the independence of the Spirit, who moves where, how, and when the Spirit wills. Symbols of wind, fire, water, oil, as well as the motif of birth, are all appropriately suggestive. Banners would be particularly meaningful if their design connoted activity rather than passivity.

In the New Testament, Jesus says, "The wind blows where it chooses, and you hear the sound of it, but you do not know where it comes from or where it goes. So it is with everyone who is born of the Spirit." This non-predictable movement, this lack of functional uniformity, could be appropriately incorporated into an asymmetrically designed worship space. The pulpit, baptismal font, Communion table/altar, lectern, etc., could be arranged in a different manner. This service is especially suitable to liturgical dance, so the arrangement could be done with the needs of the dancer(s) or dramatic celebrants in mind.

Entrance. In order to enlarge the congregation's expectations regarding the celebration of Pentecost, choose a processional hymn that acknowledges the activity of the Holy Spirit over the whole course of salvation history. This will also prepare people for the broader focus of the liturgy.

Word. The activity of the Holy Spirit as recorded in the Pentecost narrative in Acts is highly dramatic. This service seeks to remind us that our human sphere began in an equally dramatic and momentous fashion. Suitable to this drama would be a "Gloria" from, for example, one of Mozart's masses. The richness of the Genesis reading lends itself to such a response.

The Creation/Fall juxtaposition leads the congregation immediately into the tension of our salvation story, through which we must wait and listen, and to which we are called to respond. The homiletic reflection could consist of any number of samples from the Old Testament narratives and prophets; almost any combination will prove itself consistent with Jesus' teaching about the unpredictable nature of the Spirit.

The instructive portions of Scripture that are

used in this service could alternatively be chosen in order to focus on Jesus' own calling, anointing, temptation, and ministry in the Holy Spirit, or they could be chosen from highlights of the ministry of the Spirit in, say, Paul or Peter's life. An important element in the choice is that the Scripture leads the congregation to confession; to confess both where desire is lacking and where desire is blossoming into longing.

Psalm 51 is a suitable responsorial Psalm for this service since it has many references to our human spirit. And, of course, it is our human spirit which must respond to God's spirit. "Spirit of the Living God" can be sung with accompanying prayer gestures, or another similar song of beseeeching could be chosen.

Eucharist/Communion. We need God's holy table to nourish both God's and our desires to grow. At the Table we can offer up our fears or hesitations and, in faith, receive Christ's help through the bread and wine. During the receiving of Communion, the congregation could sing songs of hope and declaration of the Spirit's redeeming presence in this our fallen world.

Dismissal. The poem "God's Grandeur" may not be appropriate for all congregations, but it is a magnificent work that powerfully draws the senses to perceive the reality of fallen Creation, then steadily leads the hearer to a majestic conclusion, which is possible because of the Spirit's presence over this, our "bent world."

The benediction could be altered depending on the congregation, Scriptures, and focus of the preceding service. The recessional hymn/song should lead the people out in celebration of the Spirit that lives in and among us.

Diane S. George Ayer

301 ◆ A Convergence Pentecost Service

The following service features the use of traditional patterns and texts for Pentecost worship but provides freedom for spontaneous expressions of praise and worship and for charismatic expression of the power of God's Spirit.

Pentecost Sunday is the birthday of the church, as the Holy Spirit was poured out with his gifts and ministries upon those in the Upper Room.

Next to Easter, this should be one of the most exciting days in the life of the body. The major emphasis is the power of the Holy Spirit, sent forth to produce holy living and anointed ministry. This day can also be used as a time to publicly identify those who sense a call to Christian service.

The red theme for paraments, frontals, and vestments gives a sense of power and joy. Accents in gold and other bright colors add to the display. Banners and hangings with appropriate symbols, such as the descending dove and the tongues of fire, are especially good for this festival. Displays may even be set up around the church showing the various ministries the church is involved in. These could be placed in a fellowship hall where a common meal may be shared following the service.

This is a day when you pull out all the stops. Banners, dancers, singers, and special music should all be coordinated in a major celebration of our life and purposes as the church of Jesus Christ. Adapt the service below to local usage and style.

ACTS OF ENTRANCE

Personal Preparation
Commentary: Just as the disciples waited in the Upper Room, the people should come into a quiet sanctuary and wait upon the Holy Spirit. This is a good time all worshipers to reexamine their calling before the Lord, asking themselves searching questions.

Opening Sentences
Commentary: From the back of the sanctuary, the minister begins the service with these opening words: Thanks be to God, who gives us victory through our Lord Jesus Christ! If then you have been raised with Christ, seek the things that are above, where Christ is, seated at the right hand of God.

Processional
Commentary: The processional should be a large one, with a crucifer, banner carriers, dancers, singers, ministers, etc. The music, upbeat and victorious, should start immediately after the opening sentences.

Acts of Praise and Worship
Commentary: The hymns and choruses can especially focus around the power and fruit of the

Holy Spirit. In addition, the use of litanies, responses, directed readings, etc., can be interspersed. The gifts of the Holy Spirit should be formally invited to come forth during worship.

MINISTRY OF THE WORD

Commentary: In addition to the readings, a drama, special song, or other special form of presentation could be used to further celebrate the day of Pentecost.

Collect
O God, who on this day stirred the hearts of your faithful people by pouring upon them the gift of your Holy Spirit: grant us by the same Spirit that we might manifest the holy fruit of his life, and build up the church by his holy gifts of power through Jesus Christ your Son our Lord, who lives and reigns with you, in the Holy Spirit, one God, forever and ever. Amen.

Readings
First Lesson: Joel 2:28-32 or Acts 2:1-11
Responsive Reading: Chrysostom Litany or Psalm 104:25-37 or 33:12-15, 18-22
Second Lesson: Acts 2:1-11 or 1 Corinthians 12:4-13
Gospel Reading: John 7:37-39 or 14:8-17 or 20:19-23

Message
Commentary: Since the power of Pentecost resides in each believer through the Holy Spirit, the preaching of Pentecost can be a benchmark for the church year. The power of the Spirit is a necessity for the church, not an option. The message should be followed with an opportunity to yield and allow the Holy Spirit to be released in a person's life.

Invitation for the Release of the Holy Spirit
Commentary: At the end of the message, an invitation can be given for people who desire to have a releasing of the power of the Holy Spirit in their lives. Some call this santification, others call this the baptism in the Holy Spirit. This call can go out to those who have never allowed the Holy Spirit to take control or for those who have quenched the Spirit. The purpose is twofold: power for holy living and the release of gifts for ministry to the body of Christ. Ministry teams may need to be available to pray with people. A second call could be given for those who sense a call to full-time Christian service, setting them apart by prayer and public confession to pursue the possibilities of a life in vocational ministry.

Prayer
Commentary: O God, you have called to all the peoples of the earth through your Son Jesus Christ, sending him to preach peace to those who are far off and to those who are near: grant that people everywhere may seek after you and find you; bring the nations together as one flock; pour out your Spirit upon all flesh; build your church in this world; and hasten the coming of your kingdom; through Jesus Christ our Lord. Amen.

Prayers of the People
Commentary: Today's prayer can focus on the church's mission to reach their city. A large map could be placed on a table in the front of the sanctuary. During prayer time, representatives from the different sections of the community could be seated around the table, laying their hands on their particular part of town. This time of prayer invites the Holy Spirit to stir up our gifts and ministries for spiritual warfare and outreach to the harvest field where we have been placed.

MINISTRY OF THE TABLE

Offertory
Commentary: Pentecost Sunday can be a day of special giving for church extension. The burden could be to expand the ministries of the local church, to assist in the planting of a new work, or to take an offering for church planting in general.

Great Thanksgiving
Commentary: Communion on Pentecost Sunday should reflect the great joy of the church in receiving the Holy Spirit. While Communion is being administered, sing songs of the Holy Spirit and of the power of the Spirit. Administer the laying on of hands with the anointing of oil.

Prayer after Communion
Heavenly Father, we thank you for satisfying the hunger in our hearts through giving us the Bread of heaven. In sharing in this holy meal, may we remember his death and passion. Through your Holy Spirit, use these elements of bread and wine to strengthen us with grace and mercy that we may live a life of purity and power. This we ask through Jesus Christ our Lord. Amen.

ACTS OF DISMISSAL

Blessing/Benediction

LEADER: Now to him who is able to do exceedingly and abundantly beyond what we ask or think, according to his power that is at work within us, to him be glory in the church and in Jesus Christ throughout all generations forever and ever. Amen. Go forth to proclaim the gospel of the Lord in the power of the Holy Spirit!

PEOPLE: **Thanks be to God!**

Anointing of Believers

Commentary: The people leave the sanctuary with a song of commissioning being sung by the worship team and the congregation. The people can either be dismissed by rows or just leave slowly. The ministers are standing at the door and anointing each one with oil, making the sign of the cross on their foreheads. This symbolizes the unction of the Holy Spirit upon them as they leave to serve.

302 ✦ LITANIES FOR PENTECOST SUNDAY

The litany below may be used on Pentecost Sunday as a prayer.

The fields are white unto harvest;
Bring forth your church, O Lord.
We see the fruit of righteousness being formed on new stalks;
Bring forth your church, O Lord.
You are establishing a people unto yourself;
Bring forth your church, O Lord.
You are raising up a standard in the wilderness;
Bring forth your church, O Lord.
The root of Jesse is coming forth now in kingdom power;
Bring forth your church, O Lord.
The nations are silent, longing and expectant;
Bring forth your church, O Lord.
They wait for the Name to be spoken in word and deed;
Bring forth your church, O Lord.
They cry in their hearts for an answer;
Bring forth your church, O Lord.
They watch the heavens for a sign;

Bring forth your church, O Lord.
Speak today through us your people;
Bring forth your church, O Lord.
Raise the ensign of life before all mankind;
Bring forth your church, O Lord.
Draw us to your harvest field;
Bring forth your church, O Lord.
Let us behold the richness of new life coming forth;
Bring forth your church, O Lord.
Let us raise the sword and bring forth your bounteous harvest;
Bring forth your church, O Lord.
Call your people from the north, from the south, from the east,
and from the west;
Bring forth your church, O Lord.
Gather them as a chosen people, the apple of your eye;
Bring forth your church, O Lord.
Incline their hearts toward your throne;
Bring forth your church, O Lord.
Knit them as one in your love;
Bring forth your church, O Lord.
Bring forth your church, O Lord.
Yes, bring forth your church, O Lord.

This litany may be used as a prayer on Pentecost Sunday or on one of the Sundays immediately after.

Spirit of the Living God,
Visit us again as on the day of Pentecost.
Come, Holy Spirit.
With rushing wind that sweeps away all barriers,
Come, Holy Spirit.
With tongues of fire that set our hearts aflame,
Come, Holy Spirit.
With speech that unites the bable of our tongues,
Come, Holy Spirit.
With love that overlaps the boundaries of race and nation,
Come, Holy Spirit.
With power from above to make our weakness strong,
Come, Holy Spirit.

ALL: **In the Name of Jesus Christ Our Lord. Amen.**

Randolph W. Sly

303 • An Anthology of Hymns and Songs for the Season after Pentecost

The central focus for all congregational song for this season is the promised advent of the Holy Spirit's coming (John 15:26; 16:7-11; Acts 1:5, 8), and his actual historical arrival into the lives of believers (Acts 2:1-4). These two contexts have inspired a rich repertory of hymns and songs, from the medieval times of Venantius Fortunatus or Hrabanus Maurus to the numerous contemporary writers of gospel song and Scripture chorus. Among the traditional hymns, there is a tendency to praise the Holy Spirit in his attributes, character, and power as coeternal third person of the Trinity; while contemporary charismatic writers and writers outside of liturgical worship traditions tend to focus on the Holy Spirit's person through his dynamics of activity in the body of Christ; fellowship, love, personal and corporate infilling by the Spirit, relational wholeness, correction and spiritual healing, and the potentials of koinonia.

This section gives attention to citations to recent vintage; the notable exceptions are the best-known medieval and Reformation-age hymns and tunes within the liturgical traditions (e.g., Veni Sancte Spiritus, Veni Creator Spiritus, Komm Heiliger Geist, Herre Gott), each of which have also inspired famous choral and instrumental works of major scope, from the fifteenth century to the present.

The Pentecost season itself consists of Pentecost Eve, the day of Pentecost, and Pentecost evening; and the worship service for Pentecost celebrates the Spirit's outpouring as depicted in Acts 2. From the first Sunday after Pentecost (Trinity Sunday) through Sunday of the Fulfillment (earlier termed Christ the King) preceding the first Sunday in Advent, the entire period is made up of ordinary Sundays in the season known as the Time of the Church. This is not a meaningless term, for it signifies the age of grace that the contemporary body of Christ lives within, and which—by common grace—is extended to the world at large (Ezek. 33:11, Rom. 10:21; 2 Pet. 3:9; Acts 1:7-8; Matt. 5:45b).

TITLE	AUTHOR/COMPOSER	TUNE	STYLE	SCRIPTURE REFERENCE
Awake, Thou Spirit of Watchmen	M. Gates/S. Howard (1982)	Isleworth	Traditional	Matthew 9:37-38 John 4:35
Breathe on Me, Breath of God	E. Hatch/_Chetham's Psalmody_, 1718; E. Hatch/R. Jackson	Wirksworth, Trentham	Traditional	Ephesians 1:13-14 John 17:26
Come Down, O Love Divine	B. daSiene/R. Vaughan Williams	Down Ampney	Traditional	John 14:16-17
Come Gracious Spirit, Heavenly Dove	I. Watts/S. Dyer, 1824	Mendon	Traditional	John 16:13
Come, Holy Ghost	M. Luther/Erfurt, 1524	Komm Heiliger Geist, Herre Gott	Chorale	Acts 1:4-5
Come Holy Ghost, Our Souls Inspire	H. Maurus/J. Klug H. Maurus/Sarum Plainsong	Komm, Gott Schöpfer and Veni Creator Spiritus	Plainsong	John 16:13-14; Galatians 4:6
Come, Holy Spirit	J. Peterson (1971)		Gospel Song	Acts 2:17
The Day of Pentecost Arrived	F. Brooks/American Folk Hymn (1972)	Land of Rest	Early American	Acts 2:1

Continued...

TITLE	AUTHOR/COMPOSER	TUNE	STYLE	SCRIPTURE REFERENCE
Dwell in Me, O Blessed Spirit	M. Lankton/G. Borky	DWELL IN ME	Traditional	Ephesians 1:13-14
Every Time I Feel the Spirit	Anon./Black Spiritual		Spiritual	Romans 8:26
Fill My Cup, Lord	R. Blanchard		Southern Gospel	Romans 8:26
Filled with the Spirit's Power	J. Peacy/Anon., 1832	BIRMINGHAM		Acts 1:14; Acts 2:4
The Friends of Christ Together	D. Romig/17th c., Memingen	ES FLOG EIN KLEINS WALDVÖGELEIN		Acts 1:4-5
Get the Flame	D. Harkin (1972)		Contemporary	Romans 12:11
Gracious Spirit, Dwell with Me	T. Lynch/Basle (1745)	CASSEL	Traditional	John 16:13-14
Hail, This Joyful Day's Return	attr. Hilary of Portiers/ Claude Goudimel	GOUDIMEL 75		Acts 2:3
Hail Thee, Festival Day	V. Fortunatus/ R. Vaughan Williams	SALVE FESTA DIES	Note: also for use on Easter Sunday	Acts 2:3
Holy Ghost, Dispel Our Sadness	P. Gerhart/arr. R. Hillert	JEFFERSON		Acts 1:8
The Holy Spirit Came at Pentecost	J. Peterson	COME HOLY SPIRIT	Gospel Song	Acts 2:17
Holy Spirit, Font of Life	anon. Latin/S. Webb	VENI SANCTE SPIRITUS	Plainsong	John 14:16-17
Holy Spirit, Light Divine	A. Reed/L. Gottschalk	MERCY	Art-Song Derived	Romans 8:11
Holy Spirit, Thou Are Welcome	D. Rambo and D. Huntsinger (1976)		Scripture Chorus	Ephesians 5:18
If You Have Ears	F. Kaan/A. Wyton (1977)	LISTEN	Hymn Renaissance	Acts 1;8
In Thy Pentecostal Splendor	J. Speers/J. Stainer	CROSS OF JESUS		Acts 2:1-4
The Lone, Wild Bird	H. McFayden/arr. D. Johnson (1968)	PROSPECT		Hebrews 4:3
May the Holy Spirit's Sword	Chinese, tr. F. Price	JU MENG LING	Chinese	Hebrews 4:12-13
Not with a Spirit of Fear	D. Williams (1989)			2 Timothy 1:7
O Day, Full of Grace	Danish Folk/C. Weyse (1982)	DEN SIGNEDE DAG		Acts 1:2
O Holy Spirit, Enter In	S. Brown/W. Knapp	WAREHAM		Acts 1:8

TITLE	AUTHOR/COMPOSER	TUNE	STYLE	SCRIPTURE REFERENCE
Song of Anointing	B. Ballinger (1983)		Scripture Chorus	1 John 2:27
The Spirit Breathes upon the Word	W. Cowper/T. Hastings	ORTONVILLE		1 John 2:27
The Spirit of Jesus Is in This Place	G. and W. Gaither	SPIRIT OF JESUS	Southern Gospel	Matthew 18:19-20
Spirit of Mercy, Truth and Love	J. Cruger (1640)		Chorale	1 John 2:27
Spirit Song	J. Wimber (1979)		Scripture Chorus	Matthew 3:16; John 21:15-17
Sweep over My Soul	H. Clarke (1983)		Scripture Chorus	John 3:8; Ezekiel 39:29
Sweet, Sweet Spirit	D. Akers (1962)		Gospel Song	Job 19:21
There Is a River	D. and M. Sapp (1987)		Scripture Chorus	John 7:38-39
There's a Spirit in the Air	B. Wren/W. Rowan (1987)	FREINER	Hymn Renaissance	Ephesians 3:20
Thou, Whose Purpose Is to Kindle	E. Trueblood/R. Arnatt (1968)	LADUE CHAPEL		Hebrews 4:12
Though I May Speak with Bravest Fire	H. Hopson (1972)/ American folktune	GIFT OF LOVE		1 Corinthians 13
To Thee, O Comforter Divine	F. Havergal/ D. McK. Williams (1977)	ST. BARTHOLOMEWS		Ephesians 1:13
We Are One in the Spirit	P. Scholtes (1966)	THEY'LL KNOW WE ARE CHRISTIANS	Scripture Chorus	John 13:35; 17:20
Wind Who Makes All Wind	T. Troeger/C. Doran (1985)	FALCONE	Hymn Renaissance	Acts 2:1-13

Steve Cushman

304 ◆ PENTECOST PRAYERS

The following prayers for the Pentecost are based on images found in Scripture. Brief commentaries follow each prayer, directing worship planners to Scripture passages that can be used in conjunction with each prayer.

Invocations or Opening Prayer

Come O sovereign God, and invade and inspire us with your wind and fire. Shake loose that which binds and consume that which competes so that our tongues might be tuned to sing your praises. Enable us through your Spirit to *reclaim the power of Pentecost. In Jesus' mighty name. Amen.*

Commentary: The biblical account of the day of Pentecost (Acts 2:1-4) provides rich pictures for prayer. As was demonstrated during the Easter section, Acts 2 offers a fertile field of imagery that can be used to construct all the components of worship. For example, prayer of confession/words of assurance (vv. 21, 22-28, 37-39), prayer of illumination (vv. 17-20), offering (vv. 44-45), and pastoral prayer (vv. 5-13, 42-47).

Spirit of the living God, come be our guest and guide. Release your mighty power and fill us with a desire to speak to one another and sing to you with hearts alive with praise. May all our actions and attitudes declare our gratitude to you, Lord God, through the precious name of Jesus Christ. Amen.

Commentary: This prayer paraphrases the apostle Paul's prayer from Ephesians 1:18-20. It reminds us how the Scriptures are a rich reservoir not only for inspiring worship, but that they actually suggest specific prayers for various occasions throughout a service.

Prayer of Confession

Gracious God, we rejoice and praise you for the gift of your Holy Spirit. But as we celebrate the release of your power we would confess our own lack of power. While our need is great for your Spirit, we frequently have not taken the time to ask or pause long enough to receive your Spirit. Tragically we have often sought to do your ministry with our own might. Forgive our impatience and rebellious efforts to run the church and your kingdom on our own. We acknowledge that our actions and attitudes have often grieved you and suppressed your Holy Spirit. Cleanse us from our sins so that we might be renewed and refreshed by this liberating gift of Pentecost. Hear us now as we continue to confess our sins and needs before you . . . [opportunity for silent confession] . . . In the strong name of Jesus we pray. Amen.

WORDS OF ASSURANCE

LEADER: (reads Acts 2:38)
PEOPLE: (read 1 Peter 3:18)
ALL: (read 2 Corinthians 3:17)

Commentary: This prayer relies upon a number of scriptural strands that relate to the Holy Spirit. In particular, Luke 24:49; Acts 1:4, 8; and Ephesians 4:30 are woven together to create this confession. Further, all the scriptural references for the words of assurance are drawn from passages that relate to the Holy Spirit. It should also be emphasized that the best source for words of assurance and pardon are the Scriptures. The act of confession is an acknowledgment before God and others that we have fallen short. Therefore, the most powerful pronouncement of forgiveness is from the Scriptures that capture and communicate God's Word to us.

Prayer for Illumination

Everfaithful God, many voices tug at our hearts and summon our allegiance. But you have called us to be different from the rest of our society. Awaken us to the reading of your Scripture. Let us listen and live by your Spirit so that we might keep in step with your illuminating Spirit. In Jesus' name. Amen.

Commentary: Galatians 5:25 declares the Holy Spirit's power and ability to guide our lives. This verse suggests not only this prayer but wonderful possibilities for developing other prayers for illumination.

Offertory Prayers

Breathe on us, O breath of God, and fill our lives anew. Your amazing love has stretched and sealed our hearts so that we may praise and give you glory. Receive the offerings of our lives that we might further your ministry both here and around the globe. Gratefully we respond in Jesus' precious name. Amen.

Commentary: The first stanza of the hymn, "Breathe on Me, Breath of God," establishes the base line of this prayer. Additionally there are allusions to the metaphors of Ephesians 1:12-13.

Gracious God, you have been called our Maker, Defender, Redeemer, and Friend, and so you are. Your liberating Spirit creates and renews the face of our lives and land. You surprise us with the spectrum of your mighty acts of power and provision. May our response bring delight to you as we present our tithes, offerings, and gifts of gratitude to the honor and praise of Christ, our Lord. Amen.

Commentary: The opening theme of this prayer is drawn from the fourth stanza of Robert Grant's stirring hymn, "O Worship the King," ("Frail children of dust, . . ."). Since this hymn is based on Psalm 104, the additional imagery was also selected from this portion of Scripture. In particular, the themes are borrowed from verses thirty and thirty-four. This offers us yet another guide in the construction of worship and development of prayers. Most hymnals provide some sort of scriptural index to hymns. The careful worship planner will discover many helpful images and insights that can be employed from the original passages that gave birth to the specific hymns used in worship.

Pastoral Prayer

Sovereign Lord God, your creating Spirit first moved over the formless void and brought into being the heavens and the earth. You formed not only the land and animals but also displayed your marvel in fashioning us in your image. We are grateful that you observed your creation and pronounced it good, saving your highest joy for us who bear your own likeness. We are thankful that your same Holy Spirit has continued to create new life through your Son Jesus Christ. Ancient prophets spoke and wondered what we so often take for granted. Forgive our presumption and startle us afresh with the mighty power of your sovereign will. In our efforts to be faithful and follow Christ, may we not lose hope amidst the attempts of others to resist and reject you. Grant us the courage to withstand these temptations as we seek to bear witness to Jesus Christ.

Lord of power and might, grant us a courage that echoes the example of the early church. Unleash your pentecostal power that we might speak and act with humble boldness.

As we face the realities of life, be gracious to extend your powerful hand that your presence would be known in healing and performing miracles of wonder and new life. Help us, O compassionate God, to realize that you answer our prayers not always according to our desires but in response to the wisdom of your divine will and providence. Healing God, hear us then and be gracious to those we name as they face surgery, wait for recovery, or wrestle with the lingering effects of illness. Be present also with doctors,

nurses, technicians, and others in the medical arts. Work in and through them and guide their efforts to cooperate with you, our Great Physician. Our minds also remember that many are still imprisoned in various forms of bondage and despair. Whether it be mental or emotional illness, disabilities, the haunting nightmares of abuse, or the destructive ravages of war, release and restore those trapped in these bitter entanglements of turmoil.

Since we are never equal to our calling, we seek for the filling of your Holy Spirit. Grant us that daily dependence that converts our human efforts into that cooperative venture with you, O mighty, heavenly Father. In Jesus' name we pray. Amen.

Commentary: The scriptural prayer of Acts 4:23-31 inspires this prayer for Pentecost. This sample has tapped only a few of the available themes and images of this rich model from the early church. Additionally it seeks to remind us that not all prayers are answered exactly or as quickly as we desire. Prayer always needs to be surrendered to the mystery and greater wisdom of our triune God.

Tom Schwanda

305 • A Pentecost Creed

The creed below may be used on Pentecost Sunday or on any of the Sundays immediately after Pentecost.

One advantage to this form of the creed is that it does not require overburdened congregations to learn any new or complicated responses. In addition, it helps people understand the real meaning of "Amen." As the litany continues and the "Amen" grows in volume, a person can hear his or her individual response blend in with the full response of the community.

This type of creed offers a challenge to individuals to question their faith and reaffirm it on more mature levels. "Do I believe this or . . . ?" is the question that must be asked, and each person must come to his or her own answer.

Recovering the Pentecostal faith that fired the first disciples is not outside the reach of any of us. If we wish to change the world we must first change ourselves. Pentecost, we know, changed a motley crew of simple men and women into giants of faith and power.

LEADER: Let all those who believe that there is only one God, our all-powerful Father, respond "Amen."

Let all those who believe that God is the Creator of all that exists in the universe respond "Amen."

Let all those who believe that Jesus Christ is the Father's only son and that he is equal to the Father in every way, respond "Amen."

Let all those who believe that Jesus became a human being through the power of the Spirit and was born of the Virgin Mary, respond "Amen."

Let all those who believe that Jesus truly suffered and died and that by his death he redeemed us from the power of evil, respond "Amen."

And let all those who believe that he will come again in glory to judge the living and the dead, respond "Amen."

Let all those who believe that the Holy Spirit is equal to the Father and the Son, and is the giver of life, respond "Amen."

Let all those who believe that the Spirit came down upon the disciples at Pentecost and still works in the midst of the church today, respond "Amen."

Let all those who believe that Jesus established one, holy, universal, and apostolic church, and that it is called to share in God's eternal life, respond "Amen."

This is the faith of the church and our faith. We are proud to profess it and give thanks to God.

Arnaldo Figueroa[57]

306 ✦ PRAYER OF THANKSGIVING FOR PENTECOST EUCHARIST

The following prayer of thanksgiving for the liturgy of the Lord's Supper includes the themes of the Scripture readings for this day.

MINISTER: The Lord be with you.
PEOPLE: **And also with you.**
MINISTER: Lift up your hearts.
PEOPLE: **We lift them to the Lord.**
MINISTER: Let us give thanks to the Lord our God.
PEOPLE : **It is right to give our thanks and praise.**

MINISTER: It is truly right and our greatest joy
to give you thanks and praise,
eternal God, creator and rule of the universe.
With the majesty of your hand,
you shaped this world and all that is in it.
By your Holy Spirit,
you breathed life into human form,
and set us on the earth to praise and serve you.
When we wandered from your ways
and were lost in sin's wilderness,
your truth burned in the hearts of prophets
who called your people to return to the path of righteousness.
In the fullness of time
you sent your Son to be our deliverer.
In every age your Holy Spirit has led us in your ways.

Therefore we praise you,
joining our voices with choirs of angels
and with all the faithful of every time and place,
who forever sing to the glory of your name:

(The people may sing or say:)

**Holy, holy, holy Lord, God of power and might,
heaven and earth are full of your glory.
Hosanna in the highest.**

**Blessed is he who comes in the name of the Lord.
Hosanna in the highest.**

(The minister continues:)

You are holy, O God of majesty,

and blessed is Jesus Christ, your Son,
  our Lord.
At his baptism by John,
your Spirit came with gentle wings,
settling on him your blessing.
In the wilderness of temptation,
your Spirit stood by with power.
In his life and ministry,
our Spirit led him to serve the poor,
proclaim freedom from sin's bondage,
open eyes with faith's sight,
and befriend the friendless and the
  outcast.
In all he did and said,
he announced the coming of your
  saving might.
By his death on the cross and rising
  from the tomb,
he broke the power of death,
and led the way to eternal life.
Ascended to rule from on high,
Christ prays for us and promises the
  coming of peace and power.

(If they have not already been said, the words
of institution may be said here, or in relation
to the breaking of the bread.)

MINISTER: We give you thanks that the Lord Jesus,
on the night before he died,
took bread,
and after giving thanks to you,
he broke it, and gave it to his disciples, saying:
Take, eat.
This is my body, given for you.
Do this in remembrance of me.
In the same way he took the cup, saying:
This cup is the new covenant sealed
  in my blood,
shed for you for the forgiveness of
  sins.
Whenever you drink it,
  do this in remembrance of me.

Remembering all your mighty and
  merciful acts,
we take this bread and this wine
from the gifts you have given us,
and celebrate with joy

the redemption won for us in Jesus
  Christ.
Accept this our sacrifice of praise and
  thanksgiving
as a living and holy offering of ourselves,
that our lives may proclaim the One
  crucified and risen.

(The people may sing or say one of the following:)

1
MINISTER: Great is the mystery of faith:
PEOPLE: **Christ has died,**
Christ is risen,
Christ will come again.

2
MINISTER: Praise to you, Lord Jesus:
PEOPLE: **Dying you destroyed our death,**
rising you restored our life.
Lord Jesus, come in glory.

3
MINISTER: According to his commandment:
PEOPLE: **We remember his death,**
we proclaim his resurrection
we await his coming in glory.

4
MINISTER: Christ is the bread of life:
PEOPLE: **When we eat this bread and drink**
this cup,
we proclaim your death, Lord Jesus,
until you come in glory.

(The minister continues:)

Gracious God,
pour out your Holy Spirit upon us
and upon these your gifts of bread
  and wine,
that the bread we break
and the cup we bless
may be the communion of the body
  and blood of Christ.
By your Spirit unite us with the living
  Christ,
and with all who are baptized in his
  name,
that we may be one in ministry in
  every place.
As this bread is Christ's body for us,

send us out to be the body of Christ
in the world.

(Intercessions for the church and the world may
be included here.)

By the fire of your Spirit, O God, forge
us into one church,
many and different people, together
in Christ's embrace.
Set our hearts aflame with a love for
the truth
and the desire to do your will,
that our witness to Christ may burn
brightly
in lives of joyful discipleship.
Keep us faithful in your service
until Christ comes in final victory
and we shall feast with all your saints
in the joy of your eternal realm.

Through Christ,
all glory and honor are yours, almighty Father,
with the Holy Spirit in the holy
church,
now and forever.

PEOPLE: **Amen.**

Book of Common Worship[58]

307 ✦ A Pentecost Blessing

*This blessing combines the themes of Easter and Pente-
cost and is especially appropriate for use on Pentecost
Sunday.*

LEADER: Go forth in the power of the Holy
Spirit! Proclaim the gospel throughout the earth! Serve the Lord with
gladness in the power of the kingdom
and with deeds of justice and mercy.

PEOPLE: **We are sent in the name and power
of the Lord!**

LEADER: May the God who raised Jesus from
the dead bless you.

PEOPLE: **Amen.**

LEADER: May the God to whom our Lord ascended make his face shine upon you
and be gracious to you.

PEOPLE: **Amen.**

LEADER: May the Spirit who is the unity of love

between Father and Son, grant you
peace forevermore.

PEOPLE: **Amen. Thanks be to God.**

Randolph W. Sly

308 ✦ Bibliography for the Seasons of Lent, Holy Week, and Easter

Aho, Gerhard, Kenneth Rogahn, and Richard
Kapfer. *Glory and the Cross: Fruit of the Spirit
from the Passion of Christ.* St. Louis: Concordia,
1984. This book provides Lenten resources that
relate the "fruit of the Spirit" (Gal. 5:22-23a) to
events in the Easter Week. The material includes
sermonic studies that present a "fruit" in light
of a text from the Passion narrative; four- to five-
page homilies on a characteristic as seen in the
passion of Christ; and worship resources—liturgies that emphasize the themes being proclaimed. Includes extensive word studies,
alternative sermon outlines, and a variety of
homiletical resources with a large number of
illustrations. Ecumenical/Lutheran.

Akehurst, Peter R. *Keeping Holy Week.* Bramcote,
Notts., U.K.: Grove Books, 1976. This booklet
examines traditions and methods for keeping
Holy Week. The reader or local Christian community can use this resource to make its observance a pastoral and evangelistic event relevant
to both church and the community at large. The
text considers the historic frame of reference
for keeping the week, advocates a narrative approach, lists options for potential implementation, and presents a theological and practical
context in which decisions can be made. Ecumenical.

Berger, Rupert, and Hans Hollerweger, eds. *Celebrating the Easter Vigil.* New York: Pueblo Publishing, 1983. The authors propose to reform
the triduum and Easter celebration by deepening spiritual understanding of the event and
providing a more experiential celebration
through more intensive homiletic explanation
and sound principles of liturgical theology. Introductory chapters on biblical roots and content and form of the Easter Vigil are followed
by homily series for each of the three years in
the A, B and C cycles. Section III is devoted to
the celebration of Easter as the feast of feasts

(with pastoral and liturgical suggestions for its conduct), and an entire chapter is devoted to importance and execution of music at the event. The volume finally extends the Easter celebration to parish and family in three chapters that detail a Saturday children's celebration and provide suggestions for Easter Sunday and home observance. Ecumenical/Roman Catholic.

Chilson, Richard. *A Lenten Pilgrimage*. New York: Paulist, 1983. A guide to the season of Lent as a season of preparation for baptism. Includes reflections on both the Scripture readings and the services for the season, and a large collection of supplemental liturgical resources for the season. Roman Catholic/ecumenical.

Cotter, Theresa. *What Color is Your Lent?* Cincinnati: St. Anthony Messenger Press, 1987. Cotter explores the season of Lent by using color to symbolize various themes (green: hope; gold: gratitude and generosity; blue: responsible stewardship, justice and peace, etc.). Each devotional theme includes an explanation of the use of color related to the theme, a relevant Scripture text, prayer, and suggestions for Lenten projects. There is also a final section of more formal (classic) prayers. ecumenical/Roman Catholic.

Coughlin, Dan, Ron Lewinske, and Gabe Huck. *Parish Path through Lent and Eastertime*. Chicago: Liturgy Training Publications, 1981. A brief overview of the Lent and Easter seasons appropriate for a parish library or group study. Roman Catholic/Ecumenical.

Crichton, J. D. *The Liturgy of Holy Week*. Leominster, Herefordshire, U.K.: Fowler Wright Books, 1983. A brief essay on each service in Holy Week. Roman Catholic.

Days of the Lord. Vol. 2: Lent. Vol. 3: Easter Triduum, Easter Season. Collegeville, Minn.: Liturgical Press, 1991. These volumes are liturgical commentaries, guides for examining and understanding the structure of the post-conciliar reforms of Vatican II. Two- to three-page commentaries for each Sunday in each of the three church years (A, B, and C) are presented with exegetical, pastoral, and liturgical notes. Ecumenical/Roman Catholic.

Flood, Edmund. *Making More of Holy Week*. New York: Paulist, 1983. A commentary on each Holy Week service, with notes that suggest meaningful ways to plan and lead them. Roman Catholic.

Freeman, Eileen Elizabeth. *The Holy Week Book*. San Jose: Resource Publications, 1979. Articles on every aspect of liturgical planning for Holy Week, with information on historical background and theological implications, as well as supplemental liturgical texts, all presented in an accessible format.

Greenacre, Roger, and Jeremy Haselock. *The Sacrament of Easter*. Leominster, Herefordshire, U.K.: Gracewing Publications, 1989. A theological description and analysis of the services of Holy Week and Easter in light of the Paschal feast. Anglican/ecumenical.

Hartgen, William E. *Planning Guide for Lent and Holy Week*. Glendale, Ariz.: Pastoral Arts Associates, 1979. Suggestions for planning each of the services of Holy Week.

Hopko, Thomas. *The Lenten Spring*. Crestwood, N.Y.: St. Vladimir's Seminary Press, 1983. The author takes a refreshingly upbeat tone in this collection of forty original meditations built around scriptural and liturgical passages from Lenten services. He presents the wisdom and teaching of both ancient and modern authors, guides, and saints from many church traditions. Text includes Hopko's pastoral insights and illustrations. Ecumenical/Roman Catholic.

Huck, Gabe. *The Three Days*. Chicago: Liturgy Training Publications, 1981. Huck has prepared a very practical guide to parish celebration of the triduum. It may be used by planners and ministers in order to gain a heightened awareness of the overall movement of the liturgy and to learn detailed insight for rites and particular items that may be used in celebration. There are liturgical notes for each day as well as appendices that offer practical suggestions regarding dress, music, and decorations used in celebrations. Ecumenical/Roman Catholic.

Huck, Gabe, and Mary Ann Simcoe, eds. *A Triduum Sourcebook*. Chicago: Liturgy Training Publications, 1983. A comprehensive compilation of prayers from many sources, both ancient and modern, and from many traditions. The material is grouped under headings that relate to each of the liturgies celebrated at triduum and on Easter Sunday. Includes a large section of initiation prayers. Ecumenical/Roman Catholic.

Huck, Gabe, Gail Ramshaw, and Gordon Lathrop, eds. *An Easter Sourcebook: The Fifty Days*. Chicago: Liturgy Training Publications, 1988.

This unique volume divides the fifty days from Easter Sunday to Pentecost into seven thematic weeks that teach the significance of Easter as an initiation into the mysteries of God, salvation, and the church. Weekly themes are: Creation, Table, Ark, Pasture, Garden, Palace, and Temple. Each daily reading considers a new (often unusual and surprising) subject related to the weekly theme and consists of an opening, Scripture text, commentary, reinforcing prose/poetry and/or Scripture, and a closing element which may be used as a prayer. Ecumenical.

Irwin, Kevin W. *Lent: A Guide to the Eucharist and the Hours.* New York: Pueblo Publishing, 1985. A handbook to each service in the Lenten season, including eucharistic and daily prayer services. Roman Catholic/ecumenical.

————. *Easter: A Guide to the Eucharist and the Hours.* New York: Pueblo Publishing, 1991. A handbook to each service in the Easter season, including eucharistic and daily prayer services. Roman Catholic/ecumenical.

Lesser Feasts and Fasts. New York: Church Hymnal Corporation, 1988. This volume provides propers for the weekdays of Lent and those following the Second Sunday of Easter; a revision of the collects for the Lesser Feasts to emphasize more distinctively the person's or feast's specific contribution or character, complete with detailed biographical sketches for homiletic purposes; and brief notes on the significance of major holy days and feasts. Ecumenical/Episcopal.

MacGregor, A. J. *Fire and Light in the Western Triduum: Their Use at Tenebrae and at the Paschal Vigil.* The Alcuin Club Collection no. 71. Collegeville, Minn.: Liturgical Press, 1992. An insightful, scholarly book on the history of Tenebrae and Easter Vigil, with particular attention to the symbols of fire and light which are prominent in the texts and ceremonies of both services. Ecumenical.

Manning, Michael. *Pardon My Lenten Smile.* New York: Alba House, 1976. Manning's original homily-meditations are reflections on Scripture passages for the five weeks of Lent and Holy Week which include personal insights and experiences, short stories, parables, sometimes plays, and a prayer. They are refreshing, honest, very contemporary, and will put a smile on your face. Ecumenical.

Nocent, Adrian. *The Liturgical Year.* Vol. 2. Collegeville, Minn.: Liturgical Press, 1977. This volume covers the season of Lent and is divided into two parts: (1) biblico-liturgical reflections on Lent and (2) structure and themes of the Lenten liturgy. The elements of scriptural exegesis, historical/cultural context, and liturgical/pastoral commentary are thoughtful, scholarly, and very interesting. Material covers all three years in the church-year cycle. Ecumenical/Roman Catholic.

————. *The Liturgical Year.* Vol. 3. Collegeville, Minn.: Liturgical Press, 1977. This volume covers the period of the paschal triduum and the Easter season. The commentary is divided into two major parts: (1) biblico-liturgical reflections on the triduum and at the structure and themes of the three days of Holy Week and (2) the structure and themes of Easter Sunday and the Easter season. Scriptural exegesis, historical/cultural context, and liturgical/pastoral commentary are valuable. Ecumenical/Roman Catholic.

Nouwen, Henri. *Walk with Jesus: Stations of the Cross.* Maryknoll, N.Y.: Orbis Books, 1990. Nouwen's book is a collection of original meditations that juxtapose individual stories of contemporary suffering from many cultures with the passion of Christ at Easter. They are compassionate, moving accounts that help the modern mind to appropriate more fully the story of Jesus. Sister Helen David's beautiful artwork is an integral part of the presentation. Ecumenical.

Schmemann, Alexander. *Great Lent.* Crestwood, N.Y.: St. Vladimir's Seminary Press, 1969. This volume is an especially valuable insight into the richness of the life, thought, and worship tradition of Eastern Orthodox spirituality of the "Journey to Pascha" at Lent and Easter. Schmemann intends to "soften" our hearts for Easter in his discourses on preparation for Lent; Lenten worship, journey and lifestyle; and the sacraments and the Liturgy of the Presanctified Gifts. Ecumenical/Orthodox.

Shepherd, J. Barrie. *A Pilgrim's Way.* Louisville: Westminster/John Knox, 1989. Shepherd's book contains fifty unique meditations on Scripture for the morning and evening prayer of each day in Lent, up to and including Easter. The prayer diary is based on readings in the Common Lectionary. The author advises the reader to keep a notepad handy for the recording of additional insights. Ecumenical.

Simcoe, Mary Ann, ed. *Parish Path through Lent and Eastertime.* Chicago: Liturgy Training Publications, 1985. This concise volume is written for liturgy, clergy, and RCIA teams. It is a guide for the forty days of Lent and fifty days of Eastertime that contains an overview of the seasons, tying together the use of the lectionary, prayer texts, rites of initiation, music, environment and art, and preaching. Material covers all years in the church cycle and contains many pastoral and practical insights. Ecumenical/Roman Catholic.

Stevenson, Kenneth. *Jerusalem Revisited: The Liturgical Meaning of Holy Week.* Washington, D.C.: Pastoral Press, 1988. Stephenson reconsiders the meaning of Holy Week with a revealing and sometimes humorous look at the rituals for the purpose of lending new understandings for faith and the church through the liturgy. The prologue takes both a historical and pietistic perspective on the development of the season. Discourses on the traditions and reforms of Palm Sunday, the paschal supper and accompanying events, Good Friday and Easter—especially emphasizing the paschal liturgy—constitute the remainder of this enlightening volume. Ecumenical/Anglican.

Stuhlmueller, Carroll. *Biblical Meditations for Advent and the Easter Season.* New York: Paulist, 1980. Each meditation is "born from that fertile moment of combining the inspiration of the [first and second] Bible passages" (along with a third on Sundays) with reflective commentary and a prayer in order that new insights may be achieved and spiritual renewal take place. Weekdays of the Easter season and Sundays from Easter to Pentecost are included. Meditations may be used privately or publicly. Ecumenical/Roman Catholic.

Thompson, William. *Hands of Lent.* Lima, Ohio: C.S.S. Publishing, 1989. Using the imagery of hands, the authors have written a complete worship and preaching program for Lent and Easter day which includes services for the impositions of ashes, Good Friday Tenebrae, six children's services (with object lessons), and complete liturgies that may be duplicated. Themes include dirty hands (Ash Wednesday), seeking, hurting, nervous, angry, estranged, serving, pierced, and living hands. Ecumenical/ Lutheran.

Wangerin, Walter. *Reliving the Passion.* St. Louis: Creative Communications for the Parish, 1988. The pamphlet is a collection of brief, original, and contemporary devotional meditations with prayers on select Scripture texts for those making the Lenten journey from Ash Wednesday to Easter. The dramatic narrative style is theologically sound, offering the minister of liturgy the opportunity to use them in a larger public forum. Ecumenical.

See also article #164, the bibliography of general resources for the Christian year. All of the resources listed there include resources for Lent, Holy Week, and Easter worship.

PART EIGHT

The Season after Pentecost and Other Commemorations

One of the reasons that the Christian year is so widely used is that it is both fixed and flexible. It is firmly rooted in the Christ event, the paschal mystery. The primary Christian celebrations of Christmas and Epiphany, Easter and Pentecost call attention to the dying and rising of Christ. The Christian year also calls attention to other themes, people, and events in light of the paschal mystery. Many important commemorations occur during the long season after Pentecost. The two chapters that follow present both introductions to these topics and resources for planning worship.

✿ TWENTY-EIGHT ✿

The Season after Pentecost

The season between Pentecost and Advent is known as ordinary time, or nonfestive time. During this season, many worship traditions follow lectionaries that highlight the work of the Spirit in the mission of the church in the world. Other churches organize their worship life around a lectio continua, continuous readings from a given section of Scripture. Some worship traditions have also called this season "kingdomtide," focusing on the kingdom of God that is present now and the one that will be realized in more profound ways in the future. This chapter includes resources for planning worship during this season.

309 • AN INTRODUCTION TO THE ORDINARY TIME AFTER PENTECOST

The season from Pentecost to the beginning of Advent is ordinary, or nonfestive, time. During this season, the church focuses on its vision for witness to the world and on God's continuing work in bringing about his kingdom.

Once the festival seasons of Advent, Christmas, Epiphany, Lent, Holy Week, Easter, and Pentecost are over, a long stretch of time known as the nonfestive season, or ordinary time, spans through the summer and fall months until the festive cycle begins again.

Ordinary time has a character that is distinctly different than that of the festal season, particularly in the fact that the various Sundays are not connected by a particular theme. In Advent we await the coming of Christ; during Christmas, we celebrate his arrival; and at Epiphany, we proclaim that Christ is manifested to the world as Savior. During Lent, we prepare for the death; in Holy Week, we reenact his death;, then in Easter, we celebrate his resurrection and complete the Easter cycle with the celebration of the coming of the Holy Spirit. But in the nonfestive season of the church year, there is no unified theme that ties the Sundays together.

What is primary during the season after Pentecost is the simple but powerful meaning of Sunday. Every Sunday is the celebration of the death and resurrection of Jesus, the paschal mystery through which we and the world are saved. In this celebration is the promise of a restored human person and a re-created world. Because Christ dethroned the power of evil on the cross, we live in the expectancy of his ultimate triumph over evil and the redemption of the world from the kingdom of darkness.

The festive time of the church year is also rooted in the paschal mystery, but it concentrates on a certain aspect of that mystery: the longing of Israel, the incarnation of the Savior, the manifestation to the world, the expectancy of the death, the events surrounding Christ's death, burial, resurrection, and ascension, and the coming of the Holy Spirit. Thus while every Sunday of the festal season does celebrate the entire paschal mystery, the seasonal themes emphasizes one aspect of the whole. No such seasonal themes exist for the other half of the church year.

Nevertheless, the Common Lectionary has been laid out in such a way that sermons can move through a larger portion of Scripture in a series on a particular book of the Bible, picking up book themes. For example:

Scriptures:		O. T.	*Epistle*	*Gospel*
	Year A:	Genesis Exodus	Romans Philippians 1 Thessalonians	Matthew
	Year B:	1 & 2 Samuel	2 Corinthians Ephesians James Hebrews	Mark
	Year C:	1 & 2 Kings The prophets	Galatians Colossians Hebrews 1 & 2 Timothy	Luke

Preachers and worship planners should be aware that it is not good planning to force a unified theme out of the readings for the nonfestive time, for no such theme exists. And no particular theme is intended by the arrangement of texts in the Common Lectionary. The theme is the paschal mystery, the death and resurrection of Jesus, the central fact and proclamation of the church. And the various texts serve this theme in their own way.

Robert E. Webber

310 ✦ LECTIONARY READINGS FOR THE SUNDAYS IN THE SEASON AFTER PENTECOST

The following are the texts suggested for the Sundays of ordinary time in the Revised Common Lectionary. Brief descriptions of each lesson are provided to aid in recalling the basic theme of each passage.

Unlike the rest of the year, the lessons during the season after Pentecost call for the reading of extended continuous passages from a given book over a span of weeks (*lectio continua*). This necessarily means that the readings for a given week will not follow one particular theme.

——— Year A (1995, 1998, 2001, 2004) ———

SUNDAY	OLD TESTAMENT	PSALM	EPISTLE	GOSPEL
Trinity Sunday (First Sunday after Pentecost). If the Sunday between May 24 and 28 inclusive follows Trinity Sunday, the Proper for the Eighth Sunday after the Epiphany [8] is used.	Deuteronomy 4:32-40	Psalm 8	2 Corinthians 13:5-14, final warnings and a Trinitarian blessing.	Matthew 28:16-20, Jesus sends disciples in the name of Father, Son, and Holy Spirit.
Proper 4 [9], Sunday between May 29 and June inclusive (if after Trinity Sunday)	Genesis 6:9-22; 7:24, 8:14-19, Noah and the Flood.	Psalm 46 or Deut. 11:18-21; Psalm 31:1-5, 19-24	Romans 1:16-17; 3:22b-28, (29-31), we are justified through faith, not through the law.	Matthew 7:21-29, we are not saved by saying, "Lord, Lord."

——— **Year A (1995, 1998, 2001, 2004) cont.** ———

SUNDAY	OLD TESTAMENT	PSALM	EPISTLE	GOSPEL
Proper 5 [10], Sunday between June 5 and June 11 inclusive (if after Trinity Sunday)	Genesis 12:1-9, God calls Abram, "leave your homeland."	Psalm 33:1-12 or Hosea 5:15–16:5; Psalm 50:7-15	Romans 4:13-25, Abraham counted righteous through faith.	Matthew 9:9-13, 18-26, Jesus calls Matthew; he came to call outcasts.
Proper 6 [11], Sunday between June 12 and June 18 inclusive (if after Trinity Sunday)	Genesis 18:1-15, (21:1-7), call of Abraham, promise of a son.	Psalm 116:1-2, 12-19 or Exodus 19:2-8a; Psalm 100	Romans 5:1-8, we have been put right with God by faith.	Matthew 9:35–10:8, (9-23), Jesus preaches, heals, sends out the Twelve.
Proper 7 [12], Sunday between June 19 and June 25 inclusive (if after Trinity Sunday)	Genesis 21:8-21, rivalry of sons, Ishmael sent away.	Psalm 86:1-10, 16-17 or Jeremiah 20:7-13, Psalm 69:7-10, (11-15), 16-18	Romans 6:1b-11, we are dead to sin and alive in Christ.	Matthew 10:24-39, don't fear people, stand in awe of Christ.
Proper 8 [13], Sunday between June 26 and July 2 inclusive	Genesis 22:1-14; Abraham tested, sacrifice of Isaac.	Psalm 13 or Jeremiah 28:5-9; Psalm 89:1-4, 15-18	Romans 6:12-23, we were slaves to sin, now of righteousness.	Matthew 10:40-42, to welcome the other is to welcome Jesus.
Proper 9 [14], Sunday between July 3 and July 9 inclusive	Genesis 24:34-38, 42-29, 59-67, find a wife for Isaac: Rebekah.	Psalm 45:1-17 or Zechariah 9:9-12 or Song of Solomon 2:8-13; Psalm 145:8-14	Romans 7:15-25a, the conflict within us. Thank God for Christ!	Matthew 11:16-19, 25-30, come to me and rest, take my yoke.
Proper 10 [15], Sunday between July 10 and July 16 inclusive	Genesis 25:19-34, Jacob and Esau, pottage and birthright.	Psalm 119: 105-112 or Isaiah 25: 10-13; Psalm 65:(1-8), 9-13	Romans 8:1-11, live by the Spirit, not by our human nature.	Matthew 13:1-9, 18-23, parable of the sower and the explanation.
Proper 11 [16], Sunday between July 17 and July 23 inclusive	Genesis 28:10-19a, Jacob's dream at Bethel, covenant.	Psalm 139:1-12, 23-24 or Wisdom of Solomon 12:13,16-19 or Isaiah 44:6-8 or Psalm 86:11-17	Romans 8:12-25, since we're God's children, glory in the future.	Matthew 13:24-30, 36-43, parable of the weeds and the explanation.

continued...

——— **Year A (1995, 1998, 2001, 2004) etc.** ———

SUNDAY	OLD TESTAMENT	PSALM	EPISTLE	GOSPEL
Proper 12 [17], Sunday between July 24 and July 30 inclusive	Genesis 29:15-28, Jacob works fourteen years for wives.	Psalm 105:1-11, 45b, or I Kings 3:5-12 or Psalm 128; Psalm 119:129-136,	Romans 8:26-39, sustained in weakness, confidence is in God.	Matthew 13:31-33, 44-52, parables of mustard seed, treasure, pearl, net.
Proper 13 [18], Sunday between July 31 and August 6 inclusive	Genesis 32:22-31, Jacob wrestles angel at Jabbok river.	Psalm 17:1-7, 15 or Isaiah 55:1-5; Psalm 145: 8-9, 14-21	Romans 9:1-5, Paul's pain for his fellow Jews.	Matthew 14:13-21, feeding of the five thousand.
Proper 14 [19], Sunday between August 7 and August 13 inclusive	Genesis 37:1-4, 12-28, Joseph sold into slavery by his brothers.	Psalm 105:1-6, 16-22, 45b or 1 Kings 19:9-18; Psalm 85:8-13	Romans 10:5-15, salvation for all in Christ.	Matthew 14:22-33, Jesus walks on the water.
Proper 15 [20], Sunday between August 14 and August 20 inclusive	Genesis 45:1-15, Joseph makes himself known to his brothers.	Psalm 133 or Isaiah 56:1, 6-8; Psalm 67	Romans 11:1-2a, 29-32, God's salvation for Jew and Gentile.	Matthew 15:(10-20), 21-28, the faith of the Canaanite woman.
Proper 16 [21], Sunday between August 21 and August 27 inclusive	Exodus 1:8–2:10, Israel enslaved in Egypt; Moses is born.	Psalm 124 or Isaiah 51:1-6; Psalm 138	Romans 12:1-8, offer ourselves and our gifts to God.	Matthew 16:13-20, "Who do you say that I am?" "You are the Christ."
Proper 17 [22], Sunday between August 28 and September 3 inclusive	Exodus 3:1-15, God calls Moses from the burning bush.	Psalm 105:1-6, 23-26, 45c or Jeremiah 15:15-21; Psalm 26:1-8	Romans 12:9-21, exhortation to life in God's service.	Matthew 16:21-28, Jesus: about suffering, cost of discipleship.
Proper 18 [23], Sunday between September 4 and September 10 inclusive	Exodus 12:1-14, account of the Passover.	Psalm 149 or Ezekiel 33:7-11; Psalm 119:33-40	Romans 13:8-14, duties of Christians toward one another.	Matthew 18:15-20, discipline of followers; where two or three are, I am.

——— **Year A (1995, 1998, 2001, 2004) cont.** ———

SUNDAY	OLD TESTAMENT	PSALM	EPISTLE	GOSPEL
Proper 19 [24], Sunday between September 11 and September 17 inclusive	Exodus 14:19-31, crossing of Red Sea; songs of Moses, Miriam.	Psalm 114 or Genesis 50:15-21; Psalm 103:(1-7), 8-13 or Exodus 15:1b-11, 20-21	Romans 14:1-12, welcome the other, do not judge.	Matthew 18:21-35, parable of the unforgiving servant,
Proper 20 [25], Sunday between September 18 and September 24 inclusive	Exodus 16:2-15 , God feeds Israel manna and quail.	Psalm 105:1-6, 37-45 or Jonah 3:10–4:11; Psalm 145: 1-8	Philippians 1:21-30, "for me, to live is Christ."	Matthew 20:1-16, parable of the workers in the vineyard.
Proper 21 [26], Sunday between September 25 and October 1 inclusive	Exodus 17:1-7, God gives them water from the rock.	Psalm 78:1-4, 12-16 or Ezekiel 18:1-4, 25-32; Psalm 25:1-9	Philippians 2:1-13, the greatness of Christ, who emptied himself.	Matthew 21:23-32, questioning of Jesus' authority; parable of two sons.
Proper 22 [27], Sunday between October 2 and October 8 inclusive	Exodus 20:1-4, 7-9, 12-20, the Ten Commandments.	Psalm 19 or Isaiah 5:1-7; Psalm 80:7-15	Philippians 3:4b-14, pressing toward the goal.	Matthew 21:33-46, parable of the tenants in the vineyard.
Proper 23 [28], Sunday between October 9 and October 15 inclusive	Exodus 32:1-14, the golden calf.	Psalm 106:1-6, 19-23 or Isaiah 25:1-9; Psalm 23	Philippians 4:1-9, instructions for the faithful.	Matthew 22:1-14, parable of the wedding feast.
Proper 24 [29], Sunday between October 16 and October 22 inclusive	Exodus 33:12-23, God promises to be with Israel.	Psalm 99 or Isaiah 45:1-7; Psalm 96:1-9, (10-13)	1 Thessalonians 1:1-10, thanks for your example, others admire it	Matthew 22:15-22, the question about paying taxes
Proper 25 [30], Sunday between October 23 and October 29 inclusive	Deuteronomy 34:1-12, Moses gives final blessing and dies.	Psalm 90:1-6, 13-17 or Leviticus 19:1-2, 15-18 or Psalm 1	1 Thessalonians 2:1-8, Paul's faithfulness as their teacher.	Matthew 22:34-46, greatest commandment; the Messiah as Son of David.

continued...

──────── **Year A (1995, 1998, 2001, 2004) cont.** ────────

SUNDAY	OLD TESTAMENT	PSALM	EPISTLE	GOSPEL
Proper 26 [31], Sunday between October 30 and November 5 inclusive	Joshua 3:7-17, Ark of the covenant; waters of Jordan stop flowing.	Psalm 107:1-7, 33-37 or Micah 3:5-12; Psalm 43	1 Thessalonians 2:9-13, the witness of the Thessalonians, Paul's work with them.	Matthew 23:1-12, Jesus and the Pharisees: do what they do, not say.
Proper 27 [32], Sunday between November 6 and November 12 inclusive	Joshua 24:1-3a, 14-25, covenant at Shechem, "choose whom you will serve."	Psalm 78:1-7 or Wisdom of Solomon 6:12-16 or Amos 5:18-24; Wisdom of Solomon 6:17-20 or Psalm 70	1 Thessalonians 4:13-18, what will happen on the Day of the Lord.	Matthew 25:1-13, parable of ten girls and oil lamps.
Proper 28 [33], Sunday between November 13 and November 19 inclusive	Judges 4:1-7, Deborah and Barak.	Psalm 123 or Zephaniah 1:7, 12-18; Psalm 90:1-8, (9-11), 12	1 Thessalonians 5:1-11, be ready for the Day, which will come unexpectedly.	Matthew 25:14-30, parable of the talents.
Proper 29 [34], (Reign of Christ or Christ the King), Sunday between November 20 and November 26 inclusive	Ezekiel 34:11-16, 20-24, "I am the shepherd and will care for my sheep."	Psalm 100 or Psalm 95:1-7a or Ezekiel 34:11-16, 20-24	Ephesians 1:15-23, Paul's prayer that they will receive the Spirit.	Matthew 25:31-46, final judgment: when did we see you?

──────── **Year B (1993, 1996, 1999, 2002, 2005)** ────────

SUNDAY	OLD TESTAMENT	PSALM	EPISTLE	GOSPEL
Trinity Sunday (First Sunday after Pentecost). If the Sunday between May 24 and 28 inclusive follows Trinity Sunday, the Proper for the Eighth Sunday after the Epiphany [8] is used.	Isaiah 6:1-8, Isaiah's vision in the temple and his call.	Psalm 29	Romans 8:12-17, we live by the Spirit as children of God.	John 3:1-17, Jesus and Nicodemus, "God so loved the world."

——— **Year B (1993, 1996, 1999, 2002, 2005) cont.** ———

SUNDAY	OLD TESTAMENT	PSALM	EPISTLE	GOSPEL
Proper 4 [9], Sunday between May 29 and June 4 inclusive (if after Trinity Sunday)	1 Samuel 3:1-10, (11-20), call of Samuel; "speak, your servant hears."	Psalm 139:1-6, 13-18 or Deuteronomy 5:12-15; Psalm 81:1-10	2 Corinthians 4:5-12, preaching Christ; treasure in clay pots.	Mark 2:23–3:6, Jesus breaks the Sabbath; it was made for humans.
Proper 5 [10], Sunday between June 5 and June 11 inclusive (if after Trinity Sunday)	1 Samuel 8:4-11, (12-15), 16-20, (11:14-15), people demand a king; Saul is anointed king.	Psalm 138 or Genesis 3:8-15, (11:14-15); Psalm 130	2 Corinthians 4:13–5:1, God, who raised Jesus, will raise us too.	Mark 3:20-35, Jesus and Satan; Jesus and his family.
Proper 6 [11], Sunday between June 12 and June 18 inclusive (if after Trinity Sunday)	1 Samuel 15:34–16:13, Samuel deserts Saul; David is anointed.	Psalm 20 or Ezekiel 17:22-24; Psalm 92:1-4, 12-15	2 Corinthians 5:6-10, (11-13), 14-17, living by faith, pleasing the Lord.	Mark 4:26-34, parables of growing seed and mustard seed.
Proper 7 [12], Sunday between June 19 and June 25 inclusive (if after Trinity Sunday)	1 Samuel 17:(1a, 4-11, 19-23), 32-49, David and Goliath.	Psalm 9:9-20 or 1 Samuel 17:57–18:5, 10-16; Psalm 133 or Job 38:1-11; Psalm 107:1-3, 23-32	2 Corinthians 6:1-13, now is the time; we are God's servants.	Mark 4:35–5:13, Jesus calms the storm, heals disturbed man.
Proper 8 [13], Sunday between June 26 and July 2 inclusive	2 Samuel 1:1, 17-27, David's lament for Saul and Jonathan.	Psalm 130 or Wisdom of Solomon 1:13-15, 2:23-24; Lamentations 3:23-33 or Psalm 30	2 Corinthians 8:7-15, Christian giving and help for the poor.	Mark 5:21-43, raising young girl from the dead, healing sick woman.
Proper 9 [14], Sunday between July 3 and July 9 inclusive	2 Samuel 5:1-5, 9-10, David becomes king, establishes Jerusalem.	Psalm 48 or Ezekiel 2:1-5; Psalm 123	2 Corinthians 12:2-10, Paul's afflictions; God's vision and grace.	Mark 6:1-13, Jesus rejected at Nazareth, sends out the Twelve.
Proper 10 [15], Sunday between July 10 and July 16 inclusive	2 Samuel 6:1-5, 12b-19, ark of covenant brought to Jerusalem.	Psalm 24 or Amos 7:7-15; Psalm 85:8-13	Ephesians 1:3-14, spiritual blessings in Christ; chosen by God.	Mark 6:14-29, death of John the Baptist.

continued...

——— Year B (1993, 1996, 1999, 2002, 2005) cont. ———

SUNDAY	OLD TESTAMENT	PSALM	EPISTLE	GOSPEL
Proper 11 [16], Sunday between July 17 and July 23 inclusive	2 Samuel 7:1-16, God's covenant with David.	Psalm 89:20-37 or Jeremiah 23:1-6; Psalm 23	Ephesians 2:11-22, we are all one in Christ, who is our peace.	Mark 6:30-34, 53-56, teaches from boat, heals the sick.
Proper 12 [17], Sunday between July 24 and July 30 inclusive	2 Samuel 11:1-15, David and Bathsheba; Uriah sent to death.	Psalm 14 or 2 Kings 4:42-44; Psalm 145:10-18	Ephesians 3:14-21, Paul's prayer that we know Christ's love.	John 6:1-21, feeding of the multitude; walking on water.
Proper 13 [18], Sunday between July 31 and August 6 inclusive	2 Samuel 11:26-12:13a, Nathan's parable of the sheep: "You are that man."	Psalm 51:1-12 or Exodus 16:2-4, 9-15; Psalm 78:23-29	Ephesians 4:1-6, show your love by keeping unity of the body.	John 6:24-35, "I am the bread of life."
Proper 14 [19], Sunday between August 7 and August 13 inclusive	2 Samuel 18:5-9, 15, 31-33, David and Absalom; Absalom killed.	Psalm 130 or 1 Kings 19:4-8; Psalm 34:1-8	Ephesians 4:25–5:2, live in love as did Christ.	John 6:35, 41-51, "I am the living bread."
Proper 15 [20], Sunday between August 14 and August 20 inclusive	1 Kings 2:10-12; 3:3-14, death of David; Solomon's prayer for wisdom.	Psalm 111 or Proverbs 9:1-6; Psalm 34:9-14	Ephesians 5:15-20, instructions for living the Christian life.	John 6:51-58, whoever eats my flesh has eternal life.
Proper 16 [21], Sunday between August 21 and August 27 inclusive	1 Kings 8:(1, 6, 10-11), 22-30, 41-43, Solomon's prayer in the Temple.	Psalm 84 or Joshua 24:1-2a, 14-18; Psalm 34:15-22	Ephesians 6:10-20, put on the whole armor of God.	John 6:56-69, you have the words that give eternal life.
Proper 17 [22], Sunday between August 28 and September 3 inclusive	Song of Solomon 2:8-13, a season for love.	Psalm 45:1-2, 6-9 or Deuteronomy 4:1-2, 6-9 or Psalm 15	James 1:19-27, true religion acts on God's word.	Mark 7:1-8, 14-15, 21-23, they teach human laws as if they are God's.
Proper 18 [23], Sunday between September 4 and September 10 inclusive	Proverbs 22:1-2, 8-9, 22-23 , wisdom about the poor	Psalm 125 or Isaiah 35:4-7a; Psalm 146	James 2:1-10, (11-13), 14-17, warning over prejudice against the poor.	Mark 7:24-37, Jesus heals deaf and dumb person.
Proper 19 [24], Sunday between September 11 and September 17 inclusive	Proverbs 1:20-33, wisdom calls to the foolish ones.	Psalm 19 or Isaiah 50:4-9a; Psalm 116:1-9.	James 3:1-12, using and controlling the tongue.	Mark 8:27-38, "Who do you say I am?" Messiah must suffer.

——— **Year B (1993, 1996, 1999, 2002, 2005) cont.** ———

SUNDAY	OLD TESTAMENT	PSALM	EPISTLE	GOSPEL
Proper 20 [25], Sunday between September 18 and September 24 inclusive	Proverbs 31:10-31, the woman of the Lord.	Psalm 1 or Wisdom of Solomon 1:16–2:1, 12-22 or Jeremiah 11:18-20; Psalm 54	James 3:13–4:3, 7-8a, wisdom from above; problems arise from desires.	Mark 9:30-37, Jesus speaks of his death.
Proper 21 [26], Sunday between September 25 and October 1 inclusive	Esther 7:1-6, 9-10; 9:20-22, Esther and Haman, basis of festival of Purim.	Psalm 124 or Num. 11:4-6, 10-16, 24-29; Psalm 19:7-14	James 5:13-20, warning to the rich.	Mark 9:38-50, those not against us are for us; put away temptations.
Proper 22 [27], Sunday between October 2 and October 8 inclusive	Job 1:11; 2:1-10, Job is tested by Satan.	Psalm 26 or Genesis 2:18-24; Psalm 8	Hebrews 1:1-4, 2:5-12, God's word through the Son leads us to salvation.	Mark 10:2-16, teaching marriage and divorce; Jesus blesses children.
Proper 23 [28], Sunday between October 9 and October 15 inclusive	Job 23:1-9, 16-17, Job looks for God to present his case.	Psalm 22:1-15 or Amos 5:6-7, 10-15; Psalm 90:12-17	Hebrews 4:12-16, Word is sharper than sword: be of courage	Mark 10:17-31, rich young ruler; kingdom of God difficult for wealthy
Proper 24 [29], Sunday between October 16 and October 22 inclusive	Job 38:1-7, (34-41), God responds to Job, "I am the Creator."	Psalm 104:1-9, 24, 35c or Isaiah 53:4-12; Psalm 91:9-16	Hebrews 5:1-10, Jesus became perfect; God chose him as High Priest.	Mark 10:35-45, James and John request special treatment.
Proper 25 [30], Sunday between October 23 and October 29 inclusive	Job 42:1-6, 10-17, Job responds: "You are all-powerful. I repent."	Psalm 34:1-8, (19-22) or Jeremiah 31:7-9; Psalm 126	Hebrews 7:23-28, Jesus our High Priest always intercedes for us.	Mark 10:46-52, Jesus heals the blind Bartimaeus.
Proper 26 [31], Sunday between October 30 and November 5 inclusive	Ruth 1:1-18, Ruth to Naomi: "Where you go, I will go."	Psalm 146 or Deuteronomy 6:1-9; Psalm 119:1-8	Hebrews 9:11-14, through Christ's offering of his blood we are made clean.	Mark 12:28-34, the greatest commandment.
Proper 27 [32], Sunday between November 6 and November 12 inclusive	Ruth 3:1-5; 4:13-17, Ruth marries again; son is ancestor of David.	Psalm 127 or 1 Kings 17:8-16; Psalm 146	Hebrews 9:24-28, Jesus is High Priest, is priest forever.	Mark 12:38-44, warning about Pharisees; widow's mite.

continued...

——— **Year B (1993, 1996, 1999, 2002, 2005) cont.** ———

SUNDAY	OLD TESTAMENT	PSALM	EPISTLE	GOSPEL
Proper 28 [33], Sunday between November 13 and November 19 inclusive	1 Samuel 1:4-20, Hannah and Eli, birth of Samuel.	1 Samuel 2:1-10 or Daniel 12:1-3; Psalm 16	Hebrews 10:11-14, (15-18), 19-25, Christ takes away sins once for all.	Mark 13:1-8, warning about the end times.
Proper 29 [34], (Reign of Christ or Christ the King), Sunday between November 20 and November 26 inclusive	2 Samuel 23:1-7, David's final words, God's eternal covenant or Daniel 7:9-10, 13-14, judgment before the Ancient of Days.	Psalm 132:1-12, (13-18) or Psalm 93	Revelation 1:4b-8, Jesus the king makes us a kingdom of priests.	John 18:33-37, Jesus' kingdom is not of this world.

——— **Year C (1994, 1997, 2000, 2003)** ———

SUNDAY	OLD TESTAMENT	PSALM	EPISTLE	GOSPEL
Trinity Sunday (First Sunday after Pentecost). If the Sunday between May 24 and 28 inclusive follows Trinity Sunday, Proper for Eighth Sunday after the Epiphany [8] is used.	Proverbs 8:1-4, 22-31, God created world through Wisdom, the master worker.	Psalm 8	Romans 5:1-5, God's love poured into us through Holy Spirit.	John 16:12-15, the Spirit will guide you in all truth and glorify me.
Proper 4 [9], Sunday between May 29 and June 4 inclusive (if after Trinity Sunday)	1 Kings 18:20-21, (22-29), 30-39, Elijah and the prophets of Baal on Mt. Carmel.	Psalm 96 or 1 Kings 8:22-23, 41-43; Psalm 96:1-9	Galatians 1:1-12, preach gospel of Christ not one of human origin.	Luke 7:1-10, Jesus heals servant of a Roman officer.
Proper 5 [10], Sunday between June 5 and June 11 inclusive (if after Trinity Sunday)	1 Kings 17:8-16, (17-24), Elijah raises son of widow of Zarephath.	Psalm 146 or 1 Kings 17:17-24; Psalm 30	Galatians 1:11-24, Paul's testimony: going from enemy to apostle.	Luke 7:11-17, Jesus raises son of a widow of Nain.

—————— **Year C (1994, 1997, 2000, 2003) cont.** ——————

SUNDAY	OLD TESTAMENT	PSALM	EPISTLE	GOSPEL
Proper 6 [11], Sunday between June 12 and June 18 inclusive (if after Trinity Sunday)	1 Kings 21:1-10, (11-14), 15-21a, Naboth's vineyard; disaster to follow.	Psalm 5:1-8 or 2 Samuel 11:26–12:10, 13-15; Psalm 32	Galatians 2:15-21, Paul disputes: Gentiles saved not by law but grace.	Luke 7:36–8:3, Jesus in home of Pharisee, women followed.
Proper 7 [12], Sunday between June 19 and June 25 inclusive (if after Trinity Sunday)	1 Kings 19:1-4, (5-7), 8-15a, "Even I only am left." The still small voice.	Psalm 42 and 43 or Isaiah 65:1-9; Psalm 22:19-28	Galatians 3:23-29, law in charge until Christ, now we are saved by faith.	Luke 8:26-39, Jesus heals Gerasene man with demons.
Proper 8 [13], Sunday between June 26 and July 2 inclusive	2 Kings 2:1-2, 6-14, Elijah goes up in chariot; Elisha asks for Spirit.	Psalm 77:1-2, 11-20 or 1 Kings 19:15-16, 19-21; Psalm 16	Galatians 5:1, 13-25, don't become slaves again; what living by the Spirit does.	Luke 9:51-62, he set his face for Jerusalem; the cost of discipleship.
Proper 9 [14], Sunday between July 3 and July 9 inclusive	2 Kings 5:1-14, Elisha cures leper, Naaman, the Syrian.	Psalm 30 or Isaiah 66:10-14; Psalm 66:1-9	Galatians 6:(1-6), 7-16, it is the Cross that matters, not circumcision.	Luke 10:1-11, 16-20, sending of the seventy; harvest is plentiful.
Proper 10 [15], Sunday between July 10 and July 16 inclusive	Amos 7:7-17, vision of plumb line; Amaziah confronts Amos.	Psalm 82 or Deuteronomy 30:9-14; Psalm 25:1-10	Colossians 1:1-14, I pray you be filled with knowledge of God's will.	Luke 10:25-37, parable of Good Samaritan: Who is my neighbor?
Proper 11 [16], Sunday between July 17 and July 23 inclusive	Amos 8:1-12, vision of fruit basket; doom predicted for Israel.	Psalm 52 or Genesis 18:1-10a; Psalm 15	Colossians 1:15-28, Supremacy of Christ.	Luke 10:38-42, Jesus visits Martha and Mary.
Proper 12 [17], Sunday between July 24 and July 30 inclusive	Hosea 1:2-10, Hosea's marriage, names for the children.	Psalm 85 or Genesis 18:20-32; Psalm 138	Colossians 2:6-15, (16-19), baptized to life in Christ, who forgave our sins.	Luke 11:1-13, Lord's Prayer. God's care for all of us.
Proper 13 [18], Sunday between July 31 and August 6 inclusive	Hosea 11:1-11, God's love for the people: "How can I give you up?"	Psalm 107:1-9, 43 or Ecclesiastes 1:2, 12-14, 2:18-23; Psalm 49:1-12	Colossians 3:1-11, as you have been raised in Christ, put to death the old.	Luke 12:13-21, parable of the rich fool.
Proper 14 [19], Sunday between August 7 and August 13 inclusive	Isaiah 1:1, 10-20, God reprimands people; offerings are useless.	Psalm 50:1-8, 22-23 or Genesis 15:1-6; Psalm 33:12-22	Hebrews 11:1-3, 8-16, the nature of true faith.	Luke 12:32-40, treasure in heaven; be ready.

continued...

————— **Year C (1994, 1997, 2000, 2003) cont.** —————

SUNDAY	OLD TESTAMENT	PSALM	EPISTLE	GOSPEL
Proper 15 [20], Sunday between August 14 and August 20 inclusive	Isaiah 5:1-7, the song of the vineyard; Israel is the vineyard.	Psalm 80:1-2, 8-19, or Jeremiah 23:23-29; Psalm 82	Hebrews 11:29–12:2, surrounded by witnesses, persevere in the race.	Luke 12:49-56, came not to bring peace; a house divided.
Proper 16 [21], Sunday between August 21 and August 27 inclusive	Jeremiah 1:4-10, God calls Jeremiah.	Psalm 71:1-6 or Isaiah 58:9b-14; Psalm 103:1-8	Hebrews 12:18-29, you have come not to fearful Sinai but to living Zion.	Luke 13:24-30, many seek to enter, few will; first will be last.
Proper 17 [22], Sunday between August 28 and September 3 inclusive	Jeremiah 2:4-13, sin of Israel's ancestors, Lord's case against the people.	Psalm 81:1, 10-16 or Sirach 10:12-18 or Proverbs 25:6-7; Psalm 112	Hebrews 13:1-8, 15-16, final advice on Christian conduct: hospitality, love.	Luke 14:1, 7-14, on banquets: where to sit, whom to invite.
Proper 18 [23], Sunday between September 4 and September 10 inclusive	Jeremiah 18:1-11, the parable of the potter: "emend your ways."	Psalm 139:1-6, 13-18 or Deuteronomy 30:15-20; Psalm 1	Philemon 1:1-21, Paul returns a slave, asks for treatment for slave as if it were himself.	Luke 14:25-33, the cost of discipleship: hate family, renounce world.
Proper 19 [24], Sunday between September 11 and September 17 inclusive	Jeremiah 4:11-12, 22-28, threat of God turning Israel to a desert wasteland.	Psalm 14 or Exodus 32:7-14; Psalm 51:1-10	1 Timothy 1:12-17, "Christ came to save sinners: I am foremost."	Luke 15:1-10, parables of lost sheep and lost coins.
Proper 20 [25], Sunday between September 18 and September 24 inclusive	Jeremiah 8:18–9:1, Jeremiah's sorrow for his people; no balm in Gilead?	Psalm 79:1-9 or Amos 8:4-7; Psalm 113	1 Timothy 2:1-7, our intercession for others pleases God.	Luke 16:1-13, parable of shrewd steward; can't serve God and money.
Proper 21 [26], Sunday between September 25 and October 1 inclusive	Jeremiah 32:1-3a, 6-15, Jeremiah buys a field, a parable of hope.	Psalm 91:1-6, 14-16 or Amos 6:1a, 4-7; Psalm 113	1 Timothy 6:6-19, love of money is root of evil; fight the good fight.	Luke 16:19-31, parable of rich man and Lazarus.
Proper 22 [27], Sunday between October 2 and October 8 inclusive	Lamentations 1:1-6, the sorrows of Jerusalem during the exile.	Lamentations 3:19-26 or Psalm 137 or Habakkuk 1:1-4, 2:1-4; Psalm 37:1-9	2 Timothy 1:1-14, guard the truth, proclaim the faith.	Luke 17:5-10, "we are unworthy servants."

——— Year C (1994, 1997, 2000, 2003) cont. ———

SUNDAY	OLD TESTAMENT	PSALM	EPISTLE	GOSPEL
Proper 23 [28], Sunday between October 9 and October 15 inclusive	Jeremiah 29:1, 4-7, his letter to Jews in Babylon: "settle down there."	Psalms 66:1-12 or 2 Kings 5:1-3, 7-15c; Psalm 111	2 Timothy 2:8-15, Paul fettered; Word is not. He remains faithful.	Luke 17:11-19, healing of the ten lepers, only one gives thanks.
Proper 24 [29], Sunday between October 16 and October 22 inclusive	Jeremiah 31:27-34, God will raise them up again; "write the law on your hearts."	Psalm 119:97-104 or Genesis 32:22-31; Psalm 121	2 Timothy 3:14–4:5, Paul's charge: preach the Word.	Luke 18:1-8, parable of judge and persistent widow.
Proper 25 [30], Sunday between October 23 and October 29 inclusive	Joel 2:23-32, rejoice, God will restore fertility in the land.	Psalm 65 or Sirach 35:12-17 or Jeremiah 14:7-10, 19-22 or Psalm 84:1-7	2 Timothy 4:6-8, 16-18, "I have kept the faith. The Lord stood by me."	Luke 18:9-14, parable of Pharisee and tax collector.
Proper 26 [31], Sunday between October 30 and November 5 inclusive	Habakkuk 1:1-4, 2:1-4, prophet complains of injustice; God answers him.	Psalm 119:137-44 or Isaiah 1:10-18; Psalm 32:1-7	2 Thessalonians 1:1-4, 11-12, pray constantly.	Luke 19:1-10, Zaccheus receives Jesus, gives to poor
Proper 27 [32], Sunday between November 6 and November 12 inclusive	Haggai 1:15b–2:9, have hope, new Temple will be splendid.	Psalm 145:1-5, 17-21, or Psalm 98 or Job 19:23-27a; Psalm 17:1-9	2 Thessalonians 2:1-5, 13-17, "Day of the Lord," you are chosen for salvation.	Luke 20:27-38, Sadducees try to trap Jesus about resurrection.
Proper 28 [33], Sunday between November 13 and November 19 inclusive	Isaiah 65:17-25, "I am making a new heaven and earth."	Isaiah 12 or Malachi 4:1-2a; Psalm 98	2 Thessalonians 3:6-13, let all work; do not weary of doing good.	Luke 21:5-19, signs of the end of the age, persecutions first.
Proper 29 [34], (Reign of Christ or Christ the King), Sunday between November 20 and November 26 inclusive	Jeremiah 23:1-6, "I will choose a new king. People will live in peace."	Luke 1:68-79 or Psalm 46	Colossians 1:11-20, all things made through and for Christ.	Luke 23:33-43, Jesus crucified: "Remember me in your kingdom."

Revised Common Lectionary, descriptions by H. A. Tillinghast

311 ◆ PRAYERS FOR THE SEASON AFTER PENTECOST

The following prayers are based on themes contained in Scripture passages and hymns that are used in many worship traditions. Following this set of prayers are suggested Scripture passages on which other prayers can be based.

—— Invocations, or Opening Prayers ——

Come, almighty King, and help us your name to sing, for you are a God of love. Come, incarnate Word, and make known your wonders to our souls, for you are a God of grace. Come, holy Comforter, and bear witness within every heart that we belong to you, for you are a God who creates fellowship. Come, triune God, that we might love and adore you all the days of our lives. Amen.

Commentary: This prayer, focusing on the Trinity, is derived from the hymn "Come, Thou Almighty King," and echoes the themes from 2 Corinthians 13:14 on the specific ministry of each person of the Trinity as the successive stanzas are introduced. This illustrates how the rich language of both Scripture and hymns can interact dynamically in the formation of worship materials. This prayer would be appropriate for use on Trinity Sunday.

Loving God, do not hide your face from us or we will be lost. Speak to our longing spirits with your sustaining Spirit. Show us through the Scriptures how we are to live, for we lift our attentive souls to you. Instruct us in the way of your will, and lead us as only your Spirit can lead. In Jesus' name. Amen.

Commentary: Most of the language for this prayer is a paraphrase of Psalm 143:7, 8b, 10. This portion of Scripture lends itself well to the topic of illumination as the Scriptures are read, preached, and lived.

—— Prayers of Confession and Words of Assurance ——

CONFESSION

Almighty Lord and God, we confess that it is often difficult for us to be your people. You have called us to be the church and to continue the mission of Jesus Christ to our lonely and confused world. Yet in truth, we admit that we are more prone to apathy than action; isolation than involvement; callousness than compassion; obstinance than obedience; legalism than love; rigidness than receptiveness; pessimism than praise; self-filled than Spirit-filled. Gracious Lord, freely pour out your mercy on us and forgive our sins. Remove those obstacles that hinder us from being your representatives in a broken world. Awaken our hearts to the promised gift of your indwelling Spirit...(opportunity for silent confession)...Hear our prayer in Jesus' powerful name. Amen.*

WORDS OF ASSURANCE

UNISON: Hear what our gracious God declares to us: (Ezekiel 36:25-27).

Commentary: The images for this prayer are the result of a composite sketch of the book of Acts. Any one of many stories could be used to further enhance this prayer or create similar models. For example, Acts 12:5-17 suggests a myriad of metaphors for confession. This story captures the doubt-filled and anemic prayers the early church offered for Peter's release from prison. The underlying theme of this prayer is that our hearts are often divided and not properly focused on God. To further reinforce this reality, the words of assurance relate to God's radical heart transplant and cleansing of our lives.

PRAYER OF CONFESSION

Great and mighty God, you have graciously unleashed your Holy Spirit to live and move among us. You call us to come and grow and extend the mission of your church. While we are quick to hear these words, we are often slow to act on them. There is much in our lives that restricts our growth as we nervously cling to the familiar patterns of yesterday. Forgive our resistance, and cleanse us from the sins of disobedience that hinder the flow of your new life in us. Grant us as your children the ability to trust and be open so that we might welcome and depend upon the resources of your Spirit. Fill us, we pray, with this hope as we continue our prayer in silence . . . (opportunity for silent confession) . . . In Jesus' merciful name. Amen.

WORDS OF ASSURANCE

LEADER: (reads Romans 8:27)

PEOPLE: (read Romans 8:1-2)
ALL: (read Romans 8:10-11)

Commentary: A familiar theme for the season following Pentecost is that of the church and her mission in the world. Once again numerous biblical passages capture the tendency of the church to forget her foundation and depend upon herself. Much of this prayer reflects the warning of 1 Thessalonians 5:19 and the witness of Ephesians 5:18b.

Prayers for Illumination

Have your own way, Lord, for you are the potter and we are the clay. Release your Holy Spirit so that as we hear and ponder your Scripture we might be molded and made after the likeness of Christ. Form us with a desire to follow your will. Create within us the cooperation to wait and to surrender ourselves to the shaping of your transforming Spirit. In Jesus' name. Amen.

Commentary: The central image comes from Isaiah 64:8, which in turn has inspired the writing of the hymn "Have Thine Own Way, Lord." Here, the first stanza has been employed to engage us in the shaping power of the Scripture. Too often we read the Bible seeking only information when in reality God desires to form and transform us by the Scriptures.

Almighty God, we are grateful that you communicate your wisdom and truth to us. Prepare us now to receive with eagerness your living and active Word. Blow your Holy Spirit through these pages that they might penetrate deeply into our lives, directing us how to live. Enable us to participate in this marvel of communication as we explore and experience the good news made known in Jesus Christ. Amen.

Commentary: This prayer intentionally seeks to convey the interactive nature of Scripture. Unless God assists us, our efforts are in vain. Likewise, unless we cooperate with God the overall effect of Scripture will be diminished. The metaphors of Hebrews 4:12 and Acts 17:11 combine to create this prayer. Additionally, there is a slight echo from Isaiah 55:11, which could be developed further or used alone to form another prayer for illumination.

Offertory Prayers

Lord of Life, daily you confirm your faithfulness in supplying all our needs. You amaze us how each new challenge is met by the glorious riches that are available in Christ Jesus. May our remembrance of your goodness inspire our gratitude as we offer these gifts to bless and honor you. In Jesus' abundant name. Amen.

Commentary: In Philippians 4:19, the apostle Paul speaks from his own experience of God's faithfulness in meeting our needs. These words create numerous possibilities of which the above prayer is only one example.

Generous God, your abundant gifts stretch our hearts and inspire our joyful response. May we never limit our gratitude to one hour a week on Sunday. Rather, may our lives shine brightly as beacons to those between Sundays that they may see your good deeds at work within us and offer you praise, O heavenly Father.

Commentary: Jesus' words from the Sermon on the Mount (Matt. 5:16) provide a vivid picture of stewardship that extends beyond the four walls of the church building. This prayer could be used for stewardship Sunday or at other times to call the people of God to connect their worship life with their daily life.

Heavenly Father, unlike our society, which often seeks to mislead us with counterfeit substitutes, you always shower us with blessings that are good and perfect. Accept the gifts we offer for all your love imparts, and may we satisfy your desire with our humble, thankful hearts. We thank you, Lord, for the bounteous love you lavish on us in Jesus' name. Amen.

Commentary: This prayer, which reflects the theme of thanksgiving, owes its origin to the third stanza of "We Plow the Fields and Scatter" ("We thank you, our Creator, for all things bright and good"), which in turn was inspired by James 1:17.

Pastoral Prayers

Sovereign and sustaining Lord, we draw near to you in prayer because you have first drawn near to us. We gratefully rejoice that you have sent and continually remind us of your Holy Spirit. Too often we neglect you, O Holy Spirit, *as we endeavor to be the church through our own planning and power. Free us from this distorted practice and pour out afresh the gift of your life-giving Spirit. Everlasting God, we praise you that your commitment to continue the church involves us today. You never send us forth by our own resources but renew us through the agenda and anointing of your mighty wind and fire.*

Grant us then, O gracious God, the desire and ability to speak the gospel with passion and power. May we not neglect the poor and disadvantaged, speaking only to those people with whom we feel comfortable.

Grant us then, O healing God, the compassion and sensitivity to bind up those whose hearts have been bruised and broken.

Grant us then, O liberating God, the courage and patience to proclaim hope to those who are in bondage and freedom to those who are oppressed. May we not forget those people imprisoned in institutions or caught in armed conflict.

Grant us then, O illuminating God, the vision and clarity to see clearly so we might direct others to follow you.

Grant us then, O God of justice, the realization of our need to be responsible and prepare ourselves for the Day of Judgment. Free us from the exhausting trap of performance, and fill us with the gift of your blessing and favor.

Grant us then, O tender God, hearts that are large enough to embrace those who mourn and walk gently with those who grieve. Surround with your restorative peace those who struggle that they may continue the journey of following Jesus.

Grant us then, O renewing God, the transforming of our hearts that we might wear the crown of beauty not as a sign of boasting but rather as a reminder that we belong to you. Where we are clothed with despair, exchange this with the garment of praise that our lives might rejoice and reveal the fulfillment of your promised Scriptures. This we pray, depending upon the ever-faithful name of Christ our Lord. Amen.

Commentary: The season following Pentecost, often called ordinary time, usually turns our attention to the nature and purpose of the church.

This prayer is the result of the interaction of Isaiah 61:1-3 with Luke 4:18-19, 21. Jesus selected this passage from Isaiah as he began his public ministry. Likewise for us today it can serve as the magna carta for our ministry. One may observe from this prayer that when we take Scripture seriously and in its proper context, we are often challenged to explore areas that we would otherwise neglect. We cannot read Scripture selectively if we wish to remain faithful and continue as Jesus' disciples.

Revive us again, O holy God, for we often forget who we are. We are grateful that you do not grow weary in reminding us of our true identity. Too often we become bound by the busyness and drivenness of our consumer society. Gracious God, impress upon us once again that we are of value not because of what we produce but because of who we are. Forgive us when we deny or ignore your handwriting on our hearts. Call us to awareness as we receive your words of Scripture, remembering that we are a chosen people, a royal priesthood, a holy nation, a people belonging to you, O powerful and present God.

May we further recall that this description of who we are reminds us of our responsibility. It is not enough to simply hear these words of belonging and blessing. Rather we must declare with joy and gratitude our praises to you for freeing us from the domain of darkness and leading us into the kingdom of your marvelous light. Alert us, Lord, that our daily conduct at school, work, home, play, and in the community may be the only evidence some people may see of your gospel of love and eternal life. Help us then to walk in such a way that we might accurately live by the tender mercy you have lavished upon us.

Out of that same mercy be gracious and refresh those within our community of faith who are sick or awaiting surgery, especially those who we now name. . . . Further may your mercy accompany those for whom the wounds of grief and sorrow are raw and painful, especially . . . Heavenly Father, our prayers also reach out to include all the children and youth of this church and our city. We realize the complexity and increasing pressure that our young people face. Grant them healthy friendships and stable families in which to mature. Provide your wisdom, patience, and humor to parents as they seek to create the proper settings in which to raise our youth.

Lord God, help us to realize that we are not the only expression of the body of Christ in this city. Break down the dividing walls of competition and pride, and send forth the unifying Spirit of Christ. Assist all that call upon your great name to cooperate and reflect the transforming message of Jesus Christ, our Master. Revive us again, O triune God. Fill each of our hearts with the love of Christ, and rekindle our souls with the power of your Spirit. For the sake of Christ's great kingdom we pray. Amen.

Commentary: This prayer seeks to remind the church of her true identity and mission. The biblical model which has inspired this is 1 Peter 2:9-10. Additionally, support is given by the fourth stanza of the hymn, "Revive Us Again" ("Revive us again: fill each heart with thy love"). This prayer could be restructured to employ the refrain from this hymn as a response at various points throughout the prayer. Further, it should be observed that frequently when we speak of God, we either focus on God's transcendence or immanence. This prayer consciously seeks to integrate and blend both of these aspects of God's nature.

Writing Scripturally Based Prayers

The previous models have illustrated how Scripture can generate and enhance the prayers of worship. What follows is a seedbed of Scripture to provide additional passages for the formation of your own prayers.

INVOCATIONS or OPENING PRAYERS
Isaiah 55:1-6; Jeremiah 33:3; Matthew 11:28-30; John 7:37-38; Revelation 3:20; 22:17.

PRAYERS OF CONFESSION
Genesis 3:8-19; Psalm 51:1-14; Daniel 9:4-11; Hosea 6; Micah 7:14-20; 1 John 2:1-6.

PRAYERS FOR ILLUMINATION
1 Kings 3:9,14; Psalm 119:9-11; 33-40; 105-106; Daniel 2:22-23; Luke 11:28.

OFFERTORY PRAYERS
Psalm 51:15-17; 116:16-19; Isaiah 56:6-7; 2 Corinthians 9:6-15; Galatians 6:6-10; 1 Peter 2:4-5.

PASTORAL PRAYER
Deuteronomy 32:1-43; 1 Samuel 2:1-10; 1 Chronicles 16:7-36; Matthew 5:3-10; John 17; 1 John 3.

Tom Schwanda

312 • THE ENVIRONMENT FOR WORSHIP DURING THE SEASON AFTER PENTECOST

Trinity Sunday is celebrated on the first Sunday after Pentecost. Trinity Sunday, a principal feast day in the church, is different from other principal days in that it does not commemorate an aspect of God's saving deed in history. Instead, it celebrates the Triune God, the source of the historical action that brings our salvation. It is appropriate for the Trinity to be celebrated on the Sunday after Pentecost, for Pentecost expresses the fullness of the Godhead by revealing the Spirit. Although Trinity Sunday originated in the tenth century, it did not become a universally adopted feast until the fourteenth century. Today the church around the world celebrates the Trinity on the first Sunday after Pentecost. One tradition associated with this observance is the use of the Athanasian Creed.

For the lectionary texts for this Sunday, see the list of texts for the Sundays in the season after Pentecost earlier in this chapter.

Opening Prayers for Trinity Sunday

Almighty God, our Father, dwelling in majesty and mystery, renewing and fulfilling creation by your eternal Spirit, and revealing your glory through our Lord, Jesus Christ: Cleanse us from doubt and fear, and enable us to worship you, with your Son and the Holy Spirit, one God, living and reigning, now and forever. Amen.

Almighty and ever living God, you have given us grace, by the confession of the true faith, to acknowledge the glory of the eternal Trinity and, in the power of your divine majesty, to worship the unity. Keep us steadfast in this faith and worship,

and bring us at last to see you in your eternal glory,
one God, now and forever. Amen.

Lutheran Book of Worship[59]

Penitential Prayers for Trinity Sunday

Father, you come to meet us when we return to
    you:
Lord, have mercy.
Lord, have mercy.

Jesus, you died on the cross for our sins:
Christ, have mercy.
Christ, have mercy.

Spirit, you give us life and peace:
Lord, have mercy.
Lord, have mercy.

or

Father, you enfold us with wings of love as a bird
    protects her young.
In our sin we have spurned your love.
Lord, have mercy.
Lord, have mercy.

Jesus, you gather us around you that we may learn
    your ways.
In our sin we have strayed from your presence.
Christ, have mercy.
Christ, have mercy.

Spirit, you feed us with the seed of you holy word:
In our sin we have chosen the chaff.
Lord, have mercy.
Lord, have mercy.

Enriching the Christian Year[60]

Prayer of Thanksgiving

The following prayer of thanksgiving for the liturgy of the Lord's Supper includes the themes of
the Scripture readings for this day.

MINISTER: The Lord be with you.
PEOPLE: **And also with you.**
MINISTER: Lift up your hearts.
PEOPLE: **We lift them to the Lord.**
MINISTER: Let us give thanks to the Lord our
      God.
PEOPLE: **It is right to give our thanks and
      praise.**

MINISTER: It is truly right and our greatest joy
      to give you thanks and praise,
    eternal and triune God,
    whom we worship as Father, Son, and
      Holy Spirit.
    In Jesus Christ you spoke the word
    that brought the world into being.
    By the Holy Spirit
    you brought order out of chaos
    and breathed life into your creatures.
    In parental love,
    you stood by us in spite of our dis-
      obedience,
    correcting us with gracious reproof
    and welcoming us again into your lov-
      ing embrace.

    Therefore we praise you,
    joining our voices with choirs of angels
    and with all the faithful of every time
      and place,
    who forever sing to the glory of your
      name:

(The people may sing or say:)

    **Holy, holy, holy Lord, God of power
      and might,
    heaven and earth are full of your
      glory.
    Hosanna in the highest.
    Blessed is he who comes in the
      name of the Lord.
    Hosanna in the highest.**

(The minister continues:)

    You are holy, O God of majesty,
    and blessed is Jesus Christ, your Son,
      our Lord.
    Born of Mary, he came to dwell
      among us,
    full of grace and truth.
    To all who believed,
    he gave power to become your chil-
      dren.
    In ministry among your own
    Jesus cared for all,
    forgiving their failures,
    healing their hurts,
    and nurturing their faith,
    giving himself in utter sacrifice for
      those he loved.

He inspired ordinary folk to Spirit-
    filled living
and displayed in his life, death, and
    rising again
the power of your Spirit.

(If they have not already been said, the words
of institution may be said here, or in relation
to the breaking of the bread.)

MINISTER: We give you thanks that the Lord
    Jesus,
on the night before he died,
took bread,
and after giving thanks to you,
he broke it and gave it to his dis-
    ciples, saying:
Take, eat.
This is my body, given for you.
Do this in remembrance of me.

In the same way he took the cup, say-
    ing:
This cup is the new covenant sealed
    in my blood,
shed for you for the forgiveness of
    sins.
Whenever you drink it,
do this in remembrance of me.

Remembering your gracious acts in
    Jesus Christ,
we take from your creation this bread
    and this wine
and joyfully celebrate his dying and
    rising,
as we await the day of his coming.
With thanksgiving we offer our very
    selves to you
to be a living and holy sacrifice,
dedicated to your service.

(The people may sing or say one of the following:)

1

MINISTER: Great is the mystery of faith:
PEOPLE: **Christ has died,**
    Christ is risen,
    Christ will come again.

2

MINISTER: Praise to you, Lord Jesus:
PEOPLE: **Dying you destroyed our death,**

rising you restored our life.
Lord Jesus, come in glory.

3

MINISTER: According to his commandment:
PEOPLE: **We remember his death,**
    we proclaim his resurrection,
    we await his coming in glory.

4

MINISTER: Christ is the bread of life:
PEOPLE: **When we eat this bread and drink**
    this cup,
    we proclaim your death, Lord Jesus,
    until you come in glory.

(The minister continues:)

Gracious God,
pour out your Holy Spirit upon us
and upon these your gifts of bread
    and wine,
that the bread we break
and the cup we bless
may be the communion of the body
    and blood of Christ.
By your Spirit make us one with
    Christ
that we may be one with all who share
    this feast,
united in ministry in every place.
As this bread is Christ's body for us,
send us out to be the body of Christ
    in the world.

(Intercessions for the church and the world may
be offered here.)

Nurture us at this table, O God,
that we may grow to the stature of
    Jesus Christ.
Help us to love you above all else
and to love our neighbor as we love
    ourselves,
demonstrating that love, in deed and
    word,
toward all your children.
Keep us faithful in your service
until Christ comes in final victory,
and we shall feast with all your saints
in the joy of your eternal realm.

Through Christ, with Christ, in Christ,
in the unity of the Holy Spirit,

all glory and honor are yours, almighty Father,
now and forever.

PEOPLE: **Amen.**

Book of Common Worship[61]

Blessings for
Trinity Sunday

The Lord God Almighty, Father, Son, and Holy Spirit, the holy and undivided Trinity, guard you, save you, and bring you to that heavenly city, where he lives and reigns forever and ever. Amen.

May God, the Holy Trinity, make you strong in faith and love, defend you on every side, and guide you in truth and peace; and the blessing of God Almighty, the Father, the Son, and the Holy Spirit, be among you and remain with you always. Amen.

Book of Occasional Services[62]

313 ✦ ALL SAINTS' DAY

In the early church it became customary to remember the martyrs of the church in worship. When the list of martyrs became too great, a special day was set aside to remember their commitment to Christ, a commitment that led to their suffering and death for the sake of the gospel. Although different areas of the church celebrated the memory of these saints on different days at first, by A.D. *835 it became the custom to celebrate these martyrs on November 1. Today, All Saints' day is celebrated on November 1 or the Sunday closest to November 1.*

Scriptural Words of Greeting
for All Saints' Day

Grace be to you and peace from God, who is and who was and who is to come, and from Jesus Christ, the faithful witness, the firstborn of the dead, and the ruler of the kings of the earth. Amen. (Rev. 1:4-5)

Opening Prayers for
All Saints' Day

Almighty God, whose people are knit together in one holy church, the body of Christ our Lord: Grant us grace to follow your blessed saints in lives of faith and commitment, and to know the inexpressible joys you have prepared for those who love you, through your Son, Jesus Christ, our Lord, who lives and reigns with you and the Holy Spirit, one God, now and forever. Amen.

Lord God, you have surrounded us with so great a cloud of witnesses. Grant that we may persevere in the course that is set before us, to be living signs of the gospel and at last, with all the saints, to share in your eternal joy, through your Son, Jesus Christ, our Lord. Amen.

Lutheran Book of Worship[63]

——— Lectionary Texts for All Saints' Day ———

SUNDAY	OLD TESTAMENT	PSALM	EPISTLE	GOSPEL
Year A	Revelation 7:9-17, the crowd worshiping around the throne.	34:1-10, 22	1 John 3:1-3, we are God's children.	Matthew 5:1-12, beatitudes.
Year B	Wisdom of Solomon 3:1-9 or Isaiah 25:6-9, God prepares a banquet for all the nations.	24	Revelation 21:1-6a, "I saw a new heaven and a new earth."	John 11:32-44, Jesus brings Lazarus back to life.
Year C	Daniel 7:1-3, 15-18, Daniel's vision; saints receive kingdom forever.	149	Ephesians 1:11-23, riches of glorious inheritance of the saints.	Luke 6:20-31, blessings and woes; love your enemies.

Revised Common Lectionary, descriptions by H. A. Tillinghast

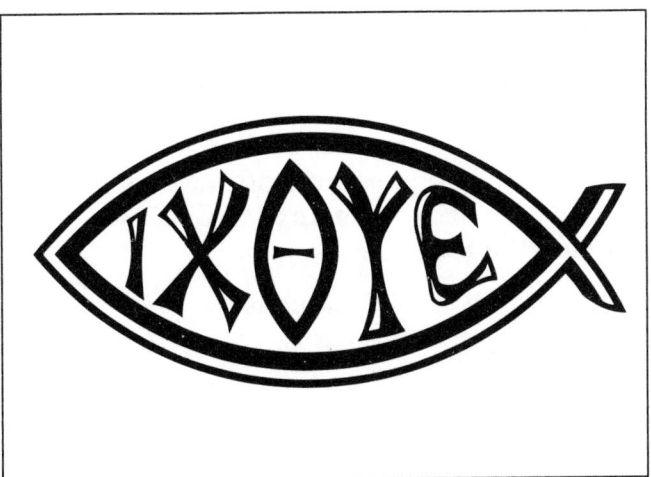

Ichthus. The ichthus, which is the Greek word for fish, *is also an acronym for the name of Jesus (ΙΧΘΨΣ—Jesus Christ, God's Son, Our Savior).*

Scriptural Statement of Faith for All Saints' Day

We believe in God, the Father, Son, and Holy Spirit. We believe that nothing—neither death, nor life; angels, nor principalities; things present, nor things to come; neither height, nor depth, nor anything in all creation—will be able to separate us from the love of God in Christ Jesus our Lord. Amen. (Rom. 8:37-39)

Blessings for All Saints' Day

May God, who has bound us together in the company of the elect, in this age and the age to come, attend to the prayers of his faithful servants on your behalf, as he hears your prayers for them. Amen.

May God, who has given us, in the lives of his saints, patterns of holy living and victorious dying, strengthen your faith and devotion, and enable you to bear witness to the truth against all adversity. Amen.

Book of Occasional Services[64]

A Service for All Saints' Day in the Free Church Tradition

The following service for All Saints' Day is designed for churches that do not follow a prescribed liturgical pattern. It is designed to highlight each of the important themes of worship on this day.

ENTRANCE

(Worshipers enter in silence for meditation.)

Statement of Purpose

Commentary: A brief explanation outlines the nature and purpose of worship on All Saints' Day.

Hymn of Praise: Te Deum

Commentary: This ancient canticle is present in many recently released hymnals in metrical form with the title "Holy God, We Praise Your Name."

LAMENT

Commentary: In this section of the service, the community remembers and laments the death of members, friends, and relatives of the community who have recently died, and takes comfort in the promise of Jesus.

Scripture Lesson: Matthew 11:28-30

Silent Meditation

Spoken Prayer

Psalm 23

Commentary: This psalm may be sung responsively or sung to a metrical setting such as "My Shepherd Will Supply My Need."

THANKSGIVING

Commentary: In this section of the service, the community gives thanks to God for the faithful witness and service of all the saints.

Scripture Lesson: Psalm 116:12-15

Litany of Thanksgiving

LEADER: O eternal God, we, your children, give you thanks
for our ancestors in the household of faith:
For Abraham, the father of the faithful,
For patriarchs and matriarchs who followed him in faith,
For Moses, who—with your guidance—led your people to freedom and gave them your law.

PEOPLE: **We bring thanks to you, O God.**

LEADER: For the prophets who declared your Word and will,

For David, the king who sang your praise,

For those who gave their lives to preserve your law,

For those disciples of Christ who left all to follow him,

For Paul, who so richly experienced the grace of the risen Lord

and brought his gospel to the nations,

PEOPLE: **We bring thanks to you, O Lord.**

LEADER: For the fathers and mothers of your church,

who guided her even in her oppressed beginning,

For the noble army of martyrs who faced death for their love of you,

PEOPLE: **We bring thanks to you, O Lord.**

LEADER: For mothers, fathers, and grandparents who ushered us into the knowledge of you

and now have been ushered into your kingdom,

For elder members of our community who mentored us,

and dear friends old and young who brought joy into our lives,

who now praise you in heavenly glory,

PEOPLE: **We bring thanks to you, O Lord.**

ALL: **Glory be to God, our Fortress and our Rock.**

Hymn: "For All the Saints"

ANTICIPATION

Commentary: In the final section of the service, the worshiping community looks forward to the coming reign of God, where all of God's saints will gather at the feast of the Lamb.

Scripture Lesson: Revelation 21:1-7

Silent Meditation

Hymn: "Love Divine, All Loves Excelling"

Blessing

John D. Witvliet

314 ♦ THE FEAST OF THANKSGIVING

The Scriptures mandate: "You shall observe the feast of the harvest of the first fruits of your labors" (Exod. 23:16). Throughout the history of the church, worshiping communities have designated certain days for common thanksgiving to God. In North America, the anniversary of the early Puritan thanksgiving feast has become the day on which Christians of every tradition gather for worship. In the United States, it is celebrated on the fourth Thursday of November; in Canada, it is celebrated on the second Monday in October.

--------- **Lectionary Texts for Thanksgiving** ---------

SUNDAY	OLD TESTAMENT	PSALM	EPISTLE	GOSPEL
Year A	Deuteronomy 8:7-18, a warning not to forget God in prosperity.	Psalms 65	2 Corinthians 9:6-15, how we sow determines how we shall reap.	Luke 17:11-19, Jesus heals the ten; one returns to thank him.
Year B	Joel 2:21-27, God restores fertility to the land.	Psalm 126	1 Timothy 2:1-7, offer thanks to God for all people.	Matthew 6:25-34, God and possessions: don't worry or fret.
Year C	Deuteronomy 26:1-11, harvest festival instructions to Israel.	Psalm 100	Philippians 4:4-9, be joyful, have a thankful heart.	John 6:25-35, Jesus as the bread of life.

Revised Common Lectionary, descriptions by H. A. Tillinghast

An Order of Worship for Thanksgiving

The following service is designed for worship in the free-church tradition. It includes elements that can be used in many worship traditions. Adapt to local use and customs.

The Approach to God

Call to Worship

LEADER: Our help is in the name of our God, who made heaven and earth.

PEOPLE: **Amen.**

LEADER: Sing to the Lord with thanksgiving. Make music upon the harp. How good it is to celebrate God's presence and sing praise throughout each day!

PEOPLE: **How good it is to sing praise and give honor to our God!**

LEADER: All of nature sings aloud God's goodness—clouds, rain, grass, creatures great and small. Our God creates and sustains our world with his ever-growing, never-ending love.

PEOPLE: **How good it is to sing praise and give honor to our God!**

LEADER: Grace and peace be yours in abundance through the knowledge of God and of Christ Jesus, our Lord.

PEOPLE: **Amen.**

Hymn of Praise: "Come, Ye Thankful People, Come"

Invocation

Prayer of Confession

LEADER: Loving God, we gather today rich in blessing, somehow believing that we merit the wealth and comforts that we enjoy. Forgive us, our God, for comfortably closing our eyes to the faces of the poor that stare blankly in our direction.

PEOPLE: **Lord, have mercy on us.**

LEADER: With bellies full of grain and meat, we offer token gestures to the hungry in our world, and we feel we have done enough. Forgive us, God, for keeping a distance between us and them, for closing our ears to the cries of the hungry.

PEOPLE: **Christ, have mercy on us.**

LEADER: With hands tightly clasping our treasure on earth, we cannot reach out to our oppressed brothers and sisters around this world. Forgive us for clinging to our own possessions rather than to you. Unite us with hearts of thanksgiving that we may work to ensure freedom and justice for all.

PEOPLE: **Lord, have mercy on us.**

Assurance of Forgiveness

LEADER: Hear what our God has to say to all people: "The Redeemer will come to Zion, to those...who repent of their sins." (Isa. 59:20)

The Law of God

LEADER: My command is this: Love each other as I have loved you. Greater love has no one than this, that he lay down his life for his friends.

Response of Gratitude and Praise: Gloria Patri (Glory Be to the Father)

The Word of God

Children's Message

Hymn: "All Things Bright and Beautiful"

Scripture Lesson: 1 Thessalonians 5:14-28; Luke 17:11-19

Message

Prayer for Blessing on the Word

The Response to God

Prayers of the People

LEADER: Let us give thanks to God our Creator for all the blessings we share this day. For all of those who have gone before, people strong and brave, willing to put their lives on the line for the causes they believed in, we give you thanks.

PEOPLE: **Grant us, our God, the courage to step out in faith for that which is true and right.**

LEADER: For freedom of speech and of the press, for the avenues open to express ourselves, and for opportunities to effect change, we give you thanks.

PEOPLE: **We pray for those who are voiceless victims of unjust governments.**

LEADER: For fertile soil, abundant rain, and seasons of refreshment, we give you thanks.

PEOPLE: **We pray for those who are hungry and tired, hopeless and wandering, finding no place to rest.**

LEADER: For strong bodies and minds, for opportunities that encourage us to grow and become more like the servants of thanksgiving you call us to be, we give you thanks.

PEOPLE: **We pray for the sick, for the stagnant who are unwilling to dream or change.**

LEADER: Help us, O God, to be responsible stewards of your blessings, people who care for the earth and all its people. Keep us connected with all humanity, even though miles and cultures tend to separate us. May we always respond to your call with a true spirit of thanksgiving.

The Lord's Prayer

(Note: In addition to the Prayers of the People, consider placing paper and pencils in the pews, asking everyone to write a prayer of thanksgiving to God.)

Confession of Faith

Offering

Doxology

Prayer of Dedication

Hymn: "Now Thank We All Our God"

Benediction

Silent Prayer of Commitment (with organ response)

Donald Jansma[65]

——— A Thanksgiving Litany ———

LEADER: Let us give thanks to the Lord, our rock, our fortress, and our deliverer. Let us remember his mercy, for he is gracious and compassionate.

PEOPLE: **We thank you for calling us to faith in Christ,**
for putting your Spirit within us,
for giving us the mind of Christ,
for gathering us into your church.

LEADER: We thank you, Lord, for extending your grace to us,
for calling us to a life of gratitude,
for calling us to service in your kingdom.

ALL: **Thanks be to God!**

LEADER: Let us give thanks to the Lord,
for he satisfies the thirsty,
he fills the hungry with good things,
and he heals the afflicted.
Let us celebrate his abundant goodness.

PEOPLE: **We thank you, gracious Father, that you provide for all our needs,**
for the food on our tables,
for the clothes on our bodies,
for the beds we sleep in,
and for the dwellings that shelter us.

LEADER: We praise you for all your gifts that go beyond our basic needs,
for the things that make our work easier, for the conveniences of modern life,
for the beauty and pleasure that you bring into our lives.

ALL: **Thanks be to God! Amen.**

——— Another Thanksgiving Litany ———

LEADER: Let us give thanks to the Lord for the people he has given us. For parents and grandparents, for sons and daughters, for brothers and sisters, for husband and wife—for all those who reflect to us the human dimension of your love,

PEOPLE: **We give you thanks, O Lord.**

LEADER: For neighbors and colleagues, for friends both far away and nearby—for all those who share the joys and sorrows of our daily lives,

PEOPLE: **We give you thanks, O Lord.**

LEADER: For those who serve us in restaurants, in repair shops, in stores, in schools, in hospitals—for all those who make our lives more comfortable,

PEOPLE: **We give you thanks, O Lord.**

LEADER: For the family of God, of the church universal, and for those who worship with us and minister to us in this church,

PEOPLE: **We give you thanks, O Lord.**

LEADER: For those who are weak and destitute, for those who need protection and support, for those who need healing and nurturing, for all those to whom we minister,

PEOPLE: **We give you thanks, O Lord. Amen.**

Paul Hesselink[66]

315 ✦ FEAST OF CHRIST THE KING OR FEAST OF THE REIGN OF CHRIST

This celebration acknowledges the lordship of Jesus Christ over all of creation. This service is always celebrated at the end of the Pentecost season on the last Sunday before Advent begins.

The Feast of Christ the King is a new festal celebration established for the Roman Catholic church by Pope Pius XI in 1925. Although Epiphany, Easter, and Ascension are already feasts of the King, Pius XI felt the need for an additional one to combat the secularization of the world and of society. Working with the older Catholic notion of a Christendom in which God rules the world through the church, Pius XI envisioned Christ the King Sunday as a proclamation for governments and institutions to submit to Christ.

Since Vatican II, the shift in Catholic thought, and thus the shift on the readings, prayers, and themes of Christ the King Sunday, is toward the cosmic and eschatological character of Christ's reign over the world. This emphasis fits well the theme of Christ's second coming in the early Sundays of Advent and prepares the worshiper for the expectant waiting of the coming season. This celebration is widely observed in many traditions of Christian worship. (The lectionary texts for this Sunday can be found in the list of texts for the Sundays in the season after Pentecost earlier in this chapter.)

Scriptural Words of Greeting

Grace be to you and peace from God, who is and who was and who is to come, and from Jesus Christ, the faithful witness, the firstborn of the dead, and the ruler of the kings of the earth. Amen. (Rev. 1:4-5)

Opening Prayer

Almighty and everlasting God, whose will it is to restore all things to your beloved Son, whom you anointed priest forever and king of all creation: Grant that all the people of the earth, now divided by the power of sin, may be united under the glorious and gentle rule of your Son, our Lord Jesus Christ, who lives and reigns with you and the Holy Spirit, one God, now and forever. Amen.

Lutheran Book of Worship[67]

Prayer of Confession

Righteous God, you have crowned Jesus Christ as Lord of all. We confess that we have not bowed before him and are slow to acknowledge his rule. We give allegiance to the power of this world and fail to be governed by justice and love. In your mercy, forgive us. Raise us to acclaim him as ruler of all that we may be loyal ambassadors, obeying the commands of our Lord Jesus Christ. Amen.

Book of Common Worship[68]

This prayer could be followed by words of assurance from Colossians 1: "For in Jesus Christ all the fullness of God was pleased to dwell, and through him God was pleased to reconcile to himself all things, whether on earth or in heaven, by making peace through the blood of the cross" (vv. 19-20).

Scriptural Statement of Faith

I believe in Jesus Christ, the Lord.
I believe that Jesus Christ is the image of the invisible God,
the firstborn of all creation;
for in him all things in heaven and on earth were created,
things visible and invisible, whether thrones or dominions or rulers or powers—
all things have been created through him and for him.
He himself is before all things; and in him all things hold together.

I believe that Jesus Christ is the head of the body,
the church;
he is the beginning, the firstborn from the dead,
so that he might come to have first place in everything.
For in him all the fullness of God was pleased to
dwell,
and through him God was pleased to reconcile to
himself all things,
whether on earth or in heaven,
by making peace through the blood of the cross.
(based on Col. 1:15-20)

I believe in Jesus Christ, the Lord.

For other scriptural statements of faith or ascrip-
tions of praise appropriate for this Sunday, see
Revelation 7:12; 1 Timothy 1:17; 6:15-16; and Revelation 5:12.

——— Prayer of Thanksgiving ———

The following prayer of thanksgiving for the liturgy of the Lord's Supper includes the themes of
the Scripture readings for this day.

MINISTER: The Lord be with you.
PEOPLE: **And also with you.**
MINISTER: Lift up your hearts.
PEOPLE: **We lift them to the Lord.**
MINISTER: Let us give thanks to the Lord our
God.
PEOPLE: **It is right to give our thanks and
praise.**
MINISTER: It is truly right and our greatest joy
to give you thanks and praise,
eternal God, Creator and ruler of the
universe.
You fashioned this world in love
and govern all the earth with grace
and peace.
Nations and monarchs rise and fall,
but your reign is for all time,
and your mercy is without end.

In love you made us to love and serve
you.
When we turned from you
and bent our knees to gods of our
own making,
you spoke through prophets
to bring us back to your ways.
You gave us a vision of your holy kingdom

that we might hunger after righteousness
and thirst for justice
and long for the day when peace will
triumph
over the pride and greed of nations.
Therefore, we praise you,
joining our voices with the servants
around heaven's throne
and with all the faithful of every time
and place,
who forever sing to the glory of your
name:

(The people may sing or say:)

**Holy, holy, holy Lord, God of power
and might,
heaven and earth are full of your
glory.
Hosanna in the highest.
Blessed is he who comes in the
name of the Lord.
Hosanna in the highest.**

(The minister continues:)

You are holy, O God of majesty,
and blessed is Jesus Christ, your Son,
our Lord.
Born as king in David's line,
he lived with the lowly
and cared for the least of your children.
His power was revealed in weakness,
his majesty in mercy.
His captors knelt to mock him,
giving him bruises instead of praise,
and piercing thorns for a crown.
His only earthly throne was a cross
on which to die.
Even there his arms stretched out
to embrace friends and foes in love.
From the grave you raised him to your
right hand,
where he rules again from heaven,
and commands true loyalty from
peoples and nations.

(If they have not already been said, the words
of institution may be said here, or in relation
to the breaking of the bread.)

MINISTER: We give you thanks that the Lord Jesus,

on the night before he died,
took bread,
and after giving thanks to you,
he broke it and gave it to his disciples, saying:
Take, eat.
This is my body, given for you.
Do this in remembrance of me.

In the same way he took the cup, saying:
This cup is the new covenant sealed
in my blood,
shed for you for the forgiveness of
sins.
Whenever you drink it,
do this in remembrance of me.

Remembering your gracious acts in
Jesus Christ,
we take from your creation this bread
and this wine
and joyfully celebrate his dying and
rising,
as we await the day of his coming.
With thanksgiving we offer our very
selves to you
to be a living and holy sacrifice,
dedicated to your service.

(The people may sing or say one of the following:)

1

MINISTER: Great is the mystery of faith:
PEOPLE: **Christ has died,**
Christ is risen,
Christ will come again.

2

MINISTER: Praise to you, Lord Jesus:
PEOPLE: **Dying you destroyed our death,**
rising you restored our life.
Lord Jesus, come in glory.

3

MINISTER: According to his commandment:
PEOPLE: **We remember his death,**
we proclaim his resurrection,
we await his coming in glory.

4

MINISTER: Christ is the bread of life:
PEOPLE: **When we eat this bread and drink**
this cup,

we proclaim your death, Lord Jesus,
until you come in glory.

(The minister continues:)

Gracious God,
pour out your Holy Spirit upon us
and upon these your gifts of bread
and wine,
that the bread we break
and the cup we bless
may be the communion of the body
and blood of Christ.
By your Spirit unite us with the living
Christ
and with all who are baptized in his
name,
that we may be one in ministry in every
place.
As this bread is Christ's body for us,
send us out to be the body of Christ
in the world.

(Intercessions for the church and the world may
be offered here.)

Lead us, O God, to conform this world
to your kingdom of love, justice, and
peace.
Help us to live as the Lord requires:
to do justice,
to love kindness,
and to walk humbly with you, our God.
Keep us faithful in your service
until Christ comes in final victory
and we shall feast with all your saints
in the joy of your eternal realm.
Through Christ, with Christ, in Christ,
in the unity of the Holy Spirit,
all glory and honor are yours, almighty
God,
now and forever.
PEOPLE: **Amen.**

Book of Common Worship[69]

316 ✦ BIBLIOGRAPHY FOR THE SEASON AFTER PENTECOST

Days of the Lord. Vols. 4, 5, and 6. Collegeville,
Minn.: Liturgical Press, 1991. These useful volumes
are liturgical commentaries, guides for

examining and understanding the structure of the postconciliar reforms of Vatican II. Two- to three-page commentaries for each Sunday in each of the three church years (A, B, and C) are presented with exegetical, pastoral, and liturgical notes. One book commences with a valuable chapter on the use of the Lukan text in Liturgical Year C, includes a helpful "practical scheme of the Gospel," and concludes with an extensive section of notes. Ecumenical/Roman Catholic.

Nocent, Adrian. *The Liturgical Year.* Vol. 4. Collegeville, Minn.: Liturgical Press, 1977. This volume covers the period of Sundays nine to thirty-four in ordinary time for years A, B, and C. The unstated theme of this volume is the church living out its faith in the paschal mystery. A brief commentary for each Scripture reading attempts to link it to the preceding or succeeding passage. Ecumenical/Roman Catholic.

See also article #161, the bibliography of general resources for the Christian year. All of the resources listed there include resources for the season after Pentecost.

TWENTY-NINE

Other Commemorations in the Christian Calendar

Throughout the history of Christianity, the church has set aside days to recall important events of the Christian faith, the contributions of heroes of the faith, and events recorded in Scripture. The following pages describe some of these observances so that readers unfamiliar with these commemorations will gain a fuller understanding of the faith of those who have gone before them. The memory of these events also challenges the church to remain faithful in its witness and to renew its vision for current ministry. Many of these observances are followed faithfully in worshiping traditions to this day.

These observances should not be an end in themselves. Rather, each commemoration should remind us of the life and work of Jesus Christ. To avoid overuse, liturgical reformers throughout history have restricted the numbers of such commemorations.

The following articles include brief descriptions of some of the most prominent observances during the season after Pentecost and the Scripture lessons that traditionally are associated with them.

317 ◆ COMMEMORATION OF EVENTS IN THE LIFE OF CHRIST

The Christian calendar is designed to focus our attention on the life of Christ. Thus, the most significant of the minor commemorations of the church are those that recall events in the life of Christ not already mentioned in earlier chapters of this volume. Some churches schedule separate services for these days; others include the events as part of their customary Sunday worship. Prayers not identified in this article are from the Lutheran Book of Worship.

Name of Jesus. This observance recalls Jesus' circumcision and naming as recorded in Luke 2:21. It is observed on January 1. Suggested readings include Numbers 6:22-27; Psalm 67; Galatians 4:4-7 or Philippians 2:9-13; and Luke 2:15-21. The following prayer is based on the theme of this observance:

Eternal Father, you gave your Son the name of Jesus to be a sign of our salvation. Plant in every heart the love of the Savior of the world, Jesus Christ, our Lord, who lives and reigns with you and the Holy Spirit, one God, now and forever. Amen.

The Presentation of Christ. This observance recalls the presentation of Jesus in the temple. It is celebrated on the fortieth day after Christmas, February 2. Suggested readings are Malachi 3:1-4; Psalm 84 or Psalm 24:7-10; Hebrews 2:14-18; and Luke 2:22-40. Especially significant in the readings are the role of Simeon and Anna. All observances should include the singing of the Nunc Dimittis, the Song of Simeon (Luke 2:29-32). The images of this canticle are included in this prayer:

Blessed are you, O Lord, our God, for you have sent us your salvation. Inspire us by your Holy Spirit to see with our own eyes him who is the glory of Israel and the light for all nations, Jesus Christ, our Lord.

The Annunciation. The angel's announcement to Mary regarding the birth of Jesus is observed on

March 25, nine months before Christmas. The lectionary readings are Isaiah 7:10-14; Psalm 45 or 40:6-10; Hebrews 10:4-10; and Luke 1:26-38. Worship on this day should include the singing of the Magnificat, the Song of Mary (Luke 1:46-55). The following is an appropriate prayer for this observance:

> Pour your grace into our hearts, O Lord, that we, who have known the incarnation of your Son, Jesus Christ, announced by an angel, may by his cross and passion be brought to the glory of his resurrection; who lives and reigns with you and the Holy Spirit, one God, now and forever. Amen.

The Visitation. This observance, celebrated on May 31, recalls the visit of Mary to Elizabeth. Suggested readings are 1 Samuel 2:1-10; Psalm 113; Romans 12:9-16b; and Luke 1:39-57. Worship on this day should include the singing of the Magnificat, the Song of Mary (Luke 1:46-55). This images of this canticle are reflected in the following prayer:

> Almighty God, in choosing the Virgin Mary to be the mother of your Son, you made known your gracious regard for the poor and the lowly and the despised. Grant us grace to receive your Word in humility and so to be made one with your Son, Jesus Christ, our Lord, who lives and reigns with you and the Holy Spirit, one God, now and forever. Amen.

Feast of the Transfiguration. In some traditions the Feast of Transfiguration is on the closest Sunday to August 6. Many churches now, however, celebrate the Transfiguration on the Sunday before Ash Wednesday.

The Feast of the Transfiguration reenacts the experience of Peter, James, and John on Mount Tabor. Since the Transfiguration took place, according to tradition, forty days before Jesus' crucifixion, the date of August 6 is fixed by the Feast of the Triumph of the Cross, which is celebrated on September 14. The Transfiguration has always been a major feast in the East. Christians of this tradition have placed great emphasis on the words in 2 Peter 1:4: "That we might become partakers of the divine nature." In the Transfiguration, Jesus shows the glory that is his with the Father, a glory that he shares with humanity by virtue of the Incarnation and the conquest of the powers of evil over human flesh. In the Eastern tradition, the Kata Basis (litany) of the cross was sung every Sunday from the Transfiguration to the Triumph of the Cross (August 6–September 13) as a way of especially celebrating the cross—the instrument that revealed Christ as Savior. Lectionary texts for this day include Exodus 34:29-35; 2 Peter 1:13-21; Luke 9:28-36; and Psalm 99. Appropriate hymns for this day include "O Word of God Incarnate," "The God of Abraham Praise," and "The Majesty and Glory of Your Name." The litany and prayer for Transfiguration that follow can be used whenever this feast is celebrated, whether in the season after Pentecost or just before Ash Wednesday.

LEADER: O Christ, before your crucifixion, Mount Tabor became like the heavens, a great cloud was spread over it like a canopy, and there you were transfigured, so that your glory with the Father became manifest. There Peter, James, and John, who were with you at your betrayal, saw the marvels of your divinity.

PEOPLE: **Make us worthy to adore you for the sake of your great mercy.**

Leader: O Christ, before your crucifixion, you took your disciples onto a high mountain, and there you were transfigured before them. You dazzled them with the rays of your glory; you showed them the glory of your resurrection.

PEOPLE: **Do the same for us, O God, for you are full of mercy and love.**

LEADER: O Christ, the old mountain which was gloomy and smoking is now honorable, for your feet have stood upon it. There the splendor of your countenance and the radiance of your garments so dazzled Peter, James, and John that they fell with their faces to the earth and covered them. And they were amazed when they saw Moses and Elijah talking to you and when they heard the voice saying, "This is my beloved son, in whom I am well pleased; hear ye him."

PEOPLE: **Come to us, Lord, and be present in all your glory.**

LEADER: O Christ, when you were transfigured on the mount, you became gloriously radiant and showed forth the virtues of your divine nature, and so, O

Christ, Peter, James, and John magnified you, the devils trembled, and hell shook in fear to see the glory that was yours with the Father.

PEOPLE: **For the heavens is yours and the earth and the seas also.**

LEADER: O Christ, come, shine in our midst and give us the light of your glory.

PEOPLE: **Even so, come, Lord Jesus. Amen.**

(Adapted from Eastern sources.)

A Transfiguration Prayer

O Lord, you prefigured your resurrection when you took three of your disciples, Peter, James, and John, and ascended Mount Tabor, and when you were transfigured, O Savior, Mount Tabor was covered with light, and your disciples, O Lord, threw themselves down upon the earth, unable to bear the sight which may not be looked upon. Angels ministered with fear and trembling, the heavens were filled with fear, and the earth shook when they saw the Lord of glory on earth. O Christ God, let your light illumine us as we, with the heavens and the earth, magnify you, the very light of the Father and the giver of light to the world. Amen. (Adapted from Eastern sources.)

318 ✦ COMMEMORATIONS OF OTHER EVENTS RECORDED IN SCRIPTURE

The following events recording in Scripture have also been commemorated throughout the history of the church. These days of commemoration call the church's attention to events and portions of Scripture that otherwise may be overlooked.

Holy Innocents. On this commemoration, observed on December 28, the church recalls the slaughter of all the innocent children by Herod, in his attempt to kill the baby Jesus. Appropriate readings include Jeremiah 31:15-17; Psalm 124; 1 Peter 4:12-19; and Matthew 2:13-18. An appropriate prayer is as follows:

We remember today, O God, the slaughter of the holy innocents of Bethlehem by order of King Herod. Receive, we pray, into the arms of your mercy all innocent victims, and by your great might, frustrate the designs of evil tyrants and establish your rule of justice, love, and peace; through Jesus Christ our Lord, who lives and reigns with you and the Holy Spirit, one God, now and forever. Amen.

Confession of St. Peter. Observed on January 18, this observance recalls Peter's stirring confession of Jesus as Lord. It also recalls the Lord's promise to Peter and to his church. Thus, this is a day for remembering God's faithfulness to the church and to the promise Jesus made to Peter. Suggested readings include Acts 4:8-13; Psalm 18:1-7, 17-20; 1 Corinthians 10:1-5; and Matthew 16:13-19. An appropriate prayer is as follows:

Almighty God, you inspired Simon Peter to confess Jesus as Messiah and Son of the living God. Keep your church firm on the rock of this faith, that in unity and peace it may proclaim one truth and follow one Lord, your Son, our Savior Jesus Christ, who lives and reigns with you and the Holy Spirit, now and forever. Amen.

Conversion of St. Paul. Observed on January 25, this commemoration recalls the riveting conversion of Paul on the road to Damascus. This is an occasion to celebrate God's faithfulness to his church, to remember the vision for Christian mission that characterized Paul's ministry, and to pray for God's blessing on the current mission of the church. Suggested readings include Acts 9:1-22; Psalm 67; Galatians 1:11-24; and Luke 21:10-19. An appropriate prayer draws on themes from these readings:

Lord God, through the preaching of your apostle Paul, you established one church from among the nations. As we celebrate his conversion, we pray that we may follow his example and be witnesses to the truth in your Son, Jesus Christ, our Lord, who lives and reigns with you and the Holy Spirit, one God, now and forever. Amen.

The Nativity of John the Baptist. Observed on June 24, this day recalls the birth of John the Baptist. Thus, it comes after the observance of the visitation described above. Lectionary texts include Malachi 3:1-4; Psalm 141; Acts 13:13-26; Luke 1:57-67. Worship on this day should include the singing of the Benedictus, the Song of Zechariah (Luke 1:68-79).

A prayer that is based on this theme is as follows:

Almighty God, you called John the Baptist to give witness to the coming of your Son and to prepare his way. Grant to your people the wisdom to see your purpose and the openness to hear your will, that we too may witness to Christ's coming and so prepare his way, through Jesus

Christ, our Lord, who lives and reigns with you and the Holy Spirit, one God, now and forever. Amen.

Prayers from the
Lutheran Book of Worship

319 ✦ COMMEMORATION OF THE APOSTLES AND SAINTS

The Christian calendar also allows for the memory of those special persons in the life of the church who were called to be instruments of the gospel. Paul speaks of all Christians as saints (Rom. 15:25), and throughout the history of the church, the lives and testimony of these people have been models for commitment, servanthood, and faith. Worship should not be ordered and organized around them, however, because worship celebrates God's saving deeds in Christ. But mention of them in prayer or in any other appropriate way is acceptable and profitable to the church for the edification of the believer and the building up of the community of faith.

The Sanctoral Calendar

Nov. 30	St. Andrew, Apostle
Dec. 21	St. Thomas, Apostle
Dec. 26	St. Stephen, Deacon and Martyr
Dec. 27	St. John, Apostle and Evangelist
Feb. 24	St. Matthias, Apostle
Mar. 19	St. Joseph
Apr. 25	St. Mark, Apostle and Evangelist
May 1	St. Philip & St. James, Apostles
June 11	St. Barnabas, Apostle
June 29	St. Peter and St. Paul, Apostles
July 22	St. Mary Magdalene
July 25	St. James, Apostle
Aug. 15	St. Mary, Mother of the Lord
Aug. 24	St. Bartholomew, Apostle
Sept. 21	St. Matthew, Apostle and Evangelist
Sept. 29	St. Michael and All Angels
Oct. 18	St. Luke, Evangelist
Oct. 23	St. James of Jerusalem
Oct. 28	St. Simon and St. Jude, Apostles

Suggestions for Planning

The purpose of commemorating apostles and saints is to remember their life, to take their faith as an example for our own, and to celebrate God's faithfulness to the church through their ministry. Worship on or near these days may accomplish this by following these guidelines:

- Read a passage of Scripture that records the ministry and life of the given apostle or saint. Consult a Scripture concordance to find these passages.

- Sing hymns that celebrate God's faithfulness through the lives of these apostles and saints. Many hymnals include texts that are appropriate for this. Consult a concordance or index of any recently released hymnal. Consider also hymns that celebrate God's faithfulness to the church such as "For All the Saints" or "The Church's One Foundation."

- Offer prayers that praise God for his faithfulness to the church. Prayers for each of these days can be found in *The Collects for the Church Year* (New York: Church Hymnal Corporation, 1985); *Lutheran Book of Worship* (Minneapolis: Augsburg, 1978); *The Proper for the Lesser Feasts and Fasts* (New York: Church Hymnal Corporation, 1980); and *The Cloud of Witnesses: A Companion to the Lesser Festivals and Holidays of the Alternative Service Book 1980* (London: Collins Liturgical Publications, 1980).

320 ✦ OTHER COMMEMORATIONS

Throughout the history of the church, other observances have developed that focus on various dimensions of Christian piety. Not all Christians recognize these commemorations, the practice of which has tended to ebb and flow during Christianity's two thousand years. This article presents descriptions of liturgical resources for some of these days.

Corpus Christi Sunday

This feast, which is celebrated on the Thursday or the Sunday after Trinity Sunday, is a memorial of the Eucharist, particularly the blood of Christ. Also called the Feast of the Precious Blood, it was established in Rome in the thirteenth century and became universal in the fourteenth century after Thomas Aquinas wrote a special liturgy for the feast. It was the custom on this day to elevate the host and hold a procession around the church. Consequently, all the people were able to see the host for their personal devotion. The extravagances related to this festival prevented it from being used in the Protestant world. Today, in the modern Roman Rite, the service is called _Corpus et sanguis_, the body and the blood, reflecting a concern to emphasize both elements celebrated in the Eucharist. While not observing this day, many Protestant traditions have emphasized the aspect of piety that this observance highlights. Think of the many Protestant (often revival) hymns focusing on the blood of Christ, such as "There Is a Fountain Filled with Blood." Lectionary texts associated with this day include Genesis 14:18-20; 1 Corinthians 11:23-26; Luke 9:11-17; and Psalm 80. The following litany gives a flavor of this observance.

A LITANY OF THE CROSS AND THE BLOOD OF CHRIST

I have heard, O Lord,
of the mystery of your ways
and have contemplated your works.
We praise your precious blood, O Christ.

O three times blessed tree,
The tree upon which Christ the King was stretched,
The same tree through which Adam fell,
You, O God, were nailed upon it.
We praise your precious blood, O Christ.

When Moses struck with his rod
The Red Sea and caused it to part and striking again
caused it to close on the enemy,
He did symbolize the weapon of the cross.
We praise your precious blood, O Christ.

When Jonah in the belly of the whale
stretched forth his hands in the form of a cross,
He foreshadowed your passion, O Lord.
And when he came out of the third day,
he symbolized the Resurrection
and illuminated the world.
We praise your precious blood, O Christ.

When the three youths were put
in the belly of the consuming fire,
They sang
Blessed art thou, God of our Fathers,
We praise, bless, and worship you, O Lord.

O ye youths equal in number to the Trinity,
Bless the Father, the God creator;
Praise the word which turned the fire to a dewy
    breeze;
and exalt more and more the all-holy Spirit,
who giveth life to everyone.
We hymn you and glorify you, O Christ.

Let all the trees of the wood rejoice,
For their nature has been sanctified
by the stretching of Christ on the tree.
We adore the elevated cross and magnify it,
And we worship him who is lifted up.
We magnify you and adore you forever and ever.
Amen.
(Adapted from Eastern Orthodox sources)

Feast of the Sacred Heart

In the Roman calendar, the Feast of the Sacred Heart is celebrated on the Friday of the week after Corpus Christi. The focus is on the symbol of the physical heart of Jesus and on the human and divine love that poured forth from his heart. While the themes of this service are found in the Scripture, the feast was developed in the medieval era, particularly in the subjective piety of that

Banners. Churches are using banners more frequently to mark important events in the Christian year.

period. Although Protestants have not observed this feast, many strains of Protestant piety have emphasized similar themes, such as the heart of Jesus, the love that flows from it, and our devotion to him and to others resulting from his heart of love. Lectionary texts associated with this day include Ezekiel 34:11-16; Romans 5:5-11; and Luke 15:3-7. A traditional prayer used on this feast day is a prayer that the love of Christ's heart may touch the world with healing and peace:

> Father, we honor the heart of your Son, broken by man's cruelty, yet a symbol of love's triumph, pledge of all that man is called to be. Teach us to see Christ in the lives we touch, to offer him living worship by love-filled service to our brothers and sisters. We ask this through Christ our Lord.

Appropriate hymns for this day include "For Heart to Praise My God," "A Perfect Heart," "Come Ye Disconsolate," "Just as I Am," "Let Your Heart Be Broken," "My Jesus, I Love Thee," "Near to the Heart of God," "O For a Heart to Praise My God," "Rejoice Ye Pure in Heart," and "Since Jesus Came into My Heart."

Triumph of the Cross

The origin of the feast celebrating the triumph of the cross goes back to the fourth century and is observed on September 14th, the date when tradition holds the cross was discovered. It may be observed on the Sunday nearest this day. Nevertheless the feast did not appear in liturgical books until the middle of the seventh century. In the East, "the universal exaltation of the precious and live-giving cross" is nearly as important as Easter. The world *exaltation,* which means "to lift up," is taken from John 3:14. The liturgical formulas praise the cross as "both the sign of God's suffering and the trophy of his victory." Lectionary texts for this day include Numbers 21:4-9; Philippians 2:6-11; John 3:13-17; and Psalm 20. Appropriate hymns include "At the Cross," "Beneath the Cross of Jesus," "In the Cross of Christ I Glory," "Lift High the Cross," "Near the Cross," and "The Old Rugged Cross."

Holy Cross Day

This day focuses on the cross of Christ and is observed on September 14, the day on which the cross of Christ was supposed to have been discovered. Suggested texts include Numbers 21:4b-

9; Psalm 98:1-5 or 78:1-2, 34-38; 1 Corinthians 1:18-24; and John 3:13-17. An appropriate prayer is as follows:

> Almighty God, your Son Jesus Christ was lifted high upon the cross so that he might draw the whole world to himself. Grant that we who glory in his death for our salvation may also glory in his call to take up our cross and follow him; through your Son, Jesus Christ, our Lord, who lives and reigns with you and the Holy Spirit, one God, now and forever. Amen.

This is an appropriate day to recall the passion of Christ. This can be an important part of the Christian journey through the year, highlighting the central reality of Christ's cross at a point in the year that is almost the farthest from Holy Week. Appropriate hymns include almost any Good Friday hymn, such as "When I Survey the Wondrous Cross."

Feast of Dedication

This ancient feast is rooted in the Jewish celebration of Hanukkah, or Dedication (John 10:22), which remembers the rebuilding and reconsecration of the temple after the victory of the Maccabees over the Syrians in A.D. 165. The church, adopting this Jewish feast to its own buildings, turned it into a feast of the church. On this Sunday, the church may celebrate its own existence. Today the celebration is not so much that of a material building, but of the spiritual building of the church itself. This feast may be celebrated on the first Sunday in October. Lectionary texts include 1 Corinthians 3:16 and 1 Peter 2:5.

321 ❖ OBSERVANCE OF A NATIONAL HOLIDAY

Although the church calendar does not include civil holidays, the message of the gospel does have important implications for life in government and society. Thus, some worship traditions have appropriated readings for selected civil holidays.

Any national holiday is an appropriate occasion for the gathering of Christians for prayer. On such days, suggested readings are Jeremiah 29:4-14 or Micah 4:1-5; Psalms 20, 33, or 107:1-32; Romans 13:1-10; and Mark 12:13-17. An appropriate prayer is as follows:

Lord of the nations, guide our people by your Spirit to go forward in justice and freedom. Give us what prosperity may be your will, but above all things give us faith in you, that our nation may bring glory to your name and blessings to all peoples, through your Son, Jesus Christ, our Lord. Amen.

Prayer from the Lutheran Book of Worship

322 ◆ OBSERVANCE OF EVENTS IN THE HISTORY OF THE CHRISTIAN CHURCH

Almost all worshiping communities recall the anniversaries of important days in their history as occasions to bless and thank God for his faithfulness to them. Some of the events are important to entire worshiping traditions; others are significant in the life of individual congregations.

An Anniversary of the Local Church. One occasion for thanksgiving and prayer is the anniversary of the founding of a local congregation. Readings for such an occasion include 1 Kings 8:22-40; Psalm 84; 1 Peter 2:1-9; and John 10:22-30. An appropriate prayer is as follows:

O God, you have promised through your Son to be with your church forever. We give you thanks for those who founded this community of believers and for the signs of your presence in our congregation. Increase in us the spirit of faith and love, and make us worthy of our heritage. Knit us together in the communion of saints, and make our fellowship an example to all believers and to all nations. We pray through your Son, Jesus Christ, our Lord. Amen.

Reformation. Prior to Vatican II, many Protestant churches celebrated Reformation Day, the anniversary of Luther's posting of his 95 theses on October 31, 1517. Since Vatican II, many churches have realized that celebrating such a day calls attention to the division in the church instead of its need for unity. This occasion is most meaningfully celebrated by calling the church to thank God for his faithfulness and by praying for and calling each other to remain faithful to the Word of God. Suggested readings include Jeremiah 31:31-34; Psalm 46; Romans 3:19-28; and John 8:31-36. An appropriate prayer is as follows:

Almighty God, gracious Lord, pour out your Spirit upon your faithful people. Keep them steadfast in your Word, protect and comfort them in all temptations, defend them against all their enemies, and bestow on the church your saving peace; through your Son, Jesus Christ, our Lord, who lives and reigns with you and the Holy Spirit, one God, now and forever. Amen.

Prayers from the Lutheran Book of Worship

World Communion Sunday. The twentieth century has witnessed unprecedented openness among Christians of various traditions. In order to celebrate the unity of the Christian church, Christians in many worshiping traditions have set aside the first Sunday in October as World Communion Sunday. On this occasion, churches could use hymns and songs from around the world. Almost every recently published hymnal includes fine examples of hymns from Asia, Africa, Latin America, and Eastern Europe. The following prayer is appropriate for this occasion.

Lord of languages and nations, we offer you our thanks for creating a new unity among the divided peoples of the earth. You have given Christians of every nation and language and race your Spirit, that your church might be one. We join Christians from around the world in voicing our praise to you. We ask that your Spirit may continue to work in us, so that the unity which we profess may be a unity which brings witness to the world. Amen.

323 ◆ BIBLIOGRAPHY FOR OTHER COMMEMORATIONS IN THE CHRISTIAN YEAR

For information about the various commemorations of apostles and saints, see:

Brown, Peter. *The Cult of the Saints.* Chicago: University of Chicago Press, 1981.

Cunningham, Lawrence. *The Meaning of Saints.* New York: Harper & Row, 1980.

Perham, Michael. *The Communion of Saints.* Alcuin Club Collections, no. 62. London: S.P.C.K., 1980. A theological discussion of the commemoration of the saints.

Wilson, Stephen. *Saints and Their Cults: Studies in Religious Sociology, Folklore, and History.* Cambridge, U.K.: Cambridge University Press, 1983. This volume contains an exhaustive bibliography.

Complete guides to individual saints can be found in:

Bentley, James. *A Calendar of Saints*. New York: Facts on File, 1986.

Butler, Alban. *Butler's Lives of Saints*. San Francisco: Harper & Row, 1987.

Delaney, John. *Dictionary of Saints*. Garden City, N.Y.: Doubleday, 1980.

Farmer, Robert Hugh. *The Oxford Dictionary of Saints*. New York: Oxford University Press, 1978.

For a liturgical guide to these feasts, see:

Baldovin, John. "On Feasting the Saints." *Worship* 54 (1980): 336–344.

Days of the Lord. Vol. 7: *Solemnities and Feasts*. Collegeville, Minn.: Liturgical Press, 1994. Ecumenical/Roman Catholic.

Erickson, Craig Douglas. "Reformed Theology and the Sanctoral Cycle." *Reformed Liturgy and Music* 21:4 (1987): 228–232.

Whalen, Michael. "Saints and Their Feasts: An Ecumenical Expression." *Worship* 63 (1989): 194–209.

For information on various feasts in the Christian year see:

Weiser, Francis Xavier. *Handbook of Christian Feasts and Customs*. New York: Harcourt, Brace, 1959.

Works Cited

1. Richard Mouw, "The Danger of Alien Loyalties," *Reformed Worship* 15 (March 1990): 8–9.

2. Geoffrey Wainwright, "Beginning with Easter," *The Reformed Journal* 38:3 (March 1988): 13–17.

3. Don E. Saliers, "The Church Year and Congregational Life," *Reformed Liturgy and Music* 20:2 (Spring 1986): 92–94.

4. William Stringfellow, "Advent as a Penitential Season," *Witness* 64:12 (December 1981): 10–12.

5. From Ralph E. Dessem, *Celebrating Advent in the Sanctuary* (Lima, Ohio: C.S.S.P.C, 1983).

6. Keith Watkins, *Thankful Praise: A Resource for Christian Worship* (St. Louis: CBP Press, 1987), 63–65.

7. Brian Hooper, "Praying the Antiphons," *Modern Liturgy* 17:10 (1990): 8-11.

8. Presbyterian Church (USA), et al., *Book of Common Worship* (Louisville: Westminster/John Knox Press, 1993), 169–171.

9. "Seasonal Blessings," in *Book of Occasional Services* (New York: Church Hymnal Corporation, 1988), 20–21.

10. Peter Mazar, "Passing over into Winter," *Environment and Art Letter* 1:8 (October 1988): 5.

11. Jill Knuth, "Advent Banners," *Modern Liturgy* 8:8 (1981): 32

12. Ronald Gagne, Thomas Kane, and Robert Ver Eecke, *Introducing Dance in Christian Worship,* (Washington, D.C.: The Pastoral Press, 1984), 101.

13. From Ralph E. Dessem and Thomas J. Tozer, *Deck the Halls: A New Service for the Hanging of the Greens* (Lima, Ohio: C.S.S.P.C, 1986).

14. *Book of Common Worship,* 180–183, 194–197.

15. *Book of Occasional Services,* 21–22.

16. Peter Mazar, "Before You Begin to Prepare the Christmastime Worship Environment," *Environment and Art Letter* 1:9 (November 1988): 5.

17. Criss Van Hof, "Choice Christmas Musicals," *Reformed Worship* 5 (Fall 1987): 32–33.

18. Published in *Reformed Worship* 9 (Fall 1988): 30–31, adapted from *Service Book: Part Three, Services of the Word and Sacraments* (Grand Rapids: CRC Publications, 1981), 24–30.

19. Originally published as *The Cross in the Christmas Tree* by Richard P. Musser (St. Louis: Concordia, 1967) and adapted by William DeVries and Charlotte Larson for *Reformed Worship* 9 (Fall 1988): 17–20.

20. Rubén R. Armendáriz, "Las Posadas," *Reformed Liturgy and Music* 22:3 (Summer 1988): 142–143.

21. Hoyt Hickman, Don E. Saliers, Laurence Hull Stookey, and James F. White, *The New Handbook of the Christian Year* (Nashville: Abingdon Press, 1993), 79–84.

22. *Book of Common Worship,* 216–219.

23. Don E. Saliers, "Ash Wednesday through Lent: Practical Considerations," *Reformed Liturgy and Music* 24:1 (Winter 1990): 16–18.

24. *Book of Common Worship,* 237–241.

25. *Book of Occasional Services,* 23–24.

26. Peter Mazar, "Decorating for Lent," *Environment and Art Letter* 1:10 (January 1989): 5.

27. Thomas S. Rambert, "Visualizing Lent," *Modern Liturgy* 8:1 (1981): 38.

28. *Book of Common Prayer* (New York: Church Hymnal Corporation, 1979), 355.

29. Robert E. Webber, adapted from "Easter: Reliving the Mystery," *Christianity Today* (March 21, 1986): 16–18.

30. John D. Grabner, "Triduum: Practical Considerations," *Reformed Liturgy and Music* 24:1 (Winter 1990): 19–22.

31. Rambert, "Visualizing Lent," 38.

32. *Book of Occasional Services,* 24.

33. Jonathan Levy Gerdan II and Fred Walhof, "The Triumphal Entry Temple Scene," *Reformed Worship* 14 (Winter 1990): 12–15.

34. Bert Polman, "The Passion of Our Lord," *Reformed Worship* 18 (Winter 1991): 16–19.

35. *Liturgical Year: The Worship of God. Supplemental Liturgical Resource* 7 (Louisville: Westminster/John Knox Press, 1992).

36. Paragraphs 1, 3, and 4 are from *The Book of Occasional Services,* 91.

37. *Book of Common Prayer,* 275.

38. Doug Adams, "Triumph and Tripudium: A Gesture of Jubilation to Avoid Passing Over the Joy of Holy Thursday," *Modern Liturgy* 5:2 (1978): 8.

39. At the time of publication, information about this article was not available. Please write Star Song Publishing Group for information regarding this drama.

40. Patrick Regan, "Veneration of the Cross," *Worship* 52 (January 1978): 2–12.

41. Adapted by Robert E. Webber from *Good Friday* (London: SPCK, 1948).

42. Virginia Kimball, "Holy Thursday: A Dramatic Liturgy of the Word," *Modern Liturgy* 5:2 (1978):10.

43. From Arlo Duba, "Keeping Vigil: Easter Vigil at Taizé," *Reformed Worship* 6 (Winter 1988), 10–14.

44. Marjorie Proctor-Smith, "A Week of Sundays: Celebrating the Great Fifty Days," *Reformed Liturgy and Music* 24:1 (Winter 1990): 23–26.

45. A complete listing of canticles can be found in the *Book of Common Prayer*, 286–287.

46. From the *Handbook of the Christian Year* (Nashville: Abingdon Press, 1986), 206.

47. Many of the headings in this section of the service as well as prayers have been adapted from the *Handbook of the Christian Year*, 196–197.

48. Adapted from "The Baptismal Covenant IV" in the *United Methodist Hymnal* (Nashville: UMC Publishing House, 1989), 50ff.

49. Betsy L. Willis, "Brining Easter Vigil Reading to Life," *Modern Liturgy* 17:2 (1990): 22–24.

50. Rick Hodson; see also Gagne, et al., *Introducing Dance in Christian Worship*, 104.

51. *Book of Common Worship*, 332–333.

52. *Book of Common Worship*, 318–320.

53. *Book of Occasional Services*, 24–25.

54. Peter Mazar, "Decorating for Easter," *Environment and Art Letter* 2:2 (February 1989): 5.

55. Robert Copeland, "Carols For Easter," *Reformed Worship* 6 (Winter 1988): 15–17.

56. Sue Mitchell Wallace, "Easter Hymn Festival," *Reformed Worship* 10 (Winter 1989): 17.

57. Arnaldo Figueroa, "A Pentecost Creed," *Modern Liturgy* 5:5 (1978): 30.

58. *Book of Common Worship*, 343–347.

59. Inter-Lutheran Commission on Worship, *Lutheran Book of Worship* (Minneapolis: Augsburg, 1978), 24.

60. Michael Perham, comp., *Enriching the Christian Year* (Collegeville, Minn.: The Liturgical Press, 1993), 68.

61. *Book of Common Worship*, 349–352.

62. *Book of Occasional Services*, 26

63. *Lutheran Book of Worship*, 36.

64. *Book of Occasional Services*, 26–27.

65. Donald Jansma, "Service of Thanksgiving," *Reformed Worship* 8 (Summer 1988): 44–45.

66. Paul Hesselink, "Thanksgiving Liturgies," *Reformed Worship* 1 (Fall 1986), 19.

67. *Lutheran Book of Worship*, 30.

68. *Book of Common Worship*, 396.

69. Ibid., 396–399.

Index

IN MEMORIAM

Larry J. Nyberg

1949–1993

Distinguished Project Editor
who suddenly entered into the kingdom
as his editorial work on
The Complete Library of Christian Worship
was nearing completion